Professional Management of Housekeeping Operations

SECOND EDITION

Professional Management of Housekeeping Operations

SECOND EDITION

Robert J. Martin

Wm. F. Harrah College of Hotel Administration
University of Nevada, Las Vegas

Thomas J. A. Jones

Wm. F. Harrah College of Hotel Administration
University of Nevada, Las Vegas

John Wiley & Sons
New York · Chichester · Brisbane · Toronto · Singapore

Library of Congress Cataloging-in-Publication Data
Martin, Robert J., 1927–
    Professional management of housekeeping operations / Robert J.
    Martin, Thomas J.A. Jones. —2nd ed.
        p.   cm.
    Includes bibliographical references and index.
    ISBN 0-471-54779-4 (alk. paper)
    1. Hotel housekeeping.   I. Jones, Thomas J. A.   II. Title.
TX928.M37   1992
    674.94 068 — dc20   91-34407
                                                                          CIP
Printed in the United States of America

10 9 8 7 6 5

To managers and executives of the future
who enter through the housekeeping door
and
to Carolyn and Terri

Preface

Much has happened in the housekeeping profession since the first edition of this text was published six years ago. Not only has the industry undergone modernizing changes, but also the managerial jobs of the executive housekeeper in hotels and the director of environmental services in the housekeeping operations of hospitals have become dramatically similar. This may be more noticeable if one happens to be a member of the National Executive Housekeeper's Association, where housekeeping and environmental service directors mingle freely.

There are numerous cases now being cited in which management personnel move freely from hospitals to hotels and vice versa. Add to this the opening of megahotels with 4000 rooms (larger ones on the drawing board) and hospitals that are now competing in quality of "hotel type services" for their patients, and there is a clearly observable need to blend the professional and technical aspects of hospital environmental service management with hotel and hospitality housekeeping management.

The first edition of this text only hinted at the similarities of the professions. This edition, however, will devote an entire chapter to environmental services. In addition, where the term executive housekeeper is used, the reader should make a mental correlation with the director of environmental services in any hospital because, from a management standpoint, the two jobs are on the same turf.

In this edition, Part II will continue to deal with the planning, organizing, and staffing of a new, soon to open, hotel facility. Although under a new banner, our model hotel is very much intact. This part of the book is relatively undisturbed and remains essentially as before since the managerial responsibilities of opening a housekeeping or environmental services department of a hotel or hospital are not far from being exactly alike.

Thanks to the constructive comments of several of our users, job descriptions heretofore found in Chapter 3 have been placed in a new Appendix A. Additionally, this second edition will blend the job descriptions and standard operating procedures of both hotels and hospitals, allowing for different models of both to be presented and compared for style. Introductory remarks regarding "organization" will now be found at the close of Chapter 2.

Thanks to our new coauthor, the chapter on material planning has been divided into four chapters, in which particular attention is paid to the more technical concerns of purchasing equipment and using products.

Old Part III has been subdivided into two parts (III and IV). New Part III deals exclusively with the basic routines and subroutines of department operation. These chapters deal with the "daily routine" as a 24-hour scenario in the activity of hotel operations. Again, thanks to our users, a section entitled "Cleaning the Guestroom" is fresh and appropriate. This section will support both the instructor who needs a reference when teaching *how to clean a guest room* and the instructor who will continue to teach how to manage the department of those who do. Part IV contains the new chapter devoted entirely to environmental services. The final subjects of the book will also be found in Part IV.

In addition to the usual and expected updating of material, the chapter on safety and security has been broadened to include the entire body of knowledge regarding the protection and safeguarding of assets. Also, the new OSHA and HASCOM regulatory requirements, which treat concerns for infectious and hazardous waste disposal and recycling, are also now included.

Computer applications for housekeeping operations remain something of a spin-off from hotel front-office property management systems (PMSs). For this reason, and because the greatest use for computers in housekeeping departmental management continues to be the common spreadsheet, the topic of computer applications for the housekeeping operator will be left to the proponents of the specific system where the manager happens to be employed. Further scenarios for the computer have, however, been advanced.

Finally, several of the appendixes have been updated thanks to their authors; others have been shortened.

The important role of women in industry is evidenced by the fact that female registration at the College of Hotel Administration, University of Nevada, Las Vegas, has increased from 20 to 50 percent. At the same time, total registration has increased threefold, indicating a need for a shift in gender-related pronouns. Terminologies containing gender assumptions, especially houseman and maid have, moreover, changed. The maid has become the section housekeeper or guestroom attendant (GRA), and the head houseman has become the senior housekeeping aide.

As with the first edition, it is important to recognize that although the order of the material parallels that of a startup operation, with proper planning and active staff involvement each and every step will bring new efficiencies in time and productivity to ongoing operations whether hospital or hotel, union or union-free.

Acknowledgments

Our special thanks to the many users of the first edition for their welcomed comments. Over the years we have maintained file folders for each chapter of the text. Into them have gone scraps of ideas, bits of papers, journal articles, book reviews, and seminar notes. Each of the folders became the basis for updated data, new ideas, clarifications, and reworked segments. The model hotel is no longer a Holiday Inn but is now the Radisson at Star Plaza in Merrilville, Indiana. Users of the book will, however, find the basic structure of the book essentially unchanged, although there is substantial change in its content.

Our special thanks also go to the many directors of environmental services who have inspired us to bring these two noble professions together.

And to the Excalibur Hotel and Casino of Las Vegas, Nevada; especially to Mr. Mike Burns, Director of Housekeeping Services, his assistant, Mrs. Chitra Hammond, for her perseverance in "getting those pictures," and all the persons willing to give of their time to set up and bring about the photo work for the segments involving cleaning of the guestroom.

Also, our thanks to Marriott's Residence Inn of Las Vegas, Nevada, especially their executive housekeeper, Ms. Cathy Ness, for her expert guidance and assistance.

Robert Martin continues to extend his appreciation to the Marriott Hotel Corporation for allowing him the opportunity to benefit from their outstanding training programs, and especially to Mr. Paul T. Reed, executive vice president, Marriott Hotel Corporation, for allowing him to get his foot in the door.

He also wishes to thank Mr. Dean V. White, owner and operator of the Holiday Inn, Merrillville, Indiana (now the Radisson at Star Plaza), for his willingness to allow him to take charge and operate his facility.

Appreciation is also extended to Mr. Bruce White, President, White Lodging Services, for allowing us to continue to use this fine property as a model hotel in this book, and to the management and staff of that property for their contribution, which was a part of the original and actual development of housekeeping systems permanently established for operations during the period 1977–1979.

Contents

PART ONE

The Housekeeping Profession and the Principles of Management

S ince people have always traveled there has always been a need for housekeepers and hospitality. The function of housekeepers has changed over the years from doing specific tasks to managing the people, material, and other resources required for task accomplishment. In Part One we trace this change and see how the developing science of management relates to the profession of executive housekeeping. We also introduce Mackenzie's ordering of the principles of management, which include the sequential functions of planning, organizing, staffing, directing, and controlling. These sequential functions will be used as the organization structure for Parts Two and Three of the book. (Part Four will address special topics and will offer a summary of the book.)

1

The Executive Housekeeper and Scientific Management

CHAPTER OBJECTIVES

1. To understand how the function of housekeepers has changed over the years.
2. To see how the science of management relates to the profession of executive housekeeping.
3. To investigate the principles of management, as presented by R. Alec Mackenzie.

Over the last 30 years the profession of executive housekeeping has passed from the realm of art to that of scientific management. Previously, professional housekeepers learned technical skills related to keeping a clean house. Now, the executive housekeeper and other housekeeping supervisory personnel are not only learning how to do such work but also how to plan, organize, staff, direct, and control housekeeping operations. They are learning how to inspire others to accomplish this with a high degree of quality, concern, and commitment to efficiency and cost control. In order to understand how the art melds with the science, we will trace the origins of professional housekeeping and of scientific management.

Origins of Hospitality and Housekeeping

Hospitality is the cordial and generous reception and entertainment of guests or strangers, either socially or commercially. From this definition we get the feeling of the open house and the host with open arms, of a place in which people can be cared for.

Regardless of the reasons people go to a home away from home, they will need care. They will need a clean and comfortable place to rest or sleep, food service, an area for socializing and meeting other people, access to stores and shops, and secure surroundings.

Americans have often been described as a people on the move, a mobile society, and in their earliest history Americans required bed and board. Travelers in the early 1700s found a hospitality similar to that in countries of their origin, even though these new accommodations might have been in road houses, missions, or private homes and the housekeeping might have included only a bed of straw that was changed weekly.

Facilities in all parts of young America were commensurate with the demand of the traveling public, and early records indicate that a choice was usually available at many trading centers and crossroads. The decision as to where to stay was as it is today, based on where you might find a location providing the best food, overnight protection, and clean facilities. Even though the inns were crude, they were gathering places where you could learn the news of the day, socialize, find out the business of the community, and rest.

With the growth of transportation—roadways, river travel, railroads, and air travel—Americans became even more mobile. Inns, hotels, motor hotels, resorts, and the like have kept pace, fallen by the wayside, overbuilt, or refurbished to meet quality demands.

Just as the traveler of earlier times had a choice, there is a wide choice for travelers today. We therefore have to consider seriously why one specific hotel or inn might be selected over another. In each of the areas we mentioned—food, clean room, sociable atmosphere, meeting space, and security—there has been a need to remain competitive. Priorities in regard to these need areas, however, have remained in the sphere of an individual property's management philosophy.

Creating Proper Attitudes

In addition to the areas of hospitality we discussed, professional housekeeping requires a staff with a sense of pride. Housekeeping staffs must show concern for guests, which will make the guests want to return—the basic ingredient for growth in occupancy and success in the hotel business. Such pride is best measured by the degree to which the individual maids (guestroom attendants or section housekeepers) say to guests through their attitude, concern, and demeanor, "Welcome, we are glad you chose to stay

with us. We care about you and want your visit to be a memorable occasion. If anything is not quite right, please let us know in order that we might take care of the problem immediately."

A prime responsibility of the executive housekeeper is to develop this concern in the staff; it is just as important as the other functions of cleaning bathrooms, making beds, and making rooms ready for occupancy. Throughout this text, we will present techniques for developing such attitudes in housekeeping staffs.

Origins of Management

While the evolution of the housekeeping profession was taking place, professional management was also being developed. In fact, there is evidence that over 6000 years ago in Egypt and Greece complex social groups required management and administration. It is even possible to derive evidence of the study and formulation of the management process as early as the time of Moses. Henry Sisk[1] reminds us that in the Bible (Exod. 18:13–26) Jethro, Moses' father-in-law, observed Moses spending too much time listening to the complaints of his people. Jethro therefore organized a plan to handle these problems that would in turn relieve Moses of the tedium of this type of administration. A system of delegation to lieutenants thus emerged. We can therefore assign some of the credit to Jethro for establishing several of the principles of management that we recognize today: the principles of **line organization, span of control,** and **delegation.**

Schools of Management Theory

Although it is beyond the scope of this book to provide an exhaustive examination and comparative analysis of all of the approaches to management theory that have appeared over the past two thousand years, the following section is an attempt to identify the major schools of management theory and to relate these theories to the modern housekeeping operation.

The Classical School

The **classical school** of management theory can be divided into two distinct concerns: **administrative theory** and **scientific management.** Administrative theory is principally concerned with management of the total organization, whereas scientific management is concerned with the individual worker and the improvement of production efficiency by means of an analysis of work using the scientific method.

These two branches of the classical school should be viewed as being complementary rather than competitive.

Administrative Theory

Considered by many to be the father of administrative theory, Henri Fayol[2] (1841–1925) was a French engineer who became the managing director of a mining company. Fayol sought to apply scientific principles to the management of the entire organization. His most famous work, *Administratim Industrielle et General (General and Industrial Management)*, first published in 1916, and later in English in 1929, is considered by many to be a classic in management theory.

Fayol asserted that the process of management was characterized by the following five functions:

1. Planning—the specification of goals and the means to accomplish those goals by the company
2. Organizing—the way in which organizational structure is established and how authority and responsibility are given to managers, a task known as **delegation**
3. Commanding—how managers direct their employees
4. Coordinating—activities designed to create a relationship among all of the organization's efforts to accomplish a common goal
5. Controlling—how managers evaluate performance within the organization in relationship to the plans and goals of that organization[3]

Fayol is also famous for his Fourteen Principles of Management and his belief that administrative skills could be taught in a classroom setting.

Scientific Management

Fayol's counterpart in the management of work was Frederick W. Taylor[4] (1856–1915), the father of scientific management. Taylor was an intense (some would say obsessive) individual who was committed to applying the scientific method to the work setting. In 1912 Taylor gave his own definition of **scientific management** to a committee in the U.S. House of Representatives by stating what scientific management *was not:*

> Scientific Management is not any efficiency device, nor a device of any kind for securing efficiency; nor is it any branch or group of efficiency devices. It is not a new system of figuring cost; it is not a new scheme of paying men; it is not a piecework system; it is not a bonus system, nor is it holding a stop watch on a man and writing down things about him. It is not time study, it is not motion study nor an analysis of the movements of men.

Although Taylor's definition of scientific management continued at length in a similar vein, he did not argue against using the aforementioned tools. His point was that scientific management was truly a *mental revolution,* whereby the **scientific method** was the sole basis for obtaining information from which to derive facts, form conclusions, make recommendations, and take action. Taylor's contribution was a basis for understanding how to administer a project and the people involved.

In his ***Principles of Scientific Management*** published in 1911, he outlined four principles that constitute scientific management:

1. Develop a science for each element of a man's work, which replaces the old rule-of-thumb method.
2. Scientifically select and then train, teach, and develop the workman, whereas in the past he chose his own work and trained himself as best he could.
3. Heartily cooperate with the men so as to ensure all of the work being done is in accordance with the principles of the science which has been developed.
4. There is an almost equal division of the work and the responsibilities between the management and the workmen, while in the past almost all of the work and the greater part of the responsibility were thrown upon the men.[5]

Taylor also pointed out that the mental revolution had to take place in the workers' as well as the managers' minds.

The School of Management Science

An outgrowth of "Taylorism" is the school of **management science,** or, as it is alternatively known, **operations research.** Management science is defined as the application of the scientific method to the analysis and solution of managerial decision problems. The application of mathematical models to executive decision making grew out of the joint U.S. and British efforts during World War II to use such models in military decision making at both the strategic and the tactical level.

The Behavioral School

A predecessor to the **human relations** school of management was the nineteenth-century Scottish textile mill operator, Robert Owen.[6] He believed that workers needed to be "kept in a good state of repair." Owen urged other manufacturers to adopt his concern over improving the human resources they employed. He claimed that returns from investment in human resources would far exceed a similar investment in machinery and equipment.

Unfortunately, it was not until the second decade of the twentieth century that the results of Elton Mayo's Hawthorne Studies affirmed Owen's position and caught the imagination of American management.

Mayo[7] (1880–1949) was a faculty member of the Harvard University School of Business Administration when he began to study workers at the Hawthorne Works of the Western Electric Company in Chicago in 1927. From this study Mayo and his colleagues concluded that there were factors other than the physical aspect of work that had an effect on productivity. These factors included the social and psychological aspects of workers and their relationships with managers and other workers.

Mayo's work effectively demonstrated to managers that in order for them to increase productivity in the work setting they must develop human relations skills as well as the scientific management methods of Taylor and the other classical theorists.

Managerial Temperament

The behavioral school does not end with Mayo. Douglas McGregor summarized certain assumptions about traditional or work-centered theory of management under the heading *Theory X*. McGregor's Theory X assumption is summarized in the following four statements:[8]

1. Work, if not downright distasteful, is an onerous task that must be performed in order to survive.
2. The average human being has an inherent dislike of work and will avoid it if he can.
3. Because of the human characteristic to dislike work, most people must be coerced, directed, controlled, or threatened with punishment to get them to put forth adequate effort toward the achievement of organizational objectives.
4. The average human being prefers to be directed, wishes to avoid responsibility, and has relatively little ambition, and wants security above all.*

*Assumptions 2, 3, and 4 are quoted directly from McGregor (Ref. 4). Assumption 1 has been added as an explicit statement of the nature of the work to which humans are reacting.

Simply stated, Theory X indicates that there is no intrinsic satisfaction in work, that human beings avoid it as much as possible, that positive direction is needed to achieve organizational goals, and that workers possess little ambition or originality.

McGregor also presented **Theory Y,** which is the opposite of Theory X. His six assumptions for Theory Y are as follows:[9]

1. The expenditure of physical and mental effort in work is as normal as play or rest. The average human being does not inherently dislike work. Depending upon controllable conditions, work may be a source of satisfaction and will be voluntarily performed.
2. External control and the threat of punishment are not the only means for bringing about effort toward organizational objectives. Man will exercise self direction and self control in the service of objectives to which he is committed.
3. Commitment to objectives is a function of the awards associated with their achievements. The most significant of such work, e.g., the satisfaction of ego and self actualization needs, can be direct products of effort directed toward organizational objectives.
4. The average human learns under proper conditions not only to accept but to seek responsibility. Avoidance of responsibility, lack of ambition, and emphasis on security are general consequences of experience, not inherent human characteristics.
5. The capacity to exercise a relatively high degree of imagination, ingenuity, and creativity in the solution of organizational problems is widely not narrowly distributed in the population.
6. Under the conditions of modern industrial life, the intellectual potentialities of the average human beings are only partially utilized.

An important point is that the opposite ways of thinking as reflected in McGregor's Theory X and Theory Y are what is actually conveyed by managers to their employees through everyday communication and attitudes.

Satisfiers and Dissatisfiers

Another leading theorist in the behavioral school was Frederick Herzberg. Herzberg and his associates at the Psychological Service of Pittsburgh[10] found that experiences that create positive attitudes toward work come from the job itself and function as **satisfiers** or motivators. In other words, satisfiers are created by the challenge and intrigue of the job itself.

A second set of factors related to productivity on the job are conditions outside of the job itself. Things such as pay, working conditions, company policy, and the quality of supervision are all a part of the working environment but are outside of the task of the job itself. When this second set of factors is inadequate, that is, when you believe that these conditions are not up to par, they function as **dissatisfiers,** or demotivators. When these factors are adequate, however, they do not necessarily motivate employees for a lasting period of time but may do so only for a short time.

Stated another way, Herzberg argued that the presence of satisfiers tends to motivate people toward greater effort and improved performance. The absence of dissatisfiers has no long-lasting effect on positive motivation; however, the presence of dissatisfiers has a tendency to demotivate employees.

Participative Management

Rensis Likert,[11] another leading behaviorist, introduced the term **participative management,** (which is characterized by worker participation in discussions regarding decisions which ultimately affect them).

Participation occurs when management allows hourly workers to discuss their own observances and ideas with department managers. (Such techniques have been seen as being one of the greatest motivators toward quality performance in a housekeeping operation.) More about this technique will be said when we discuss employee morale and motivation. **Theory Z**[12], the highly vaunted Japanese management model, is heavily based on this participative management model.

The Managerial Grid

Blake et al.[13] presented a revolutionary idea concerning the methods that underlie the thinking process involved in decision making. They found that a **managerial grid** could be established whereby a maximum or minimum concern for production could be equated with a maximum or minimum concern for people. The managerial grid attempts to define the various ways in which people think through decisions. Knowing why people think or feel the way they do can have a great influence on the quality of commitment from a group decision, especially when it comes to resolving conflicts. Blake and Mouton held that the best managers have both a high concern for production and a high concern for people in the organization.

One of the most recent attempts at group involvement in decision making has come out of a major concern for the loss of U.S. prestige in its own automobile market. Specifically, Japanese managers and workers have coined the term **"quality circle,"** which is a way of explaining total worker involvement in the processes as well as in the management decisions about production and quality that will ultimately affect worker welfare. Quality circles are now undergoing heavy scrutiny in the United States and are being used to help rekindle automobile production.

Situational Leadership

Situational leadership[14] or the **contingency approach**[15] to management asserts that there is no one universally accepted approach to a management problem. It maintains that different problems require different solutions. This approach perhaps best reflects the complex nature of management in the organizational setting. Adherents to this approach agree that there is no "one best" way to manage; flexibility is the key to successful management. The works of Fred Fiedler,[16] Victor Vroom,[17] and Ken Blanchard and Paul Hersey[18] have contributed to this model.

Principles of Management

Executive housekeepers today recognize the need for a clear understanding and successful application of management principles. They may, however, feel overwhelmed by the many terms in the field of scientific management, both from the past and in the present. It is important for executive housekeepers to be familiar and comfortable with these terms and principles, since there is no department within the hospitality industry in general and hotels in particular that will provide a greater opportunity for applying management skills.

In order to help you understand the concept of management, we will present an ordering of the management process as developed by R. Alec Mackenzie[19] Building on the works of Fayol, he has created a three-dimensional illustration relating the elements, continuous and sequential functions, and activities of managers. Refer to Figure 1.1, Mackenzie's diagram, when reading the following material.

Elements

According to Mackenzie, the **elements** that today's managers work with are ideas, things, and people.

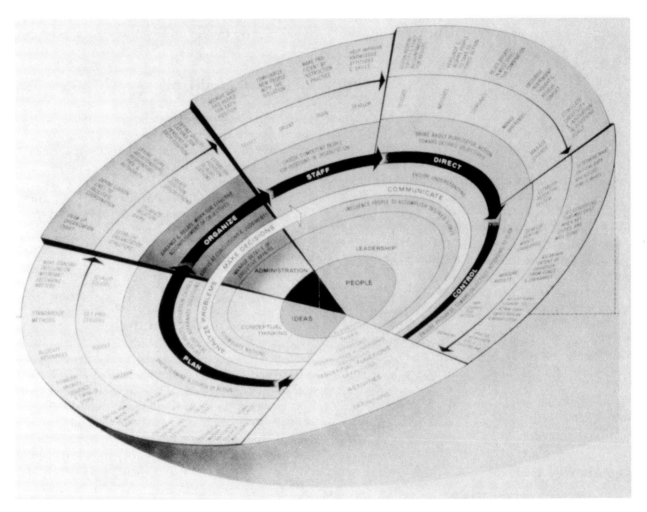

Figure 1.1 Mackenzie's management process, showing the elements, functions, and activities that are part of the executive's job. (R. Alec Mackenzie,) *The Management Process in 3-D,* Harvard Business Review (Copyright©, November-December 1969 by the President and Fellows of Harvard College; all rights reserved.)

These are the main components of an organization and are in the center of the figure. The manager's task that is related to **ideas** is to think conceptually about matters that need to be resolved. The task related to **things** is to administer or manage the details of executive affairs. The task related to **people** is to exercise leadership and influence people so that they accomplish desired goals.

Functions

The **functions** of a manager can be thought of as continuous functions and sequential functions. Many times a question may be asked: "But what does the manager do?" The manager should be seen to do several continuous functions, as well as several sequential functions.

The **continuous functions** relating to ideas and **conceptual thinking** are to *analyze problems.* Those related to things and **administration** are to *make decisions,* and those related to people and **leadership** are to *communicate* successfully. Problems are analyzed, facts gathered, causes learned, alternative solutions developed, decisions made, conclusions drawn, communications generated, and understanding assured.

The **sequential functions** of management are more recognizable as a part of the classical definition of management. They involve the planning, organizing, staffing, directing, and controlling of ideas, things, and people. Mackenzie sets forth various activities in each of these sequential functions that should be studied and recalled whenever necessary.

Activities of Sequential Functions

According to Mackenzie, a manager's sequential functions are divided into five areas—planning, organizing, staffing, directing, and controlling.

Planning

The **management plan** involves seven basic activities:

1. *Forecasting:* Establishing where present courses will lead
2. *Setting objectives:* Determining desired results
3. *Developing strategies:* Deciding how and when to achieve goals
4. *Programming:* Establishing priorities, sequence, and timing of steps
5. *Budgeting:* Allocating resources
6. *Setting procedures:* Standardizing methods
7. *Developing policies:* Making standing decisions on important recurring matters

Organizing

Getting **organized** involves arranging and relating work for the effective accomplishment of an objective. Managers organize by making administrative or operational decisions. The four activities involved in getting organized are as follows:

1. *Establishing an organizational structure:* Drawing up an organizational chart
2. *Delineating relationships:* Defining liaison lines to facilitate coordination
3. *Creating position descriptions:* Defining the scope, relationship, responsibilities, and authority of each member of the organization
4. *Establishing position qualifications:* Defining the qualifications for people in each position

Staffing

The third sequential function, **staffing,** involves people. Leadership now comes into play and communication is established to ensure that understanding takes place. There are four activities:

1. *Selecting employees:* Recruiting qualified people for each position
2. *Orienting employees:* Familiarizing new people with their environment
3. *Training:* Making people proficient by instruction and practice
4. *Developing:* Improving knowledge, attitude, and skills

Directing

The first three sequential functions of management—planning, organizing, and staffing—might be performed before an operation gets underway. The last two sequential functions—directing and controlling—are carried out after the operation has begun or is in process. As with other managerial relationships involving people, leadership is accomplished through communication. In the **directing** of operations, there are five basic activities:

1. *Delegating:* Assigning responsibility and exacting accountability for results
2. *Motivating:* Persuading and inspiring people to take a desired action
3. *Coordinating:* Relating efforts in the most efficient combination
4. *Managing differences:* Encouraging independent thought and resolving conflict
5. *Managing change:* Stimulating creativity and innovation in achieving goals

Controlling

The final sequential function of management is to **control** organizations and activities to ensure the desired progress toward objectives. There are five basic activities in the controlling of operations:

1. *Establishing a reporting system:* Determining what critical data are needed
2. *Developing performance standards:* Setting conditions that will exist when key duties are well done
3. *Measuring results:* Ascertaining the extent of deviation from goals and standards
4. *Taking corrective action:* Adjusting plans, counseling to attain standards, replanning and repeating the several sequential functions as necessary
5. *Rewarding:* Praising, remunerating, or administering discipline

Management Theory and the Executive Housekeeper

The question now is, "How can the executive housekeeper apply these diverse management theories to the job at hand, that being the management of a housekeeping department?"

Before we attempt to answer that rather encyclopedic question, perhaps we should first turn our attention to some of the inherent organizational and employee-related problems facing many housekeeping departments.

To begin, housekeeping is not a "glamorous" occupation. Cleaning toilets for a living is not, nor has it ever been, the American dream. No one wishes for his or her child to become a guestroom attendant or a housekeeping aid. Housekeeping is viewed by a majority of the American public as being at the bottom of the occupational hierarchy in terms of status, pay, benefits, and intrinsic worth.

Even in the hotel industry, housekeeping employees are among the lowest-paid of all workers in the hotel. Thus, the housekeeping department has traditionally attracted individuals who possess minimal levels of education, skills, and self-esteem.

Even the management positions in the housekeeping department have an image problem. In hospitality education, students normally tend to gravitate to the front office, marketing, food and beverage, and even human resource areas before they will consider housekeeping.

Normative Characteristics Exhibited by Housekeeping Employees

In order to more effectively manage housekeeping employees, we must attempt to understand their cultural, psychological, and social makeup. The following employee characteristics are commonly found in many housekeeping departments.

- Cultural diversity abounds in most housekeeping departments. Racial minorities, particularly black and Hispanic employees, are to be found in numbers that are disproportionate to their representation in the general population.

    The reason for this situation is obvious; the doors of opportunity have been closed to these Americans for generations (many of these doors are not yet fully open). Consequently, these Americans have gravitated to those few areas of employment left open to them.

- In many parts of the country, particularly the Southwest, Florida, New York, and many major urban centers, English is not the predominant language spoken in the housekeeping department. In fact, in many housekeeping departments many workers can neither speak nor write in English.

- Housekeeping often attracts individuals with little formal education. Many workers are functionally illiterate, and others can be classified as being "math illiterate." This can have a particularly telling effect upon departmental efficiency and communications.

- Many of the employees come from lower socioeconomic backgrounds. These environments can often be a major factor in the formation of employee attitudes and behaviors that are not compatible with traditional corporate values. For instance, these individuals tend to have a work ethic that is far different from that of middle America. These employees often need to be taught such fundamentals as the need for punctuality, personal hygiene, and how to communicate with the guest.

- A worker may often have emotional or economic problems, or may even have a dependency problem. It is not suggested that the executive housekeeper is the only manager within the hotel who faces these problems, but many would argue that the frequency of these problems is higher in housekeeping than in other areas. Housekeeping often attracts displaced housewives, single parents, and former welfare recipients who have a higher incidence of these problems.

Although there may be numerous properties throughout the United States where these traits and characteristics are not found in the employees of the housekeeping department, they do appear frequently enough to require the astute housekeeping manager to prepare for such eventualities.

Motivation and Productivity

Motive is defined by Webster's[20] as "something (as a need or desire) that leads or influences a person to do something." The **motivation** of employees is accomplished by the manager having created an environment in which employees can motivate themselves. Managers cannot hope to directly motivate other human beings; however, they can provide a climate where self-motivation will take place.

What we as managers want our employees to do is to become more **productive.** We want them to accomplish their duties in a more effective and efficient manner. We want to substantially reduce **turnover,**

absenteeism, and **insubordination** in the organization. We want our organization to be populated with happy, competent people that believe, as Douglas McGregor postulated, that "work is as natural as play or rest."[21]

To do that we must empower our employees with the abilities and inspiration to accomplish the mutually held objectives of the organization and the individual. There is no magic formula to achieve this goal. It takes dedication, perseverance, a plan, and plain hard work. What follows is not a fail-safe prescription for leadership success, but a series of approaches, methods, procedures, and programs that incorporates the best that the previously discussed schools of management theory have to offer the housekeeping department. Although not all of these applications may work in every setting, they have been shown to positively affect the productivity of a number of housekeeping departments.

Researching the Motives

First, find out what motivates your best long-term employees to perform as well as they do. Find out why they stay with you. This can be best done by interviewing these people one-on-one (this is also a great opportunity to personally thank your best employees) in a distraction-free setting.

Second, find out why others leave. Conduct **exit interviews** with all persons being separated, but do not do it yourself and do not do it at the time of separation. Employees will be less than honest with you about the real reason for their resignation if you are part of the problem. Interviewing at the time of separation may also provoke the employee to be less than honest. They may give an "acceptable" reason for separation, such as more money, so they do not jeopardize a potential reference source.

The best approach is to have a third person call on the former employee a month after the separation. Make sure that the interviewer is able to convey an image of trust to the former employee.

Third, find out what current employees really want regarding wages, benefits, and working conditions. Administer a survey that assures the anonymity of the respondent. If English is not the predominant language of the employees in your department, take the extra time to have a bilingual survey prepared. Also, form a committee of employees to assist you in designing the survey. This will help to lessen the effects of management bias and ensure that the survey reflects the attitudes of your department.

Have the employees mail the survey back to the company (be sure that the form has a stamp and return address), or have a ballot box for the forms. You may even want a third party, such as an outside consulting firm, to administer the survey.

Finally, administer this survey on a periodic basis—for example, twice a year—in order to remain current with the prevailing employee attitudes.

Use the information you have collected to assist you in strategic policy-making decisions and in the day-to-day operation of your department.

Selection

Far too often in housekeeping we take the first warm body that applies for the job. Recruiting is often viewed as a costly and time-consuming process for the management and the property. It is an endeavor fraught with failure; prospective employees don't show for interviews, newly hired workers quit during their first week on the job, and so on.

There is one method that can help to substantially reduce the cost and time involved in recruiting prospective employees. It can also help to reduce employee turnover and its associated costs.

This method is employee referral; that is, asking your employees (your best employees in particular) to refer people whom they know (friends, family, and acquaintances) for entry-level position openings. In order for this procedure to work, the employer must be ready to pay a significant reward when a suitable candidate is presented. Typically, the reward is paid in installments over a time span of several months to a year or more to ensure the continued presence of both the employee who recommended the candidate and, of course, the candidate. One benefit to this system is that most conscientious employees will only recommend candidates whom they honestly feel will be good employees and will not reflect negatively on their recommendation.

However, safeguards must also be established to prevent unscrupulous employees from taking advantage of the system.

This author once observed an employee in a large hotel in Las Vegas asking an applicant, a stranger, who was in the waiting room of the personnel office in the hotel to put down his name on the referral line of the application blank. If the applicant was hired, the employee would then receive a bonus, which he offered to split with the applicant.

Other nontraditional sources of applicants for the housekeeping department include tapping into the disabled worker pool. Most communities have rehabilitation agencies where contacts can be established and cooperative programs initiated.

Senior citizens, young mothers, and legal immigrants are other potential sources of nontraditional labor.

Training

A formal training program, as most housekeeping administrators know, is an indispensable element in achieving productivity goals. There are, however, certain training approaches and concerns that are not being addressed by all housekeeping administrators.

These concerns include the educational background of the staff. As was mentioned earlier, many housekeeping workers may be illiterate or may not be able to communicate in English. Written training materials, such as manuals, posters, and written tests, are quite useless when the staff cannot read, write, or speak the English language. Special audio/visual training materials are often required in housekeeping departments, and the written training materials must often be made available in Spanish or other languages to the workers.

The introduction of these materials does not rectify the problem, however. Consequently, many housekeeping departments have initiated remedial educational programs so that employees can not only learn to read and write in English, but can also earn their high school diplomas.

The executive housekeeper does not have to implement these remedial programs from scratch; he or she can turn to a number of sources of assistance found in most communities, such as the public school or the community college system. These sources can often provide qualified bilingual adult instruction at little or no cost to the company. Another tactic is to reimburse employee tuition if they complete remedial classes at the local community college.

The payoff to the housekeeping department is twofold. First, productivity benefits because the level of communication has increased. Second, the esteem level of the employees should certainly increase when they begin to achieve their personal educational goals, and a self-assured workforce will ultimately become a more competent and productive workforce.

Delegation: The Key to Managerial Success

According to Mackenzie, delegation is one of five activities of direction. Others view **delegation** as the most valuable activity. The other activities—motivation, coordination, managing differences, and managing change—can be seen as stemming from a manager's ability to delegate properly.

Too often, we hear the phrase, "delegation of responsibilities and authority." In fact, it is impossible to delegate a responsibility. To delegate actually means to pass authority to someone who will act in behalf of the delegator. The passing of such authority does not relieve the delegator of the responsibility for action or results, although there is an implied accountability of the person to whom power has been delegated to the person having that power. The responsibility of a manager for the acts or actions of his or her subordinates is therefore absolute and may not be passed to anyone else.

When an executive housekeeper is assigned overall responsibility for directing the activities of a housekeeping department, carrying out this responsibility may require the completion of thousands of tasks, very few of which may actually be performed by the executive housekeeper. It is therefore a responsibility of management to identify these tasks and create responsibilities for subordinates to carry them out. (The creation of these responsibilities is done during organization through the preparation of job and position descriptions; see Appendix A.) A good operational definition of delegation is the creation of a responsibility for, or the assignment of a task to, a subordinate, providing that person with the necessary authority (power) to carry out the task and exacting an accountability for the results of the subordinate's efforts. The lack of any one of the three elements of this definition creates a situation whereby the manager abdicates the responsibility to manage.

Thorough and complete delegation, where possible, will free the manager from tasks that can be performed by subordinates, allowing the manager time to manage the operation. The manager is then left free to (1) coordinate the activities of subordinates, (2) manage change (implies that the manager now has time to be creative and search for changes that will improve operations), and (3) manage differences (a form of problem solving).

How does one delegate? There are several methods, all of which will be useful to the executive housekeeper.

Methods of Delegation

1. *By results expected:* The manager can make a simple statement of the results that are to be obtained when the task has been completed properly.
2. *By setting performance standards:* The manager can create conditions that will exist when a task has been performed satisfactorily. An example of this type of delegation is found in inspection forms, which specify conditions that exist when the tasks are adequately performed. Figure 1.2 shows a room inspection form that sets forth

```
┌─────────────────────────────────────────────────────────┐
│              GUEST ROOM INSPECTION FORM                  │
├─────────────────────────────────────────────────────────┤
│  Name: _____   Date: _____  Room: _____   │
│                                          ┌──┐ Not        │
│                          Score: _____   │  │ acceptable │
│                                          ├──┤            │
│                                          │  │ Acceptable │
│                                          └──┘            │
└─────────────────────────────────────────────────────────┘
```

☐	Door	Clean, no dust on front, back, or top
☐	Door frame	Clean, no dust
☐	Connecting door	Clean, no dust, bolt locked
☐	Door chain	Fastened
☐	D.N.D. sign	Good condition
☐	Coat rack	Clean, no dust, no hangers missing, two laundry bags
☐	Carpet	Vacuumed, no debris (including behind drapes, between beds, and under spread, no dust around edges or under furniture, clean between connecting doors *report all spots and gum to supervisor*
☐	Furniture	No dust on tops or sides, include kneehole under desk, chair legs, and cushions, cushion turned regularly so the cover stays in place, drawers clean in c/o room, all furniture in proper position
☐	Pictures and mirror	No dust on frames, no streaks on mirror
☐	Wall lamps	No dust on bulbs, bulbs working, no dust on dish under bulb, seam on shade turned to the back, shade straight, correct wattage bulb
☐	Floor lamp	No dust (on arm, stand, or base) bulb working, no dust on bulb, in proper position (12 inches from either wall with light extending over the chair) seam on shade turned to the back, shade straight, correct bulb
☐	TV	No dust on screen, front, back, stand, and restaurant ad on top
☐	Air conditioner	No dust on front, top, or control box; turned off

Figure 1.2 Guest Room Inspection Form. Acceptable conditions are specified which, if met, indicate satisfactory performance. Checkmarks in boxes indicate satisfactory performance; N.I., needs improvement; U, unsatisfactory condition (must be corrected before renting the room).

standards that, if met, signify satisfactory performance.

In hospitals and health care institutions, standards may become more strict and even require that the institutions meet agency approval. Figure 1.3 is a list of standards, prepared by Charles B. Miller, that could be used as a guide in establishing standards, adding or deleting them as necessary in hospitals, health care institutions, and hotels.

3. *By establishing procedures:* The major technique in dealing with routine matters is to prepare **standard operating procedures (SOP)** in which the tasks to be performed are set forth in a routine procedure. The SOP also indicates who will do what in the procedure, thus allowing for the delegation of appropriate tasks to people.

Another simple and equally important technique of delegation is to take all tasks that must be done and

☐	Tracks and patio door	Clean, no dust, locked
☐	Beds	Neat and smooth appearance, clean linen, sheet tucked under head of mattress, hospital corners, top sheet folded over blanket 6 inches from top edge of mattress, pillowcase seams turned to the wall, blanket clean, spread clean, mattress and box springs positioned properly on frame, no dust on head board
☐	Night stand	No dust (top, sides, and inside), phone book neat, name card
☐	Phone	No grease, makeup, or hair on receiver, clean dial and sides, clean cord, no dust at the back
☐	Waste basket	Clean and in good condition
☐	Desk drawer	Proper number of each in proper place (map, A.M. express, choose your credit, advance registration, stationery, two plastic bags, fly swatter)
☐	Dresser supplies	Proper number in proper places (Bible, we care, room service, menu, guest services directory, correct ashtray with matches, tray placed longway against back of right hand dresser with four glasses and pitcher cleaned and turned upside down)
Remarks:		**Work orders:**

Figure 1.2 Guest Room
Inspection Form (*continued*)

divide them into three separate groups. Group 1 contains tasks that may be done by someone else immediately. Group 2 contains tasks that may be assigned to other people as soon as they have been properly trained. Group 3 contains tasks that must be done *only* by the manager. People are assigned group 1 tasks as soon as staff is available. Training is started for people to undertake group 2 tasks. As soon as training is complete and competence is shown, the tasks in group 2 are assigned. Group 3 tasks remain with the manager. The number of tasks remaining in group 3 is usually a measure of the manager's confidence to train people and let them become involved.

Why Managers Do Not Delegate

Often managers do not delegate tasks properly. The reasons can be summed up as follows:

1. *Some managers do not understand their roles as managers.* This happens most often with newly appointed managers who have been promoted from within as a reward for outstanding service. For example, the section housekeeper who has been doing an outstanding job as a room attendant is rewarded by being promoted to the position of supervisor, although he or she is given no supervisory training. Having been physically very busy in the act of cleaning guest rooms, the person is now in charge and as such feels out of place. The new supervisor (manager) has been moved from a realm in which he or she was very competent to a position in which he or she has little or no expertise. In Figure 1.1 we saw that a manager should be continually analyzing problems, making decisions, and communicating. Failing to understand this new role, the new supervisor

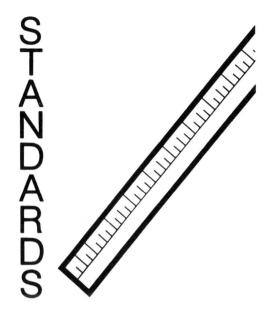

STANDARDS

1. Ceilings - Clean, free of dust and spots, paint intact, vents clean and free of dust and lint, lights replaced.

2. Room Walls - Clean, no lint, paint intact, free of finger marks and stains.

3. Floors - Clean, free of dust, lint, and stains; no wax buildup or accumulation of soil in corners; free of heel and scuff marks; free of discolored wax.

4. Cove Bases - Clean and clear, no wax buildup, no mop marks, no accumulation of soil in corners, intact around room (firmly affixed to wall with no signs of being loose at juncture with floor).

5. Doors - Clean, free of marks, finish intact, kickplate clean and shiny, top free of dust and lint, edges clean, handle or knob clear and clean, hinge facing and door frame clean, door vent clean and free of dust and lint, window and frame clean and free of dust and lint (inside and outside).

6. Windows - Clear and clean, not in need of immediate washing, frame clean; glazing intact; sill clean; paint in good condition.

7. Window Drapes - Free of lint; properly hung on tracks; not faded; no stains, yellowing, or tears; pulleys and pull cords intact and working; pins installed correctly in drapes and on carriers.

8. Cubicle Curtains - Clean and free of stains, not faded, pull freely in tracks, properly mounted, no tears, adequate length and width.

9. Beds - Headboards and footboards clean, metal upright and horizontal frame members clean, control unit and cord clean and working, linen clean and free of stains and tears, bed properly made, undercarriage free of lint and soil, wheels clean and free of lint.

10. Mattresses - Clean, free of stains and lint, in good repair without rips or tears, thoroughly deodorized, mattress turned on each discharge.

11. Overbed Tables - Clean and free of dust; elevation controls working properly, drawer and drawer mirror clean and free of dust, lint, and streaks; base, frames, and wheels clean and free of dust and lint.

12. Bedside Console Units - Counter top, shelves, and facings clean and free of dust and spots; no accumulation of soil in corners; stainless steel sink and plumbing fixtures clean and free of spots and streaks; clothes closet clean and free of dust and lint.

13. Chairs - Clean, free of lint and dust.

14. Television Sets - Clean, free of dust and lint; shelf clean, free of dust and lint.

15 Toilets - Toilet bowl clean inside and outside; no stains, streaks, or residue, toilet seat clean, free of spots, stains, or streaks, and tightly fastened to toilet; plumbing fixtures clean, free of dust, spots, and streaks; plumbing connections to toilet free of alkali buildup and dirt; base of toilet free of soil buildup and stains.

16. Sinks - Clean, inside, outside, and underneath, free of spots and streaks; plumbing fixtures on top and underneath free of dirt, spots, and streaks; base of plumbing fixtures free of alkali buildup.

17. Mirrors - Clean, free of spots and streaks; frame top and edges free of dust and lint; shelf clean, free of spots and streaks.

18. Shower Stalls - Walls clean, free of soil buildup on caulking, caulking intact; fixtures free of spots and streaks; door frame and glass free of dust, lint, spots, and streaks, horizontal cross bars above door free of dust, lint, spots and streaks.

19. Dispensers - Soap, paper towel, and seat cover dispensers clean, free of dust and lint on top and underneath, free of spots and streaks, supplies replenished.

20. Refrigerators - Clean, free of dust spots and stains; shelves and facing clean and free of spots, spills, and stains, freezer clear and free of stains; motor vent clean and free of dust and lint.

21. Ovens - Stainless steel top, sides and metal or glass door clean and free of spots and streaks; interior shelf, sides and top free of stains; no accumulation of soiled food on surface of oven (interior).

22. Counter Tops - Clean, free of dust, stains and finger marks.

23. Telephones - Clean, free of dust and lint; receiver, mouthpiece and dial free of dust and lint.

24. Drinking Fountains - Stainless steel free of spots and streaks.

Figure 1.3 A list of items that may be used as a basis for establishing standards, adding or deleting them as necessary for adaptation to a specific institution. This list can be used to develop an inspection form. (Reprinted with permission from *How to Organize and Maintain an Efficient Hospital Housekeeping Department,* by Charles B. Miller, published by American Hospital Publishing, Inc., © 1981.)

does someone else's work. For this reason supervisory training is an absolute must when promoting first-line workers into the positions requiring managerial performance such as supervising.

2. *Managers who enjoy physically doing work are sometimes reluctant to let go of such tasks.* Again, this is a matter of training. The new manager needs to be reminded that doing the task is not what he or she is being paid to do. A new manager may need to be reminded that, by doing physical work that should be delegated, situations requiring management decisions may go unnoticed because the manager is too busy to observe, evaluate, and direct operations.

3. *Less competent people fear the consequences of being outperformed.* There are managers who refuse to delegate routine tasks for fear that their own incompetence will be magnified. Surprisingly enough, their incompetence will be in managing the activities of others, not in their ability to perform the task that they do not delegate. These people are uneasy because they fear that a stronger person will eventually be able to perform their jobs. What some managers forget is that they cannot be pro-

moted themselves until someone is available and competent enough to replace them.

4. *Some managers feel that delegation is an all or nothing situation.* This may occur in spite of the fact that there are several **degrees of delegation.** Imagine the situation in which a manager needs to investigate a situation, decide if action is needed, and, if so, take the appropriate action. This task, or portions of it, may be delegated to another person, depending upon the degree of training and demonstrated ability of the person. Here are several degrees of delegation, any one of which might be used, depending upon the skill level and reliability of the subordinate.

   a. Investigate and report back
   b. Investigate and recommend a course of action
   c. Investigate and advise of intended action
   d. Investigate, take action, and keep manager informed
   e. Investigate and take action

5. *Some managers feel that if they do not do the task themselves, it will not be done properly.* This is synonymous with the often heard phrase, "If you want something done right, do it yourself." Sometimes it is ego that prompts this type of thinking, but more often it is the mark of a Theory X thinker. This type of attitude encourages inaction on the part of the employees and a feeling that they are not trusted with important matters. More importantly, it is counter productive to the creation of good morale-building environments. Many managers fear the possibility that some subordinate will rise to the occasion of being able to replace the manager. Said another way, some managers keep themselves in the position of being indispensable. Other managers recognize that until someone is capable of replacing them, they themselves are not promotable. What is important to remember is that until the manager trains people to act in his or her behalf and delegates as much as possible to subordinates, the manager need not think of promotion, vacation, or even becoming ill, lest the operation crumble.

Rewards and Motivation

Recognizing and rewarding proper employee performance is essential. Virtually all employees want to know if their performance meets management expectations, and most want to see a linkage between that performance and rewards.

The question that is often asked by managers is, "What form should these rewards take?" Some experts believe that although certain intangible rewards, such as recognition for achievement, may be nice, they are not as crucial to raising productivity as are the more tangible rewards (that is, money).[22]

This theory seems to be borne out by some recent experiments linking pay to productivity levels. The Country Lodging by Carlson chain, a subsidiary of the Carlson Hospitality Group, pays their housekeepers by the rooms they clean rather than by the hour.[23] This approach has reduced their need for full-time housekeepers and it has reduced the turnover and hiring costs in the housekeeping department. Housekeepers earn more and they earn it, on average, in a shorter workday.

Three cautions regarding the implementation of a pay-per-room program should be addressed. First, management must not take advantage of the employee by raising the benchmark standards of how many rooms ought to be cleaned in an hour. As Country Lodging's Vice President Kirwin says, "The goal is to get your rooms cleaned, not to take advantage of people."[24] They have set the productivity standard at 2.25 rooms per hour at Country Lodging.

Second, an incentive room inspection program should be part of the program so that the hotel's room cleanliness standards do not erode because of the pay-per-room program.

Third, it is doubtful that this program could be adopted in most union environments at this time.

We stated in the beginning of this section that intangible rewards, such as recognition, may not be as crucial to the improvement of productivity as the more tangible effects of money. While we believe this to be true, we certainly hold that recognition for employee achievement is an essential management technique.

One outstanding example of employee recognition in housekeeping is the annual Hotel Association of New York City Bed Making Contest.[25] Forty-five New York hotels participated in this event in 1989. The final contest was held in the Grand Ballroom of the New York Hilton with representatives of the broadcast and print media from the United States and Europe in attendance.

The 1989 winner, Ms. Hazel Maye, won an all-expense-paid trip to the Fontainebleau Resort Hotel and Spa in Miami Beach and a brass bed trophy. Ms. Maye's picture appeared in hundreds of newspapers and on dozens of television stations.

Here is an excellent example of a promotional vehicle that engenders a sense of pride and accomplishment in a hotel's housekeeping staff.

Management Theory and Housekeeping Administration

We have looked at the role of employee participation, management delegation, training, and rewards in influencing productivity in housekeeping. Each of these practices evolved from management theories. The answer, then, to the question of which theory should be applied in the housekeeping department is none of them, and at the same time, all of them. Each of them is appropriate at different times and under different circumstances (situational leadership).

Current research also seems to favor the situational leadership or contingency approach. Studies[26] have indicated that different circumstances demand different management approaches; the same **leadership style** does not work as effectively as a flexible style. The key variable that influences a manager's style, according to the situational leadership theorists, is the ability and attitude of the follower.

Although a manager's behavior may change, or an approach to a problem may be dictated by the ability and attitude of the follower, we believe that a manager should always maintain a high level of concern for both the organization and the employee; this concern should be reflected in everything that is said and done by management.

New Horizons in Management

Recent attempts to gain better guest acceptance of the service product being presented have yielded reports that the root problem noted by the guests was usually centered around the employee failing to perform adequately. Employee attitudes and motivations were also highly suspect; this was noticed when guests were asked to rank their most common complaints when visiting a hotel. Appearing at the top of most lists were the guests' concerns about employee attitudes. More detailed studies, however, have indicated that a clear 85 percent of all guest and service quality problems were the result of systems, policies, and procedures that were either outdated, inappropriate, or restrictive to the need to take care of the guest. Only 15 percent of quality problems were associated directly with the employee's failure to perform properly in the employee's relationship with the guest.

Other studies addressed the issue of quality assurance in hotel operations. Such was the case of the American Hotel and Motel Association's sponsored study conducted at the Sheraton Scottsdale in Scotts-

dale, Arizona.[27] This study was primarily concerned with problem solving in areas where guest comments indicated a quality problem in rendering service to the guest.

Theory Z technique was applied at the Sheraton Scottsdale and several focus groups (created from among several first-line employees who would be most conversant with the particular problem being discussed) were formed to address the problem areas identified by guest comments. (The term *focus group* and *quality circle* are interchangeable). The focus group concept, once and for all, took recognition of the fact that it was the front-line employee who was actually delivering the product or service being offered; not the company, general manager, or the middle management of the property, or even the first-line supervisor. It is the front-line employee who, having the greatest contact with the guest, actually represents the entire organization to the guest. Too often in the past, when talking to the guest, the only answer available to the employee was, "you will have to talk to the manager."

By placing the guest's problem in front of those employees (focus group) who had the greatest knowledge about how to solve a problem (because they did the work in the area of the problem) quality standards would be raised. Having been involved in creating the new and better-quality standard, the employees would be more inclined to personally commit themselves to meeting the new standards. These new standards then became the benchmarks for training or retraining of all employees: standards set by employees and agreed to by management.

The results of the changes developed through this sponsored study, as reported by Sheraton Scottsdale general manager Ken MacKenzie, included "growth in revenue of twenty-eight percent in the first year of the program, twenty-five percent in the second year, and a group of supportive employees. You don't buy them or hire them, you develop them."[28]

Employees Renamed and Empowered

Further recognition of the results obtained with Theory Z and focus groups has resulted in many hotel companies referring to their employees no longer as employees but as **"associates."**

In addition, associates are being **empowered** to do whatever is necessary to resolve problems for the guest, rather than to refer problems up to management.

Empowerment is actually a form of ultimate delegation that allows the person who is delivering the product and is most closely in touch with the problem to do (within certain boundaries) whatever is necessary to "make it right" for the guest.

Empowerment as a program is not reflected by the employee taking power but by being granted power from the supervisor after being properly trained to meet written standards that have been prepared by the associates, and have been accepted by management. Should an employee make a mistake through empowerment, he or she may be counseled or retrained.

These quality and empowerment concepts are now being developed by several hotel organizations into what is becoming known as Total Quality Management (TQM). According to Stephen Weisz, Regional Vice-President, Middle Atlantic Region, Marriott Hotels, Inc., "TQM encompasses having an understanding of customer requirements, and modifying product and service delivery to meet these re-

quirements, customers being both external and internal to the company."

Summary

In this chapter we briefly traced the origins of hospitality and housekeeping, as well as the development of management theory and its application to the housekeeping function.

Our exploration of housekeeping and management theory has by no means been exhaustive. It is impossible to discuss all of the contributors and their contributions to management here, but we will be referring to some of the major contributors throughout this text, particularly the sequential functions of management as revised and expanded by R. Alec Mackenzie. Keep these principles in mind and refer to them as you read this text.

KEY TERMS AND CONCEPTS

Hospitality
Line organization
Span of Control
Delegation
Classical School
Administrative theory
Scientific management
Scientific method
Management science
Operations research
Behavioral school
Human relations
Theory X
Theory Y
Satisfiers
Dissatisfiers
Participative management
Theory Z
Managerial grid
Situational leadership
Contingency approach
Quality circle
Elements
Ideas

Things
People
Functions
Continuous functions
Conceptual thinking
Administration
Leadership
Sequential functions
Management plan
Organize
Staffing
Directing
Control
Motivation
Productive
Turnover
Absenteeism
Insubordination
Exit interviews
Standard Operating Procedures
Degrees of Delegation
Leadership Style
Associates
Empowered

DISCUSSION AND REVIEW QUESTIONS

1. How has the function of executive housekeepers changed over the years?
2. Discuss the contributions of the following people to the science of management:
   Henri Fayol
   Frederick W. Taylor
   Douglas McGregor
   Frederick Herzberg
   Rensis Likert
   R. R. Blake

3. Explain Theory X and Theory Y. Why are these theories significant in the development of worker morale and job enrichment?
4. What are the three elements of delegation? Discuss the importance of each element. What are some of the reasons why managers do not delegate?
5. Alex Mackenzie provides us with a matrix that relates many management principles, terms, functions, and activities. Recall as many as you can from memory. Identify them as elements, continuous functions, sequential functions, or activities of these functions. In your opinion, which ones are the most important?
6. Discuss the difference between managers and leaders.

NOTES

1. Henry L. Sisk, *The Principles of Management: A Systems Approach* (Ohio: Southwestern Publishing Co., 1969), p. 24.
2. Louis E. Boone & David L. Kurtz, *Principles of Management* (New York: Random House, 1981), pp. 82–83.
3. Patrick Montana & Bruce Charnov, *Management* (New York: Barron's Educational Series, Inc., 1987), p. 14.
4. H. F. Merrill (ed.), *Classics in Management* (New York: American Management Association, 1960), p. 77. The passage quoted is from Frederick W. Taylor's testimony at hearings before the special committee of the House of Representatives to investigate Taylor and other systems of shop management, January 25, 1912, p. 1387.
5. Louis E. Boone & David L. Kurtz, *Principles of Management,* p. 36.
6. Robert Owen, *A New View of Society* (New York: E. Bliss and F. White, 1825), pp. 57–62. Reprinted in H. F. Merrill (ed.), *Classics in Management* (New York: American Management Association, 1960), pp. 21–25.
7. Patrick Montana & Bruce Charnov, *Management,* pp. 17–19.
8. Douglas McGregor, *The Human Side of Enterprise* (New York: McGraw-Hill Book Co., 1960), pp. viii, 33–34, 246.
9. Ibid., pp. 47–48, 246.
10. Frederick Herzberg, Bernard Mausner, and B. Snydeman, *The Motivation to Work,* 2nd ed. (New York: John Wiley & Sons, 1959).
11. Rensis Likert, *New Patterns of Management* (New York: McGraw-Hill Book Co., 1961), pp. 222–236.
12. Patrick Montana & Bruce Charnov, *Management,* pp. 26–28.
13. R. R. Blake, J. S. Mouton, L. B. Barnes, and L. E. Greiner, "Breakthrough in Organization Development," *Harvard Business Review,* vol. XXXXII, November-December 1964, pp. 133–155. For a complete description of the managerial grid, see Robert R. Blake and Jane S. Mouton, *The Managerial Grid* (Houston: Gulf Publishing Co., 1964).
14. Kenneth H. Blanchard & Paul Hersey, *Management of Organizational Behavior: Utilizing Human Resources* (Englewood Cliffs, New Jersey: Prentice Hall, 1988).
15. J. M. Shepard & J. G. Hougland, Jr. "Contingency Theory: 'Complex Man' or 'Complex Organization'?" Academy of Management Review, July 1978, pp. 413–427.
16. Fred E. Fielder, *A Theory of Leadership Effectiveness* (New York: McGraw-Hill Book Co., 1967).
17. Victor Vroom & Phillip W. Yetton, *Leadership and Decision-Making* (Pittsburgh: University of Pittsburgh Press, 1973).
18. Kenneth H. Blanchard & Paul Hersey, *Management of Organizational Behavior.*

19. R. Alec Mackenzie, "The Management Process in 3-D," *Harvard Business Review,* November–December 1969.

20. *Webster's New Ideal Dictionary,* rev. ed. (1978), s.v. "motive."

21. Douglas McGregor, *The Human Side of Enterprise,* p. 47.

22. Timothy Weaver, "Theory M: Motivating with Money," *The Cornell Hotel and Restaurant Administration Quarterly,* Vol. 29, No. 3, November 1988.

23. Paul Kirwin, "A Cost-Saving Approach to Housekeeping," *The Cornell Hotel and Restaurant Administration Quarterly,* Volume 31, No. 3, November 1990.

24. Ibid., p. 27.

25. Margaret Rose Caro, "N.Y. Housekeepers' Egos Bolstered by Competition," *Lodging,* Vol. 15, No. 5, January 1990.

26. Kenneth H. Blanchard & Paul Hersey, *Management of Organizational Behavior:* pp. 197–199.

27. Pearson, James, "A.H. & M.A. Observation Hotel in Quality Assurance. The Sheraton Scottsdales in Scottsdale, Arizona," *Lodging Magazine,* April and May, 1985.

28. Ibid., p. 58, April.

PART TWO

*Planning,
Organizing, and
Staffing the New
Organization*

I n Part One we introduced five sequential steps of
management—planning, organizing, staffing,
directing, and controlling. In Part Two you will
see how the first three steps apply to the management
functions of a newly assigned executive housekeeper
in a soon-to-open hotel. Chapters 2–9 will take you
through the management tasks of planning for a
new hotel, establishing position and job descriptions
for both environmental services departments in hospitals and for housekeeping departments in hotels,
scheduling workers, planning for necessary materials,
staffing for housekeeping operations, and operational
planning.

2

Conceptual Planning

CHAPTER OBJECTIVES

1. To find out how executive housekeepers begin planning
    for a soon-to-open hotel.
2. To learn about setting priorities.
3. To consider what may have already taken place in a new
    facility before the executive housekeeper comes on the
    scene.
4. To learn about the House Breakout Plan, Department
    Staffing Guide, and Table of Personnel Requirements.
5. To become aware of the team system of staffing.

As noted in Chapter 1, there are five sequential functions of management: planning, organizing, staffing,
directing, and controlling. Planning to administer a
housekeeping department affords one of the most classical experiences that might be found in the management profession. It is for this reason that Chapter 1 was
devoted primarily to landmarks of professional management development. It would therefore be a good
idea for you to refer to Mackenzie's chart of management terms, activities, and definitions while studying
this chapter on conceptual development.

The New Executive Housekeeper

Being appointed **executive housekeeper** of an ongoing operation has its challenges. After a brief introduction and orientation, the new manager would
normally be expected to improve upon and bring
about changes in operations related to the management potential for which he or she might have been
selected. Any executive housekeeper who has had
this experience might comment about how trying
the task of bringing about change can be and how
much easier it would have been if the operation could

be started over. There is considerable truth in such a statement.

Begin involved in a soon-to-open operation in which department planning has yet to be undertaken gives a manager the opportunity to influence how a department will be set up. Involvement in such an experience is both rewarding and enlightening and, once experienced, can prepare managers to bring about changes in an ongoing operation systematically and efficiently. The important point to remember, as stated by John Bozarth, is, "Good results without planning is good luck, NOT good management."[1] It is therefore essential that planning any operation, change, system, organization, or procedure be allotted a proper portion of the manager's energies.

Chapters 2–9 will place you in the role of a newly assigned executive housekeeper in a soon-to-open hotel. You will learn about the management planning that must take place to initiate operations, as well as about organizing and staffing a new operation. Once systems are developed and understood, you will see how they may be applied systematically and efficiently to ongoing operations.

The Executive Housekeeper's Position within the Organization

In the model hotel that we present in this text the executive housekeeper will be in the position of a **department head.** This position and level of responsibility is not uncommon in most transient hotels or hospitals that range in size from 200 to 3000 rooms. On the other hand, some executive housekeepers are below the department head level, whereas others may rank even higher. Many become executive committee members (top management within the facility) and others reach corporate executive levels. Many seek careers that develop along housekeeping lines, and others choose to be executive housekeepers and oversee the entire maintenance function of their hotels or health care facilities. Still others see an involvement in housekeeping as an entry into the hospitality or health care field. Regardless of position, all should have the freedom to communicate within channels to every level of the enterprise.

For all illustrative purposes in this text, we will presume that our newly assigned executive housekeeper will operate from the department head level and will report to the hotel **resident manager.**

The Model Hotel

Recognizing that the major hotel market in the United States is the corporate transient market, we selected a commercial transient hotel with resort flare—the Radisson Hotel at Star Plaza in Merrillville, Indiana (Figure 2.1)—as a **model hotel** to illustrate the systems and procedures that you will study.

The Radisson Hotel at Star Plaza

Located in the northwest corner of Indiana at the intersection of Interstate Highway 65 and U.S. 30, this Radisson originated as a typical roadside Holiday Inn, a franchised operation, located 6 miles south of the heart of the Midwest steel-producing region near Gary, Indiana. Strategically located on the main southern interstate highway south of the Chicago area, the Radisson at Star Plaza is the result of the vision of its owner and founder Dean V. White. In 1969 he constructed the first increment of this property, as a typical 120-room Holiday Inn, with a small restaurant, a cocktail lounge, and several small meeting rooms. In 1972 the property underwent its first enlargement by having 128 rooms and 6700 square feet of ballroom space added.

In 1979 the property's second enlargement took place, adding 105 guest rooms, more than doubling the size of meeting and convention space, adding an indoor pool and recreation area (Holidome), renovating all older guest rooms and food facilities, and joining a 3400-seat performing arts theater to the hotel. As a result of the 1979 expansion, the property became a system award winner and in 1983 changed its name from Holiday Inn, Merrillville, to Holiday Star Resort and Conference Center. In early 1990 the hotel franchise was changed from Holiday Inn to Radisson. The theater is now known as the Star Theater. Unless otherwise noted, we will use this 353-room commercial and resort hotel to show you the basis for housekeeping department planning and systems development.

Reporting for Work

Assume that you are in the position of the newly assigned executive housekeeper of the model hotel and have been told to report for work only 6 weeks before first opening. It is necessary for you to set priorities for your first activities. Recognizing that the housekeeping department consists of only one person (the executive housekeeper), you readily see that planning, organizing, and staffing functions

Figure 2.1 The Radisson Hotel at Star Plaza. The facility has 353 deluxe guest rooms, including 20 suites and two bilevel suites, seven restaurants and lounges, 18,000 square feet of convention space, and a 3300-seat theater. The hotel and convention center are connected to the theater (left) and to a Twin-Towers office complex (right) by enclosed overhead walkways. The conference center is owned and operated by White Lodging Services, a subsidiary of Whiteco Industries in Merrillville, Indiana. (Rendering courtesy of Whiteco Hospitality Corporation.)

are of first importance, and the efficient use of time is paramount. Not only is the planning of people functions important, but the design of systems, the establishment of procedures, the determination of supply and equipment needs, and reporting and coordinating relationships must be considered.

The executive housekeeper's experience usually begins by having the person to whom he or she will report (resident manager) introduce him or her to other on-board members of the hotel staff. These people are usually located in temporary hotel quarters such as a nearby office building.

It is at this time that the executive housekeeper will most likely be given the tentative chart of hotel organization, showing the positions of principal assistants to department heads. Figure 2.2 is an example of a hotel **organization chart** for our model hotel, showing the executive housekeeper position as that of department head in middle management.

Note the positions of the **executive committee** members at the top of the chart—this is the policy-making body of the hotel organization. Pay special attention to the positions of chief engineer and personnel director, which appear to be above the department heads and below the other members of the executive committee. The incumbents of these two positions are actually department heads, but by virtue of the fact that their staff functions cross all departments to which they will provide a staff service, they are (ex officio) members of the executive committee. They are in fact middle managers with department head status.

The executive housekeeper is on equal rank with the front office manager, with both reporting to the resident manager. The executive housekeeper will

have an assistant, tentatively titled **housekeeping manager.** In addition, operation of the property's laundry will be placed under the direction of the executive housekeeper, requiring another junior manager, **laundry manager,** to report to the executive housekeeper.

Considering that we have a new property under construction that has not yet begun hotel operations, it is important to note the probable advance time when different members of the hotel organization may have reported. The director of sales and marketing is usually the first major manager on the site, being there since ground breaking because advanced group room sales were begun at that time. The next major manager on site would probably be the chief engineer. This manager reports about the time the new building's foundation is completed and the first electrical and plumbing development has started. The chief engineer must monitor the birth of the mechanical systems, since this person will be expected to know these systems with great thoroughness. Sometimes the chief engineer will work as an assistant to the construction manager until construction is near completion. The third manager to report will probably be the general manager (six months before opening), followed by the resident manager and director of food and beverage (four months before opening), and the balance of the department heads (between six and eight weeks before opening). Junior management will report about four weeks before opening.

The significance of knowing who reports when becomes evident when we realize that the executive housekeeper must learn in six weeks what several others have been exposed to for a far greater time. For example, the executive

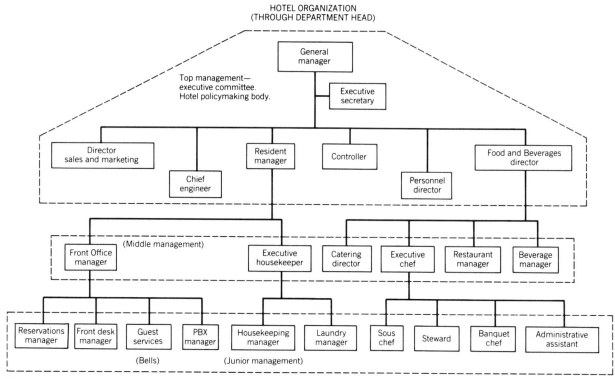

Figure 2.2 A hotel organization chart (through department heads and assistants) that might be presented to the executive housekeeper of our model hotel six weeks before opening. Note the position of the executive housekeeper in middle management and the expectation that the executive housekeeper will manage the laundry as well as the housekeeping department. The junior manager position, tentatively called housekeeping manager, would be the assistant to the executive housekeeper.

housekeeper has to learn about available supply, storage, and security spaces before distribution of these spaces is undertaken to make sure that the housekeeping department is not slighted in the assignment of such space.

Reporting relationships also are significant. Coordination between housekeeping and front office personnel requires the respect and understanding of each of the department managers for the others' responsibilities. In addition, the executive housekeeper will have many occasions to relate to other members of the total hotel organization. It is therefore important to know and become known to each of these managers, and a respect and understanding needs to be developed for each of them and their functions. Others should in turn develop an understanding and respect for the functions of the housekeeping department and its significance in the total operation.

Becoming acquainted with the new surroundings includes obtaining a set of working architectural drawings of the rooms portion of the hotel. Such drawings will allow the executive housekeeper to study the physical layout of the facility and will provide the basis for determining the scope of involvement and delineation of responsibilities of the

various managers' areas. In addition, working drawings will assist the executive housekeeper when onsite inspections are begun.

Once the executive housekeeper has an understanding of who is who in the organization; has a knowledge of how long each person has been on site, how knowledgeable certain managers are, and how helpful they can be; has met all the members of the management team thus far assembled; and has a copy of the working architect's drawings of the rooms department and related areas, he or she is ready to be shown the temporary working area in which departmental planning may begin.

Early Priority Activities

Given the various activities that make up the functions of planning, organizing, and staffing, there will be a mixture of activities that take place at the same time. Whereas there is an obvious need to determine what is to be done and how to go about doing it, there is an equal and urgent need to define the need for, establish the requisite qualifications of, and recruit the housekeeper's two principal assistants as soon as possible—the housekeeping manager and the laundry manager. Until these two managers are present, the entire planning, organizing, and staffing function rests on the shoulders of the executive housekeeper. Thus we see the immediate need to specify the qualifications of these two managers to the personnel director in order that advertisements may be placed and recruitment begun. Recruitment is an immediate concern and will remain a part of the daily concern of the executive housekeeper until these people are hired, usually within 10 days to 2 weeks.

Division of Work Document

The work that must actually be accomplished for the entire property needs to be recognized and identified as soon as possible. The executive housekeeper should make regular daily tours of the property under construction and, as soon as possible, draw up what is known as the **Division of Work Document**. This document is a recognition of what will be required in cleaning the property; all departments must become aware of this. The division of work document should include, but not necessarily be limited to, the care and maintenance of the following:

Rooms Department Includes guestrooms, room corridors, elevators, elevator landings, stairwells, storage areas

Public Areas Associated with the sale of guestrooms; the front desk, main entrance, public thoroughfares, public restrooms, storage areas and similar locations

Recreation Areas Indoor and outdoor pools, health clubs, saunas, game rooms, public restrooms, storage areas

Restaurants Dining areas and service areas

Cocktail Lounges Bar area, service areas, liquor storage areas

Meeting Rooms Each by name, indicating the number of square feet in service and storage areas

Banquet and Ballrooms Each by name, indicating the number of square feet in service and storage areas

Kitchen Areas Main kitchen, banquet kitchens, salad preparation areas, refrigerators, freezers, holding boxes, food storerooms

Employee Areas Includes locker rooms, employee restrooms, employee cafeteria

Offices All offices, such as sales, reservations, and executive offices, that the public might be expected to frequent

Maintenance Shops Main engineering work area; TV workshops; electrical, plumbing, refrigeration, and paint shops

Building Exterior

Landscaping

Lighting

Laundry

Other

Once completed, the executive housekeeper should present the division of work document to the executive committee for review, listing the areas by name, noting anything unusual about expected cleaning requirements, and offering a recommendation as to who should be responsible for cleaning and maintaining each area.

Whereas most executive housekeepers are involved only in the guestroom portion of the hotel and related public areas, it is not unusual to be assigned the responsibility for nightly cleaning of kitchens, afterevent ballroom cleaning, swimming pool maintenance, and similar tasks. There is essentially nothing wrong with inheriting such responsibilities *provided* sufficient funds and staff are allocated to compensate for the additional workload. Many times trade-offs are reasonable, such as the food and beverage department maintaining the employees' cafeteria at no cost to other departments and the housekeeping departments maintaining all public restrooms regardless of where they are. However, if the housekeeping department is expected to clean an area foreign to the rooms department, such as kitchens, banquet space, restaurants, or cocktail lounges, then budgetary compensation and personnel must be provided to the housekeeping department and charged to the department receiving the service. It is always proper that costs be levied against the revenue generated in each of the various departments.

A Recommendation for Clean-As-You-Go

It might seem most efficient to place all cleaning responsibilities under one manager for control, but employees are inclined to be more careful and make less mess if they are required to clean up after themselves. Thus departments charged with cleaning their own facilities create their own cost category for cleaning expense, which is to be charged against revenue generated rather than to another department.

At any rate, if the housekeeping department is to be responsible for cleaning any area aside from the actual rooms department, monetary and personnel compensation is in order.

Area Responsibility Plan

Once the division of work document has been submitted to the executive committee for review and the executive housekeeper has made recommendations to the resident manager (member of the executive committee), the **Area Responsibility Plan** can be drawn up by the executive committee. This plan is an assignment of responsibility of the various areas mentioned in the division of work document and shows various cleaning area boundaries on a copy of a floor plan blueprint. Such boundary lines are important to ensure that no space is left unassigned and that no overlaps in cleaning responsibilities occur. The area responsibility plan is usually the result of the advance thinking and planning by an experienced executive housekeeper who makes regular tours of the property. The plan should be forthcoming from the executive committee within the first week of the housekeeper's tenure.

Continuous Property Tours

An important reason for regular and frequent tours of the property before actual operation is to learn the various locations of storerooms and service areas. There is little question regarding the main linen room, the laundry, and major storage areas. However, most hotels have small storage or service areas located in secluded places throughout the facility. It is important that the executive housekeeper note these out-of-the-way areas in order that enlightened negotiations for their use can take place when the time comes. For example, the executive housekeeper will need satellite (floor) linen rooms and the chief engineer will need storage area and TV repair space. Joint tours are highly recommended in order that department heads can reason with one another about the use of such space.

Housekeeping Department Organization

The next task of the executive housekeeper is to develop the **housekeeping department organization.** Let us assume that the Area Responsibility Plan indicates that the housekeeping department personnel will be responsible for cleaning the rooms and associated public facilities areas, the offices, the recreation facilities, and all public restrooms. Figure 2.3 sets forth an organization chart that indicates the assignment of such responsibility.

Note that a portion of the organization devoted to cleaning rooms is not yet firm and may undergo considerable change before the final departmental organization is arrived at. However, assistant managers are clearly in place, and the task of organizing the laundry will be delegated to the laundry manager as soon as he or she is selected. The first-line hourly supervisory structure provides for evening operations (3:30 P.M. to midnight), linen room operations (communication central), public area and utility personnel supervision, and supervision of recreation areas (two swimming pools, whirlpool, game room, sauna, and associated public restrooms). The actual size of the largest part of the organization (that which is associated with pure guestroom cleaning and servicing) is accommodated by applying a technique known as **zero-base budgeting.** Zero-base budgeting refers to worker use that takes into account actual occupancy on a specific day or for a specified period of time. Worker staffing and eventual scheduling are limited on a daily basis to the service of that specified occupancy and no more.

House Breakout Plan

The next major planning step that the executive housekeeper must undertake is the development of the **House Breakout Plan.** In order to ensure maximum familiarity with the facility, it is highly recommended that the executive housekeeper personally develop this pictorial representation of every guestroom as it is located within the hotel. This is done by making a line drawing of the guestroom portion of the hotel, showing the relative positions of guestrooms, corridors, service areas, and other areas significant to guestroom cleaning. Figures 2.4 through 2.7 are examples of such drawings for our model hotel.

Criteria for Workloads

As the house breakout plan is being created, certain criteria must be established: specifically, the workload of room attendants. The U. S. national average for rooms cleaned per day by one person ranges from 14 to 16 rooms, but the actual number may range from 13 rooms per day (eight-hour shift) to a high of 20 rooms per day, depending upon the type and nature of hotel activity. In resort hotels with many metal surfaces to polish, mirrors to clean, and multiple occupancy guests who sleep in late, the workload of a room attendant may be only

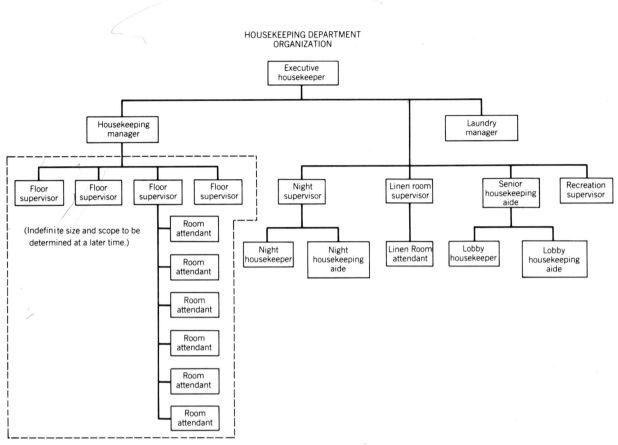

Figure 2.3 Housekeeping department organization. The executive housekeeper's first conception of department organization. Note the separation of tasks to be performed under various supervisors. The number of floor supervisors and the floor worker organization remains to be determined.

13 rooms per day. In transient operations of standard size rooms, where room occupancy consists primarily of business people (usually single occupancy) who arise and vacate early each day, room attendants can clean as many as 20 rooms per day—and clean them well if properly equipped and trained for efficient operation. (It is not a matter of working harder, just smarter.) In our model hotel, experience dictates that approximately 18 rooms per day would not be unreasonable, taking into account special areas of the hotel in which cleaning loads might be dropped to 17 rooms per day.

Room Sections and House Divisions

Based upon the workload criteria, the house breakout plan can now show the facility divided up into room sections. A **room section** is a group of 13 to 20 guest rooms, reasonably contiguous to each other, that may normally be cleaned and serviced by one person in one eight-hour shift. The room section will normally be assigned a number and for purposes of illustration will be cleaned by a person called a **section housekeeper.**

In order for the room sections to be grouped into logical units for supervisory and control needs, **house divisions** will be used. A **house division** is a group of four to six room sections with associated and/or specified corridors, elevators, stairwells, service areas, and storage areas. It may be assigned a color or letter designation and placed under the charge of a supervisor. For demonstration purposes with our model hotel, house divisions will be color coded and placed under a supervisor known as a **senior housekeeper.**

We can use the pictorial drawings in Figures 2.4–2.7 to determine the room sections and house divisions in the model hotel. We have the 18-room-per-day criteria and 353 rooms that must be cleaned under 100 percent occupancy conditions. If we divide 353 rooms by 18 rooms per day, we get 19.6 room sections. Since a partial section is not practical or economical, we divide the house into 20 sections of either 17 or 18 rooms each. Additionally, five section housekeepers will form a house division for supervisory and control purposes.

The house breakout plan may now be completed by considering the size of sections, assembly of house

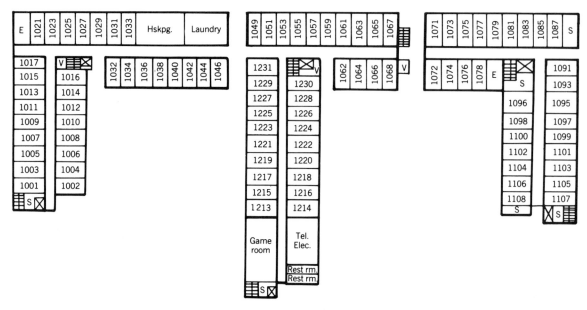

Figure 2.4 Floor plan layout house breakout plan of the model hotel; 94 first-floor rooms. Abbreviations for Figures 2.4–2.7: S, storage; V, vending; E, electrical switch room; X, elevator; GL, guest laundry.

divisions, location of contiguous rooms, position of elevators, and transportation from room to room.

Figure 2.8 shows how the first floor of the model hotel in Figure 2.4 has been divided into room sections 1 to 5, of 18 rooms each. In addition, the entire first floor of the model hotel has been combined to form the red division, which contains a total of 90 rooms for supervision and control by the senior housekeeper. Note the four excess rooms on the first floor (rooms 1023, 1025, 1027, and 1029). At 100 percent occupancy, these rooms are not a part of

the red division but will be cleaned by a section housekeeper from the second floor who will pick up these rooms as part of another section. Figures 2.9, 2.10, and 2.11 show the same planning procedure used in Figure 2.8 for Figures 2.5, 2.6, and 2.7, respectively.

Note that the number of rooms on the second and third floors is much greater than that on the first floor. This requires consideration when forming the remaining house divisions. Figures 2.9, 2.10, and 2.11 show the creation of the yellow division on the second floor (composed of sections 6 through 10—

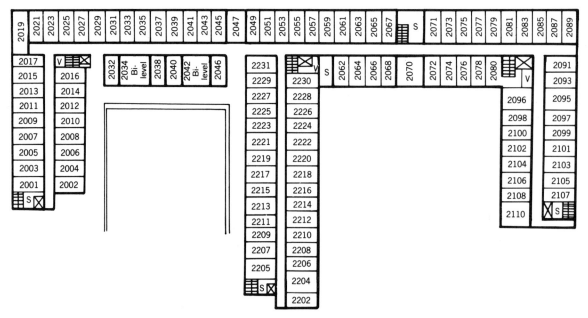

Figure 2.5 Floor plan layout of the model hotel; 114 second-floor rooms.

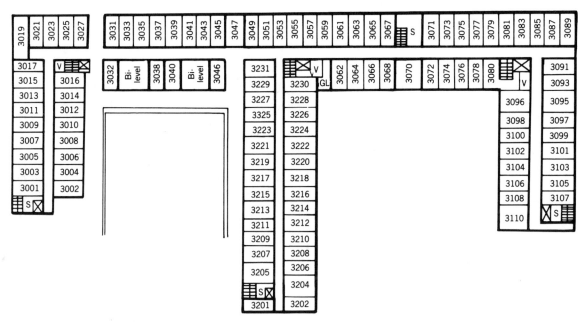

Figure 2.6 Floor plan layout house breakout plan of the model hotel; 112 third-floor rooms.

west end of second floor), the brown division on the third floor (composed of sections 11 through 15—west end of third floor), and the green division on the fourth floor (composed of sections 16 through 19—east end of the building). Section 7 is completed by including the four rooms on the first floor that are not a part of the red division. Note the proximity of these rooms to section 7 (directly below and adjacent to an elevator).

The house breakout plan developed in this chapter is by no means the only way the model hotel can be broken into logical work units. It does, however, reflect an efficient method of division of the workload. This particular technique also lends itself to a form of work scheduling (known as team scheduling, which will be dealt with in Chapter 3).

Staffing Considerations

Most hotel housekeeping departments will hire and individually schedule section housekeepers on an as-needed basis depending on occupancy. Whereas union operations may require the guarantee of a 40-hour work-week for **regular employees,** most union houses have few such regular employees. Union operations have considerably more people, referred to as **steady extras,** who can be called upon on an as-needed basis (when occupancy exceeds 25 to 40 percent).

Nonunion operations seldom guarantee a 40-hour workweek but will staff in such a way (based on expected occupancy) so as to provide between 35 and 40 hours of work each week for their regular employees.

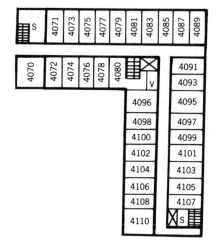

Figure 2.7 Floor plan layout house breakout plan of the model hotel; 33 fourth-floor rooms.

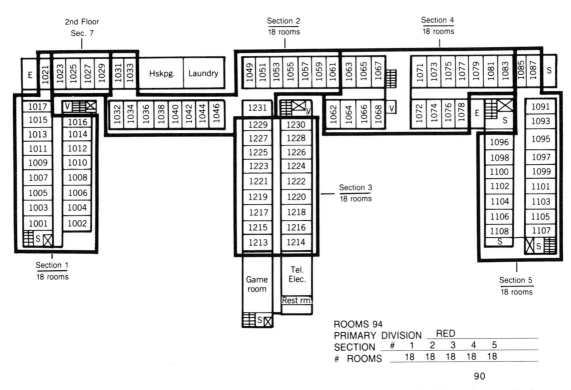

Figure 2.8 House breakout plan of the model hotel; first floor. S, storage; V, vending; E, electrical switch room; X, elevator; GL, guest laundry.

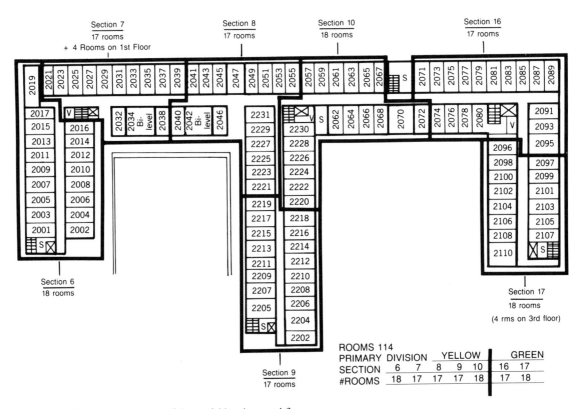

Figure 2.9 House breakout plan of the model hotel; second floor.

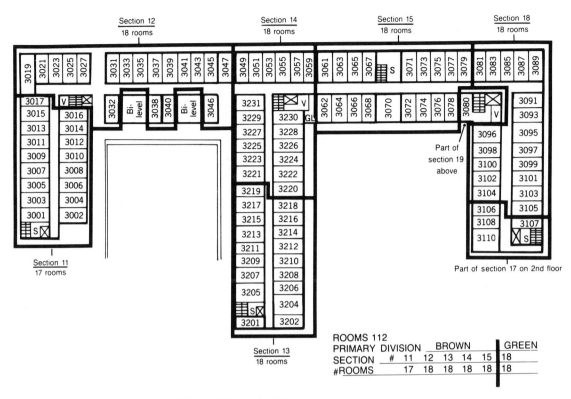

Figure 2.10 House breakout plan of the model hotel; third floor.

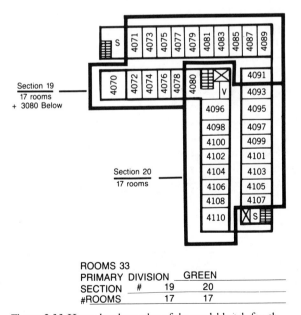

Figure 2.11 House breakout plan of the model hotel; fourth floor.

Recognizing that labor costs within a housekeeping department are the highest recurring costs in a rooms department budget, it is highly inefficient to guarantee a set number of regular employees 40 hours when occupancy is low. For this reason a practical number of employees will be hired based on expected occupancy for a given period of time.

Section housekeepers are scheduled on an individual but rotating basis to ensure a fair and equal spread of the available hours. Sometimes the size of the hotel might warrant the scheduling of several hundred such employees on a daily basis. Such scheduling techniques are time consuming and tedious. As a result, we will use a different scheduling concept that has been tested and proven to have many advantages over individual housekeeper scheduling.

Team Concept in Staffing

Rather than scheduling housekeepers on an individual basis, **housekeeping teams** may be formed. A housekeeping team consists of one supervisor (senior housekeeper) who is in charge and one section housekeeper for each section within a division. Since a house division includes the cleaning and care of corridors, stairwells, elevators, and designated service areas as well as associated guestrooms, the additional position of **section housekeeping aide** is required on a team. (This is the nonsexist term for houseman.) This position may be filled by any person capable of performing the work set forth in the job description (see job description of the section housekeeping aide in Appendix A). Teams consisting of one senior housekeeper, five section housekeepers, and one housekeeping aide can now be formed, identified by a corresponding color designation, and assigned to corresponding house divisions (for instance, red team to the red division; yellow team to the yellow division). Recall that the team system of organization thus far only deals with the subject of staffing. The actual day-to-day scheduling within teams will be based on actual occupancy and will be discussed in Chapter 3.

Swing Teams

The assignment of regular teams to house divisions for staffing purposes satisfies the need for division cover age, but it becomes obvious that the hotel operating on a seven-days-per-week basis will require additional personnel to work when regular teams have days off. To accommodate days off, **swing teams** may be formed.

Consider the requirement that no employee may work more than a 40-hour week without the provision of overtime. It becomes prudent to assume that a 40-hour week consisting of five regular eight-hour days will be the standard and that the sixth and seventh day of work in a house division must be accomplished by using additional employees.

Recall that the housekeeping department in the model situation will also operate a laundry. The laundry has about the same staffing requirements and will face the same situation of a seven-day operation, with employees requiring two days off each week. By combining the total workforce of the section housekeepers and laundry attendants (20 section housekeepers, five laundry attendants, supervisor and aides for each group), a relief situation can be developed as follows:

$$20 \text{ section housekeepers} + 5 \text{ laundry attendants} = 25 \text{ employees}$$

$$25 \text{ employees} \times 7 \text{ days/week} \text{ requires } 175 \text{ man-days of effort}$$

$$175 \text{ man-days} \div 5 \text{ maximum number of days allowed} = 35 \text{ employees needed}$$

This same formula can be applied to supervisors and section housekeeping aides.

The original 25 employees will require an additional 10 employees to relieve them if a five-day workweek is to be adhered to. By forming two extra teams from the 10 extra employees, with each team having a supervisor and a housekeeping aide, a staffing rationale may be created as follows

REGULAR ASSIGNED EMPLOYEES	RELIEF
Red team	Swing team 1 relieves two days per week
Yellow team	Swing team 1 relieves two days per week
Brown team	Swing team 2 relieves two days per week
Green team	Swing team 2 relieves two days per week
Laundry team	Each swing team relieves in the laundry one day per week

As you can see, not only are the four regular teams and the laundry staff now regulated to five days each week for staffing purposes, each swing team is also staffed for a five-day week. It should be remembered that the development of the above criteria pertains to staffing only. The actual day-to-day scheduling and employee needs based on occupancy considerations will be discussed in Chapter 3.

Completion of the Department Organization

The staffing requirement of the housekeeping department may now be completely defined. The incomplete department organization shown in Figure 2.3 may be completed by the addition of six teams—four regular teams (identified as red, yellow, brown, and green), each having one supervisor, one section housekeeping aide, five section housekeepers, and two swing teams (identified as swing teams 1 and 2). The swing teams will each work four days in the rooms section of the hotel and one day in the laundry.

The Staffing Guide

A major phase of personnel planning may now be completed by formulation of the **Department Staffing Guide.** Table 2.1 sets forth a staffing guide showing each and every position that must be filled within the department using the team concept of staffing.

The department staffing guide provides for personal and numerical identification of every person who must be hired for the department. A copy may be given to the personnel department and the resident manager for review and critique of staffing plans. Note that space is provided for writing in the employees' names opposite the position numbers. When vacancies oc-

Table 2.1   Department Staffing Guide

POSITION NO.	TITLE	NAME ASSIGNED
Management Team		
1	Executive housekeeper	_____
2	Housekeeping manager	_____
3	Laundry manager	_____
Fixed Team		
4	Linen room supervisor	_____
5	Linen room attendant	_____
6	Senior housekeeping aide (public area supervisor)	_____
7	Public area housekeeper 1 (male)	_____
8	Public area housekeeper 2 (female)	_____
9	Public area housekeeper (relief)	_____
Evening team		
10	Night supervisor	_____
11	Night section housekeeper	_____
12	Night housekeeping aide	_____
13	Night (public area) housekeeper 1 (male)	_____
14	Night (public area) housekeeper 2 (female)	_____
15	Night (public area) housekeeper (relief)	_____
Regular Rooms Cleaning Teams: *Red Team*		
16	Senior housekeeper (supervisor)	_____
17	Section housekeeping aide	_____
18	Section housekeeper 1	_____
19	Section housekeeper 2	_____
20	Section housekeeper 3	_____
21	Section housekeeper 4	_____
22	Section housekeeper 5	_____
Yellow Team		
23	Senior housekeeper (supervisor)	_____
24	Section housekeeping aide	_____
25	Section housekeeper 6	_____
26	Section housekeeper 7	_____
27	Section housekeeper 8	_____
28	Section housekeeper 9	_____
29	Section housekeeper 10	_____

Table 2.1   Department Staffing Guide *(continued)*

POSITION NO.	TITLE	NAME ASSIGNED
Brown Team		
30	Senior housekeeper (supervisor)	_____
31	Section housekeeping aide	_____
32	Section housekeeper 11	_____
33	Section housekeeper 12	_____
34	Section housekeeper 13	_____
35	Section housekeeper 14	_____
36	Section housekeeper 15	_____
Green Team		
37	Senior housekeeper (supervisor)	_____
38	Section housekeeping aide	_____
39	Section housekeeper 16	_____
40	Section housekeeper 17	_____
41	Section housekeeper 18	_____
42	Section housekeeper 19	_____
43	Section housekeeper 20	_____
Laundry		
44	Laundry supervisor (washman)	_____
45	Laundry helper/sorter	_____
46	Laundry attendant (ironer)	_____
47	Laundry attendant (ironer)	_____
48	Laundry attendant (folder/stacker)	_____
49	Laundry attendant (folder/stacker)	_____
50	Laundry attendant (folder/stacker)	_____
Swing Team 1		
51	Senior housekeeper (swing supervisor)	_____
52	Section housekeeping aide (ST-A)	_____
53	Section housekeeper A-1	_____
54	Section housekeeper A-2	_____
55	Section housekeeper A-3	_____
56	Section housekeeper A-4	_____
57	Section housekeeper A-5	_____
Swing Team 2		
58	Senior housekeeper (swing supervisor)	_____
59	Section housekeeping aide (ST-B)	_____
60	Section housekeeper B-1	_____
61	Section housekeeper B-2	_____
62	Section housekeeper B-3	_____
63	Section housekeeper B-4	_____
64	Section housekeeper B-5	_____

cur, they will occur by position numbers and may be readily identified. Should projected occupancy be less than 90 percent for the upcoming year, certain established positions may be left unfilled until such time as increased occupancy is forecast.

Table of Personnel Requirements

After developing the house breakout plan and the staffing guide, the executive housekeeper can develop one of the most important day-to-day tools

for effective management of the housekeeping department—the Table of Personnel Requirements—illustrated in Table 2.2. This table has been developed for the model hotel in which there are 353 rooms and in which each section housekeeper will clean an average of 18 rooms per day.

At each percent of occupancy, the table establishes the number of rooms that will require service, the number of housekeepers required at the rate of 18 rooms cleaned per day each working eight hours a day, the number of housekeeper-hours required in an eight-hour workday, the number of housekeeper-

Table 2.2   Table of Personnel Requirements[a]

PERCENT OF OCCUPANCY	NUMBER OF ROOMS	NUMBER OF HOUSEKEEPERS PER DAY	HOUSEKEEPER HOURS/DAY	HOUSEKEEPER HOURS/WEEK	HOUSEKEEPER HOURS/28 DAY PERIOD
100	353	20	160	1120	4480
99	350	20	160	1120	4480
98	346	20	160	1120	4480
97	343	20	160	1120	4480
96	339	19	152	1064	4256
95	336	19	152	1064	4256
94	332	19	152	1064	4256
93	329	19	152	1064	4256
92	325	19	152	1064	4256
91	322	18	144	1008	4032
90	318	18	144	1008	4032
89	315	18	144	1008	4032
88	311	18	144	1008	4032
87	308	18	144	1008	4032
86	304	17	136	952	3808
85	300	17	136	952	3808
84	297	17	136	952	3808
83	293	17	136	952	3808
82	290	17	136	952	3808
81	286	16	128	896	3584
80	283	16	128	896	3584
79	279	16	128	896	3584
78	276	16	128	896	3584
77	272	16	128	896	3584
76	269	15	120	840	3360
75	265	15	120	840	3360
74	262	15	120	840	3360
73	258	15	120	840	3360
72	255	15	120	840	3360
71	251	14	112	784	3136
70	248	14	112	784	3136
69	244	14	112	784	3136
68	241	14	112	784	3136
67	237	14	112	784	3136
66	234	13	104	728	2912
65	230	13	104	728	2912
64	227	13	104	728	2912
63	223	13	104	728	2912
62	220	13	104	728	2912
61	216	12	96	672	2688
60	212	12	96	672	2688
59	209	12	96	672	2688
58	205	12	96	672	2688
57	203	12	96	672	2688
56	199	12	96	672	2688
55	195	11	88	616	2464
54	191	11	88	616	2464
53	187	11	88	616	2464
52	184	11	88	616	2464
51	181	11	88	616	2464

[a] This table is for a 353-room hotel with a work criteria of 18 rooms per day to be cleaned by one section housekeeper.

Table 2.2 Table of Personnel Requirements *(continued)*

PERCENT OF OCCUPANCY	NUMBER OF ROOMS	NUMBER OF HOUSEKEEPERS PER DAY	HOUSEKEEPER HOURS/DAY	HOUSEKEEPER HOURS/WEEK	HOUSEKEEPER HOURS/28 DAY PERIOD
50	177	10	80	560	2240
49	173	10	80	560	2240
48	169	10	80	560	2240
47	166	10	80	560	2240
46	162	9	72	504	2016
45	159	9	72	504	2016
44	156	9	72	504	2016
43	152	9	72	504	2016
42	149	9	72	504	2016
41	145	9	72	504	2016
40	142	8	64	448	1792
39	138	8	64	448	1792
38	135	8	64	448	1792
37	131	8	64	448	1792
36	127	8	64	448	1792
35	124	7	56	392	1568
34	121	7	56	392	1568
33	117	7	56	392	1568
32	114	7	56	392	1568
31	110	7	56	392	1568
30	106	6	48	336	1344
29	103	6	48	336	1344
28	99	6	48	336	1344
27	96	6	48	336	1344
26	91	6	48	336	1344
25	89	5	40	280	1120
24	85	5	40	280	1120
23	82	5	40	280	1120
22	78	5	40	280	1120
21	75	5	40	280	1120
20	71	4	32	224	896
19	67	4	32	224	896
18	64	4	32	224	896
17	60	4	32	224	896
16	57	4	32	224	896
15	53	3	24	168	672
14	50	3	24	168	672
13	46	3	24	168	672
12	43	3	24	168	672
11	39	3	24	168	672
10	36	2	16	112	448
9	32	2	16	112	448
8	29	2	16	112	448
7	25	2	16	112	448
6	22	2	16	112	448
5	18	1	8	56	224
4	15	1	8	56	224
3	11	1	8	56	224
2	7	1	8	56	224
1	4	1	8	56	224
0	0	0	0	0	0 base

hours per week, and the number of housekeeper-hours per 28-day period.

Construction of the table starts at zero base (see end of table), noting that at zero occupancy no housekeepers are required. Occupancy through 18 rooms requires one section housekeeper working an eight-hour day, occupancy through 36 rooms requires the addition of the second section housekeeper, and so on until occupancy above 96 percent requires the addition of the twentieth section housekeeper.

Every executive housekeeper must have a table of personnel requirements in order that the number of section housekeepers and the number of housekeeper's hours per day, per week, and per period may be determined quickly for every given occupancy. Such information becomes vital to the efficient scheduling and administration of any housekeeping department.

Job Descriptions

Along with the development of the Table of Personnel Requirements, a set of **Job Descriptions** and/or **Position Descriptions** must also be developed. This is done by developing a sequence of individual tasks for operations that may be grouped and then assigned to a single person. The grouping of such tasks is the creation of the position and job description.

If one is to take full advantage of the **motivators of achievement**—growth, responsibility, and recognition—one must examine every job very closely in order to see to it that the factors that make up the job itself will form the **"satisfiers"** referred to by Herzberg in Chapter 1. All too often, jobs are designed around people of special ability. This is not necessarily unprofessional, provided there is *no* possibility of losing the person for whom the job was designed. In most situations, however, this is not possible. When a person of special quality leaves or is transferred, we hope to fill the position with someone of equal capability. If no one can be found with the same abilities, the job must be redefined. This is often time consuming and may cause some reorganizing. It is a much wiser course of action to first specify the tasks that must be accomplished and then to group these tasks into logical units that have the lowest per unit cost.

When there is a choice about which tasks should be combined into a single job, the criterion of *lowest per unit cost* is applied. Since cost is to be minimized, it is logical to design tasks and combine them in such a fashion that the lowest level of skill is required. For example, we would not want to combine the

task performed by a guestroom attendant with those of a supervisor, because different skill levels are required. Similarly, the tasks involved in the job of a guestroom attendant should not be combined with those involved in the job of a lobby housekeeper. The rationale is that it would not be cost effective to have people cleaning rooms one minute and fulfilling other maintenance tasks in the lobby the next.

The objectives of a study of Job Descriptions must therefore be:

1. To find out what the individual tasks of operations are that make up the work of a housekeeping or environmental services department.
2. To see how these tasks are grouped into positions and job descriptions.
3. To understand the difference between Position Descriptions and Job Descriptions, and how each is used.
4. To see what goes into writing such documents.

Appendix A contains two complete sets of job descriptions: one for a hotel housekeeping department, and the other for a hospital environmental services department. The method by which the systems are to be presented differ only for the purpose of showing several different styles of presentation. One style can work just as easily as the other for either of the presentations being made.

Even though job descriptions may be written for unskilled, semiskilled, and skilled employees, they may also be written for supervisors, managers, and executives.

Position and Job Descriptions (Hotel Housekeeping Departments)

Position Descriptions are sometimes written for managers, or for those who have management prerogatives. Such people hire, fire, set wages, and make policy. The Position Description type of document sets forth the **basic function** of the manager and defines the **scope** of the manager's responsibilities and authority. **Specific responsibilities** that have been created for the manager and the **relationships to responsibility** they have with other members of the organization are listed. There is usually a statement, referred to as **work emphasis**, about how a manager should allot his or her time and efforts.

In the first examples of position descriptions for the executive housekeeper and housekeeping manager in Appendix A, note that the basic function listed in each position description is a simple statement of overall responsibility. The scope helps the manager define the limits of managerial authority. What usually follows the scope is a group of specific responsibilities (actual tasks that must be accomplished). Note that the terms "coordinate," "administer control," and "be responsible for" are used frequently. They imply that the specific tasks have been delegated to someone who is working for the manager.

Note also the *standard form,* first of the position descriptions for the department managers, then of the job descriptions for the working line personnel of the housekeeping department. These will differ when compared with those for the environmental services department.

Job Descriptions (Hospital Environmental Services Departments)

In the second half of Appendix A, the **environmental services department** of a hospital will be the subject of the presentation. Notice that position descriptions in this set do not come into play. The same form for the **job description** (*JD*) is used whether for manager or for worker. The documents remain an essential ingredient for all departments within the hospital and all departments will use the same format. The *JD* provides a synopsis of the requirements for each job classification. It is used by the personnel department when they recruit to fill an open position, as reference for a current employee, and as a resource in conducting performance evaluations.

The structure and number of job descriptions depends on the individual facility. The personnel or human resources department often has a preferred format for job assignments; the number needed will depend on the size and structure of the department. Those presented herein are working job descriptions for an environmental services department in a medium-to-large facility. Departments that are structured differently may require more, fewer, or have differing types of job descriptions. The uniqueness within each facility must be taken into consideration when developing the job description.

Summary

Although the day-to-day operation of a hotel housekeeping department can be interesting and rewarding, it also has its limitations. Many of the systems and procedures used in day-to-day operations are already developed. For this reason, we began from the point of view of a newly assigned executive housekeeper for a soon-to-open hotel. This situation required that planning be started from the beginning.

In this chapter, we selected a model hotel and showed many of the first plans that must be established. We also saw that priorities for activities become paramount. The executive housekeeper must quickly become familiar with the first hotel organization, which has been created before his or her arrival; making acquaintances with staff members already present can be valuable sources of information, including where future road blocks may occur. The executive housekeeper must quickly obtain a set of architect's drawings and begin planning staffing requirements and methods of operation. Daily property tours are a must in order that the executive housekeeper quickly learn every space with which future contact will be made. Departmental organization must be started, division of work documents created, an area responsibility plan recommended and approved, and the house breakout plan created.

First personnel planning is finished when the staffing guide is complete and a table of personnel requirements has been constructed. At this time the executive housekeeper is in a position to provide first labor budgets and actual staffing requirements. Immediate steps can be taken to acquire the two junior managers noted in the organization and to make the department ready to hire personnel at least two weeks before opening.

In this chapter, you were also introduced to the team system of staffing. Much more will be said about this method of staffing when you study scheduling, supervisory direction of effort, and morale-building environments. The scenarios presented here should in no way detract from other techniques that are workable and have been proven efficient and effective. Conversely, other departments outside of housekeeping, which must schedule in a manner sensitive to occupancy changes, would do well to consider team staffing as explained herein.

The third activity of Mackenzie's sequential functions of getting organized involves the creation of position and job descriptions. In order to take full advantage of Herzberg's satisfiers (see Chapter 1), position and job descriptions need to be designed based on the job, and not on the talents of specific people.

Job descriptions are written for unskilled, semiskilled, and skilled employees, as well as for supervisors, managers, and executives. The job descriptions in this chapter are for hourly employees; included here are first-line workers and supervisors who perform hands-on work.

Position descriptions are written for employees with management prerogatives who hire, fire, and set wages. Each position description gives the basic function, scope, specific responsibilities, relationships to responsibilities, and work emphasis. Examples were presented.

Appendix A contains a complete set of Job and Position Descriptions for a hotel housekeeping department and a complete set of Job Descriptions for a hospital environmental services department.

KEY TERMS AND CONCEPTS

Executive housekeeper
Department head
Resident manager
Model hotel
Organization chart
Executive committee
Housekeeping manager
Laundry manager
Division of Work Document
Area Responsibility Plan
Housekeeping department
  organization
Zero-base budgeting
House Breakout Plan
Room section
Section housekeeper
House division
Senior housekeeper
Regular employees

Steady extras
Housekeeping team
Section housekeeping aide
Swing team
Department Staffing Guide
Table of Personnel Requirements
Job description
Position description
Motivators of achievement
Satisfiers
Lowest per unit cost
Basic function
Scope
Specific responsibilities
Relationships to responsibility
Work emphasis
Environmental Services Department

DISCUSSION AND REVIEW QUESTIONS

1. Assume you are a newly assigned executive housekeeper for a soon-to-open hotel. Develop a priority list of action items to be completed before opening. How would you modify this list if the operation were already in progress?
2. In your own words, define zero-based staffing.
3. Discuss reasons why the executive housekeeper should develop a Division of Work Document. What is its relation to an Area Responsibility Plan?
4. The House Breakout Plan is developed from a line drawing of a floorplan of the guestroom portion of a hotel. Why should the executive housekeeper *personally* prepare this drawing?
5. Give four reasons why the executive housekeeper should make daily tours of a new facility before opening. Should these tours be made alone? If not, who should accompany the executive housekeeper?
6. What is the difference between a job description and a position description? Outline the elements of each.
7. Would it be inappropriate to indicate a wage or pay scale on a position description? On a job description? Justify your answer.
8. What is a management prerogative? Give several examples in addition to those listed in the text.
9. The preparation of a set of job descriptions is a part of which sequential function of management?
10. Using the job and position descriptions found in this chapter as a guide, prepare a position description for a laundry manager, a recreation supervisor, and a management trainee who is trained within the housekeeping department for six weeks.

NOTES

1. John Bozarth, C. E. H., "Leadership Styles—Where Do You Fit In?" *Executive Housekeeping Today*, May 1983, p. 20.

3

Planning to Schedule Workers: A Major Advantage of Housekeeper Team Staffing

Conventional Methods of Worker Scheduling
A Word About Team Staffing
    Promoting Teamwork
    Teamwork and Swing Teams

Standing Rotational and Tight Scheduling Systems
    Standing Rotational System
    Tight Scheduling System
Union Contracts and Their Effects on Scheduling

CHAPTER OBJECTIVES

1. To learn about conventional methods of worker scheduling.
2. To find out what team staffing is.
3. To learn what a standing rotational system of scheduling is and how to construct one.
4. To learn what tight scheduling is, how it fits in with a standing rotational system, and how to develop one.
5. To understand how to construct workweeks based on the standing rotational system.
6. To see how union contracts can affect worker scheduling.

Conventional Methods of Worker Scheduling

Not many hotels or hospitals close on Saturdays, Sundays, and holidays. **Worker scheduling** would be greatly simplified if such were the case. Everyone would have weekends and holidays off, and when doors of the department were closed, workers and managers alike could relax knowing that nothing was happening at the office.

In hotels, hospitals, restaurants, and other seven-day operations, however, worker scheduling is a major task that must be performed with absolute regularity. Not only must the manager and supervisor devote time and forethought to the task of scheduling, but they must also take into account the needs of people whom they schedule. For example, some workers may not be able to work on Tuesdays and others want weekends off; family demands and illness must also be recognized and accommodated. Add to these concerns the problem of fluctuating occupancy, which has the greatest effect on housekeeper scheduling, and the manager has a full-time task that may not allow time for other less repetitive but more creative tasks.

The manager who schedules a group of individual workers on a weekly basis and who must adjust schedules on a daily basis may well earn the label "tied down." In order to improve this routine of scheduling and in so doing greatly reduce the time that management has to spend performing these tasks, you should try the team system of organization and scheduling.

A Word About Team Staffing

The **team system of organization** presented in Chapter 2 has many advantages. A principal advantage to the manager is in being able to schedule a group of people as though it were one entity. It is true that not every person in the department can be handled in such a manner, but the majority of employees in a housekeeping department can be grouped for scheduling purposes. Another advantage of the team system of organization is the fact that co-operation and workers' morale will be higher as part of a small unit than as one in a large group of people. A worker who is a member of a seven-person team is much more likely to relate to team performance to which he or she can see a personal contribution than to a large organization in which he or she is but one of many.

The system of **team scheduling** and **staffing** also embraces the idea that the team will work together and will regularly be off together. Having assigned teams to work in specific areas of the hotel (red team in the red division, yellow team in the yellow division, and so on), the teams become responsible for the entire cleaning function in their areas. The team—which has a supervisor (senior housekeeper) in charge, several section housekeepers who clean guest rooms, and a section housekeeping aide who assists and also cleans other areas of the division such as corridors, stairwells, and elevators—becomes totally responsible for the entire division of the hotel. Cleaning performance within the division becomes a primary responsibility of the entire team under the supervisor, and performance is measured on a team basis rather than an individual basis.

If the premise that each individual worker wants to be a part of a worthwhile operation is true, team spirit will cause the entire group to excel. There will always be a few above-average section housekeepers who excel in rooms cleaning and take personal pride in their individual work; however, in the eyes of the guest, the reputation of the best housekeeper will never be better than the reputation of the poorest section housekeeper in the entire group. Section housekeepers, once they understand that their individual reputation is judged by performance of the poorest in the team, will become more willing to help the poorer performers to improve. It should not be surprising, therefore, to find many small disciplinary problems such as absenteeism and tardiness resolved at the team level because to be absent or late could have a negative effect on the team's reputation.

Promoting Teamwork

Even though the entire department is one team and teamwork must be fostered at every turn, promoting teamwork within each individual team requires special effort. Susan C. Bakos[1] offers the following observation:

> Most people, management and employees alike, pay lip service to the teamwork concept. "Teamwork" looks good in company slogans and fits nicely into speeches. But the word usually means getting someone else to cooperate with you. Unfortunately, everyone on the "team" feels the same way!
>
> Individuals work for the achievement of personal goals; promotions, raises, benefits, and recognition. Today's economy has made competition for these goals more fierce, with the obvious result; workers are even less willing to be team players than ever before. And managers often contribute to this situation by espousing "teamwork" yet rewarding individual performance.

Bakos continues by saying that managers who follow a teamwork approach should reward cooperation and suggests a **Manager's Teamwork Checklist**, which includes the following:

- Rewarding teamwork through (team) praise, choice assignments, raises, and promotions just as we would reward individual performance
- Including teamwork as a part of performance appraisals
- Rotating special assignments, allowing everyone an opportunity to shine as an individual occasionally
- Considering team ideas as well as individual ideas
- Sharing information, decision making, *and* credit for jobs well done
- Setting an example by cooperating with others

Bakos concludes by indicating that such a Teamwork Checklist helps make competitive individuals part of a goal-oriented group and helps individuals put self-interest aside and make company goals first priority.

Teamwork and Swing Teams

Swing (or **relief**) **teams**, although not assigned to a regular division of the hotel, are as accountable as regular teams for performance and for condition of jointly used equipment on the days they are scheduled to work in a given division. This helps resolve problems that come up. For example, section housekeepers on occasion complain about the condition of "their" section after returning from scheduled days off or about the condition of "their" maids' cart, vacuum cleaner, or other equipment. Such complaints are often resolved when the regular section housekeeper knows exactly who will be cleaning in the section when the regular team is off. Problems are much easier to talk out when the same workers face each other and are held accountable for the condition of jointly used equipment.

As another example, let's consider the regular section housekeeper in the red team who works in section 1 five days each week. When the red team is off, swing team 1 works in the red division, and Jane from that swing team regularly works in Mary's section. On a different day, swing team 1 relieves the yellow team, and Mary and Jane both work in the hotel. Both of them, as well as their supervisor, thus have the opportunity to talk about section 1 and to discuss and resolve any problems. Also, when plaudits are offered for the condition of section 1, both the red team and swing team 1 receive equal praise.

Other advantages of team staffing and scheduling will be discussed later in the text. Of primary concern at this time is the scheduling of the staff for work. You can see that scheduling four regular teams, two swing teams, and the laundry team as a group is simpler than scheduling 49 individual workers. In our model hotel, team scheduling will take care of the scheduling of 49 workers' positions. Twelve workers' positions, however, will still require individual scheduling.

Standing Rotational Scheduling and Tight Scheduling (Two Parts to the Total System)

There are two major tasks that must be accomplished in order for the following complete scheduling system to work. One is the task of constructing a system for **standing rotational scheduling.** (The word "standing" is used to denote a continuous system, and the word "rotational" to denote the cyclical nature of the system that provides for two regular days off for people each week and for staff to cover a full seven-day workweek at 100 percent occupancy.) The other task is that of providing **tight scheduling,** which is a modification of the rotational system to account for reduced occupancy. This will be accomplished by assigning extra days off when occupancy is low. The tight schedule is actually a daily modification of the standing rotational schedule based on occupancy.

In new operations, these two systems are designed before opening and are then easily implemented on a given start date. In ongoing operations, these systems may be used, but they require a thorough briefing of staff and an understanding by employees before they are implemented. Usually several weeks must pass after training employees on the scheduling system in order that the one-time shock of shifting from one system to another can be accommodated. Once the system is designed and employees are properly prepared, the standing rotational system is implemented on a given start date, which usually falls on the first day of the property workweek.

Standing Rotational System

Using the model hotel, assume the following work situation:

1. The hotel workweek has been established as beginning on Saturdays and ending on Fridays.
2. Workers may work no more than five days in any workweek without drawing overtime pay.
3. Days off will be consecutive unless the employee can be shown an advantage for having split days off.
4. A condition of employment will be that all team employees must be willing to work their share of weekends. (This can be a condition of employment provided it is specified at the time of employment.)

The Work Calendar

The **work calendar** is divided into seven distinct workweeks. In each week, teams (or individual employees) will be assigned two regular days off. Each following week, the days that are assigned off will rotate forward one day. For example, if the red team is scheduled to be off on Friday and Saturday of workweek 1, then it will be off Saturday and Sunday of workweek 2, and Sunday and Monday of workweek 3. This form of rotation (off days moving forward) continues through the seventh workweek. The eighth workweek is a repetition of the first workweek, creating a cycle of workweek schedules that repeats every seventh week. Figure 3.1 is an illustration of this system.

Note the seven workweeks, with each day of the week indicated (workweeks are separated by a vertical line). Note also the horizontal bar under the regularly assigned days that the worker is scheduled off. As the weeks progress, the bar moves to the next succeeding days until the day off are Friday and Saturday. Here the days off split to the opposite ends of the week. Although days off are split in a particular week, each of these split days joins the two adjacent days off in the prior week or the succeeding week, causing the worker to have three days off in a row. This will happen twice in seven weeks. Note that there are never more or fewer than two days off in any workweek, even though in most cases the worker is working six days straight. Now that we have explained the cyclical method of days off, we can construct workweek 1.

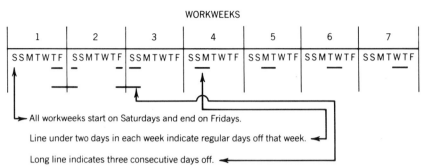

Figure 3.1 The standing rotational scheduling system. Each week in the seven-week system begins on a Saturday and ends on a Friday. Underlines indicate regularly assigned days off. Days off rotate forward one day each succeeding week. In workweek 2, when days off are Friday and Saturday, they must be split with Saturday being the first day off in the week and Friday being the last day off in the same week. Thursday and Friday of workweek 1 join with Saturday of workweek 2, providing three consecutive days off. The same happens when workweeks 2 and 3 are combined. This offers a strong selling point for the system. When the employee's days off are on the weekend, there are three days off in a row, yet only two days off in any one workweek, allowing for a full 40 hours of work in each week. The eighth workweek is a repeat of workweek 1, hence the cyclic character of the system.

Construction of Workweek 1

First, let us look at Figure 3.2—the **Housekeeping Standing Schedule Form** that has been specifically designed for the model hotel. The four regular teams, laundry staff, two swing teams, and individual positions that must be staffed are listed. Note that it is the **position** that is scheduled, not a specific person.

The color designations—red, yellow, brown, and green—in the column "Team Position Person" correspond with the divisions of the hotel described in the House Breakout Plan. If there is *no* indication in a schedule block, it means that the team designated by a specific color is working in the division of that same color designation; for example, the red team working in the red division will

HOUSEKEEPING STANDING SCHEDULE
WEEK _____

TEAM/POSITION PERSON	SATURDAY	SUNDAY	MONDAY	TUESDAY	WEDNESDAY	THURSDAY	FRIDAY
RED							
YELLOW							
BROWN							
GREEN							
LAUNDRY							
SWING TEAM 1							
SWING TEAM 2							
LINEN ROOM SUPERVISOR							
LINEN ROOM ATTENDANT							
SENIOR HSKPG. AIDE							
PUBLIC AREA HOUSEKEEPER #1							
PUBLIC AREA HOUSEKEEPER #2							
A.M. PUB AREA (RELIEF)							
NIGHT SUPERVISOR							
NIGHT HOUSEKEEPER							
NIGHT P.A. HOUSEKEEPER #1							
NIGHT P.A. HOUSEKEEPER #2							
NIGHT P.A. (RELIEF)							

Figure 3.2 Housekeeping standing rotational schedule form.

HOUSEKEEPING STANDING SCHEDULE
WEEK _____ *ONE* _____

TEAM/POSITION PERSON	SATURDAY	SUNDAY	MONDAY	TUESDAY	WEDNESDAY	THURSDAY	FRIDAY
RED						Off / ST-1	Off / ST-1
YELLOW							
BROWN							
GREEN							
LAUNDRY							
SWING TEAM 1						Red	Red
SWING TEAM 2							

Figure 3.3 Beginning of preparation of the standing rotational schedule for workweek 1. The red team is scheduled to work Saturday through Wednesday and to be off Thursday and Friday. Swing team 1 (ST-1) is scheduled to work in the place of the red team where indicated.

be indicated by a blank schedule block. For the swing teams, it is necessary to specify, in the appropriate schedule block, exactly where the swing team is to work. In the standing rotational system, all members of a given team will be considered as scheduled to work if the team schedule block is left blank.

We can now construct workweek 1, using Figure 3.2 as the scheduling form.

Step 1. As a starting point, assume that in workweek 1 the red team will work in the red division on Saturday, Sunday, Monday, Tuesday, and Wednesday and will be off on Thursday and Friday. On the days off, swing team 1 will work in place of the red team. This is indicated on the schedule sheet in Figure 3.3

In the Thursday and Friday schedule blocks, note the "off" and the "ST-1," indicating that swing team 1 is working in place of the red team. Note also that "red" must be placed opposite the Thursday and Friday schedule blocks for swing team 1.

Step 2. Now that swing team 1 has been scheduled to work on Thursday and Friday for the red team, it is necessary that the team be *kept working* five consecutive days. Given that swing team 1 also relieves the yellow team two days and works in the laundry one day, its schedule may now be completed as shown in Figure 3.4.

At this point the scheduling of the red team, yellow team, and swing team 1 has been completed, and one day off for the laundry personnel has been designated.

Step 3. Swing team 2 is next introduced to give the laundry team its second day off. The team will also work two days for the brown team and two days for the green team, giving it five consecutive workdays. (Note that the off days for both swing teams are now established.) Figure 3.5 shows the completion of the scheduling for all regular teams, the laundry, and both swing teams.

HOUSEKEEPING STANDING SCHEDULE
WEEK _____ *ONE* _____

TEAM/POSITION PERSON	SATURDAY	SUNDAY	MONDAY	TUESDAY	WEDNESDAY	THURSDAY	FRIDAY
RED						Off / ST-1	Off / ST-1
YELLOW	Off / ST-1	Off / ST-1					
BROWN							
GREEN							
LAUNDRY			Off / ST-1				
SWING TEAM 1	Yellow	Yellow	Laundry	Off	Off	Red	Red
SWING TEAM 2							
LINEN ROOM SUPERVISOR							
LINE							

Figure 3.4 Continuation of scheduling system preparation for workweek 1. Swing team 1 is kept working five days straight by swinging in for the yellow team on Saturday and Sunday and for the laundry on Monday.

HOUSEKEEPING STANDING SCHEDULE

WEEK _____ *ONE* _____

TEAM/POSITION PERSON	SATURDAY	SUNDAY	MONDAY	TUESDAY	WEDNESDAY	THURSDAY	FRIDAY
RED						Off / ST-1	Off / ST-1
YELLOW	Off / ST-1	Off / ST-1					
BROWN					Off / ST-2	Off / ST-2	
GREEN	Off / ST-2						Off / ST-2
LAUNDRY			Off / ST-1	Off / ST-2			
SWING TEAM 1	Yellow	Yellow	Laundry	Off	Off	Red	Red
SWING TEAM 2	Green	Off	Off	Laundry	Brown	Brown	Green
LINEN ROOM SUPERVISOR							
LINEN ROOM ATTENDANT							
SENIOR HSKPG. AIDE							
PUBLIC AREA HOUSEKEEPER #1							
PUBLIC AREA HOUSEKEEPER #2							
A.M. PUB AREA (RELIEF)							
NIGHT SUPERVISOR							
NIGHT HOUSEKEEPER							
NIGHT P.A. HOUSEKEEPER #1							
NIGHT P.A. HOUSEKEEPER #2							
NIGHT P.A. (RELIEF)							

Figure 3.5 Completion of team scheduling for workweek 1. Swing team 2 is scheduled to work for laundry team on its second consecutive day off; then it works two days for the brown team and two days for the green team. Having completed five consecutive days of work in relief, swing team 2 is then off for two days.

Step 4. The next step is to schedule individual positions for workweek 1. Note that individual positions are normally referred to as **fixed positions**, since their scheduling does not fluctuate based on occupancy. It is logical for the linen room supervisor and the linen room attendant to be off on different days. It is also reasonable to have one day in between their days off to facilitate routine communication and continuity between the two positions. Similarly, the senior housekeeping aide should not be scheduled off on the same day as the linen room supervisor. (Even though management positions do not show on the hourly worker schedule, it is illogical to schedule them off at the same time. Management positions are therefore assigned two consecutive days off in such a way that either a manager can cover for the one who is off or who has important obligations for part of each workday.) Note also that in the case of public area (PA) housekeepers, the third position provides a relief for the first two positions, provided the relief is not scheduled off on the same day as public area housekeepers 1 and 2. There will be one day out of seven when all three public area housekeepers are on duty. On this particular day, many special projects can be scheduled and completed that would otherwise require the hir-

ing of additional personnel. Figure 3.6 is a logical completion of the design of workweek 1.

Even though the total staff may be reduced at times, cross-training and overseeing by other supervisors is used to keep staffing at an optimum. For example, on days that the night supervisor is off, the head housekeeping aide or the linen room supervisor might be scheduled to come in late, thereby being available to take over part of the night supervisor's duties. Another possibility is that management might be scheduled to cover for the night supervisor. The balance of the scheduling for workweek 1 as indicated is therefore one of several logical arrangements.

Construction of Workweeks 2 through 7

Recalling the standing rotational system illustrated in Figure 3.1, we can now construct the balance of the workweeks. By using the identical form as shown in Figure 3.2, the days off expressed in workweek 1 are, in each and every case, advanced one day on each of the six remaining workweeks. Similarly to how Figure 3.6 shows the complete workweek 1, Figure 3.7 represents the complete workweek 2. Once again, in the case in which days off are Friday and Saturday, they are at opposite ends of the schedule.

HOUSEKEEPING STANDING SCHEDULE
WEEK _____ ONE _____

TEAM/POSITION PERSON	SATURDAY	SUNDAY	MONDAY	TUESDAY	WEDNESDAY	THURSDAY	FRIDAY
RED						Off ST-1	Off ST-1
YELLOW	Off ST-1	Off ST-1					
BROWN					Off ST-2	Off ST-2	
GREEN	Off ST-2						Off ST-2
LAUNDRY			Off ST-1	Off ST-2			
SWING TEAM 1	Yellow	Yellow	Laundry	Off	Off	Red	Red
SWING TEAM 2	Green	Off	Off	Laundry	Brown	Brown	Green
LINEN ROOM SUPERVISOR	Off	Off					
LINEN ROOM ATTENDANT				Off	Off		
SENIOR HSKPG. AIDE						Off	Off
PUBLIC AREA HOUSEKEEPER #1	Off	Off					
PUBLIC AREA HOUSEKEEPER #2			Off	Off			
A.M. PUB AREA (RELIEF)					Off	Off	
NIGHT SUPERVISOR			Off	Off			
NIGHT HOUSEKEEPER					Off	Off	
NIGHT P.A. HOUSEKEEPER #1	Off						Off
NIGHT P.A. HOUSEKEEPER #2		Off	Off				
NIGHT P.A. (RELIEF)				Off	Off		

Figure 3.6 Completed standing rotational scheduling system for workweek 1. Days off have been assigned to individual workers not considered part of housekeeping teams.

HOUSEKEEPING STANDING SCHEDULE
WEEK _____ TWO _____

TEAM/POSITION PERSON	SATURDAY	SUNDAY	MONDAY	TUESDAY	WEDNESDAY	THURSDAY	FRIDAY
RED	Off ST-1						Off ST-1
YELLOW		Off ST-1	Off ST-1				
BROWN						Off ST-2	Off ST-2
GREEN	Off ST-2	Off ST-2					
LAUNDRY				Off ST-1	Off ST-2		
SWING TEAM 1	Red	Yellow	Yellow	Laundry	Off	Off	Red
SWING TEAM 2	Green	Green	Off	Off	Laundry	Brown	Brown
LINEN ROOM SUPERVISOR		Off	Off				
LINEN ROOM ATTENDANT					Off	Off	
SENIOR HSKPG. AIDE	Off						Off
PUBLIC AREA HOUSEKEEPER #1		Off	Off				
PUBLIC AREA HOUSEKEEPER #2				Off	Off		
A.M. PUB AREA (RELIEF)						Off	Off
NIGHT SUPERVISOR				Off	Off		
NIGHT HOUSEKEEPER						Off	Off
NIGHT P.A. HOUSEKEEPER #1	Off	Off					
NIGHT P.A. HOUSEKEEPER #2			Off	Off			
NIGHT P.A. (RELIEF)					Off	Off	

Figure 3.7 Workweek 2 of the standing rotational system. Compare workweeks 1 and 2 and note how regular days off have been rotated forward one day for each entity to be scheduled. Workweeks 3–7 are prepared in a like manner by continuing to move days off forward one day each week.

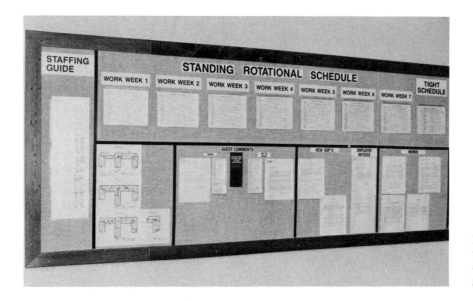

Figure 3.8 Bulletin board display of the standing rotational scheduling system and the department staffing guide.

System Posting and Initiation

After the standing rotational system has been designed, all that remains is posting and initiation. The schedules should be posted on a bulletin board next to a copy of the **Department Staffing Guide** on which the incumbents to all positions are indicated. Remember, these schedule forms are to become permanent and should therefore be typed and protected with coverings. The worker only needs to know what position he or she is filling and what workweek is in effect to know his or her regular days off. Figure 3.8 shows how a Department Staffing Guide and seven weeks of standing rotational schedules might be displayed on an employee bulletin board within a housekeeping department.

System initiation is begun on any upcoming day that is designated by management as the beginning of the workweek (it is Saturday in our example). Once initiated, the system is in perpetual rotation, requiring only that someone move a marker every week to indicate what workweek is in effect.

In a new operation, the system should be initiated several days before opening. In an ongoing operation, the system should be explained several weeks before changing to it because of the effect the change may have on day-off rotation.

Tight Scheduling System

Whereas the standing rotational schedule is a *permanent* system that, once established and initiated, continues to cycle on its own, the tight scheduling system is an *operational* system. It provides simple day-by-day modifications of the standing rotational schedule that are needed because of fluctuations in

occupancy. The tight schedule pertains only to team scheduling; it has no effect on the individual positions scheduled (bottom portion of the standing rotational schedule), since all positions other than teams are considered fixed and are not affected by occupancy.

Figure 3.9 is a form especially designed for the model hotel on which the tight schedule modifications will be shown. Note especially the space for tomorrow's date, day, and workweek and the columns labeled "area" (division), to which tomorrow's schedule refers, "team scheduled," indicating which team is to work, and "bring in," which is for a directive issued to the appropriate supervisor as to how many section housekeepers within the indicated team are to be used. In this way, management is *delegating* to the team supervisor the task of determining which people within the team are to be brought in; said another way, it indicates which team members are to be scheduled for an extra day off.

Developing the Tight Schedule for a Typical Day

For illustrative purposes, assume that the following hypothetical situation exists regarding the 353-room model hotel:

1. Tomorrow's day and date are Thursday, June 16.
2. Tomorrow's date falls at a time when the standing rotational schedule is cycling through workweek 2 (Figure 3.7)
3. Today's occupancy was 95 percent, and tomorrow's occupancy is forecasted to be 76 percent (268 rooms expected to be occupied tonight; see Table 2.2, Table of Personnel Requirements).

The following steps are required to operationally develop a tight schedule for tomorrow.

TIGHT SCHEDULE FOR _____ / _____ / _____
    (date)   (day)   (work week)

EXPECTED OCCUPANCY % _____ # ROOMS _____

AREA	TEAM SCHEDULED	BRING IN	SUPERVISOR ASSIGNMENT	EXTRA DAY OFF	OTHERS ON CALL
RED	SUPERVISOR:		1._____ 2._____ 3._____ 4._____ 5._____	1._____ 2._____ 3._____ 4._____ 5._____	
YELLOW	SUPERVISOR:		6._____ 7._____ 8._____ 9._____ 10._____	6._____ 7._____ 8._____ 9._____ 10._____	
BROWN	SUPERVISOR:		11._____ 12._____ 13._____ 14._____ 15._____	11._____ 12._____ 13._____ 14._____ 15._____	
GREEN	SUPERVISOR:		16._____ 17._____ 18._____ 19._____ 20._____	16._____ 17._____ 18._____ 19._____ 20._____	
LAUNDRY	SUPERVISOR		1._____ 2._____ 3._____ 4._____ 5._____	1._____ 2._____ 3._____ 4._____ 5._____	

Figure 3.9 Form used for the model hotel to prepare the tight schedule.

Step 1. At about 4 P.M. on the afternoon of Wednesday, June 15, one of the managers of the housekeeping department refers to the standing rotational schedule (Figure 4.7) and notes the following teams scheduled to work on that date (in workweek 2): red team in red division, yellow team in yellow division, swing team 2 in brown division, and green team in green division (the brown team and swing team 1 are scheduled for a regular day off, and the laundry crew is scheduled to work in the laundry). This information is then transferred to a copy of the form for tight scheduling (Figure 3.9).

Step 2. The manager contacts the front desk manager and asks for an estimate of tonight's occupancy (tomorrow's workload for the housekeeping department). The manager is informed that 268 of the hotel's 353 rooms are expected to be occupied.

Step 3. The housekeeping manager refers to the table of personnel requirements (Table 2.2) and notes that 268 rooms reflects a 76 percent occupancy, requiring the use of 15 housekeepers.

Step 4. In the "bring in" column, on the tight schedule, the housekeeping manager indicates as close to an equal distribution as possible of the 15 housekeepers required to service tomorrow's occupancy. For example, three teams bring in four and one team

brings in three of the five section housekeepers who are permanent members of the indicated teams.

Step 5. The laundry will be working to service the soiled linen workload created by *today's* occupancy (95 percent), requiring a full laundry staff of all five members.

Step 6. Within a period of about five minutes, the housekeeping manager has developed the directive portion of tomorrow's tight schedule, which is now posted in a specially designed place adjacent to the standing rotational schedule. Figure 3.10 is a copy of the tight schedule prepared for tomorrow's workday.

Step 7. Within the next 10 or 15 minutes, each senior housekeeper (supervisor) will note the bring-in requirement for tomorrow and will, on a fair and equitable basis, determine who (by name) among the team members will be assigned to work. Similarly, they will indicate who will be assigned an extra day off. Such indications are made on the tight schedule (Figure 3.11), which all employees may refer to for tomorrow's staffing needs before the end of today's workday.

Tight scheduling is now complete for Thursday's workday and is available for all to see. (Note that the regular laundry staff was off the previous day.) It will be necessary for the laundry supervisor to call in and ask about tomorrow's requirement for

TIGHT SCHEDULE FOR 6/16/, Thursday, 2

EXPECTED OCCUPANCY % 76%   # ROOMS 268

AREA	TEAM SCHEDULED	BRING IN	SUPERVISOR ASSIGNMENT	EXTRA DAY OFF	OTHERS ON CALL
RED	Red SUPERVISOR: Miller	4	1. ___ 2. ___ 3. ___ 4. ___ 5. ___	1. ___ 2. ___ 3. ___ 4. ___ 5. ___	
YELLOW	Yellow SUPERVISOR: Jones	4	6. ___ 7. ___ 8. ___ 9. ___ 10. ___	6. ___ 7. ___ 8. ___ 9. ___ 10. ___	
BROWN	Swing Team 2 SUPERVISOR: Foster	3	11. ___ 12. ___ 13. ___ 14. ___ 15. ___	11. ___ 12. ___ 13. ___ 14. ___ 15. ___	
GREEN	Green SUPERVISOR: Smith	4	16. ___ 17. ___ 18. ___ 19. ___ 20. ___	16. ___ 17. ___ 18. ___ 19. ___ 20. ___	
LAUNDRY	Laundry SUPERVISOR Thomas	5	1. ___ 2. ___ 3. ___ 4. ___ 5. ___	1. ___ 2. ___ 3. ___ 4. ___ 5. ___	

Figure 3.10 Tight schedule form based on tomorrow's forecast occupancy for our hypothetical situation.

TIGHT SCHEDULE FOR 6/18/, Thursday, 2

EXPECTED OCCUPANCY % 76%   # ROOMS 268

AREA	TEAM SCHEDULED	BRING IN	SUPERVISOR ASSIGNMENT	EXTRA DAY OFF	OTHERS ON CALL
RED	Red SUPERVISOR: Miller	4	1. Julia 2. ___ 3. Yvonne 4. Billie 5. Margaret	1. ___ 2. Gladys 3. ___ 4. ___ 5. ___	
YELLOW	Yellow SUPERVISOR: Jones	4	6. Dianne 7. Vivian 8. Marie 9. ___ 10. Mildred	6. ___ 7. ___ 8. ___ 9. Janice 10. ___	
BROWN	Swing team 2 SUPERVISOR: Foster	3	11. Harriet 12. ___ 13. Mannie 14. Jane 15. ___	11. ___ 12. Elvira 13. ___ 14. ___ 15. Mary	
GREEN	Green SUPERVISOR:	4	16. ___ 17. Georgia 18. Tommy 19. Donna 20. Louise	16. Lillian 17. ___ 18. ___ 19. ___ 20. ___	
LAUNDRY	Laundry SUPERVISOR Thomas	5	1. Jane 2. Marie 3. Wilma 4. Helen 5. Laura	1. ___ 2. ___ 3. ___ 4. ___ 5. ___	

Figure 3.11 Supervisors complete the tight schedule by indicating who from among the indicated teams will be working and who will be scheduled for an extra day off. The completed tight schedule is posted daily next to the standing rotation scheduling system (see Figure 3.8, extreme right).

workers. The supervisor will specify by phone how many laundry employees will work from among the members of the laundry team. The supervisor will then call the team members and specify tomorrow's requirement for workers.

When it is known that an annual occupancy less than about 90 percent is forecast, 100 percent staffing is not required; that is, teams need not be staffed to capacity and may be reduced in size to provide more scheduled workdays for the staff. If staffing is reduced and occupancy exceeds the capabilities of the staff, people who are regularly scheduled off may be offered overtime to fill the gaps.

Control over the Tight Schedule

Recall that the task of specific designation as to who works within each team has been delegated to each team supervisor. Although this delegation is job enriching to each supervisor, control must be maintained to ensure equitable and fair rotation of the assignment of extra days off for team members. For this reason, each supervisor should be required to maintain a notebook indicating rotational assignment of extra days off for each member of the specified team. If questioned by any employee regarding fairness of assignment, the supervisor must be able to produce a record of fairness in the designation of extra days off. In many cases, if a team is to be scheduled down, a request for volunteers to accept an extra day off is usually all that is needed; in other cases, the extra day off must be assigned. Records must be kept to indicate that this assignment has been performed in a fair manner.

Equipment Use Related to the Tight Schedule

There are two major pieces of equipment that are associated with each room section—maid's cart and vacuum cleaner. This equipment should be identified by a number corresponding to the section to which it belongs. At 100 percent occupancy, each of the section housekeepers working in one of the 20 assigned sections will have the exclusive use of the specified equipment. In this manner, a specific housekeeper from a regular team and a swing team may be held accountable for the condition and care of the equipment. At less than 100 percent occupancy, however, several sections will not have a section housekeeper assigned. Note that in Figure 3.11 sections 2, 9, 12, 15, and 16 have no one assigned. This does not mean that there will be no work to perform in those sections, only that the workers scheduled are to use their assigned equipment. At a later time, the actual placement of the section housekeeping in a specific work area will be covered by a procedure known as *opening the house.*

Union Contracts and their Effects on Scheduling

We have shown you one of the most efficient scheduling techniques available to executive housekeepers. In real-life situations, however, **union contracts** can have an overwhelming effect on scheduling techniques. They may insist on a guaranteed 40-hour week and the requirement of additional positions on the labor force rather than cross-trained employees to perform more than one type of task (e.g., housekeeping and laundry).

Executive housekeepers thus have the challenge of presenting to unions plans that guarantee fairness to current employees as opposed to plans that pad staffs with unnecessary workers. In most cases, the best argument in favor of cross-training and scheduling of employees is that a 40-hour job does not exist and the company will not hire a full-time employee to work where only eight or 16 hours of work actually exist. Many union houses are able to deal with this problem by having a very small cadre of full-time employees and a majority of workers who are considered **steady extras** (workers who are not guaranteed 40 hours).

Where union contracts are in force, the executive housekeeper should work to ensure fairness to employees. If union contracts are not in force, executive housekeepers should do everything possible to ensure that workers have fair treatment and adequate wages and benefits.

Summary

Although there are several ways to schedule workers in seven-day operations, the best techniques are simple methods that use manager's time wisely, ensure fairness to workers, provide adequate coverage, and are understandable. A combination of two systems—the standing rotational system which, once initiated, operates in a cyclic manner for a indefinite time, and a tight scheduling system, which modifies the standing system daily to accommodate for hotel occupancy—has been presented in this chapter. The model hotel provided the vehicle by which these systems have been demonstrated.

The standing system defines regular days off from scheduled positions, and the tight system defines extra days off due to hotel occupancy being reduced below 100 percent. Both systems are displayed on the department bulletin board next to a copy of the department staffing guide.

Both systems are adaptable to hotels of 100 rooms or more. The systems are in fact adaptable to any departments in which scheduling is based on a fluctuating occupancy or workload. The team method of staffing and scheduling allows for friendly competition and the delegation of more tasks to supervisors.

The executive housekeeper of the soon-to-open hotel should consider the type of scheduling presented in this chapter during the planning stage. If scheduling techniques are dealt with after opening, many overtime hours could result and workers and management will be adversely affected by the lack of a good scheduling system. In an existing operation the system should be introduced, the staff trained, and a specific date chosen on which to institute the system. The best plan is to develop scheduling techniques before hiring the first employee.

KEY TERMS AND CONCEPTS

Worker scheduling
Team system of organization
Team staffing
Team scheduling
Manager's Teamwork Checklist
Swing teams
Relief teams
Standing rotational scheduling
Tight scheduling

Work calendar
Housekeeping Standing Schedule Form
Fixed position
Staffing Guide
System initiation
Union contract
Steady extra

DISCUSSION AND REVIEW QUESTIONS

1. Assume that a state law will not allow a worker to work more than five consecutive days without paying the person overtime. Design a standing rotational system (similar to the one described in Figure 3.1) that will meet the criteria of working five days in a row but will not require paying the overtime premium.
2. How does a tight scheduling system take advantage of the directional activity of delegation?
3. Assume that a standing rotational system and a tight scheduling system have been designed for an ongoing operation. What must be done before it may be initiated? Why?
4. Assume an ongoing operation that is currently cycling through workweek three. A new employee has been hired to fill a vacancy in a housekeeping team. How would you explain the system to the new employee?
5. Are standing rotational and tight scheduling systems feasible in a union environment?
6. Assuming your answer to question 5 is yes, how would you go about justifying the system to union officials?

NOTES

1. Susan C. Bakos, "Promoting Teamwork," *Executive Housekeeping Today*, September 1982, p. 26.

4

Material Planning: Administration of Equipment and Supplies

CHAPTER OBJECTIVES

1. To discover that executive housekeepers are administrators and what that means.
2. To learn about planning for materials.
3. To become familiar with the budgets involved in a housekeeping operation.
4. To learn about inventories, equipment, assets, and costs.
5. To obtain a general knowledge of materials, that is, guestroom furniture and guestroom fixtures needed for a housekeeping operation.

The executive housekeeper's time appears thus far to have been occupied only with people matters, giving the impression that other forms of planning are of no consequence. Although staff planning may require great human engineering and is assuredly the most costly part of housekeeping operations, there is also the necessity to plan for and become organized in material administration. **Administration** refers to the selection, purchasing, use, and control of items; **material** refers to the various product items that will be used by the department, all of which must be properly classified and categorized.

Planning for material acquisition and use parallels staff planning and must also be initiated when the new executive housekeeper joins the organization. In the case of linen and **software items**, it would be expected that some initial planning and procurement might already have taken place due to long lead times required for acquiring such material. In this chapter, we will continue planning for the opening of the model hotel. However, all knowledge gained through understanding these procedures and concepts is applicable to ongoing operations. We will begin with a discussion about budgeting and inventory control and will then present a complete analysis of materials.

Material Budgets

Budgets are the plans by which resources required to generate revenues are allocated. There are many different types of budgets. Some allocate personnel; others deal with person-hours or with dollars. Plans that allocate material resources associated with generating revenue are a significant part of many budgets.

Two types of budgets most commonly used in hotel operations are capital expenditure budgets and operating budgets. When new properties are opened, preopening budgets are designed to guide the expenditure of resources through the event. Budgets should be prepared by the management of the departments to which they will apply. A review procedure normally takes place whereby upper levels of management comment, return for revision, and finally endorse departmental budgets for top management's approval. Once budgets are approved, they are used to guide departments to successful operations over the course of the year or period of time to which they apply.

Capital Expenditure Budgets

Capital expenditure budgets allocate the use of capital assets that have a life span considerably in excess of one year; these are assets that are not normally used up in day-to-day operations. Because such items of material are capital in nature, they are considered to add to the capital investment of the company and are therefore subject to some form of **depreciation**. The hotel building is a capital asset that may be depreciated over a period of 25 or 30 years. **Furniture, fixtures, and equipment (FFE)** are capital assets whose depreciation schedules are somewhat shorter (three, five, or seven years) but are nonetheless depreciable. In hotel operations, the term **software** is sometimes used to describe certain types of depreciable fixtures.

In ongoing operations once each fiscal year there is a call for capital expenditure budgets from the various departments. At this time the housekeeping department management is required to specify needs for funds to purchase FFE. Capital expenditure budgets might also include requests for funds to support renovation and modernization programs, since both add to the asset value of the property. Once budgets are approved and funds are made available, capital expenditure budgets are implemented by the various departments.

If unexpected needs arise for FFE during the budget year, the general manager usually must submit supplementary justification to ownership before making such expenditures. Depending on company policy, some general managers have authority to spend a finite amount of money in excess of capital expenditure budgets, but such spending is quite con-

strained. As an example, for one major hotel corporation whose capital expenditure budget may range in the millions of dollars for a given property, the authority of its general managers for excess spending without approval from higher authority is limited to $500.

Before a specific item of equipment may be **capitalized**, there could be a requirement that the item have a life expectancy in excess of one year and that the cost be in excess of $100. Should a specific item not meet these criteria, it would be **expensed** (converted into the cost of doing business) rather than capitalized.

Operating Budgets

Operating budgets are prepared annually for a fiscal year period. Operating budgets relate day-to-day **operating costs** to the **revenue** resulting therefrom. **Labor costs** (salaries and wages), **employee costs** (health, welfare, and benefit programs), and **controllable costs** make up the total expenditure relating to specific revenue being generated; **control profit** (or **loss**) is the result of the comparison.

Revenue is generated by a hotel rooms department, and costs are incurred by two subdepartments—front office and housekeeping. The front office manager and the executive housekeeper are therefore responsible for controlling the costs associated with revenue generated from the sale of guestrooms. That portion of controllable cost administered by the executive housekeeper includes but is not limited to items such as cleaning supplies, guest supplies, linen expense, uniform costs (for staff), and laundry costs. A detailed analysis of a rooms department operating budget is in Chapter 11.

Since department managers are charged with holding operating costs in check in order that profit may be maximized, the purchase of small items of equipment on a one-at-a-time basis should be curtailed. Foresight in planning can and will maximize departmental control profit.

Preopening Budgets

Preopening budgets are usually thought of as allocating money and resources to opening parties, advertising, and initial good will. Preopening expenses actually go far beyond such expenditures and usually include initial cost of employee salaries and wages and supplies, food, china, glass, silver, and similar items. Recall that in our hypothetical opening many managers have been on the payroll for several months. Other employees will soon be on the payroll for training and orientation. Preopening budgets normally include the cash and inventory requirements to meet these needs, along with others for getting the property open and operating. Preopening budgets are quite sizable and as a result are usually amortized over a three-year period from the date of opening. Preopening expenses are therefore not quite so devastating to corporate profits in the first year of operation. Most professionally sound hotel companies understand the need for substantial preopening budgets and plan such expenses into **pro formas**. Hotel companies that do not plan ahead are plagued with unplanned-for last-minute costs, and departments end up undersupplied and underequipped. The preopening budget forces the planning necessary for a smooth opening. The executive housekeeper can play a major role in establishing sound preopening budgets.

Inventory Control

Inventory control is the management function of classifying, ordering, receiving, storing, issuing, and accounting for items of value. The executive housekeeper for new and ongoing operations must not only perform tasks in controlling various classifications of inventories but must be technically competent in the selection, use, and maintenance of material items such as textiles, sleep equipment, furnishings, department equipment, and supplies. In addition, top management might dictate the degree of quality of certain material items to be used in the hotel guestroom. In some cases, for example, the room rate charged will be an indicator of expected quality of items such as bath towels or of the number and type of bars of soap to be found in each guestroom.

As initial planning for opening takes place, systems and procedures must be designed to facilitate inventory control, and personnel training plans must be generated to familiarize the staff with how to care for equipment, use supplies, and account for items of value. Storage must be organized and allotted to the various categories of material; **pars** (required on-hand amounts) must be established, accounting methods must be coordinated with the controller's office, and fiscal inventory rules and procedures must be established. Most of all, organization, system, and forethought (inventory control) are needed to preclude unnecessary loss and waste. (We will discuss more about inventory control in Chapter 11.)

Material Classification

Basic Application to Principles of Accounting

The **classification of material** is the first step in the process by which items of value will be accounted for and controlled. Recall the general principles of accounting where **assets** of the company are stated. Under the broad term **assets**, there are current and fixed assets. **Current assets** include items such as cash, accounts receivable, and inventories. **Fixed assets** include land, building, and equipment. (In the case of hotels, the broad term **equipment** also includes furniture and fixtures— FFE). **Inventories** are an asset until they are *used*, and FFE are carried as assets until they are fully depreciated. Capital expenditure budgets are the plans by which fixed (depreciable) assets are acquired; operating budgets are the plans by which inventories are acquired.

As portions of inventories are used up in day-to-day operations to generate revenue, they are expensed and will appear as subtractions from revenue on income statements.

Table 4.1 lists some material items under the control of the executive housekeeper that are normally carried on the hotel **books of account** as fixed assets. These items are listed under various depreciation categories indicating their **life expectancy**. Since these items are fixed assets, they are not charged against routine day-to-day operations.

Table 4.2 lists material items that might be found in inventory assets under the control of the executive housekeeper. These items are regularly used up in the course of generating revenue and are therefore considered cost items and are carried as period expenses on operational and financial performance statements.

As inventory items are purchased, their invoices become payables (**liabilities**) that must be paid for with cash from the asset account cash. The result is the conversion of one asset, cash, into another form of current asset, inventories. As material is requisitioned from inventories to support day-to-day operations, inventory assets are used up and period expenses are recognized through adjusting entries. We hope that revenue is being generated in the process. Even though the executive housekeeper is responsible for control and use of both fixed and current assets, it is the day-to-day expenditure of current assets (cash for wages and inventories for material) as guided by operating budgets that will have the greatest effect on the department control profit.

Table 4.1 Material Classification of Fixed Assets for the Housekeeping Department

GUEST ROOM FURNITURE AND FACILITY EQUIPMENT	SOFTWARE	DEPARTMENT EQUIPMENT

7-Year Category
Carpet
Sleep equipment
  Boxsprings
  Mattresses
  Sofa beds
  Studio couches
  Chair-beds
  In-wall beds
Furniture
  Chests of drawers
  Tables
  Chairs
  Desks
Fixtures
  Paintings
  Accessories
  Lamps and lighting
    fixtures
Other equipment
  Telephones
  Radios
  Message
    equipment
  Televisions
  In-room safes
  Minibars
	5-Year Category
	Roll-away beds
	Accent drapes
	Blackout drapes
	Sheer curtains
	Pillows (regular and
	  nonallergenic)
	Bedspreads
	
	2-Year Category
	Blankets
	Shower Curtains
		7-Year Category
		Laundry equipment
		Permanent shelving
		Glass washer
		
		5-Year Category
		Maid's carts
		Corridor vacuums
		Space vacuums
		Pile lifter
		Wet vacuum
		Rotary floor scrubbers
		High-pressure hot water
		  carpet shampoo equipment
		Sewing machines
		Convertible mobile linen
		  shelving
		
		3-Year Category
		Maid's vacuums
		Backpack vacuums
		Electric brooms
		Rubbish handling conveyors
		Wheelchairs
		Baby beds

Ongoing Operations

Classification of material accounts for ongoing operations is similar to those for new operations. In ongoing operations, preopening budgets do not come into play, but capital expenditure budgets and operating budgets are presented on an annual basis. If the hotel has been in operation for some time, first operating budgets are planned and approved, and then capital expenditure budgets follow. The executive housekeeper should remember that income statements reflect progress toward attainment of the operating budget. Minor or small items of equipment that will be capitalized should not be purchased so as to be charged against operating costs (miscellaneous expenses). This type of purchase should be planned far enough in advance so as to be charged against capital expenditures.

Ongoing operations will include the routine and periodic purchase of all inventory items, requiring that systems for research, ordering, receipt, storage, issue, and the accounting for use of items of value be developed.

Preopening Operations

Temporary Storage

By now the executive housekeeper has been involved in selecting and purchasing items of material that are arriving daily for the opening of the hotel.

Although preopening budgets do not include the cost of fixed assets (FFE), it will be necessary to prepare to receive and temporarily store *all* material ordered, regardless of whether they are capital items (Table 4.1) or part of inventories (Table 4.2). Some hotel companies arrange for the contractor to install guestroom furniture and equipment before acceptance of the facility by operations. In any

Table 4.2 Material Classification of Inventory Assets

CLEANING SUPPLIES	GUEST SUPPLIES	LINENS	UNIFORMS
All-purpose cleaner	*Guest Expendables*	Sheets	Section
Disinfectants	Matches	Pillow cases	housekeeper
Germicidals	Laundry bags	Bath towels	Senior
Window cleaners	Laundry tickets	Hand towels	housekeeper
Acid bowl cleaners	Stationery	Washcloths	Section
Metal polishes	Pens	Bath mats	housekeeping
Furniture polish	Notepads	Specialty towels	aide
(lemon oil)	Postcards		Other
Applicators (all	Magazines		supervisors
kinds)	Plastic utility bags		
Spray bottles	Disposable slippers		
Rubber gloves	Emery boards		
Scrubbing pads	Table tents (in-house		
Steel wool	advertising)		
Brooms	Individual packs of coffee		
Mops	Candy mints		
Cleaning buckets	Toilet tissue		
Mop wringers	Toilet seat bands		
Floor dust mops	Facial tissue		
Cleaning rags	Sanibags		
	Bath soaps (bar)		
	Facial soaps (bar)		
	Guest Essentials		
	Clothes hangers		
	Plastic trays		
	Ice buckets		
	Water pitchers		
	Fly swatters		
	Glasses (or plastic		
	drinking cups)		
	Ashtrays		
	Waste baskets		
	Shower mats (rubber)		
	Do-not-disturb signs		
	Bibles		
	Guest Loan Items		
	Ironing boards		
	Irons		
	Hair dryers		
	Heating pads		
	Hot water bottles		
	Razors		
	Electric shavers		
	Ice packs		
	Alarm clocks		
	Bed boards		

case, furniture items are relatively easy to safeguard since they are either massive in size or are attached to the facility. Smaller movable (or removable) items are much more pilferable and should be kept in secure storage until operations is in control of the facility.*

Moving onto the Property

Several days before opening (after operational personnel have moved into the facility), a **move-in day** is established for all material. The move-in day requires detailed planning for the staging of material (from warehouse to ballroom to permanent setup and storage) so that nothing is misplaced or lost. Every item of inventory or equipment that has been purchased and placed in temporary storage must now be accounted for as it is transferred into the hotel. Depending on the size of the hotel, this process may take several days. The planning for move-in day will determine the efficiency and effectiveness by which the operation will take place and whether or not significant losses will occur.†

Disposition of Spares

Because guestroom furniture fixtures and equipment will normally be put in place by the contractor, many hotel companies buy capital items with a 1 to 10 percent **spare component**. Spares are turned over to operations, and inventory responsibility must be assumed at that time. Storage is then allotted and future use controlled.

In many cases, the chief engineer of the hotel will be held accountable for inventory and storage of items such as carpet and furniture spares. The execu-

---

*I participated in the opening of a major 1000-room hotel in which there was no provision for temporary storage of movable equipment and items of initial inventory. As these items were received, they were stored in the open, in the hotel garage, and in hallways as arranged for by the contractor. After operations took control of the building, it was determined that material valued in excess of $60,000.00 had disappeared, far outweighing the expense of having provided temporary storage in a bonded warehouse.
†I participated in several move-ins while employed by Marriott Hotels. The Marriott system requires that bonded warehouses be used for temporary storage and that move-in day use hotel ballrooms to stage all movable equipment and inventory items temporarily. From ballroom staging areas, equipment is assembled, marked as necessary for identification and, with other inventory items, moved to permanent storage. All this takes place according to detailed plans. Hundreds of thousands of items were thus controlled with an absolute minimum of loss. For example, in 1973 move-in day for the Los Angeles Marriott Hotel involved the staging of more than a million dollar material inventory into two ballrooms of more than 20,000 square feet without the reported loss of a single corn broom, vacuum cleaner, or bed sheet.

tive housekeeper is usually responsible for designating replacement of such items when the need arises in the future. Because carpet is a large bulk item, it is not uncommon for hotels to employ carpet companies for carpet repair and, in such cases, have these carpet companies hold spare carpet and provide periodic inventory of spares to the hotel for validation.

Guestroom Furniture and Fixtures

The items listed in Tables 4.1 and 4.2 are typical of those found in most hotel material inventories. Executive housekeepers in new and ongoing operations are involved in the purchase of such material inventories and are expected to research current literature, study samples, investigate sources of supply, decide characteristics and quality issues, and know the reputations of selected vendors for service and repair. The executive housekeeper must have a general knowledge of materials. The information in the rest of this chapter on guestroom furnishings and the information contained in the following three chapters can be used as a reference for housekeeping-related materials and their use.

Mattresses and Beds

Most hoteliers would agree that one of the most important elements of a guest's comfort is the quality of the bed. There is little that the hotel can do to make up for a guest's discomfort caused by a sleepless night on an uncomfortable bed.

Unfortunately, there is no unanimity of thought as to what makes a comfortable bed. Although some guests might disagree, the prevailing thought holds that a comfortable bed is one that is firm on the inside, but has a soft exterior.

Mattress Construction

Three types of mattresses are used in hotels today: innerspring, foam, and water. Mattresses range in size from twin to California King, as shown in Table 4.3. Average to high quality hotels are using the oversize double as a standard in most rooms because of the extra 4-inch (10.2 centimeter) length. It is better to have a mattress that is at least 6 inches (15.2 centimeters) longer than the average height of the sleeper.

Mattresses may be medium, firm, extra firm, or super firm. Innerspring mattresses are constructed like a sandwich, with insulating material and padding on both sides of a coil unit. Each coil should give support and at the same time conform to body contours. The number of springs in a coil unit can range from 150 to as many as 1000 coils, with 250 to 300 being the standard, depending on degree of firmness desired.

Table 4.3 Mattress Sizes

	WIDTH (IN.)	LENGTH (IN.)	WIDTH (CM)	LENGTH (CM)
Twin	38	× 74	96.5	× 188.0
Double	54	× 74	137.2	× 188.0
Oversize double	54	× 80	137.2	× 203.2
Queen	60	× 80	152.4	× 203.2
California king	72	× 84	182.9	× 213.4
Eastern king	76	× 80	193.0	× 203.2

Design of the coil unit is important in mattress construction. The resiliency, temper, number of turns in each coil, gauge of steel in individual springs, and the manner in which the springs are tied are of great importance in evaluating the quality of an innerspring mattress. Independent spring action and latex or baked enamel coating of coils provide longevity and noiseless operation. There should also be ventilators on the side of the mattress to ensure a fresh airflow into the coil unit.

Good mattresses have a layer of tough insulation to separate padding from springs. A layer of upholstery cotton or foam before ticking is applied provides a smooth surface and complies with government flame-spread regulations. The current federal fire-safety standard for mattresses holds that a lighted cigarette should not be able to ignite the mattress's insulation or ticking.

Mattress manufacturers have responded to the industry's and the public's concern over fire safety by developing mattresses that do not release toxic fumes when flame is applied; other manufacturers have created mattresses that will not support direct flame.

Ticking is the upholstered cover used in mattress construction. Ticking is found in all colors and patterns. It should be a tightly woven fabric that is well quilted to improve wearing qualities. Good quality innerspring mattresses should last for more than 10 years.

Foam mattresses are found in two types of materials—latex foam and urethane. Latex foam is a slab of 100 percent pure rubber, formed in one of two types of molds—pincore (small) holes or honeycomb (larger hole pattern). Polyurethane is less expensive than latex. Both are usually manufactured in $4\frac{1}{4}$- to 6-inch (10.8 to 15.2 centimeter) thickness, depending on the height of the foundation and box spring unit. The advantage of foam over regular innerspring mattresses is that foam is nonallergenic, less expensive, and easier to roll up for storage. Foam, however, does not have the longevity of innerspring mattresses.

Water-filled mattresses or "waterbeds" made their debut onto the hotel scene during the 1960s. They were not well received initially because they leaked, the water had to be heated, they required special (and costly) sheets, and they were prohibitively heavy for some multistory structures. Waterbeds were soon relegated to bridal suites and "theme" guestrooms.

Waterbeds today bear little resemblance to their 1960s predecessors; in fact, many of them resemble the traditional innerspring mattresses in appearance. Mattress manufacturers such as Simmons have designed waterbeds that have water-filled cells in the center of the mattress. The cells are covered with a vinyl-covered urethane foam and the perimeter of the mattress has a row of innerspring coils that provides support to an occupant sitting on the side of the bed. The mattress uses standard sheets and the water-filled cells do not have to be heated because of the insulating foam layer. The ticking can be removed via a zipper on the top of the mattress so that the cells can be serviced.

All mattresses should have reinforced sides to prevent sagging caused by people sitting on the sides. Such reinforcement is formed by tape being stitched to the top and bottom edges and sides of the ticking.

When purchasing new mattresses, the executive housekeeper should insist on viewing a cutaway model of the mattress prior to purchase.

Box Springs

Box springs and mattresses should be purchased simultaneously. Box springs are like shock absorbers. They cushion the weight and sleep movements of the sleeper and provide a large portion of the experienced sleep comfort. Box spring coils are much heavier-gauge steel than that found in mattresses. Springs are positioned on wooden or metal slats running laterally across the frame, giving fixed support to the underside of the unit. Box spring coils should be tied to the base, sides, and each other. The best test for a set of box springs is to stretch out on it and see if you experience firm support in all areas of the body.

Bed Frames

There are two basic styles of bed frames available to the housekeeper, metal and platform. The metal frame consists of four lengths of angle iron and a metal leg attached to each corner. Queen-size, king-size, and waterbeds will also have one or two cross bars added for extra support.

Platform frames are made from either metal or solid wood and provide the box springs and mattress with a platform or box on which to rest. The advantage to platform frames is twofold; carpet does not have to be laid under the platform, thus saving a considerable amount of carpet in a large hotel, and housekeepers need not worry about cleaning under the box frame. The sides of the frame are often carpeted to eliminate unsightly scuffing by vacuums.

Care and Maintenance of Beds

Preventive maintenance begins with mattress covers. Every bed should be covered with a moisture-proof mattress cover. The better-quality mattress covers are made of vinyl materials and are stain resistant, non-allergenic, flame retardant, as well as being moisture proof. A washable mattress pad that is also nonallergenic and flame retardant is placed above the mattress cover. Its purpose is to provide the guest with a cushioning layer between the sheets and the mattress. Many mattresses, especially tufted mattresses that have buttons, need mattress pads.

Innerspring mattresses should be turned regularly; head to foot for one turn, and side to side for the next turn. Mattresses that are turned regularly may have their life expectancy extended by as much as 50 percent. To help monitor mattress rotation, labels can be affixed to the corners of the mattress. On one side, the label "January, February, and March" can be affixed to one corner with "April, May, and June" affixed to the opposite corner. On the reverse side of the mattress the label "July, August, and September" can be sewn and on the opposite corner the label "October, November, and December" can be affixed. Inspections can then reveal whether or not a particular mattress has been rotated.

Roll-Aways, Cots, and Cribs

The demand for mobile beds will vary in proportion to guest type. Vacationing families and youth groups will generate the greatest demand for these items.

Cots or folding beds have disappeared from the scene because they are cumbersome to transport from storage to the guest's room. They have been replaced by the roll-away, a bed on wheels. The quality of roll-aways varies greatly by model and manufacturer. Standard roll-aways have a latex foam mattress that rests on flat bed springs attached to a folding frame. The better roll-away beds have specially designed innerspring mattresses. Roll-aways should have plastic covers to protect them from dust while in storage.

Cribs should meet all federal construction guidelines. Most hotel cribs are collapsible in order to save storage space. To ensure that they do not collapse while occupied by an infant, they should be inspected regularly and the staff should be instructed on how to prepare the crib. The lowest mattress level should always be used when setting up a crib to forestall the possibility of an overactive toddler crawling over the side and tumbling onto the floor.

Dual-Purpose Sleep Equipment

Dual-purpose sleep equipment provides extra sleeping capacity in guestrooms that otherwise would become crowded with a roll-away bed. Sofas, love seats, and formal chairs with ottomans convert into sleep equipment at night. There are basically five types of dual sleep equipment:

1. The sofa bed converts from a sofa into a bed by removal of the cushions. A small handle in the center of the seat unit releases the bed, which unfolds revealing a full (double size) mattress. This type of equipment may be found in either sofa or love seat configuration.
2. The jack-knife sofa converts to sleep configuration by dropping the back to the level of the seat.
3. The single studio couch converts by removing the bolsters and cover.
4. The chair bed and ottoman back drop to form a bed that is about 28 inches wide.
5. In-wall beds are becoming more the rule than the exception. Many hotels are now using the in-wall bed to conserve area in rooms normally used as sitting rooms and parlors during daytime. Outstanding queen size sleep equipment may now be found concealed in a wall, which by day gives the appearance of a paneled wall with table and chair placed against it. Well-balanced swing equipment allows the foot of the bed to drop to the floor with a gentle pull on a handle usually concealed in a picture frame. In-wall beds provide outstanding sleeping comfort, with no possibility of retracting into the wall with the sleeper, regardless of the impression given by old comedies.

Furniture

Furniture must be both functional and attractive. Furniture should be well constructed and easy to maintain. The variety of furniture available for hotel use today is as great as the number of companies manufacturing institutional furniture.

Most hotel furniture is a combination of wood and plastics made to look like wood. (Many times, close examination of the facades of what looks like French provincial carved wood will reveal a molded plastic exposure.) Hardwoods are scarce and expensive; therefore, substitutes such as surfaced plywood and pressed particleboard are used extensively in the manufacture of institutional furniture. Little if any metal furniture will be found in hotels.

The executive housekeeper should examine samples to ensure that furniture is well designed, constructed with corner blocks (Figure 4.1) to withstand hard and abusive use, well finished, and refinishable. Joints are major factors in the strength and durability of well-made furniture. Figure 4.2 shows examples of various types of furniture joints. Mortise and tenon joints or double doweled joints are used in well-made furniture. Desks, luggage racks, chests of drawers, and pieces that provide storage are known as case furniture and are primarily constructed with dovetail joints. Some metal pieces will be used in the construction of case furniture for drawer guides and luggage receivers. Drawer construction in case furniture should always have concealed dovetail joints in the front piece to ensure that constant motion of the drawer will not cause the drawer front to become detached. Laminated tops are an essential element of most institutional furniture. Spilled drinks and beverage rings would quickly mar the finish and stain ordinary wood furniture.

Figure 4.3 shows an example of institutional guestroom furnishings and Figure 4.4 is an example of institutional room furnishings for a senior living center.

Upholstery Fabrics

Most fabrics are constructed of fibers. These fibers are of two general classifications—natural fibers and synthetic fibers. Table 4.4 lists examples of each type of fiber. Most synthetic fabrics are made from either cellulose or coal-tar derivatives.

Natural fibers are strong, long wearing, available in many finishes, and easily dyed. They must, however, be treated for insects and not be allowed to remain wet. Natural fibers are usually expensive when woven into fabrics for upholstery.

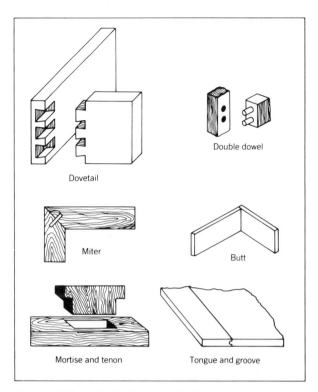

Figure 4.2 Methods of joining wood in furniture construction.

Synthetic fabrics are less expensive, not subject to damage by insects or moisture, and clean easily, but they are more likely to create static electricity and are difficult to dye. Dark color synthetics also show lint badly.

Many upholstered fabrics are blends of natural and synthetic fibers. Industrial upholstery fabrics are being woven into stretch knits that are dense, full bodied, and strong and into earth textures. Some are double knit and are woven into a jacquard texture; others are woven into fine textured materials.

Plastic Fabrics. Plastic fabrics have a leatherlike finish and are used in furniture construction. They may be wiped clean with a soapy cloth or sponge. Plastic

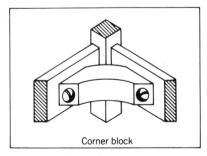

Figure 4.1 Corner block used in the construction of well-made chairs.

Table 4.4 Fibers Used in Upholstery Fabrics

NATURAL FIBERS	SYNTHETIC FIBERS
Cotton	Rayon
Wool	Acetate
Linen	Acrilan
Silk	Arnel
	Dacron
	Dynel
	Fiberglass
	Nylon
	Orlon
	Vicara

Figure 4.3 Guestroom contract (institutional) furniture from the Broyhill Corporation. (Photo courtesy of Jacqueline & Associates, Las Vegas.)

fabrics may also be found in mattress ticking and blackout drapes.

Fixtures

The broad category of fixtures associated with hotel guestrooms includes decorative accessories, pictures and paintings, and lighting treatment.

Accessories, Pictures, and Paintings. Most often, the designer who is responsible for the appearance of the room will have planned the accessories and paintings. The best use of accessories is for there to be a few that give the desired impact. Accessories, like furniture, must be selected to conform to the size of the room and should not be overdone.

Balance of color and fundamental style is essential to achieve the proper feeling. Formal balance is a term used to describe formal appearance (for example, two candlesticks flanking a similar style bowl of flowers). Informal balance occurs when assembly of dissimilar, unequally sized and shaped objects are assembled into groupings that appear balanced.

Framed hanging mirrors (with pronounced frames) give glamour to a room and are effective. Such mirrors might be used in place of a picture or painting. Usually the room designer will also select paintings that conform to the room decor. Most hotel paintings will be lithographs in order that volume economy in purchase may be attained. Colors in wall hangings are used to make room decor a pleasing experience.

The universal rule about hanging mirrors and paintings is that the geometric center of the item should be at eye level. Since viewers are of different height, discretion must be used so as to balance the room properly.

BROYHILL CONTRACT
SENIOR LIVING/WESTPORT

Figure 4.4 Nursing home contract (institutional) furniture from the Broyhill Corporation. (Photo courtesy of Jacqueline & Associates, Las Vegas.)

Lighting

Proper lighting heightens the beauty of a room and adds to guest comfort. Lighting can create a desired effect by flattering the occupant as well as the room furnishings. Lighting should never be an afterthought but should be considered in the total design of the room. The sconce in Figure 4.5 would look completely out of place in a guestroom decorated in an Early American motif.

In many modern decors the source of lighting is concealed. Contemporary decors also use table, wall, and hanging lamps, which are securely fastened to the facility to reduce theft and avoid accidents. Table lamps should have their on/off switches located at their base. This reduces scorched fingers and the prospect of groping about in

the dark for the switch. Floor lamps are seldom, if ever, used in modern hotel construction because of the space used and the tripping hazard created by unsightly cords.

Fluorescent lighting used in concealed lighting fixtures should never be of the cool variety because of the harshness resulting in the tone of light. Only warm fluorescent lighting should be used. Fluorescent lighting, like incandescent lighting, may be controlled by rheostat to create a feeling of comfort and softness. Pink incandescent bulbs provide warmth and give a rose-colored glow to skin tones. Orange or amber incandescent lighting causes an unflattering harsh gray skin tone. Warm fluorescent bulbs controlled by the proper type of rheostat can be energy saving and reduce power consumption by as much as 75 percent. Furthermore, they can last up to ten times

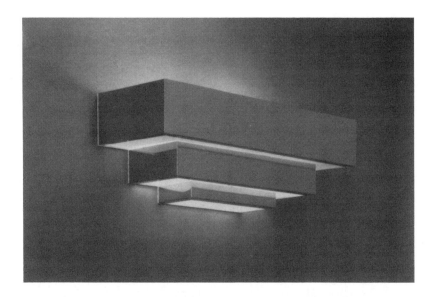

Figure 4.5 Sconce by Visa Lighting Corporation (Photo courtesy of Jacqueline & Associates, Las Vegas.)

longer than ordinary incandescent bulbs. Compact fluorescents will screw into almost any light socket. Finally, sufficient light for reading must be provided in the room. Both hanging lamps over work tables and bed lamps for reading should have bulbs of sufficient wattage.

Guestroom Safes

A recent newcomer to the guestroom fixture scene is the guestroom safe. Introduced for the first time in 1983 by Elsafe, guestroom safes are now available from companies offering dozens of models with hundreds of features. There are two main varieties available: electronic and manual. Access to many electronic safes is monitored from a panel at the front desk, and if the hotel charges a fee for their use, the system can electronically post the charge to a guest's folio. Guestroom safes come wall mounted, floor mounted, and hidden inside nightstands and armoires. Normal access to the safe may be through a common key, a keypad, the use of a special card, or even a standard credit card. Other features to look for when selecting guestroom safes are interior dimensions and fire ratings.

Minibars

A new and potentially very profitable fixture in the modern guestroom is the minibar. Stocked with sodas, juices, liquor, and snacks, the minibar is a tempting convenience that few guests can resist. As with guestroom safes, there are dozens of companies and hundreds of models from which to choose. Minibars can either be leased or purchased outright by the hotelier. A number of companies lease the equipment

out to the hotel for a fee and/or a share in the profits. Minibars range from manual systems to fully automated units.

The fully automated systems can electronically sense when an item is removed from the shelf and can automatically post the charge for the item to the guest's folio. At the same time, it can print out a stock list for each room, thus letting the staff know what needs to be restocked in every room. Automated systems can also be electronically locked when the room is rented to minors or when the room is rented to paid-in-advance guests.

Other systems require housekeeping to take a physical inventory and relay the information via a hand-held computer to the front desk. The manual systems often rely on the honor system, which may or may not be effective, depending on location and guest profile. Stories abound of guests having filled vodka bottles with water or running out to grocery stores the next day to replace used sodas and beers.

Audio-Visual Equipment

Audio-visual guestroom equipment includes telephone systems, radios, televisions, and video cassette recorders (VCRs).

The room telephone with its red message light has undergone immense technological changes at some properties over the past few years. Now, the telephone serves as a communication and room control system. The television, radio, heat, lighting level, and air conditioning can be controlled from one central console. The telephone can be directly linked to the hotel's property management system, allowing housekeepers to inform the linen room and the front desk of the status of the room directly through the guest's telephone.

Televisions have changed over the years as well. Although 19-inch color televisions are still the normal size, the television of today is commonly equipped with a guest-pay programming device that allows first-run movies to appear on the guestroom television.

Guestroom televisions often come with no on-set secondary controls that can be broken. All tuning is done through the anchored remote on the night-stand or through a special set-up transmitter that the hotel controls so the color and tint cannot be altered by guests. Many guestroom TVs have AM/FM clock radio modules attached to the set, while others have installed compact video cassette recorders. Many hotels rent recently released movies either from the front desk or from special cabinets located inside the guestrooms.

Summary

The executive housekeeper must be not only a planner but also an administrator with a basic knowledge of budgeting procedure, furniture, fixtures, equipment, cleaning products, and supply inventories.

Material planning for hotel operations begins with an understanding of budgeting systems by which material resources will be allocated. Capital expenditures, operating budgets, and preopening budgets were defined and discussed in this chapter. Classification of material resources must be understood. Knowledge of those material items that are part of the fixed assets and of other items that are part of inventories that will be used up in the generation of revenue is also important if costs are to be controlled. Inventory control is more than the mere counting of items; it is the entire process by which material is classified, ordered, received, stored, issued, and otherwise accounted for. The executive housekeeper involved in opening a hotel is involved not only with establishing certain material accounts and inventories, but also with arranging physical layouts to store materials, developing systems to account for supply use, making arrangements to purchase products, and establishing relationships with vendors and purveyors.

In this chapter and the following three chapters, a complete analysis of the material inventories with which the executive housekeeper may be involved is presented. A continuation of the topic of inventory control will be presented as the management functions of direction and control are developed.

KEY TERMS AND CONCEPTS

Administration
Material
Software items
Budgets
Capital expenditure budgets
Depreciation
Furniture, fixtures, and equipment (FFE)
Software
Capitalized
Expensed
Operating budgets
Operating cost
Revenue
Labor costs
Employee costs
Controllable costs

Control profit
Control loss
Preopening budgets
Pro formas
Inventory control
Pars
Classification of material
Assets
Current assets
Fixed assets
Equipment
Inventories
Books of account
Life expectancy
Liabilities
Move-in day
Spare component

DISCUSSION AND REVIEW QUESTIONS

1. Some items of material are capitalized; others are expensed. What is the difference between these two terms?
2. Explain the difference between capital expenditure budgets and operational budgets. In an ongoing operation, how many times in a fiscal year is each prepared? Which is usually prepared first? Why?
3. Preopening budgets usually include items such as funds for opening ceremonies and parties, advertising, and public relations. List several

other important items that should be funded in a preopening budget. Why should the preopening budget be amortized, and over what period of time?

4. Define these terms:
   Inventory control
   Minibar
   Material classification
   Dual-purpose sleep equipment
   In-room Safe

5. Explain the concept of using temporary storage when opening a hotel.

6. Discuss the differences, including advantages and disadvantages, between innerspring mattresses and foam mattresses.

5

Material Planning: Floors, Walls, and Windows

CHAPTER OBJECTIVES

1. To identify the various types of floor coverings and to be able to describe the relative advantages and disadvantages of each type.
2. To describe the standard procedures employed in cleaning a floor.
3. To identify the elements of carpet construction.
4. To describe standard carpet-cleaning procedures.
5. To identify standard window-washing techniques.
6. To describe materials used in wallcoverings and window treatments.
7. To obtain a general knowledge regarding the care and treatment of walls, windows, and floors.

This chapter examines the materials used in the construction of floors and floor coverings. The specific properties of appearance, durability, cost, and ease of maintenance for each type of floor will be covered. The treatment of each floor type (methods that are used in the cleaning, sealing, and refinishing of floors) will also be examined.

Particular attention will be given to carpeting. Carpet composition, construction, and design will

be addressed, and alternative cleaning methods for carpets will be evaluated.

Wallcoverings and window treatments will also be described. The different types of wall coverings, their durability, relative cost, ease of maintenance, and proper cleaning procedures will be explored.

In window treatments, the construction of, cleaning of, and materials used in drapes, shades, and blinds will be studied.

Floor Types and their Care

Whether for a facility under construction or for the remodeling of an existing property, the executive housekeeper is often called upon to assist in the selection of the floor or floor coverings.

There are a multitude of variables that must be considered when selecting the appropriate floor or floor covering. The floor must meet the aesthetic requirements of the architect and/or interior designer. Floors must coordinate with wall and window coverings. They must also coordinate with the room's furnishings.

Floor and floor covering selection is not predicated only upon design and aesthetic considerations, however; many other factors, such as durability, installation cost, maintenance cost, and ease of maintenance should also be considered in the selection process.

The amount and type of traffic to which a particular floor will be subjected must be determined before selecting the flooring. Next, the durability of the proposed floor materials to be subjected to the expected traffic must be considered. In other words, one must project how long each floor material under consideration can be expected to last when it is subjected to the expected wear.

The executive housekeeper should then estimate the cleaning and maintenance costs for each of the prospective floor materials over the life of the floor. These costs will include labor, chemicals, and equipment.

Installation costs should then be added to the maintenance costs. This sum should be divided by the expected life of the floor (estimated in months). The monthly cost of each of the prospective floor materials can be compared, and this comparison can be used in the decision-making process. Certainly, other variables, such as how the intended flooring complements the overall design and the relative ease of maintenance, should be weighed against the cost considerations.

Floor Care Methods

Floor care is a four-step process, according to Saunders and Mazzoli of Glit Inc. (Figure 5.1). In this section we shall explore each phase of the Saunders and Mazzoli FPMR floor care model.[1]

Foundation

The first phase of the FPMR model is **foundation**. Floor finishes are not permanent fixtures. Periodically, a floor must be stripped of its old **finish** and a new finish must be applied to the floor. Saunders and Mazzoli list four reasons to strip a floor of its existing finish:

1. When there is a breakdown in the floor surface and there are definite worn traffic areas that are beginning to show. These areas are indicated by a worn-away finish and/or seal, and the bare floor becomes exposed.
2. A noticeable flaking or chipping of the surface of the finish from too much old finish. This mainly occurs when the wet scrubbing procedure has not been followed.
3. When the "wet look" begins to show definite dark shadowy areas as you look into the surface of the floor. This is usually blamed on burnishing the floor without wet mopping first. The result? Shiny dirt!
4. When there is a staining from spills or from inadequate pick-up of the cleaning solutions while mopping the floors.[2]

Once the decision has been made to refinish the floor, the first stage is to strip the floor of its existing finish. Figure 5.2 lists the equipment required to perform this task.

The purpose of **stripping** is to remove both the old floor finish and all of the dirt that has been embedded in that finish. This is accomplished in the following way: First dust-mop the floor to remove all loose dirt and dust. Then get two clean mops and two clean mop buckets and fill the buckets half full

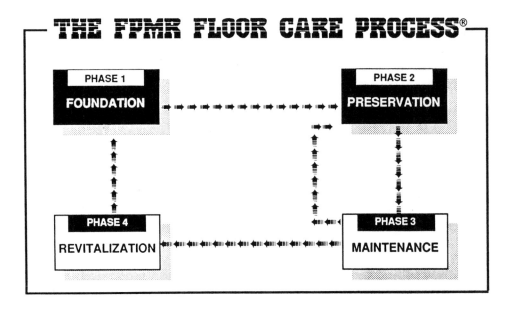

Figure 5.1 Mazzoli and Saunders' "FPMR Floor Care Process Model." (Used with permission of the authors.)

with hot water. Add the recommended amount of stripping solution to one of the buckets. Rope off the areas to be stripped and place warning signs at appropriate locations. Place mats at the exits to the area being stripped so that the stripping solution is not tracked to other floors.

Lay down a generous amount of the stripping solution in a small area of the floor and let stand for approximately five minutes. Do not allow the solution to dry. If allowed to dry, the stripping solution, mixed together with the old finish, will turn into a dirty grey paste, and the entire process must be begun again.

After the solution has stood for five minutes, start by scrubbing along the baseboards or in the corners with a scrubbing pad. Then start scrubbing with a floor machine using a black or brown pad. Use a machine that runs between 175 and 350 rpm; do not use a high-speed buffer. Be careful not to splash the walls with the stripping solution. Using the floor machine, scrub in a straight line along the baseboard; then scrub

Required Supplies & Equipment

Clean dust mop
Dust pan and brush
Standard speed floor machine with pad drive assembly or stripping brush
Clean floor stripping pads
Wet pick-up vacuum
Set of "Wet Floor" signs
2 clean mop buckets with clean wringers
2 wet mop handles with clean looped-end banded mops
Putty knife
Doorway mats
Hand pads and holder for edge cleaning
Floor stripping concentrate
Stripper neutralizer concentrate

Figure 5.2 Required floor stripping supplies and equipment. (Used with permission of the International Sanitary Supply Association, Inc.)

from side to side. When a section of the floor has been covered, go back over the area in the opposite direction.

Once the area has been thoroughly scrubbed, the old finish can be picked up from the floor. The best way to perform this task is to use a wet/dry pick-up vacuum, but if one is not available, you must have an additional pick-up bucket. The same mop that was used for laying down the solution can be used to pick up the dirty solution. Rinse that mop in the pick-up bucket and change the water when it gets dirty.

The next step is to completely rinse and dry the floor using a clean mop and clear hot water in the rinse bucket. Then either pick up the rinse water with the mop, or use the wet/dry vacuum to remove all rinse water from the floor.

Once the floor dries, check to see if there is a grey film on the floor by rubbing your hand over the dried floor. If a film is present, there is still old finish on the floor; the stripping procedure should then be repeated.

When finished, clean up all buckets and wringers, wash all mop heads, and wash the pad on the floor machine and all other equipment used.

The second phase involves the application of floor finish, or **sealer**. Sealers include the permanent type, penetrating solvent-based sealers, used on concrete, marble, **terrazzo**, or other stone surfaces. Floor stripping does not remove these types of sealers. A second type is a water emulsion stripper that is placed on certain kinds of asphalt and tile floors. This type of sealer has to be replaced after floor stripping.

On today's market there is quite a variety of floor sealer/finishes, and many of them work quite well on the modern floors for which they were intended. For older floors, however, the application of a sealer, followed by a finish, is the standard approach.

A floor sealer/finish serves three purposes. First, it protects the floor from wear and staining caused by traffic, inadvertent spills, and chemicals used in the cleaning process. Second, it provides a safe surface upon which to walk. The appropriate finish should make the floor more slip resistant. Third, the finish has an aesthetic appeal. It makes the floor shine, conveying a positive impression to both customers and employees. Today, the buzzword in floor care is the "wet look," which is an extremely high gloss on tile, wood, and stone floors. Floors of today must not only look clean enough to be noticed; they must positively shine. Interestingly, this current trend toward the "wet look" may appear dangerous to the uninitiated, but, in reality, these floor surfaces are often less slippery than a dull surface.

Figure 5.3 is a listing of the required supplies and equipment to seal/finish a floor.

The first step is to inspect the floor and make sure that it is completely dry and clean. The International Sanitary Supply Association then recommends that the mop bucket be lined with a plastic trash liner to save clean-up time.[3]

Using either a clean nylon mop, a lamb's wool applicator, or a mechanical applicator designed for the task, first apply the finish next to the baseboard in smooth strokes (see Figure 5.3). Then apply the finish to the center area with figure-8 strokes if using the mop. Be sure that the first coat and all subsequent coats are *thin* coats. Thick coats of finish do not last as long and can make for a very slippery surface. Four thin coats are far better than two thicker coats.

After the first coat is dry to the touch, let the floor sit for at least the length of time that it took the first coat to dry before applying a second coat. Repeat this procedure for each coat.

To avoid finish buildup in corners and along the baseboards, do not apply more than two coats within 12 inches of the walls.

Finally, allow the floor to dry as long as possible before buffing or burnishing, and keep the floor closed to traffic as long as possible. Seventy-two hours is the optimal drying time for most floor finishes.

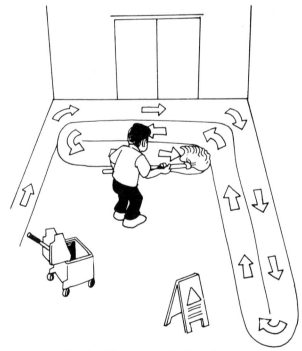

Required Supplies & Equipment

Clean mop bucket and clean wringer
Set of "Wet Floor" signs
Floor finish
Clean plastic trash bag
Clean "Floor Finish" mop

Figure 5.3 Required floor sealing supplies and equipment. (Used with permission of the International Sanitary Supply Association, Inc.)

Buffing (or polishing) the floor is done with a floor machine that delivers up to $1\frac{1}{2}$ horsepower and turns at 175 to 350 rpm. **Burnishing** is accomplished with a different type of floor machine that places less weight on the floor, which allows it to turn at speeds in excess of 1000 rpm. This higher speed, which creates more friction, creates the high-gloss "wet look" in floors that has become so popular.

Whichever type of machine is issued, the type of pad used is the same (white in color). There is a universal color code that is adhered to by all pad manufacturers to ensure that the proper type of pad can be used for each application. Black and brown pads are used for stripping, blue and green pads for scrubbing, red for spray cleaning, and white for polishing.

Once the finishing process is completed, all equipment should be washed immediately. Washed mop heads should be segregated by their original use and should not be used for any other application.

A tile or terrazzo floor beginning to turn yellow indicates that too much finish has been applied to the floor, and it then becomes necessary to strip one or two of the layers off the floor in order to restore it to its original luster. One positive note is that the new polymer finishes do not yellow like the old wax finishes.

Preservation

The second phase of the FPMR model is preservation.[4] This is accomplished through three techniques: sweeping/dust mopping, spot mopping, and the use of walk-off mats.[5]

Sweeping is done only when the floor surface is too rough for a dust mop. Push brooms are used for large areas and old-fashioned corn brooms are best for corners and tight spaces. A practiced sweeper develops a rhythm and "bounces" the push broom to avoid rolling under the bristles.

Dust mopping is the preferred way to remove dust, sand, and grit from a floor. If these substances are not removed from a floor on a daily basis, they will scratch the surface of the finish, diminishing its luster, and will eventually penetrate down to the floor itself.

Use the largest dust mop that is manageable. When mopping, keep the mop head on the floor at all times and do not move it backwards. When you reach the end of a corridor, swivel the mop around, and on the return pass, overlap the area that you have dusted by about 8 inches. Use a dust pan to sweep up accumulated trash, and pick up gum with a putty knife.

Clean the mop frequently by vacuuming the mop in the custodian's closet or by shaking the mop in a plastic bag. The time to treat a mop is at the end of dusting, not at the beginning, so that the mop will have a chance to dry out. Never use oil-based dust mop treatments; these can discolor a stone floor. The mop head should be periodically removed and washed when it becomes saturated with dirt.

When finished, hang the mop up with the yarn away from the wall. Do not let the mop stand on the floor or touch a wall surface because it may leave a stain.

Spot mopping is essential to the preservation of a floor's surface. Liquids and solids that are spilled on the floor's surface, if left for any length of time, may penetrate the finish and stain the floor. Even acids from fruit juices may wreak havoc on a floor if they are not immediately cleaned up. A mop and bucket should be made available to take care of these accidents.

When spot mopping, clean cold water should be used so that the finish on the floor is not softened. Detergents should be avoided unless they become a necessity, that is, when a substance has been allowed to dry on the floor. If they are necessary, use a pH neutral detergent, avoid abrasives, and dilute the detergent to a level that will accomplish the task but will not harm the finish.

The use of walk-off mats is the third preservation method. Their purpose is to prevent dirt and grit from being tracked onto the floor's surface from outside sources. There are three considerations when using walk-off mats: (1) make sure that the mat is large enough so that everyone will step on the mat at least twice with the same foot; (2) select a mat that correlates to the type of soil that is being tracked into the area; and (3) change out dirty mats. A mat that is saturated with dirt and soils will be a source of floor contamination rather than a cure for that contamination.

Maintenance

The third phase of the FPMR model is maintenance.[6] This involves the periodic removal of stains, dirt, and scuffs that appear on the surface of the finish. Its purpose is to produce lustrous, shiny, clean floors. Maintenance encompasses **damp mopping**, spray buffing, and burnishing. These techniques are done sequentially, and each technique is often performed immediately after the preceding one.

Before the floor can be damp mopped, it must first be dust mopped. After the floor is dusted, the equipment listed in Figure 5.4 must be assembled. Add neutral or mildly alkaline detergent to the mop water. The detergent used may be the variety that needs no rinsing. If not, the floor will need to be rinsed after the detergent solution is applied. Immerse the mop in the bucket and wring it out until it is only *damp*. Use the same pattern in the damp mopping of a floor that was used in the application of stripper to the floor.

Required Supplies & Equipment

Clean dust mop
Dust pan and brush
Automatic floor machine with pad driving assembly or brush
Clean mop bucket with clean wringer
Wet mop handle with clean looped-end banded mop
Squeegee with handle
Floor pads
Putty knife
Approved detergent solution appropriate to the area
Set of "Wet Floor" signs
Clean wipers

Figure 5.4 Required damp mopping supplies and equipment. (Used with permission of the International Sanitary Supply Association, Inc.)

The solution in the bucket should be changed when the water becomes dirty. A brush or a floor machine may be used for stubborn spots and a squeegee may be used to help speed the drying of the floor. Baseboards should be wiped off immediately if solution is splashed on them.

As in the foundation section, all equipment should be cleaned upon the completion of a task.

Spray buffing may follow the damp mopping procedure. Spray a section of the floor (approximately 4' × 6') with the buffing solution and buff the floor with a floor machine using a red buffing pad. Buff the area with a side-to-side motion until the floor begins to shine. Allow the machine to overlap the previously buffed area and change the dirty buffing pads frequently. Figure 5.5 is a list of the required supplies and equipment needed for spray buffing.

Burnishing or dry buffing uses a high-speed machine that produces from 300 rpm to 1500 rpm, depending on the particular model. This machine is operated in a straight line rather than a side-to-side motion. The white floor pad is used for dry buffing and should be changed frequently. As with spray buffing, it is wise to overlap completed areas when burnishing to ensure a uniform finish.

Required Supplies & Equipment

Clean dust mop
Dust pan and brush
Floor Machine (175-400 rpm) with pad drive assembly or brush
Clean floor polish pads
Clean mop bucket with clean wringer
Wet mop handle and clean looped-end banded mop
Approved detergent solution appropriate for the area
Spray buff solution in dispensing container
"Wet Floor" signs

Figure 5.5 Spray buffing supplies and equipment. (Used with permission of the International Sanitary Supply Association, Inc.)

Revitalization

The fourth phase in the FPMR model is revitalization.[7] Revitalization or deep scrubbing involves removing one or more layers of the old finish and applying new finish. The first step is to combine cool water with a neutral or mildly alkaline cleaning solution, which is then applied to the floor and scrubbed with a floor machine using a black pad. The floor machine is passed over the floor once to lessen the chance of removing too much finish, and cool rather than hot water is used because hot water would soften all the layers of finish.

The dirty water is picked up with a wet vac or mop, and the floor is rinsed using a clean mop and clean rinse water. Once the floor is dry, one or two coats of finish are applied, and the floor can then be buffed to a renewed shine.[8]

In the next section we shall review the major varieties of floors and the floor care requirements peculiar to each variety. The following suggested floor care techniques are only meant to be general guidelines for specific types of floors. Readers are cautioned to follow the guidelines of the manufacturer in regard to cleaning supplies and techniques.

Nonresilient Floors

Nonresilient floors are those floors that do not "give" underfoot. Their hardness ensures their durability. Dents are not a problem with these types of floors. However, the hardness of these types of floors is also a major drawback. They are extremely tiring to those who must stand on them for any length of time.

Brick

Brick is not commonly used as flooring material for interiors, except to convey a rustic theme. Brick floors are normally left in their natural unglazed state and color, but they can be sealed and finished for some interior applications.

Unglazed bricks are a highly porous material, and they provide a highly durable, fairly slip-resistant floor, but the mortar used between the bricks can deteriorate rapidly if it is not properly maintained. Deteriorating mortar and loose bricks can quickly become a serious hazard for slip-and-fall accidents.

Another caution is not to use bricks where there may be grease spills. Since an unglazed brick is very porous, spilled grease and oil will be absorbed into the brick and will be very hard to remove. If the floor then becomes wet, the surface of the brick will have this oil and water mixture, making for a very slippery surface.

Cleaning Procedures. Brick floors create special problems in cleaning. If the bricks are the specially-made type of slip-resistant brick, they will cause cotton mop heads to fray. Also, unglazed bricks tend to become very dusty.

The best approach to cleaning a brick floor is to vacuum it with a brush and, when mopping, use a bristle brush in combination with a wet/dry vacuum.

Sealing, Finishing, Stripping. Although the bricks themselves are not always sealed, the mortar between the bricks needs to be sealed and maintained on a regular basis. Be sure to select a sealer that is designed for this application.

Finishes, such as waxes and acrylics, are not normally applied to brick surfaces; because of this, there is no need for stripping.

Ceramic and Terra Cotta Tiles

Like brick, ceramic and terra cotta tiles are made from clay that is fired in a kiln. However, ceramic tile differs from brick in that a coating is applied to one side of the tile and the tile is then fired in a kiln, creating a surface that is almost totally impervious to soil and liquids. Figure 5.6 is an example of glazed ceramic floor tiles.

Terra cotta tiles, typically six inches square, resemble bricks because they are left in their natural color, and they do not have the glaze coat that is commonly applied to ceramic tile. The color of terra cotta is traditionally a reddish-brown. One variety of terra cotta is often used in kitchen floor applications because it is marketed with a rough surface that makes it slip resistant in greasy conditions.

These tiles can also be classified as completely nonresilient surfaces, and since there is no "give" to the tile, care must be taken not to drop heavy, hard objects on the floor that could pit or crack the surface.

Ceramic tile comes in a multitude of colors and can have either a matte or glossy surface. Care must be taken when selecting ceramic tile because certain solid colors will show dirt quite easily. Ceramic tile also appears on walls and countertops, as well as on interior and exterior floors.

Finally, here is one note of caution regarding ceramic tile and its use on certain types of floors: Unless a special slip-resistant surface is employed, tile surfaces that are wet, greasy, or icy make for a very dangerous floor surface.

Cleaning Procedures. The tiles must be cleaned frequently to remove dust and grit that could damage the glaze on the tile. Cleaning procedures might include dust mopping, damp mopping, and light scrubbing when needed. Cotton mop heads should

Figure 5.6 Glazed ceramic tile from the Dal-Tile Corporation. (Used with permission of Jacqueline & Associates, Las Vegas.)

not be used on tiles that contain slip-resistant surfaces, because these surfaces will quickly shred a traditional mop head. Scrubbing should be done with brushes and the water should be picked up with a wet/dry vacuum.

Sealing, Finishing, and Stripping. The tile does not need to be sealed because it already has a scratch and stain resistant surface; however, the grout between the tiles has to be sealed with a sealer that is specifically designed for ceramic tile grout.

Finishes are not normally applied to ceramic tiles, so stripping is not a concern.

Concrete

The concrete floor is employed for its utility, not for its attractiveness or its resiliency. A concrete floor is composed of cement, rocks, and sand, to which water is added to initiate a chemical reaction that changes the ingredients into a stonelike material.

Cleaning Procedures. The cleaning procedures that may be used on a concrete floor range from a daily dust mopping, to damp mopping, to heavy scrubbing to remove grease and soils. Since concrete, and especially unsealed concrete, is so porous, an immediate effort must be made to clean up spilled liquids before they are absorbed into the concrete and cause unsightly stains.

Sealing, Finishing, and Stripping. Concrete definitely requires sealing. An unsealed concrete floor will be constantly dusty and will absorb dirt and any liquid that is spilled on it.

The sealer used on a concrete surface must be a permeable sealer. Moisture and acids in the concrete percolate to the surface as the concrete dries. A permeable sealer is one that allows moisture and acids to evaporate from the surface of the concrete. If a nonpermeable sealer is used, the moisture and acids will be trapped on the surface just under the sealer. As the acids and moisture begin to concentrate, the surface of the concrete will begin to disintegrate.

The concrete must be completely clean before a sealer is applied; if it is not, the sealer will not adhere to the surface of the concrete. If the concrete is new, special sealers must be used to allow the concrete to continue to "cure."

Finishes may be applied to concrete floors, but they should be compatible with porous floors and permeable sealers. Color sealers and paints should be avoided because once they start to show wear, they become unsightly and are almost impossible to repair. However, on a cured floor, epoxy sealers and paints can be applied to help diminish the effects of heavy wear. Finishes can be buffed with a rotary floor machine.

Stripping the finish from a concrete floor normally requires an alkaline stripping agent that has been properly diluted with water. The stripping solution is then applied to the floor surface using a rotary floor machine with an abrasive pad.

After the old sealer is removed and before a new sealer is applied, the floor is often treated with a special acidic solution that will "etch" the surface of the floor, providing greater adhesion for the new sealer.

Epoxy

The **epoxy** floor is a compound of synthetic resins that provides an extremely durable, seamless floor. These floors are an ideal choice when a floor is required to withstand massive loads. Decorative particles can be mixed into the epoxy resin to provide an attractive, yet highly utilitarian, flooring.

Epoxy floors are ideal for trade show facilities, locker rooms, loading docks, and shower areas.

Cleaning Procedures. Exotic procedures and techniques are not necessary when cleaning an epoxy floor; sweeping, mopping, and scrubbing with an alkaline cleaner diluted with water is sufficient.

Sealing, Finishing, and Stripping. Epoxy floors should be sealed, and they can receive a finish; however, finishing is not necessary to the maintenance of an epoxy floor. Stripping is accomplished with commercial alkaline strippers used in conjunction with a rotary floor machine.

Stone Floors

Common types of natural stone flooring include marble, travertine, serpentine, granite, slate, and sandstone (see Figure 5.7). All natural stone products share certain properties that must be taken into consideration by the professional housekeeper to ensure the proper care of this type of flooring.

Natural stone flooring may look impervious to the elements, but it is decidedly not as resistant to damage as it looks. Acids and moisture can have disastrous effects on natural stone. Some acids are present naturally in the stone, but even the acid from spilled orange juice can have a deleterious effect on stone floors, causing pitting, cracking, and **spalling**. These floors need to have moisture-permeable sealers applied so moisture and acids do not build up under the sealer and destroy the floor's surface. Oils and grease can permanently stain untreated stone floors because these floors are extremely porous.

Cleaning Procedures. To prevent the staining of stone floors, the dust mops should be free of all oil-based dusting compounds. Dusting should be carried out on a daily basis because grit, sand, and other abrasives that are tracked onto a stone floor will quickly mar the floor's finish.

A pH neutral detergent is recommended to clean all natural stone floors. Highly alkaline cleaners as well as acidic compounds will damage stone floors. When mopping stone floors, do not let water or chemicals remain on the floor. A final rinse of clean water should be applied and then immediately picked up with a mop or a wet/dry vacuum.

Figure 5.7 Agglomerate marble, a fabricated marble composed of natural marble stones blended with polyester resins from Dal-Tile Corporation. (Used with permission of Jacqueline & Associates, Las Vegas.)

Sealing, Finishing, and Stripping. Most stone floors need to be protected with a moisture-permeable sealer. Finishes should normally be applied in one or two thin layers and buffed. Applying heavy layers of finish does not work well because it causes stone floors to become slippery.

When stripping the finish off of a stone floor, make sure that the stripping agent is either neutral or mildly alkaline. Acids and strong alkalines can damage virtually all types of stone floors.

Terrazzo

A terrazzo floor is a mosaic flooring composed of Portland cement that has been embedded with marble and/or granite chips. See Figure 5.8, where a terrazzo floor is being burnished with a high-speed burnisher. Once the floor has set, it is then ground by progressively finer grit stones until a perfectly smooth and polished surface is obtained. The chips used in a terrazzo floor can differ in both size and color, creating a variety of colorful and attractive floors.

With proper care, a terrazzo floor will hold its original luster and will last indefinitely. What de-

stroys most terrazzo surfaces is not use, but improper maintenance.

Cleaning Procedures. Terrazzo should be dusted daily to remove harmful grit and sand that can wear down the surface, but dust mops should not be treated with oil dressings because oil is the archenemy of a terrazzo floor. Once oil or grease penetrates a terrazzo floor, it is virtually impossible to remove.

Steel wool should not be used on the surface of a terrazzo floor because the steel wool may put rust stains on the marble chips.

When selecting detergents and cleaners for terrazzo floors, stay away from acid cleaners, abrasives and scrubbing powders, and preparations that have an alkalinity above a pH 10. Always rinse a freshly scrubbed floor and do not allow water or cleaners to remain on the floor surface.

Sealing, Stripping, and Finishing. All terrazzo floors must be sealed with a sealer designed for this particular type of floor. The sealer must be water-permeable so that moisture can evaporate from the surface of the terrazzo but will also help to prevent the absorption of oils and chemicals into the terrazzo.

When deep scrubbing or stripping a terrazzo floor, avoid highly alkaline strippers.

Since the floor has a natural sheen, finish is often thought to be unnecessary, but if a mirrored finish is desired (often referred to as the "wet look") then one or two thin coats of finish burnished with a high-speed buffer will produce the sought-after result.

Resilient Surfaces

Resilient floors have various degrees of "give" to their surfaces. This degree of resiliency ranges from asphalt floors, which are almost as hard as a concrete or stone surface, to carpeted and padded floors. Under this classification we have included asphalt tile, cork, linoleum, rubber, vinyl, vinyl composition tile, and wood. Because the care and maintenance of carpet is such an involved and complex topic, the treatment of carpet has its own section in this chapter. Finally, some universal precautions to take with all resilient floors is to limit static loads to no more than 250 lbs. per square inch, remove those little metal domes from furniture legs, and use rubber rollers on chairs.

Asphalt Tile

Asphalt tile is one of the lowest-cost resilient floor coverings available, and it is quite durable under most normal conditions. It will, however, become brittle when exposed to prolonged periods of low temperature and will also dent when heavy objects

Figure 5.8 Burnishing a terrazzo floor. (Used with permission of the Advance Machine Company.)

are present on its surface, particularly when the ambient air temperature is above 80° Fahrenheit.

Asphalt tile is also fire resistant; in fact, it is one of the most mar resistant of all floorings in regard to cigarette burns.

Cleaning Procedures. Dust mopping, damp mopping, and scrubbing, as described in the floor care methods section, will maintain and preserve the asphalt tile floor. One important item to remember when wet mopping is to never let water stand for any length of time on an asphalt tile floor. Standing water will attack the adhesive cement and will cause tiles to curl and loosen.

Sealing, Stripping, and Finishing. Asphalt tile is normally given several thin coats of finish and burnished or buffed with a floor machine. Never let stripping solution remain on the floor; always pick up the dirty solution immediately after scrubbing with a floor machine to avoid curling or loose tiles.

Cork Tile

Cork tile is made from the outer bark of cork oak trees grown in Spain and Portugal. The cork is ground into large granules, mixed with synthetic resins, and pressed into sheets, which are then cut into tiles. Contemporary cork tiles for floors usually have a top layer of clear vinyl applied to them (see Figure 5.9). This vinyl layer protects the cork from staining and wear.

Cork tiles traditionally have had limited application in industrial or institutional settings. One reason is that cork is susceptible to staining because it is one of the most porous of all floor coverings. Another limitation is that it is not durable; it is highly susceptible to abrasion. Cinders, sand, and gravel tracked on to a cork floor will severely shorten its life span. Finally, it is expensive. Cork rivals ceramic tiles in cost and does not have nearly the useful life of ceramic tile.

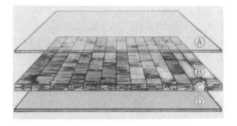

A. Pure transparent vinyl bonded wear surface
B. Natural Cork
C. Edges sealed against moisture
D. Bonded vinyl moisture barrier

Figure 5.9 How a vinyl bonded cork floor from Permagrain Inc. is constructed. (Used with permission of Jacqueline & Associates, Las Vegas.)

Although the use of cork has its drawbacks, it has three favorable properties that make it an attractive floor covering in limited settings: It absorbs sound, it is attractive, and most importantly, it is the most resilient of all floorings. This resilience has one drawback: Heavy objects resting on small weight-bearing surfaces will easily dent cork tile floors.

Cleaning Procedures. Natural cork tile floors are one of the most expensive of all floors to maintain. Cork tile floors should be swept daily, or more often, depending on usage. Natural cork tiles should only be damp mopped without detergents on infrequent occasions.

Vinyl-coated cork tiles can be wet mopped, providing that detergent solutions are not allowed to remain on the tiles for any length of time.

Stripping, Sealing, and Finishing. To remove the seal from a natural cork floor and repair any staining or discoloration, a special solvent is first applied and removed along with the seal and finish. Then the floor is sanded to remove surface stains. This is followed by successive coatings of seal followed by several thin coats of finish. The floor is then buffed.

Vinyl-covered tiles need not be sealed but can be given a few thin coats of finish and buffed with a floor machine.

Linoleum

In modern buildings, the use of vinyl has replaced **linoleum**, but on occasion, linoleum floors can still be found in older facilities. Linoleum was once so pervasive that many still use the term *linoleum* to indicate any continuous flooring material, such as solid vinyl flooring.

Linoleum was composed of oxidized linseed oil, resins, embedded cork, and wood flour with pigments pressed on a backing. Its properties included a remarkable degree of resiliency. Next to cork and rubber and, of course, padded carpeting, linoleum is considered to have the greatest degree of resiliency. Linoleum was quite durable, was resistant to oil and grease, and did not shrink.

The negative aspect of linoleum was that it was highly susceptible to water. The linoleum would absorb water and would then soften, causing it to lose its abrasion resistance and become more susceptible to indentation. Even high humidity would have a negative effect upon this material.

Cleaning Procedures. Frequent dusting is essential to the preservation of linoleum. The flooring can also be dry mopped using a pH neutral cleaner. Harsh abrasives and scouring powders should be avoided and water or detergent solutions should not be left in contact with the floor for any length of time.

When the floor is mopped, it should be allowed to dry completely before foot traffic is allowed upon it.

Stripping, Sealing, and Finishing. If the finish/sealer needs to be stripped from the floor, the stripper should be a neutral or mildly alkaline stripper. It should again be mentioned that water should not be permitted to remain on the floor's surface longer than it is absolutely necessary.

The floor should be sealed with a nonpermeable sealer applied in several thin coats. Once the sealer is completely dry, thin coats of finish can be applied and buffed using a standard floor machine or a high-speed buffer.

Rubber Floors

All modern rubber floors are made from synthetic rubber, such as **styrene butadiene rubber** (SBR). Rubber tiles are cured or vulcanized by the application of heat. Rubber floors are nonporous, waterproof surfaces. One major advantage is that they are quite resilient and will remain resilient over a considerable temperature range.

Rubber flooring is susceptible to alkalines, oils, grease, solvents, ultraviolet light, and ozone in the air. When attacked by these components, a rubber floor will often become tacky and soft. It will then become brittle and begin to crack and powder.

Rubber tiles will often have knobs on the surface or will have a tread pattern to improve traction, especially if liquids are frequently spilled on the surface.

Cleaning Procedures. Highly alkaline cleaning solutions should be avoided; it is best to use pH neutral detergents whenever possible. Cleaning solvents such as naptha and turpentine should never be used on a rubber floor.

Rubber floors are fairly easy to maintain. Daily dust mopping and an occasional damp mopping are all that is needed to maintain the floor.

Stripping, Sealing, and Finishing. Rubber floors need not be sealed, so the task of stripping is not necessary. A water emulsion floor polish can be applied, but it also is not necessary. The rubber floor will buff to a nice shine without the use of hard finishes. If a finish is used, it should be the type that is tolerant of a flexible floor surface and will not be susceptible to powdering. A high-speed floor burnishing system is not recommended because it may leave abrasion or burn marks on the floor.

Vinyl Floors

There are several types of vinyl floorings and tiles. The major varieties include vinyl asbestos tiles, vinyl composition tiles, homogeneous or flexible vinyl tiles, and laminated vinyl flooring.

Vinyl asbestos tiles are no longer made and have been removed from numerous commercial and residential settings because the **asbestos** in the tile is a known **carcinogen**. Improper cleaning of vinyl asbestos tile can release deadly asbestos fibers into the air and present a very real health hazard.

Laminated vinyl flooring is less expensive to manufacture than vinyl composition or **homogeneous** vinyl floors. The low initial cost may be deceiving, however, for once the top wear layer is worn through, the floor will have to be replaced. Some laminated floorings are only guaranteed for three years with moderate use. The cost of laminated vinyl flooring will vary in proportion to the thickness of the top vinyl wear layer.

In addition to the vinyl resins, vinyl composition tiles contain mineral fillers such as asphalt and pigments. Homogeneous vinyl tile may be either flexible or solid, and it has become the preferred standard for resilient tile flooring. It is practically unaffected by moisture, oils, and chemical solvents. The wearability of top grade vinyl tile is in direct proportion to its thickness, as the colors and patterns of the tile are present throughout the thickness of the tile. Less expensive vinyl tiles will only carry the pattern and color on the surface of the tiles.

Today, vinyl tiles come in a wide variety of colors and textures. Vinyl tiles are made to resemble wood, marble, granite, travertine, brick, and ceramic tiles. Some of these faux tiles are extremely good facsimiles and they sell for far less than the actual product.

Cleaning Procedures. Modern homogenous vinyl needs only to be dusted and damp mopped to restore its lustre. Daily dusting to remove sand and grit is extremely important to the care of vinyl because most types will scratch under heavy foot traffic. Some tiles are specially treated with a scratch resistant seal that is applied at the factory.

Modern vinyl is unaffected by alkaline detergents, but pH neutral detergents are recommended over heavy alkaline products.

Stripping, Sealing, and Finishing. Sealing, finishing, and stripping are not recommended for "no-wax" vinyl floors. Vinyl is nonporous, so sealing is not necessary and finish does not adhere well to "no-wax" vinyl flooring. "No-wax" vinyls are particularly susceptible to abrasion and should only be used in areas where the foot traffic is light to moderate. Purchasers of "no-wax" vinyl should look for "scratchguard" or other similar claims of protection.

On regular vinyl tile, finish is applied in thin coats and buffed. The finish is stripped by using recommended detergent strippers as described in the previous section on floor maintenance techniques.

Never allow a vinyl asbestos floor to become dry when stripping. Always keep the surface of the floor wet when operating the floor machine and use the least abrasive strip pad possible. Also, never buff or burnish a vinyl asbestos floor that does not have a protective coat of finish. Dry stripping or buffing without a finish will release the harmful asbestos fibers into the air, which then can be inhaled and cause lung disorders.

Wood Floors

There is nothing quite as attractive as the warmth and richness of wood floors (see Figure 5.10). Most hardwood floors are made from oak, but other popular woods include ash, beech, birch, hickory, maple, teak, and walnut. In addition to its attractiveness, hardwood floors are extremely durable if they are properly finished and maintained.

Unfinished wood floors will quickly deteriorate under even light use, as wood is an extremely porous surface. Unfinished woods are susceptible to dirt lodging in the grains, splintering of the wood fibers, abrasions caused by normal foot traffic, and, of course, moisture, the bane of wood floors. Too much moisture will cause a wood floor to warp, while too little humidity will cause wood floors to shrink and crack.

To help forestall damage, most wood floors made today receive a factory applied finish. In some instances the wood is heated to open the pores of the wood. **Tung oil** and **carnuba wax** are then applied to seal the wood.

In another process, **polyurethane** is used to seal the wood. One firm uses liquid **acrylics** that permeate and protect the wood. One company even sells a wood veneer floor that is sandwiched between layers of vinyl to make it impregnable to water and as easy to install and maintain as a pure vinyl floor.

Since there is a degree of resiliency in even the hardest of hardwood floors, precautions should be taken to protect the floor from furniture legs that may dent the flooring. Wood floors are particularly susceptible to metal or hard plastic rollers and to those small metal domes that are often found on the legs of office furniture.

Cleaning Procedures. Preventive maintenance is the key to attractive and durable wood floors. One of the best prevention techniques is to use walk-off mats at exterior entrances and use rugs and carpet runners in high-traffic areas.

Wood floors should be dusted, but do not use an oily dust mop on a wood floor. The oil from the mop head may darken or stain the floor. Water is one of the most deleterious substances to a wood floor; consequently, it should not be used to clean most wood floors. Dusting, vacuuming, buffing, and, on limited occasion, a light damp mopping is all that is necessary to maintain a wood floor on a daily basis.

Stripping, Sealing, and Finishing. When a wood floor becomes badly stained or damaged, the floor is sanded to remove stains and marks. A sealer is then applied to the floor. There are many commercial wood sealers on the market today. Types of wood sealers include oil-modified urethane sealers, moisture-cured urethane sealers, the "Swedish-type" sealers, and water-based sealers. In most instances, the same sealer that was initially used on the floor must be used for subsequent applications. Repeated applications of certain types of sealers will darken the color of the floor over time. Sanding and sealing a floor is not a frequent occurrence; most modern wood floors can only tolerate a maximum of

Figure 5.10 A Mannington wood floor. (Used with permission of Jacqueline & Associates, Las Vegas.)

three to five sandings before the entire floor must be replaced.

Surface finishes such as urethane, **varnish**, and **shellac**, are not recommended for many modern wood floors. Most only require an occasional waxing and buffing, while certain modern treated wood floors may never require refinishing.

Again, it is always wise to follow the manufacturer's recommendations regarding the maintenance of any flooring or floor covering.

As we have previously stated, carpets and rugs are unquestionably the most resilient of all flooring materials and it is to this area that we now turn our attention.

Carpets and Rugs

The use of carpets and rugs can be traced back three thousand years to the Middle Eastern kingdoms of Babylon, Sumeria, and Assyria.

Carpet is typically installed wall-to-wall to eliminate the maintenance of hard flooring surfaces around the edge of a carpet. Rugs, on the other hand, are often used to accentuate a tile or wood floor. In areas where there is heavy foot traffic, rugs can be used to equalize wear and to help prevent tracking onto other floor coverings.

Carpet offers a number of benefits over hard and resilient flooring materials. Carpet prevents slipping; it provides an additional source of insulation—thus making it less expensive to heat an interior in winter—it has acoustical properties that can effectively lower noise levels; and it is the most resilient of all floor coverings, which is a major benefit to individuals who must remain on their feet for extended periods.

Carpet Components

Generally, carpet is composed of three elements: **pile, primary backing**, and **secondary backing**; it is often accompanied by a fourth element, **padding**.

Pile is the yarn that we see and can readily touch. The fibers can be either synthetic or natural in composition. Pile density is one hallmark of carpet quality; the greater the density of the pile, the better the carpet. Carpets with greater pile density hold their shape longer and are more resistant to dirt and stains. One common test of density is to bend a piece of carpet, and if the backing can readily be seen, the carpet is of an inferior quality. Density of pile is measured by the number of pile ends or tufts across a 27″ width called the *pitch* in woven carpets or *gauge* in tufted

varieties. Another indicator of durability is the carpet's face weight. The **face weight** is the weight of the carpet's surface fibers in ounces or grams per square yard. The greater the face weight, the higher the quality. The height of the pile is a third measure of carpet quality; longer fibers are better than shorter fibers. A fourth measure is the amount of twist the pile fibers have received. The tighter the twist, the better the carpet.

The backing is on the underside of the carpet; it secures the tufts of pile and gives additional strength and stability to the carpet. Most carpets have a double backing, a primary backing to which the yarn is attached and an outer backing called the secondary backing. A layer of latex adhesive is sandwiched between the two layers to seal the pile tufts to the primary backing.

Types of backing include **jute**, a natural fiber imported from India and Bangladesh, **polypropylene**, a synthetic thermoplastic resin, and foam rubber. The foam backing is often attached to the primary backing to provide a carpet with its own built-in padding, thus eliminating the need for separate padding. This is often done with less expensive carpeting. With more expensive carpeting, rubber-covered jute is the preferred material for the secondary backing. However, synthetic backings are more resistant to mildew, odor, and dry rot, and are non-allergenic.

Padding can be placed under carpet to provide extra insulation, deaden sound, add comfort, and extend the life of the carpet by serving as a "shock-absorber." Common types of padding include foam rubber, urethane foam, and natural materials such as jute and hair blends. The natural paddings are firmer than the synthetic materials. The choice of padding depends on the type of carpet being used, the level of comfort sought, and the amount and type of wear that the carpet will be subjected to under normal conditions.

Some experts recommend that no padding be used and that the carpet be glued directly to the floor in high-traffic areas or where carts with heavy loads will be used. Heavy padding is thought to increase friction and cause buckling and ripping, thus prematurely wearing out the carpet.

There are three sizes of carpets available on the market. Broadloom carpets are normally 12 feet in width, but they can be ordered up to 15 feet in width. Carpet runners come in widths from 2 feet to 9 feet. Carpet squares or tiles are 18 inches square. Carpet tiles are becoming quite popular for public areas such as halls, lobbys, and meeting rooms. New adhesives for carpet tiles make tile removal less of a chore than it has been in past years. Standard rug sizes vary from $3' \times 5'$ to $10' \times 12'$. Custom sizes may be even larger.

Carpet Construction

Carpet construction describes the method by which the carpet is manufactured. It involves how the face yarns are anchored in the backing and the type of backing that is used. Today, well over 90 percent of all carpet produced is tufted carpet. Tufted carpet is produced by forcing needles, threaded with pile yarn, through the primary backing (usually polypropylene) to form tufts. A coating of latex adhesive is then applied to the backing to secure the tufts. The tufting process can be used to produce a multitude of carpet textures, including:

- **Cut loop**   The carpet yarn is tufted into islands of high-cut tufts and lower loop tufts to form a sculptured pattern.
- **Level loop**   A simple loop pile with tufts of equal height, it is appropriate for high-traffic areas.
- **Multi-level loop**   A loop pile carpet with two or three tuft levels.
- **Plush**   The loops of the pile are cut, which makes for a relatively plain, clean, and formal effect. Pile that is 1/2″ or less in height is called Saxony plush, while pile with a height above 1/2″ is called textured plush.
- **Frieze**   Straight tufts are mixed with tufts that are given a built-in curl. The carpet does not show footprints and can be classified as being informal in texture.
- **Random shear**   A mixture of cut and uncut loops. This approach creates a highly textured appearance.

Needle punched carpets are produced by a manufacturing method that punches the fibers into a structural backing and then compresses the fibers into a feltlike fabric. It is used mainly in indoor-outdoor carpets.

Flocked carpets are produced by electrostatically embedding short carpet fibers into a backing, producing a velvety-look cut pile surface.

Knitted carpets are produced by a method that uses a specialized knitting machine with different sets of needles to loop together the pile, backing, and the stitching yarns.

Weaving is the traditional way of making carpet on a loom. Interlaced yarns form the backing and the pile. Lengthwise yarns are called the *warp* and the yarns going across the carpet are the *weft*. Pile is part of the warp. There are three basic types of looms: the velvet, the Axminster, and the Wilton.

Woven and knitted carpets are the two most expensive types of carpet to construct.

Carpet Fibers

Wool is the standard by which all synthetic carpet fibers are judged. Independent studies have shown that wool effectively outperforms fourth-generation nylon in soiling and appearance.[9] Wool is extremely durable and resistant to soiling, but it does have its share of negative properties. Since it is a natural material, wool provides a better breeding ground for bacteria, molds, and mildew. It is also more susceptible to damage from harsh or abrasive cleaners. Wool has very poor abrasion resistance. In low humidity, untreated wool generates more static electricity than synthetic fibers. Finally, it is quite costly. Not only is the wool itself more costly than synthetic fibers, wool carpets are normally woven or knitted, processes that are much more costly than tufting.

The most widely-used carpet fiber is nylon; over 90 percent of all carpets made today are nylon carpets. The fourth-generation nylon fibers in use today are quite resilient, fairly soil resistant, and easy to clean, and they come in a variety of colors and textures. Nylon fibers can also be protected by fluorochemical treatments, as in the case of Dupont's "Stainmaster" carpets, which are treated with "Teflon" to improve their soil and stain resistance.

Another synthetic in use today is polypropylene (Olefin), which wears very well and is not susceptible to sun fade, but it is not as comfortable underfoot as nylon.

Other minor synthetic fibers include acetates, acrylics, polyesters, and rayons. Although each of these have outstanding positive qualities, they do not possess all of the positive features shared by wool, nylon, and Olefin.

Selecting the Appropriate Carpet

Different settings suggest different carpet specifications. Color, texture, pattern, and padding requirements will vary from location to location. What follows is a series of carpet specifications based on aesthetic considerations.

- Solid colors magnify the effects of dirt, litter, and stains.
- If you wish to project excitement use warm colors; if relaxation is your aim, use cool colors in the darker shades.
- Avoid precise geometric patterns in dining rooms; use organic, free-flowing designs. These hide the dirt.
- Using low-level loop pile carpet tiles with no padding is the preferred approach for high-traffic areas.

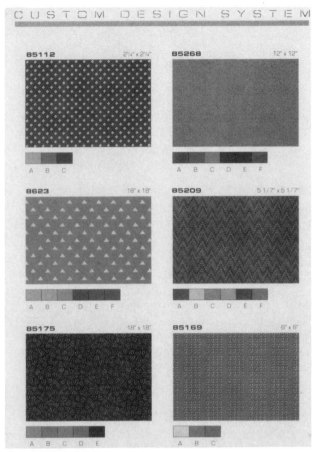

Figure 5.11 Modern geometric carpet patterns. (Used with permission of Jacqueline & Associates, Las Vegas.)

- Multi-level loop and cut loop carpets are more difficult to clean.
- Use big patterns in big rooms and small patterns in small rooms.

Figure 5.11 shows a representative sampling of modern geometric carpet patterns.

Carpet Installation

Executive housekeepers should resist all temptation to install new carpet. Laying carpet, resilient flooring, and hard floors is a job for professionals. An installation performed by amateurs often ends up costing the facility far more than was saved by not hiring professionals.

The installers should be brought back on the premises six months after the original installation to correct any buckles or bulges that have appeared in the carpet.

Carpet Maintenance

Carpet maintenance is actually four related procedures that occur at intermittent times during the life cycle of the carpet.

Inspection and Prevention

The most frequent activity is carpet inspection, which should occur on a continual basis. Carpets need to be inspected for spills and stains, which are far easier to remove if they are treated before they have a chance to set. Staff in all departments, from engineering to food and beverage, should be instructed to report all carpet and floor spills to housekeeping as soon as they are discovered.

Prevention includes the use of mats to absorb dirt and spills around food preparation areas and the use of grates, track-off mats, and carpet runners to absorb dirt and grit and control wear at entrances and in high-foot-traffic locations.

Interim Cleaning Methods

Interim cleaning methods include carpet sweeping, vacuuming, bonnet cleaning, and spot stain removal. Interim carpet care is absolutely necessary to remove gritty soil and spots before these elements become embedded in the carpet, causing the pile to wear prematurely. According to *Cleaning Team Management* there are three sources of soils: tracked particulate soils from the exterior; spots, spills, and settling dust from the interior; and animal and vegetable oils, which are by-products from the dining room and kitchen areas.[10]

Soil build-up occurs at three levels of the carpet. At the top are light soils, dust, gummy sugars, and oily soils. In the middle are the heavier particles of dust and organic matter. At the base of the pile are the heaviest particles, such as sand and grit. Although the sand and grit are not necessarily seen, they do the greatest damage to the pile because they actually erode the pile fibers.[11]

It is estimated that an average of 79 percent of all soils can be removed by a regular policy of vacuuming.[12] However, the gummy and oily substances will continue to build up while binding the dry particulates to the carpet fibers, causing carpet erosion. Although vacuuming is the most critical factor in extending the life of the carpet, vacuuming alone is not enough. All carpet must be subjected to restorative cleaning methods on a periodic basis.

Standard vacuuming with an upright machine or hose vacuum is begun by plugging the cord into the electrical outlet. The plug should be a grounded three-prong plug. Inspect the cord and plug for wear. Begin vacuuming on the wall where the machine is plugged in and work away from the plug to prevent cord entanglement. A three-foot-long push-pull stroke should be employed (see Figure 5.12). Normally, only two passes over the carpet are necessary. Care should be taken not to vacuum too fast; the beater brushes and suction should be allowed to do their job. Overlap

Figure 5.12 Vacuuming with the "AdVac 14XP" from Advance Machine Company. (Used with permission.)

Figure 5.13 Bonnet cleaning using the "All-Purpose Matador" from Advance. (Used with permission.)

strokes slightly and vacuum so that the nap (fuzzy side of the carpet) of the carpet is laid by the pull stroke. Move furniture as little as possible and avoid bumping both furniture and the wall.

When finished, inspect and replace worn brushes and belts if necessary, and empty the filter bag.

Vacuuming should be done after furniture has been dusted.

Bonnet cleaning is often categorized with other restorative cleaning methods, but it should properly be categorized as an interim cleaning method.

Figure 5.13 is an example of bonnet cleaning using an all-purpose floor machine. Bonnet cleaning utilizes a standard floor machine equipped with carpet bonnets, bonnet shampoo, a sprayer, clean water, and a bucket and wringer.

First vacuum the area to be cleaned, and then spray a $4' \times 8'$ area with the shampoo; also spray the bonnet with the solution. Then pass the machine, with the bonnet attached, over the area. This procedure is repeated until the entire carpet is cleaned. Once the bonnet begins to show dirt, it should be turned over to the clean side. When the entire bonnet is dirty, rinse it in the bucket and wring it out with the mop wringer.

When finished, completely rinse all of the equipment, then wash the carpet bonnets and hang them up to dry. Do not replace furniture until the carpet is completely dry.

Bonnet cleaning does cause a modest amount of wear on the carpet fibers and, to reiterate, it should not be viewed as a restorative cleaning method.

Finally, carpet sweepers are used to clean up dry soils and particulates on rugs before they have a chance to penetrate the surface of the carpet and lodge in the carpet's pile. They are especially handy in dining room areas where the waitstaff can use the for touch-ups under tables and in the aisles.

Restorative Cleaning Methods

Interim cleaning methods do not remove the gummy, sticky residues and the dry particulates that have become stuck to them. Deep cleaning methods must be employed to restore the carpet to a near original condition. There are four restorative carpet cleaning systems: water extraction, dry foam, dry powder, and rotary shampoo. There is quite a bit of disagreement in the industry as to which of these four systems is the single "best" method. However, all would agree that it is best to remove dry soil by vacuuming the carpet before a restorative cleaning method is attempted.

Water extraction, also referred to as hot water extraction or "steam cleaning," is a system that sprays a solution on the carpet and then picks it up with an attached wet/dry vacuum. The term "steam cleaning" is really a misnomer, as live steam is never used, only hot or cold water. The machine normally has two storage tanks, one for the solution to be sprayed on the carpet and one for the dirty picked-up solution.

An operator of a hot water extractor should avoid over-wetting the carpet and should overlap two to three inches on each pass. On problem spots the operator may need to presoak the area for a few minutes before using the pick-up vacuum. All carpet should be totally dry before the furniture is replaced or it is open to foot traffic.

Many experts consider this system to be the best approach to deep cleaning. However, hot water extraction can have a number of negative effects if improperly done. Wet carpet can shrink and seams can split if the water used is too hot or if too much solution is applied. The temperature of the water should never be over 150°F, and when cleaning wool carpet, it is best to use cold water. Most of the extractors on the market can be used with either cold or hot water. Although water extractors minimize problems associated with other wet shampooing techniques, such as mildewing and other bacteria, growth can happen in a humid environment. Use fans and the building's air conditioning or heating system to speed carpet drying time. If the operator does not put an excess amount of solution on the carpet, it should be dry within one hour.

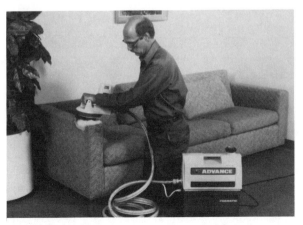

Figure 5.14 The "Foamatic" from Advance. Dry foam can be used on upholstery as well as carpets with the proper attachments. (Used with permission.)

Dry foam is another method used in carpet restoration. The foam is brushed into the carpet and taken up almost immediately with a wet/dry vacuum. After the carpet is completely dry, it is vacuumed once again to remove more of the residue (see Figure 5.14).

Dry foam is often used in high-traffic areas on even a daily basis to remove tracked-in soil. The biggest negative factor with dry foam is that it leaves the highest amount of detergent residue behind on the carpet, which will cause the carpet to become prematurely dirty. If the carpet is not rigorously vacuumed after laying down the foam, the carpet can, in a few days, look worse than it did before the treatment.

Dry powder has the advantage of minimal down time for a carpeted area. Once the procedure is completed, the area can reopen for use. Since water is not used, the problem of mildew, odor, carpet stretching, and seam splitting is not present.

Dry powder cleaning is done by laying down a powder or crystal on the carpet; this binds with the dirt, which is then removed through vacuuming while the carpet is agitated with a beater brush (see Figure 5.15).

Dry powder may leave some residue behind in the carpet and it may not remove all types of soils from the carpet.

Wet shampooing is accomplished through the use of a rotary floor machine, which normally has a tank attached that contains the shampoo solution. A special brush attachment agitates the carpet as the solution is dispersed onto the carpet. The carpet is then vacuumed with a wet/dry vacuum that contains a defoaming agent. Once the carpet is dry, it may be vacuumed again with a dry vacuum.

With this system, the danger exists of over-wetting the carpet, causing mold, mildew, and other bacterial growth. The carpet may also stretch and then shrink, causing seams to split, and the brushes from the floor machine may damage the carpet pile if they are allowed to remain on one spot for too long. Rotary shampooing is thought by many experts to cause the most wear to a carpet.

Spot Cleaning

Spots and spills call for immediate action. If allowed to set, many substances can permanently stain a carpet, especially one that is made of nylon or wool. The following are a few general procedures that should be followed regardless of the type of stain, carpet, or cleaner:

1. Carefully scrape away excess soiling materials such as gum and tar from the carpet.

Figure 5.15 The Host Dry Powder System. The powder applicator is on the right and the dry cleaning machine on the left brushes the powder into the carpet. (Used with permission of Racine Industries.)

2. Blot the excess liquid that is spilled before it has a chance to soak into the carpet. Do not rub the stain; this action may actually force the stain into the fibers. Use only clean rags to blot the carpet.
3. Apply the cleansing agent to the carpet. If the spot remover is a liquid, remove the excess spot remover by blotting with clean rags or a clean sponge.
4. After the spot remover has had an opportunity to work, vacuum up the spot remover and dry the treated area.

Many reputable companies have developed some remarkable spot removers that can effectively remove dozens of different types of spots. Figure 5.16 is an example of one of these commercial spot removal systems.

Finally, certain harsh chemicals, such as chlorine bleaches, should not be used on spots because they will often remove the dye from the carpet along with the offending stain.

Ceilings and Wallcoverings

The selection of materials to cover walls and ceilings should be predicated on the following five consider-

ations: cost of maintenance, appearance, fire safety, initial cost, and acoustics.

Although the product and installation cost of ceiling materials or wallcoverings materials must be within budgetary guidelines, consideration must be also given to the other four factors. For example, the maintenance cost of a wallcovering must be part of the cost equation. Daily maintenance costs may make the product prohibitively expensive, even though the initial costs are within budget.

The ability of a wall, floor, or ceiling material to reduce sound is a major factor when considering guest comfort, whether it be in a conference room, dining room, or guestroom. Most commercial materials have a rating, called the noise reduction coefficient, that can be used in material selection. However, improper maintenance may adversely affect a material's acoustics, such as when acoustical ceiling panels are painted, destroying most of their noise reduction ability.

Fire safety is a major concern, especially in highrise hospitals and hotels. Many communities have passed stringent laws concerning the use of fireresistant materials. In fact, many fire codes specify the use of only Class A materials in hotels and hospitals. Manufacturers have responded to this fire safety

Figure 5.16 Photo 1

Figure 5.16 Spot removal using the Host Dry Powder System. In the first photo, the "SPONGES" dry cleaning powder is scattered on the spot. In the second photo, the cleaner is brushed into the spot, using a circular pattern to blend the newly-cleaned area into the surrounding carpet. Then, as shown above in the third photo, the spot is vacuumed up. (Used with permission of Racine Industries.)

concern by manufacturing wallcoverings and ceiling panels that will emit harmless gases, which will trigger smoke detectors when heated to 300°F.

There are wall materials on the market that will emit toxic gases when burned. Many city fire codes forbid the use of these materials in guestrooms and public areas in hospitals and hotels. The National Fire Protection Association (NFPA) sets standards on fire retardancy and the toxicity of burning materials. The astute housekeeper should become familiar with these specifications.

Finally, hotels and even hospitals are concerned with the image they project. Wallcovering, ceilings, and flooring materials should be selected to enhance that image. It could be said that these materials are indeed one of the hotel's most important marketing tools.

Types of Wall and Ceiling Coverings and their Maintenance

The maintenance of wallcoverings and ceilings resembles floor maintenance in that there are three

Figure 5.16 Photo 2

distinct approaches: interim maintenance, restorative cleaning, and spot removal.

Interim cleaning methods include daily or weekly dusting and vacuuming. Restorative cleaning encompasses the use of detergents and solvents, which is done on a periodic basis, and spot removal, which is performed as the need arises.

The following section will examine the advantages and disadvantages of the most common wall and ceiling coverings and their specific maintenance requirements.

Cork

Cork has excellent sound absorption properties and has a rich and luxurious appearance, but it is a delicate surface material that can be easily damaged by improper cleaning methods. Today, it is often bonded between sheets of clear vinyl, which serve to protect it from wear, but the vinyl does impair its acoustical ability. Natural cork may be vacuumed using a soft brush attachment. Natural cork walls should never be washed with water. Spot removal may require light sanding to remove stains. It is sometimes easier to replace a damaged cork tile than to attempt to restore it to its original condition.

Fabrics

Although linens, silks, and leathers may initially provide an extremely attractive wall surface, as a rule, they should not be used for wallcoverings because of the difficulty involved in their cleaning, particularly in the case of spot removal. If fabrics are used they must be fire resistant, and it is also advisable to use only stain-resistant materials.

Fabrics are also highly susceptible to mold, mildew, and other odor-causing bacteria.

A recommended alternative to fabrics is the new vinyl wallcoverings that have fabric sandwiched between sheets of vinyl. They have the beauty of fabrics but are far easier to clean and are much more durable.

Standard fabric wallcoverings may be vacuumed to remove dust. Water should never be used on fabrics because it may cause the fabric to shrink and split. Spots and stains should only be removed with chemicals recommended by the fabric's manufacturer. Some cleaning solutions will adversely affect the fire-resistant characteristics of the fabric.

Fiberglass

Fiberglass walls are often made to resemble other construction materials, such as brick. Fiberglass can be vacuumed to remove dust, and it can be deep cleaned using water and a neutral detergent.

Painted Surfaces

Paint is still one of the most popular wallcoverings because of its relatively low initial cost and the wide range of colors available.

When selecting paint, the housekeeper should consider drying time, odor, and durability. The objective is to reduce costly down time caused by these factors.

Painted surfaces can be dusted, vacuumed, and washed using a mild detergent and water. Scrubbing and use of chemicals such as trisodium phosphate will remove the paint as well as the dirt.

Plastic Laminate

One of the easiest materials to maintain, plastic laminates come in $4' \times 8'$ panels that are nailed directly to the wall studs. Plastic laminate often has a wood grain effect or a faux tile appearance. All that is required to maintain its appearance is periodic vacuuming with a soft brush.

Tile

Tile walls demand the same care as the tile floors previously covered in this chapter. Most manufacturers carry two grades of tile, tile for wall applications and tile for floor applications. Tile walls are most often found in bathrooms and kitchens. Ceramic tiles are also used to accent stucco walls.

Vinyl

Next to paint, vinyl is indisputably the most popular form of wallcovering. It can be purchased in a wide variety of colors and textures that can fool even the trained observer into believing that the wall covering is not vinyl, but marble, rubber, fabric, metal, or even ceramic tile.

Vinyl is resistant to molds and mildew, easy to clean, considered to be four times more durable than paint, and easy to install and remove. According to government specifications, vinyl is divided into three categories by weight per square yard. Type I is normally reserved for noncommercial applications. Type II is the category most often selected for guestrooms, halls, and lobbies. Type III is the most durable and the best choice for heavy wear areas, such as elevators and other high-contact areas.

The most negative aspect of vinyl wallcovering is the fact that it can rip and tear, so it is wise to buy extra rolls when installing vinyl. With practice, torn vinyl can be repaired.

Wallpaper

Vinyl has made old-fashioned wallpaper obsolete. Vinyl wallcoverings can duplicate the effect of wallpaper while providing a surface that can be easily cleaned with mild detergent and water, which is not an option with wallpaper.

Wallpaper should be vacuumed to remove dirt and dust. Some types of stains can be removed from wallpaper using dough-type cleaners, and a few wallpapers can be damp mopped with a sponge.

Wood

Wood or wood-veneered walls demand the same treatment afforded wood floors. Water should not be used on a wood-surfaced wall. Dust frequently and when needed, and oil and polish wood wallcoverings according to the manufacturer's recommendations.

Windows and Window Treatments

Window Cleaning

Window cleaning is one of the easiest tasks to perform if the housekeeping crew has the proper tools at its disposal. What is needed is a synthetic lambswool window washing tool, a bucket that will accommodate the tool (approximately 12″ × 24″), a squeegee, and a clean lint-free cloth. The better squeegees have quick release mechanisms and angled heads.

A low sudsing cleaning solution, often containing a little ammonia, is prepared with cold or warm (never hot) water. The first step is to remove all window coverings to facilitate the cleaning and to avoid the possibility of spilling cleaning solution on the drapes and curtains.

Begin by applying the cleaning solution to the top of the window, working the dirt toward the center of the window from the outside edges. Do not over-wet the window and cause the excess solution to run and pool on the sill or floor. Before the window has a chance to dry, squeegee the window, starting at the top corner. Make one pass across the glass and angle the blade so that the dirty solution runs down onto the dirty part of the window rather than back onto the cleaned portion. Wipe the blade clean with the cloth after each pass of the blade.

Finally, never attempt to clean windows in the hot sun. The sun will cause the window to dry before it can be squeegeed, causing streaking.

Exterior window cleaning, especially on high-rise buildings, should best be left to professional window washers.

Window Treatments

When selecting window treatments, function and appearance should both be considered. The appropriate window covering provides privacy to the guest and insulation; it is a significant design element.

Window treatment can be divided into three categories: drapery, shades, and blinds.

Drapery and curtain fabric should be fire resistant, soil and wear resistant, resistant to sun damage, resistant to molds and mildew, and wrinkle resistant. Delicate fabrics and loose weaves will quickly lose their shape, will snag and wrinkle, and will wear prematurely. One increasingly popular style of drapery is vinyl-lined fabric, because of its increased durability.

Drapery should be vacuumed daily. Dry cleaning is the preferred method of restorative cleaning. Most experts agree that dry-cleaned drapes will hold their shape better than laundered fabrics.

Shades are available in a multitude of styles and materials. Their purpose is to provide a customized look to the window while affording privacy to the guest. Shades should also be vacuumed daily. Restorative cleaning methods will depend on the material composition of the shade.

Popular blind styles of today include the mini-horizontal blind and the vertical blind. The verticals are much easier to maintain and provide greater control of glare and light into the room. Cloth panels can even be inserted into some types of vertical blinds to add additional color and texture to the room.

Summary

The maintenance of floors, floor coverings, wall coverings, and windows consumes an overwhelming majority of any housekeeping department's budget. For this reason, the astute housekeeper must develop a comprehensive understanding of these materials and how they are to be maintained. This knowledge must also be communicated to the department's staff so that they may responsibly carry out the policies of the department and see to it that standards of cleanliness and repair are maintained.

KEY TERMS AND CONCEPTS

Foundation
Finish
Stripping
Sealer
Terrazzo

Buffing
Burnishing
Damp mopping
Spray buffing
Nonresilient floors

Epoxy

Spalling

Resilient floors

Linoleum

Face weight

Jute

Polypropylene

Cut loop

Level loop

Multi-level loop

Plush

Styrene butadiene rubber

Asbestos

Carcinogen

Homogeneous

Tung oil

Carnuba wax

Polyurethane

Acrylics

Varnish

Shellac

Pile

Primary backing

Secondary backing

Padding

Frieze

Random shear

Bonnet cleaning

Water extraction

Dry foam

Dry powder

Wet shampooing

DISCUSSION AND REVIEW QUESTIONS

1. When contemplating the installation of a new floor, what concerns should an executive housekeeper take into consideration?
2. Explain the relative advantages and disadvantages of the different approaches to restorative carpet care.
3. Given the following areas in a hotel—ballroom, lobby, dining room, kitchen, laundry, executive office—make recommendations for appropriate floor coverings for each area.
4. Describe the steps in the FPMR model.
5. Assume that the decision has been made to carpet the hotel's main ballroom. What suggestions would you make as to the type of carpet to use in the ballroom?
6. How would you ensure the cooperation of other departments in the hotel to report spots and spills on carpet and floors to the housekeeping department?
7. The rooms division manager wants to install an "accent wall" in each guest room. This wall would have a wallcovering that is unlike the other painted walls in the room. What wallcoverings would you suggest for this accent wall?

NOTES

1. Bill Saunders and Rick Mazzoli, "The FPMR Process of Floor Care," *Sanitary Maintenance*, October 1989, pp. 144–45.
2. Ibid., p. 144.
3. John P. Walker, *Fourteen Basic Custodial Procedures*, (Lincolnwood, IL: International Sanitary Supply Association, Inc., 1989), p. 21.
4. Bill Saunders and Rick Mazzoli, "The FPMR Process of Floor Care," *Sanitary Maintenance*, November 1989, pp. 76–77.
5. Ibid., p. 76.
6. Ibid., p. 77.
7. Ibid., p. 78.
8. Ibid., p. 79.
9. Ray Draper, "Wool Performance—Better Cleanability and Soil Resistance Than 4th Generation Nylons," *Executive Housekeeping Today*, March 1990, pp. 8–10.
10. John Phillip Walker and L. Kent Fine, *Cleaning Team Management: Custodial Management for Increased Productivity and Safety*, (Salt Lake City: ManageMen, 1990), Carpet Care: p. 2.
11. Ibid., p. 2.
12. Ibid., p. 2.

6

Material Planning: Supplies and Equipment

CHAPTER OBJECTIVES

1. To be able to categorize the chemicals used in the house-keeping department and state their intended purpose.
2. To define the properties of housekeeping chemicals.
3. To describe how to establish a Hazardous Communication Program.
4. To describe commonly used housekeeping equipment and generate standards for their purchase.
5. To describe common guest amenities that the hotel provides to its guests.

In this chapter we will continue our examination of material planning by the executive housekeeper. We now turn our attention to housekeeping supplies and equipment.

Housekeeping Chemicals

The contemporary executive housekeeper would never be able to meet the daily environmental challenge of cleaning and preserving the modern hotel,

nursing home, dormitory, or hospital without the aid of chemical products. Chemicals used by the house-keeping department include those that are intended to remove soils, those that kill **pathogenic microorganisms** and disease-carrying pests, and those that preserve, protect, and beautify the property.

The astute housekeeper knows the intended purpose of every chemical in the department's inventory. The housekeeper is also ultimately responsible for the correct handling and storage of each chemical so that it does not adversely affect either the user, the public, or the environment.

Chemical Terminology

When attempting to select the proper chemical for a particular housekeeping application, the executive housekeeper is often at the mercy of the sales staff of the local chemical supply firm because he or she is not familiar with basic chemical terminology and the chemistry of cleaning.

The environmental services chapter of this text (Chapter 12) has an entire section devoted to the chemistry of cleaning; the purpose of this section, however, is to acquaint the reader with a few basic terms that will aid in the proper selection and use of these chemicals.

Although there are a number of chemicals in the housekeeping department that are used to protect and beautify floors, walls, and furniture, the majority of housekeeping chemicals are intended to clean, disinfect, and sanitize the environment.

The intended use of **detergents** is to remove soil from a surface through a chemical action. Synthetic detergents dissolve solid soils and hold the soils in a suspension away from the environmental surface, thus allowing them to be easily removed from that surface. Most detergents used in housekeeping are synthetic detergents that are derived from a number of basic minerals, primarily sulfonated hydrocarbons. Many detergents have a neutral pH, which means that they are neither an acid nor an alkaline compound. The degree of alkalinity or acidity is indicated on the pH scale. The scale runs from 1 to 14. One through 6 on the scale indicates acidity. Position 8 through 14 on the scale indicates alkalinity. Seven indicates a neutral compound. Alkalies are often used to enhance the cleaning power of synthetic detergents. Strong alkaline detergent cleaners should not be used on certain surfaces. (For more information on this topic, see Chapter 5.)

Disinfectants are chemical agents that have been tested by the federal government and have been proven to destroy pathogenic microorganisms on inanimate surfaces. They are said to have a bacteriostatic effect. A **bacteriostat** prevents microbes from multiplying on a surface. Disinfectants are not intended to be used directly on humans or animals. Other similar terms used to describe specific disinfectants are bactericides, fungicides, germicides, and virucides. The purpose of disinfectants is not to remove soils from surfaces, but there are a number of products on the market that combine a synthetic detergent with a disinfectant so that a surface can be cleaned and disinfected at the same time. The use of a disinfectant alone on a soiled surface is ineffective, as the soil serves to protect the bacteria from the germicidal action of the disinfectant. Combined detergent-disinfectant chemicals such as the ones pictured in Figure 6.1 are quite effective if they are used according to directions. In certain instances, however, particularly in a hospital environment, it is necessary to first apply a detergent to remove soil buildup and then apply a disinfectant solution after the surface has been cleaned. In most hotel applications, it is perfectly acceptable to use combined

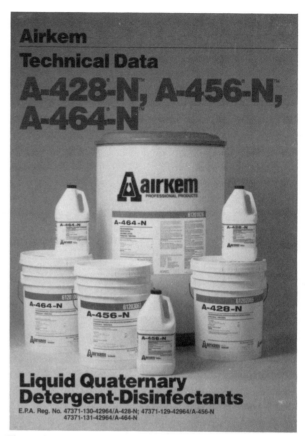

Figure 6.1 Three liquid quaternary detergent-disinfectant products that remove soils and disinfect the surface at the same time. Photo by Airkem Professional Products. (Used with permission of JB Chemical Co. Inc., Las Vegas.)

detergent-disinfectants. The great advantage to using detergent-disinfectant solutions rather than separate solutions is the labor saved from not having to wash the surface twice.

Common disinfectants include **quaternary ammonium compounds**, **idophors**, **hypochlorites** and **phenolic compounds**. These compounds are discussed in greater detail in Chapter 12.

It should be noted here that a few hotel housekeepers might fail to see the relevance of disinfectants to hotel housekeeping. This attitude is based on a common misconception that only hospitals need to worry about the control of pathenogenic microorganisms. Unfortunately, hotels and restaurants provide a superb environment for the breeding and transmission of disease. For example, according to the Center for Disease Control, 77 percent of all cases of food-borne illness originate in commercial food service establishments. It is also estimated that Hepatitis A is transmitted to thousands of restaurant customers annually from infected workers.[1] Finally, who can forget that the dreaded Legionnaires' disease originated in the air-conditioning system of a hotel?

In many areas of a hotel, the intention is not to maintain totally disinfected surfaces, as is required in a hospital environment, but merely to maintain a sanitized surface. A **sanitizer** is a chemical that kills microorganisms to an accepted, or what is generally regarded as a safe, level. Sanitizers are not intended to provide a bacteriostatic surface. Sanitizers may be specially formulated chemicals or they may be disinfectants that have been diluted to serve as sanitizers. Sanitizers are used on such surfaces as carpets, walls, and floors, and may also be used in conjunction with room deodorizers to sanitize the air.

Potentially dangerous chemical reactions can take place in the housekeeper's mop bucket as well as in the chemist's laboratory. One of the most dangerous types is when an ammoniated product is mixed with a hypochlo rite (such as bleach) or when a bleach is mixed with an acid-based cleaner. In both cases potentially deadly chlorine gases are released.

Selection Considerations

A number of variables must be considered to ensure that the most appropriate chemical product is chosen. One crucial factor is the relative hardness of the water at the site. Water hardness refers to the amount of calcium and magnesium found in the water. Most disinfectants and sanitizers that are quaternary-based are negatively affected by water hardness. Look on the product label for claims of effectiveness in hard water.

A second concern is the particular type of soil that is to be removed from the environment. Grease and oils may call for solvent cleaners that normally have a petroleum base, whereas scale and lime deposits on bathroom fixtures may require an acid-based cleaner. In the next section of this chapter, we shall explore the merits of using all-purpose cleaners.

A third consideration is the initial cost of the product. Since different chemicals are diluted to different concentrations, always base your calculations on the cost per usable gallon of solution.

A fourth factor is the cost of labor and equipment. Some chemicals are much more "labor intensive" than others; that is, they require a greater degree of physical force in their application in order to be effective. That force requirement can translate into expensive equipment and more man-hours to effectively do the job.

A fifth factor is the relative availability of the product. Is the distributor always ready, willing, and able to provide the product? Or have there been numerous instances of **stock-outs**? If the chemical is not always available when you need it, you should seriously think of changing either brands or distributors.

Finally, does the distributor give good service? Is the vendor willing to demonstrate the proper use of the product? Is the vendor willing to conduct comparison tests of chemicals at your site? Is the company also willing to help train your staff in the proper use of the product? Also, if the product fails to meet expectations, will the distributor take back the unused product and issue a credit memo?

Good service certainly adds value to the product. Sometimes this value more than compensates for an extra penny or two in cost per usable gallon.

All of these variables must be carefully weighed when purchasing chemical supplies.

All-Purpose Cleaners

One innovation in housekeeping chemical use has been the increasing use of **all-purpose cleaners**. Most all-purpose cleaners are pH neutral, so they are safe for most surfaces that can be cleaned with a water-based product. All-purpose cleaners normally do not need to be rinsed, they do not leave a haze, and they do not streak. The relative cleaning effectiveness of an all-purpose cleaner is normally

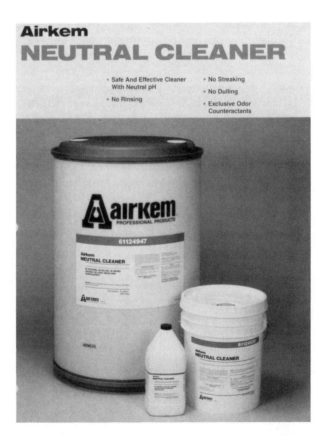

Figure 6.2 An all-purpose neutral pH cleaner. Note that the cleaner can be purchased in one-gallon, five-gallon, and economical 55-gallon sizes. Photo by Airkem Professional Products. (Used with permission of JB Chemical Co, Inc., Las Vegas.)

determined by its dilution strength, which can be set for different jobs. An example of an all-purpose cleaner can be seen in Figure 6.2.

An all-purpose cleaner is one effective way to reduce inventory product, and reducing inventory usually means bringing more dollars to the bottom line. Using an all-purpose cleaner also can translate to quantity buying, which can mean greater savings.

However, there are disadvantages to all-purpose cleaners. Perhaps the greatest disadvantage is that an all-purpose cleaner is inadequate for certain cleaning tasks. One example would be in the cleaning of bathroom equipment where a disinfectant is needed. Most all-purpose cleaners do not contain disinfectants. Another concern is whether employees are properly diluting the all-purpose cleaner for the specific task at hand. Far too often, employees will assume the attitude that "more is better" and will fail to properly dilute the detergent. This action inevitably drives up costs.

Single-Purpose Cleaners

There are numerous instances where an all-purpose cleaner is inadequate. In this section, we will examine the relative merits of a variety of single-purpose cleaners.

Abrasive Cleaners

Abrasive cleaners normally contain a detergent combined with a bleach and an abrasive (usually silica, a quartz dust that can scratch glass). The abrasiveness of the cleaner is determined by the percentage of abrasive in the cleanser. Abrasive cleansers can be found in either a powder or paste format. The paste is preferred because it will cling to vertical surfaces. Figure 6.3 is an example of a mild abrasive paste cleanser. Under no circumstances should abrasive cleaners be used on fiberglass tub and shower enclosures; furthermore, abrasives are not recommended for porcelain fixtures.

Degreasers

Degreasers or emulsifiers are usually found in most commercial kitchens. They are concentrated detergents that are formulated to remove heavy grease buildup. Figure 6.4 is an example of a concentrated degreaser from S.C. Johnson. Petroleum solvents have degreasing properties, but because of their flammability and toxicity they are rarely used on kitchen surfaces.

Deodorizers

Deodorizers, if properly used, can improve a facility's public image and improve employee morale.

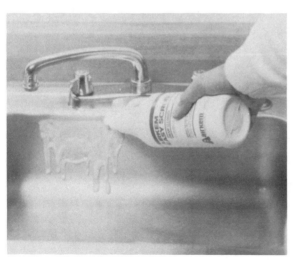

AIRKEM EASY SCRUB™

Airkem EASY SCRUB™ Cream Cleanser is a pleasantly fragranced mild abrasive detergent with superior clinging action. Ideal for use on vertical as well as horizontal surfaces.

Excellent for removing stubborn spots, soap scum build-ups, scuffs, grease, rubber marks, and numerous other tough cleaning jobs. Safe for use on porcelain, ceramics, stainless steel, chromium, formica and other surfaces not harmed by abrasive cleaners. USDA classification—Category A-6.

Figure 6.3 A mild abrasive cleanser from Airkem Professional Products. Note the squeeze bottle and built-in applicator. Photo by Airkem Professional Products. (Used with permission of JB Chemical Co. Inc., Las Vegas.)

AccuMix A1 Grease Release Food Service Cleaner. A super concentrated, general purpose degreasing cleaner formulated to remove grease, fats, protein and grimy soils, conveniently packaged in a unique portion-dose bottle. Product is ideal for use in every department of the supermarket where heavy, greasy soils are found. Also recommended for use in restaurants, institutional kitchens and food processing plants. 32 oz. bottles (6 per case).

Figure 6.4 The AccuMix Grease Release Food Service Cleaner. Note the Accumix measuring spout. (Photo used with permission of S.C. Johnson Wax, Racine, Wisconsin.)

Some deodorizers counteract stale odors, leaving a clean, air-freshened effect through the principle of **odor-pair neutralization**. These deodorizers leave no trace of perfume cover-up. This approach is preferred in restrooms, guestrooms, and public areas. Most guests react negatively to cheap cover-up deodorant perfumes in hotel lobbys or guestrooms.

However, where there are particularly strong odors, such as a garbage dumpster or a pet kennel, a deodorant formula that contains fragrances may be appropriate. Methods of deodorant application include aerosol sprays, time release systems (see Figure 6.5), "stick-up" applicators, liquids, powders, and hand pump sprays.

Drain Cleaners

Drain cleaners contain harmful acids and lyes and should not be applied by the regular housekeeping staff. They should only be used by management or by staff who have been specially trained in their application. Drain cleaners are hazardous and can corrode pipes; consequently, many properties have banned

their use in favor of pressurized gases or drain-cleaning augers.

Furniture Cleaners and Polishes

Furniture cleaners and polishes are normally wax or oil-based products that contain antistatic compounds. The best polishes contain lemon oil, which serves to replenish the moisture that is lost from the wood.

Hand Soaps and Detergents

Hand washing is an important component of personal hygiene for all employees. One of the biggest preventatives of **nosocomial infection** in hospitals is the practice of handwashing.[2] Unfortunately, many employees do not wash their hands often enough because they believe that repeated handwashing will cause skin dryness and cracking. Since the housekeeping department is often in charge of purchasing handsoaps, the housekeeper should only stock disinfectant lotion soaps that prevent dryness and cracking.

Laundry Chemicals

Laundry chemicals include synthetic detergents, concentrated bleaches, **antichlors**, **sours**, and fabric softeners. The detergents will often be **nonionic detergents** that contain fabric brighteners and antiredeposition agents. The active ingredient in most laundry bleaches is sodium hypochlorite. Antichlors are added to remove excess chlorine from the fabric. Sours are added to lower the pH and may also contain bluing and whiteners. Suitable sours include ammonium silicofluoride, sodium silicofluoride, zinc silicofluoride, and acetic acid. Excessive use of sours may result in a sour odor remaining on the clothes. Softeners are usually **cationic** products that contain antistatic and bacteriostatic agents. Their purpose is to leave the laundered product fresh, soft, and with no static cling. When bacteriostatic agents are present, they help to reduce the growth of pathenogenic organisms on the fabric. Figure 6.6 shows representative examples of premeasured laundry chemicals. The packets of chemicals dissolve in the wash water.

Metal Cleaners and Polishes

Metal cleaners and polishes are usually paste-type cleaners that contain mild acidic solutions. Some contain protective coatings that inhibit tarnishing.

Solvent Cleaners

Solvent cleaners are used to clean surfaces that are badly soiled by grease, tar, or oil. Solvents are made from pine oils, kerosene, and alcohols. Some types will not adversely affect paint, acrylics, and metals. Nonflammable solvents like carbon tetrachloride are extremely toxic and should only be used by trained

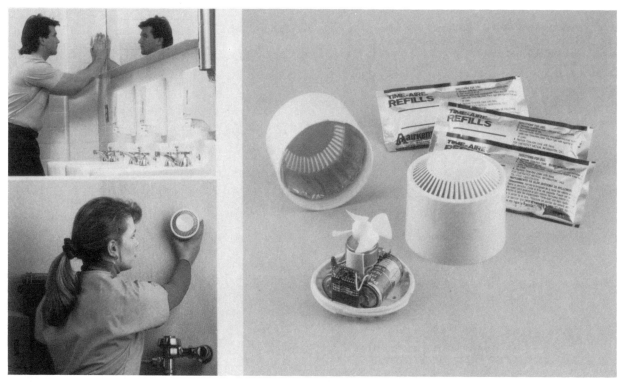

Figure 6.5 A timed-release odor counteractant system. Photo by Airkem Professional Products. (Used with permission of JB Chemical Co. Inc., Las Vegas.)

staff members. Flammable cleaners are less toxic. Housekeeping departments should seek to purchase only those **petroleum naptha solvents** that have a high **flash point**. The higher the flash point, the less likely a cleaner will ignite.

Bathroom Cleaners

To clean away lime encrustations in washroom fixtures, remove rust stains, and remove organic soils, the chemical industry has produced clean-

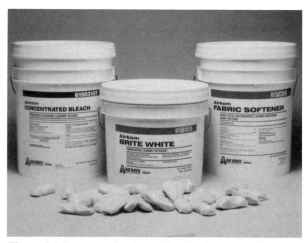

Figure 6.6 Premeasured packets of laundry detergents. Photo by Airkem Professional Products. (Used with permission of JB Chemical Co. Inc., Las Vegas.)

ers that meet these unique needs. The emulsion toilet bowl cleaner normally contains acid, which is necessary to remove rust and corrosion, and detergents that remove fecal material, urine, and bacterial colonies. Hydrochloric acid has been the acid of choice in these cleaners, but it has been replaced by the milder phosphoric acid in some products. Figure 6.7 is an example of a hydrochloric and a phosphoric acid bowl cleaner. Acidic bowl cleaners should not come into contact with metal fixtures, especially chrome.

Other emulsion bathroom cleaners, called all-purpose bathroom cleansers, are often milder versions of the toilet bowl cleaner. Bathroom cleaners should not be used on other floor or wall surfaces. Stone floors and tiles react very negatively to even mildly acidic cleaners.

Carpet Cleaners

Carpet cleaning chemicals, whether they are sprays, foams, dry powders, or shampoos, contain essentially the same types of chemicals in slightly different forms. Common chemicals include neutral water-soluble solvents, emulsifiers, **defoamers**, optical brighteners, and deodorizers. Many also contain sanitizers; however, some of these may have an adverse effect on fourth- and fifth-generation nylon carpets. Soil and stain repellents may also be included in

Figure 6.7 Two varieties of bowl cleaners. Photo by Airkem Professional Products. (Used with permission of JB Chemical Co., Inc., Las Vegas.)

the cleaners. When selecting a particular brand, look for these chemicals in the product and do a comparison test between your present carpet cleaner and the proposed alternatives.

Floor Care Products

The chemical formulation of a floor care product is dependent on the product's function.

Strippers

Strippers are used to remove the worn finish from floors. They may have either an ammoniated base or may be a nonammoniated product. Nonammoniated strippers are not as effective in removing **metal cross-linked polymer finishes**, but they do not have the harsh odor associated with the ammoniated product. A neutralizing rinse is often applied after the stripper. These rinses neutralize alkaline residues left from the stripping solution that may affect the performance of the new finish.

Floor Cleaners

Floor cleaners are mild detergents that work in cool water to remove soils without affecting the existing floor finish. Many floor finishes are **thermoplastic**; hot water tends to soften the finish. Most floor cleaners also have a neutral pH and many require no additional rinsing.

Sealers and Finishes

Sealers and finishes are applied to most floor surfaces to protect the flooring material from wear, cleaners, and liquid spills. The chemical composition of the sealer or finish will vary according to the type of flooring material for which it is intended. The preferred product for most resilient floors and some stone floor applications has been the metal cross-linked floor finishes (particularly zinc cross-linked polymers) because of their abil ity to give floors the popular "wet look." Recently, the use of these heavy metal finishes has fallen into disfavor because of environmental concerns. A number of states have prohibited their sale because of the perceived danger from emptying these heavy metals into the sewer when these finishes are stripped from the floors. Companies such as Airkem, as shown in Figure 6.8, are now producing a line of sealers and finishes that do not contain these heavy metals.

Many of the same concerns are being voiced about wood sealers and finishes that have solvent bases. A water-based finish for wood is now available that is considered by many experts to be environmentally safe (see Figure 6.9).

Pesticides

Pesticide applications should be left to the expert. Housekeeping departments are advised to seek out the services of a reliable pest control company rather than attempting to control pests themselves. If there is a perceived need to keep pesticides in inventory, it is strongly suggested that only natural pyrethrins be used if at all possible. Pest and rodent control is discussed in greater detail in Chapter 12.

PATH for Programmed Applications to Hygiene and is Air-kem's answer to the major issues and concerns that face our markets in the 1990's. Our PATH mission is to develop technological systems and products aimed at:

- Providing a safer workplace
- Providing a safer environment
- Lowering the cost and cash flow in chemical purchases

- Lowering labor cost associated with hygiene
- Improving morale, lowering turn-over and making people proud of their profession
- Producing real aesthetic value that improves first impressions
- Insuring public health protection

Division of Ecolab, Inc., Ecolab Center, St. Paul, MN 55102

Printed in U.S.A.
©1990   21370/8900/0890

Figure 6.8 "PATH." One company has responded to the public concern regarding the use of metal cross-linked finishes by producing a new line of sealers and finishes. Airkem Professional Products. (Used with permission of JB Chemical Co. Inc., Las Vegas.)

Handling and Storage of Chemicals

Manufacturer guidelines should be strictly adhered to when storing and handling chemicals. All chemicals should be routinely kept under lock and key. A system of inventory control should be established and followed. Chemicals are expensive and employees should be held accountable for their misuse. If bulk chemicals are used, employees should be taught how to properly dilute those chemicals.

Chemical Packaging

Bulk Chemicals

Bulk chemicals offer the housekeeping department the greatest potential for savings, but the executive housekeeper should beware of overbuying chemicals. One problem is that large quantities of chemicals

cannot always be stored properly. The cost of storing large quantities of chemicals may offset any potential cost savings from bulk purchases. Chemicals may deteriorate while in storage. The expiration dates that appear on some chemical supplies should be noted. The executive housekeeper should also compare the cost savings of bulk buying with the potential interest that would be generated if a minimal amount of chemical is purchased and cost difference between the minimal amount and the bulk amount invested. If the savings from buying in bulk would be greater than the amount of interest that would be generated, then the bulk purchase is a wise investment. But if the interest generated would be greater than the cost savings from buying in bulk, then the wise choice is to buy the lesser amount and invest the difference.

Another problem with bulk chemicals occurs when employees do not dilute the chemical to its

PROPERTIES	HYDROLINE FINISH	OIL-MODIFIED FINISHES	MOISTURE-CURED FINISHES	SWEDISH-TYPE FINISHES
ODOR	MILD	OBJECTIONABLE	OBJECTIONABLE	OBJECTIONABLE
PROTECTIVE EQUIP	NOT REQUIRED	NOT REQUIRED	RESPIRATOR	RESPIRATOR
DRYING TIME	TWO HOURS MAXIMUM	OVERNIGHT	SIX TO EIGHT HOURS	TWO TO FOUR HOURS
CLEAN-UP	WATER CLEAN-UP	XYLOL & MINERAL SPIRITS	STRONG SOLVENTS	STRONG SOLVENTS
INITIAL COLOR	CLEAR	AMBER	LIGHT STRAW	CLEAR
COLOR UPON AGING	STABLE	WILL DARKEN WITH AGE	WILL DARKEN WITH AGE	STABLE
DURABILITY	EXCELLENT	GOOD	EXCELLENT	EXCELLENT
CHEMICAL RESIST	EXCELLENT	GOOD	EXCELLENT	EXCELLENT
SLIP RESISTANCE	EXCELLENT	GOOD	GOOD	GOOD
FLAMMABILITY	NON-FLAMMABLE	COMBUSTIBLE	FLAMMABLE	FLAMMABLE
RECOATABILITY	WITH ALL PRODUCTS	OTHER OIL-MODIFIED FIN.	OTHER MOISTURE-CURED FIN.	WITH SWEDISH FINISH

Figure 6.9 Basic Coatings' "Hydroline" finish is water-based so there are no objectionable solvents present that might harm employees or the public. (Used with permission of Jacqueline & Associates, Las Vegas.)

appropriate level. If the dilution process is not rigorously monitored, the tendency of most employees is to use too much chemical, which drives up cost. An alternative to this costly practice is the new in-house chemical mixing stations as pictured in Figure 6.10. These systems automatically mix bulk chemicals, thus eliminating guesswork and improper dilution levels.

Premeasured Chemicals

Many chemical and detergent manufacturers produce premeasured (packaged) products in filament containers that dissolve when placed in a prescribed amount of water, yielding the proper amount of chemical in solution[3] (see Figure 6.11). Although these products are higher in unit price, the use of such premeasured products provides a high degree of cost control, better inventory procedures and quality in cleaning. In addition, housekeeping managers and hospital administrators desiring documentation on cleaning costs are more likely to accept cost documentation when premeasured chemicals and detergents are used, since exact quantities may be determined.

Figure 6.11 Premeasured chemicals in a water-soluble packet. Photo by Airkem Professional Products. (Used with permission of JB Chemical Co. Inc., Las Vegas.)

Aerosols

Aerosol chemicals have received considerable negative press in recent years from a variety of sources. Housekeeping managers often react negatively because of the higher net product cost associated with aerosols. Packaging and propellants drive up the cost of the product.

Environmentalists have negatively reacted to the use of aerosols for years. In the 1970s the issue was the widespread use of chlorofluorocarbons (CFCs) that were linked to ozone depletion and global warming. Although CFCs are not used anymore, substitutes have been accused of contributing to acid rain and smog formation, and in one case, the propellant (methylene chloride) is suspected of being a carcinogen.[4]

Aerosols continue to be used, however, because in certain limited instances, they simply perform better than hand pump sprays and they are more convenient to apply.

Compatibility in Chemical Product Design

One reason why housekeeping managers consider the purchase of only one brand of housekeeping chemical products is chemical compatibility. Chemical manufacturers often formulate their chemicals to perform better with other chemicals in their product line than with the chemical products made by competitors. One example of this would be a floor stripper that works best in removing a floor finish made by the same manufacturer.

When selecting any new chemical, a housekeeper should ask to have the vendor demonstrate the product at the site where it will be used so that comparisons between or among brands can be drawn.

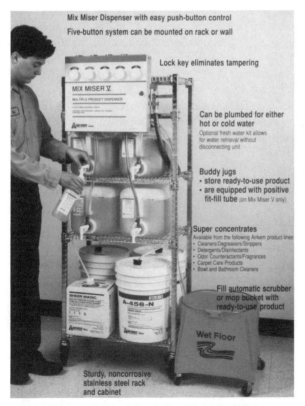

Figure 6.10 A chemical mixing station. Photo by Airkem Professional Products. (Used with permission of JB Chemical Co. Inc., Las Vegas.)

OSHA's Hazard Communication Standard

Since 1988, hotels have been required to comply with the Occupational Safety and Health Administration's Hazard Communication (**HazComm**) Standard, which applies to the handling and storage of hazardous chemical materials. Hazardous chemicals include but are not limited to aerosols, detergents, floor chemicals, carpet chemicals, flammable chemicals, cleaners, polishes, laundry chemicals, bathroom cleaners, and pesticides.

To be in full compliance, the management must read the HazComm standard. A HazComm kit that shows an employer how to be in compliance with the standard is available from the federal government. To obtain a kit, send a check for $18 to:

> Superintendent of Documents
> Government Printing Office
> Washington, DC 20402-9325

and ask for the kit. The reference number is 929-022-00000-9. Mention this reference number in your correspondence.

The hotel must also inventory and list all hazardous chemicals on the property. The company must then get **material safety data sheets** (MSDS) from the chemical manufacturers. These MSDS's should explain the chemical's characteristics, recommended handling use and storage, information on flammability, ingredients, health hazards, first-aid procedures, and what to do in case of a fire or explosion. This information must be disseminated to employees and should be made available to them at all times.

The hotel must also formulate a HazComm program for the property and establish a training program for all employees who use or come into contact with hazardous chemicals. Finally, the property must provide all necessary protective equipment to its employees.[5]

Cleaning Supplies and Equipment

Chemicals are only part of the housekeeping department's arsenal of weapons in its war against dirt. The professional housekeeper must develop standards for the equipment and supplies used by the property and must incorporate those standards into written purchase specifications. The following section is intended to aid the housekeeper in formulating those specifications.

Cleaning Supplies

Nonchemical cleaning supplies include brushes, brooms, buckets, mops, pads, rags, and wringers. Although these supplies look fairly straightforward and simplistic, there are a number of features to look for when selecting these supplies.

Brooms and Brushes

Common varieties of brooms include push brooms, corn brooms, and whisk brooms. The role of a broom is to remove large particles of soil from hard and resilient floors. Good push brooms will have two rows of bristles. The front row will have heavy-duty bristles designed to remove stubborn, large particles of dirt and debris. The second row will have fine, split tip, bristles designed to remove fine particles of dirt and debris. Many good push brooms have a steel brush hood that allows the operator to change worn brushes. One company even has a built-in shock absorber between the brush hood and the handle to prevent broken wooden handles.

The better scrub brushes have U-joints so that they can be used at any angle. This is particularly helpful when cleaning baseboards. Some models have rubber blades for drying surfaces.

Mop Buckets

Buckets are made out of three basic materials: galvanized steel, stainless steel, and structural foamed plastic. Plastic buckets do not rust and they are the most inexpensive to make, but they scratch, and dirt builds up in the scratches, making them permanently "grungy." "Stainless steel buckets are the 'Cadillacs' of the industry and predictably, they are also the most expensive."[6] Mop buckets range in size from 16 quarts up to 50 quarts. "The most popular sizes are 26 quarts and 35 quarts. . . . Round buckets track in a straight line when pushing them down hallways while oval buckets tend to wander."[7] Well-designed buckets have three-inch casters and rubber bumpers to protect furniture and walls. The best have no seams. For washing and rinsing, a two-bucket system saves valuable labor costs.

Wringers

Mop wringers squeeze in one of two directions, sideways and downward. Downward wringers are better, but more expensive. Wringers are made out of either steel or plastic. Plastic is less expensive, but it wears out much faster than the metal wringers. Wringers can be purchased by size or in a "one-size-fits-all" size.[8]

Wet Mops

Wet mop heads can be made of cotton, rayon, or a rayon/cotton blend. Cotton is best for scrubbing and is the most economical material. Rayon is best for the application of floor finishes. Rayon/cotton blends are an excellent compromise. Choose mops that are loop-end rather than cut-end. Loop-end mops hold liquids better, are more durable, and do not lint. All quality mops have a tailband that helps the mop to spread evenly and retain its shape.

Wash wet mops after each use and do not apply bleach to the mop; bleach will speed the disintegration of the fibers. Wet mops can be purchased in a variety of colors for color-coding purposes. There are now mops on the market that have a permanent antimicrobial treatment that prevents the spread of germs that cause disease and mop deterioration.[9]

Mop Handles

Mop handles can be made from wood, metal, and plastic and come with a variety of features. Quick change clamps are one welcome option. Handles are available in 54-inch, 60-inch, and 63-inch lengths.[10]

Dust Mops

Dust mops are meant to be used daily to remove dust and small particles of soil from the floor. Daily dusting helps to protect the floor's finish by removing small abrasive particles that erode the finish. Dust mops range in size from 12-inch to 60-inch widths. Dust mops can be made of cotton or synthetic yarns. Cotton mops are normally treated with chemicals that attract and hold dust particles. Oil treatments should be avoided because they can stain stone and wood floors. Dust mops should be treated at the end of the job, not the beginning, in order to allow the treated mop to dry. Synthetic yarns do not need to be treated and may be the best alternative in many instances. Disposable mops last for approximately 100,000 square feet.[11]

Squeegees

There are two types of squeegees, floor and window. Floor squeegees have a much heavier rubber than the window variety. Window squeegees come with a number of attractive features, from telescoping handles that enable a worker to clean a third story exterior window without the aid of scaffolding or a ladder, to U-joints that allow a worker to squeegee a window at an angle.

Pads, Bonnets, and Brushes

Floor machines and burnishers use floor pads, bonnets, and brushes. Pads are made from either natural or synthetic fibers. Floor pads have a universal color code so that users can tell at a glance if they are using the right pad for a particular application (see Chapter 5). Bonnets are made of yarn and are intended to be used on a floor machine

to spray clean carpets. Floor machine brushes are used to shampoo carpets. The fibers are synthetic.

Cleaning Equipment

When purchasing housekeeping equipment, it should be remembered that there are many products that will seem to fulfill a requirement but will fall short of lasting needs. The challenge is to find the right piece of equipment, one that is of a quality that will withstand continuous use with limited maintenance, and that will be the most cost effective in use of resources.

The decision as to what equipment best meets the needs of the department is usually made as job descriptions are being written. Quality, however, becomes another issue. Some managements stress price of purchase rather than quality of product and do not consider the overall value of more substantial equipment. Other managements will demand a high quality of equipment for employees and will then expect the highest standards of cleanliness. The executive housekeeper should presume that management desires the highest level of cleanliness possible and expect that workers be supplied with the wherewithal to accomplish the task.

Many product suppliers also act as equipment representatives. When new hotels open, suppliers will seek an appointment to present their product and equipment lines. A manufacturer's representative who can be depended upon is an asset worth considering when purchasing equipment.

The executive housekeeper should have the final say regarding the type, quantity, and quality of equipment required for cleaning the guestrooms and public areas of the rooms department. Equipment purchases will be substantial and will therefore require the utmost care and consideration in selection. An analysis of the various items of equipment listed in Table 4.1 is appropriate for a hotel the size of our hypothetical model. General information about this equipment follows.

Housekeeper's Cart

The housekeeper's cart is a most significant piece of equipment. There should be one cart for each section of rooms. This cart must be large enough to carry *all* of the supplies that the section housekeeper might readily be expected to use in the workday. (Repeated trips to the main or satellite linen room for two extra sheets or three more glasses is distracting and will decrease work efficiency.) Since the cart is large and may be heavily loaded, it must be maneuverable and capable of being pushed by some one weigh-

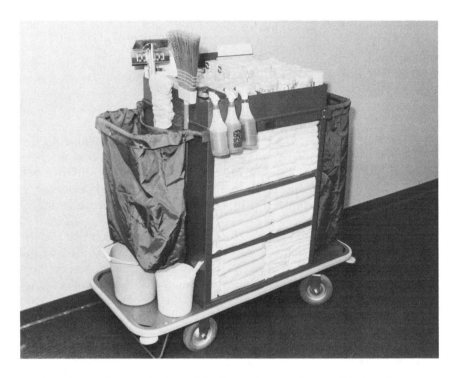

Figure 6.12 Section housekeeper's cart loaded with enough linen to service 20 guestrooms. Note three deep shelves and trash and soiled linen containers. Carts should be of high quality with good casters and neoprene bumpers. (Photo used with permission of Forbes Industries.)

ing less than 100 pounds. Surprisingly, such carts do exist. Quality housekeeper's carts are maneuverable with fixed wheels at one end and castered wheels at the opposite end. The solution lies in quality caster and ball-bearing wheels.

Carts should have three deep shelves, facilities to handle soiled linen sacks and rubbish sacks that are detachable, storage for a maid's vacuum, and a top that is partitioned for small items. Figure 6.12 shows a three-shelf housekeeper's cart that, when fully loaded, will service 20 guest rooms (30 beds).

Notice the neoprene bumper guard that surrounds the cart and protects corridor walls and door casings. These bumper guards should not leave unsightly marks if they come in contact with walls. The cart in Figure 6.12 weighs over 500 pounds when fully loaded. Figure 6.13 shows a cart-top basket used with a housekeeper's cart and various small, highcost guest supply items needed during the workday at a hotel.

The partitioning of the top of the cart is best accomplished on a local basis when the specific items to

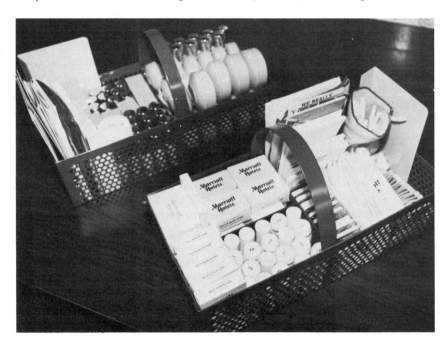

Figure 6.13 A cart-top basket used in conjunction with a housekeeper's cart. (Photo courtesy of Los Angeles Airport Marriott Hotel.)

be carried are available for sizing. The hotel carpenter should be able to make the appropriate partitions.

Small service carriers are also available to support the work of lobby and public area housekeepers.

Housekeeper's Vacuum

There are many ways to provide vacuums for cleaning guestrooms. Some hotels have tank-type vacuums for guestroom attendants. Others have tank-type vacuums installed on the housekeeper's carts with 24-foot vacuum hoses that will reach from the hotel corridor through the entire room. The main concern about tank vacuums being permanently installed on the housekeeper's cart, however, is the noise that permeates the hallway when one or more vacuums are in use. The vacuum most readily seen in hotel operations remains the upright vacuum with bag and belt-driven beater brush. Figure 6.14 is a photograph of such a vacuum cleaner.

An improved variation of the single-motor upright vacuum pictured in Figure 6.14 is the dual-motor vacuum shown in Figure 6.15. One motor drives the beater brush and a second motor provides

Figure 6.15 The "Carpetwin," a dual-motor housekeeper's vacuum. This vacuum is available in 14-, 16-, and 20-inch models. (Photo courtesy of Advance Machine Company.)

Figure 6.14 Standard single-motor housekeeping vacuum with a 12-inch brush. (Photo courtesy of Advance Machine Company.)

the suction. These dualmotor varieties often have a convenient built-in hose for cleaning corners and upholstery.

There are many commercial grade vacuums of varying degrees of quality ranging in price from just over $100 to in excess of $500. (I have yet to find $400 worth of significant difference in vacuum cleaners and am thus disposed toward the less expensive.) The horsepower of the vacuum motor, ease of emptying and changing of beater belts, and routine maintenance are either criteria upon which to judge vacuums. Whether inexpensive or top line, housekeeper's vacuums will receive heavy use and at times abuse. If the less-expensive vacuum can withstand the heavy use (and it can) it is better to use it and have a higher replacement schedule when machines wear out than to pay a higher price and only be able to replace vacuums one-fifth as often. There should be one vacuum cleaner for each section housekeeper, one for each public area housekeeper, and a 10 percent complement of spare vacuums.

Corridor Vacuum

Housekeeping teams have section housekeeping aides whose responsibilities include vacuuming extensive sections of hotel corridors. Such areas have open expanses of carpet that require an efficient form of vacuuming. The section housekeeping aide should have a vacuum that can do this heavy and time-consuming task. A motor-driven vacuum with an 18-inch to 28-inch foot, shown in Figure 6.16, is appropriate for this type of work.

All manufacturers of commercial equipment make models of this type and size and each should be investigated and compared before purchase.

Space Vacuums

Space vacuums (Figure 6.17) look like lawn mowers. Approximately 30 inches (76.2 centimeters) wide, motor driven, and capable of picking up large items of debris, space vacuums are best suited for vacuuming the large expanses of carpet found in ball-

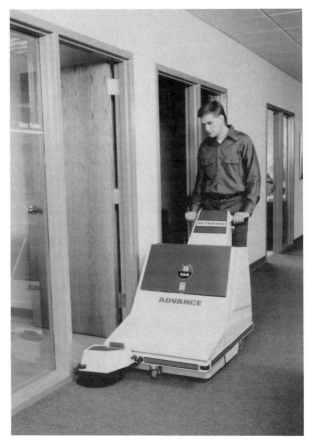

Figure 6.17 The 34-inch "Retriever" space vacuum. This is a battery-powered, self-propelled model that has a side broom for cleaning along side walls. (Photo courtesy of Advance Machine Company.)

rooms, meeting rooms, and corridors. In a hotel the size of our model, both the banquet and housekeeping departments need space vacuums. On occasion, one space vacuum can substitute for the other if one is out of commission. There will be times when the catering department will need to use both space vacuums.

Pile Lifter

Pile lifting, as the term implies, means lifting carpet pile that has become packed. This process usually occurs in conjunction with shampooing. The Rugavator (Figure 6.18) is an example of a machine that is capable of returning carpet pile to its vertical orientation.

A pile lifter used before shampooing assists in cleaning the carpet and, if used after shampooing, assists in drying the carpet. Pile lifters are another form of vacuum cleaner, having a very heavy vacuum and large rotary brush that is operated by pulling the machine across the carpet. One pile lifter is usually found in the arsenal of equipment of every hotel with over 300 rooms.

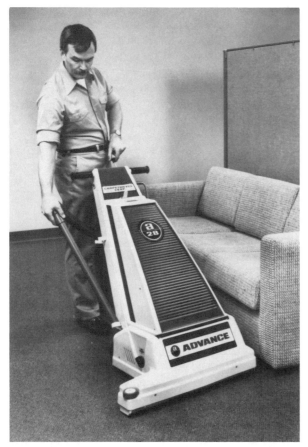

Figure 6.16 The "Carpetriever" vacuum from Advance. Note the hose attachment on this model. (Photo courtesy of the Advance Machine Company.)

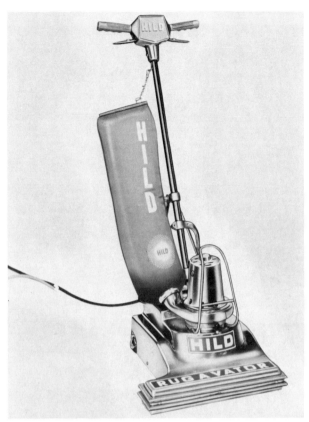

Figure 6.18 Rugavator is used to vacuum carpet and restore vertical orientation to carpet pile. It is especially good for use before and after shampooing. The Rugavator is highly maneuverable, may be used in restricted areas, and may be adjusted to different pile heights. (Photo courtesy of HILD Floor Machine Co., Inc.)

Figure 6.19 "Tip & Pour" wet vacuum model from Advance. No lifting is required to empty this wet vacuum. (Photo courtesy of the Advance Machine Company.)

Wet Vacuums

Wet vacuums (Figure 6.19) are an absolute necessity in hotel operations. Even though wet vacuums can be used for both wet and dry vacuuming, they are usually maintained in their wet configuration and are therefore ready for any spill emergency. There should be two wet vacuums on the property, one in the banquet department and one in housekeeping, both clean and ready for use. Wet vacuums are also required when large areas of noncarpeted floor are being stripped and cleaned. They greatly aid in water removal, making such operations more efficient.

Backpack Vacuums

Backpack vacuums (Figure 6.20) are very efficient for cleaning curtains, drapes, ceiling corners, and other areas requiring high dusting. The vacuum unit straps to the user's back and has a handheld wand with various attachments that provide flexible cleaning methods without having to configure the vacuum. Two backpack vacuums are sufficient in a housekeeping department that services 350 rooms.

Electric Brooms

Electric brooms are very lightweight vacuums that have no motor driven beater brush. Electric brooms are used primarily for very light vacuuming and are sometimes used in place of the housekeeper's vacuum. Electric brooms are excellent for quick touch-ups on carpet and hard floors or for sand and spills when full vacuuming is not required. They should not be relied upon to replace the housekeeper's vacuum.

Single-Disc Floor Machines

The single-disc floor machine, also known as the buffer or scrubber, is the most versatile item of equipment in the housekeeper's inventory. This machine can scrub floors, strip floor finishes, spray buff floors, sand wood floors, polish floors, and shampoo carpets. Machines are available in 17, 18, 19, 20, and 21-inch models. These machines will accommodate pads, brushes, and bonnets. As it has been already noted, different pads are designed for different jobs from stripping to buffing (see Figure 6.21).

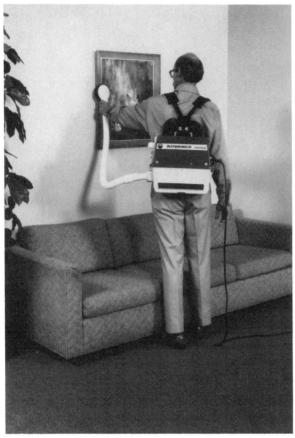

Figure 6.20 The "Papoose-On-the-Back Vac" from Advance converts to tank-type vacuum by snapping on a set of wheels. (Photo courtesy of the Advance Machine Company.)

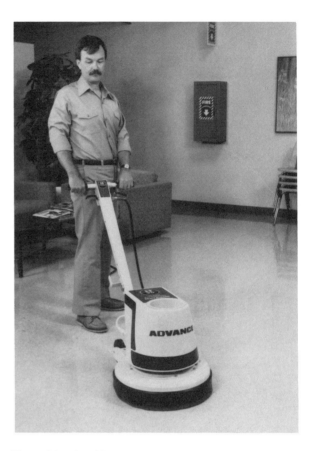

Figure 6.21 The "All-Purpose Matador" can polish floors, strip and scrub floors, and shampoo rugs with the proper attachments. (Photo courtesy of the Advance Machine Company.)

Brushes are used to scrub floors and shampoo carpets and bonnets are used to "bonnet clean" carpets (described in Chapter 5). When selecting a standard single-disc scrubber, do not select too small a scrubber. A larger machine will cover an area faster, thus reducing labor costs. Table 6.1 is a comparison of labor costs for a 17-inch and a 20 inch floor machine. Depending on the model, a single disc floor machine will operate between 175 rpm and 350 rpm.

Burnishers

Burnishers or ultra-high-speed (UHS) buffers resemble single-disc floor machines, but they operate between 350 rpm and 2,500 rpm. They were developed to polish the new harder floor finishes that had been recently introduced into the market. Unlike single-disc floor machines, the pad of a UHS buffer does not rest entirely upon the floor. Only the front part of the pad comes into contact with the floor; the rest of the weight is distributed to the wheels. Many models have caster wheels in the front of the machine to distribute the weight. UHS buffers operate in a straight line, while traditional scrub-

bers operate from side-to-side. There are battery and propane models that enable the operator to cover vast areas without the need for troublesome electric cords. Propane models are noisy, they create noxious fumes, and they present a possible fire hazard. They are illegal in some municipalities. Pictured in Figure 6.22 are two UHS buffers.

Automatic Scrubbers

The purpose of the automatic scrubber is to scrub or strip hard and resilient floors. The units apply a cleaning or stripping solution, scrub the floor, and vacuum up the dirty floor solution in one continuous operation. Most units are self-propelled. Some have attachments that turn them into a wet/dry vacuum, while others can also be used to buff dry floors. In addition to AC electric-cord models, there are battery-driven models. The better battery-driven models are preferred because the constant plugging and unplugging of electric cords is an inconvenience and reduces employee productivity. Automatic scrubbers come in a wide variety of sizes, from a width of 17 inches to widths over four feet.

Table 6.1 Labor Cost Comparisons for 17-inch and 20-inch Floor Machines

TIME PER 1000 SQ. FT.	*Hourly Labor Cost per 1000 Sq. Ft.*					
	$5/HR.	$6/HR.	$7/HR.	$8/HR.	$9/HR.	$10/HR.
17"—23 min.	$1.91	$2.30	$2.67	$3.06	$3.44	$3.82
20"—16 min.	$1.33	$1.60	$1.86	$2.13	$2.39	$2.66

(Table courtesy of the Advance Machine Company.)

When purchasing a machine to clean halls and aisles, consider the number of passes necessary to clean a hall. If a machine cleans aisles in the same number of passes as a smaller machine, then there is no benefit in paying the additional cost for the larger machine. Figure 6.23 shows an automatic scrubber in action.

Wet-Extraction Systems

Wet-Extraction is sometimes referred to as a "steam" or hot water carpet machine. These terms are actually misnomers, for steam is never produced by these machines and hot water is often not used because of the shrinkage and fading risk.

There are three varieties of extractors on the market today. The first type is the least expensive. It consists of two tanks, one holds the cleaning solution, a second tank holds the dirty pick-up water, and a wand that connects to the two tanks through two hoses. As the wand is pulled across a carpet, the operator sprays the clean detergent solution onto the carpet. On the same stroke, the solution is immediately vacuumed up into the waste tank.

The second variety of extractor is virtually identical to the first, but it incorporates an invaluable attachment. A beater brush is attached to the wand that works the detergent solution into the carpet and

Figure 6.22 Left, the "Whirlamatic 2500B," a 2500-rpm burnisher that is battery-powered for big jobs. Above, the "Whirlamatic 17/20 UHS," an AC cord-electric burnisher that operates at 1500 rpm. (Photos courtesy of the Advance Machine Company.)

Figure 6.23 An automatic scrubber replaces time-consuming hand mopping. (Photo courtesy of the Advance Machine Company.)

Figure 6.24 The "Aquatron 16XP," a tank-type extractor with a power-head brush. (Photo courtesy of the Advance Machine Company.)

physically breaks down the clinging soils before vacuuming. This option (see Figure 6.24) is definitely worth the higher price.

The third variety is unquestionably the best, for it reduces operator fatigue and effectively eliminates the extra effort required to periodically reposition the hose and tank unit. This variety is called a self-contained carpet extractor. These units (see Figure 6.25) eliminate the wand and hoses, and battery models also eliminate the bothersome electric cord. The smaller self-contained units work quite well in guestrooms and the larger walk-behind models can clean up to a 3-foot swath of carpet in one pass. Some of these models have a hose and hand tools for cleaning stairs and upholstery.

Dry foam carpet cleaners brush a low moisture foam into the carpet that is vacuumed up after it has been allowed to briefly dry. It does leave a residual amount of foam in the carpet. Units come in a variety of width sizes, from 12 inches to over 28 inches (see Figure 6.26). Many have attachments for upholstery.

Dry Powder Systems

Dry powder systems normally use three pieces of equipment. First, the dry powder is laid down on the carpet with an applicator. Then a brush unit works the powder into the carpet; this dislodges the soil from the carpet fibers. The powder is then vacuumed up using a standard vacuum cleaner. Pictured in Figure 6.27 is the Host dry extraction carpet cleaning system. As mentioned in Chapter 5, this system allows the carpet to be walked on immediately following cleaning.

Convertible Mobile Shelving

Convertible mobile shelving is unique in its versatility and construction. (A typical convertible mobile shelving unit, shown in Figure 14.5, is discussed further in Chapter 14.)

A shelving unit in a satellite linen room, with shelves adjusted to receive soiled linen, acts as a storage hamper for used linen. At the end of the day the soiled linen is moved to the laundry in its own conveyor. In the meantime, another unit, with shelves adjusted to receive clean linen being processed in the laundry, may be moved to the satellite linen room so section housekeepers can load their housekeeper's carts for the next day's operation. Once emptied, the shelves are repositioned for a repeat of the cycle the next day. Mobile convertible shelving not only removes the need for permanent shelving in the laundry and satellite linen rooms, it reduces the three-step

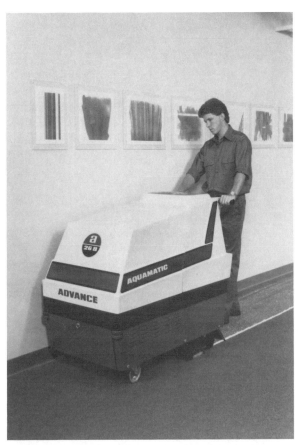

Figure 6.25 The Advance "Aquamatic" battery-powered walk-behind extractor. (Photo courtesy of the Advance Machine Company.)

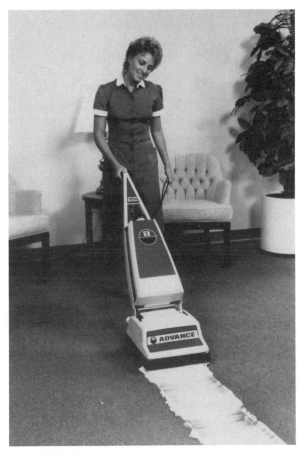

Figure 6.26 The Advance "Minitron" dry foam shampooer. (Photo courtesy of the Advance Machine Company.)

task of moving linen from shelf to conveyor to shelf to a one-step loading process. There should be at least two units for each satellite linen room.

Trash-Handling Equipment

Another piece of equipment used by the section housekeeping aide is some form of conveyor whereby rubbish and other materials may be moved from various sections of the hotel to a disposal area.

A conveyor similar to that produced by Rubbermaid (Figure 6.28), known as a hopper, is recommended. The hopper may be used to remove soiled linen several times each day from housekeeper's carts to the satellite linen room, or it may be used to carry rubbish sacks from maid's carts for emptying. A great deal of moving of material supplies and rubbish occurs each day in each section of the hotel. Each housekeeping team (section housekeeping aide) will therefore need a conveyor for moving material.

Sewing Machines

A sewing machine of commercial quality is useful in the main linen room. This sewing machine will be used to repair drapes and bedspreads and may be used to make certain fabric items. The machine must be of commercial quality since one item requiring repair will be heavy blackout drapes. No automatic or multiple stitch machines are required.

Glass Washers

Depending on whether guestroom drinking glasses will be made of plastic or glass and depending upon the availability of the hotel dish room dishwasher, the housekeeping department may need its own glass washer. In hotels of major size (1000 rooms) a properly equipped linen room should have a glass washer to prevent using labor to move 15 or 20 cases of glasses to the kitchen each night.

Glass washers are expensive and are major items of equipment. The use of real glasses as opposed to plastic ones is a matter of quality as well as economics, and the multiple uses of glasses justifies the expense of a glass washer.

Guest Supplies

A guest supply is any item that is conducive to the guest's material comfort and convenience. The term

Figure 6.27 The Host Dry Extraction Carpet Cleaning System. (Photo courtesy of Racine Industries, Inc.)

Figure 6.28 A tilt truck (Hopper) is suitable for moving supplies from place to place, for removing soiled linen from housekeepers' carts, and fro removing rubbish. The model shown here will carry 1,000 pounds and has $\frac{1}{2}$ cubic yards capacity. (Photo courtesy of RUBBERMAID®Commercial Products Division)

amenity is commonly used to identify luxury items that a hotel gives away to its guests at no extra charge, although the cost of those items are often hidden in the room rate.

There are also those guest supplies that are expected to be used up by the guest that cannot be classified as luxuries even at the most spartan budget property. We shall categorize those items as **guest expendables**.

Then there are items essential to the guestroom that are not normally used up or taken away by the guest. These items shall be referred to as **guest essentials**.

Guest loan items are those guest supplies that are not normally found in the guestroom, but are commonly available to the guest when requested.

These categories of guest supplies are fairly arbitrary, but they represent an attempt to distinguish those items that are necessary in every room from those items that are discretionary purchases.

Quite often the rate to be charged for each guestroom will have a bearing on the quantity and quality of these guest supplies. Although these guest supplies are not particularly expensive if considered on an item-by-item basis, their aggregate can add substantially to a hotel's costs. Today, many budget prop-

erties are scaling back on their amenity packages. On the other hand, luxury hotels can ill afford to reduce their amenity pack ages. Many think that a reduction in the amenity package would seriously reduce the perceived value of many luxury hotel rooms.[12]

Guest supplies are a major storage and security concern. Some items such as guest pens, stationery, and envelopes appear in such great quantity and appear to be of such little significance that employees who are not well trained may feel that their use at home is quite acceptable. Other items of higher value (such as portion packages of guest laundry detergents and bleaches) may require even greater security in storage. In such cases, locked-cage storage (inside of storage rooms) is in order. If not properly controlled, the indiscriminate use and negligent storage of guest supplies can become a costly expense.

Amenity Packages

Although amenities extend well beyond the guestroom (free breakfasts, recreation facilities, and so on), our discussion encompasses only those amenities that are found in the guestroom.

Bath Amenities

When the general public thinks of guestroom amenities, they typically think of bathroom amenity packages. Table 6.2 contains a listing of common amenity items.

There are two opposing schools of though when it comes to bathroom amenities. One camp believes that the guest appreciates seeing name-brand products on the vanity counter, while the other camp is of the opinion that the product should be "branded"

Table 6.2 Bathroom Amenity Items

Aftershave	Glycerin soap
Bath gel	Hair conditioner
Bath salts	Hand lotion
Body oils	Loofa sponges
Body powder	Mouthwash
Bubble bath	Nail clippers
Colognes	Perfumes
Cosmetics	Razors
Deodorants	Scissors
Deodorant soap	Sewing kit
Emery boards	Shampoo
Fabric wash	Shaving creme
Face lotions	Shoe horn
Face soap	Shoe mit
Facial mud packs	Shower cap
	Tanning lotion

Table 6.3 Guestroom Amenities

Bathrobes	Flowers
Chocolate	Free in-room beverages
Clothes sachets	Free snacks
Coffee maker	In-room movies
Corkscrews	Luxury stationery
Expensive pens	Quality pens

with the hotel's logo. Fortunately, a number of suppliers can arrange (for a price) to print both.

What should be of even greater concern to the hotel is the cost/benefit relationship of amenities. Far too often the management of a hotel believes that customer loyalty can be won by throwing money into an amenity program. Management would be better served if they first analyzed what is truly important to their guests. Perhaps, just perhaps, far too much money is being spent in American hotels on guest amenities that are of marginal concern to the guests of those hotels.

Guestroom Amenities

These amenities are items that can be found in the guest's bedroom. Table 6.3 is a list of common guestroom amenities.

Guest Essentials

Guest essentials are intended to remain with the hotel after the guest departs. Unfortunately, this is not always the case. One particularly troublesome area for guests and the hotel revolves around the clothes hanger. Years ago, hotels eliminated the standard wooden hanger because these hangers frequently found their way into the guest's luggage. They were replaced by the knob-headed hanger, which was not stolen, but it was and continues to be a source of irritation to the guest. Enter the hanger with an undersized hook. This compromise item has a hook that is too small to fit over a standard clothes rack, but it is far easier to use.

A colleague of the author's, who is a designer by trade and a frequent business traveler, once suggested a guest essential that would warm the heart of any traveler who uses a suit bag: a small but well-anchored hook opposite the clothes rack or closet in a hotel room. These hooks would be placed approximately 6 feet 6 inches from the floor and would serve as hooks for suit bags. Unloading a suit bag from inside the closet or from the bed, contends the designer, is extremely inconvenient. Although a few hotels have recognized this need, they are an extremely small minority.

One final note on guest essentials: the hotel logo will often make these items souvenirs and, as such, will cause them to disappear at alarming rates. If it is decided that this is an effective form of "advertising," then perhaps the cost for these items should be shared with other departments in the hotel, particularly the marketing department.

A list of guest essentials appears in Table 4.2.

Guest Expendables

Guest expendables, those items expected to be used up or taken by the guest, are sometimes supplied by organizations other than the housekeeping department. For example, laundry bags and laundry slips are usually supplied by the cleaning establishment that provides valet service. Many guest expendable items (such as soaps) are not necessarily used up or taken away upon guest departure but are replenished when the room is made ready for a new guest. All expendable items are normally inventoried and stored by the housekeeping department.

Guest expendables are also listed on Table 4.2.

Guest Loan Items

Guest loan items are not maintained in the guestroom but are available if requested by the guest on receipted loan basis. Guest loan items are usually stored in the main linen room (housekeeping center of operations) and when requested are delivered to the guest with a receipt form. Such receipts should specify when the item may be picked up so as not to convey the idea that they are free for the taking.

Summary

The financial success of any institution is not necessarily the result of a few isolated strategic decisions. It is often accomplished through hundreds of small decisions concerning such minutiae as the selection of the right soap cake for the guestroom, the purchase of the right size of floor machine, and using a bathroom cleaner that will not harm fixtures. The professional housekeeper must stay abreast of technological developments in housekeeping supplies and equipment and must base all purchase and use decisions on objective fact finding, not on the hype of smooth-talking vendors.

KEY TERMS AND CONCEPTS

Pathogenic microorganisms
Detergents
Disinfectants
Bacteriostat
Quaternary ammonium compounds
Idophors
Hypochlorites
Sours
Nonionic detergent
Cationic
Petroleum naptha solvents
Flash point
Defoamers
Metal cross-linked polymer finishes

Phenolic compounds
Sanitizer
Stock-outs
All-purpose cleaners
Odor-pair neutralization
Nosocomial infection
Antichlors
Thermoplastic
HazComm
Material safety data sheets
Amenity
Guest expendables
Guest essentials
Guest loan items

DISCUSSION AND REVIEW QUESTIONS

1. What amenities would you feature in an budget hotel property? In a mid-sized property? In a luxury property?
2. Explain the advantages and disadvantages of relying primarily on an all-purpose chemical cleaner.
3. In what areas of the hotel should a housekeeper use a disinfectant cleaner? In what areas would a sanitizer be appropriate?
4. List the applications for a single-disc floor machine.
5. Define these terms:
   disinfectant
   sanitizer
   detergent
   sour
   antichlor
   amenity
6. Explain the benefits of using convertible mobile shelving.

NOTES

1. John J. Dykstra and Andrew R. Schwarz, "Sanitation and Disinfection Key to Infection Control," *Executive Housekeeping Today*, November 1990, p. 4.
2. "Handwashing: The Most Effective Method in Preventing Nosocomial Infection," *Executive Housekeeping Today*, May 1990, p. 12.
3. "Premeasured Detergents and Costs," *Executive Housekeeping Today*, November 1982, p. 12.
4. Ron Gillette, "Aerosols Under Pressure," *Sanitary Maintenance*, June 1990, p. 22.
5. Christine O'Dwyer, "Chemical Warfare," *Lodging*, December 1990, pp. 59–60.
6. Buzz Flannigan, "Mopping Equipment," *Sanitary Maintenance*, May 1989, p. 42.

7. Ibid.

8. Ibid.

9. Joseph Wilen, "Wet Mops," *Sanitary Maintenance*, May 1989, pp. 37–38.

10. Buzz Flannigan, "Mopping Equipment," *Sanitary Maintenance*, May 1989, p. 80.

11. Mark Friedman, "Dust Mops," *Sanitary Maintenance*, May 1989, p. 40–41.

12. Christine O'Dwyer, "Should You Cut Amenities?" *Lodging*, October 1990, pp. 73–75.

7

Material Planning: Bedding, Linens, and Uniforms

Bedding
> *Sheets and Pillow Cases*
> *Blankets*
> *Bedspreads, Comforters, and Dust Ruffles*
> *Pillows*
> *Mattress Covers*

Bath and Table Linens
> *Bath Linens*
> *Table Linens*
Uniforms

CHAPTER OBJECTIVES

1. To be able to generate purchase specifications for all bedding, including sheets, pillows, mattress pads, blankets, and bedspreads.
2. To develop purchase criteria for table linens, including the proper size, fabric content, and method of construction.
3. To be able to generate standards of selection for employee uniforms.
4. To describe criteria used to judge bath linens for a commercial operation.

This chapter is the fourth and final chapter devoted to the examination of material administration. In this chapter we will explore **bedding, linens,** and **uniforms**. These items are the highest annual cost items in hotel operational supply inventories. Initial supplies required to support operations of a commercial hotel the size of the model hotel can well exceed $150,000.

Before deciding on the requirements for an initial supply of bedding, linens, and uniforms, the professional housekeeper must have a thorough knowledge of the composition and construc-

tion of these items. The professional housekeeper must then establish purchase specifications for these items so that the purchased items complement the property rather than detract from it.

The intention of this chapter is to acquaint the housekeeper with the range of materials and manufacturing methods used to construct these textiles.

Bedding

Bedding encompasses all materials used in the making of a bed. This includes sheets, pillow cases, blankets, pillows, bedspreads, **dust ruffles**, comforters, and mattress covers.

Sheets and Pillow Cases

Many small (inexpensive) hotels change linen once a week or when the guest departs, whichever occurs first. Quality hotels change linen daily regardless of whether the guest departs.

Fabric Materials and Construction

While 100 percent cotton sheets are available, the overwhelming majority of hotels use a cotton/polyester (Dacron) blend. A 50/50 dacron/cotton blend is thought to provide the optimum qualities of the natural and the synthetic fibers.

Cotton/polyester blends are more durable than straight cotton. After 100 launderings, cotton loses 35 to 40 percent of its tensile strength. Cotton/polyester blends lose 3 to 7 percent. Expected wear increases three and one-half times with a blend.

Blends do not shrink as much as cotton. If cotton is tumbled dry, it will shrink from 5 to 8 percent. A blend will shrink from 0 to 3 percent.

Blends are more economical to launder. They will retain from 15 to 50 percent less water than a full cotton sheet after extraction. This feature means a faster drying time for blends.

The cotton fibers in the sheet can be either combed or carded before spinning. If the fibers are carded, the fabric is rough and dull looking. Sheets that are made in this manner are called **muslin** sheets. If the fibers are combed the fabric is much smoother and has a greater tensile strength. Sheets made from this process are called **percale** sheets.

The threads running lengthwise through the sheet are called the **warp**. The threads that run crosswise (horizontally) are called the **weft** or **filling**. The most common weave for sheets is called the plain weave. In this weave the warp and weft threads are perpendicular to each other.

Textiles are graded by the **thread count** and **tensile strength**. Housekeeping managers should specify a sheet that has a thread count of at least a T-180. This means that there are 180 threads in a one-inch square piece of sheet. Ideally, there should be 94 threads in the warp and 86 in the weft. In any event, the number of warp and weft threads should be fairly close. The tensile strength is determined by the amount of weight it takes to tear a 1 inch × 3 inches piece of fabric.

Fabrics that come directly from a loom are called **gray goods**. This means that the fabric has not received a finishing treatment and is unsuitable for most purposes. Finishing is an all-inclusive term that is applied to a number of treatments that can be applied to a freshly woven fabric. Finishing includes washing, bleaching, and a process, called **mercerizing**, in which the fabric is treated with caustic soda. Mercerizing swells the cotton fibers, increasing the strength and luster of the cloth. Fabric may also be sanforized. **Sanforizing** preshrinks the cloth to prevent it from shrinking more than one percent during regular laundering. Cotton/polyester sheets are normally chemically modified during manufacturing to provide what is often called a "durable press" or "no-iron" effect. This fabric is smooth to

begin with, stays smooth after laundering, and stays smooth while in use. Some finishing treatments are patented processes.

Sheets may be dyed, but white is the color choice for most hotels. If sheets are to be dyed, the best process is to dye the threads in a vat before weaving, but most of the time the completed fabric is dyed. White sheets will often have a colored thread or colored piping in the sheet to indicate the sheet's size for sorting. White sheets are preferred because they do not fade after laundering, nor do they require extra handling for sorting.

Sheets that have minor imperfections are called **seconds** and are usually marked with an "S" or have the manufacturer's tag cut off. Most seconds are perfectly acceptable in the majority of hotels.

Sheets and pillow cases are shipped in case lots. A case may have from a dozen to 12 gross in its contents, depending on the size of an order and a manageable weight per case. An example of how a linen case is marked would be as follows: "2F/11S–81 × 104." This information is translated as follows: 2 dozen first quality, 11 dozen second quality, double sheets.

Size

There are two sheet measurements. The **torn sheet** size is the size of the sheet before hemming. The **finished sheet** has a top and bottom hem. Institutional sheets normally have a two-inch hem on the top and the bottom of the sheet. This is done so that the sheet does not require extra handling when folding or making the bed. Also, since the sheet can be reversed, it is hoped that both hems will wear evenly.

In Table 7.1 recommended sheet sizes for each mattress size are given in inches.

Table 7.1 Recommended Sheet Sizes (in inches)

NAME	MATTRESS SIZE	TORN SHEET SIZE	FINISHED SHEET SIZE
Roll-away	33 × 76	66 × 104	66 × 99
Twin	39 × 76	66 × 104	66 × 99
Long twin	39 × 80	66 × 108	66 × 103
¾ twin	48 × 76	66 × 104	66 × 99
Double	54 × 76	81 × 104	81 × 99
Long double	54 × 80	81 × 108	81 × 103
Queen	60 × 80	90 × 108	90 × 103
King	78 × 80	108 × 110	108 × 105
California king	72 × 80	108 × 115	108 × 110
Pillow case	Standard	42 × 36	20½ × 30
Pillow case	King	42 × 46	20½ × 40

Fitted sheets are never used in commercial applications because they tear at their corners, they take up to three times the space in storage, and they can only be used as the bottom sheet. On the other hand, standard sheets are more flexible, and larger standard sheets can be substituted for smaller sheets.

Par Levels

The term **par** refers to standard, specific, or normal levels of stock. Linen pars are the standard levels of linen inventory required to support operations. "One par linen" is that quantity of each item required to completely outfit the guestrooms of the hotel one time. Since one pare is hardly enough to have an efficient operation, a par number must be established to ensure adequate supply for smooth operations. (The section housekeeper who has to wait for the laundry to finish laundering linen before a bed can be made hardly represents the efficient use of costly personnel or shows proper guest service. In addition, freshly laundered sheets should be allowed to "rest" for 24 hours before being put back into service. This will ensure their durability.)

Hotel properties having their own linen supply need to have 3 $\frac{1}{2}$ par linen on hand (1 par in the guestroom, 1 par soiled for tomorrow's laundry work requirement, 1 par clean for tomorrow's work in the guestrooms, and $\frac{1}{2}$ par new in storage). Hotels that must send their linen out to be laundered require 1 additional par due to out-and-in transit time.

Blankets

A blanket is an insulator; it keeps body heat in and cold air out. The best blanket is light in weight for comfort, but at the same time it should be a highly effective thermal insulator. Adding weight to a blanket does not necessarily make it a better insulator. The way a blanket is woven (how it traps the body heat) is what makes a blanket warm.

Fabric Materials and Construction

Although wool blankets have extremely high heat retention, they are much heavier than synthetic blankets. Synthetics such as polyester, acrylics, and nylon are the preferred fabrics for commercial blanket construction.

Another positive aspect of synthetic blankets is that they can be laundered as well as dry-cleaned. However, repeated launderings will tend to make blankets fade over time. If blankets are to be laundered, care must be taken to ensure that the blanket binding is made of the same material so that different fibers do not shrink at a different rate.

Blankets can be woven, needle punched (similar to carpet tufting), or made through an electrostatic process. Woven blankets are normally more expensive, but they are not necessarily a better insulator. One popular blanket variety is the thermal blanket. Thermal blankets are light woven blankets that have large air pockets for insulation. A regular blanket or sheet is placed on top of this blanket to increase its insulation coefficient.

Care should be taken to select blankets that are moisture permeable. A blanket that cannot transfer moisture will make the guest feel clammy and uncomfortable.

Above all, blankets should be fire retardant.

Some hotels provide electric blankets in their rooms. One school of thought holds that electric blankets are a service feature appreciated by many guests and that their use will decrease the hotel's heating costs. Other hoteliers believe that the theft rate of electric blankets is higher than that of ordinary blankets, that electric blankets are potential fire hazards, and that some of their guests hold that sleeping under an electric blanket is dangerous, unhealthy, or both.

Size

A blanket that is too short for a bed will wear prematurely from constant tugging by the guest. A blanket should be the length of the mattress, plus the thickness of the mattress, plus an additional six inches for tucking. The width of the blanket should be the width of the mattress, plus double the mattress' thickness, plus six additional inches for tucking.

The weight of a standard blanket will vary from two and one-half to three and one-half pounds. Lighter blankets should be used in the Southeast and Southwest and the heavier blankets should be reserved for northern climates.

Par Levels

Blankets should be set at one par plus ten percent in southern climates. In some northern climates the par level may be as high as two and one-half par, where an extra blanket is placed in the room for each bed. This policy, however, often results in a higher theft rate.

Bedspreads, Comforters, and Dust Ruffles

The bed is the focal point in most guestrooms; consequently, the bedspread is extremely important from a design perspective. The bedspread should complement the colors and other design elements in the room, but it should be durable and easy to maintain.

There are two main styles of bedspreads, throw spreads and tailored spreads. Tailored spreads fit the corners of the mattress snugly, whereas throw spreads bulge at the corners at the foot of the bed.

A bedspread may reach to the floor, covering the mattress, box springs, and the frame; or it may be a coverlet that only covers the mattress. If a coverlet is used, a dust ruffle is added to the bed to cover the box springs and the frame. A dust ruffle is a pleated cloth skirting that extends around the sides and foot of the bed. This decorative fabric is often sewn on to a muslin fabric that is placed between the mattress and box springs, thus holding the dust ruffle securely in place. The dust ruffle is normally cleaned when the bedspread is cleaned.

In a formal setting the bed is also decorated with **shams**. Shams are pillow covers that match the fabric used in the bedspread.

In an informal setting, the bed is often covered with a quilted comforter that does double duty as a bedspread and a blanket.

Fabric Materials and Construction

Synthetic materials such as polyester have come to dominate the commercial bedspread market. Dust ruffles are often cotton/polyester blend products.

Most hotels would prefer to have a washable bedspread fabric that is guaranteed to maintain its shape through repeated washings. When purchasing new bedspreads, use one for a trial sample to ensure that it does not shrink, fade, or wrinkle. All spreads should be fire retardant.

Size

As has already been mentioned, a full-sized bedspread just touches the floor, while a **coverlet** covers the top of the dust ruffle. Coverlets are easier to handle and they fit better into the washer and dryer, but to place a dust ruffle on the bed requires the mattress to be removed.

Par Levels

The par level for bedspreads, coverlets, comforters, and dust ruffles should be one plus 10 percent.

Pillows

It seems as though everyone has a different opinion as to what is a good pillow. Some prefer soft pillows while others prefer hard pillows. One camp holds that to be truly comfortable a pillow must be filled with goose down, while others contend that polyester will do just as well.

Natural Fills

The standard by which all other fills are measured is down—specifically, goose down from the European variety of goose. Goose down consists of the small soft feathers found on a goose or duck. Duck down is considered to be inferior to goose down. Using goose down alone to fill a pillow is prohibitively expensive, so the larger down feathers from ducks are blended together with the goose down in most instances.

Down or down/feather blends are only found in the most upscale hotels.

Synthetic Fills

Synthetic fiber pillows have become the widely accepted norm throughout the United States. Polyester fibers lead the market in the synthetic category. In addition to the aforementioned cost advantage, synthetic fibers can be laundered, and fewer individuals are allergic to them when compared to down and feathers. A few rare individuals are allergic to synthetic fills, so every property should have a few down/feather pillows in its inventory.

A well-made pillow should be resilient, evenly filled (no lumps), and not too heavy (heavier pillows are an indication of inferior synthetic fibers); the fill and cover should be fire retardant, and the **ticking** should be stain- and waterproof.

The materials used in the construction of a pillow are printed on a label that is required by law.

Mattress Covers

Mattress covers serve two purposes; they provide a padded layer between the guest and the mattress, making for a more restful sleep, and they protect the mattress from stains resulting from spills and from incontinent or sick guests.

Mattress covers should be changed whenever the guest checks out.

Quilted Pads

All cotton quilted pads are very expensive. One problem associated with quilted pads is the tendency of the diagonal threads to break after a few washings, which allows the fill to shift and the pad to become lumpy.

All cotton pads tend to shrink from 15 to 20 percent, so it is imperative to allow for this skrinkage when purchasing pads.

Felt Pads

The preferred pad for hotels is the 100 percent polyester felt pad. There is less than two percent shrinkage with this pad. The pad does not pucker or become lumpy. This pad is also far less expensive than any quilted pad, and it can be moisture proofed.

All mattress covers should meet the federal standard FF-4-72 for fire retardancy.

Vinyl

Vinyl covers are more appropriate for hospital applications. The newer generation of vinyl covers can even be washed like cloth and can be sterilized.

Bath and Table Linens

The quality of hotel's bath and table linen is a remarkably accurate indicator of the hotel's class and price level. The thicker the towels, the more expensive the accommodations.

Bath Linens

The intended purpose of a bath towel is to absorb water, but a towel is often used by the guest as a rag to wipe up spills or as a shine cloth for shoes. Considering the abuse that hotel towels receive, it really is a wonder that, according to one major linen manufacturer, the average hotel room uses only 12 towels for one hotel room per year. This figure represents loss from normal wear and tear, permanent staining, and theft. In this section we will also examine cloth bath mats and shower curtains.

Fabric Materials and Construction

The standard hotel bath linen is a white terry cloth towel that is a blend of cotton/polyester fibers.

Terry cloth towels are woven on a loom. The fibers running lengthwise in the towel (the **ground warp**) are usually a blend of two parts polyester and one part cotton. Polyester in the warp gives the towel its strength and helps to minimize shrinkage.

Pile warp is the yarn that runs lengthwise in the towel that make the terry loops on both sides of the towel's surface. These fibers should be 100 percent cotton for absorbency. The filling or weft is the yarn that runs horizontally across the towel. The filling should be 100 percent cotton. The **selvage** is the side edge of a towel or other woven fabric. It is a flat surface with no pile warp.

Towels, like sheets, can be sold as either firsts or seconds. Seconds are usually caused by a thick filling thread, a dropped warp or filling thread, or an uneven hem or border. These types of defects in no way impair the absorbency or durability of a towel. Therefore, many hotels willingly use towel seconds.

Bath mats are made in the same way as a terry towel, but the material is much heavier.

The best type of shower curtain for a commercial operation is a curtain made of 260 **denier** nylon. This type of curtain is better than any plastic curtain because it is easier to maintain, it resists mildew, it does not become stiff or brittle over time, it does not show soap stains as readily, and it is available in a multitude of colors.

The best protection against soap stains and mildew is to use a vinyl liner with a curtain. Do not use a clear vinyl liner because these will show soap stains. Use a white or pastel-colored vinyl. The vinyl should be a minimum six gauge thickness. Plastic snap hooks are better than other types of plastic hooks or metal hooks.

Size

The standard size for a good quality towel is 25 inches × 50 inches. An average size for a face towel is 16 inches × 27 inches. A good bath mat will measure 22 inches × 34 inches and decent size for a washcloth is 12 inches × 12 inches.

Towels and washcloths can be found in larger or smaller sizes than the above recommendations. The selection of a particular towel size should be based on marketing considerations.

Par Levels

A reasonable bath linen par level for a hotel with its own laundry is three and one-half. If the laundry must be sent off the premises, the par level should be increased to four and one-half.

The information given in Table 7.2 refers to the model hotel. Room configuration and other criteria, including approximate prices per item, are given. Use this information as an exercise to determine linen pars and to develop an approximate cost of initial supplies.

Table Linens

In the food business, first impressions are lasting ones. Since success in this business depends so heavily on repeat business, the astute operator wants to make a first-time impression that will cause customers to come back again and again.

The focal point in most food service operations is the tabletop. It should look as pleasing as the menu, and nothing adds to this scene more than crisp, clean **napery** (table linens).

Fabric Materials and Construction

There are two dominant types of materials used for tablecloths and napkins: momie cloth and damask.

Table 7.2 Model Hotel Par Requirements

| | ROOMS | Rooms Breakdown | | |
		FURNITURE	TOTAL BEDS	PILLOW REQUIREMENT
Suites	5	1 king bed		3/Bed
Kings	13	1 king bed		3/Bed
Parlors	15	1 queen bed		2/Bed
Double-Doubles	320	2 double beds		2/Bed
Total	353	20 roll-away beds (use double sheets)		1/Bed
				Total pillows + 10 percent

| | Bath Linen | | | |
	1 PAR	3.5 PAR	PRICE	COST
Sheets				
King			$ 9.00	
Queen			7.00	
Double			6.00	
Pillowcases			1.50	
Bath towels			3.00	
Hand towels			1.50	
Washcloths			.10	
Bath mats			2.50	
1/Room				
Bed pads			6.50	
(1 par + 10 percent)				
Blankets			25.00	
(1 par + 10 percent)				
Pillows			10.00	
(1 par + 10 percent)				
Totals				

Momie cloth is normally a 50/50 cotton/polyester plain weave cloth that is relatively inexpensive, durable, and fairly colorfast, and does not pill or attract lint.

Damask is made using a twill weave. It can be divided into three categories, linen damask, cotton damask, and cotton/polyester damask blend. Linen is superior in appearance to the other two, but it is considerably more expensive. The cotton/polyester damask has the same advantages of the 50/50 momie cloth, but it has a better appearance and it looks better after laundering.

Cotton/polyester blends are expected to shrink an average of three percent, as compared to cotton alone, which will shrink an average of 12 percent. Blended napery is expected to last up to four times as long as cotton alone. Ordinary cotton napkins should last for 34 launderings and cotton tablecloths should last for 32 launderings on the average. Blends dry faster and are easier to iron.

Size

The drape of a tablecloth should be a minimum of 8 inches all around the table. the following table (Table 7.3) is a listing of some of the standard sizes for tables and tablecloths. This table is meant only to serve as a guide; only a designer or table manufacturer can give you a plan that you can depend upon.

Table 7.3 Tabletop and Tablecloth Sizes

SEATING	TOP SIZE	CLOTH SIZE
Table for 2	36″ × 36″	54″ × 54″
Table for 4	45″ × 45″	64″ × 64″
Table for 6	54″ × 54″	72″ × 72″
Table for 8	60″ round	90″ × 90″
Table for 10	66″ round	90″ × 90″

Par Levels

Par levels will vary depending on the number of covers forecasted, hours of operation, number of meal periods open, and frequency of the launderings.

However, as a rule of thumb in a new operation, there should be a par of four tablecloths per table and nine to twelve napkins per table. These par levels should do if the restaurant is open for two meals and a 24-hour laundry service is available.

Uniforms

Many hotel departments have uniformed employees. In some cases, each department maintains its own individual supply inventories of uniforms; in other cases the housekeeping department is custodian of uniforms used throughout the hotel. If the housekeeping department is custodian of all uniforms, a large secure storage space, along with work tables and repair capability, are necessary.

Uniforms may be processed in the laundry daily and issued each workday as the employee reports to work. Some uniforms may be subcustodied to specific employees who maintain their own uniforms. Some hotels have uniform services provided by companies who purchase, launder or dry clean, and provide five par of uniforms for each employee on a weekly basis. The hotel must pay a premium for this service, since the servicing company must purchase 11 uniforms for each new employee when hired.

The simplest, most cost-effective method of administering a uniform program is for each department to maintain its own uniforms and to subcustody them to employees at the time of employment, allowing each employee to care for the uniforms issued.

Housekeeping uniforms need not be unattractive or uncomfortable. They should fit well and allow for freedom of movement, since much reaching and bending is involved in housekeeping work. Sleeveless uniforms are a must and a pocket or two is always helpful. Cotton is best for comfort, but polyester fabrics are the most plentiful. The quality of the section housekeeper's and senior housekeeper's uniform should be similar, but color

distinctions may be made. An inventory of four different uniforms is appropriate for housekeeping personnel: section housekeeper (female), section housekeeping aide (male), supervisor (female), supervisor (male).

A reasonable uniform program would allow for the issue of two uniforms to each employee upon employment and an issue of a third uniform after completion of a probationary work period. Should uniforms become damaged or worn out as a result of work, they should be replaced. Carelessness causing destruction of uniforms should be the subject of counseling or disciplinary action.

The law requires that employees who are required to clean their own uniforms be compensated. The law suggests that laundry service in the hotel laundry might be a reasonable alternative to an outlay of cash. A total inventory of uniforms should include about five par, the balance being available to fit new employees or to provide replacements for the staff. Sizes range from very small (4–6–8) to very large (22–24). It is a difficult task, however, to maintain a correctly sized inventory.

Summary

Decisions that are made regarding the purchase and use of assets without a sufficient investigation into the characteristics and qualities of those assets can seriously affect the profit picture.

Costs for linens and their maintenance need to be continually assessed in order to determine if the right decisions were reached and to avoid the repetition of costly mistakes. In addition, the costs for linens should always be based on a cost per room per day basis, never on a cost per pound basis. If linen costs are evaluated on a cost per room per day basis, the level of consumption by the guest can also be addressed in the formula.

Linen maintenance and replacement is an ongoing cost of doing business; it is the housekeeping manager's responsibility to ensure that these costs remain reasonable while continuing to meet the guest's expectations.

KEY TERMS AND CONCEPTS

Bedding
Linens
Uniforms
Dust ruffles
Muslin
Percale
Warp

Weft
Filling
Thread count
Tensile strength
Gray goods
Mercerizing
Sanforizing

Seconds
Torn sheet
Finished sheet
Par
Shams
Coverlet

Ticking
Ground warp
Pile warp
Selvage
Denier
Napery

DISCUSSION AND REVIEW QUESTIONS

1. Draw up a list of specifications for a guestroom attendant's uniform.
2. Explain the criteria that you would use to evaluate the performance of bedding materials for a hotel.
3. What are the advantages to all-white bath linens that have no logo? Can you see any disadvantages to this type of product?
4. How would you establish a par level for the napery in a new dining room? What criteria would you use to set the same par level for an existing operation?

8

Staffing For Housekeeping Operations

CHAPTER OBJECTIVES

1. To learn how to staff housekeeping positions.
2. To understand job specifications and employee requisitions.
3. To become familiar with the following processes:
   a. Selecting and interviewing employees.
   b. Providing an orientation program.
   c. Training newly hired employees.
   d. Developing employees.
   e. Maintaining training and development records.
   f. Using objective performance evaluations.

Prelude to Staffing

Staffing is the third sequential function of management. Up until now the executive housekeeper has been concerned with planning and organizing the housekeeping department for the impending opening and operations. Now the executive housekeeper must think about hiring employees within sufficient time to ensure that three of the activities of staffing—selection (including interviewing), orientation, and training—may be completed before open-ing. Staffing will be a major task of the last two weeks before opening.

The development of the Area Responsibility Plan and the House Breakout Plan before opening led to preparation of the Department Staffing Guide, which will be a major tool in determining the need for employees in various categories. The housekeep-ing manager and laundry manager should now be on board and assisting in the development of various job descriptions. (These are described in Appendix A.) The hotel human resources department would also have been preparing for the hiring event. They would have advertised a mass hiring for all categories of personnel to begin on a certain date about two weeks before opening.

Even though this chapter reflects a continuation of the executive housekeeper's planning for opening operations, the techniques described apply to any on-going operation, except that the magnitude of selec-tion, orientation, and training activities will not be as intense. Also, the fourth activity—development of existing employees—is normally missing in open-ing operations but is highly visible in ongoing oper-ations.

Job Specifications

Job specifications should be written as job descriptions (see Appendix A) are prepared. Job specifications are simple statements of what the various incumbents to positions will be expected to do. An example of a job specification for a section housekeeper is as follows:

Job Specification—Example

Section housekeeper (hotels) [Sometimes—Guest Room Attendant—GRA] The incumbent will work as a member of a housekeeping team, cleaning and servicing for occupancy of approximately 18 hotel guest rooms each day. Work will generally include the tasks of bed making, vacuuming, dusting, and bathroom cleaning. Incumbent will also be expected to maintain equipment provided for work and load housekeeper's cart before the end of each day's operation. Section housekeepers must be willing to work their share of weekends and be dependable in coming to work each day scheduled.

[Any special qualifications, such as ability to speak a foreign language might also be listed.]

Employee Requisition

Once job specifications have been developed for every position, **employee requisitions** are prepared for first hirings (and for any follow-up needs for the human resources department). Figure 8.1 is an example of an Employee Requisition. Note the designation as to whether the requisition is for a new or a replacement position and the number of employees required for a specific requisition number. The human resources department will advertise, take applications, and screen

```
┌─────────────────────────────────────────────┐
│          EMPLOYEE REQUISITION                │
│                                              │
│                  Requisition no. _____     │
│   Date _____    Department _____  │
│   Position _____  │
│          (Number and Title)                  │
│    New _____   Replacement _____   Number required _____ │
│   Classification _____   │
│           (Full-time, Part-time, Temporary, Pool) │
│   Working hours _____  Estimated no. of hours/week _____ │
│   Desired starting date _____   │
│   Starting rate of pay _____  Base rate _____ │
│                                              │
│   Specification (General description of duties) │
│   _____  │
│   _____  │
│   _____  │
│   _____  │
│   _____  │
│   _____  │
│                                              │
│   Special qualifications (desired or required) │
│   _____  │
│   _____  │
│   _____  │
│   _____  │
│                                              │
│                 _____ Department Manager │
└─────────────────────────────────────────────┘
```

Figure 8.1 Employee Requisition used to ask for one or more employees for a specific job.

to fill each requisition by number until all positions are filled. For example, the first requisition for section housekeepers may be for 20 section housekeepers. The human resources department will continue to advertise for, take applications, and screen employees for the housekeeping department and will provide candidates for interview by department managers until 20 section housekeepers are hired. Should any be hired and require replacing, a new employee requisition will be required.

Staffing Housekeeping Positions

There are several activities involved in staffing a housekeeping operation. Executive housekeepers must select and interview employees, participate in an orientation program, train newly hired employees, and develop employees for future growth. Each of these activities will now be discussed.

Selecting Employees

Sources of Employees

Each area of the United States has its own demographic situations that affect the availability of suitable employees for involvement in housekeeping or environmental service operations. For example, in one area an exceptionally high response rate from people seeking food service work may occur and a low response rate from people seeking housekeeping positions may occur. In another area the reverse may be true, and people interested in housekeeping work may far outnumber those interested in food service.

Surveys among hotels or hospitals in your area will indicate the best source for various classifications of employees. Advertising campaigns that will reach these employees are the best method of locating suitable people. Major classified ads associated with mass hirings will specify the need for food service personnel, front desk clerks, waiters, waitresses, housekeeping personnel, and maintenance people. Such ads may yield surprising results.

If the volume of response for housekeeping personnel is insufficient to provide a suitable hiring base, the following **sources** may be investigated:

1. Local employment agencies
2. Flyers posted on community bulletin boards
3. Local church organizations
4. Neighborhood canvass for friends of recently hired employees
5. Direct radio appeals to local housewives

6. Organizations for underprivileged ethnic minorities, and mentally handicapped or retarded people. (It should be noted that many mentally retarded persons are completely capable of performing simple housekeeping tasks and are dependable and responsible people seeking an opportunity to perform in a productive capacity.)

If these sources do not produce the volume of applicants necessary to develop a staff, it may become necessary to search for employees in distant areas and to provide regular transportation for them to and from work.

If aliens are hired, the department manager must take great care to ensure that they are legal residents of this country and that their green cards are valid. More than one hotel department manager has had an entire staff swept away by the Department of Immigration after hiring people who were illegal aliens. Such unfortunate action has required the immediate assistance of all available employees (including management) to fill in.

Processing Applicants

Whether you are involved in a mass hiring or in the recruiting of a single employee, a systematic and courteous procedure for **processing applicants** is essential. For example, in the opening of the Los Angeles Airport Marriott, 11,000 applicants were processed to fill approximately 850 positions in a period of about two weeks. The magnitude of such an operation required a near assembly-line technique, but a personable and positive experience for the applicants still had to be maintained.

The efficient handling of lines of employees, courteous attendance, personal concern for employee desires, and reference to suitable departments for those unfamiliar with what the hotel or hospital has to offer all become earmarks for how the company will treat their employees. The key to proper handling of applicants is the use of a **control system** whereby employees are conducted through the steps of **application, prescreening,** and if qualified, **reference to a department** for interview. Figure 8.2 is a typical **processing record** that helps ensure fair and efficient handling of each applicant.

Note the opportunity for employees to express their desires for a specific type of employment. Even though an employee may desire involvement in one classification of work, he or she may be hired for employment in a different department. Also, employees might not be aware of the possibilities available in a particular department at the time of application or may be unable to locate in desired departments at the time of mass hirings. Employees who perform well should therefore be given the opportunity to transfer to other departments when the opportunities arise.

**PROCESSING RECORD FOR
EMPLOYEE CANDIDATE**

Name _____   Position desired

Address _____   _____

Phone _____   Date of application

Hours when can be reached _____   _____

Record of human resources department prescreening

Date _____   By _____   Recommended for _____
                                                        (Position)

          Screening code _____

Department interview endorsement

Date interviewed _____   Interviewed by _____

Comments _____

_____

Recommendation _____

          Hire _____   Refer to _____   Department—File

References checked by interviewing department _____
                                                        (Yes/No)

Who was contacted?
1. _____
2. _____
3. _____

Note: References will be checked on all people offered employment.
The human resources department will make reference checks on
all candidates before making offers *if requested by the interviewing
departments*. No offers will be extended before completion of satisfactory
reference checks.

Disposition

Offer extended _____   Accepted/Denied _____
              (Date)

                              Will report to work on _____

Application filed _____
              (Date/By)

Figure 8.2 Processing Record for Employee Candidate used to keep track of an applicant's progress through the employment process.

According to laws regulated by federal and state Fair Employment Practices Agencies (FEPA), no person may be denied the opportunity to submit application for employment for a position of his or her choosing. Not only is the law strict on this point, but companies in any way benefiting from interstate commerce (such as hotels and hospitals) may not discriminate in the hiring of people based on race, color, natural origin, or religious preference. Although specific hours and days of the week may be specified, it is a generally accepted fact that hotels and hospitals must maintain personnel operations that provide the opportunity for people to submit applications without prejudice.

Prescreening Applicants

The **prescreening interview** is a staff function normally provided to all hotel or hospital departments by the *human resources* section of the organization. Prescreening is a preliminary interview process in which unqualified applicants—those applicants who do not meet the criteria for a job as specified in the job specification-special qualifications—are selected (or screened) out. For example, an applicant for a secretarial job that requires the incumbent to take shorthand and be able to type 60 words a minute may be screened out if the applicant is not able to pass a relevant typing and shorthand test. The results of prescreening are usually coded for internal use and are indicated on the Applicant Processing Record (Figure 8.2).

If a candidate is screened out by the personnel section, he or she should be told the reason immediately and be thanked for applying for employment.

Applicants who are not screened out should either be referred to a specific department for interview or, if all immediate positions are filled, have their applications placed in a department pending file for future reference. All applicants should be told that hiring decisions will be made by individual department managers based on the best qualifications from among those interviewed.

A suggested agenda for a prescreening interview is as follows:

1. The initial contact should be cordial and helpful. Many employees are lost at this stage because of inefficient systems established for handling applicants.
2. During the prescreening interview, try to determine what the employee is seeking, whether such a position is available, or, if not, when such a position might become available.
3. Review the work history as stated on the application to determine whether the applicant meets the obvious physical and mental qualifications, as well as important human qualifications such as emotional stability, personality, honesty, integrity, and reliability.
4. Do not waste time if the applicant is obviously not qualified or if no immediate position is available. When potential vacancies or a backlog of applicants exists, inform the candidate. Be efficient in stating this to the applicant. Always make sure that the applicant gives you a phone number in order that he or she may be called at some future date. Because most applicants seeking employment are actively seeking immediate work, applications over 30 days old are usually worthless.
5. If at all possible, an immediate interview by the department manager should be held after screening. If this is not possible, a definite appointment should be made for the candidate's interview as soon as possible.

The Interview

Interviews should be conducted by a manager of the department to which the applicant has been referred. In ongoing operations, it is often wise to also allow the supervisor for whom the new employee will work to visit with the candidate in order that the supervisor may gain a feel for how it would be to work together. The supervisor's view should be considered, since a harmonious relationship at the working level is important. Although the acceptance of an employee remains a prerogative of management, it would be unwise to accept an employee into a position when the supervisor has reservations about the applicant.

Certain personal characteristics should be explored when interviewing an employee. Some of these characteristics are native skills, stability, reliability, experience, attitude toward employment, personality, physical traits, stamina, age, sex, education, previous training, initiative, alertness, appearance, and personal cleanliness. Although employers may not discriminate against race, sex, age, religion, and nationality, overall considerations may involve the capability to lift heavy objects, enter men's or women's restrooms, and so on. In a housekeeping (*or environmental services*) department, people should be employed who find enjoyment in housework at home. Remember that character and personality cannot be completely judged from a person's appearance. Also, it should be expected that a person's appearance will never be better than when that person is applying for a job.

Letters of recommendation and references should be carefully considered. Seldom will a letter of recommendation be adverse, whereas a telephone call might be most revealing.

If it were necessary to select the most important step in the selection process, interviewing would be it. Interviewing is *the* step that separates those who will be employed from those who will not. Poor **interviewing techniques** can make the process more difficult and may produce a result that can be both frustrating and damaging for both parties. In addition, inadequate interviewing will result in gaining incorrect information, being confused about what has been said, suppression of information, and, in some circumstances, complete withdrawal from the process by the candidate.

The following is a well-accepted list of the steps for a successful interview process.

1. *Be prepared.* Have a checklist of significant questions ready to ask the candidate. Such questions may be prepared from the body of the job description. This preparation will allow the interviewer to assume the initiative in the interview.

2. *Find a proper place to conduct the interview.* The applicant should be made to feel comfortable. The interview should be conducted in a quiet, relaxing atmosphere where there is privacy that will bring about a confidential conversation.

3. *Practice.* People who conduct interviews should practice interviewing skills periodically. Several managers may get together and discuss interviewing techniques that are to be used.

4. *Be tactful and courteous.* Put the applicant at ease, but also control the discussions and lead to important questions.

5. *Be knowledgeable.* Be thoroughly familiar with the position for which the applicant is interviewing in order that all of the applicant's questions may be answered. Also, have a significant background knowledge in order that general information about the company may be given.

6. *Listen.* Encourage the applicant to talk. This may be done by asking questions that are not prone to be answered by a yes or no. If people are comfortable and are asked questions about themselves, they will usually speak freely and give information that specific questions will not always bring out. Applicants will usually talk if there is a feeling that they are not being misunderstood.

7. *Observe.* Much can be learned about an applicant just by observing reactions to questions, attitudes about work, and, specifically, attitudes about providing service to others. Observation is a vital step in the interviewing process.

Interview Pitfalls

Perhaps of equal importance to the interviewing technique are the following **pitfalls**, which should be avoided while interviewing.

1. Having a feeling that the employee will be just right based on a few outstanding characteristics rather than on the sum of all characteristics noted.

2. Being influenced by neatness, grooming, expensive clothes, and an extroverted personality—none of which has much to do with housekeeping competency.

3. Overgeneralizing, whereby interviewers assume too much from a single remark (for instance, an applicant's assurance that he or she "really wants to work").

4. Hiring the boomer, that is, the person who always wants to work in a new property; unfor-tunately, this type of person changes jobs whenever a new property opens.

5. Projecting your own background and social status into the job requirement. Which school the applicant attended or whether the applicant has the "proper look" is beside the point. It is job performance that is going to count.

6. Confusing strengths with weaknesses and vice versa. What is construed by one person to be overaggressiveness might be interpreted by another as confidence, ambition, and potential for leadership, the last two traits being in chronic short supply in most housekeeping departments. These are the very characteristics that make it possible for management to promote from within and develop new supervisors and managers.

7. Being impressed by a smooth talker—or the reverse: assuming that silence reflects strength and wisdom. The interviewer should concentrate on what the applicant is saying rather than on how it is being said. Then decide whether his or her personality will fit into the organization.

8. Being tempted by overqualified applicants. People with experience and education that far exceed the job requirements may be unable for some reason to get a job commensurate with their background. Even if such applicants are not concealing skeletons in the closet, they still tend to become frustrated and dissatisfied with jobs far below their level of abilities.

The application of the techniques and avoidance of the pitfalls will be valuable tools in the selection of competent personnel for the housekeeping and environmental service departments.

For many years, the approach of many managers was to write a job description and then fill it by attempting to find the perfect person. This approach may overlook many qualified people, such as disadvantaged people or slow learners. Job descriptions may be analyzed in two ways when filling positions: (1) what is actually required to do the work, and (2) what is desirable. Is the ability to read or write really necessary for the job? Is the ability to learn quickly really necessary? A person who does not read or write or who is a slow learner can be trained and will make an excellent employee. True, it may take additional time, but the reward will be a loyal employee as well as less turnover. It has been proven many times that those who are disadvantaged or slightly retarded, once trained, will perform consistently well for longer periods. There are agencies who seek out companies that will try to hire such people.

Results of the Interview

If the results of an interview are negative and rejection is indicated, the candidate should be informed as soon as possible. A pleasant statement, such as "others interviewed appear to be more qualified," is usually sufficient. This information can be handled in a straightforward and courteous manner and in such a way that the candidate will appreciate the time that has been taken during the interview.

When the results of the interview are positive, a statement indicating a favorable impression is most encouraging. However, no commitment should be made until a *reference check* has been conducted.

Reference Checks

In many cases, **reference checks** are made only to verify that what has been said in the application and interview is in fact true. Many times applicants are reluctant to explain in detail why previous employment situations have come to an end. It is more important to hear the actual truth about a prior termination from the application than it is to hear that they simply have been terminated. Reference checks, in order of desirability, are as follows:

1. Personal (face-to-face) meetings are the least available but provide the most accurate information when they can be arranged.
2. Telephone discussions are the next best and most often used approach. For critical positions, an in-depth conversation by telephone between the potential new manager and the prior manager is most desirable; otherwise a simple verification of data is sufficient to ensure honesty.
3. The least desirable reference is the written recommendation, since managers are extremely reluctant to state a frank and honest opinion that may be later used against them in court.

Applicants who are rated successful at an interview should be told that a check of their references will be conducted, and, pending favorable responses, they will be contacted by the personnel department within two days. Applicants who are currently employed will normally ask that their current employer not be contacted for a reference check. This request should be honored at all times. Applicants who are currently working will usually want to give proper notice to their current employer. If the applicant chooses not to give notice, chances are no notice will be given at the time he or she leaves your hotel.

In some cases, the applicant gives notice and upon doing so is "cut loose" immediately. If such is the case, the applicant should be told to contact the department manager immediately in order that the employee may be put to work as soon as possible.

Interview Skills versus Turnover

There is no perfect interviewer, interviewee, or resultant hiring or rejection decision of an applicant. We can only hope to improve our interviewing skills in order that the greatest degree of success in employee retention can be obtained. The executive housekeeper should expect that 25 percent of initial hires into a housekeeping department will not be employed for more than three months. (This is primarily because the housekeeping skills are easily learned and the position is paid at or near minimum wage.) Some new housekeeping departments have as much as a 75 percent turnover rate in the first three months of operation. Certainly this figure can be improved upon with adequate attention to the interviewing and selection processes. However, regardless of the outcome of the interview, the processing record (Figure 8.2) should be properly endorsed and returned to the personnel department for processing.

Orientation

A carefully planned, concerned, and informational **orientation program** is significant to the first impressions that a new employee will have about the hospital or hotel in general and the housekeeping department in particular. Too often, a new employee is told where the work area and restroom are, given a cursory explanation of the job, then put to work. It is not uncommon to find managers putting employees to work who have not even been processed into the organization, an unfortunate situation that usually is discovered on payday when there is no paycheck for the new employee. Such blatant disregard for the concerns of the employee can only lead to poor reception of the company. A planned orientation program will eliminate this type of activity and will bring the employee into the company with personal concern and with a greater possibility for a successful relationship.

Every good orientation program is usually made up of four phases: employee acquisition, receipt of an employee's handbook, tour of the facility, and an orientation meeting.

Employee Acquisition

Once a person is accepted for employment, the applicant is told to report for work at a given time and place, and that place should be the personnel department. Preemployment procedures could take as much as one-half day, and department

---

EMPLOYMENT CHECKLIST

Name _____ Social Security number _____

Address _____

City _____ State _____ Zip _____

Item   Complete

Application   _____
Employment history   _____
Security identification   _____
  (Health card/Work permit)
Health and welfare documents   _____
W-4 forms submitted   _____
Deductions from pay (if any)   _____
  (union, state income tax)
Hotel employee handbook issued   _____
  (acknowledgment received)
Data processing
  Personnel action form filled out   _____
  Employee payroll number assigned   _____
  Wage dept. classification number   _____
Application for name tag
  (First name only except for management)   _____

Employee has been turned over to _____
in the _____ department for training and department
orientation.

Property orientation meeting has been scheduled for this employee on

_____ .

Personnel supervisor   Receiving department

_____   _____
Signature   Supervisor signature

Figure 8.3 Employment Checklist. Once an applicant has been prescreened and interviewed, has had references checked, and has received an offer of employment, the checklist is used to ensure completion of data required to place the employee on the payroll.

managers eager to start new employees to work should allow time for a proper **employee acquisition** into the organization. Figure 8.3 is an **Employment Checklist** similar to those used by most personnel offices to ensure that nothing is overlooked in assimilating a new person into the organization.

At this time it should be ensured that the application is complete and any additional information pertaining to employment history that may be necessary to obtain the necessary work permits and credentials is on hand. Usually the security department will record the entry of a new employee into the staff and will provide instructions regarding use of employee entrances, removing parcels from the premises, and employee parking areas. All documents required by the hotel's health and welfare insurer should be completed, and instructions should be given about im-

mediately reporting accidents, no matter how slight, to supervisors. The federal government requires that every employer submit a W-4 (withholding statement) for each employee on the payroll. The employee must complete this document and give it to the company. Mandatory deductions from pay should be explained (federal and state income tax and Social Security FICA), as should other deductions that may be required or desired. At this time, some form of personal action document is usually initiated on the new employee and is placed in the employee's permanent record. Figure 8.4 is an example of such a form.

Figure 8.4 is a computer-printed document called a **Personnel Action Form** (PAF) indicating all data that is required about the new employee. Note the permanent information that will be carried

PERSONNEL ACTION FORM

DATE PRINTED | SEQ

PAYROLL CHANGE

COMPANY

SOCIAL SECURITY NO. | NO. | DIVISION

LAST NAME | FIRST NAME | M.I.

ADDRESS | CITY | STATE | ZIP CODE

TELEPHONE | BIRTHDATE | EMPLOYMENT DATE | EEO | WORKMAN'S COMP | TYPE | STATUS

PERM TEMP | FULL PART | POOL

PRIMARY RATE

JOB NO. | JOB DESCRIPTION | JOB RATE | ACCT NO | PAY CLASS | REASON CODE | EFFECTIVE DATE | NEXT REVIEW | PAY CODE | SCHEDULE HRS

HOURLY SALARY | WEEKLY BI-WEEKLY | SEMI MONTH

LAST JOB RATE

LAST REVIEW | STATE EMPL | STATE RES | MARITAL STATUS | FED DEP | STATE DEP

NEXT TO LAST JOB RATE

MARRIED SINGLE

TAX INFORMATION

FEDERAL | STATE | MUNICIPAL | COUNTY | OTHER

AMOUNT | % | STD | AMOUNT | % | STD | AMOUNT | % | STD | AMOUNT | % | STD | AMOUNT | % | STD

DISTRIBUTION | **EDUCATION** | **GROUP INSURANCE**

COST CENTER | REPORT | DEPT NO | DEPARTMENT | LEVEL | YRS | GRAD | DED AMOUNT | CLASS | EFFECTIVE DATE | TYPE COVERAGE

GRADE HIGH | COLLEGE POST

DEDUCTIONS | **CHANGE TO**

NO. | DESCRIPTION | FIXED AMOUNT | % | LIMIT | FIXED AMOUNT | % | LIMIT | EMPLOYEE OK

TERMINATION | **LEAVE OF ABSENCE**

LAST DAY WORKED | REASON | REHIRE | VOL | EFFECTIVE DATE | REASON | LOA RETURN DATE | DATE RETURNED TO WORK

YES NO COND | YES NO

REASON CODES

RATE CHANGE
10. PERFORMANCE REVIEW
11. PROBATIONARY INCREASE
12. EMPLOYMENT AGREEMENT
13. MERIT
14. WAGE ADJUSTMENT
15. LATERAL TRANSFER
16. ADDED DUTIES
17. PROMOTION
18. DEMOTION
19. INCREASE DENIAL
20. CORRECT OR CHANGE INFORMATION

VOLUNTARY TERMINATION
21. ACCEPT OTHER EMPLOYMENT
22. SEEK OTHER EMPLOYMENT
23. GO INTO OR OPERATE OWN OR FAMILY BUSINESS
24. TRANSFER TO ANOTHER DIVISION/SUBSIDIARY
25. ATTEND SCHOOL
26. DISSATISFIED WITH JOB (SALARY, HOURS, DUTIES, CONDITIONS)
27. UNABLE TO COPE WITH PRESSURES OF JOB
28. UNABLE TO RELATE WITH SUPERVISOR, SUBORDINATES OR CO-WORKERS
29. QUIT AFTER REPRIMAND OR UNFAVORABLE REVIEW
30. QUIT WITHOUT NOTICE/REASON UNKNOWN
31. FAILURE TO APPEAR OR CALL OFF ON THREE CONSECUTIVE SHIFTS
32. FAMILY OR DOMESTIC OBLIGATIONS
33. TO BE MARRIED
34. RELOCATE TO MORE DESIRABLE AREA
35. SPOUSE TRANSFERRED
36. TRANSPORTATION DIFFICULTIES
37. MENTAL/PHYSICAL CONDITION
38. PREGNANCY
39. MILITARY
40. FAILURE TO RETURN FROM LEAVE OF ABSENCE
41. VOLUNTARY RETIREMENT
42. DEATH

INVOLUNTARY TERMINATION
50. CHRONIC TARDINESS OR ABSENTEEISM
51. VIOLATION OF COMPANY RULES
52. DOCUMENTED UNSATISFACTORY PERFORMANCE
53. NOT QUALIFIED FOR POSITION
54. INSUBORDINATION
55. MISCONDUCT
56. UNAUTHORIZED POSSESSION OR REMOVAL OF COMPANY PROPERTY
57. REASONS OF CHARACTER OR INTEGRITY
58. LACK OF INTEREST AND/OR ATTITUDE
59. UNABLE TO RELATE TO SUPERVISOR, SUBORDINATES OR CO-WORKERS
60. END OF TEMPORARY POSITION
61. JOB ELIMINATION
62. MANDATORY RETIREMENT
63. PLANNED REDUCTION IN FORCE/PERMANENT LAYOFF
64. RESIGNATION IN LIEU OF DISCHARGE/MUTUAL AGREEMENT
65. TRANSFER TO ANOTHER DIVISION/SUBSIDIARY
66. WORK RELATED ACCIDENT/ILLNESS
67. UNSATISFACTORY COMPLETION OF PROBATIONARY PERIOD
68. POOL STATUS/HAS NOT WORKED IN THREE MONTHS

LEAVE OF ABSENCE CODES
81. STD – PREGNANCY
82. STD – MEDICAL
83. UNPAID MEDICAL
84. UNPAID PERSONAL
85. UNPAID PREGNANCY
86. MILITARY
87. JURY/COURT SERVICE
88. WORKMANS COMP
89. TEMPORARY LAYOFF
90. LTD

SUPERVISOR | DATE SIGNED

AUTHORIZED APPROVAL | DATE SIGNED | WDS | DATE

Figure 8.4 Personnel Action Form (PAF) is a data-processing form used to collect and store information about an employee. Note the various bits of information collected. (Courtesy of White Lodging Services.)

carried on file. The PAF is serially numbered and is created from data stored on magnetic discs and is maintained in the employee's personnel file. When a change has to be made, such as job title, marital status, or rate of pay, the PAF is retrieved from the employee's record, changes are made *under* the item to be changed, and the corrected PAF is used to change the data in the computer storage. Once new information is stored, a new PAF is created and placed in the employee's record to await the next need for processing. A long-time employee might have many PAF's stored in the personnel file.

When either regular or special **performance appraisals** are given, the last (most current) PAF will be used to record the appraisal. Figure 8.5 is a standard form used to record such appraisals, as well as written warnings and matters involving terminations. These forms are usually found on the reverse side of the PAF. Since performance appraisals may signify a raise in pay, the appropriate pay increase information would be indicated on the front side of the PAF (Figure 8.4). All recordings on PAFs, whether on one side or both, require the submission of data, storage of information, and creation of

Strengths			
Objectives			
1.	MET	NOT MET	N/A
2.	MET	NOT MET	N/A
3.	MET	NOT MET	N/A

Weaknesses

Counseled action

   What the employee will do to improve performance.

   What the supervisor will do to assist in improving performance.

Estimate ready for promotion on _____

Written warning ☐   reevaluate not later than _____

Termination reason _____

Signature of evaluator _____ Date _____
Action reviewed by _____ Date _____
Employee signature _____ Date _____

Employee comment

Figure 8.5 The reverse side of the PAF may be used to record performance appraisals, written warnings, or matters involving terminations.

a new PAF (Figure 8.4) to be stored in the employee's record.

The PAF and performance appraisal system should be thoroughly explained to the new employee, along with assignment of a payroll number. The employer should also explain how and when the staff is paid and when the first paycheck may be expected.

The Employee Handbook

The new employee should be provided with a copy of the **Hotel or Hospital Employee's Handbook** and should be told to read it thoroughly. Since the new housekeeping employee is not working just for the housekeeping department but is to become integrated as a member of the entire staff, reading this handbook is extremely important to ensure that proper instructions in the rules and regulations of the hotel are presented. The handbook should be developed in such a way as to inspire the new employee to become a fully participating member of the organization. As an example, the Employee's Handbook for the Radisson Hotel at Star Plaza is presented in Appendix

B. Note the tone of the welcoming letter and the manner in which the rules and regulations are presented.

Familiarization Tour of the Facilities

Upon completion of the acquisition phase, a **facility tour** should be conducted for one or all new employees. For new facilities, access to the property should be gained within about one week before opening, and many new employees can be taken on a tour simultaneously. It is possible for employees to work in the hotel housekeeping department for years and never have visited the showroom, dining rooms, ballrooms, or even the executive office areas. A tour of the complete facility melds employees into the total organization, and a complete informative tour should *never* be neglected.

For ongoing operations, after acquisition the new employee may be turned over to a department supervisor, who becomes the tour director. An appreciation of the total involvement of each employee is strengthened when a facilities tour is complete and thorough. If necessary, the property tour might be postponed until after the orientation meeting; however, the orientation activity of staffing is not complete until a property tour is conducted.

Orientation Meeting

Orientation meetings should not be conducted until the employee has had an opportunity to become at least partially familiar with the surroundings. After approximately two weeks, the employee will have many questions about experiences, the new job, training, and the rules and regulations listed in the Property and Department handbooks (see section on training). Employee orientation meetings that are scheduled too soon fail to answer many questions that will develop within the first two weeks of employment.

The meeting should be held in a comfortable setting with refreshments provided. It is usually conducted by the director of human resources and is attended by as many of the facility managers as possible. Most certainly, the general manager or hospital administration members of the executive committee, the security director, and the new employees' department head should attend. Each of these managers should have an opportunity to welcome the new employees and give them a chance to associate names with faces. All managers and new employees should wear name tags. In orientation meetings, a brief history of the company and company goals should be presented.

A planned orientation meeting should not be concluded without someone stressing the importance of each position. Every position must have a purpose

behind it and is therefore important to the overall functioning of the facility. An excellent statement of this philosophy was once offered by a general manager who said, "The person mopping a floor in the kitchen at 3:00 A.M. in the morning is just as valuable to this operation as I am—we just do different things."

The orientation meeting should be scheduled to allow for many questions. And there should be someone in attendance who can answer *all of them.*

Although the new employee will be gaining confidence and security in the position as training ends and work is actually performed, informal orientation may continue for quite some time. The formal orientation, however, ends with the orientation meeting (although the facility tour may be conducted after the meeting). Finally, it should be remembered that good orientation procedures lead toward worker satisfaction and help quiet the anxieties and fears that a new employee may have. When a good orientation is neglected, the seeds of dissatisfaction are planted.

Training

General

The efficiency and economy by which any department will operate will depend on the ability of each member of the organization to do his or her job. Such ability will depend in part on past experiences, but more commonly it can be credited to the type and quality of **training** offered. Employees, regardless of past experiences, always need some degree of training before starting a new job.

Small institutions may try to avoid training by hiring people who are already trained in the general functions with which they will be involved. However, most institutions recognize the need for training that is specifically oriented toward the new experience and will have a documented training program.

Some employers of housekeeping personnel find it easier to train completely unskilled and untrained personnel. In such cases, bad or undesirable practices do not have to be trained out of an employee. Previous experience and education should, however, be analyzed and considered in the training of each new employee in order that efficiencies in training can be recognized. If an understanding of department standards and policies can be demonstrated by a new employee, that portion of training may be shortened or modified. However, skill and ability must be demonstrated before training can be altered. Finally, training is the best method to communicate the company's way of doing things, without which the new employee may do work contrary to company policy.

First Training

First training of a new employee actually starts with a continuation of *department* orientation. When a new employee is turned over to the housekeeping or environmental services department, orientation usually continues by familiarizing the employee with *department rules and regulations.* Many housekeeping departments have their own **Department Employee Handbooks.** For an example, see Appendix C, which contains the housekeeping department rules and regulations for Bally's Casino Resort in Las Vegas, Nevada. Compare this handbook with that of the Radisson Hotel at Star Plaza (Appendix B). Although these handbooks are for completely different types of organizations, the substance of their publications is essentially the same; both are designed to familiarize each new employee with his or her surroundings. Handbooks should be written in such a way as to inspire employees to become team members, committed to company objectives.

A Systematic Approach to Training

Training may be defined as those activities that are designed to help an employee begin performing tasks for which he or she is hired or to help the employee improve performance in a job already assigned. The purpose of training is to enable an employee to begin an assigned job or to improve upon techniques already in use.

In hotel or hospital housekeeping operations, there are three basic areas in which training activity should take place: **skills, attitudes,** and **knowledge.**

Skills Training. A sample list of skills in which a basic housekeeping employee must be trained follows:

1. *Bed making:* Specific techniques; company policy
2. *Vacuuming:* Techniques; use and care of equipment
3. *Dusting:* Techniques; use of products
4. *Window and mirror cleaning:* Techniques and products
5. *Setup awareness:* Room setups; what a properly serviced room should look like
6. *Bathroom cleaning:* Tub and toilet sanitation; appearance; methods of cleaning and results desired
7. *Daily routine:* An orderly procedure for the conduct of the day's work; daily communications
8. *Caring for and using equipment:* Housekeeper cart; loading
9. *Industrial safety:* Product use; guest safety; fire; and other emergencies

The best reference for the skills that require training is the job description for which the person is being trained.

Attitude Guidance. Employees need guidance in their attitudes about the work that must be done. They need to be guided in their thinking about rooms that may present a unique problem in cleaning. Attitudes among section housekeepers need to be such that, occasionally, when rooms require extra effort to be brought back to standard, it is viewed as being a part of rendering service to the guest who paid to enjoy the room. Carol Mondesir,[1] director of housekeeping, Sheraton Centre, Toronto states that

> A hotel is meant to be enjoyed and, occasionally, the rooms are left quite messed up. However, as long as they're not vandalized, it's part of the territory. The whole idea of being in the hospitality business is to make the guest's stay as pleasant as possible. The rooms are there to be enjoyed.

Positive relationships with various agencies and people also need to be developed.

Below is a list of areas in which attitude guidance is important.

1. The guest/patient
2. The department manager and immediate supervisor
3. A guestroom that is in a state of great disarray
4. The hotel and company
5. The uniform
6. Appearance
7. Personal hygiene

Meeting Standards. The most important task of the trainer is to prepare new employees to **meet standards.** With this aim in mind, sequence of performance in cleaning a guestroom is most important in order that efficiency in accomplishing day-to-day tasks may be developed. In addition, the *best method* of accomplishing a task should be presented to the new trainee. Once the task has been learned, the next thing is to meet standards, which may not necessarily mean doing the job the way the person has been trained. Setting standards of performance will be discussed in Chapter 11 under operational controls.

Knowledge Training. Areas of knowledge in which the employee needs to be trained are as follows:

1. Thorough knowledge of the hotel layout; employee must be able to give directions and to tell the guest about the hotel, restaurants, and other facilities
2. Knowledge of employee rights and benefits
3. Understanding of grievance procedure
4. Knowing top managers by sight and by name

Ongoing Training

There is a need to conduct **ongoing training** for all employees, regardless of how long they have been members of the department. There are two instances when additional training is needed: (1) the purchase of new equipment and (2) change in or unusual employee behavior while on the job.

When new equipment is purchased, employees need to know how the new equipment differs from present equipment, what new skills or knowledge are required to operate the equipment, who will need this knowledge, and when. New equipment may also require new attitudes about work habits.

Employee behavior while on the job that is seen as an indicator for additional training may be divided into two categories: events that the manager witnesses and events that the manager is told about by the employees.

Events that the manager witnesses that indicate a need for training are frequent employee absence, considerable spoilage of products, carelessness, a high rate of accidents, and resisting direction by supervisors.

Events that the manager might be told about that indicate a need for training are that something doesn't work right (product isn't any good), something is dangerous to work with, something is making work harder.

Although training is vital for any organization to function at top efficiency, it is expensive. The money and man-hours expended must therefore be worth the investment. There must be a balance between the dollars spent training employees and the benefits of productivity and high-efficiency performance. A simple method of determining the need for training is to measure performance of workers: Find out what is going on at present on the job, and match this performance with what should be happening. The difference, if any, describes how much training is needed.

In conducting **performance analysis**, the following question should be asked: Could the employee do the job or task if his or her life depended on the result? If the employee *could not* do the job even if his or her life depended on the outcome, there is a **deficiency of knowledge** (DK). If the employee could have done the job if his or her life depended on the outcome, but did not, there is a **deficiency of execution** (DE). Some of the causes of deficiencies of execution include task interference, lack of feedback (employee doesn't know when the job is being performed correctly or incorrectly), and the balance of consequences (some employees like doing certain tasks better than others).

If either deficiency of knowledge or deficiency of execution exists, training must be conducted. The approach or the method of training may differ, however. Deficiencies of knowledge can be corrected by training the employee to do the job, then observing, correcting as necessary until the task is proficiently performed. Deficiency of execution is usually corrected by searching for the underlying cause of lack of performance, not by teaching the actual task.

Training Methods

There are numerous methods or ways to conduct training. Each method has its own advantages and disadvantages, which must be weighed in the light of benefits to be gained. Some methods are more expensive than others but are also more effective in terms of time required for comprehension and proficiency that must be developed. Several useful methods of training housekeeping personnel are listed and discussed.

On-the-Job Training. Using **on-the-job training** (OJT), a technique in which "learning by doing" is the advantage, the instructor demonstrates the procedure and then watches the students perform it. With this technique, one instructor can handle several students. In housekeeping operations, the instructor is usually a section housekeeper who is doing the instructing in the rooms that have been assigned for cleaning that day. The OJT method is not operationally productive until the student is proficient enough in the training tasks to absorb part of the operational load.

Simulation Training. With **simulation training**, a model room (unrented) is set up and used to train several employees. Whereas OJT requires progress toward daily production of ready rooms, simulation requires that the model room not be rented. In addition, the trainer is not productive in cleaning ready rooms. The advantages of simulation training are that it allows the training process to be stopped, discussed, and repeated if necessary. Simulation is an excellent method provided the trainer's time is paid for out of training funds and clean room production is not necessary during the workday.

Coach-Pupil Method. The **coach-pupil method** is similar to OJT except that each instructor has only one student (a one-to-one relationship). This method is desired provided that there are enough qualified instructors to have several training units in progress at the same time.

Lectures. The **Lecture** method reaches the largest number of students per instructor. Practically all training programs use this type of instruction for certain segments. Unfortunately, the lecture method can be the dullest training technique and therefore requires instructors who are gifted in presentation capabilities. In addition, space for lectures may be difficult to obtain and may require special facilities.

Conferences. The **conference** method of instruction is often referred to as **Workshop Training**. This technique involves a group of students who formulate ideas, do problem solving, and report on projects. The conference or workshop technique is excellent for supervisory training.

Demonstrations. When new products or equipment are being introduced, **demonstrations** are excellent. Many demonstrations may be conducted by vendors and purveyors as a part of the sale of equipment and products. Difficulties may arise when language barriers exist. It is also important that no more information be presented than can be absorbed in a reasonable period of time; otherwise misunderstandings may arise.

Training Aids

Many hotels will use **training aids** in a conference room or will post messages on an employee bulletin board. Aside from the usual training aids such as chalkboards, bulletin boards, charts, graphs, and diagrams, photographs can supply clear and accurate references for how rooms should be set up, maid's carts loaded, and routines accomplished. Most housekeeping operations will have films on guest contact and courtesy that may also be used in training. Motion pictures speak directly to many people who may not understand proper procedures from reading about them. Many training techniques may be combined to develop a well-rounded training plan.

Development

It is possible to have two students sitting side by side in a classroom, with one being trained and the other being developed. Recall that the definition of training is preparing a person to do a job for which he or she is hired or to improve upon performance of a current job. **Development** is preparing a person for advancement or to assume greater responsibility. The techniques are the same, but the end result is quite different. Whereas training begins after orientation of an employee who is hired to do a specific job, upon introduction of new equipment, or upon observation and communication with employees indicating a need for training, development begins with the identification of a specific employee who has shown potential for advancement. Training for promotion or to improve potential is in fact development and must always include a much neglected type of training—**supervisory training**.

Many forms of developmental training may be given on the property; other forms might include sending candidates to schools and seminars. Developmental training is associated primarily with supervisors and managerial development and may encompass many types of experiences.

Figure 8.6 is an example of a **developmental training program** for a junior manager who will soon become involved in housekeeping department management. Note the various developmental tasks that the trainee must perform over a period of 11 months.

Development of individuals within the organization looks to future potential and promotion of employees. Specifically, those employees who demonstrate leadership potential should be developed through supervisory training for advancement to positions of greater responsibility. Unfortunately, many outstanding workers have their performance rewarded by promotion but are given no development training. The excellent section housekeeper who is advanced to the position of senior housekeeper without the benefit of supervisory training is quickly seen to be unhappy and frustrated and may possibly become a loss to the department. It is therefore most essential that individual potential be developed in an orderly and systematic manner, or else this potential may never be recognized.

While undergoing managerial development as specified in Figure 8.6, both student and management alike should not lose sight of the primary aim of the program, which is the learning and potential development of the trainee, not departmental production. Even though there will be times that the trainee may be given specific responsibilities to oversee operations, clean guestrooms, or service public areas, advantage should not be taken of the trainee or the situation to the detriment of the development function. Development of new growth in the trainee becomes difficult when the training instructor or coordinator is not only developing a new manager but is also being held responsible for the production of some aspect of housekeeping operations.

Records and Reports

Whether you are conducting a training or a development program, suitable **records** of training progress should be maintained both by the training supervisor and the student. Periodic evaluations of the student's progress should be conducted, and successful com-

---

**HOTEL HOUSEKEEPING MANAGMENT TRAINEE PROGRAM
DEVELOPEMENT TRAINING SCHEDULE**

Dates   For _____
                                      (Name)

ADVISOR   PROJECT TASKS

Linen room attendant   Time: 1 Month

                       Concepts:
                       Maintenance orders
                       Handling and processing telephone calls, including
                          communication with guest and other hotel
                          departments
                       Handling of C/O, VIP Rooms, preregistration
                          rooms and in-order as well as out-of-order
                          rooms

A.M. Room attendant   Time: 2 weeks

                       How to clean a guest room.

P.M. Room attendant   Time: 2 weeks

                       Daily procedure and night turndown service

Floor supervisor   Time: 3 months

                       How to inspect a room
                       Opening and closing and other daily procedures

Training supervisor

                       Training of four new girls
                       Follow-up procedure
                       Orientation booklet

Head supervisor

                       Additional duties and responsibilities

Laundry manager   Time: 3 months

                       Concepts:
                       Products, equipment, costs, profit, maintenance
Washer   Products used, equipment breakdowns
Linen sorter   Poundage figures
Valet presser   Priorities and procedures
Valet runner   Duties
Laundry worker   Counting

Figure 8.6 Hotel housekeeping management trainee program Development Training Schedule used to cycle the trainee through the various functions involved in a hotel housekeeping department. Note the position of the person who will coach the development in the various skills and the time expected to be spent in each area.

pletion of the program should be recognized. Public recognition of achievement will inspire the newly trained or developed employee to achieve standards of performance and to strive for advancement.

Once an employee is trained or developed and his or her satisfactory performance has been recognized and recorded, the person should perform satisfactorily to standards. Future performance may be based on beginning performance after training. If an employee's performance begins to fall short of standards and expectations, there has to be a reason other than lack of skills. The reason for unsatisfactory performance must then be sought out and addressed. This type of follow-up is not possible unless suitable records of training and development are maintained and used for comparison.

Chief engineer   Time: 2 months

        Concepts:
        To learn all duties and responsibilities of all
            housekeepers and public area personnel

Head housekeeper

	Scheduling
	End-of-month ordering of supplies
A.M. cleaner	Restaurant and lobby cleaning
P.M. housekeeper	Gamedeck procedure
	Second floor and front office cleaning
Groundspeople	Waterfall and pool cleaning
	Tennis courts and garden court
Window washer	Procedure
Floor housekeeper	Stocking linen rooms on floors
Lobby attendant	Detailed lobby procedure

Assistant director of housekeeping   Time: 1 month

        Concepts:
        Payroll—Time cards
        Daily labor analysis
        Daily scheduling of room attendants
        Employee interviews

Director of housekeeping   Time: 1 month

        Concepts:
        Staffing
        Renovation programs
        Budget and capital improvement items
        Selection and ordering of supplies
        Maintaining records—inventory—maintenance
            status
        Exit interviews
        Training and retraining subordinates
        Handling employee grievances
        Guest complaints
        Employee disciplinary action and work
            performance history
        Motivation of employees (incentive programs)
        Safety programs
        Linen ordering, sizes, and storage
        Uniform ordering
        Purchase of equipment
        Procedures for monthly and yearly general
            cleaning

Figure 8.6 (*continued*)

Evaluation and Performance Appraisal

Although **evaluation and performance appraisal** for employees will occur as work progresses, it is not uncommon to find the design of systems for appraisal as part of organization and staffing functions. This is true because first appraisal and evaluation occurs during training, which is an activity of staffing.

Once trainees begin to have their performance appraised, the methods used will continue throughout employment. As a part of training, new employees should be told how, when, and by whom their performances will be evaluated and should be advised that questions regarding their performance will be regularly answered.

Probationary Period

Initial employment should be **probationary** in nature, allowing the new employee to improve efficiency to where the designated number of rooms cleaned per day can be achieved in a probationary period (about three months). Should a large number of employees be unable to achieve the standard within that time, the standard should be investigated. Should only one or two employees be unable to meet the standard of rooms cleaned per day, an evaluation of the employee in training should either reveal the reason why or indicate the employee as unsuitable for further retention. An employee who after suitable training cannot meet a reasonable performance standard should not be allowed to continue employment. Similarly, an employee who has met required performance standards in the specified probationary period should be continued into regular employment status and thus achieve a reasonable degree of security in employment.

The Subject of Evaluation

Evaluation of personnel is an attempt to measure selected traits, characteristics, and productivity. Unfortunately, evaluations are generally objective in nature, and raters are seldom trained in the art of subjective evaluation. Initiative, self-control, and leadership ability do not lend themselves to measurement; therefore such characteristics are estimated. How well they are estimated depends to a great extent on the person doing the estimating. Two raters using the same form and rating the same person will probably arrive at different conclusions.

Certain policies on the use of evaluations should be established so that they are understood by both the person doing the evaluating and the person being evaluated. These policies must be established and disseminated by management. In order to establish such policies, the following questions, among others, must be answered and communicated to all those involved in the evaluation: What will evaluations be used for? Will evaluations influence promotions, become a part of the employee's record, be used as periodic checks, or be used for counseling and guidance? What qualities are going to be evaluated? Who is going to be evaluated? Who will do the evaluating?

Reliable evaluations require careful planning and take considerable time, skill, and work. An evaluation must be understood by the employee.

Evaluation should be used at the end of a probationary period, and the employee must understand at the beginning of the period that he or she will be observed and evaluated. Each item, as well as what impact the evaluation will have on future employment, should be explained to the employee. People undergoing periodic evaluations, such as at the end of one year's employment, should also know why evaluations are being conducted and what may result from the evaluation. In both situations, the evaluation should be used for counseling and guidance so that performance may be improved upon or corrected if necessary. Certainly, strong points should be pointed out. An employee should be made aware of good as well as not-so-good evaluations.

Evaluations should be made for a purpose and not for the sake of an exercise. They should ultimately be used as management tools. Evaluations should be developed to fit the policies of the particular institution using it and the particular position being evaluated. The same evaluation may not be suitable for every position.

An example of an evaluation—a performance appraisal form—was presented in Figure 8.5 (the backside of the PAF—Figure 8.4). More will be mentioned on the subject of performance appraisal in Chapter 11 when we discuss subroutines in the housekeeping department.

Summary

Staffing for both hospital and hotel housekeeping operations involves the activities of selecting, interviewing, orienting, training, and developing personnel to carry out specific functions in the hotel organization for which they are hired. Each activity should be performed with consistency, dispatch, and individual concern for each employee brought into the organization. Whereas the major presentation of staffing in this text has been developed for the model hotel where a mass hiring has been performed, each and every aspect of selecting, orienting, and training new employees applies equally to situations in which replacement employees (perhaps only one) are brought into the organization.

Job specifications are the documents that indicate qualifications, characteristics, and abilities inherently needed in applicants. The Employee Requisition is the instrument by which specific numbers and types of candidates for employment are sought by the personnel department for each of the operating departments.

The next step is interviewing, which should be done by people from various departments. Actual selection, however, should only be performed by the department manager for whom the employee will work.

The employee acquisition phase is vital to the successful orientation of a new employee and should not be omitted. Upon acquisition of the new employee, presentation of an Employee's Handbook (Appendix B & C) is appropriate. This handbook should contain major company rules, procedures, and regulations, along with relevant facts for the employee. Orientation is the basis for allowing the new employee to become accustomed to new surroundings. The quality of orientation will determine whether the new employee will feel secure in a new setting, and it will set the stage for the relationship that is to follow.

As training begins, orientation continues but is now conducted by the specific department in which the new employee will work. There are several methods of training, each of which should be used so as to gain the best effect for the least cost. Employee performance in training should be evaluated by methods similar to those used in evaluating operational performance that will follow. After new employees receive approximately 24 hours of on-the-job training in the cleaning of rooms, they should become productive and be able to clean a reasonable number of rooms (about 60 percent efficient). Continued

application of skills will develop greater productivity as the new employee spends each day working at the new skills.

As preliminary training ends, orientation should be completed by ensuring that an employee orientation meeting and a tour of the entire facility has taken place. Failure to complete an orientation or to provide sufficient training can plant the seeds of employee unrest, discontent, and possible failure of the employee relationship with the company that might well have been prevented.

Whether conducting training or development, adequate records of employee progress should be maintained. Records of training that have been successfully completed establish a base for future performance appraisal. Measurement of growth in skills and promotion potential may not be recalled if training records and evaluations are not initiated and continued. Employees have a right to expect evaluations and usually consider objectively prepared statements about their performance a mark of management's caring about employees.

KEY TERMS AND CONCEPTS

Staffing
Job specification
Employee requisition
Sources of employees
Processing applicants
Control system
Application
Prescreeening
Reference to a department
Processing records
Prescreening interview
Interview
Interviewing techniques
Interview pitfalls
Reference checks
Orientation program
Employee acquisition
Employment checklist
Deficiency of execution (DE)
On-the-job training (OJT)
Simulation training
Coach-pupil method
Lectures
Conferences
Workshop training
Demonstrations

Personnel action form
Performance appraisal
Hotel or hospital employee's
  handbook
Facility tour
Orientation meeting
Training
First training
Department employee's
  handbook
Skills
Attitudes
Knowledge
Meeting standards
Ongoing training
Performance analysis
Deficiency of knowledge (DK)
Training aid
Development
Supervisory training
Developmental training program
Records
Evaluation and performance
  appraisal
Probationary period

DISCUSSION AND REVIEW QUESTIONS

1. When should a job specification be prepared? What should it contain?
2. What services should the personnel department of an organization perform in the hiring process? What services should department managers for whom employees will be working perform?

3. Draw up an interview plan. What questions would you ask? What questions should be avoided?
4. After reviewing the hotel handbook in Appendix B and the departmental handbook in Appendix C, discuss the differences in approach offered in these two documents.
5. There are three basic areas in which housekeeping employees should receive training. What are these areas? List several elements found in each area.

NOTES

1. Dan Wilton, "Housekeeping: Cleaning up Your Hotel's Image." Reported in an interview with Carol Mondesir, in *Canadian Hotel and Restaurant*, March 1984, pp. 36–37.

9

Operational Planning

CHAPTER OBJECTIVES

1. To learn about operational planning for the direction and control of hotel housekeeping operations.
2. To understand the opening the house routine.
3. To discover the advantages of using forms to standardize procedures and communicate with employees.
4. To find out about standard operating procedures and see how they are used to delegate tasks.

The subject of planning for the opening of a hotel has thus far included staffing, scheduling, preparing job descriptions, using materials, and hiring, orienting, and training employees. Even though the who, what, and when may have been decided, procedures for the *how* of operations still remain to be established. The executive housekeeper may have, through past experience, established a mental plan of daily operations as they should be conducted. Much remains to be done, however, in standardizing specific procedures and routines for the new property. This chapter deals primarily with procedures for direction and control of housekeeping operations in hotels.

Recall MacKenzie's three-dimensional management chart (Chapter 1), which includes the sequential management functions of direction and control. Certain activities of direction and control must be planned for in advance of opening. These are delegating work (an activity of direction) and establishing reporting systems, developing performance standards, measuring results, and taking corrective action (activities of control). These activities cannot take place without having procedures designed and communicated to employees. since most of the work of the housekeeping department is a routine that recurs on a daily basis, communication for direction and control is best done with **forms.**

The day-to-day delegation of tasks as to which rooms require service and who will actually service them is performed through a routine commonly known as **opening the house.** This delegation takes place by the creation and use of several forms that are developed in advance of opening and are made available in sufficient quantity as to provide this communication on a daily basis. Additional forms relating to communication, control of information about progress, and timely reporting of information are also necessary. The technique by which such forms are explained is usually that of documents known as **standard operating procedures (SOPs).** The SOPs not only establish and describe routines for normal daily operations, but they cover a variety of other procedures such as key control, room inspections, inventory procedures, standards of performance, and lost-and-found operations. Several procedures associated with housekeeping operations will be presented in this chapter, including examples of the SOPs that control the operations.

Procedures for Opening the House

Opening the house is a procedure by which the following events take place.

1. Front desk provides information to housekeeping as to which rooms will require service on a given day.
2. Information received by housekeeping is transferred to **working and control documents** for senior housekeepers (team leaders or supervisors) to use that day to control work progress.
3. Information is provided showing room sections with specific housekeepers assigned and any **open sections** (sections with no housekeepers assigned due to occupancy being less than 100 percent).
4. If occupancy is less than 100 percent, the information is used to establish **18-room workloads** for those housekeepers who are scheduled to work on the specific day. This is accomplished by taking occupied rooms from open sections and marking them as **pickup rooms** for housekeepers whose regular sections are less than fully occupied. Total pickup rooms combined with the regular rooms of sections that are occupied form the 18-room workloads. (With 100 percent occupancy, all sections have housekeepers assigned and there are no pickup rooms.)
5. After all occupied rooms have been assigned to a specific housekeeper and information is cross-checked on all team leader documents, the daily planning is transferred to documents, whereby section housekeepers are informed of individual work assigned.
6. Because the House Breakout Plan (Chapter 2) divided the model hotel into four divisions of five sections each, daily opening-the-house exercises require the preparation of 24 documents (forms) to convey information from the front desk to the workers and supervisors who will be responsible for performing the work.
7. Once all forms are properly filled out, placed on a clipboard, and positioned on the main linen room counter, room keys associated with appropriate work areas are prepared for issue. When this is done, opening the house planning for that specific day is considered complete.

Note: It is important to recognize that all planning relating to opening the house may be computerized, and the specific documents referred to in this section can be obtained through hotel computers.

A detailed look at forms and how they are to be used will now be presented. All forms relate specifically to the 353-room model hotel.

Night Clerk's Report to Housekeeping

The document whereby early morning information is passed from the front desk to housekeeping is called the **Night Clerk's Report to Housekeeping.** Figure 9.1 is an example of this form; it has been completed with information from the hotel room rack at the front desk. The position of room numbers on the form is identical to the order in which rooms appear on the front desk room rack.

Note the columns next to the ones with room numbers. Check marks in columns "OCC" indicate rooms that were **occupied** last night and will require service during the upcoming day. Check marks in columns "C/O" will not only require service, but occupants of these rooms are expected to **check out** of the hotel sometime during the day. If there are no check marks in any of the columns next to a room number, the rooms are considered **ready rooms (R)** and will not require the services of a section housekeeper that day. Rooms marked "OOO" are **out of order** and will also not require service until the engineering department reports their status as being ready for cleaning service.

At the top of the report is the date and a summary of total rooms occupied, total rooms vacant, checkouts expected, rooms in which guests are expected to stay over, and rooms that are out of order. In Figure 9.1 note that stay overs (176) plus checkouts (72) equal total rooms occupied (248); and that total rooms occupied (248) plus total rooms vacant

**NIGHT CLERK'S REPORT
TO HOUSEKEEPING
(Rooms Requiring Service)**

Total Rooms Occupied ___248___ Date ___10/1/___

Total Rooms Vacant ___102___

Check Outs ___72___ Prepared By ___A.B. Clark___

Stayovers ___176___

Out of Order ___3___

Room	OCC	R	C/O	Room	OCC	R	C/O	Room	OCC	R	C/O	Room	OCC	R	C/O	Room	OCC	R	C/O	Room	OCC	R	C/O	Room	OCC	R	C/O	Room	OCC	R	C/O
1001	✓			1068	✓			1228	✓			2051	✓			2110	✓			3015	✓			3079	✓			3222			
1002				1071	✓			1229			✓	2053	✓							3016				3080				3223	✓		
1003	✓			1072			✓	1230			✓	2055			✓	2202	✓			3017	✓			3081				3224	✓		
1004	✓			1073			✓	1231			✓	2057			✓	2204	✓			3019				3083				3225			
1005				1074			✓					2059			✓	2205			✓	3021	✓			3085	✓			3226			
1006	✓			1075	✓							2061	✓			2206				3023				3087				3227			
1007	✓			1076	✓			2001	✓			2062	✓			2207				3025				3089				3228	✓		
1008	✓			1077	✓			2002	✓			2063				2208	✓			3027				3091	✓			3229	✓		
1009	✓			1078	✓			2003				2064	✓			2209	✓			3031	✓			3093				3230			
1010	✓			1079	O-O-O			2004	O-O-O			2065	✓			2210				3032				3095	✓			3231			✓
1011			✓	1081			✓	2005	✓			2066				2211				3033	✓			3096				4070			
1012	✓			1083			✓	2006	✓			2067				2212				3035			✓	3097				4071			✓
1013	✓			1085	✓			2007	✓			2068	✓			2213	✓			3037			✓	3098	✓			4072			
1014	✓			1087	✓			2008				2070	✓			2214	✓			3038	✓			3099				4073	✓		
1015				1091			✓	2009	✓			2071	✓			2215	✓			3039			✓	3100	✓			4074	✓		
1016				1093				2010	✓			2072	✓			2216	✓			3040			✓	3101	✓			4075			
1017	✓			1095	✓			2011	✓			2073				2217	✓			3041	✓			3102				4076	✓		
1021	✓			1096	✓			2012	✓			2074			✓	2218	✓			3043	✓			3103	✓			4077			✓
1023	✓			1097			✓	2013				2075			✓	2219	✓			3045	✓			3104			✓	4078			✓
1025	✓			1098				2014	✓			2076				2220			✓	3046	✓			3105			✓	4079			✓
1027			✓	1099	✓			2015	✓			2077	✓			2221			✓	3047				3106				4080	✓		
1029	✓			1100	✓			2016	✓			2078	✓			2222	✓			3049	✓			3107				4081	✓		
1031			✓	1101	✓			2017	✓			2079			✓	2223	✓			3051	O-O-O			3108			✓	4083	✓		
1032	✓			1102	✓			2019				2080				2224	✓			3053				3110	✓			4085	✓		
1033			✓	1103			✓	2021	✓			2081	✓			2225				3055	✓			3201				4087	✓		
1034	✓			1104			✓	2023	✓			2083			✓	2226	✓			3057				3202				4089			✓
1036	✓			1105	✓			2025	✓			2085	✓			2227				3059				3204	✓			4091	✓		
1038			✓	1106	✓			2027				2087	✓			2228			✓	3061	✓			3205	✓			4093			✓
1040			✓	1107	✓			2029	O-O-O			2089	✓			2229				3062				3206	✓			4095	✓		
1042	✓			1108	✓			2031			✓	2091	✓			2230	✓			3063	✓			3207				4096			
1044	✓			1213				2032			✓	2093	✓			2231			✓	3064	✓			3208			✓	4097			✓
1046	✓			1214	✓			2033			✓	2095	✓			3001	✓			3065	✓			3209			✓	4098	✓		
1049	✓			1215				2034				2096	✓			3002	✓			3066	✓			3210	✓			4099			
1051				1216				2035	✓			2097				3003	✓			3067				3211				4100			✓
1053				1217	✓			2037	✓			2098	✓			3004	✓			3068	✓			3212	✓			4101	✓		
1055	✓			1218				2038			✓	2099	✓			3005			✓	3070				3213				4102	✓		
1057	✓			1219				2039	✓			2100				3006	✓			3071	✓			3214				4103			✓
1059	✓			1220	✓			2040				2101				3007			✓	3072			✓	3215	✓			4104			✓
1061	✓			1221			✓	2041	✓			2102				3008			✓	3073	✓			3216				4105			✓
1062	✓			1222			✓	2042			✓	2103				3009	✓			3074				3217			✓	4106	✓		
1063	✓			1223				2043	✓			2104	✓			3010				3075				3218	✓			4107	✓		
1064	✓			1224	✓			2045	✓			2105			✓	3011	✓			3076	✓			3219				4108	✓		
1065	✓			1225			✓	2046			✓	2106			✓	3012	✓			3077				3220	✓			4110	✓		
1066			✓	1226			✓	2047	✓			2107				3013				3078	✓			3221							
1067			✓	1227				2049				2108	✓			3014	✓														

Figure 9.1 The Night Clerk's Report to Housekeeping indicates which rooms will require service as a result of being occupied or being vacated and not being serviced. Check marks in the "OCC" column indicate an expected stay-over guest, and check marks in the "C/O" column indicate a guest in residence who is expected to check out sometime during the upcoming day.

(102) plus out-of-order rooms (3) equal total rooms in the hotel (353).

This summary information is provided as a backup check and must agree with the totals of the individual marks. The report is usually available at about 6:30 each morning and is picked up by a housekeeping supervisor or manager who then proceeds to the housekeeping department to open the house. The Night Clerk's Report to Housekeeping is one of several forms referring to today's specific date that will later be collected and filed as a permanent record of work performed today.

After the supervisor has the Night Clerk's Report, the first task is to compare the actual rooms occupied with the Table of Personnel Requirements (Table 2.2) and to determine the number of section housekeepers needed to clean the 248 rooms requiring service. From the table we see that 14 section housekeepers are required to service 248 rooms; the next immediate concern is to determine whether or not 14 section housekeepers were told to report to work that day. Quick reference to the tight schedule (Chapter 3) will answer this question. If not enough section housekeepers are expected in, phone calls are made to standby workers telling them to come to work. If there is an excess of workers indicated on the tight schedule, workers may be called early and told not to report that day, preventing an unnecessary trip. If scheduled workers call to say they will not be in while the supervisor is in the process of opening the house, standby workers may be called to work.

Senior Housekeeper's Daily Work Report

The information contained on the Night Clerk's Report to Housekeeping is transferred to the **Senior Housekeeper's Daily Work Report.** Figures 9.2 through 9.5 show this report for the four divisions of the model hotel—red, yellow, brown, and green. The four forms are created by reference to the House Breakout Plan that was developed in Chapter 2.

Next to each division name is the total number of rooms in that division. Note also that there are five room sections in each division and that there are either 17 or 18 rooms in each section. At the top of the report there are spaces for the name of

the senior housekeeper, day, and date. There are also spaces for the name of the section housekeeper who will be assigned to each section. The check marks next to certain rooms, along with an indication of which rooms are expected to be vacated that day (CO), are transferred information from the Night Clerk's Report. This transfer of information can be a tedious task until the opening supervisor is familiar with the two reports and how they relate to each other. The organization of numbers on one form does not necessary relate to the organization of numbers on the other. (The Night Clerk's Report is a reflection of the room rack, and the Senior Housekeeper's Daily Work Report is designed around the House Breakout Plan.)

After the transfer of information is made, housekeepers' names from the tight schedule are now placed against specific section numbers. Housekeepers reporting to work should, in most cases, be assigned their regular sections according to the staffing guide in order that they will be working with their regularly assigned equipment. Since occupancy only

---

SENIOR HOUSEKEEPER'S DAILY WORK REPORT

RED — Division (90)

Senior Housekeeper _Georgia_ — Day _Wednesday_ — Date _11/4_

Section 1		Section 2		Section 3		Section 4		Section 5	
Hskpr _Julia_		Hskpr _(Open)_		Hskpr _Yvonne_		Hskpr _Billie_		Hskpr _Marjorie_	
1001	✓	1031	✓ CO	1213		1062		1091	✓ CO
1002		1032	✓	1214	✓	1063	✓	1093	
1003	✓	1033	✓ CO	1215		1064	✓	1095	✓
1004	✓	1034	✓	1216		1065	✓	1096	✓
1005		1036	✓	1217	✓	1066	✓ CO	1097	✓ CO
1006	✓	1038	✓ CO	1218		1067	✓ CO	1098	
1007	✓	1040	✓ CO	1219		1068	✓	1099	✓
1008	✓	1042	✓	1220	✓	1071	✓	1100	✓
1009	✓ CO	1044	✓	1221	✓ CO	1072	✓ CO	1101	✓
1010		1046	✓	1222	✓ CO	1073	✓ CO	1102	✓
1011	✓ CO	1049	✓	1223		1074	✓ CO	1103	✓ CO
1012	✓	1051		1224	✓	1075	✓	1104	✓ CO
1013	✓	1053		1225	✓ CO	1076	✓	1105	
1014	✓	1055	✓	1226	✓ CO	1077		1106	
1015		1057	✓	1227		1078	✓	1107	✓
1016		1059		1228	✓	1079	OOO	1108	
1017	✓	1061	✓	1229	✓ CO	1081	✓ CO	1085	
1021	✓	1231	✓ CO	1230	✓ CO	1083	✓ CO	1087	✓

Figure 9.2 Senior Housekeeper's Daily Work Report: red division. This report contains the transferred information from the Night Clerk's Report to Housekeeping regarding rooms that are a part of the five sections of the red division.

SENIOR HOUSEKEEPER'S DAILY WORK REPORT

YELLOW — Division (87)

Senior Housekeeper: *Katy* Day: *Wednesday* Date: *11/4*

Section 6		Section 7		Section 8		Section 9		Section 10	
Hskpr *Dianne*		Hskpr (*Open*)		Hskpr (*Open*)		Hskpr *Janice*		Hskpr *Mildred*	
2001	✓	2021		2040	✓ CO	2202		2220	✓ CO
2002	✓	2023	✓	2041	✓	2204	✓	2222	✓
2003		2025	✓	2042	✓ CO	2205	✓	2224	✓
2004		2027		2043	✓	2206		2226	✓
2005	✓	2029	o-o-o	2045	✓	2207		2228	✓ CO
2006	✓	2031	✓ CO	2046	✓ CO	2208	✓	2230	✓
2007	✓	2032	✓ CO	2047	✓	2209	✓	2057	✓ CO
2008		2033	✓ CO	2049		2210		2059	✓ CO
2009		2034		2051	✓	2211	✓	2061	✓
2010	✓	2035	✓	2053	✓	2212		2062	
2011	✓	2037	✓	2055	✓ CO	2213	✓	2063	
2012		2038	✓ CO	2221	✓ CO	2214	✓	2064	✓
2013		2039	✓	2223	✓ CO	2215	✓	2065	✓
2014	✓	1023	✓	2225		2216	✓	2066	
2015	✓	1025	✓	2227		2217	✓	2067	
2016	✓	1027	✓ CO	2229		2218	✓	2068	✓
2017	✓	1029	✓	2231	✓ CO	2219	✓	2070	✓
2019								2072	✓

Figure 9.3 Senior Housekeeper's Daily Work Report: yellow division.

SENIOR HOUSEKEEPER'S DAILY WORK REPORT

BROWN Division (89)

Senior Housekeeper _Jesse_   Day _Wednesday_   Date _11/4_

Section 11 Hskpr _Florence_		Section 12 Hskpr _Wilma_		Section 13 Hskpr _Marilyn_		Section 14 Hskpr _(Open)_		Section 15 Hskpr _Susie_	
3001	✓	3019		3201		3220	✓	3061	✓
3002	✓	3021	✓	3202	✓ CO	3221		3062	
3003	✓	3023		3204	✓	3222		3063	✓
3004	✓	3025		3205	✓ CO	3223	✓	3064	
3005	✓ CO	3027		3206	✓	3224	✓	3065	✓
3006	✓	3031	✓	3207		3225		3066	✓
3007	✓ CO	3032		3208	✓ CO	3226		3067	
3008	✓ CO	3033	✓	3209	✓ CO	3227		3068	✓
3009	✓	3035	✓ CO	3210	✓	3228	✓	3070	✓
3010	✓	3037	✓ CO	3211		3229	✓	2071	✓
3011	✓	3038	✓	3212	✓ CO	3230		3072	
3012	✓	3039	✓ CO	3213	✓	3231	✓ CO	3073	✓
3013		3040	✓ CO	3214		3049	✓	3074	✓
3014	✓	3041	✓	3215	✓	3051	O-O	3075	
3015	✓	3043	✓	3216	✓ CO	3053	✓	3076	✓
3016		3045	✓	3217	✓ CO	3055	✓	3077	
3017	✓	3046	✓	3218	✓	3057	✓	3078	✓
		3047		3219		3059	✓	3079	✓

Figure 9.4 Senior Housekeeper's Daily Work Report: brown division.

SENIOR HOUSEKEEPER'S DAILY WORK REPORT

GREEN Division (87)

Senior Housekeeper _Heidi_   Day _Wednesday_   Date _11/4_

Section 16 — Hskpr Harriet	Section 17 — Hskpr (open)	Section 18 — Hskpr (open)	Section 19 — Hskpr Jane	Section 20 — Hskpr Mary
2071 ✓	2096 ✓	3081	3080	4080 ✓
2073	2097	3083	4070	4093 ✓ CO
2074 ✓ CO	2098	3085 ✓	4071 ✓	4095 ✓
2075 ✓ CO	2099 ✓	3087	4072	4096
2076	2100	3089	4073 ✓	4097 ✓ CO
2077 ✓	2101	3091 ✓	4074 ✓	4098 ✓
2078 ✓	2102	3093	4075	4099
2079 ✓ CO	2103	3095 ✓	4076 ✓	4100 ✓ CO
2080	2104 ✓	3096	4077 ✓ CO	4101 ✓
2081 ✓	2105 ✓ CO	3097	4078 ✓ CO	4102 ✓
2083 ✓ CO	2106 ✓ CO	3098 ✓	4079 ✓ CO	4103 ✓ CO
2085 ✓	2107	3099	4081 ✓	4104 ✓ CO
2087	2108 ✓	3100 ✓	4083 ✓	4105 ✓ CO
2089 ✓	2110 ✓	3101 ✓	4085 ✓	4106 ✓
2091	3106	3102 ✓	4087 ✓	4107 ✓
2093 ✓	3107	3103	4089	4108 ✓
2095	3108 ✓ CO	3104 ✓ CO	4091 ✓	4110 ✓
	3110 ✓	3105 ✓ CO		

Figure 9.5 Senior Housekeeper's Daily Work Report: green division.

requires 14 section housekeepers, six sections will not have a housekeeper assigned. These six sections will be listed as open sections even though they contain rooms that will require service.

The next step in the process requires a throrough knowledge of the hotel layout—positioning of rooms in relation to each other and elevator location. The best written reference for this information is, again, the House Breakout Plan shown in Chapter 2. At this step, occupied rooms in open sections are assigned to section housekeepers who have been assigned to regular but partially unoccupied sections. Rooms so assigned are referred to as pickup rooms.

The technique of assigning pickup rooms will be illustrated for the red division and will involve the readjustment of sections 1 through 5 only. (In some cases, the reassignment of workload rooms may require the transfer of occupied rooms in a section in which a seciton housekeeper is assigned, to a section in which another housekeeper is assigned. This is due to the proximity of certain rooms in one section to those of another and to a desire to balance the workload.) Refer to Figure 9.6, which is a continuation of the opening process for the red division (Figure 9.2). Note the small circled number to the left of the section housekeeper's name. This is the number of rooms in the regular section that require service and is a reference for the opening supervisor.

Assignment of Pickup Rooms

The assignment of pickup rooms requires specific reference to the House Breakout Plan. Note first that sections 1 and 2 are adjacent. Section 1 has a section housekeeper (Julia) assigned; Section 2 is open. Also note that at 100 percent occupancy, rooms 1023, 1025, 1027, and 1029 are located in section 7 (directly above on the second floor). Since occupancy is less than 100 percent and since section 1 is not a full section, first consideration should be to remove the need for an elevator trip by anyone assigned to section 7. Hence the four rooms mentioned (if in need of service) are assigned as pickup rooms for Julia. This is indicated by writing the four room numbers at the bottom of the column marked section 1. The work-load for Julia has now increased from 13 to 17 rooms. Note also that room 1031 in section 2 is adjacent to room 1029, making it a logical pickup choice to complete the workload of 18 rooms for section 1.

SENIOR HOUSEKEEPER'S DAILY WORK REPORT

_____ R E D _____ Division (90)

Senior Housekeeper _____ Georgia _____ Day Wednesday Date 11/4

Section 1 (13) Hskpr Julia (18)		Section 2 (15) Hskpr (open) (0)		Section 3 (11) Hskpr Yvonne (18)		Section 4 (16) Hskpr Billie (18)		Section 5 (12) Hskpr Marjorie (17)	
1001	✓	1031	✓CO ←	1213		1062		1091	✓
1002		1032	✓ →3	1214	✓	1063	✓	1093	
1003	✓	1033	✓CO →3	1215		1064	✓	1095	✓
1004	✓	1034	✓ →3	1216		1065	✓	1096	✓
1005		1036	✓ →3	1217	✓	1066	✓CO	1097	✓
1006	✓	1038	✓CO →3	1218		1067	✓CO	1098	
1007	✓	1040	✓CO →3	1219		1068	✓	1099	✓
1008	✓	1042	✓ ↗4	1220	✓	1071		1100	✓
1009	✓ CO	1044	✓ ↗4	1221	✓CO	1072	✓ CO	1101	✓
1010		1046	✓ ↗4	1222	✓CO	1073	✓ CO	1102	✓
1011	✓ CO	1049	✓ ↗4	1223		1074	✓ CO	1103	✓ CO
1012	✓	1051		1224	✓	1075	✓	1104	✓ CO
1013	✓	1053		1225	✓CO	1076	✓ →5	1105	
1014	✓	1055	✓ ↗4	1226	✓CO	1077	✓ →5	1106	
1015		1057	✓ ↗4	1227		1078	✓ →5	1107	✓
1016		1059		1228	✓	1079	ooo	1108	
1017	✓	1061	✓ ↗4	1229	✓	1081	✓ →5	1085	
1021	✓	1231	✓CO →3	1230	✓	1083	✓ →5	1087	✓
1023,1025,1027,1029 1031				1231,1032,1033,1034,1036 1038,1040		1042,1044,1046,1049,1055 1057,1061		1076,1077,1078,1079 1081,1083	

Figure 9.6 Senior Housekeeper's Daily Work Report: red division. Specific room-scheduling information has been added by the supervisor during opening operations for that day. Similar information is added to the Senior Housekeeper's Daily Work Reports for the yellow, brown, and green divisions.

Section 2 has been listed as an open section; therefore, all occupied rooms in section 2 must be reassigned for service. Remember that we moved 1031 in section 2 into the workload for section 1. Rooms 1032, 1033, 1034, 1036, 1038, 1040, and 1231 have been transferred to section 3, where Yvonne is assigned, since the House Breakout Plan shows that these rooms are contiguous to section 3. The remaining rooms in section 2 (1042, 1044, 1046, 1049, 1055, 1057, and 1061) are more closely associated with section 4, where Billie is assigned, and are transferred there. Note the techniques for showing how the movement of the rooms into the various sections is indicated. The supervisor must remember to write the room numbers of pickup rooms in both the original and new sections.

All rooms in the open sections have now been reassigned. However, in doing so, Billie in section 4 has been given an overload. To remedy this, rooms 1076, 1077, 1078, 1081, and 1083 are taken out of Billie's regular section and reassigned as pickups for Marjorie in section 5. The

planning for the red division workload is now complete. The numbers in parentheses to the right of each section housekeeper's name refer to the final number of rooms assigned to each employee. Note the even distribution of work: three sections with 18 rooms and one section with 17.

Planning the workload of the other three divisions proceeds as with the red division. There is no one correct answer to the placement of pickup rooms. There is, however, "the best" answer, which can only be arrived at through practice. The best indication that planning for opening has been satisfactory is the lack of complaints from employees who have to work according to the plan.

Section Housekeeper's Daily Report

Figures 9.7–9.11 are the **Section Housekeeper's Daily Report** forms for the five sections of the red division. These particular forms will serve two functions: (1) to pass the workload information about pickups to each section housekeeper, and

SECTION HOUSEKEEPER'S DAILY REPORT

SECTION _____1_____ (18) RMS.   AM.   PM.

Housekeeper __*Julia*_____ Day *Wednesday* Date __*11/4*__

ROOM #	C/O	OCC	R	REMARKS	PICK-UP
1001					*1023*
1002					*1025*
1003					*1027*
1004					*1029*
1005					*1031*
1006					
1007					
1008					
1009					
1010					
1011					
1012					
1013					
1014					
1015					
1016					
1017					
1021					

Figure 9.7 Section Housekeeper's Daily Report for section 1, which has been assigned to Julia. Julia will be expected to clean all guestrooms requiring service from the list of rooms printed in the left column, plus rooms specifically listed as pickup rooms. The fact that five rooms have been listed as pickup rooms is an indication to Julia that five of the 18 rooms listed in the left column will not require service. Julia will also be given a blank copy of the Section Report for use later in the day when the P.M. room check is conducted.

(2) to provide a duplicate copy of the blank form to each section housekeeper in order that a **P.M. Report** of the regular section rooms (rooms whose numbers are printed) may be performed in the afternoon. Note that on copy number 1 of the form, nothing is given except pickup rooms and special notes or remarks. (Note that in Figure 9.10—section 4—Billie is informed that Marjorie will do rooms 1076, 1077, 1078, 1081, and 1083. In this particular case, regular rooms in section 4 would have normally been done by the assigned section housekeeper. However, there was an overload in this section due to pickups being assigned; therefore, rooms at the opposite end of section 4 were passed to the section housekeeper in section 5.)

The form has columns headed "C/O," "OCC," and "R." These columns become significant as the second use of the form develops (covered in detail in Chapter 10). The significant point to remember at this time is that a duplicate blank copy of the form with the section housekeeper's name and date are provided in the morning as a part of opening the house.

SECTION HOUSEKEEPER'S DAILY REPORT

SECTION _____2_____ (18) RMS.   AM.   PM.

Housekeeper _____*(Open)*_____ Day *Wednesday* Date __*11/4*__

ROOM #	C/O	OCC	R	REMARKS	PICK-UP
1031					
1032					
1033					
1034					
1036					
1038					
1040					
1042					
1044					
1046					
1049					
1051					
1053					
1055					
1057					
1059					
1061					
1231					

Figure 9.8 Section Housekeeper's Daily Report for Section 2. This is an open section, indicating that no housekeeper has been assigned on this day. The form, however, will be given to the senior housekeeper, red division in order that a P.M. room check can be performed later in the day. All occupied rooms in section 2 have been reassigned to other housekeepers working in the vicinity of section 2 and are referred to as pickup rooms for other housekeepers.

Preparing for Arrival of Employees

Planning the workload distribution for the day has now been completed. Note that the forms used are in fact routine directives for the accomplishment of work for the day. They are the delegation of tasks to employees based upon the specific occupancy requirements for the servicing of guestrooms on a specific day. All that remains to be done now is to prepare for the arrival of employees.

A duplicate copy of the four senior housekeepers' work schedules are made and displayed on the linen room counter near the telephone and the elec-trowriter (an electrical device that transmits and receives facsimiles of handwritten messages between housekeeping, front office, and engineering). Original Senior Housekeepers' Daily Work Reports are attached to clipboards and placed on the linen room counter to await employee arrivals at about 8:00 A.M. A copy of the Section Housekeeper's Daily Report for *open* sections is also attached to the senior housekeepers' clipboards. All other Section Housekeeper's Daily Reports with pickups assigned are attached to smaller clipboards, along with a blank copy of the same form (to be used later in the day for a room report). Pass keys associated with work areas are put

SECTION HOUSEKEEPER'S DAILY REPORT

SECTION _____3_____ (18) RMS.   AM.   PM.

Housekeeper _Yvonne_ _____ Day _Wednesday_ Date _11/4_

ROOM #	C/O	OCC	R	REMARKS	PICK-UP
1213					1231
1214					1032
1215					1033
1216					1034
1217					1036
1218					1038
1219					1040
1220					
1221					
1222					
1223					
1224					
1225					
1226					
1227					
1228					
1229					
1230					

Figure 9.9 Section Housekeeper's Daily report for section 3, which has been assigned to Yvonne, who will have seven pickup rooms.

next to the clipboards on the linen room counter. Opening the house operations are now considered complete and the department awaits 8:00 A.M. and the arrival of employees for work.

Other Forms for Direction and Control: Standard Operating Procedures

Standardization

Standard operating procedures (SOPs) are written instruments that set forth specific recurring ac-

tions. They are the devices by which procedures are standardized and are the basis for ready reference as to how to accomplish specific tasks. The opening-the-house procedure just described is a prime example of a procedure requiring documentation. The existence of an SOP on a given subject tacitly prevents deviation from standard activities until such time as a controlled change takes place. At that time a new or revised SOP may be promulgated. SOPs are similar in form, are numbered, and are usually kept in a reference journal (manual) available for anyone who will have any responsibility regarding a specific procedure. SOPs are coded into various departments

SECTION HOUSEKEEPER'S DAILY REPORT

SECTION _____4_____ (18) RMS.   AM.   PM.

Housekeeper ___*Billie* (18)___ Day *Wednesday* Date __11/4__

ROOM #	C/O	OCC	R	REMARKS	PICK-UP
1062					*1042*
1063					*1044*
1064					*1046*
1065					*1049*
1066					*1055*
1067					*1057*
1068					*1061*
1071					
1072					
1073					
1074					
1075					
1076					*Marjorie will do*
1077					*" " "*
1078					*" " "*
1079					
1081					*" " "*
1083					*" " "*

Figure 9.10 Section Housekeeper's Daily Report for section 4, which has been assigned to Billie, who has seven pickup rooms. The supervisor opening the house recognizes that the pickup rooms given to Billie create an overload. Rooms 1076, 1077, 1081, and 1083 have therefore been reassigned to Marjorie working in Section 5, because they are adjacent to Marjorie's regular section.

of the hotel and may be collected into a master SOP notebook available to the general manager and others interested in reviewing operational techniques. All SOPs usually begin with a simple statement of policy, followed by paragraphs indicating directives, procedures, explanation of forms, records to be kept, positional responsibilities, and coordinating relationships.

Structured versus Unstructured Operations

Some managers feel that large numbers of controlled SOPs form an organization that is too highly structured, creating an environment that stifles ini-

tiative. On the contrary, organizations that do not have controlled processes and procedures usually have as many ways to perform an operation as there are people working at the tasks. Some employees may present better ways of accomplishing a task than the manner prescribed in an SOP. If such is the case, testing of a new procedure may well warrant the promulgation of a change in procedure, again standardizing to the better way. SOPs can therefore present a challenge to employees to find better ways to accomplish tasks. If such participation results, employees may be given credit for their participation in improving operations.

SECTION HOUSEKEEPER'S DAILY REPORT

SECTION _____5_____ (18) RMS.　　AM.　　PM.

Housekeeper _*Marjorie*_ (17) Day *Wednesday* Date _11/4_

ROOM #	C/O	OCC	R	REMARKS	PICK-UP
1085					*1076*
1087					*1077*
1091					*1078*
1093					*1081*
1095					*1083*
1096					
1097					
1098					
1099					
1100					
1101					
1102					
1103					
1104					
1105					
1106					
1107					
1108					

Figure 9.11 Section Housekeeper's Daily Report for section 5, which has been assigned to Marjorie, who has five pickup rooms.

Suitable Subjects for Standard Operating Procedures in Hotels

The following are procedural items that are suitable for presentation by SOPs. Note that these procedures recur regularly, are suitable for delegation of tasks, allow for communication by forms, and are the foundation upon which change may be made if warranted.

Opening the house

Daily routine

Night activities

Key control

Lost-and-found operations

Inventory control procedures

Linen-handling procedures

Time card control

Dilution control for chemicals used in cleaning

Inspection checklists

Standards of performance

Maintenance work-order program

Control of guest loan items

Examples of Standard Operating Procedures for Hotels

There are many procedures that may warrant the publication of an SOP. As examples we will present three typical procedures that are standard in almost all housekeeping departments.

LOST-AND-FOUND OPERATIONS

Hskpg Dept
SOP-1
6/91

**Your Hotel
Anywhere, USA
Standard Operating Procedure 1
Lost-and-Found Operations**

Responsibility

A hotel lost-and-found will be operated by the housekeeping department. No department other than the housekeeping department will maintain a collection of found items. Any employee finding an item anywhere in the hotel that appears to be of value will follow his or her supervisor's instructions regarding lost items, and each departmental supervisory staff will ensure that its internal procedures provide for the orderly flow of found items to the housekeeping department for proper storage and disposal. The housekeeping department has also been assigned the task of controlling and coordinating the return of found property to rightful owners, *if such property is inquired about.* Under no circumstances will any employee of the hotel attempt to contact who they think might be a rightful owner for the return of the property. (For property to be returned, it must be inquired about.) Nor will any employee admit to seeing an item or suggesting that such an item may be in the lost-and-found unless they have the item in their hand.

Procedure (Items Found)

1. When an item is found during day shift operations (8:00 A.M.–4:00 P.M.) it will be taken to the linen room office for logging and custody control.
2. At other times, items will be turned into the front desk for custody control.
3. The linen room supervisor will take any item left at the front desk booth during the swing or grave shift to the linen room for proper storage and logging.

4. If a purse or wallet is found, it will be inventoried by two (2) managers, the contents noted in the log book (later described), and the book signed by both managers.

The Lost-and-Found Log

All property turned into the housekeeping department for safekeeping will be logged in a Lost-and-Found Log Book containing the following columnar entries: Date/Serial Number/Description of Item/Where Found/By Whom/Department/Disposition/Cross Reference/Signature/Remarks

1. Each item turned into the housekeeping department will be logged with the information indicated above, noting the date found. The entry will be assigned a serial number, and a description of the item will be recorded along with where it was found, by whom, and in what department the finder may be located.
2. The item will then be placed in an opaque bag if possible and the bag marked with *The Log Book serial number only.*
3. The item will then be placed into the lost-and-found storeroom using a sequential numbering system to make for easy location.
4. The linen room supervisor or linen room attendant will be responsible for making all log entries and for maintaining the Log Book and the lost-and-found storeroom.
5. The linen room supervisor or attendant will ensure that at the close of the day shift, the Lost-and-Found Log Book is locked *inside the lost-and-found.*

Lost-and-Found Inquiries

1. All inquiries about items lost or missing will be referred to the housekeeping department linen room supervisor or attendant for processing. Any inquiry made to any employee in the hotel about a lost item will be referred to the housekeeping office. The business hours of the lost and found will be from 9:00 A.M. to 5:00 P.M., Monday through Friday.
2. Upon the inquiry of a guest about a lost item during day operations, the linen room supervisor will first check the Lost-and-Found Log Book. If the item is recorded, he or she will proceed to the lost and found and actually locate the item. Once the supervisor has the item in hand, he or she may then tell the guest that the item is in the lost and found. If the guest is in the hotel, he or she will be told how to come to the lost and found. Upon presenting him- or herself and

after properly described the item, the guest will be required to sign the Lost-and-Found Log Book under the column marked Disposition. A name, address, and phone number will be recorded in the Disposition column. The guest may then be given the item. A reward should *never* be sought; however, if a reward is offered, it will be noted in the Remarks column of the Log Book. (The finder may then be called to the housekeeping office to receive the reward.) Under no condition will a person be told that the item is in the lost-and-found solely on the strength that it is noted in the lost-and-found log. The item must be personally in hand before an acknowledgment is made that the item is in the lost-and-found.

3. Any inquiries during swing and grave shift operations will be noted on a lost-and-found inquiry form and left for the linen room supervisor. If property is located, the linen room supervisor will mail the item(s) to the rightful owner.

Items to Be Mailed

When a lost item has been positively identified by an inquirer and the item must be mailed, the item will be packaged for mailing by the housekeeping department linen room attendant. The mail room will then be requested to pick up the package for mailing. The person taking the package for mailing will sign the Lost-and-Found Log Book, assuming temporary custody of the item.

Control of the Lost-and-Found Storeroom

Strict control of the lost-and-found storeroom will be maintained. The executive housekeeper or assistant and the linen room supervisor or attendant will be the only people permitted in the lost-and-found storeroom. These people will be the only ones permitted to release property from the lost-and-found storeroom. At the end of each day shift, the linen room supervisor will ensure that the lost-and-found door is locked.

Disposition of Items Not Claimed

Any item maintained in the lost and found will be held for 90 days. If at the end of this time period the item has not been properly claimed by its rightful owner, it will be offered to the finder as his or her personal property. If the finder desires the item, he or she will be issued a hotel property pass by the housekeeping department authorizing the removal of the property from the hotel. Should the person not desire the item, it will be given to a charitable organization such as Opportunity Village or any other charity that may be designated by the management. Disposition will be so noted in the lost-and-found log.

Proper Guest Relations

Proper handling of lost-and-found matters for our guests is one of our best opportunities to further our public image. Every effort should be made to recognize the concern of our guests and grant them that concern by offering prompt and efficient service regarding lost items.

CHANGING DOOR LOCKS

Hskpg Dept
SOP-2
6/91

Your Hotel
Anywhere, USA
Standard Operating Procedure 2
Procedure for Changing Door Locks

Procedure

Whenever the need arises to request a room lock change, the following procedure will be followed:

1. The manager requesting the lock change will fill out the new lock change request form indicating the room number, the lock cylinder number, the date, time, and a housekeeper's name.
2. A security officer will also date and approve the request on the line provided.
3. If request is made on the day shift, the lock change request form will be hand-carried to the locksmith, who will sign and receipt for same. The pink copy will then be left with the locksmith.
4. If request is made on swing or grave shift, the request form will be brought to the security office. The secretaries will be responsible for taking the form to the locksmith's office the next day.

A notation will be made on the report indicating that a lock change request has been made.

The lock change request form is a three-part form, and the distribution is as follows:

White copy   Retained by security office
Yellow copy   Forwarded to front desk and house-
              keeping
Pink copy   Given to locksmith

There will be occasions when the maintenance of proper security will require the changing of door locks.

KEY CONTROL

Hskpg Dept
SOP-3
6/91

Your Hotel
Anywhere, USA
Standard Operating Procedure 3
Key Control

General

The control of keys is basic to the security of the hotel and to the safety of the employees and guests. The security department holds a number of emergency keys, master keys, and special keys that are subcustodied to employees authorized to use them on specific occasions. Tight security of these keys is required, and the security department will establish procedures for the maintenance of security of these keys.

Procedure

1. The housekeeping department will maintain floor master keys in a locked key control cabinet.
2. Each of these keys will be identified by a stamping and a tag as to their use and level of entry and will be listed on the Master Key Control Chart in the security office.
3. People who have a legitimate need or those involved in an emergency that warrants the use of such keys will contact the housekeeping linen room supervisor for assistance.
4. Keys must be signed for on the Master Key Control Chart.
5. Keys returned will be receipted for on the Master Key Control Log Sheet.

Found Keys

Employees finding keys on the premises must turn them in to the security department. Employees having knowledge of an unauthorized person in possession of any key must report such information to the security department. Employees in possession of an unauthorized key will be subject to disciplinary action.

Key Assistance for Guests

1. If a guest is locked out of his or her room, has no key, and asks for assistance, a security officer or manager should be notified.
2. Upon arrival at the guest's room, the security officer should ask the guest his or her name and home residence.

3. The security officer may then enter the room, leaving the door open and asking the guest to remain outside until positive identification may be obtained.
4. The security officer will then call the front desk and ask *the name and home town of the guest in the designated room.*
5. If the information received by the security officer over the phone from the front desk coincides with what the security officer was told by the guest, then the guest may be allowed to enter the room.

There should be no exceptions to this policy. Security officers will write an incident report any time they are required to let a guest into a room.

Examples of Standard Operating Procedures for Hospitals

The following pages show the SOP in a different format. Four examples of hospital SOPs are shown to illustrate the changed format; however, a complete set of typical hospital SOPs are presented in Appendix D. Most traditional environmental service SOPs are presented in the Appendix and should likely cover 95 percent of the environmental service workload. Many procedures in the Appendix are also suitable for use in the hotel industry. Both the examples provided in this chapter and in Appendix D were provided by Janice Kurth, author of *Environmental Services Policy and Procedure Manual,* published by Aspen Publishers, Inc. Greatful appreciation is extended to both author and publisher for allowing this work to be reprinted.

General Procedures

SUBJECT: **Cart Setup**
DEPARTMENT: **Environmental Services**   DATE ISSUED:_____
APPROVED BY:_____   DATE EFFECTIVE:_____
ORIGINATED BY:_____   SUPERSEDES DATE:_____
Page 1 of 1.

Purpose: To provide the Environmental Technician with a checklist of equipment and supplies that will be needed to complete a routine job assignment. (Project work assignments will require different and/or additional equipment and supplies.)
The following items should appear on a properly equipped cleaning cart:
    1 dust mop handle
    1 wet mop handle
    5 (or more) wet mop heads
    1 (or more) dust mop head
    An adequate supply of 23″ plastic bags
    An adequate supply of 15″ bags
    1 plastic bottle equipped with trigger sprayer
    1 bottle liquid abrasive cleaner
    1 bottle toilet bowl cleaner
    1 toilet swab

    1 high duster
    1 dust pan
    1 small broom
    1 5-gallon mop bucket
    1 small wringer
    1 10-quart plastic bucket
    6 containers liquid hand soap
    An adequate supply of toilet tissue
    An adequate supply of paper towels
    1 gallon of disinfectant with pump dispenser or measuring device
    Rags
Environmental Technicians are expected to keep cleaning carts clean and orderly at all times.
All cleaning solutions and chemicals must be labeled clearly as to contents.

Use of Machines

SUBJECT: __Use and Care of Wet Vacuums__

DEPARTMENT: __Environmental Services__   DATE ISSUED:_____

APPROVED BY:_____ DATE EFFECTIVE:_____

ORIGINATED BY:_____ SUPERSEDES DATE:_____

Page 1 of 1.

Purpose: To provide supplemental instruction to the employee on using and caring for a wet pickup vacuum safely and efficiently.

The Environmental Services Department has several models of vacuums designed for wet pickup. They have stainless steel tanks and are mounted on wheels.

Procedure:

1. Place the motor onto the tank and fasten securely; if the motor is not fastened properly, the machine will not operate properly.
2. Place a section of hose (not to exceed 50 feet) into the opening at the front of the machine and fit securely; the hose will fall out if not fastened properly.
3. Fit the metal extension into the hose at one end and the squeegee attachment to the other end below the curved section.
4. Plug the machine in, turn on the on/off switch, and place the squeegee onto the floor extended in front of you.
5. Pull the hose toward you for maximum effect; lift, extend, and pull toward you; repeat.
6. Be alert as to when the machine is full; the automatic float valve will operate and the machine will not pick up any more liquid. There also will be a change in the sound of the motor when the tank is full.
7. Turn off the machine, disconnect the hose, unplug (be careful not to lay plug on a wet surface), and empty the tank.
8. Clean and dry the inside of the machine to prevent rust before returning it to its proper storage area.
9. Run clear water through the hose to clean it out.
10. Damp wipe the hose, cord, squeegee, and outside of the tank and motor.
11. Report any irregularities or maintenance problems to your Area Manager.
12. Store properly.

Floor, Wall, and Window Care

SUBJECT: __Dust Mopping__

DEPARTMENT: __Environmental Services__   DATE ISSUED:_____

APPROVED BY:_____ DATE EFFECTIVE:_____

ORIGINATED BY:_____ SUPERSEDES DATE:_____

Page 1 of 1.

Purpose: To relocate dust, dirt, and debris to a central area for removal while limiting dispersal into the air.

Assemble needed equipment:

Handle and frame for dry mopping (use small mop head in patient rooms or offices; long heads in corridors or other open, unobstructed areas)

A clean dust mop head to fit frame (sizes vary so be sure to check for fit)

Broom and dust pan or vacuum cleaner

Procedure:

1. Place dust mop onto frame and attach securely.
2. Begin at the farthest point in a room and work back out, or begin at one end of a corridor and work toward the other.
3. Push the dust mop, keeping it in front of you; as the frame has a swivel feature, turning and/or changing directions is done easily.
4. Cover the entire floor surface for best results.
5. Do not pick up dust mop until area is completed as particles will become airborne and redeposit themselves.
6. Pick up the accumulation, using either a broom and dust pan or a vacuum cleaner, when entire area has been covered.
7. Do not shake dust mop at any time.
8. Change mop heads as needed; never use a dust mop head from a previous day.
9. Place soiled mop heads in a plastic bag, tie securely, and take it to Laundry or drop it down a laundry chute.
10. Clean equipment and store properly.

Carpet and Upholstery Care

SUBJECT: **Carpet Cleaning–Using a Bonnet**[*]
DEPARTMENT: **Environmental Services**   DATE ISSUED:_____
APPROVED BY:_____   DATE EFFECTIVE:_____
ORIGINATED BY:_____   SUPERSEDES DATE:_____

Page 1 of 1.

Purpose: To clean the surface of a carpeted area quickly with little interference in the operation of the area, with minimum wetting and minimum drying time.

Assemble needed equipment:
Vacuum cleaner
Rotary floor machine
Spin yarn pads
Carpet shampoo
Pressure sprayer and/or 2 large buckets with one wringer

Procedure:

1. Vacuum area to be cleaned thoroughly, first across width of the room, then lengthwise; this is a crucial step—do not omit.
2. Mix shampoo solution in large bucket following label directions carefully for proper dilution ratios.

Method A:

1. Pour solution into the pressure sprayer.
2. Work 4-foot squares, spraying the area thoroughly, but avoid overwetting.
3. Soak the yarn pad in clear water and wring out thoroughly. Place on carpet and center floor machine over it.
4. Move the machine across the square widthwise, then lengthwise, taking care to agitate the entire area.
5. Repeat this procedure in overlapping four-foot sections until completed, turning the pad when soiled; for large areas, you may need to rinse the pad to remove excess soil and/or use several pads.
6. Allow to dry before allowing foot traffic.
7. Clean equipment and store properly.

Method B:

This differs from A only in application of solution.

1. Prepare solution in a large bucket.
2. Fill a second large bucket with clear water.
3. Soak the yarn pad in the detergent solution and wring thoroughly.
4. Follow the procedure outlined above to clean the carpet, rewetting and turning the pad frequently.
5. Rinse pad in the clear water to remove excess soil and prolong its use.

[*]A bonnet, also called a spin yarn pad, is a thick yarn pad made of cotton or cotton polyester that fits onto the pad holder of a standard floor machine.

Standard Operating Procedures Are Not to Restrict Initiative

The extent to which housekeeping department managers choose to document procedures for reference, standardization, and use in training is a matter of personal preference, and, in most cases, company policy. Most companies requiring the promulgation of SOPs are usually quick to emphasize that such SOPs are to be used primarily as guidelines for operations and should not stifle **initiative** in the investigation of ways and means to improve operations. Many hotels are quick to reward employees who find better ways of performing tasks; some even offer incentive awards for improvement of procedures. The SOPs may very well become the framework for operations and, simultaneously, the tool whereby controlled change may take place.

Summary

In this chapter we saw how preparation for opening the new hotel moves into the operational planning phase. Although the hotel is not yet in operation, preliminary techniques for routines, delegation, and control have been constructed as were other systems involving concept development, organizing, staffing, and material planning. Although direction of operations has not yet begun, preparation for the routine communication of daily activities must be conceptually developed and standardized.

One of the first routines by which daily activities are directed—opening the house—has been developed in detail, as have the necessary forms by which this direction is communicated. In addition, a system of standard operating procedures has been presented, with examples, by which the opening the house and other routines may be standardized. Topics for the SOP approach are listed but are only the beginning of such a list.

KEY TERMS AND CONCEPTS

Forms
Standard Operating Procedures (SOPs)
Opening the house
Working and control documents
Open sections
18-room workload
Pickup rooms
Night clerk's report to housekeeping

Occupied
Checkout
Ready rooms
Out of order
Senior housekeeper's daily work report
Section housekeeper's daily report
P.M. report
Initiative

DISCUSSION AND REVIEW QUESTIONS

1. Discuss how operational planning is related to delegation and why preplanning an operation is so important.

2. Explain why forms are important in the operation of a housekeeping department. Explain how these forms are used in opening the house:
   Night Clerk's Report to Housekeeping
   Senior Housekeeper's Daily Work Report
   Section Housekeeper's Daily Report

3. Define the following terms and give their symbols if appropriate:
   Ready room
   Occupied
   Checkout
   Out of order
   Pickup room
   Open section

4. Some people say that standard operating procedures (SOPs) restrict initiative. Explain why this is not necessarily true.

5. Explain the meaning of controlled change.

PART THREE

Directing and Controlling Ongoing Housekeeping Operations

In Part Two, the planning, organizing, and staffing principles of management we discussed were applied before the opening of a new hotel or similar operation. In Part Three, we will concentrate on the direction and control functions as applied to ongoing operations of housekeeping management.

We will begin by discussing the hotel housekeeper's daily routine of department management. We will then present "subroutines," that is, other functions of hotel housekeeping management that are not necessarily daily routines but are essential routines nonetheless.

Other special concerns regarding environmental services, protection of assets, linen and laundries will be addressed, and a conclusion presented, in Part Four.

10

The Hotel Housekeeping Daily Routine of Department Management

CHAPTER OBJECTIVES

1. To learn about the hotel's daily routines that occur in ongoing operations.
2. To see how routine activities of the housekeeper's day are segmented by time and who is responsible for the routines during each time period.
3. To learn how to clean a guestroom.
4. To understand how forms are used to record and transfer information among housekeeping shifts.
5. To find out how computers are used in housekeeping operations.

In Part Two we opened the house. The stage is now set for presentation of the primary daily routine that occurs in ongoing operations. In fact, opening the house is the first step of the daily routine in the ongoing cycle known as the housekeeping day.

The Housekeeping Day

The chronology of the **housekeeping day** may be divided into several distinct parts. This chronology differs depending on the type of property to which it is related and whether or not a computer application is in effect. For the purpose of illustration, the model hotel (commercial transient type; uncomputerized in housekeeping communication to the front desk) will continue to be the basis for system development. You should recognize, however, that destination resorts and resorts that are located in the center of activities may present different chronologies due to different types of markets.

A **daily routine chronology** for the model hotel housekeeping department might be as follows:

6:30 A.M. to 8:00 A.M.	Opening the house
8:00 A.M. to 1:00 P.M.	Morning activities (also cleaning the guestroom)
1:00 P.M. to 3:00 P.M.	Resolution of Do Not Disturbs (DNDs)
3:00 P.M. to 3:30 P.M.	The P.M. room check
3:30 P.M. to 4:30 P.M.	Shift overlap: first and second shift coordination
At 4:30 P.M.	Housekeeper's Report is transmitted to the front desk
4:30 P.M. to 6:00 P.M.	*Discrepancies generated* (Identification of those rooms in which front desk status is different from that noted on the Housekeeper's Report.) Many discrepancies will be resolved by close investigation of guest accounts at the at the front desk. *Rechecks Generated* (Unresolved discrepancies published to housekeeping.) Rooms on recheck list are again viewed to ensure correct status. P.M. housekeeping workload is finalized.
6:00 P.M. to midnight	Evening activities (until housekeeping closes)

Opening the House (6:30 A.M. to 8:00 A.M.)

Opening the house is the first step in the chronology of the housekeeping department day. Information communicated from the front desk to housekeeping via the Night Clerk's Report to Housekeeping is transcribed onto working forms for the housekeeping department. Adequate staffing is assured, and preparation is made for the arrival of workers. Figures 9.6 through 9.11 were examples of the means by which the direction and delegation of daily tasks for the routine conduct of work by a portion of a housekeeping staff (red team for our model) might normally be conveyed on a typical day. The conveyance of direction and delegation to other segments of the housekeeping staff (yellow, brown, and green teams) occur in a similar manner. As we discuss the daily chronology of events, the forms used in Figures 9.6 through 9.11 for direction to the red team will continue to be used.

Morning Activities (8:00 A.M. to 1:00 P.M.)

Most housekeeping departments start their daily routine at about 8:00 A.M. The time for the start of

morning activities may vary based on the ability of section housekeepers to gain access to guestrooms. In commercial transient properties in which weekend packages might be offered to families, the start of work may be delayed until 9:00 A.M. or even 10:00 A.M., depending on how late guests are known to sleep in. In hotels in which business people are the major occupants, however, there are sufficient numbers of early risers to allow section housekeepers to start work at about 8:00 A.M. Such will be assumed for the morning activities in the model hotel, which commence at 8:00 A.M. (The examples of communication that follow will again relate to the red team as presented in Chapter 9.)

In small properties, employees simply clock in for work and proceed directly to their central housekeeping area to pick up their assignments. Frequently employees come to work in their uniforms and are essentially ready to pick up their assignments and proceed directly to their floors.

Some hotels, however, do not allow their employees to take uniforms off the property. Others do not even have locker rooms where street clothing can be stored during working hours. In these latter cases, **changing rooms** are provided adjacent to **wardrobe departments**, which help facilitate large numbers of employees reporting to work at the same time.

For example, at the Excalibur Hotel in Las Vegas, Nevada, employees clock in at a time clock area as they enter the building. The employees then proceed some distance to a wardrobe department where they pick up preassigned **plastic hang-up bags**. The hang-up bag has one of four or five uniforms that have been purchased for each employee. (A wardrobe department containing in excess of five thousand hang-up bags is depicted in Figure 10.1). The suit bags with the fresh uniforms are then checked out by the employees, who proceed to the changing room. Upon changing into the **costume** the employees then place their street clothing into the hang-up bag, then return the bag to the wardrobe department for storage while the employees are at work. At the end of the workday the procedure is reversed and the soiled uniforms are returned to the wardrobe department. The employees will be resupplied with fresh uniforms for the next workday.

Figure 10.2 shows Excalibur guestroom attendants (GRAs) arriving at a sign-in area outside of housekeeping central where they are actually "reporting for work in uniform." According to the work rules at that hotel, it is at this time that the eight-hour work day will commence.

As workers arrive, section housekeepers and senior housekeepers pick up work assignments and

Figure 10.1 Wardrobe storage of employee uniforms. The uniforms are hung on moving racks beside suit bags to be used for storage of the employees' street clothing. (Photo courtesy of the Excalibur Hotel, Las Vegas.)

sign for keys on the Passkey/Beeper Control Sheet (Figure 10.3). Each of the four teams in the model hotel then moves to the satellite (floor) linen room areas associated with its particular work area. Before leaving the main linen room, senior housekeepers will check with the linen room attendant for specific information relating to actual check-outs

Figure 10.2 Signing in for work prior to receiving key cards and work assignments. (Photo courtesy of the Excalibur Hotel, Las Vegas.)

that may have occurred in their areas since the opening-the-house process began.

The Senior Housekeeper's Daily Work Report (Figure 9.6) had notations of rooms expected to be checked out of that day. The question now is this: Have any of these or other rooms actually been vacated as of 8:00 A.M.? If checkouts have actually occurred, the front desk would have conveyed this information as soon as possible to housekeeping. This type of information (rooms actually vacated) will flow all during the day from the front desk, to the main linen room, and on to each senior housekeeper, who in turn will pass it on to the appropriate section housekeepers in order that the latter may efficiently move into these rooms as soon as it is appropriate to do so.

Figure 10.4 shows how the Senior Housekeeper's Daily Work Report (Figure 9.6) is used to record *actual* checkouts against those rooms that had heretofore only been *expected* to check out. Note that some rooms that had been expected to remain occupied (such as Rooms 1228 and 1096) are now showing checkout status. These guests were early and unexpected departures, resulting in additional checkout rooms. In either event, the actual checkout is recorded by circles around the C/O notation. This information is passed to the section housekeeper in order that she or he might immediately enter the rooms to service them for reoccupancy.

Upon arriving at the satellite linen room, the senior housekeeper ensures that members of the team are properly prepared and move toward their assigned work stations as soon as possible. Section housekeeper's carts should have been properly loaded the day before and should require only slight attention before being completely in order for work. Each section housekeeper now moves toward the assigned area of room cleaning responsibility.

The section housekeeping aide begins a routine inspection of corridors, elevators, stairwells, and other public areas to determine if any place needs emergency attention as a result of some accident during the night (spills, cigarette urns turned over, and so on). The section housekeeping aide records what, if any, attention is needed on the inspection form such as that shown in Figure 10.5. The aide also notes any project work that will become a part of the regular day's cleaning assignment or of a future plan. Figure 10.6 shows an Excalibur housekeeping aide (houseman) cleaning up a previous night's spill, which was discovered in an elevator during morning inspection of an assigned area. Otherwise, the section housekeeping aide commences work in accordance with the job description as noted in Appendix A. The senior housekeeper begins a morning room check.

PASSKEY/BEEPER CONTROL SHEET

Day _____   Date _____

Issued to	Floor	Keys	Beep no.	Time out	Returned by	Keys	Beeper in	Time in	Accepted by

Figure 10.3
Passkey/Beeper Control Sheet. All issues and turn-in receipts of communication beepers and passkeys should be recorded as they occur. Such records keep close control over these objects. (Form courtesy of MGM Hotel, Las Vegas.)

A.M. Room Check

Daily A.M. **room checks** are performed to determine whether the status of rooms reported by the front desk is in fact the correct status from the preceding night. For example, if the front desk reports certain rooms as **occupied** (with guest or with luggage) and in need of service, the A.M. room check determines if these rooms are actually occupied or the status is incorrect. The report verifies rooms reported as **ready to rent** or **on change** (in the process of being serviced for reoccupancy; sometimes called checkouts or simply C/O) are as reported. Are these rooms in fact ready to rent and vacant? Or has a **discrepancy** been uncovered in the status held by the front desk?

Since this information is needed and must be accurate, room checks are conducted in the early morning in most hotels. Room attendants and section housekeepers knock on doors and, where necessary, enter rooms. Some hotels do not even use an opening-the-house routine. Daily routine simply starts with someone in the housekeeping department entering every room to determine if service is needed.

SENIOR HOUSEKEEPER'S DAILY WORK REPORT

_____ **R E D** _____ Division (90)

Senior Housekeeper _Georgia_   Day _Wednesday_   Date _11/4_

Section 1 — Hskpr (13) Julia	Section 2 — Hskpr (15) (Open) (0)	Section 3 — Hskpr (11) Yvonne (18)	Section 4 — Hskpr (16) Billie (18)	Section 5 — Hskpr (12) Marjorie (17)
1001 ✓	1031 ✓ CO ←	1213	1062	1091 ✓
1002	1032 ✓ →3	1214 ✓	1063 ✓	1093
1003 ✓	1033 ✓ CO →3	1215	1064 ✓	1095 ✓
1004 ✓	1034 ✓ →3	1216	1065 ✓	1096 ✓ (CO)
1005	1036 ✓ →3	1217 ✓	1066 ✓ CO	1097 ✓
1006 ✓	1038 ✓ CO →3	1218	1067 ✓ CO	1098
1007 ✓	1040 ✓ (CO) →3	1219	1068 ✓	1099 ✓
1008 ✓	1042 ✓ ↗4	1220 ✓	1071 ✓	1100 ✓
1009 ✓ (CO)	1044 ✓ ↗4	1221 ✓ CO	1072 ✓ (CO)	1101 ✓
1010	1046 ✓ ↗4	1222 ✓ (CO)	1073 ✓ CO	1102 ✓
1011 ✓ CO	1049 ✓ ↗4	1223	1074 ✓ CO	1103 ✓ CO
1012 ✓	1051	1224 ✓	1075 ✓	1104 ✓ CO
1013 ✓	1053	1225 ✓ CO	1076 ✓ →5	1105
1014 ✓	1055 ✓ ↗4	1226 ✓ (CO)	1077 ✓ →5	1106
1015 ✓	1057 ✓ ↗4	1227	1078 ✓ →5	1107 ✓
1016	1059	1228 ✓ (CO)	1079 ooo	1108
1017 ✓	1061 ✓ ↗4	1229 ✓	1081 ✓ →5	1085
1021 ✓	1231 ✓ CO →3	1230 ✓	1083 ✓ →5	1087 ✓
1023,1025,1027,1029, 1031		1231,1032,1033,1034,1036 1038,1040	1042,1044,1046,1049,1055 1057 1061	1076,1077,1078, 1079 1081,1083

Figure 10.4 Senior Housekeeper's Daily Work Report, red division, as it may appear at 8:00 A.M. Note circles around COs, indicating that rooms expected to be vacated have in fact now been vacated.

A.M. Housekeeper's Report.   In some cases an A.M. room check is conducted (Figure 10.7), and the results are assembled into an A.M. Housekeeper's report. The report is submitted to the accounting department as a cross-reference and audit check on the revenues reported by the front desk from occupied rooms. The primary function of an A.M. Housekeeper's Report, then, is to ascertain that revenue is reported for every room that was occupied last night.

Quick Discrepancy Check.   There is a simpler way to ascertain the status of rooms for which revenue should be reported than to disturb every guest in the hotel every morning. Rooms that are thought to be occupied have been scheduled for service. Rooms that are thought to be vacant and ready to rent have not been scheduled for service and their boxes are blank on the Senior House keeper's Daily Work Report (Figure 10.4). Since the primary concern is whether or not there are rooms

occupied for which no revenue is being received, there is no need to check rooms known to be occupied; senior housekeepers need to inspect only those rooms thought to be vacant and/or ready to rent. Such rooms in this category that are found occupied (or obviously not ready) need to be investigated immediately to determine why their statuses are incorrectly held by the front desk. A discrepancy report may therefore be generated from the inspection of ready rooms only.

There are several reasons why discrepancies occur:

1. A guest was to have been in room 2204 but was inadvertently handed the key to room 2206. A simple error in key selection went unnoticed by the clerk and the guest went to the address (2206) found on the key. At this point the front desk thought that room 2204 was to have been occupied when it will actually be discovered at morning room check that 2206, thought to be vacant, is the one that

HOUSEKEEPING AIDE—EARLY A.M. CHECK

Date: _____

Area	Location and Condition
Satellite Linen Rooms	
Stairwells	
Hallways	
Elevators	
Vending areas	

Figure 10.5 Housekeeping Aide—Early A.M. A check form is used to record results of early inspections of public areas in the guestroom section of the hotel. This report will form the basis for special work that must be performed.

Figure 10.6 A housekeeping aide (houseman) cleans up a late night spill discovered in an elevator on early morning inspection. (Photo courtesy of the Excalibur Hotel, Las Vegas.)

Figure 10.7 A guestroom attendant begins her day with a morning room check. (Photo courtesy of the Excalibur Hotel, Las Vegas.)

is occupied. This type of error is of no major consequence involving revenue; however, the possibility of inadvertently **double rooming** another person into room 2206 can occur, which may prove embarrassing to both hotel and guest.

2. Another and more major concern is the possibility that the room may have been given away by someone who did not have the authority to do so. (No records kept, therefore no questions asked!)
3. Finally, there is the possibility that some member of the hotel staff (bellperson, night security watch, desk clerk) who had access to guestrooms keys did, without proper authority, use a guestroom for an unauthorized night's rest—or whatever.

Regardless of the reasons for rooms that have been used and not recorded for revenue, they must be uncovered and corrective measures taken to prevent such happenings in the future.

A Matter of Quality Service. It is indeed unfortunate that many hotels cling to the notion that it is necessary to knock on every guestroom door at 8:00 A.M. in order to conduct an accurate room check. Other hotels recognize that it is not necessary to disturb a guest in a room thought to be occupied in order to determine whether a room thought to be vacant is in fact vacant. It is not necessary to disturb a guest only to conduct a room check; A.M. room checks should be confined to rooms thought to be vacant and ready or vacant and on change (checked out of). If this procedure is followed, section housekeepers need not approach any room in the morning until they are ready to clean that room. A.M. room checks may then be left to the senior housekeeper, who will open every door of guestrooms thought to be vacant to assure their status.

Techniques of Keeping Track. Figure 10.8 illustrates a technique of recording A.M. room check informa-

SENIOR HOUSEKEEPER'S DAILY WORK REPORT

RED Division (90)

Senior Housekeeper *Georgia* Day *Wednesday* Date *11/4*

Section 1 (13) Hskpr *Julia* (18)	Section 2 (15) Hskpr *(Open)* (0)	Section 3 (11) Hskpr *Yvonne* (18)	Section 4 (16) Hskpr *Billie* (18)	Section 5 (12) Hskpr *Marjorie* (17)
1001 ✓	1031 ✓ CO	~~1213 R~~	~~1062 R~~	1091 ✓
~~1002 R~~	1032 ✓ → 3	1214 ✓	1063 ✓	~~1093 R~~
1003 ✓	1033 ✓ CO → 3	~~1215 R~~	1064 ✓	1095 ✓
1004 ✓	1034 ✓ → 3	(1216) DISC (CO)	1065 ✓	1096 ✓ (CO)
~~1005 R~~	1036 ✓ → 3	1217 ✓	1066 ✓ CO	1097 ✓
1006 ✓	1038 ✓ CO → 3	~~1218 R~~	1067 ✓ CO	(1098) DISC (✓)
1007 ✓	1040 ✓ (CO) → 3	~~1219 R~~	1068 ✓	1099 ✓
1008 ✓	1042 ✓ ↗ 4	1220 ✓	1071 ✓	1100 ✓
1009 ✓ (CO)	1044 ✓ ↗ 4	1221 ✓ CO	1072 ✓ (CO)	1101 ✓
~~1010 R~~	1046 ✓ ↗ 4	1222 ✓ (CO) R	1073 ✓ CO	1102 ✓
1011 ✓ CO	1049 ✓ ↗ 4	~~1223 R~~	1074 ✓ CO	1103 ✓ CO
1012 ✓	~~1051 R~~	~~1224 ✓ R~~	1075 ✓	1104 ✓ CO
1013 ✓	~~1053 R~~	1225 ✓ CO	1076 ✓ → 5	~~1105 R~~
1014 ✓	1055 ↗ 4	~~1226 ✓ (CO) R~~	1077 ✓ → 5	~~1106 R~~
~~1015 R~~	1057 ✓ ↗ 4	~~1227 R~~	1078 ✓ → 5	1107 ✓
~~1016 R~~	~~1059 R~~	1228 ✓ (CO)	1079 OOO	~~1108 R~~
1017 ✓	1061 ✓ ↗ 4	1229 ✓	1081 ✓ → 5	~~1085 R~~
1021 ✓	1231 ✓ CO → 3	1230 ✓	1083 ✓ → 5	1087 ✓
1023, 1025, 1027, 1029, 1031		1231, 1032, 1033, 1034, 1036 1038, 1040	1042, 1044, 1046, 1049, 1055 1057, 1061	1076, 1077, 1078, 1079 1081, 1083

Figure 10.8 Senior Housekeeper's Daily Work Report for the red division, indicating results of the morning room check. Rooms supposedly ready to rent and found in that condition are marked with an R; a line is drawn through the entry to indicate that no more service is required for that room that day. Rooms 1215 and 1098 are found to be discrepancies; that is, they are *not* ready rooms as reported by the front desk.

tion. Note the R placed opposite each room found to be ready, thus verifying correct status (for example, see rooms 1002, 1005, and 1010). A line is drawn through the room number and the space next to it, indicating that there is no further service required from the housekeeping department in that room for that day. Also note how discrepancies uncovered during A.M. room check are recorded. For rooms 1215 and 1098, circles are drawn around the room numbers indicating these discrepancies. An immediate call is then made to the front desk pointing out the discrepancies in order that the front desk personnel might resolve the matter immediately. The only action required of housekeeping department personnel is recognition by the senior housekeeper that an additional room in the division will require service. This room may then be assigned to one of the section housekeepers; or the room may be "sold" to any section housekeeper desiring to work an overload; or the senior housekeeper may actually do the room.

A.M. room check is normally completed in about 30 minutes, depending on the number of unoccupied (ready or checkout) rooms listed. Once morning room check is completed, the senior housekeeper is free to resume her supervisory responsibilities with the team.

Communication and Supervision.   The senior housekeeper circulates throughout the assigned division, communicating with section housekeepers and section housekeeping aides and **progressing work** during the day. The senior housekeeper is constantly receiving information and conveying it to section housekeepers. The senior housekeeper receives information about rooms having been vacated by communicating with the main linen room. This information is passed on to section housekeepers so that these rooms may be cleaned as soon as possible. Also, information—about rooms that are cleaned and ready for reoccupancy—that is received from section housekeepers is conveyed back to the main linen room attendant, who in turn passes it on to front desk personnel.

In Figure 10.8, room 1222 has been reported to the senior housekeeper as having been cleaned by the section housekeeper and is now ready to be reported to the front desk. The senior housekeeper places an R after the circled CO indication, thereby keeping track of all rooms reported as having been cleaned (whether occupied or checked out). The supervisor may make an inspection of the room or, if confident that the room will meet standards, simply mark the Senior Housekeeper's Daily Work Report as indicated by room 1222 on Figure 10.7. Since the room

is *actually reported* to the main linen room as a ready room, the senior housekeeper draws a line through the entire entry opposite the room number. This has been done for room 1226, noting that all routine interest in that particular room has now been completed for that day.

Similar action may be applied to occupied rooms in which there are stayover guests. Room 1224 (Figure 10.8) required service as a result of a stayover guest (the room did not have a CO indication and therefore was not expected to be vacated). Since the room did require service, the section housekeeper should report when service has been completed. The R also indicates that an occupied room has been serviced, and the line drawn through the entry indicates that no further routine service is necessary.

Communication Symbols.   The following list is a summary of the **communication symbols** regarding the progress of work for each room on the Senior Housekeeper's Daily Work Report.

1. A check mark indicates a room requires service.
2. The symbol CO indicates that the room is expected to be vacated at some time today.
3. A circle around the CO indicates that the room has actually been vacated (section housekeeper notified).
4. The symbol R indicates that the room has been reported serviced by the section housekeeper to the senior housekeeper.
5. A line drawn through the entire entry indicates that the room has been reported to the main linen room as a ready room (no further routine action required in that particular room that day).

The senior housekeeper is capable of progressing a large number of rooms each day and can keep up with this progress by a simple system of symbols used to indicate varying degrees of status change. When every room has a line drawn through its entry, all routine services have been concluded.

Progressing Work in the Main Linen Room. (Sometimes referred to as "Housekeeping Central").   A duplicate copy of each of the four division's Senior Housekeeper's Daily Work Reports has been displayed in the main linen room on the counter (or may be viewed on video monitors, where computer status boards are in operation). Therefore, the linen room attendant, who is in contact with the front desk, can forward relayed information concerning recently cleaned ready rooms. (If the hotel has an electrowriter, which we mentioned previously, it transmits a facsimile of the sender's handwriting. The numerous communications sent in both directions by housekeeping and the front desk are thereby preserved.) As ready rooms are reported to the linen room attendant by each senior housekeeper, the linen room attendant also marks a copy of the Daily Work Report with a symbol R. As these rooms are reported to the front desk, a line is drawn through the room number and a completed record of work is therefore available in the linen room for all departmental managers to review any time during the day.

Priority for Cleaning Rooms

In what order should rooms be cleaned by each section housekeeper? It would seem that nothing could be more convenient for each section housekeeper than to begin cleaning rooms at one end of an assigned section and proceed from room to room down the corridor until reaching the other end, at which time all rooms in the assigned section are completed. Although this may seem to be the most efficient way of proceeding through the work day, it does not take into consideration concern for guests who do not want to be disturbed or who may want their rooms cleaned first or last.

As the section housekeepers first move into their work areas each day, they should survey each room assigned for cleaning (both regular and pickup rooms) to determine rooms in which the guest has indicated "Do Not Disturb," and rooms in which the guest has indicated "Maid please make ASAP." (Rooms in which the guest has put the night latch on the door will normally be in evidence by a small pin that will protrude through the doorknob. This small pin is easily discerned by feeling the center of the doorknob. When the pin is out, the section housekeeper should consider the room occupied and not to be disturbed until the night latch is taken off or until a later time of the day.)

A priority for cleaning rooms can be established as follows:

1. Rooms in which the guest has requested early service
2. Early morning checkouts that are specially requested by the front desk (usually required for preblocking of preregistered guests expected to arrive)
3. Other checkouts
4. The balance of occupied rooms requiring service
5. Requests for late service

A proper priority for cleaning rooms provides the greatest concern for the guest's needs and desires. While it is true that some occupied rooms (stay overs) will be the last to be cleaned each day (about 4:00 P.M.), the guests who wonder why their rooms are not serviced until the afternoon need only be reminded that a phone call to housekeeping or a sign on the door requesting early service will be accommodated as soon as possible. Otherwise, a room occupied by a stay-over guest might indeed be the last room cleaned that day in a particular section.

Occasionally, especially on weekends and holidays, many guests will indicate that they do not wish to be disturbed until late in the morning. A large number of such rooms could interfere with a particular section housekeeper being able to enter *any* of the assigned rooms. If such is the case, a notification to the senior housekeeper may warrant the section housekeeper helping another housekeeper in a different part of the division until such time as rooms begin to open up. At the later time the "favor" can be returned. This is another example of the significance of teamwork and team operation within the division.

Many times during the morning the section housekeeper may visibly notice rooms being vacated. When such is the case, that room immediately becomes a checkout and can be entered next, provided there are no rooms of a higher priority (guest requests or front desk requests) that have yet to be serviced.

Cleaning the Guestroom

At this point the "Housekeeping Day" scenario will be suspended temporarily and the specific techniques and systems on how to clean a guestroom will be addressed. We will first look at the large hotel where all guestrooms are quite similar in size and furnishings. Then we will investigate the "suite type" hotel, where more than one room may be involved in an individual unit. Finally, we will consider those guestrooms that have such items as fireplaces, cooking facilities, and kitchenettes.

As mentioned in an earlier chapter, the national standard for numbers of rooms cleaned in one eight-hour shift by one person can vary from 13 to 20 rooms per day. This is usually dependent on the type of market being served, the type of furniture and bathroom that is involved, and the facility itself. The numbers of rooms cleaned each day will not, therefore, be at issue in this section.

Most hotels have set routines for guestroom cleaning based on their own objectives and experiences. There are many hotel corporations that have had years of experience to build upon in their procedures. Through experience they have developed and honed their procedures until they become quite unique. Other hotels take a different approach by letting their executive housekeepers start from scratch and develop new room cleaning procedures based on their own individual experience.

What follows, then, is not necessarily unique or generic, but an example of the systematizing of routines that must take place in any individual hotel if the operations are to become systematic, effective, and efficient. Although the following procedural examples are specific, they do not rule out the possibility that other examples can be made as to the best way to clean a guestroom.

Special thanks are extended to the Excalibur Hotel and Casino of Las Vegas Nevada for allowing the use of their hotel (4120 rooms) systems relative to rooms cleaning and to the Marriott's Residence Inn of Las Vegas, Nevada, as we investigate the suite hotel with kitchen facilities.

Entering the Guestroom

The room attendant should knock softly with the knuckles, not with a key. (Over a period of time a key can damage the door finish.) The attendants should announce themselves either as "Housekeeper," "Room Attendant," or simply "Housekeeping." After waiting about fifteen seconds, if there is no response, they should repeat the procedure and insert their key or card entering device into the door lock. Figure 10.9 shows a housekeeper as she knocks, waits, then inserts her entry card into the door. If there is still no answer, after another five seconds, she should open the door announcing once again "Housekeeper, may I come in please?" If there is a guest in the room who failed to answer the door previously, then the guest should be addressed as follows: "I am sorry I disturbed you. When would it be convenient for me to service your room? I will be glad to come back at a later time if you wish."

The guest's answer should prevail as to whether the room is to be cleaned now or the attendant should come back at a later time. If the guest indicates it is all right to service the room now (while the guest remains in the room), the attendant might start a conversation by asking, "Did you have a nice sleep last evening?" or offer any remark which will allow pleasant conversation to develop.

The attendant might also ask, "Will you be staying another night with us, or will you be leaving later today?" The answer to this question will determine whether only the bed should be made and the room **tidied** with the intent of returning later to finish the work for a new guest. The attendant might also conclude this remark by saying (if the guest is leaving later today), "All right, I will just make the beds and

Figure 10.9 This housekeeper has knocked and waited for an answer. She now prepares to enter the room by inserting her card entry device into the door. As she opens the door she should again announce herself and ask, "May I come in, please?" (Photo courtesy of the Excalibur Hotel, Las Vegas.)

tidy the room and bathroom for you now, and I'll return later to finish after you have departed."

If the guest is staying another night, simply continue with a complete servicing of the room.

If there is no guest in the room at the time of entry, continue with the cleaning procedure.

Leave the door wide open. The attendant should pull the housekeeping cart across the doorway, positioning the linen side towards the room and as close to the wall as possible. Figure 10.10 shows a housekeeping floor manager admonishing the housekeeper to cover the entire door with her cart. The cart should be positioned in such a way that no one could enter the room without being discovered.

The vacuum cleaner should be taken into the room, not left in the hallway. As the attendant enters the room, he or she should turn on all lights and open all drapes for proper light. If the TV was left on, it should be turned off.

The attendant should check around the room for items missing, damaged, or broken. If noticed, they should call the main linen room central and notify a supervisor in order that an engineer or security person can be dispatched immediately.

The attendant should be sure to inspect the following items in every room, regardless of whether

Suggested Cleaning Methods

Before actually entering into the servicing of a guest-room, a list of cleaning methods should be reviewed. All dusting should be done with a damp washcloth or a cloth treated with an en-dust type chemical. Here are several suggested methods of cleaning specific items:

Mirror—Rinse with hot water and finish with a dry cloth.

Lampshades—Brush lightly with a dry cloth or feather duster.

Shower stalls—Use an **all-purpose cleaner** and dry with a towel.

Bath Floor—Scrub wet floor with all-purpose cleaner and dry with a towel.

Shower Doors—Scrub with all-purpose cleaner, rinse, and dry with a towel.

Sinks—Use all-purpose cleaner, rinse, and dry with a towel.

Tubs—Scrub with all-purpose cleaner or scouring powder, rinse, and dry with a towel.

Chrome—Use all-purpose cleaner, rinse, and dry with a towel; make sure there are no water spots.

Toilet Bowl—Wash the toilet inside and out. Use a **germicidal cleaner** and dry with a towel.

The following items should be dusted with a damp, or treated, washcloth: luggage rack, drawers and shelves, wastebaskets, lamp bulbs, air conditioner, thermostat, pipes under sink, tables and chairs, TV and stand, headboards, nightstands, picture frames, and window sills.

Special considerations in cleaning may require special products. When this happens, the supervisor should closely control the use of **special cleaning compounds**. All employees should be cautioned against "becoming chemists" and mixing chemicals, thinking a better solution can be attained if a few products are mixed together. For example, **acid bowl cleaner** used to remove spots and build-ups in toilet bowls, when mixed with Clorox, can create deadly chlorine gas. In addition, some people may be allergic to certain kinds of products in concentrated form. All-purpose cleaners are supposed to be used at **specified dilution ratios** for specific cleaning jobs. Employees should be trained in this area and should be required to comply with the manufacturer's specifications for dilution.

For protection, it is advised that rubber gloves be worn for all cleaning duties to guard against

Figure 10.10 A floor manager reminds a section housekeeper to make sure her cart completely blocks the door so that she will not be surprised by someone entering without her knowledge. (Photo courtesy of the Excalibur Hotel, Las Vegas.)

or not the room is a check-out or a stay-over. They should report immediately to **linen room central** any **discrepancies** found with the following items that cannot be immediately attended to:

1. Check all lights in the room, replace burned-out bulbs in the **swag lamp**, dresser lamp, or nightstand lamp. Report any other burned-out lamps to linen room central.
2. Check drapes, cords, and pulleys.
3. Check shower doors or shower curtains for serviceability.
4. Check shower, toilet, and sink for leakage or other problems.
5. Check TV for proper sound and picture.

If any room service or bar items need to be returned, remove them to an assigned location or to the hallway and notify a housekeeping aide so that they can be further positioned for retrieval by the appropriate department. The supervisor should see to their quick removal from the hallway since they are unsightly and can begin to smell. If these items are not removed in a reasonable period of time, notify linen room central by phone.

If the room is an occupied room, pick up magazines and newspapers, fold neatly and place on the table or dresser. Never throw away these items unless they are in the wastebasket.

germs, infection, and possible chemical reaction. Although few products are used which can cause harm in cleaning, as mentioned elsewhere in the text, **HAZCOMM requirements** direct that the dangers of each product used should be clearly labeled on each container. This information must be made available to the users of such products.

The Bedroom

Get all trash out of the room. The attendant should collect all waste and trash, remove it, and empty it into the trash receptacle bag on the cart. Take trash receptacles into the bathroom for cleaning. Collect all ashtrays in smoking rooms and empty into the toilet. Flush, then wash all ashtrays and wipe dry. Damp wipe all trash receptacles, then replace ashtrays and trash receptacles.

Bring clean linen and any other supplies needed to service the room into the room. Do not place clean linen on the floor while preparing to make the bed.

Shake all bed linen carefully when stripping the bed. Guests tend to leave articles and valuables in and under the bed and in pillow cases. Notify the floor supervisor and follow **lost-and-found procedures** for any item left behind by the guest.

Check mattresses and box springs for soiled or torn spots. Also check for wires that may be sticking outside of the box springs. The mattress and box spring should be straight on top of each other and should be placed firmly against the headboard. check bedframes where used (a dangerous item if out of place). If adjustment is needed, notify the floor supervisor. Any bedding in need of replacement (wet mattresses, soiled bed pads, torn or soiled bedspreads, damaged or soiled pillows, soiled, damaged, or torn blankets) should be reported to the floor supervisor and replacement items secured immediately in order that work can continue efficiently.

Fresh linen should be placed on every bed that was used or turned down the night before. Do not use torn or spotted linens. Place any rejected linen in the reject linen bag in the linen locker (satellite linen room).

The bottom sheet should now be placed on the mattress so as to facilitate tucking in the top at the head of bed with a **mitered corner** (see Figure 10.11). The bottom sheet should also be tucked in on both sides of the bed, but not necessarily at the foot.

The second sheet should be placed on the bottom sheet with the smooth fabric finish down (so as to be next to the body), with the major hem (if any) placed "jam-up" against the head board. This should leave plenty of top sheet at the foot of the bed to perform

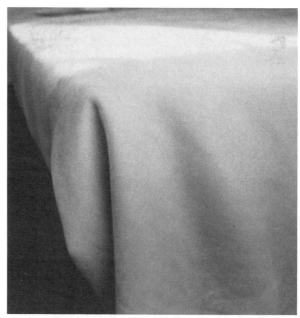

Figure 10.11 The technique of making a bed using the mitered corner. In photo A (above), the top sheet and blanket have been tucked in across the foot of the bed and the sides hang free. In photo B (below), sheet and blanket are picked up together at approximately a 45-degree angle and placed tight against the side of the bed. In photo C (next page), the bottom selvage is now tucked under the mattress while the top is still held up at the 45-degree angle. In photo D (next page), the top is now allowed to fall and is smoothed. Photo E (next page) shows the side being tucked under the mattress. Depending on company policy, the sides could be left hanging down. The bottom sheet should also be mitered by itself at the head of the bed.

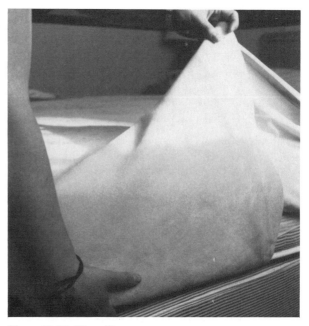

Figure 10.11, Photo B

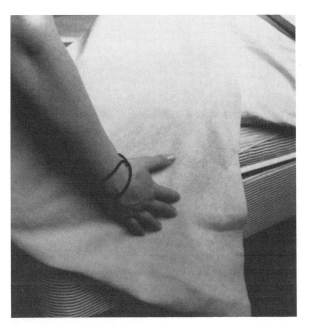

Figure 10.11, Photo C

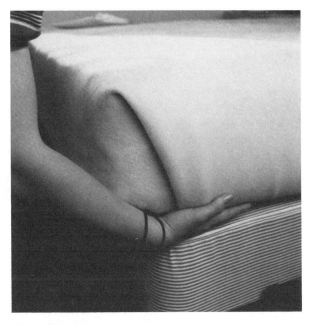

Figure 10.11, Photo E

another mitered fold after the blanket is placed in the proper position.

The blanket should now be placed on top of the second sheet, nine inches from the head of the bed. When the blanket is properly squared on the bed, the top sheet should be folded back across the top of the blanket. The top sheet and the blanket should now be tucked in together at the foot of the bed, and a mitered fold (Figure 10.11) made on both sides of the foot of the bed.

Figure 10.11, Photo D

Some hotels employ a *snooze sheet*, (a third sheet placed precisely on top of the blanket). This step also gives a quality application to the appearance of the bed if the spread is turned back or removed, but it is primarily done to protect the blanket from spills and spots. If a snooze sheet is employed, it will be tucked in at the foot of the bed simultaneously with both the blanket and the second sheet before the mitered corner is made.

Some hotels now *tuck in* the second sheet, blanket, and snooze sheet on both sides of the bed. Other hotels leave both sides untucked. When sides are tucked in, the guests will more than likely "unmake" the bed when they try to get into it. As top sheet and blanket are pulled back, the bottom sheet becomes untucked also.

This writer suggests the best of both methods. Tuck in the top sheet and blanket on the side of the bed opposite to the side the guest is more likely to use when entering the bed. Leave the side that the guest will most likely use to enter the bed untucked.

The bedspread. Because the bed is most often the major focal point of the guestroom, the bedspread must be properly positioned, smoothed, and without lumps upon completion of the make-up. Assuming the spread is properly fitted, it should just miss touching the floor on three sides and be properly tucked in at the head of the bed. The corners of the spread at the foot of the bed should either be tucked or pleated.

The spread at the head of the bed is easily dressed by first turning the spread back about 12 inches

Figure 10.12 The housekeeper turns the spread back about 10 inches in preparation for rolling the pillows as a unit. (Photo courtesy of the Excalibur Hotel, Las Vegas.)

from the headboard. The pillows should be placed about fifteen inches from the headboard on top of the turned back spread. Once done, the front edge of the spread can be carried back over the pillows on both sides of the bed, and then the entire unit can be rolled together toward the headboard. Figure 10.12 shows the housekeeper turning back the spread about 10 inches from the head of the bed.

In Figure 10.13 she has placed three pillows on the turned back spread and is now turning the spread back over the pillows. Once done on the other side of the bed, the entire unit can be "rolled" toward the head of the bed.

The spread should then be smoothed as necessary for a complete and dressed look. This technique of making the head of the bed is easily mastered with practice and is especially useful when one person is making up a king bed with three pillows.

Portable beds are to be made with clean linen and, unless otherwise instructed, no bedspread is used. Most are made with a snooze sheet, which will act as a bedspread. If the room is a "check-out" the bed is to be made up, pillow strapped vertically under the retaining strap and stood up on its rollers. Once standing upright, the bed can be replenished under the retaining strap with one bath towel, one

Figure 10.13 The housekeeper now rolls three pillows and the bedspread toward the headboard. This is an efficient way for one person to handle three pillows. (Photo courtesy of the Excalibur Hotel, Las Vegas.)

hand towel, one washcloth and two fresh bars of soap neatly tucked in with the pillow. A housekeeping aide can now be called to remove the bed from the room and have it properly stored. Remember, portable beds are to be made up before being moved into the hallway.

Clean (**damp-wipe**) chairs, tables, dresser tops, window sills and tracks, head boards, air conditioner, thermostats, hanging swag lamps, pictures, luggage racks, and closet shelves. Figure 10.14 shows a housekeeper using a solution diluted and prepared especially for damp-wiping furniture. Also dust all light bulbs and lamp shades. Properly adjust lamp shades and move the shade so that the shade seam is located in the rear of the light as would be seen by the guest. Dust bar areas (if applicable) and clean all mirrors in the bedroom.

Replace and/or reposition all literature, ash trays, and hotel guest service directories or PR items. Matches should be carefully *placed* in ashtrays (not thrown into them) striker side up with advertisement facing the front of the table or desk where they are supposed to be located according to hotel specifications.

Drawers should be opened in "check-out" rooms and damp wiped. Check carefully for any items the previous guest may have left behind. Do not go into drawers of **stay over rooms**.

Dust the desk area, including lamp and chairs. Check the phone directory. If the cover is torn or is marked or bent, replace it. All literature on and in the desk drawer should be checked for completeness, and writing items should be clean and unmarked.

Damp-wipe the phone and use a disinfectant to wipe the mouthpiece.

Check all drawers and closet shelves. Figure 10.15 shows a housekeeper using a special dusting tool to dust the top shelf in a closet. Also check safes (if provided) and check underneath beds for items left behind. If any item is found, complete a lost-and-found slip, place the item and the slip into a plastic bag, and turn into the lost-and-found at the end of the shift. Remove any clothes hangers not belonging to the hotel; replace hotel clothes hangers as necessary.

Clean the guestroom mirror. Figure 10.16 shows the housekeeper using an all-purpose product that has been properly diluted for cleaning glass. The final wipe should always be with a dry cloth.

Adjust as necessary all drapes, light fixtures, and any other item that may be moved out of position.

For the *final dusting* step, if the room is a connecting room, open the connecting door and damp-wipe inside of the door and wipe the door sill. Damp-wipe inside the entrance door around the lock area. Damp-wipe the door sill. Clean the entire area and damp-wipe plastic covers (if applicable) on any signs on the back of the room door.

Some hotels require that every room be *vacuumed* every day. Others call upon the judg-

Figure 10.14 A housekeeper uses specially prepared and properly diluted product for damp wipings. (Photo courtesy of the Excalibur Hotel, Las Vegas.)

Figure 10.15 A housekeeper uses a special duster, which has replaced the feather duster. It can be washed and retreated with a dust collection product. (Photo courtesy of the Excalibur Hotel, Las Vegas.)

Figure 10.16 A housekeeper uses all-purpose cleaner, properly diluted, to clean a guestroom mirror. (Photo courtesy of the Excalibur Hotel, Las Vegas.)

Figure 10.17 Vacuuming as a final step in cleaning the guestroom. (Photo courtesy of the Excalibur Hotel, Las Vegas.)

ment of the room attendant to make this decision based on a standard set of appearance criteria and a critical look at the floor by the housekeeper. Most times the room attendant's judgment is well founded and time can be saved in the room cleaning routine. If the attendant's judgment is not good, the supervisor must work with the guestroom attendant regarding their power of observation. Figure 10.17 shows the housekeeper vacuuming as a final step to cleaning the guestroom.

Cleaning the Bathroom

Turn on all lights and flush the toilet. Clean the inside and the outside of the toilet with the designated cleaner and a **johnny mop**. Make sure to clean under the rim where the flushing water emerges. Figure 10.18 shows the housekeeper properly gloved and using the johnny mop to clean under the commode ring.

To clean the Tub/Shower area, first place a dry towel inside the tub/shower. Then, with the designated cleaner, clean the shower walls, soap dish, and shower doors inside and out. In Figure 10.19 another housekeeper demonstrates the proper technique of stepping into the tub/shower to clean it. She is properly gloved and is standing on a cloth towel to keep from slipping. Wipe chrome fixtures clean, including the shower head. Use a soft scouring product to

Figure 10.18 The Housekeeper is properly gloved while cleaning the bathroom commode with a johnny mop. (Photo courtesy of the Excalibur Hotel, Las Vegas.)

Figure 10.19 A gloved housekeeper demonstrates the proper way to clean the chrome inside a shower. She is standing on a piece of soiled linen to make sure she does not slip or scratch the tub surface. (Photo courtesy of the Excalibur Hotel, Las Vegas.)

Figure 10.20 A housekeeper dries the door inside and out as a finishing touch on the tub/shower area. (Photo courtesy of the Excalibur Hotel, Las Vegas.)

clean the inside of the tub. Pull the tub stopper out of the tub and clean it thoroughly. Replace. Dry all surfaces and wipe all water spots from chrome fixtures. The shower and tub area are completed by the housekeeper drying the shower door (Figure 10.20).

Clean the sink with the designated product and a soft scrub applicator. Pull the sink stopper and clean thoroughly. Wipe clean and dry all faucets.

Check other chrome fixtures, including the toilet tissue, facial tissue holders, and chrome towel rods. Damp-wipe and ensure they are free from water spots. "Re-point" the toilet tissue and facial tissue (the first extended sheet of paper from each fixture should be folded so as to present a neat triangle-pointed tip for the next user of the bathroom).

Clean the mirror, and damp wipe the sides of the mirror frame (if applicable). The mirror should be spotless. A damp cloth with no cleaner will usually give the best results. Wipe all chrome plumbing fixtures underneath the sink and behind the toilet.

The toilet should be cleaned with a germicide cleaner. Clean the outside of the toilet tank, the toilet, lid, seat, and base. With a johnny mop, clean the inside of the bowl. Flush; rinse the johnny mop carefully so as not to drip on the floor and return it to the housekeeper's cart.

The floor should first be wiped with a damp cloth to remove any hair and dirt. Wipe the floor (using the germicidal cleaner), including all corners, behind the toilet and the door. Damp-wipe the waste basket and reposition.

Check the supplies. Replace as needed. (Most guestrooms should be equipped with one bath towel, one hand towel, and one washcloth for every pillow in the guestroom.) Also include at least one bar of bath soap and one bar of facial soap. Some hotels use two bars of each kind of soap in every guestroom. Still others are using the **amenity package** for soaps, shampoos, softeners, and powders (additional rolls of toilet paper and boxes of facial tissue are also included). Do not replace the toilet tissue in the fixture until the roll is less than one-fourth full. Fold towels properly and set up the bathroom as instructed.

For the *Final bathroom check*, recheck all lights in the bathroom. Check room once more before leaving and lightly spray with air freshner. Turn off all lights in the bathroom.

For the *Final inspection of the bedroom*, the guestroom attendant should move to the front of the room next to the entrance door and observe the entire room. Remember, what is now seen is what the guests will see as they enter the room. The attendants should also be prideful about their work. They should leave behind what they would be willing to enter upon if they were paying what the guest is going to be paying.

If the guest is present while the room is being cleaned, the attendant should remember that they actually deliver hospitality more than any other person. In general, the room attendant will come into more contact with the guest than will their department head or even the general manager. For this reason the attendant should remember to wish their guest a happy visit with us, and invite them back again. After all, the guest pays everyone's salary.

Remember also to fill out the documentation required by the hotel housekeeping room cleaning system. The attendant should now back out of the room, ensuring that the door is completely locked, and either move to the next room to be cleaned or, when finished with the shift, move to the satellite linen room and restock the housekeeper's cart for the next day.

Suite Hotels (with Kitchens, Fireplaces, and Patios)

There are many different types of hotel offerings that involve standard but, in their own way, unique routines. A good example of this type of hotel would be a **suite hotel** where more than the standard bedroom and bath are offered. Such facilities might include a formal sitting room or parlor, bedroom, kitchen and dining area, fireplace, and formal patio. A good example of such a facility would be the chain of hotels known as Marriott's Residence Inns.

The Marriott Corporation reaches into several market areas of the hotel industry; the Marquis and Full Service Hotels are at the top of the line, Marriott Courtyards and Fairfield Inns are upper-scale apartment type accommodations to guests expecting to stay anywhere from one night to six months. This type of operation is designed to reach the guest who might be moving into a community or someone working in a community for a limited period of time. Because this operation caters more to the individual who is having to maintain a home away from home, it is not unreasonable to find that linen would not be changed as often as in a full scale hotel, where guests are expected to come and go almost daily.

What follows is the daily routine of the guestroom attendant for this unique type of hotel. The reader should assume that the room attendant is equipped as before with the necessary cleaning equipment and supplies. Specific details on how to clean or make beds will not be repeated.

Grateful appreciation is extended to Marriott's Residence Inn, Las Vegas, Nevada, for allowing part of their systems to appear in this text.

Cleaning the Suite Areas

Daily Cleaning (Vacant and Ready Rooms) is accomplished as before, by observing the proper protocol for entering the room. The **suite attendant** will then turn on all lights to check for burned-out bulbs; replace as necessary, then clean all light switches, lamps, and lampshades.

Any carpet stains present will be treated.

Wastebaskets, trash containers, and ashtrays will be emptied. After emptying, clean and damp-wipe all wastebaskets as necessary, wipe and dry ashtrays. Replace liners in wastebaskets, if applicable, and reposition.

Furniture and shelves will be damp-wiped and the carpet vacuumed as necessary. Make sure that all furniture out of place is restored to its proper position.

Check patio doors and the outside door. Make sure they are locked and the **security bar** is set and in place with **security chain** in place.

Check for finger smears or dirt on the sliding glass doors or windows; clean as needed.

Clean all window sills, windows, curtain rods, and doors, including the door tracks.

Ensure that the telephone is restored to its proper place and that the phone cord is not tangled.

All pretreated spots on carpets should now be scrubbed, rinsed, and dried as necessary.

Entrance Area and Closets

Using a damp cloth, wipe the inside and outside of the entrance door, door facing, the threshold plate, door knob, and all door hardware. (Abrasive cleanser is not to be used on hardware.) Clean and vacuum the entrance mat.

Ensure that a flyswatter is positioned on the closet shelf. Check also that the proper type and amount of clothes hangers are in the closet. Foyer closet has four hangers, main closet has four to six regular/skirt hangers. Vacuum interior of closet. Ensure that the **room rate card** is properly in place.

Living Area

If the fireplace has been used, notify a houseman to come and clean the residue. Clean all fireplace tile, the black face plate, flue handle, screen, and poker. Close the flue and clean the picture above the fireplace. Such routines become instinctive after repeatedly following the prescribed procedures. Figure 10.21 shows a suite attendant following an instinctive procedure.

Ensure that all reading and PR materials are in place. The radio should be tuned to an "easy listening" channel.

Dry-wipe the TV screen. Damp-wipe the TV stand and face plate. All cords to standing lamps should be dust-free and placed safely out of the way.

Ensure that the candy jar is clean and has the required candy pieces. Make sure that the live plant is in its proper place.

Beds

Empty and clean the bed bench and nightstand drawers. Return all phone books to their proper place. Damp-wipe the telephone mouthpiece with disinfectant and replace in the phone cradle (Figure 10.22).

Check the spread for stains, topside and underside. Replace with a clean spread if necessary.

Check blankets for holes, stains, and tears. If a hole is smaller than two fingers, triple sheet the bed.

Mattress pads should be stain free. Make the bed.

Sheets should be changed at least twice a week in stay-over rooms. All check-out rooms must have linen changed.

Check the alarm clock and ensure that the time is accurately set.

Bathroom

Wipe and dry the shower curtain and rod with a cloth dampened with all-purpose cleaner. Cleaner the tub enclosure with the assigned product.

Clean all mirrors and polish chrome with glass cleaner.

Clean the toilet bowl. Check holes under the rim. Disinfect weekly or upon check-out. Clean the toilet seat/lid hinges, base, and caps with all-purpose cleaner.

Figure 10.21 A suite attendant damp-wipes the picture frame above the fireplace as part of her servicing routine. Such procedures become instinctive with repetition. (Photo taken with permission.)

Figure 10.22 Another suite attendant damp-wipes the telephone mouthpiece with a germicidal disinfectant as she cleans and services one of her suite bedrooms. (Photo taken with permission.)

Clean sinks with all-purpose cleaner. Remove any burn marks.

Reset the shower area with clean bathmat and fresh soap. Figure 10.23 shows the proper setup display for the suite bathroom.

Replace other soaps and tissues as necessary. If facial tissues are low, leave extra supplies on the vanity. Always leave an extra roll of toilet tissue.

Place clean bath towels, hand towels, and washcloths in the bathrooms according to Placement Standards.

Kitchen

Wipe clean the front, controls, and crevices of the dishwasher. Check inside the dishwasher for objects left behind by the guest, or for any small items that may have fallen into the bottom. If dirty dishes have been left by the guest, load them in the dishwasher (Figure 10.24) and turn on or, if the dishes do not make a full load, wash them by hand.

Place any clean dishes and utensils in their proper place according to the **Quest for Quality Standards Placement Guide** (this is a small publication of photographs indicating the proper setup of

Figure 10.24 In cleaning the kitchen of an occupied suite, the suite attendant loads all soiled dishes into the dishwasher and turns it on. If there are only a few dishes, she will wash them in the sink. (Photo taken with permission.)

every item in the kitchen and other parts of the suite. Every dish, pot, pan, knife, fork, and spoon has its place).

Pots and pans should be cleaned daily; make sure that any black marks or stains are removed.

Check the inside of the refrigerator and freezer:

—Wipe up any spills.

—Remove any items left behind.

Clean the outside, top, hinges and the door gaskets of the refrigerator door. Clean and leave dry.

Check oven burners for operation; check inside the oven for spills; clean as necessary. Damp-wipe the oven front and control panel as necessary. Clean the oven hood and air cleaner.

Cupboards: Wipe all shelves. Ensure that all dishes and glasses are clean and free of water spots. Wipe the fire extinguisher and store properly.

If small appliances have been used (toaster, coffee maker, popcorn popper), clean and/or polish the exteriors or wash as needed. Replace in appropriate positions. Wipe any crumbs off the bottom of the toaster tray.

Figure 10.23 The tub/shower area; clean, dry, and properly set up with a cloth bath mat and fresh soap. (Photo taken with permission.)

Figure 10.25 The "first-nighter kit" is being checked for an income guest. It contains small amounts of kitchen soaps and small packets of coffee, creamers, sugar, and sweeteners. Note the dining area setup. (Photo taken with permission.)

Wash down counter tops and behind sinks and ledge. Clean sink and polish chrome.

Check dishwasher soap supply. Replenish as needed; no less than one third of a small box is to be left.

Replace the **first-nighter kit**. Figure 10.25 shows a suite attendant replenishing the first-nighter kit with the dining area properly set for a newly arriving guest.

Gather dirty napkins and replenish the clean napkin supply as necessary.

Place a clean kitchen towel and dish cloth by the sink according to standards.

Replace all ashtrays in their proper position. Figure 10.26 shows the suite attendant checking a final setup in the desk area of the suite.

Before Leaving the Room

On check-outs, set the thermostat; air conditioning at 75 degrees, heat at 65 degrees. Ensure that the fan is left on "auto."

Turn off all lights except over the kitchen sink.

Figure 10.26 A suite attendant places a clean ashtray in its proper place at the desk. (Photo taken with permission.)

When completed, stand back and observe your work. Complete any maintenance request forms and turn in to the supervisor.

When servicing suites where guests are present, experience has shown that guests will more than likely remain out of your way, allowing you to get on with the work. This does not rule out the opportunity to be pleasant and extend hospitality to the guest. All suite attendants are encouraged to participate in friendly conversation when the opportunity presents itself. Figure 10.27 reflects the suite attendant's opportunity to extend hospitality in a personal way.

Daily Cleaning Guide for Stay-Overs is essentially the same except that in the kitchen, soiled dishes are placed in the dishwasher and the machine started.

Check the refrigerator and freezer for any spills. Clean as necessary.

The H.O.M.E.S. Manual

The above steps involving suite hotels are contained in one of the Residence Inns' *Hospitality Operations Manual for Excellent Service (H.O.M.E.S.)*. There are other H.O.M.E.S. manuals for procedures involving the Front Office, Maintenance Department, Hotel and Housekeeping Management, Uniform and Grooming, and **Commitment to Quality**. There is also a "Quest for Quality Placement Standard Guide" for every item in a suite. Additional guidance is offered when working in guest contact areas.

As should now be evident in the scenarios just presented, there is great detail in the step-by-step procedures involved in cleaning the guestroom. At first glance, what has been shown might seem almost insurmountable. What appears to be overwhelming becomes quite instinctive, however, with training and practice. At the Residence Inn, the experienced housekeeper cleans over 16 rooms a day.

Let us now return to the scenario of the "Daily Routine."

The Housekeeping Day Continued

As the section housekeepers complete each room, they should make a written record of each room cleaned in order to know when the daily work assignments have been completed. In addition, the section housekeepers should reevaluate the priority of cleaning rooms after each room is finished. A new request for early service may have appeared or checkouts may have been noticed while cleaning a particular room; these situations can cause a small change in the order in which the work schedule should be progressed.

During "opening of the house" the senior housekeeper was notified on the Daily Work Report which rooms were expected to check out that date. However, the section housekeeper was not so notified. When the section housekeeper is told about expected checkouts, it is important to know whether to wait for those rooms to be vacated before rendering service. What if a room is scheduled to be vacated and the outgoing guest requests early service? The room might have to be serviced twice in the same day; once by special request of the guest for early service

Figure 10.27 A suite attendant locates and presents a piece of reading material to a guest. The opportunity to show hospitable concern is reflected in the smiles being exchanged. (Photo taken with permission.)

and then again after the guest departs. A reasonable compromise can exist provided the early service request is honored. The section housekeeper asks all guests requesting early service, "Will you be staying another night with us?" Then expected departures will be noted and the section housekeeper may say, "Very well then, I will just spread up your bed and tidy the bathroom until after you have left, then I will come back and completely service the room. In this way, your room will be straight and I need not disturb you for any great length at this time." Such an answer is usually well received by any guests expecting to have visitors in their rooms and are departing later.

The section housekeeper continues throughout the day cleaning each room assigned in a priority order as described above until the last room on the schedule has been serviced. Likewise, the section housekeeping aide and the senior housekeeper continue with their functions as described above and as further set forth in their job descriptions.

The working team takes a 15-minute break from work in the morning, a 30-minute lunch break, and a 15-minute break in the afternoon. Most housekeeping departments operate in such a way that lunch breaks are on employee time—that is, employees punch out for lunch and are on their own time—and the 15-minute morning and afternoon breaks are on company time. During the rest breaks and lunch periods it is advisable that some member of the team stay behind in the general work area until the main portion of the work team returns. This staggering of break time allows for someone always to be present in the event of some emergency or priority of work requirement. The priority of work and chronology of the day continue very much as described until 1:00 P.M., at which time those rooms heretofore noted as "do-not-disturb" must be resolved.

Resolution of Do Not Disturbs (1:00 P.M. to 3:00 P.M.)

Let us assume that no prior specific notification has been received by the housekeeping department regarding a known late sleeper and that no specific request for late service has been received. (If such had been the case, a specific time would have been arrived at for the receipt of daily room cleaning service.) It then becomes necessary to resolve the status of those rooms which have heretofore been noted as **do not disturb (DND)**. This also involves determining the status of rooms in which pins have been out on doors. It would not be uncommon for section housekeepers to have several such rooms in their sections each day.

Since 1:00 P.M. is checkout time, this is a reasonable time to resolve the DND status of such rooms. Room doors with pins out are simply knocked on. Since it is difficult to knock on a door in the face of a sign indicating do not disturb, a more practical method of resolving this dilemma is to call the room. This call may be made from a vacant room possibly as close as across the hall. Before actually making the call, it is appropriate to consider all of the possibilities you could face by making such a call:

Case 1: The answering guest either

    (a) was awakened, or

    (b) was not awakened but was not aware that the DND sign was on the door

Case 2: The guest does not answer

In case 1 it would be appropriate to open the conversation as follows: "Good afternoon, this is Mary from the housekeeping department. I am calling to find out at what time you would like to have your room serviced today." Most answers to such a question asked over the telephone fully resolve what is to be accomplished in the DND rooms. Such answers as, "You may come now" or "Come in about one hour" or "Do not come until 6:00 P.M." or even "I do not want service today" resolve the problem. However, any guest not desiring service today should prompt the following type of reply: "Very well; however, I have a housekeeper on her way up to your room with some fresh towels. She will be there in just a moment."

What has been accomplished with such a scenario is that even though the guest has paid for a room that comes with daily service, including a change of bed linen, you cannot force service on a guest. It is imperative, however, that someone get a peek into the room in question to verify that nothing illegal is happening in the room. (Most illegal acts being performed in hotel rooms are covered by a DND sign and a statement that no service is desired that day.) The peek will be obtained under the guise of delivering the fresh towels into the room. In every case in which service is being refused, the supervisor and a housekeeping manager should be notified. The supervisor or manager might deliver the towels to verify that service was in fact being refused, as well as to engage the guest in conversation to ensure that no illegal activity is taking place within the room.

In case 2, in which there is no answer to the phone call, the section housekeeper should go immediately to the room, knock on the door, and enter the room. In most cases in which a phone call has received no answer, entering the room will reveal only that the guest is out of the room or has checked out. In either case, the guest has usually left the room forgetting to remove the DND sign from the door.

If the door pin is out and the guest has failed to answer a knock on the door or a phone call, immediate management attention is warranted. The main concern in this case is that someone in the room has locked him- or herself in and is now incapacitated to the extent that he or she cannot answer the door. Without delay, this room requires a manager with an emergency key that will allow immediate entry.

A similar situation exists if the section housekeeper attempts to enter a room with the floor master key after a phone call to a room and, as the door is opened slightly, the chain lock is found to be on the door. Concern in this situation is great enough to warrant calling a manager and an engineer with a bolt cutter in preparation for cutting the chain on the door.

There are two specific exceptions to the concerns stated, both of which should be considered before using the emergency master key or the bolt cutters. The room may have been sold as a part of a suite that adjoins the adjacent room. Quite often when guests have two rooms, they will chain lock and/or bolt latch one room and enter the locked room through the internal door of the adjacent room. A quick check at the front desk will reveal whether or not this has happened. The other exception occurs when the room is on the first floor and is capable of being vacated through a sliding glass door. It is not unusual to find that guests have chain locked and placed the latch bolt on the hall door, left a DND sign on the door, and checked out, departing through the sliding glass door to the street. This possibility should always be investigated before cutting chains and using emergency keys on first-floor room doors.

Although the possibility might seem remote, guests have been found dead in the hotel guestrooms, and this possibility will always confront the section housekeeper when access to guestrooms cannot be immediately gained. The fact that a deceased person could be discovered in a guestroom should be covered well in training sessions.

Having resolved all rooms previously seen as DNDs, the section housekeeper continues cleaning guestrooms, following the same priority as in the morning. The first part of afternoon cleaning of guestrooms will find heavier involvement with checkout rooms, since most checkouts would have departed by 1:00 P.M. The overload of vacant and checkout rooms will be eliminated within about two hours, leaving mostly occupied stayover rooms to be finished in late afternoon. After-

noon rooms cleaning will be interrupted only by the necessity to make a P.M. room check.

The P.M. Room Check

Unlike the A.M. room check during the morning activities, there is now a need to obtain a factual "look" at the status of *every* room in the hotel and report this status in order that the front desk may purify the room rack in preparation of selling out the house each night. The P.M. **room check** is carried out by each section housekeeper, at a specific time and as quickly as possible, checking every room in the normally assigned section.

There are exceptions to the need to knock on every door. Should the section housekeeper see a guest vacate a room a short time before the room check, there is no need to open that door since the room is known to be vacant. Likewise, should the section housekeeper see a guest check in just a short time before room check, the room will obviously be occupied. Sometimes stay-over guests make themselves known to their housekeepers. Again, known occupancies do not require the guest to be unnecessarily disturbed. However, accuracy must take precedence over bypassing a room at the P.M. status inspection.

Recall from Chapter 9 that the section housekeepers were given a blank copy of their section reports and that the senior housekeepers were given a blank copy of the open section reports. Thus, in the model hotel there are 20 section P.M. Report sheets available in the house each day upon which to record the results of the P.M. Report. At approximately 3:00 P.M., most expected checkouts have departed (there could be exceptions) and a majority of today's arrivals have not yet arrived. Therefore, 3:00 P.M. is an appropriate time to conduct the P.M. room check and prepare the report. The P.M. inspection is conducted in such a way as to ensure accuracy. Except for the situations mentioned earlier, every door in each section will be opened between 3:00 P.M. and 3:10 P.M.

There are many different ways of knocking on room doors and announcing the housekeeper's presence. The worst possible situation occurs when the section housekeeper knocks on the door with the key (thus damaging the woodwork finish on the door) and yells "Maid," thereby disturbing everyone within hearing distance. There is a much more professional manner in which to proceed.

It should be standard practice that the housekeeper knock on guestroom doors only with the knuckles, never with an object of any kind that could damage the door with repeated abuse. The term "housekeeper" should be used in place of "Maid."

The following is a professional procedure that may be followed:

1. Knock on the door with the knuckles.
2. Announce yourself as "Housekeeper." If there is an answer, say; "Please excuse the knock, I am conducting a room status check. Thank you, have a nice stay with us." Then go to the next room. If there is no answer, continue the procedure.
3. Knock on the door again.
4. Insert the key in the door.
5. Announce again "Housekeeper."
6. Open the door and, as the room is entered, say, "May I come in, please?"

Someone who may not have heard the first knock usually hears the key enter the door. At any time there is a reply, simply apologize and indicate that a room status check is being conducted. When no one answers, enter the room to determine the room status.

The person conducting the room check observes the room to determine the following:

Ready Rooms (R): Rooms that are clean and ready to rent

Occupied (OCC): Rooms that have a guest in residence (rooms that contain luggage are also considered to be occupied.)

Checkout (C/O) or on change: Rooms that have been vacated and have not yet been made ready for a new occupant.

Figures 10.28 and 10.29 show the Section Housekeeper's Daily Report for the P.M. for sections 1 and 2, respectively. Julia was assigned to section 1 and she therefore conducts the inspection for that section. Section 2 was an open section, so the senior housekeeper will conduct the room inspection. One of the three defined statuses—C/O, OCC, R—will be indicated for each room by placing a check mark in the appropriate column. Any special remarks that need to be forwarded will be noted. Those rooms provided to Julia in the morning as pickup rooms are not checked by Julia since they will appear on another section sheet. It is therefore only the printed room numbers (left column) that need to be checked. Each room should always have *one* of the three statuses marked next to it—*never more than one.*

After each section housekeeper has completed a room check for the section and filled in the P.M. Report, the report is placed on the housekeeper's cart to await pickup. After the senior housekeepers have completed checking all open sections within the division, they circulate among their teams and pick up the completed room reports. In the four divisions in the model hotel there will be 20 reports, all of which should be brought to the main linen room by about 3:30 P.M. It is at about this time that the second, or evening, shift will be reporting for work; there will be a shift overlap of about one hour.

Other Activities During the Shift

There are many other activities associated with cleaning guestrooms that are not as obvious as those done by the room attendant.

The guestroom attendant is assisted by someone keeping soiled linen and trash off the housekeeper's cart. That person is a **section housekeeping aide** and is usually a member of the team working in the area.

Other matters of resupply are also significant. Having the necessary linen to resupply the housekeeper's cart along with the other supplies needed to service the guestroom requires a whole new army of support personnel involved in total linen handling, especially when linen must be sent out from large hotels to commercial laundries.

There is the resupply of major cleaning chemicals, most of which must be diluted to **specified dilution ratios**. To maintain control of dilution, it is usually accomplished in a separate place by one person qualified to do so.

Figures 10.30 through 10.37 depict some of these activities.

Shift Overlap: First and Second Shift Coordination (3:30 P.M. to 4:30 P.M.)

When the night supervisor and night housekeeper report to work at about 3:30 P.M., their first task will be to accept the 20 Section Housekeeper's Daily reports. They will then transcribe the information from each of these 20 Section Reports onto the **Housekeeper's Report** for later forwarding to the front desk and the controller's office. This report is somewhat tedious to transcribe because of the different order in which rooms will be arranged on the Housekeeper's Report (which follows a pattern laid out on the front desk room rack).

Figure 10.38 is a Housekeeper's Report prepared from the information received from each of the Section Reports. (Rooms that are first indicated as C/O and then changed to R will be explained below.) Note that where applicable, the information received from Julia in section 1 and from the senior housekeeper in the red division coincides with the information contained in the Housekeeper's Report. Note also that

ROOM #	C/O	OCC	R	REMARKS	PICK-UP
SECTION HOUSEKEEPER'S DAILY REPORT					
SECTION ___1___ (18) RMS. AM. (PM.)					
Housekeeper _Julia_ Day _Wednesday_ Date _11/4_					
1001		✓			
1002	✓				
1003		✓			
1004		✓			
1005			✓		
1006			✓		
1007		✓			
1008		✓			
1009	✓			Engineer working on A/C	
1010	✓				
1011		✓		Request 8:00 P.M. late service	
1012			✓		
1013			✓		
1014		✓			
1015			✓	L & F item removed	
1016		✓			
1017		✓			
1021	✓				

Figure 10.28 Section Housekeeper's Daily Report for section 1. Form used to record results of the 3:00 P.M. room check. Markings are the result of that room inspection.

the form on which the Housekeeper's Report is prepared is identical to the form on which the night clerk prepared the report early in the morning that was used to open the house. However, on the Housekeeper's Report, every room will have an indication next to the printed room number of the status in which it was seen over a time span of about 10 minutes (between 3:00 and about 3:10).

The report will normally take about 30 minutes to transcribe. No sooner will the transcription be completed than the report will need to be updated before forwarding. Between 3:00 and 4:00 P.M.

many things happen to cause the status reported at 3:00 P.M. to change. Guests are checking into ready rooms; a few guests will be departing after 3:00 P.M.; but most significant is that the rooms reported as checkout rooms will now have been made ready. (It is quite possible that a section housekeeper who had reported three rooms as checkouts would have been able to service all of them between 3:00 and 4:00 P.M.) As each section housekeeper leaves the floor at 4:00 P.M., he or she notifies the senior housekeeper of the rooms previously reported as checkouts that are now ready. As the section

SECTION HOUSEKEEPER'S DAILY REPORT					
SECTION ___2___ (18) RMS. AM. (PM.)					
Housekeeper _Open_ Day _Wednesday_ Date _11/4_					
ROOM #	C/O	OCC	R	REMARKS	PICK-UP
1031			✓		
1032	✓				
1033			✓		
1034		✓		*Luggage Only*	
1036		✓			
1038			✓		
1040		✓			
1042			✓		
1044		✓			
1046	—	—	—	*ooo*	
1049			✓		
1051			✓		
1053		✓			
1055	✓				
1057			✓		
1059		✓		*Request 10:00 P.M. late Service*	
1061			✓		
1231			✓		

Figure 10.29 Section Housekeeper's Daily Report for section 2, which was an open section and was therefore inspected by the senior housekeeper for the red division.

housekeeper moves to the satellite linen room to resupply the cart with linen for tomorrow's work effort, each senior housekeeper carries the updated information to the main linen room. The night supervisor uses this information to update the Housekeeper's Report.

In Figure 10.38 there are update corrections that have been made to many of the rooms originally showing checkout status. There is also an update recap at the top of the page. What had been originally noted as 45 checkout rooms has now been reduced to 13. Also, the vacant and ready rooms have been increased from 158 to 190. It is not uncommon to erase the

original indications and replace them with the correct indication. However, passing the updated information on to the front desk in both its original and corrected forms may help front desk personnel resolve discrepancies, since they will know which rooms were rented or vacated between 3:00 and 4:00 P.M.

At 4:30 P.M.

The Housekeeper's Report should be completed *no later than 4:30* P.M. It is reviewed by a manager (and signed), a copy is made and retained, then the original is taken immediately to the supervisor or manager at the front desk.

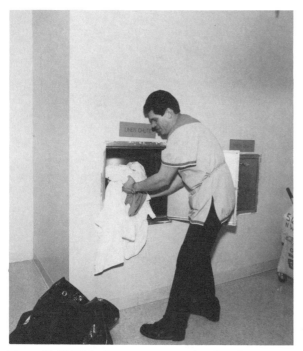

Figure 10.30 While the guestroom attendant does the rooms, section housekeeping aides are busy removing soiled linen from the housekeeper's cart and placing it in a linen chute. (Photo courtesy of the Excalibur Hotel, Las Vegas.)

Figure 10.32 A clean supply of linen is returned to the property. The utility person restocks each of various satellite linen rooms where guestroom attendants reload their carts for the next day. (Photo courtesy of the Excalibur Hotel, Las Vegas.)

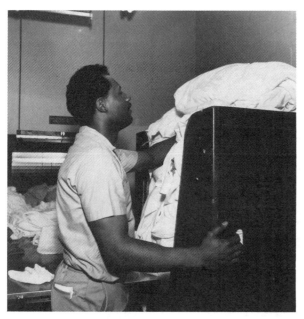

Figure 10.31 In the linen chute room, a utility person gathers all the soiled linen and packs it into large rolling hampers used to transport it to a commercial laundry. (Photo courtesy of the Excalibur Hotel, Las Vegas.)

Figure 10.33 The guestroom attendant loads her cart with a fresh supply of linen. Some hotels require that carts be loaded at the end of the work shift; others reload in the morning. Usually this depends on whether or not a clean supply of linen is available at the end of the shift. Large properties that send their linen out to commercial laundries usually have to wait until satellite linen supply rooms have been restocked during the night. (Photo courtesy of the Excalibur Hotel, Las Vegas.)

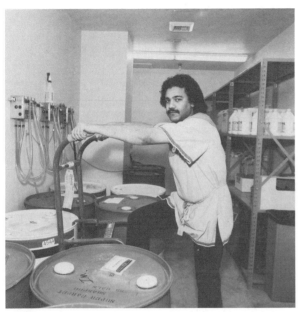

Figure 10.34 A utility person rolls a fresh drum of all-purpose cleaner into a chemical mixing room, where products are premixed and loaded into plastic spray bottles. (Photo courtesy of the Excalibur Hotel, Las Vegas.)

Figure 10.36 Other supplies needed by the guestroom attendant are made available in storerooms where carts are loaded. (Photo courtesy of the Excalibur Hotel, Las Vegas.)

Figure 10.35 Another chemical and another mixing station located near a mop sink, in a satellite storeroom allowing users easy access. Note the labeling of containers, now required by the Hazardous Communications laws. Information regarding hazards connected with a product must be clearly specified on the container. (Photo courtesy of the Excalibur Hotel, Las Vegas.)

Figure 10.37 A happy storekeeper ready for business. This utility person issues products to housekeeping aides who replenish their assigned satellite storerooms from a central storeroom. (Photo courtesy of the Excalibur Hotel, Las Vegas.)

HOUSEKEEPER'S REPORT

Total Rooms Occupied ___147___ Date ___11/4___
Total Rooms Vacant ___~~158~~ 190___
Check Outs ___~~45~~ 13___ Prepared By ___R. J. Housekeeper___
Stayovers _____
Out of Order ___3___

Room	OCC	R	C/O	Room	OCC	R	C/O	Room	OCC	R	C/O	Room	OCC	R	C/O	Room	OCC	R	C/O	Room	OCC	R	C/O	Room	OCC	R	C/O	Room	OCC	R	C/O
1001	✓			1068		✓		1228		✓		2051	✓			2110		✓		3015		✓		3079			✓	3222	✓		
1002			✓	1071	✓			1229	✓			2053	✓							3016		✓		3080	✓			3223	✓		
1003	✓			1072		✓		1230	✓			2055		✓		2202		✓		3017		✓		3081	✓			3224	✓		
1004	✓			1073			✓	1231		✓		2057			✓	2204	✓			3019		✓		3083	✓			3225	✓		✗
1005		✓		1074	✓							2059	✓			2205	✓			3021	✓			3085		✓		3226	✓		
1006		✓		1075	✓							2061		✓		2206		✓	✗	3023	✓			3087		✓	✗	3227	✓		
1007	✓			1076		✓		2001		✓		2062		✓		2207	✓			3025	✓			3089	✓			3228	✓		
1008	✓			1077		✓		2002		✓		2063		✓		2208		✓		3027		✓		3091	✓			3229	✓		
1009		✓	✗	1078		✓		2003		✓		2064	✓			2209		✓		3031		✓		3093	✓			3230	✓		
1010		✓	✗	1079	O	O	O	2004			✓	2065		✓		2210	✓			3032	✓			3095	✓			3231	✓		
1011	✓			1081		✓		2005	✓			2066		✓	✗	2211	✓			3033		✓	✗	3096		✓		4070	✓		
1012	✓	✓		1083	✓			2006	✓			2067		✓	✗	2212		✓		3035	✓			3097	✓			4071	✓		
1013		✓		1085		✓		2007		✓		2068		✓		2213	✓			3037	✓			3098		✓	✗	4072	✓		
1014	✓			1087	✓			2008	✓			2070	✓			2214		✓		3038		✓	✗	3099	✓			4073		✓	✗
1015		✓		1091		✓	✗	2009	✓			2071	✓			2215		✓		3039	✓			3100	✓			4074	✓		
1016	✓			1093	✓			2010		✓	✗	2072			✗	2216	✓			3040		✓		3101	✓			4075	✓		
1017	✓			1095		✓	✗	2011		✓		2073	✓			2217	✓			3041	✓			3102	✓			4076	✓		
1021		✓	✗	1096	✓			2012		✓		2074			✓	2218		✓		3043	✓			3103	✓			4077	✓		
1023		✓		1097	✓			2013	✓			2075	✓			2219		✓		3045		✓		3104		✓	✗	4078	✓		
1025		✓		1098	✓			2014		✓	✗	2076		✓		2220	✓			3046				3105	✓			4079	✓		
1027			✓	1099	✓			2015		✓		2077		✓		2221		✓	✗	3047	✓			3106	✓			4080		✓	
1029	✓			1100	✓			2016		✓		2078	✓			2222	✓			3049	✓			3107		✓		4081	✓		
1031	✓			1101	✓			2017		✓		2079	✓			2223		✓	✗	3051		✓	✗	3108	✓			4083	✓		
1032		✓	✗	1102	✓			2019	O	O	O	2080	✓			2224		✓		3053	✓			3110	✓			4085	✓		
1033		✓		1103	✓			2021	✓			2081		✓		2225	✓			3055	✓			3201	✓			4087	✓		
1034	✓			1104		✓	✗	2023	✓			2083	✓			2226		✓		3057		✓		3202	✓			4089	✓		
1036	✓			1105		✓		2025		✓		2085		✓	✗	2227		✓		3059		✓		3204		✓	✗	4091	✓		
1038		✓		1106	✓			2027	✓			2087		✓		2228		✓		3061	✓			3205	✓			4093			✓
1040	✓			1107	✓			2029	✓			2089	✓			2229			✓	3062	✓			3206		✓		4095	✓		
1042	✓			1108	✓			2031		✓		2091	✓			2230	✓			3063	✓			3207	✓			4096	✓		
1044	✓			1213	✓			2032		✓		2093	✓			2231	✓			3064	✓			3208	✓			4097	✓		
1046	O	O	O	1214		✓	✗	2033		✓	✗	2095	✓			3001		✓		3065		✓		3209	✓			4098	✓		
1049		✓		1215	✓			2034	✓			2096	✓			3002		✓		3066		✓		3210	✓			4099	✓		✗
1051		✓		1216		✓		2035		✓		2097		✓	✗	3003	✓			3067	✓			3211	✓			4100	✓		
1053	✓			1217		✓		2037		✓		2098	✓			3004		✓		3068		✓		3212	✓			4101	✓		
1055		✓	✗	1218	✓			2038	✓			2099	✓			3005		✓		3070	✓			3213	✓			4102		✓	
1057		✓		1219		✓		2039		✓		2100	✓			3006		✓		3071	✓			3214	✓			4103	✓		
1059	✓			1220		✓		2040	✓			2101	✓			3007			✓	3072	✓			3215	✓			4104	✓		
1061		✓		1221			✓	2041	✓			2102	✓			3008	✓			3073	✓			3216		✓		4105	✓		
1062	✓			1222		✓		2042	✓			2103	✓			3009		✓		3074	✓			3217		✓		4106	✓		
1063		✓		1223		✓		2043	✓			2104		✓		3010	✓			3075		✓	✗	3218			✓	4107	✓		✗
1064	✓			1224		✓		2045		✓		2105	✓			3011	✓			3076		✓		3219	✓			4108	✓		
1065		✓		1225		✓		2046	✓			2106	✓			3012		✓		3077		✓		3220	✓			4110	✓		✗
1066		✓		1226	✓			2047	✓			2107			✓	3013		✓	✗	3078		✓		3221	✓						
1067			✓	1227		✓		2049			✓	2108	✓			3014	✓														

Figure 10.38 The Housekeeper's Report combines information from 20 Section Housekeeper's Daily Reports into one consolidated report. The changes in original recordings reflect what happened between 3:00 P.M., when the original data were collected, and 4:00 P.M., thus updating the information.

In the meantime, section housekeepers should have finished loading carts for tomorrow's work schedule. There is a fresh supply of linen that the section housekeeping aide brought from the laundry and placed in the satellite linen room before 4:00 P.M. The section housekeeping aide collects all soiled glasses in cases, places them on rolling dollies, and moves them to the main linen room for washing and rebagging by the night crew. The senior housekeeper returns to the satellite linen room to see that all carts are properly loaded and stowed for the night.

Finally, all linen rooms are checked to ensure that trash has been removed and the linen room has been left in an orderly and locked condition. If top caddies are used on carts, they are returned to the main linen room for restocking. All workers who started work at 8:00 A.M. clock out at 4:30 P.M., having concluded an eight-hour workday in $8\frac{1}{2}$ hours lapsed time. (Recall that each employee was not on the clock during a 30-minute lunch break.) Before leaving the facility, each employee checks the Tight Schedule (See Chapter 3) to see if he or she is scheduled to work on the next day.

Discrepancies and Rechecks Generated (4:30 P.M. to 6:00 P.M.)

After the A.M. shift has departed, some member of department management or one of the day supervisors inspects all corridors and service areas to ensure that no piece of equipment, soiled linen, trash, or debris of any kind has been left in any hallway. Satellite linen rooms are spot checked to ensure that no trash cans (fire hazard) have been left unemptied and that all service doors are properly locked. Before the departure of the last department manager, the lost and found is chain locked (see lost and found, SOP, Chapter 9).

Barring any late administrative work or the need to remain behind to visit and/or work with the night crew, management's day can now be considered at an end. Evening operation of the department is now left in the control of the night supervisor, who will direct the activities of the night section housekeeper, night section housekeeping aide, and night public area housekeepers.

A short time after the Housekeeper's Report is delivered to the front desk, the night supervisor would have transcribed all checkouts remaining on the Housekeeper's Report to the **Night Supervisor's Report of Evening Activities** form (Figure 10.39).

NIGHT SUPERVISOR'S REPORT
OF
EVENING ACTIVITIES

DAY _____ DATE _____ SUPERVISOR _____

C/O	Make-up late	Recheck		Tidies		Turn down		Guest request	
Rm no.	Rm no.	Rm no.	Stat	Rm no.	Stat	Rm no.	Comp.	Rm no.	Item
1002	1011 8pm	1007	C/O /T	1007	MR	1005		1034	Iron Ret
1027	1059 10pm	2013	C/O	2083	MR	1067		2217	Foam Pillows
1067		2083	C/O /T	3055	MR	1103		2064	Bed Board
1073		3055	C/O /T	4105	MR	2040		3067	Iron Ret
1221		3068	R			2059		3225	Hair Dryer Ret
2004		3207	C/O			3018		3051	Sewing Kit
2057		3214	R			3108		2012	Bed Board
2072		4072	C/O			3222		1021	Roll-Away Bed
2229		4099	OCC			4080		2105	Crib
3007		4105	C/O /T			4107		2224	Roll-Away Bed
3066								1023	Razor Ret
3218								3067	Crib
4093								4075	Sick Guest
2013									
3207									
4072									

Other nightly duties	Completed
Vacuum front office, reservations, res. mgr's office, exec office	
Shampoo site entry carpet	
Shampoo soft furniture in Div F&B office	

Figure 10.39 Night Supervisor's Report of Evening Activities is used to record the activities of the evening crew. The report specifies checkout rooms not finished as of 4:00 P.M., the results of rechecks, room requiring a light tidying, the fulfillment of guest requests during the evening, and any special project work completed during the evening. Codes: R, ready; C/O, checkout; T, tidy; MR, made ready; OCC, occupied; RET, returned; COMP, completed; STAT, status.

Figure 10.40 Night section housekeeper provides turn-down service for guestroom at the Los Angeles Airport Marriott Hotel. During turn-down, the bedspread may be removed or folded down with the top sheet and blanket, exposing pillows, as shown. A touch of elegance includes placing a candy mint on the pillow with a small card saying "Have a pleasant night's sleep, and a good day tomorrow." (Photo taken with permission of the Los Angeles Airport Marriott Hotel.)

Recall that there were 13 rooms indicating checkout status on the Housekeeper's Report. These room numbers are transferred into the first column of the Night Supervisor's Report. Rooms 1011 and 1059, which had been listed on Section Housekeeper's P.M. Reports for sections 1 and 2 as requesting late service, are inserted on the Night Supervisor's Report with the time that they should be cleaned.

Note the column marked "Turn down." This information is received from the front desk and refers to rooms that are to have one or more beds turned back for night use. Turn-down service is usually begun when guests are out of their rooms during the evening dinner hour and continues until all rooms are completed. It is a service once reserved for V.I.P. guests but is now provided in many higher-priced hotels as a routine function in all guest rooms. Figure 10.40 shows an example of turn-down service being provided in a guest room in the Los Angeles Airport Marriott Hotel. Figure 10.41 shows a "butterfly" turn-down being folded by an Excalibur guestroom attendant.

The last column of the Night Supervisor's Report, **Guest Requests**, indicates services specifically requested by guests during the evening hours; room numbers and the services needed are recorded. If a guest loan item is needed, a receipt should be made out for the guest to sign and the item logged out of the linen room in the Guest Log Book to ensure proper return of the item.

By 6:00 P.M. the front desk would have had the opportunity to use the Housekeeper's Report to **purify the room rack**. This is a procedure in which the status of each room as reported on the Housekeeper's Report is compared to the status of each room as indicated on the room rack. There will be numerous discrepancies, primarily because of the changing of room status that has been occurring between 3:00 and 6:00 P.M.

Figure 10.41 A special touch is the "butterfly turn-down." (Photo courtesy of the Excalibur Hotel, Las Vegas.)

Most discrepancies can be resolved at the front desk by comparing arrival times of those guests for whom the front desk is showing the room as occupied (OCC) and the Housekeeper's Report is showing the room as ready (R). What might have happened is that at 3:00 P.M. the section housekeeper saw a ready room (R); however, at 6:00 P.M. the front desk room rack showed an occupied (OCC) room.

Discrepancies may also show the opposite condition. The front desk can show a checkout, whereas the Housekeeper's Report shows an occupied room. This type of discrepancy may have occurred as a result of a late checkout or of a departure *after* the room had been cleaned. Such discrepancies must be **rechecked**.

All discrepancies that cannot be reconciled by the front desk and all rooms that the front desk indicates are checkouts must be physically rechecked. The room numbers of guestrooms to be rechecked are sent to housekeeping via the electrowriter or in writing. Each recheck is listed on the Night Supervisor's Report of Evening Activities in the first half of column three. The evening supervisor or night section housekeeper should immediately recheck the status (take another look) of each of the rooms so listed and record the results of the recheck in the second half of the column.

As an example, refer to the Housekeeper's Report (Figure 10.38) to note the first status listed for each room in which there is a discrepancy. Rooms 1007, 2083, 3055, and 4105 were first listed as OCC but upon recheck were found to be CO/T; the T refers to a condition requiring a tidying. A **tidy** is a room that had been serviced earlier in the day when it was occupied but has now been vacated. Tidies require only a very light service; removal of small amounts of litter, replacing a glass, cleaning an ashtray, or perhaps smoothing a bed. A change of linen is required if a bed has been turned back and slept in or on. Night section housekeepers must check to make sure that the departing guest did not remake the bed after sleeping on what had been clean linen, leaving an unwelcomed surprise for the next guest. The bathroom might also require a light touch-up. A tidy requires two to five minutes of service, provided the guest did not get back into bed before departing.

All rooms listed in the recheck column that are showing checkout and tidy (CO/T) are also listed in the tidies column. As soon as they are **made ready (M/R)** they are so listed and phoned to the front desk as ready rooms in order that they may be sold as soon as possible.

Rooms 2013, 3207, and 4072 were simply listed as CO in the recheck column. These rooms will require a complete makeup, similar to those rooms originally listed in the C/O column. They are therefore added to the CO column if they were not already listed.

Rooms 3068 and 3214 were originally listed as R and upon recheck were found in that same status. The front desk must continue to research these two rooms to determine why the front desk status remains in error, since on two occasions both rooms were viewed by housekeeping as ready rooms. Possibly a **room found vacant (RFV)** has occurred, which happens when a customer intends to pay the account with a credit card and expects the hotel to find the room vacant, total the bill, and send through a voucher for what is owed. The other possibility is that someone has **skipped** without paying the account. Room 4099 was originally reported as R and is now found to be occupied. The front desk shows this room vacant, and must continue researching until the discrepancy is resolved.

In the manner prescribed above, all rechecks will have their status determined for the day. Most rechecks will need a light tidy. On many occasions, these tidies can be completed as they are discovered and the room reported as a ready room immediately by phone to the front desk. The final status of all rechecks is recorded and sent back to the front desk in writing or on the electrowriter.

Evening Activities (6:00 P.M. to Midnight)

The workload of the evening crew can be summarized as follows:

1. To transcribe the Housekeeper's Report and then update the report.
2. To transcribe the remaining checkouts to the Night Supervisor's Report of Evening Activities and the night housekeeper to begin cleaning these checkouts.
3. Public area housekeepers to assume responsibility for public area cleaning and servicing.
4. Evening crew to begin providing special services as requested by the guests and to note each service on the report.
5. At about 6:00 P.M. to receive rechecks and to check the statuses of rooms listed for recheck to determine what, if anything, must be done by the housekeeping department to service these rooms. Many rechecks will require a light tidy; some rooms will require a complete makeup; others require only the verification of correct status. Rooms tidied and any other special projects required of the night crew are noted on the report.

6. Turn-downs are begun at about 7:00 P.M. and are continued until completed.

7. The night housekeeping aide usually washes all guestroom drinking glasses and helps repackage them in sanitary containers for use during the next day. These glasses are delivered to satellite linen rooms at night.

8. The night supervisor, assisted by other members of the night crew, may restock cart-top baskets with the proper par of guest supplies; these baskets will be picked up the next day by section housekeepers as they proceed to work.

Of greatest significance is the fact that the night supervisor is *in charge* and must *take charge* of the evening activities of the housekeeping department. She or he must therefore wear a beeper and not be confined to an office. Electrowriter messages are reviewed upon return to the office, and telephone messages are intercepted and relayed by the PBX operator. The supervisor works closely with the night supervisor at the front desk to ensure that all rechecks are properly resolved and that every room is left clean and salable. The hotel should *never* lose room revenue because the housekeeping department failed to clean a room.

The night supervisor must also make inspections of public rest rooms to ensure that they are being properly maintained. A night guestroom attendant may service ten or fifteen rooms each night to ensure their availability for guests who arrive late (Figure 10.42). The night supervisor should see to it that the main linen room is cleaned and properly prepared for the oncoming supervisor who will be opening the house the next morning. Of greatest importance is that the night supervisor keep an eye out for the unexpected. A change in the weather at 10:00 P.M. can have a surprising effect on tomorrow's schedule. Any unusual change in expected occupancy may warrant notification to the executive housekeeper in order that special direction may be forthcoming for the unusual occasion.

When all vacant rooms are clean and ready to rent, turn-downs are completed, linen room is clean and ready for the oncoming shift, glasses washed and packaged for use the following day, and cart-top caddies replenished for section housekeepers to pick up in the morning, the evening activities are essentially finished. The final step in each evening's activity is for the supervisor to assemble all reports, records, forms, and paperwork associated with the day's activities for filing chronologically according to date. The following is a list of documents that should be filed:

1. Night Clerk's Report to Housekeeping (used to open the house that day)

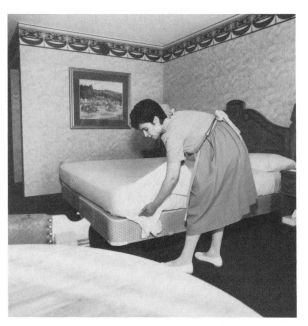

Figure 10.42 The night guestroom attendant services a late check-out to make the room ready for a late arriving guest. (Photo courtesy of the Excalibur Hotel, Las Vegas.)

2. Original and copies of all Senior Housekeeper's Daily Work Reports (original was given to each senior housekeeper; copy was used on the linen room counter to progress work by each division)

3. All Section Housekeeper's P.M. Reports

4. Copy of the Housekeeper's Report

5. Completed passkey/beeper control sheet

6. Night Supervisor's Report of Evening Activities

There will be numerous occasions when the above information will need to be researched. It is therefore imperative that it be retained for at least one year.

Computers Come of Age in the World of Housekeeping

The subject of **computers** and their application to the techniques of rooms management in hotel operations has at last come of age. Once confined to the realm of top management, statistical analysis, corporate planning payroll, and the like, state-of-the-art development of computer application to property management systems is now commonplace. The race to devise and provide economical information-handling and reporting systems has been nothing short of spectacular. Although the race goes on, **hardware** (input terminals, microprocessors, disk drive components, and printers) and hotel **software packages** (programs by which computers assimilate information) once thought to be out of reach of housekeeping personnel have become part of the daily routine of housekeeping operations. Computers are now just another tool to help housekeeping departments become more efficient in handling management information.

The development of computers is currently seen to be in its fifth generation. With each step into the future, computers have become less expensive, allowing even the smallest hotel the opportunity to modernize the efficient handling of information.

Although the hotel industry seems as ageless as history, the 1980s have introduced not only the computer into housekeeping information-handling, but also the **telephone switch** (system) as the vehicle by which computer technology is applied. Since every guestroom has one, the telephone has become the chief instrument for housekeeping to use in accessing the computer. This technique greatly reduces the cost of updating existing facilities since major expenses can be avoided in adding wiring to each individual room.

For example, an **interface** is created between the telephone system and the **central processing unit (CPU)** of the computer network. This is accomplished by the guestroom attendant dialing a specific sequence of numbers on the phone from a specific guestroom. Once connected, the computer immediately recognizes the room number to which it is being connected. After the connection, a specific list of **dial-up codes** becomes available to the GRA by which he or she can now transmit information. (Figure 10.43) shows the GRA dialing the special code from a room.

Assume the following scenario:

1. The GRA in Housekeeping Section 54 is currently in room [2025] and she wants to communicate with the computer. The special phone number of the computer is [71555].
2. GRA dials [71555] and hears a new and different dial tone. This tells her that she is connected to the computer.
3. The following list of three-digit codes are now available by which she can input information:

STATUS CODE	INFORMATION TRANSMITTED
111	Room is a *ON CHANGE* (A Check-Out - C/O)
112	Room is *Occupied* (Clean)
113	Room is *Occupied* (Dirty)
114	Room is *Vacant & READY* (Ready to Rent)
115	Room is *OUT OF SERVICE* (Maintenance) (This code can be read and acknowledged in the Maintenance Department and a maintenance person dispatched immediately.)
116	Room is Out-Of-Order (OOO) (This code is available only to the Maintenance Department to ensure that the Chief Engineer, who is ultimately responsible for returning [OOO] back to a service status, is aware of the situation.)
117	Room returned to operative status— Needs Housekeeping. (This code is available only to the Maintenance Department. It does *not* return the room to rentable status. Only housekeeping can do that after checking the room following whatever had to be done by Maintenance.)

Figure 10.43 Preparing to input information into the computer about a room ready for occupancy. (Photo courtesy of the Excalibur Hotel, Las Vegas.)

4. After dialing one of the codes (111–115), the GRA then dials his or her three-digit section number [027] which identifies him or her as the initiator of the message. If the message is a Code 116 or 117, a **special initiator code** must be assigned to a maintenance person before a code will be accepted by the computer.

After inputting information, room #2025 is identified as being in a specific **Rooms Inventory**. For example, this specific room now becomes identified in numerical order with other rooms in the same category such as ROOMS READY FOR SALE, OCCUPIED ROOMS NOT AVAILABLE FOR SALE, ROOMS THAT ARE ON CHANGE. (Between departing and newly arriving guest, not yet serviced (C/O)).

The GRA is not the only person who can make a status change entry for a guestroom. When the front desk clerk rents a room, a selection is made from the inventory of rooms identified as being READY FOR SALE. In the process of inputting check-in information for a guest, the desk clerk, through a **computer terminal**, changes the status of the room to OCCUPIED NOT (no longer) AVAILABLE FOR SALE. The front desk clerk can also put rooms into a special status, such as RUSH. Rooms in this status are rooms which have been **preassigned** and have guests waiting for them. These rooms are given priority attention by housekeeping from among other ON-CHANGE Rooms.

Housekeeping central operations can also make inputs into the system. Many times a status change needs to be reported that cannot be directly inputted from a guestroom (guest might be using the telephone, or is a *Do Not Disturb*). Status changes can be phoned into the *status board operator* in housekeeping. This information can then be inputted by the status board operator. (Figure 10.44).

At different times during the day, or on call, the status board operator can print out the status of all guestrooms at a given instant and provide floor supervisors information regarding their particular sections. Also, management can review total rooms status at any time by calling for a printout. (Figure 10.45).

This is an example of only one of many ways a computer can be employed in the management of guestroom information. New hotels can be wired for different types of systems that can give not only housekeeping information, but can turn on air conditioning systems and lights when a room becomes rented, tell whether or not the GRA is currently in a specific room, and, through the door-locking system, tell who were the last 24 persons to enter the room.

The *Night Clerk's Report*, opening the house, and the scheduling of work for supervisors and GRAs are now available through computers. Information about rooms not to be disturbed, rooms out of order, and late check-outs are updated and available, and P.M. Reports and information about rooms requiring immediate service or about turn-down requirements

Figure 10.44 The status board operator can also input information into the computer. (Photo courtesy of the Excalibur Hotel, Las Vegas.)

on specific rooms are created instantly. Room status discrepancies are handled efficiently, allowing for the cleaning of questionable rooms for reoccupancy earlier in the day.

As for spectacular advancement in the realm of computers for housekeeping, consider the following scenario:

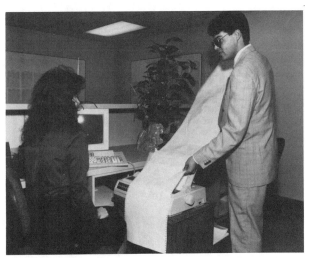

Figure 10.45 The assistant housekeeping manager reviews a status printout of all rooms at 4:00 P.M. (Photo courtesy of the Excalibur Hotel, Las Vegas.)

A supervisor or manager inspects a guestroom and records the findings vocally into a handheld tape recorder. Upon completion of the inspection, the recorder is *plugged into* a receptacle located in the guestroom. The inspection information is immediately transmitted to a **microprocessor** where it is voice read into a data memory bank. At any time from that moment on, a printout of inspection results for all rooms inspected is immediately available to the manager. Microprocessors have the capability to sort, codify, and classify information in such a fashion that inspection comments requiring maintenance work requests to engineering would be immediately transmitted. As work is completed, additional input from the guestroom would cause reports to be updated. Should rooms be necessarily held in out-of-order status, information would be available indicating the nature of the problem, corrective action being taken, and expected time the room will be back in service.

This is only one of many possible uses of computer applications in the housekeeping department. After you read Chapter 11, you will see many places in which computer application will also be beneficial. Remember, however, that before computer application becomes a reality, a thorough understanding of systems as they might be conducted *by hand* is most important; otherwise extraneous capability might be purchased when what might have been needed can only be found installed in the hotel across the street.

Summary

Recognizing that direction and control requires the communication of directive instructions and the accomplishment of many procedures, the simplest method of accomplishing direction of routine tasks is to communicate through forms. In this chapter the principal daily routine for the housekeeping department associated with the model hotel has been segmented and presented in a chronological manner. This is the major routine of the department that *recurs on a daily basis.*

First, routine information regarding which rooms would require service was communicated by a form to the housekeeping department. This in-

formation was then converted into meaningful information according to the plan of work established for the housekeeping department. Workers were then specifically assigned to work tasks according to the volume of work that had to be accomplished. This too was done through the use of forms in a procedure called opening the house. All of this was accomplished before workers reported for work. The workday was then segmented into several parts.

Morning activities included an explanation of the various activities of each member of the housekeeping team, the A.M. report and how the morning room inspection generated discrepancies in room status that had to be resolved with the front desk, the priority of room cleaning by the section housekeeper, and a technique of using forms and symbols for keeping up with the constantly changing status of rooms during the day. Procedures on how to clean a guestroom were also presented.

Then early afternoon presented a need to resolve the status of rooms that had been tagged do not disturb (DND) in the morning. A technique was presented to accomplish this task that gave primary consideration to the guest and guest safety.

In the afternoon the P.M. Report was conducted, which formed a basis for the executive housekeeper's report to the front desk as to the current an up-to-the-minute status of all guest rooms in the hotel as of about 3:00 P.M. This report was assembled under the direction of the supervisor of the second work shift who would later be required to recheck the status discrepancies of certain rooms that could not be resolved by the front desk. As these discrepancies were resolved, the balance of the workload for the day was finalized for the housekeeping department, and the second shift completed the workday about 11:00 P.M.

Other evening activities were presented including turn down service, servicing guest requests, and the collecting of all the day's paperwork into a package for filing.

There are many other procedures known as subroutines that are equally important but do not necessarily occur on a daily basis. Several of these subroutines will be addressed in Chapter 11. Once the routines are understood, any and all of them are capable of being adapted to computer operation.

KEY TERMS AND CONCEPTS		
	Housekeeping day	Plastic hang-up bag
	Daily routine chronology	Costume
	Opening the house	A.M. room check
	Morning activities	Occupied
	Changing rooms	Ready to rent
	Wardrobe departments	On change

Discrepancy
Double rooming
Progressing work
Communication symbols
Tidied
Linen-room central
Swag lamp
All-purpose cleaner
Germicidal cleaner
Special cleaning compounds
Acid bowl cleaner
Specified dilution ratios
HAZCOMM requirements
Lost-and-found procedures
Mitered corner
Snooze sheet
Portable beds
Damp-wipe
Stay-over rooms
Johnny mop
Amenity package
Suite hotel
Suite attendant
Security bar
Security chain
Room rate card
Quest for Quality Standards
    Placement Guide
First nighter kit

H.O.M.E.S. manual
Commitment to quality
Do Not Disturb (DND)
P.M. Room check
Section housekeeping aide
Specified dilutions ratios
Housekeeper's Report
Night Supervisor's Report of
    Evening Activities
Guest requests
Purify the room rack
Rechecked
Tidy
Made ready (M/R)
Room found vacant (RFV)
Skipped
Computers
Hardware
Software Packages
Telephone switch
Interface
Central processing unit (CPU)
Dial-up codes
Special initiator codes
Rooms inventory
Computer terminal
Pre-assigned
Micro-processor

DISCUSSION AND REVIEW QUESTIONS

1. Explain the different purposes of the A.M. and P.M. room checks. How can A.M. room checks be conducted so as to show maximum concern for guests?

2. Why are forms and symbols so important to the progressing of the daily routine in housekeeping departments? Define the following symbols: R, OCC, OOO, MR, T, CO, DND, RFV.

3. Explain the term discrepancy. What is the difference between a discrepancy and a recheck?

4. What are the reasons for maintaining a Night Supervisor's Report of Evening Activities?

5. During an A.M. room check, a senior housekeeper discovers two rooms thought to be ready rooms that have actually been occupied. What alternatives are available to facilitate this unexpected and additional workload?

6. List as many tasks as you can that are a part of the evening crew's responsibility. What is the last function normally performed by the night supervisor before securing the housekeeping department for the night? As part of the daily routine, what is the primary objective of the evening?

11

Hotel Housekeeping Subroutines

CHAPTER OBJECTIVES

1. To learn about other vital functions of the hotel house-keeping department—subroutines.
2. To understand that subroutines differ from the daily routine only in that they are performed from time to time rather than daily.
3. To learn how subroutines can be standardized and systematized by using standard operating procedures.
4. To see why preplanning of subroutines is important.

In Chapter 10 the primary housekeeping function of the department was presented as a chronology of events that normally constitutes the daily routine. There are many other functions, however, with which the housekeeping department may become involved. They are also best presented as routines, even though they do not all take place on a daily basis. These routines, which we call **subroutines**, are vital to total operations and should be given equal planning attention with the daily routine.

Subroutines can be presented through standard operating procedures (SOPs), several of which have been shown in Chapter 9 (lost-and-found procedures, key control, and procedures for changing door locks). It may appear that much of what will be described in this chapter cannot be delegated without abdication of responsibilities. This is not a correct assumption, as the astute professional manager will realize. Budgeting, for example, occurs so seldom (once a year) that junior managers may never have an opportunity to become involved before they are transferred and/or promoted. Every manager within the department therefore must become involved at every opportunity if professional development is to take place.

Table 11.1 contains topical areas and associated routines that will be encountered in most housekeeping operations from time to time, and, rather than be considered exceptions to the daily routine, should be thought of as subroutines. A detailed analysis of each of the subroutines in Table 11.1 is worthy of the executive housekeeper's time and effort in order that they also become routines rather than exceptions to the daily routine.

As with the daily routine, subroutines lend themselves to control by forms. Some require only limited planning and policy formulation regarding their substance, whereas others need detailed planning and careful implementation. We will now look at each of these subroutines, keeping in mind the importance of proper delegation on overall department morale, effectiveness, and efficiency of operation.

Cleaning and Maintenance

Public Area Cleaning

Section housekeepers are efficiently used when their efforts are confined to the guestroom areas of the hotel. The section housekeeping aide provides sup-

port to the housekeeping team and performs certain duties related to the maintenance of guestroom corridors (Figure 11.1), stairwells, elevators, vending areas, and satellite linen room stocking and maintenance. There are, however, other areas that require cleaning and maintenance throughout a facility and for which the executive housekeeper is responsible.

In the Division of Work Document presented in Chapter 2, we saw that there may be many **public areas** under the executive housekeeper's umbrella of responsibility that require daily if not hourly attention. Hotel lobbies, public restrooms, lobby thoroughfares, offices, banquet area restrooms, employee locker rooms, and assorted service areas require scheduled cleaning and maintenance. Such functions normally fall under the supervisory responsibility of the senior housekeeping aide, who should be a specialist in unique cleaning and maintenance tasks. Recalling the established organization for the model hotel, the lobby housekeepers, housekeeping aides, and utility housekeeping personnel normally report to the senior housekeeping aide and are available for the large number of specialized tasks that must be performed. Such personnel should be uniquely uni-

Table 11.1 Topical Areas and Routines

TOPICAL AREA	SUBROUTINE
Cleaning and maintenance	Public area cleaning
	General cleaning of guest rooms
	Projects
	Maintenance work-request programs
Operation controls	Room inspections
	Total property inspections
	Inventories
	Personnel use (forecasting and analysis)
	Period statement critiques
Purchasing	Cleaning and guest supplies
	Linens
Personnel administration	Time card control
	Payroll administration
	Performance appraisals
Communication and training	Departmental meetings
Long-range planning	Budget formulation

Figure 11.1 While the guestroom attendants are servicing guestrooms, the housekeeping aide vacuums a hallway in the guestroom area. (Courtesy of the Excalibur Hotel.)

formed and temperamentally suited for work among the general public.

Cleaning and maintenance circuits (rounds) need to be established in order that all areas of concern are kept under control. The straightening and repositioning of furniture, the emptying of ash urns and ashtrays, the cleaning of smudges from glass doors and mirrors, and the servicing of public restrooms can require attention as little as once every eight hours and as often as once every 15 minutes, depending upon the circumstances (See Figures 11.2 through 11.5). Employees functioning under the senior housekeeping aide must be trained to respond to these needs without immediate and direct supervision.

Special initiative might be expected of the lobby housekeeper to modify the cleaning circuit based on observations of crowds as they migrate through the hotel. For example, lack of activity in the lobby during certain hours of the day would indicate that less attention is required once an area has been properly serviced. Times of heavy check-in may warrant the prolonged and continued attention of the lobby housekeeper to the point that this person cannot leave the specific lobby area until the crowd subsides.

Supplies and equipment must be suitable and, where necessary, specialized for the tasks. Standard equipment for lobby personnel is a specially designed cart that is stocked with necessary supplies. Kex floor mops (special hard floor mops treated with a dust-attracting chemical), vacuum cleaners, and dusting materials are carried on carts with good

Figure 11.3 A public area housekeeping aide polishes a drinking fountain. (Courtesy of the Excalibur Hotel.)

trash-handling capability and paper supply transport. The lobby housekeeper and aide should be equipped to handle not only routine tasks, but they should have specialized equipment on hand, such as paint scrapers to keep ahead of (or behind) those who deposit chewing gum on concrete walks, hard floors, or even carpets. Indoor hard surfaces such as decorative Mexican clay tile or terrazzo floors require specialized equipment for cleaning and maintenance. In most cases, carpet shampooing requires the use of special equipment and skills in equipment maintenance. Normally, specially trained employees who

Figure 11.2 Public area housekeeping aides may work on a cleaning circuit. Here is one touching up a public restroom sink. (Courtesy of the Excalibur Hotel.)

Figure 11.4 Back to the restroom for another touch-up. The public area housekeeping aide may pass this way many times during his shift. (Courtesy of the Excalibur Hotel.)

Figure 11.5 The night lobby housekeeper services an employee dressing room. (Courtesy of the Excalibur Hotel.)

perform work such as carpet shampooing will be under the direction of the senior housekeeping aide.

After the day shift has been relieved by the second shift, the night supervisor is responsible for public area cleaning and maintenance as well as guestroom cleaning. The senior housekeeping aide and the night supervisor are therefore vital to the success of the overall housekeeping operation. The executive housekeeper should work to establish, then strengthen the technical and supervisory skills of these two employees. Most of all, the executive housekeeper should delegate properly and then allow these supervisors the opportunity to do their jobs and not interfere other than to coach and counsel in the performance of assigned tasks.

Both the senior housekeeping aide and night supervisor should be involved in establishing the standard operating procedures for performance of public area housekeeping and in developing job descriptions for employees under their control. Although actual employment is a management decision, these two supervisors should be allowed to question and give indication of their approval of any employee considered for assignment to areas under their supervisory control.

General Cleaning of Guestrooms

The routine servicing of guestrooms normally includes removing rubbish, changing linens, thoroughly cleaning bathrooms, vacuuming floors (when necessary), lightly dusting or damp-wiping flat sur-

faces, and setting up and supplying the room for the next stay-over guest. Guestrooms also need a periodic **general** or **deep cleaning**.

Tasks such as high dusting, vacuuming drapes and casements, wiping down walls, cleaning carpet edges and vent filters, moving beds and furniture, and turning mattresses must be performed on a regular but not daily basis. The frequency of such general cleanings depends on heaviness of use, weather conditions, and quality of routine maintenance.

General cleaning can be performed by the section housekeeper or by a special team of employees who do nothing other than general cleaning of rooms. I have been involved with operations in which guestrooms were general cleaned by section housekeepers assisted by section housekeeping aides, as well as with operations in which a specialized team was used to do nothing but general clean guestrooms. My experience strongly favors general cleaning by regular personnel; the added workload is not necessarily so difficult that additional personnel must be added to the staff for this task.

A good general cleaning should take approximately twice as long as a routine room servicing. For example, consider a typical day of 8½ hours. Remember that each employee has 30 minutes for lunch and two 15-minute breaks, leaving 7½ hours for work. Let us assume that a section housekeeper can service three rooms routinely in one hour and needs ½ hour to service the housekeeping cart at the end of the day. Depending on the nature of the hotel and its clientele, each section housekeeper can service from 14 to 20 rooms per day. This leaves 15 minutes to add to one room for deep cleaning. If each section housekeeper general cleans one assigned room each day, each room will receive a deep cleaning once every 15–20 days.

The section housekeeping aide also becomes involved in general cleaning because of the need to move furniture and perform high dusting of several rooms. A section housekeeping aide may be required to help more than one section housekeeper. If the section housekeeping aide becomes overloaded, a utility housekeeping aide might be employed to assist in the general cleaning of guestrooms. Senior housekeepers (team supervisors) should keep records of rooms that have received general cleaning in order that each room receive such cleaning on a regular basis.

Projects

The management of every housekeeping department requires the performance of occasional special **projects**. Periodic shampooing of a specific carpeted area, stripping and refinishing a hard surfaced floor, removing scuff marks on a seldom-used but accountable space, and cleaning and sanitizing rubbish-handling equipment are projects that must be scheduled from time to time based on someone's observation during an inspection. These projects are usually the purview of the senior housekeeping aide. The results of an early morning inspection conducted by the senior housekeeping aide (see Figure 10.5) may lead to such projects.

Special projects are performed by utility personnel under supervision. Records of projects should be maintained and reviewed periodically to determine the extent of man-hours being expended on this type of work. Many projects can be eliminated in the future by making them part of routine work. Additionally, projects justify the maintenance of man-hour expenditure records that can later be used to substantiate the need for additional budgeted hours in the staffing of the department.

Maintenance Work-Request Programs

Many times the quality and condition of a facility can be assessed by investigating the relationship that exists between the executive housekeeper and the chief engineer. When this relationship is positive and the people are mutually respectful of each other's responsibilities and workload, the physical appearance of a hotel will be excellent. When such positive relationships do not exist, property inspections will reveal little in addition to what might be expected—a substandard facility.

I recall a philosophy told to me by a ruddy up-through-the-ranks chief during my initial housekeeping training:

> You keep the place clean, and if you can't clean it like it was new, let me know and I'll replace it or repair it so you can; but I need your *eyes* in the hotel because I can't be everywhere at one time and I don't have the staff to look for problems.

Specifically, the chief engineer is charged with the **repair and physical maintenance** of a hotel facility (maintenance not referring to guestroom servicing). The executive housekeeper is responsible for cleanliness and maintenance (servicing) of specific areas. The housekeeping department staff is much larger than the engineering department and is therefore in a better position to look for and find areas in need of repair and maintenance. The major concern is to have a reporting and follow-up system between the two departments that allows for the orderly flow of information. Figure 11.6 is a standard form used for requesting repair and maintenance services not available through normal cleaning.

YOUR HOTEL

○

Maintenance work request   Serial no. 0261248

Requested by _____ Date _____
Dept _____
Location _____
Problem _____
_____
_____
_____
_____

Assigned to _____
Date completed _____
Completed by _____
Work time required   Hrs. _____ /Min. ____
Remarks _____
_____
_____
_____

Figure 11.6 A typical Maintenance Work-Request Form, which has two soft copies and one hard copy. These serialized records are kept for the disposition of all problems and discrepancies.

The **Maintenance Work-Request Form** is composed of two soft copies and one hard copy and is serialized for easy reference when communicating about a reported discrepancy. The top copy (usually soft white) is filled out and kept by the department initiating the report; the other two copies are forwarded to engineering, where the request is logged in so that materials can be ordered and work scheduled. When work is completed, the balance of the form is filled in and the second (soft blue) copy is returned to the initiating department for comparison and progressing of the original request. Work is then inspected, and, if completed satisfactorily, the soft (white and blue) Work Request Forms may be destroyed. The hard (bottom) copy remains with the engineering department as a record of time and materials expended.

The system is simple, but in many cases it is not used in a manner that will ensure that repair and maintenance are properly accomplished. The secret to a successful maintenance and repair program stems from understanding two important precepts: (1) the executive housekeeper will not be allowed to dictate the priorities of the chief engineer's workload, and (2) paper is cheap.

If the discrepancy is not corrected in a reasonable period of time, write it out again and mark it **second request**. Should there be a parts or material problem, the chief engineer may communicate this fact to the executive housekeeper and indicate that further Maintenance Work Request forms will be unnecessary. Additionally, second requests might indicate that the priority of the engineer's workload precludes the immediate response to certain types of requests, or that the engineering department will schedule certain service requests with others of a similar nature (such as vinyl repairs, furniture repairs, and painting). Items that will cause a guestroom to be out of order should be given the highest priority by the chief engineer.

If a property is to be kept in a proper state of repair, there will be an abundance of Maintenance Work Requests, many of which will be repeated. The age of a property will determine how many requests from the housekeeping department might be in the pipeline at any given time. The prime consideration is remembering that personnel in the housekeeping department are the "eyes" of the engineering department in areas under the responsibility of the executive housekeeper and that *everything not in order and not cleanable must be repaired* if the property is to be maintained in a like-new condition.

The executive housekeeper must develop a system that fosters the writing of Maintenance Work Requests. It is best to *require* that a certain number of Maintenance Work Requests be written by the department each week. Such specific requirements help ensure that every defect has a chance of being reported. Examples of what should be reported are minor tears in hallway and room vinyl, chips and scratches in furniture, leaky faucets, broken lamp switches, and burned-out light bulbs (not under the purview of housekeeping). Areas in need of paint, noisy air conditioners, bad TV reception, minor carpet repair problems (seams coming unglued), doors that rattle when closed, and unsightly tile caulking in bathtubs are also subject to Maintenance Work Requests.

I recall systems whereby all supervisors and department managers were required to write a minimum of 10 work orders each week. Such a requirement forced the "look" so greatly needed by the engineering department. When I was an executive housekeeper, I wrote 40 work orders each week. Those 40, in addition to ones written by other department managers and supervisors, totaled over 100 work orders each week. The property was six years old but looked new because the systems described here were meticulously followed.

Another system whereby the executive housekeeper and chief engineer would cooperate is combining the general cleaning program with the maintenance program. Clarence R. Johnson[1] suggests that each month 25 percent of the rooms receiving a general deep cleaning should also receive a thorough **maintenance inspection**. Every room would therefore be completely checked three times a year and maintained in a near-perfect condition. Figure 11.7 is an example of a **Maintenance Checklist** proposed by Johnson that could be used in such a program.

Proper relationships inspiring mutual cooperation between the executive housekeeper and the chief engineer may at times be difficult to maintain. This usually stems from differences in background. This fact, however, should in now way detract from the *professional effort* necessary to make a relationship work for the good of the property. Gentle persistence and persuasion are usually the key and can cause strong relationships to grow.

Operational Controls

Room Inspections

Methods of conducting **room inspections** of guestrooms may take many forms. Additionally, room inspections may be given great, varied, or no emphasis, depending on the management style of the hotel's

MAINTENANCE CHECKLIST

☐ CHECKED   ☐ NEEDS REPAIR   ■ REPAIR COMPLETED

Room No. _____

AIR CONDITIONERS

☐ 1. Switches/controls/valves—check operation

☐ 2. Thermostat dial positioned, works correctly

☐ 3. Thermostat probe secure, calibrated, working

☐ 4. Filter—clean

☐ 5. Fan & fan motor—clean, lubricated, secure

☐ 6. Evaporator and condenser—clean

☐ 7. Condensation pan & drain—clean

☐ 8. Exterior grill—clean, maintained to complement building exterior

☐ 9. Compressor—clean

☐ 10. Check for leaks in refrigeration system

☐ 11. Check electric plug, receptacles, cord

☐ 12. Heating unit, clean & operating correctly

ELECTRICAL

☐ 13. Lamp switches on/off-3 way working correctly

☐ 14. Lamp sockets & swivels, tight, in good repair

☐ 15. Lamp shades, clean, no holes, secure

☐ 16. Light bulb—replace burned, check wattage

☐ 17. Plugs, cords & connections, repair as needed

☐ 18. Lamp base/body in good repair

☐ 19. Light switches on/off—working and in good repair

☐ 20. Switch & outlet wallplates—good repair and match in color

☐ 21. Wall sockets/receptacles operate, no shorts

☐ 22. Timer switches work correctly, knob secure

☐ 23. Heat lamps, correct wattage, clean, good repair

☐ 24. All light fixtures are clean, dust free, complementary to room decor

TELEVISION

☐ 25. Audio—clear (radio and television)

☐ 26. Visual—in focus (check each station)

☐ 27. Knobs—replace, if necessary

☐ 28. Fine tune—color contrast, horizontal, vertical

☐ 29. Antenna—cable connections secure

☐ 30. Chassis/screen—clean, dust-free, no apparent damage—security mounts secure

TELEPHONE

☐ 31. Overall appearance & condition—clean, good repair

☐ 32. Dialing instructions—replace if faded

☐ 33. Defects (good connections, audio good, bell works, etc.) report to telephone company

FURNITURE

☐ 34. Drawer handles, knobs tight, good repair and drawer guides lubricated

Figure 11.7 Maintenance Checklist identifies furniture, fixtures, and equipment in the guestroom. Each month 25 percent of the rooms should be inspected and necessary repairs made. Thus, every room would be completely checked three times a year. Records should be kept of the date the room is checked and work completed. (Reprinted with permission of Lodging Magazine.)

department heads and general managers. Some hotels employ **inspectors and inspectresses**—people whose only operational function is to inspect guestrooms and report their findings. Other hotels never inspect guestrooms, and still others have sophisticated inspection procedures.

A project for students in a senior housekeeping management class in the Las Vegas area was for them to survey inspection techniques of several hotels. Students had to describe the results and effectiveness of the inspection programs they surveyed. Certain hotels employed inspectors and inspectresses, others used floor supervisors to inspect every room

before its being reported ready for occupancy, others had periodic room inspections by a general manager, and some had no inspection programs at all.

Results were measured by the appearance and cleanliness of guestrooms inspected. Surprisingly, those hotels employing inspectresses did not fare well in the surveys; nor did hotels with elaborate inspection forms used regularly by supervisors. Hotels with well-maintained and very clean rooms were those that were intermittently inspected, or **spotchecked**, by people in the operational supervisory chain (floor supervisors, section managers, the executive housekeeper, sometimes section housekeepers,

☐ 35. Mattresses and box springs, good repair, turned clean, etc.

☐ 36. All furniture surfaces—stains, scratches, damages, repair

☐ 37. Chairs (cushions, legs, brace springs) repair/replace as needed

☐ 38. Tables/desks—tops and bases tight, stable and in good repair

☐ 39. Headboards—secure, clean top and front

☐ 40. Nightstands—stable, stain and scratch-free

☐ 41. Bedbox/bedrails and castors clean and in good repair

☐ 42. Pictures secure, clean, good condition, color coordinated with room

WINDOW AND MIRRORS

☐ 43. Window guides and latches clean, work easily

☐ 44. Window trim clean, caulk in good repair

☐ 45. Drapery hardware (rod, pulls, cord, mounting, pin, hooks) all in good repair

☐ 46. Mirror(s) condition, hangers secure, no scratches or mars

SLIDING DOORS/WINDOWS

☐ 47. Tracks clean and in good repair

☐ 48. Guides, wheels are clean to slide freely

☐ 49. Doorstop and bumpers present so doors close quietly and securely

☐ 50. Latches—primary and secondary security—are effective

DOORS, ENTRANCES

☐ 51. Handles—check and secure

☐ 52. Lock cylinder, key hole, condition & operation

☐ 53. Hinges, hinge pins lubricated, secure

☐ 54. Door chain/deadbolt, securely attached, and working correctly

☐ 55. Lock striker and check plates secure to prevent unauthorized entry

☐ 56. Door frame, bumpers, replace as necessary

☐ 57. Weatherstripping in good repair, replace as needed

☐ 58. Threshold is secure, replace rubber inserts if needed

☐ 59. Door fit (security, energy and noise control) smooth and tight

☐ 60. Peepholes correctly installed, clean

☐ 61. Door condition—check for holes, need of cleaning, repair

☐ 62. Door stops in place to prevent damage to handle or wall

BATHROOM/VANITIES

☐ 63. Bathtub safety strips, clean and in good condition

☐ 64. Tub and lavatory drain, plugs, popups, strainer clean and working

☐ 65. Shower head secure, clean, has correct spray pattern

☐ 66. Bath tile and walls—check for loose tiles, grout holes, need for caulking

☐ 67. Toilet flush and drain—no excess noise, leaks

☐ 68. Toilet tank, tank top, clean, no cracks, secure to base

☐ 69. Seat, hinges, bumpers all in good repair—replace if in doubt

☐ 70. Toilet seal—check evidence of leaks

☐ 71. Hot, cold faucets—check for leaks.

☐ 72. Shower/mixing valve doesn't leak

☐ 73. Chrome fixture appearance is bright—clean/replace if needed

☐ 74. Shower rod, curtain, clean, chrome or plastic sleeve

☐ 75. Basin "P" trap is clean, no leaks

☐ 76. Tub and basin appearance is free of scratches

☐ 77. Toilet paper holder, properly mounted, clean

☐ 78. Facial tissue holder secure and clean

☐ 79. Soap dish & grab bars are secure, good repair

☐ 80. Towel racks—fastened securely, good repair

☐ 81. Vanity top/cabinet not marred, clean, attractive

Figure 11.7 *(continued)*

occasionally someone outside the department, and especially the hotel general manager). Inspection forms that stated simple and reasonable standards of performance were also in evidence in these hotels. (Refer to Figure 1.2, noting a guestroom inspection form whereby *standards* are indicated for the several areas of concern that might be encountered in a guestroom. A simple check mark indicates that the standard is being met, that items need improvement, or that an item was unsatisfactory. An indication of "unsatisfactory" must be corrected before the room is rented.)

Inspectresses outside of the operational framework for cleaning guestrooms (floor supervisors and section housekeepers) risk nothing if they complain heavily about substandard items or conditions, since

☐ 82. Floor(s) clean & in good repair

☐ 83. Light switches, heat lamp & timer switch work correctly

☐ 84. Bath privacy lock works correctly

☐ 85. Exhaust fan is clean, lubricated, operating correctly and efficiently

GENERAL ITEMS

☐ 86. Coat racks/hangers clean, secure, sufficient number

☐ 87. Baseboards, secure to wall, clean, free of scratches

☐ 88. Carpets—no stains, holes repaired, no ripples or loose curls

☐ 89. Wall covering/paint condition—all holes, scratches, tears repaired

☐ 90. Ceiling—check if clean; no cracks, peeling paint, stains

☐ 91. Smoke detectors checked, batteries replaced

☐ 92. Air leaks or insulation effectively repaired

☐ 93. Hot water set at correct temperature (120°)

GENERAL AREAS

☐ 94. Emergency exit lights, signs in good condition

☐ 95. Fire extinguishers in place, fully charged

☐ 96. Automatic door closers working properly

☐ 97. Luggage carts clean & in good repair

☐ 98. Stairway handrails are secure

☐ 99. Sidewalk, exterior walkways, good repair, clean

☐100. Interior hallways—well lighted, carpet clean and in good repair

☐101. Stairs free of debris, no loose treads, handrails, etc.

☐102. Emergency lighting system—checked & operating

☐103. Background music/public address system is effective

☐104. Emergency exits kept clear of hazards, panic bars work correctly

Figure 11.7 (*continued*)

they would not be held accountable for correcting them. These inspectresses are therefore resented by those having to do the work. Human dynamics dictates that the inspectresses would be better liked if they did not complain heavily about discrepancies. Floor supervisors who spot-check employees assigned to operational control are much more likely to find solutions to substandard performance and, as a result, improve the performance of employees. Spot-checking two or three rooms each day from each section seems to give all the indication needed to bring about top quality performance from each employee. Such action also allows each section housekeeper to report her or his own rooms ready for reoccupancy, thus enriching the job and improving efficiency of communication between housekeeping and the front desk.

There is also much to be said about displaying trust and confidence in employees, which is a great motivator for proper performance. Additionally, most section housekeepers are proud of their work and look forward to exposing the results of their efforts to those in authority. It is for this reason that the executive housekeeper and the resident and/or general manager should regularly inspect guestrooms. The importance of managers inspecting guestrooms regularly cannot be overemphasized. Not only is the inspection of the room paramount, but the opportunity for the manager to associate with his or her employees on the job is of great importance.

There are over 600 employees in the housekeeping organization at the Excalibur Hotel in Las Vegas. Such a large number of employees can present a layering problem within the organization that might be hard to overcome. There will always be a few problem employees, but those who are outstanding need the "positive stroke" of the manager who cares about his or her employees as individuals. When the work is well done, some well-placed humor helps to express warmth and acknowledge the value of a good employee (Figure 11.8 applies).

Such expectation of inspections by higher authority usually brings about an added emphasis on total work quality on **inspection day** and, as a result, tends to improve the appearance of each room cleaned.

A technique of inspection that has merit in areas in which specific employees are not performing up to standard is to let the section housekeeper conduct the inspection in the presence of the designated inspector and supervisor. Specifically, the person inspecting invites the person who cleaned the room to inspect and report while the manager or supervisor writes notes on the inspection form. This technique has proved enlightening to many section housekeepers who must, in the presence of their supervisor and manager, expose not only their questionable work but also their quality work.

Inspection programs for guestrooms should be conducted in such a way that quality performance is amply noted and publicized. Programs involving

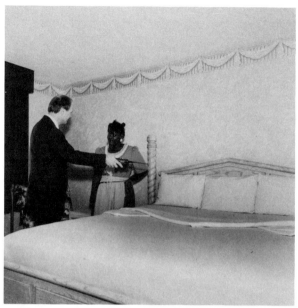

Figure 11.8 Mike Burns, Executive Housekeeper, Excalibur Hotel in Las Vegas, adds a touch of humor to his comment to one of his guestroom attendants during a room inspection. Burns asks, "I see the nice 'Butterfly Turndown'; now how many butterflies did you put *under* the covers?"

"the housekeeper of the week" who earns points toward a meaningful prize over some given time period is effective in motivating employees to excel. Section housekeepers must understand that their reputation as a rooms attendant will never be better than the weakest of all room attendants. This information reminds each of them that they need and must support each other to accomplish quality work and fosters commitment to standards.

Another technique whereby room appearance and cleanliness can be made to flourish is with a team system of reward. In earlier chapters the team system of scheduling for guestroom maintenance was presented for the model hotel. Performance systems were designed whereby each section housekeeper was expected to clean 18 guestrooms in each eight-hour shift. There are programs whereby each team that properly finishes its work has rooms spot-checked by an outside supervisor or manager and, given proper results, is provided with an added incentive of leaving early and receiving credit for the full eight-hour shift. (This would only be allowed on a team basis, never on an individual basis; otherwise the team aspect of performance could be destroyed.)

In summary, room inspections are essential to quality guestroom cleanliness and servicing and should be conducted regularly. The more efficient systems do not involve the total inspection of every guestroom cleaned. Spot inspections, properly recorded by floor supervisors, department managers,

and the general manager have proven to be the most effective form of room inspection program. Recognition should be given for quality work, and work incentives should be created to encourage high-quality performances, especially team performance.

Total Property Inspections

If hotels are to be maintained as top quality facilities, it is not enough that the executive housekeeper inspect only guestrooms or, for that matter, be the only one who does inspect rooms. Not only does the entire property require a thorough, regular, and carefully orchestrated **property inspection program**, but guestrooms need to be looked at by more than one management person. A **fresh look** is needed to ensure that items viewed but not seen are eventually picked up for correction. Managers above the executive housekeeper in the table of organization may delegate the task of rooms maintenance to the executive housekeeper but may not abdicate their own responsibility of ensuring that the hotel is properly maintained.

Other departments also have cleaning responsibilities. The restaurant manager, bar manager, chef, and catering manager have large areas for which they are held accountable for proper cleaning, maintenance, and safe operation. The chief engineer may be held accountable for the entire outside area of the facility, including shrubs, grounds, and parking areas.

In the Division of Work Document in Chapter 2, the executive housekeeper was instrumental in ensuring that each part of the property was permanently assigned to a specific department manager for upkeep. Thus, there should be a manager responsible for every square foot, corner, and crack of the hotel. The Division of Work Document should in fact be used to establish a zone inspection program (see below) whereby every part of the property is identified and periodically looked at to ensure that proper maintenance, cleanliness, and safety of both space and operation are being maintained.

Finally, the fresh look we mentioned not only brings another pair of eyes into an area, it also allows for orientation and development of management personnel in areas in which they may not normally be operationally involved. A property inspection that uses the front office manager to inspect housekeeping and the executive housekeeper to inspect kitchens is good training for future growth and development of managers for promotion and greater responsibilities.

Zone Inspection

There are many inspections that might be conducted on a subroutine basis, but none should be more thorough and, as a result, more beneficial to total property maintenance than the **zone inspection program**. **Zones** are usually created by dividing the entire facility into equal parts, whereby each inspector is responsible for an equal workload in a given period of time. Zone inspections should be conducted in not more than three hours, otherwise they lose effectiveness.

The inspection should be **documented**, and a technique must be developed whereby the person or persons responsible for each zone of the inspection may react to items found deficient and corrective measures taken before the next inspection. Documentation about unsafe conditions is also important. Liability in claims regarding negligence may be greatly reduced if it can be shown through documentation that regular, thorough, and controlled inspections of an entire property are conducted and that there is adequate follow-up on significant items.

In 1982, while acting as consultant to the Tropicana Hotel in Las Vegas, Nevada, I was instrumental in establishing a zone inspection program for that property. This particular program not only inaugurated the use of senior managers as chief inspectors, but it also involved junior managers in the inspection of each zone. Because of the size of this property, junior managers, who might otherwise never come in contact with operations other than those of their primary concern, had a vehicle for learning about, understanding, and respecting the contributions of other employees. The inspection program was developed into a standard operating procedure and is in use today. This inspection program is presented in Appendix E. Study the format, analyzing the delegation, communication, and control of this procedure as a subroutine.

Weekly Maintenance Inspections

Although zone inspections are all-encompassing for the entire property, there may be times when a particular zone is not inspected because of prior superior condition. This does not preclude public area portions of the rooms department from receiving a regular **weekly maintenance inspection** that is conducted by the senior housekeeping aide or a department manager. Figure 11.9 is an example of a Weekly Maintenance Inspection form that could be used by the rooms department supervisor at the end of each week, usually on Friday evenings, to ensure that the property was in proper condition before the weekend.

Figure 11.9 can also be used to record "quality points" for work well done. People assigned to clean public areas in a rooms department can thus be included in an incentive program with other housekeeping department personnel.

Inventories

In Chapters 4 through 7, we listed various categories of **inventories** with which the executive housekeeper might become involved. There are some subroutines related to ordering and keeping track of these inventories. Items of furniture, fixtures, and equipment (identified as FFE) along with software items (bedspreads and so on) form the basis of capital expenditures. These items have limited useful lives and are depreciated over several years. Other material items are operational in nature and are expended over much shorter business cycles (usually a four-week or monthly period); they are part of the cost of doing business in the production of revenue over the same period of time. Items such as cleaning supplies, guest supplies, and the amortized cost of basic bed and bath linens are among costs that occur monthly. Not only must the expenditure of such supplies and linens be expensed against revenue produced, such items that are on hand form the basis of balance sheet assets and must be periodically accounted for. Thus, use, balances on hand, and supply levels are critical **control information** that must be routinely maintained to ensure availability of materials when needed.

Figure 11.10 is a **Cleaning and Guest Supply Inventory** for a typical property. Note the units by which certain supply items are purchased and/or shipped. Note also the column marked "Par Stock." This column might also be marked "Minimum on Hand," allowing the manager to review counts and determine if stock levels are falling too low. According to this example, ice buckets are normally shipped in case lots (CS), each case containing six dozen items (6 DZ). It has a .5 par, which indicates that supply on hand should not fall below one-half case before reordering.

Figure 11.10 can also be used as a **count sheet** when conducting a routine inventory. The last column would be used to indicate how many of an item should be ordered at the next available opportunity.

Figure 11.11 is an **Inventory Record Log** that can be used to record information in an inventory logbook or journal. This type of log describes usage during a given period, how supplies were used, current pricing information, and the value of supplies on hand. Hotel **controllers** expect that these types of records are maintained and that inventories are conducted on a regular and routine basis.

The cost of operations should include only that portion of inventory that has been used up during the period. Such costs should not include the value of amounts purchased but still on hand. Most hotel controllers agree that unopened cases of supplies on

```
SENIOR HOUSEKEEPING AIDE
WEEKLY MAINTENANCE INSPECTION

                              Date _____ Time _____
                              Inspected by _____

Linen Room                    Vending
  Linen carts—well              Waste cans (clean, not
  supplied            _____      full)                  _____
  Floor               _____    Floor                    _____
  Shelves—neat        _____    Vending machine (top,
  No extras—Wire                side, front)            _____
  hangers             _____    Ice machine             _____
            Glasses            Elevator
            Trays                Door (inside and out)  _____
            Trash                Walls                  _____
  Neat general appearance _____  Stainless steel        _____
Hallway                          Carpet                 _____
  Carpet edges        _____      Ceiling                _____
  Carpet              _____
  Baseboards          _____
  Fire extinguisher   _____
  Fire boxes and bells _____
  Ashtrays            _____
  Wall guards         _____
  Windows (inside)    _____
  Window sills        _____
  Air conditioner     _____
  No cobwebs          _____
  Neat general appearance _____
Stairway/Stairwell
  Handrails and pipes _____
  Floor               _____
  Corners             _____
  Doors               _____
  Neat general appearance _____  Total points _____
```

Figure 11.9 Senior housekeeping aide's Weekly Maintenance Inspection form provides a checklist of areas to be surveyed during an inspection, which is usually performed on Friday evenings. The form has a place to record quality points so that housekeeping aides may be included in performance competition.

hand will be valued at full price in inventory. Once a case is opened, however, items are considered expended. There may be exceptions to this rule, allowing departments to account for individual items remaining in storage in opened cases at full price. Individual items out of the main storeroom that can be sighted in satellite linen rooms may also be considered in inventory. Once established, whatever accounting systems are specified by the controller must be followed.

Storage

Operational supply storage rooms must be closely controlled and access to storerooms limited only to personnel in charge. Certain items of high unit cost or high usage such as specialty soaps might even warrant cage storage to prevent pilferage. Operations in which storage rooms are thrown open for the day

usually have inordinate supply costs, and profits are proportionally affected. Tight storeroom controls are usually evidenced by cleaning supply costs that do not exceed three-tenths of 1 percent of revenues and guestroom supply costs that are within six-tenths of 1 percent.

Personnel Utilization

Another important subroutine is the weekly (or sometimes daily) **forecasting of man-hour requirements**—the most expensive operational cost in the entire rooms department. Executive housekeepers should be involved in the annual budgeting process (discussed later) whereby they help determine man-hour requirements based on budgeted occupancies. Once the budget has been established, it is imperative that a weekly forecast of expected

CLEANING AND GUEST SUPPLY INVENTORY

Date _____   Inventoried by _____

Item	Units	Units on hand	Par stock	Reorder (X)
Laundry bags	BDL/500		2	
Laundry lists	EA/250		250	
Room service menus	EA		500	
Stationery bags	CS/1000		1	
Stationery	CS/10 PK		1	
Envelopes	CS/1000		1	
Postcards	CS/10 BX		1	
"Tell us" forms	CS/500		1.5	
Sanitary bags	CS/1000		1	
Utility bags	CS/1000		1.5	
Guest services directory	EA/		500	
"Choose your credit"	EA/		500	
Advance reg. forms	EA/		1000	
Hotel maps	CS/		1000	
Facial tissue	CS/36 BX		3	
Toilet tissue	CS/96 RL		2	
Bath soap	CS/500		5	
Toilet seat strips	CS/10,000		.5	
Name cards	CS/		1	
AM EX. Applications	CS/		.5	
100W	CS/		.5	
Light bulbs 60W	CS/		.5	
Phone books	EA/		25	
Bibles	EA/		12	
Wood	CS/50		.5	

Figure 11.10 Cleaning and Guest Supply Inventory form, indicating units by which items are ordered and shipped, par stock, units on hand, and quantities to be reordered.

CLEANING AND GUEST SUPPLY INVENTORY

Date _____   Inventoried by _____

Item	Units	Units on hand	Par stock	Reorder (X)
Hangers (plastic)	CS/50		.5	
Ashtrays	CS/48		2	
Ashtrays (gold)	CS/6		.5	
Ice buckets	CS/6 DZ		.5	
Trays	CS/12		2	
Waste baskets	CS/12		1.5	
Matches	CS/50 BX		1	
Phone pads	CS/500		.5	
Do-not-disturb signs	PK/100		.5	
Garbage bags	CS/100		2	
Glass wrap	CS/12 RL		2 RL	
Dust mop treatment	GAL/		.25	
Bathroom cleaner	DRUM/55 G		.25	
Tablecloths	EA/		12	
Glasses	CS/36		24	
Scrubbing sponge	CS/40		.5	
Brooms	CS/12		.5	
Vinegar	CS/6 G		.5	
Trigger sprayers	CS/12		1.5	
Pint spray bottles	CS/12		1	
Stock solution btls.	EA		6	
Portion pac 202	CS/4 BX		4 BX	
Portion par 265	CS/4 BX		4 BX	
Vacuum bags (paper)	CS/250		25 BAGS	

Figure 11.10 (*continued*)

INVENTORY RECORD LOG											
1	2	3	4	5	6	7	8	9	10	11	12
Item	Par	Prior inventory	Purchases	Issues	Condemned	Due on hand	Actual count	Variance	Price	Inventory valuation	Reorder

Figure 11.11 The inventory Record Log is a method for recording information about each item of inventory carried. Due on hand = prior inventory + purchases − issues − condemned. Variance = due on hand − actual count. Inventory valuation = actual count × price.

man-hour utilization be developed and substantiated based on the weekly forecast of occupancy. Forecasts must be in line with expected occupancies and workload, or higher management must be notified.

Figure 11.12 is an example of a **Weekly Wage Forecast** form based on occupancies expected during the third week of the fourth period in the model hotel. **Forecast occupancy** refers to the expected percentage and number of occupied rooms out of the 353 rooms in the model hotel. For example, on Tuesday, 94 percent or 332 rooms are expected to be occupied. **Wage departments** refer to the accounting classifications assigned to various types of labor. In Figure 11.12, department 02 is for supervisors, 06 is for fixed-hour employees such as lobby housekeepers and utility housekeeping aides, 07 is for section housekeepers, and 08 is for section housekeeping aides.

The man-hours for supervisors in the model hotel are the total hours of the four team leaders, the linen room supervisor, the night supervisor, and the senior housekeeping aide (minus hours of those scheduled off). The man-hours for section housekeepers are obtained from the Table of Personnel Requirements in Chapter 2.

Planned number of hours for each day is listed. Hours are totaled both for the seven-day week for each wage department and for the four wage departments for each day. Revenue for the expected 2276 rooms (see 7-day forecast in Figure 11.12) is predicted for the week, and **target statistics** are developed involving sales per man-hour and section housekeeper hours per expected number of occupied rooms. Forecast statistics are then compared with those budgeted to determine whether man-hour forecasts are **in control**. Once the forecast is prepared, it is submitted to top management, who eval-

uates whether planned operations for the upcoming week appear to be in control.

Weekly Wage Analysis

Not only should wages be forecast, but actual expenditures of man-hours should be analyzed after the week has been completed. The **weekly wage analysis**, Figure 11.13, is a near replica of Figure 11.12; however, the information reflects **actual expenditures**, which should now be compared with the same week's forecast to evaluate forecast accuracy and to determine where variances may be occurring.

Note the variations between Figures 11.12 and 11.13. In situations in which occupancies were not as predicted, the executive housekeeper would have made the necessary adjustments during the week through the Tight Schedule, which would compensate for actual occupancies being less than or more than expected. Note that Wednesday had been expected to be a 100 percent day but was not by a considerable amount. Adjustments were made to accommodate the lower occupancy, and section housekeeper man-hours were adjusted to keep labor utilization in line, thereby keeping statistical targets in line. Executive housekeepers who do not forecast and analyze man-hour utilization run the risk of having uncontrollable wage costs telegraph the department into an unfavorable labor–cost situation for the year that cannot be recuperated.

Statement Critiques

Period statements provide results of period operations, especially results in attempts to control costs during these operating periods. Efficient hotel organizations require that costs be kept in line with revenues and that statements be analyzed to determine where unacceptable variations may be occurring.

WEEKLY WAGE FORECAST

Period ___4___   Week of period ___3___   Week ending ___4/18___
(Date)

Forecast occupancy	91%/322	84%/297	97%/343	94%/332	100%/353	100%/353	78%/276	92.1%/2276
Wage department	Saturday	Sunday	Monday	Tuesday	Wednesday	Thursday	Friday	Total
02	40	48	48	40	48	40	32	296
06	56	56	56	56	56	56	56	392
07	144	136	160	152	160	160	128	1040
08	32	32	32	32	32	32	24	216
Total	272	272	296	280	296	288	240	1944

Submitted by

___Housekeeper___

Estimated revenue **$ 136,560 00**   (60.00 average rate forecast)

Estimated sales/man-hour **$ 70.24**

Budgeted sales/man-hour **$ 69.55**

Section housekeeper's hours/occupied room : Budget ___.46___ Actual ___.45___

Figure 11.12 Weekly Wage Forecast report used for forecasting man-hours in various wage departments during the upcoming week. Wage departments refer to the accounting classifications assigned to various type of labor: 02—supervisors; 06—fixed hours (employees such as lobby housekeepers, utility housekeeping aides); 07—section housekeepers; 08—section housekeeping aides. Forecast occupancy refers to percent and number of occupied rooms expected out of a total model hotel availability of 353 rooms. Forecast includes statistical targets (sales per man-hour and section housekeeper hours per occupied room), indicating comparisons of what was budgeted against what is being forecast.

Many hotel organizations require that statements be **critiqued** to determine where revenues and cost are out of prescribed tolerances.

Critiques are usually required by top management within five days after statements are received. Typical standards for cost control may require that a critique be made at any time a cost variance is greater than one-tenth of 1 percent of revenue. Such critiques must explain why costs are out of tolerance and what will be done to bring them back into tolerance. (A period statement will be analyzed in detail in Figure 11.25.)

Purchasing

Cleaning and Guest Supplies

Purchasing is a subroutine that can take up a part of each day for the executive housekeeper. Even though some hotel chains have centralized national purchasing of items that bring quantity discounts, for the most part cleaning and guest supplies will be purchased either by the **purchasing agent** in the hotel (if there is one) or by the department heads for their respective departments.

Considering the size and variability of the housekeeping cleaning and guest supply inventory, there will be many suppliers and purveyors who will do their best to obtain the business from the executive housekeeper. Suppliers can be outstanding allies in the conduct of services within the housekeeping department, or they can be outstanding nuisances. Competitively shopping for suppliers or vendors will simplify the question as to who will be used and for what products. Figure 11.14 is an example of a **Competitive Shopping form** that can be used to determine the various attributes of vendors.

A separate shopping form should be maintained for each and every product that is used in the cleaning and guest supply inventory. Product prices should be reviewed at least once every six months. Comments such as how well the vendor or purveyor services the account and how well products are understood and demonstrated by the vendor are significant when selecting vendors. Price, although important, should not be the only criterion for selecting a product. Quality, suitability, storage requirements, and lot sizes each play an important part in making the right selection.

It is not unusual to find that one vendor will be selected for all paper products, another vendor for

WEEKLY WAGE ANALYSIS

Period ___4___ Week of period ___3___ Week ending __4/18__
(Date)

Actual occupancy	347	306	242	319	285	353	270	2122
Wage department	Saturday	Sunday	Monday	Tuesday	Wednesday	Thursday	Friday	Total
02	42.1	47.9	48.1	40.2	40.2	40.4	30.8	289.7
06	56.0	54.5	55.6	56.2	50.4	56.1	56.0	384.8
07	162.4	137.5	113.4	144.9	136.6	164.6	126.1	985.5
08	32.1	32.1	32.3	30.8	30.9	32.1	32.2	222.5
Total	292.6	272.0	249.4	272.1	258.1	293.2	245.1	1882.5

	Budget	Forecast	Actual	
Revenue	135,500	136,560	132,073	(Actual average rate 62.24)
Sales/man-hour	69.55	70.24	70.15	
Section housekeeper's hours/occupied rm	.46	.45	.46	

Explanation of major variances *Forecast Sales/MH were missed slightly but both SLS/MH & Section Hskpr Hr/Occ Rm were within tolerance of budget.* NO SIGNIFICANT VARIATIONS

Submitted by *Housekeeper*
Executive housekeeper

Figure 11.13 Weekly Wage Analysis Form resembles the Weekly Wage Forecast but reports actual expenditures as opposed to what was forecast. The Weekly Wage Analysis for the concluded week along with a forecast for the upcoming week are submitted to higher management.

cleaning chemicals, and another for mops, brooms, and the various and sundry items used in day-to-day cleaning. If the number of salespeople being dealt with can be limited, more efficient use of time is possible. Some suppliers call on the executive housekeeper on a weekly basis; others will call less often. Orders might be placed by phone, whereby suppliers will visit only occasionally to ensure that the account is being properly maintained. Periodic or drop shipments might be arranged, whereby the supplier rather than the hotel retains the storage problem.

There are two major areas of caution that need be mentioned at this point. Most suppliers budget funds to service the customer. Some will offer prizes and personal discounts to executive housekeepers for allowing them to have the hotel's account. Great caution is necessary to ensure that it is the hotel that is receiving the discount, not the executive housekeeper. Said more simply, watch out for offers of kickback. Every executive housekeeper should know and thoroughly understand company policy about accepting gifts before Christmas time or other periods of benevolence when suppliers are generous with their clients. Usually, hotel organizations have set guidelines about what should or should not be accepted.

On one particular occasion when I was executive housekeeper, I received a long distance phone call from a supplier who indicated that "their new all-purpose cleaner was meeting with spectacular success" and that "if I would allow the product to be tested on my property, I would receive *at my home address* a complete home entertainment center with stereo and TV. Of significant note was the fact that this new product was $7.80 a gallon to be purchased in 55-gallon drums. The product currently being used, and with satisfactory results, had been purchased on a national contract for $1.20 a gallon. You should immediately recognize who would be paying for the home entertainment set.

Linens

As you will recall from Chapter 6, in housekeeping operations the term "linens" normally refers to items

COMPETITIVE SHOPPING FORM								
Item	Qt/size	Price	Vendors					Remarks

Figure 11.14 Competitive Shopping Form used to compare vendor prices for a given item of supply inventory. Vendors should be evaluated periodically to ensure that the best price is being paid for items purchased.

associated with guestroom beds and bathrooms—sheets, pillowcases, bath towels, hand towels, washcloths, and fabric bathmats. Several subroutines concerning linens might be developed. Some might warrant simple policies and standard operating policies describing the movement of linens to and from the laundry and floor areas each day, whereas others might relate to routines involving condemnation, storage, repair, and normal care of linens. Linens rank second, next to wages, in departmental costs. For this reason, particular interest must be taken in the subroutines associated with the inventory and ordering of linens.

Linen Inventories

As mentioned in Chapter 6, the initial supply of house linens might be a part of preopening expenses, whereby initial requirements would be placed in position for operational use and amortized over an extended period. Replacement of this initial supply, however, is an operational expense. Because of relative costs (labor versus linens) the total supply of linens should never be so small as to cause employees to have to wait for linens to service rooms. Overall linen supplies therefore should be in amounts several

times that required to cover all rooms one time (one par).

If the hotel has an on-premise laundry, an initial supply of linens includes the following:

1 par	*To cover all beds* and baths (after daily service is complete)
1 par	*Soiled* or just removed from beds and baths after daily service (tomorrow's workload for the laundry)
1 par	*Clean* and ready to use in servicing guest rooms the next day
½ par	*New*, in storage to be used as replacements when necessary
3½ par	Total

If the property does not have an on-premise laundry, add one par for linen in transit to and from a commercial laundry.

Because an unnoticed reduction in the supply of linens can cause a reduction in efficient service to guestrooms, **physical linen inventories** should be conducted regularly and accurate records should be maintained to ensure forewarning of additional needs. Many hotels inventory linens monthly. In situations in which inventories are under good control and count systems are accurate, inventories may be conducted on a quarterly basis.

Let us assume that a 3.5 par is to be maintained for the model hotel and that linen usage and control are stabilized, allowing for a quarterly inventory. A linen inventory log book should be maintained, with headings similar to the Inventory Record Log described in Figure 11.11. Periodic needs for resupply are determined upon the completion of each physical inventory.

On days when inventories are conducted, special care must be taken to ensure that every piece of linen can be located for counting. Inventories should be conducted at the end of the normal workday when linen movement is at a minimum. (After the laundry has completed work, usually all guestroom regular servicing has been completed and each section housekeeper's linen cart has been loaded for the next day's routine.) Figure 11.15 is an example of a **Linen Count Sheet** used by employees taking the inventory.

The more employees involved in counting linens, the faster the inventory process can be completed. Additionally, when employees are involved

in the actual count, they become more aware of the significance, importance, and value of the linen. Each section housekeeper counts linens loaded on his or her cart; senior housekeepers count linens found on mobile linen trucks and shelves in satellite linen rooms. The linen room supervisor and assistant count all items found in the main linen room. Section housekeeping aides count linens on made-up roll-away beds. Laundry workers count soiled linen in the laundry, which will comprise the next day's laundry workload, as well as any clean linen that might be lingering after the day's workload has been completed. The senior housekeeping aide and assistants count new linen in storage.

When counting bed sheets, differentiation must be made in sizes of sheets (See Figure 11.15). For convenience, other items not necessarily a part of linens, such as pillows, blankets, bedpads and bedspreads, might also be counted at this time.

Where items were located when counted and who counted them at that location should be noted on the Count Sheet so that managers might audit certain counts. (It would not be unusual for the hotel

LINEN COUNT SHEET	
Count location _____	Counted by _____
	Date _____
Item	**Number counted**
Sheets K	
Q	
D	
T	
Pillowcases	
BT	
HT	
WC	
BM	
Bed pads	
Blankets (optional)	
Pillows (optional)	

Figure 11.15 Linen Count Sheet used by employees counting linen in various locations of the hotel.

controller to participate in the inventory by auditing certain count sheets.)

When counts have been completed, Count Sheets are collected and recorded in a **Period Linen Inventory Count Record**, such as the one in Figure 11.16. The Count Record is used to compile all count sheets and record **total linen in use** and **total new linen on hand**. Once total counts have been determined, they are compared with the prior inventory to determine usages (same as in Figure 11.10). The separation of linen in use and new linen is done to assign a proper value to the inventory. Most hotel operations will value new linen (linen in unopened boxes) at full price and linen in use at half price. Total **linen valuation** is thus determined as follows:

$$\left(\frac{\text{Linen in use} \times \text{Price}}{2}\right) + (\text{New linen} \times \text{Price})$$

$$= \text{Linen valuation}$$

Care should be taken in counting linen to ensure that unexplained growths do not occur in specific items. For example, a prior inventory indicates 1000 double sheets on hand. Between inventory periods there were 500 double sheets purchased. Total availability of double sheets thus should not exceed 1500. A current inventory, however, reveals that 1724 double sheets are now on hand, giving an unexplained growth of 224 sheets. When such growth occurs, either the prior inventory or the current inventory is suspect, requiring that a recount be made. When such unexplained growths occur, inventories

need to be conducted more frequently until inventory subsystems are under control.

Linen Purchases

Linen inventories reveal the need for purchases, and there are many **linen brokers** who gladly service this type of need. When linen must be purchased from a linen broker, however, it should be expected that a premium will be paid. Savings of up to one-third may be available when the services of a linen broker are not used and linens are purchased directly from **linen mills**. Direct purchases from mills require long-range planning and purchase arrangements contracted up to 1½ years in advance, allowing the mill to produce ordered linens at their convenience.

Such planning may seem impossible, but the **annual linen reorder plan** illustrated in Figure 11.17 is quite feasible. Note how quarterly inventories are conducted and compared to an on-hand requirement of 3.5 par. Linen orders may be made up for a one-year period, one-half year before effective date of the order; the order is then drop shipped on a quarterly basis. The vertical axis in Figure 11.17 indicates the number of a particular item of inventory. Heavy black vertical lines indicate the increase of linen inventory caused by the receipt of drop shipments. The horizontal axis indicates the passage of time from one quarter to the next. Diagonal lines between quarters indicate the linen shortage generated due to linen loss, use, and condemnation that might occur between inventories. The shortages determined in each of four quarterly inventories gen-

1 Item	2 Beds	3 Laundry soiled	4 Laundry clean	5 Housekeeping soiled	6 Main linen room	7 Satellite linen rooms	8 Housekeeper carts	9 Roll beds	10 Total in use	11 New in storage	12 Grand total

PERIOD LINEN INVENTORY COUNT RECORD

Figure 11.16 Period Linen Inventory Count Record used to record the results of linen inventories. Columns 2 through 9 equal column 10. Columns 10 plus 11 equal column 12. Results are transferred to a Linen Inventory Record Log so that comparisons can be made with prior inventories to determine usage and variances.

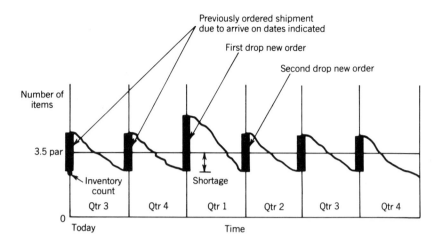

Figure 11.17 Annual linen reorder plan shows the supply and replenishment of a given item of linen inventory. Appropriate replenishment orders for quarters 1, 2, 3, and 4 for the upcoming year may be determined at the beginning of the third quarter of the current year. The formula for this plan is as follows: Linen on hand (today) + Linen expected to arrive (already ordered) − Shortages (forecast to occur at the end of the current order) − Annual usage − 3.5 par = Order ÷ 4 (quarters) × Case lot size = expected quarterly drop shipments in the future year.

erate annual linen usage that must be replaced each year. A horizontal line at some given value indicates the count of a given item when being maintained at 3.5 par. The count levels are then seen to vary equally above and below 3.5 par value.

As an example, let us assume that a linen order for double sheets (DS) is to be developed on 30 June and will be initiated on 1 January for the upcoming year, said order to be drop shipped on a quarterly basis during the year the order is in effect. The 3.5 par value of DS is given at 2000. On 30 June, inventory counts reveal 1750 DS on hand (250 short of 3.5 par). Shortly after the 30 June inventory, a drop shipment (prior order) of 500 DS is expected to arrive that will raise the count of DS to 2250. Prior quarterly shortages indicate that a forecast shortage in September may be expected, but a second drop shipment of 250 DS (already ordered) will again arrive that will return the inventory count on 1 October to a value of about 1950 DS. A similar quarterly usage is then forecast for the final quarter of the year, creating a forecast shortage on 31 December of 225 sheets. An order may now be created on 30 June, which will include annual usage (four prior quarterly shortages) plus the shortage forecast to exist on 31 December. This annual order may then be divided into four quarterly drop shipments and the order placed directly with a mill a full six months before the effective commencement of the order. Hence the formula

Linen on hand (today) + Linen expected to arrive (prior orders) − Shortage (expected at the end of the current order) − Annual usage − 3.5 par = future order (a negative number)

Order ÷ 4 × case lot size = expected quarterly drop shipments to commence six months hence

As has been shown, the preplanned purchase of linens for future use can produce great economies of operation. Whereas linen brokers are available and willing to fill linen needs, the profits made by such brokers represent true cost savings for housekeeping departments who order linens directly from mills. Linen brokers should therefore be used only in an emergency.

Personnel Administration

Time Card Control

Another subroutine requiring the daily attention of management is **time card control**. Employees should be counseled at the time of employment as to how many hours constitute the work shift each day. Some organizations specify an eight-hour shift, including time off for work breaks and lunch. Others require that employees clock out for lunch, thus leaving them on their own time for lunch. A housekeeping operation may be arranged in such a way as to have employees on the property for 8½ hours, including two work breaks of 15 minutes each on company time, but require the employee to clock out for lunch, creating a net eight-hour workday. The above arrangement is specified; however, employees are still required to punch a time clock at the beginning and end of each shift, as well as clock out for lunch and back in after lunch. Federal regulations require that time card records be maintained on each employee to guarantee fair wage administration.

Some employees, although understanding that their shifts begin at 8:00 A.M., may clock in early (7:45) and then expect to be paid for all time worked as indicated on the time card. Employees must not be allowed to enter times on a time card indiscriminately and expect to be paid for these times. It therefore behooves department managers to set specific ground rules about overtime and the time spread in which employees may punch in and out each day. Then, should employees be available and needed before the normal working day, they may be asked to clock in early and can expect to be paid for this early time; otherwise, clock-ins between 7:55 and 8:05 A.M. will be considered 8:00 A.M. clock-ins. Similar policies apply to clock-out times.

Many hotels have two time card racks for each employee; one is for time cards when employees are off the property, and the other is for time cards when employees are on the clock. In large operations, quick note of where the time card is located can determine whether or not an employee is actually at work.

While the employee is on the property, there should be a record of a clock-in with no clock-out yet showing. During this time, managers can audit clock times on cards from the previous day and indicate the number of hours that are to be paid based on the punched indications. This allows employees to note exactly how many hours they may expect to be paid for the previous day. Any questions that arise may then be immediately resolved. Also, indications of overtime authorization can be noted.

Figure 11.18 shows an example of a time card upon which several days of clock time have been recorded. Note the penciled indications wherein the manager has audited the card and indicated the amount of time for which the employee will be paid. On Wednesday the early punch, and hence overtime, was authorized. On Tuesday, overtime was not authorized and the employee may need to be reminded of rules and procedures for clocking in and out. This type of audit of time worked by employees is a subroutine that should be done on a daily basis. It is easy to audit time cards using a 24-hour time clock that records hours and hundredths of hours.

Payroll Administration

The proper payment of wages due an employee is a matter requiring great attention to detail by the department manager. Employees have a right and do expect to be paid for work performed. It is therefore vital that department managers ensure that hours worked during a given workweek be properly recorded on **time sheets** from which actual pay will be calculated.

Figure 11.18 The daily time card audit. This time card has been used with a time clock that registers in Navy time hours and hundredths of hours. It is actually easier to audit in hours and tenths of hours than in A.M. and P.M. hours and minutes. Note the example for Thursday: The first clock-in time is registered as 15.56 (or about 3:34 P.M. — $^{56}/_{100}$ of an hour past 3:00 P.M.). The last clock out is 23:99 ($^{1}/_{100}$ of an hour before midnight). By subtracting the smaller time from the larger, the total time that the employee was on the property is determined. The two intermediate times register out and in times for the dinner break. Subtracting the smaller from the larger time determines the amount of time taken for dinner. Finally, subtracting the dinner break time from the overall time determines actual time on the clock for pay purposes. Note that the audit of time on Tuesday indicates a total of 8.5 hours because of an early clock-in time. This early time was not authorized; therefore, only the normal eight-hour shift will be allowed. John Smith would have noticed this reduction on Wednesday during the normal work shift. If there were any questions about the audited reduction, John would have been counseled not to clock in early unless requested to do so. On Wednesday, overtime was authorized; hence the nine hours were allowed. Some states require that overtime be paid after the eighth hour worked on any given day; others require the payment of overtime only after 40 hours have been worked in one workweek. In the first instance, John worked 39.5 regular hours and one overtime hour. In the second instance John worked a total of 40.5 hours; hence only the excess over 40 hours should have been paid at the overtime rate.

Time sheets are normally given to department managers by the payroll department before the end of each workweek. Time sheets contain an alphabetical listing of all employees on the payroll. Employees hired after time sheets are originated may be added. Assuming there has been a daily audit of time cards at the conclusion of the workweek, the time cards must be totaled and their values entered on time sheets (Figure 11.19), which will be submitted to the personnel department timekeeper or paymaster.

Weekly time sheets indicate the number of hours for which employees will be paid. Days off are also indicated so that no blanks are noted for any day; special forms of pay are entered where appropriate. Items such as sick pay, vacation pay, total regular time, overtime, and wage rates are entered, as are the wage department classification under which the employee is to be paid. Some employees may have a secondary job code for which they may be paid at a secondary rate. For example, the section housekeeper in wage department (07) may work one day during the week as a relief for a senior housekeeper in wage department (02). The employee should then be paid at the higher wage rate for that particular day. After all time has been correctly recorded, summaries of information are included on Weekly Wage Analysis reports (Figure 11.13).

Proper wage administration includes orientation of the employee in understanding when wages will be paid. Given a workweek that runs from Saturday through Friday, time sheets would normally be prepared at the end of work on Friday. Lapse time, which ranges from 5 to 10 days, is required to prepare checks. Depending on methods of payroll preparation, pay due an employee for the week ending Friday, June 5, for example, may not be presented until Wednesday, June 15, creating what is known as **time in the hole**.

The employee must be counseled at the onset of employment that pay for work completed on the upcoming Friday of the first week worked will not be received until Wednesday, 10 days hence. Even though this procedure may be burdensome for some employees, it is better to have a payday far enough delayed to guarantee that paychecks will be available on the stated payday than have earlier stated paydays that are *not* met due to late arrival of paychecks. Late paychecks tend to produce major uproars and should be avoided.

Employees need to understand that upon termination of employment, pay owed will be received and termination will not affect amounts owed. Employees who quit their jobs should expect to wait for scheduled paydays to receive their pay. It is best if employees who are terminated by the company be paid off immediately with a special paycheck in order that they need not return to the property after termination.

Since the department manager is controlling the employee's working time and pay, the passing out of paychecks is the department manager's responsibility, which should not be passed on to any other department (such as the personnel department).

Employees whose names appear on time sheets for which no pay is entered constitute two categories of personnel; those on legal and granted **leaves of absence (LOA)** and those who have been terminated but for which no terminating paperwork has been received by the payroll division. This latter category requires the immediate attention of the department manager to ensure that time sheets do not contain the names of employees who no longer work for the company.

The subroutine of **time sheet preparation** is a tedious and time-consuming one requiring great attention to detail. With proper training, however, the task can be delegated on a rotating basis to all department supervisory personnel. An authenticating signature of the department manager (or acting manager) should be required on all time sheets.

Performance Appraisals

One subroutine that must never be neglected is **performance appraisals** of all employees within the department. Every employee has a right to know management's expectations and to receive appraisals of how well responsibilities and tasks are being carried out. Performance appraisals should be conducted at stated intervals and at other times when appropriate.

The first regular appraisal occurs at the end of a **probationary period of employment**. Employees are usually hired for probationary periods, which may last from three to six months. An employee should be notified at the end of probationary periods that his or her performance has been satisfactory and that he or she is now considered full-time permanent, temporary, or pool employee in good standing. Or the employee should have been advised well in advance of the end of the probationary period that the performance was lacking. Managers who wait until the end of a probationary period to inform an employee that performance has been unacceptable are being insensitive to the human dynamics of supervisory responsibilities.

WEEKLY TIME SHEET   Week Ending __3/15__

Name (Primary Wage Dept.) (Secondary Wage Dept.)	Rate	Hours							Total hours	Earnings			
		SAT	SUN	MON	TUE	WED	THR	FRI		Reg	OT	SPEC	Total
ADAMS, Sarah (07)	5.50	8	8	8.1	7.9	OFF	OFF	8	40.0	220.00	—	—	
													220.00
BROWN, Betty (07)	5.75	9.	—	—	8	7.9	OFF	OFF	24.9	143.18	7.43	—	
	6.25		8	8					16.0	—	—	100.00	250.61
CARTER, Louis (06)	5.50	9.0	8.0	OFF	OFF	8v	8v	8v	41.0	88.00	8.25	132.00	
													228.25
GREEN, Martha (02)	6.50	OFF	EDO	8s	8	8	8	OFF	32.0	156.00	—	52.00	
													208.00
JONES, Thomas (08)	5.50	LOA			LOA				—				
(02)													—
KING, Mary (07)	5.00	8.2	8.1	8s	8s	OFF	OFF	8	40.3	120.00	2.25	80.00	202.25
SMITH, John (08)	5.25	8	OFF	OFF	8	9	7.9	7.6	40.5	210.00	3.93	—	213.93
THOMAS, William (08)	5.00	8	8	OFF	OFF	T	T	T	16.0	80.00	—	—	80.00
WHITE, Jane (06)	5.50	8	8	8	7.4	8A	OFF	OFF	39.4	172.70	—	44.00	216.70
(02)	6.00												
Totals (Primary)		58.2	40.1	32.1	47.3	40.9	23.9	31.6	274.1	1189.88	21.86	408.00	1619.74
(Secondary)		—	8.0	8.0	—	—	—	—	16.0				

Special codes
S—Sick pay
V—Vacation pay
J—Jury duty pay
A—Administrative pay

LOA—Leave of absence
OFF—Regular day off (without pay)
EDO—Extra day off (without pay)
T—Terminated

Prepared by _Supervisor_

Approved by _Housekeeper_

Figure 11.19 Weekly time sheet prepared by the payroll department illustrating a computer-printed page of an alphabetical listing of employees on the payroll. An entire department payroll may be made up of many such pages. Explanations for entries on the weekly time sheet are as follows:

Adams: Worked five regular days as a section housekeeper (07); was off on Wednesday and Thursday. A total of 40 hours worked that week at a pay rate of $5.50/hour for total weekly earnings of $220.00.

Brown: A section housekeeper; worked three regular days under a primary job classification (07) and two days under a secondary job classification (02) (standing in for a supervisor). Also worked nine-tenths of an hour overtime for which she will be paid time and a half.

Carter: Worked two regular days as a public area housekeeper, had two regular scheduled days off, had requested and was granted three days vacation pay.

Green: Worked three regular days; was scheduled off for an extra day and was granted eight hours sick leave.

Jones: Has been on leave of absence for several weeks. (leave was authorized, therefore benefits continue to accrue.)

King: Worked three regular days; requested and was granted two days sick leave. Also worked three-tenths of an hour overtime.

Smith: Similar schedule to Adams; off Sunday and Monday.

Thomas: Worked two regular days, was off two days, then failed to return to work. Thomas was terminated. He will be paid monies due on the next regular payday. Had Thomas been fired, he would have been paid off immediately and a cross reference made on the time sheet that he had already been paid.

White: Worked four regular days, asked for and was granted one day administrative leave (without pay). Also had a secondary job classification but did not work in that capacity during the workweek.

Routine performance appraisals should occur at stated intervals. After successfully completing periods of probationary performance, the time of the next performance appraisal should be made known to the employee (usually one year hence). When probationary periods are successfully concluded it should be presumed that the employee is capable of performing the task assigned properly. Failure to continue to perform in a like manner is an indication of unsatisfactory performance and becomes worthy of a special performance evaluation. When performance is noted as being routinely outstanding, it should also be made the subject of a special performance evaluation.

Satisfactory and outstanding performance evaluations should offer consideration of **pay increases** in accordance with company policy. Assuming that an employee has successfully passed from a probationary status, a raise in pay is appropriate. One year later, given satisfactory performance, another pay increase might be expected.

Many companies have **pay scales** that allow for a start rate, base rate, one-year rate, and maximum rate for each job classification. For example, for the section housekeeper the following rates might apply:

Start rate	$6.00/hour
Base rate	$6.50/hour
One-year rate	$7.00/hour
Maximum rate	$9.00/hour

The start rate is applied when the person begins employment. Given satisfactory performance at the end of a three-month probationary period, pay will be increased to the base rate. Satisfactory performance throughout the year warrants an additional pay increase at the end of the year if for no other reason than inflation. The same might occur for the next three years. Upon reaching the maximum rate, no further increases may be obtained, other than for changes in wage scales due to cost-of-living increases or promotion increases.

Essentially satisfactory performances warrant standard increases to the limit specified by the type of work performed, not years in service in a specific job category. The wage scale might be expected to increase each year due to cost-of-living increases, not seniority. To achieve better-than-standard wage increases, the worker must be above average or be promoted to the next higher classification.

Technique of Performance Appraisal

Performance appraisals should be personal between the manager and the employee. The manager may consult with other supervisors, but the actual appraisal should come only from one of the department managers.

In Chapter 8 a Personnel Action Form (PAF) was instituted on each employee who was hired. The front side of the PAF (Figure 8.4) contains all pertinent identifying data on the employee, and the back (Figure 8.5) is used for performance appraisal. Long-time employees might have several PAFs in their personnel jackets, which had been completed any time the employees had significant personal data changed or when performance was appraised. The front side of the most recent PAF contains the most current data on the employee, with the back page blank awaiting the next needed action (change of data or performance appraisal).

The human resources department helps the executive housekeeper recall when performance appraisals are due on each employee by pulling the most recent PAF and sending it to the housekeeping department. The subroutine of performance appraisal requires action when such appraisals are sent to the department (usually within one week). A set time each week might be scheduled for writing and presenting these appraisals to employees.

As Figure 8.5 showed, the appraisal form requires the following:

1. A statement of observed strengths
2. An indication of whether objectives assigned have been met
3. A statement of observed weaknesses. (It is highly doubtful that an employee's performance will be perfect. Weaknesses therefore should be noted in order that the employees know where they need improvement. A performance appraisal indicating no weaknesses is an implied statement that improvement cannot be made in any aspect of performance.)
4. A statement of counseled action—what the employee should do to improve performance and what the employer will do to assist
5. An estimate of when the employee should be ready for promotion (does not guarantee that promotion will be gained)

Once the appraisal has been prepared, a conference with the employee should be scheduled. The written appraisal is used to discuss the employee's performance. After discussion and assured understanding, the employee should sign the appraisal as an acknowledgment that he or she has in fact received the appraisal and is aware of the meaning of its contents. The signature is not an acknowledgment of the accuracy of the contents of the appraisal, only that it has been received and understood as the appraiser's view. The employee should then be allowed to comment in writing in the space provided on the appraisal. Should the appraisal warrant an increase in pay, such notation would be made on the front side of the PAF, as should a notation as to when the next appraisal is due.

Special Appraisals

Special appraisals should be conducted in a similar manner as regular appraisals, except that the occasion would be to either note routinely outstanding performances or substandard performances. Poor performance should be appraised *before* the employee's performance becomes unsatisfactory. This allows for corrective action before the possibility of termination. The PAF may be used to document that a verbal warning has been issued or to document an official written warning. When poor or questionable performance must be appraised, a technique known as leveling should be used. The **leveling technique** is carried out as follows:

1. Conduct leveling sessions on a one-to-one basis. There are rare exceptions when a third person should be present to validate conditions or observations; one-on-one is usually more open and conducive to agreement and future commitment.
2. Be completely honest and straightforward. Do not use the leveling technique if less than total honesty is contemplated.
3. Deal with the problem as soon as possible. Immediate action is much better than delayed action. Delays in dealing with a problem infer a weakness on the part of management and a lack of willingness to deal with unpleasant issues when they occur in hopes that problems will go away. They usually do not.
4. Set up the room so that nothing is between the evaluator and the employee. Move out from behind a desk and sit as an equal with the employee. Do not stand while the employee sits, or vice versa.
5. Go immediately to the problem. No small talk or jokes are appropriate.
6. Send "I" messages. "I" messages show concern without inferring that the employee is necessarily a bad person. Statements such as "I am concerned about your repeated tardiness for work" or "I am troubled because you are having difficulty adjusting to your fellow workers" are not

so likely to put the employee on the defensive but will likely cause the person to open up and talk about problem areas.

7. Give honest positive reinforcement when deserved, but never patronize.
8. Listen. Half of communication requires listening, understanding meanings, and determining where people are coming from when they talk.
9. Avoid references to past mistakes if they are not relevant to current issues. (Past mistakes should have been dealt with in the past. *It is now that counts.*)
10. Arrive at a mutual decision or understanding as to what future actions or behavior may be expected.
11. Reconfirm understandings by providing written notes of discussions and decided actions; do this for the record and provide a copy of such notes to the employee (may be a copy of a written warning).
12. Keep the entire encounter professional and free of emotion on the part of the evaluator. Should the employee become emotional, allow the employee to calm down before proceeding with the appraisal.

Employee performance appraisal is one of the most important aspects of personnel administration in which the executive housekeeper will become involved. A manager gets things done through people. To understand this requires a commitment to the understanding of human dynamics and a desire to be a professional in the task of supervision.

Communication and Training

Good management requires an absolute understanding of proper delegation and how such delegation brings about commitment and involvement on the part of employees. Successful commitment cannot be attained by being secretive about matters that employees have a *need to know* out of concern for jobs to be performed or about matters that they *want to know*, which indicate that employee performance is contributing to the success of the company. Commitment and involvement stem from thorough orientation, individualized training, and regular meetings through which the employees get the word.

Departmental Meetings

On a regular basis (at least monthly), **departmental meetings** should be scheduled. They should be interesting, informative, and productive. Praise for jobs well done is always appropriate in departmental meetings where individual praiseworthy performances may be recognized in front of others.

Announcements about upcoming events and the success (or failure) of past events are appropriate, as well as management observations about certain happenings. A portion of meetings should be devoted to the presentation and discussion of new hotel policies, as well as the regular and periodic review of existing policies.

Guest comments as to service (both good and bad) need to be presented; however, specific comments about poor individual performance are best presented in private. Meetings should allow time for questions from employees, whereby management may learn about matters concerning employees.

The executive housekeeper should allow junior managers and supervisors to chair meetings but should always be present to convey management's control over meetings. Team leaders should conduct regular (simplified) meetings with team members, keep notes of such meetings, and discuss the results with the executive housekeeper.

Long-Range Planning

Budget Formulation (The Once-a-Year Subroutine)

There are many cases in which budgets are presented to executive housekeepers that dictate how much labor and supplies will be expended in the performance of tasks. Such budgets, which originate with top management and are handed down, seldom draw the commitment of operational managers because little or no planning was contributed at the department level. The participation of the executive housekeeper in formulating the **operational budget for the housekeeping department** is essential if managers are to commit themselves to successful accomplishment of the long-range plan known as the budget.

Top Management's Input to the Budget

Top management must be involved in the budgeting process: Company expectations should be stated and national trends analyzed; criteria should be established regarding standards to be met in the use of supplies; marketing plans must be finalized for the upcoming year; and budget guidance is essential. Once these tasks are done, however, each department

of the hotel should begin the task of assembling from a zero base, requirements for the expenditure of man-hours, materials, and money to produce the service or product that will be creating revenue. After identifying expected sales and related costs, top management should critique the budget, indicating where adjustments must be made in order that company or corporate objectives will be met. If modification of the budget is necessary, it should be revised by the operating departments until agreement is reached.

The Budget Cycle

The **operational budget cycle** usually requires several months from the onset of planning until critiques and adjustments are finalized. The budgeting process must therefore be begun well in advance of the beginning of the budget (fiscal) year.

Operational budgets usually reflect **periods** of the fiscal year. Some hotel operating budgets are constructed with each of the 12 months reflecting a period. Other systems reflect 13 (28-day) periods, each of which is made up of four consecutive weeks. The 13-period system seems most appropriate because periods will start on the first day of a scheduled workweek and will end on the last day of the following fourth workweek. It allows for the comparison of revenues and costs on a consistent basis each period.

Budget periods based on calendar months create two months out of 12 where an extra payday will occur, causing a distorted comparison of wage cost against revenues. Such distortion will not occur in 13-period systems. In addition, set days of each period will always occur on the same days of the week in each period, allowing for systematic comparisons of similar days. For example, assume that workweeks begin on Saturdays and end on Fridays. The first day of every period will then occur on a Saturday. The sixteenth day of every period will similarly always be the third Sunday of each period. Except for special holiday periods, hotel revenues and resultant costs of operations will more likely reflect similarity by days of the week than any other statistical criteria.

The Budgeting Subroutine

Each budget planning cycle is commenced by those involved in budgeting room sales. Schedules indicating the volume of room sales to be expected on each day of the upcoming year are prepared and finalized before operational cost budgeting is begun by any department affected by fluctuating occupancy (such as housekeeping). Most schedules of expected room sales will also show a comparison of the upcoming budget year with the existing year in order that growth can be analyzed. Not only will growth in the sale of guestrooms be significant, but changes in average room rate and expected period revenues will later prove significant in the development of statistical targets for the housekeeping department. Figure 11.20 is an example of a typical **consolidated room sales summary** from which the housekeeping department will clue department (cost) budget formulation.

Wage Classification

Since man-hour utilization represents the highest housekeeping cost of operation, the greatest detail in justification will be required in the development of man-hours to be expended. Recall that man-hours for the various types of work performed within the housekeeping department are classified for accounting purposes. In our earlier example, man-hours worked by section housekeepers were classification (07), hours worked by section housekeeping aides were (08), those worked by supervisory personnel were (02), and those worked by public area, linen room and utility personnel do not fluctuate and are therefore classified as fixed hours (06). Other classifications of man-hours to be performed in a rooms department include front office personnel (01, 03, 05), which would be under the control of the front office manager. Figure 11.21 illustrates a system whereby man-hours are classified into **wage departments**.

	% OCC	# Rooms	Ave Rate	Sales Dollars	% Inc. in Rooms	% Inc. in Dollars
CURRENT Year 1	73	7215	5121	369480		
Actual 2	74	7314	5143	376159		
3	77	7611	5139	391129		
4	73	7215	5404	389898		
5	82	8105	5408	438318		
6	79	7808	5395	421241		
7	85	8401	5399	453569		
8	89	8797	5402	475213		
9	83	8203	5410	443782		
(Forecast) 10	82	8105	5394	437183		
(Forecast) 11	81	8006	5406	432804		
(Forecast) 12	69	6820	5404	368552		
(Forecast) 13	60	5931	5413	321045		
Total	77.5	99531	5343	5318373		
BUDGET Year 1	75	7413	55–	407715	2.7	10.3
Budget 2	78	7709	55–	423995	5.4	12.7
3	86	8500	55–	467500	11.7	19.5
4	86	8500	55–	467500	17.8	19.9
5	88	8697	55–	478335	7.3	9.2
6	92	9093	57–	518301	16.5	23.0
7	93	9192	57–	523944	9.4	15.5
8	93	9192	57–	523944	4.5	10.2
9	92	9093	57–	518301	10.8	16.8
10	89	8797	57–	501429	8.5	14.7
11	89	8797	57–	501429	9.9	15.8
12	80	7907	57–	450699	15.9	22.3
13	63	6227	57–	354939	5.0	10.5
Total	85.0	109117	5625	6138031	9.6	15.4

Figure 11.20 Consolidated room sales summary presents the expected room sales, percent occupancy, average room rate, and sales dollars to be generated by the annual budget. Current statistics are provided for comparison, and percent increases in number of rooms to be sold and revenue dollars are given in relation to the current year. The consolidated room sales summary must be developed and distributed to all departments before cost budgeting can be initiated. Since the budget cycle must be begun about the tenth period of the active year in progress, figures listed as "Actuals" for the tenth through thirteenth periods are "forecast" since they have not yet occurred. As the budget process continues, these last-period forecasts of the active year will be updated. For illustrative purposes, however, assume that all periods of the current year have been completed.

Wage department no.	Wage category
00 *	Management
01 **	Front office supervisory
02 ***	Housekeeping supervisory
03 **	Front office/reservations clerks
04 **	Front office cashiers
05 **	Bell staff
06 ***	Housekeeping (fixed)
07 ***	Section housekeepers
08 ***	Section housekeeping aides
09 ****	Recreation attendants

Figure 11.21 A wage classification system for budgeting and accounting purposes is necessary in order that man-hours in specific wage categories may be budgeted, collected, and analyzed.

Budget Justification

The executive housekeeper needs to explain how man-hour requirements are established for each wage department. Usually a standard form for **man-hour justification** is prepared and included as part of the budget submission package. Figure 11.22 is an example of a budget justification of man-hour form explaining utilization of section housekeeper man-hours (wage department 07), which is one wage department for which the executive housekeeper in our example was responsible.

Considering the expected occupancies noted in Figure 11.20, the executive housekeeper refers to the Table of Personnel requirements (Table 2.1) to determine exactly how many man-hours will be required to service this occupancy for the model hotel. Statements about method of operation as related to the section housekeeper wage department (07) is based on the least number of man-hours that will accomplish the servicing of budgeted occupied guestrooms.

Figure 11.22 illustrates the detail of the budget justification, although justification sheets for other wage departments may not be so detailed. Note that night operations are identified separately; training costs are also identified separately but are not included at this point. Training cost will be added with other property training costs and summarized separately. In the example, it is estimated that four employees will be replaced each period at a training cost of 24 nonproductive hours per employee replaced per period.

If a critique challenge is made by top management to the detail expressed in the budget justification, a clear statement as to what service will be discarded or downgraded before hours can be reduced must be made. If profits must be increased but

services maintained at the level specified in budget justifications, average room rates would have to be increased to improve revenues and resultant profits. Such may be the topic of discussion during budget critiques.

Wage Summaries

Figure 11.23 is a summary statement of all man-hour and wage cost information for the entire rooms department. At the bottom of Figure 11.23 is the calculation of the **sales per man-hour**. This is an efficiency calculation referring to the number of wage department (07) man-hours to be expended for each dollar of sales revenue generated. Once the statistic is accepted, it becomes an efficiency target to be maintained or bettered in each period. Later, comparisons of sales per man-hour for the budget year with that for the current year indicate whether efficiencies are being maintained, exceeded, or lessened over the prior year.

In our example, revenue for the budget year is reflected as $6,138,031. Section housekeeper hours (Wage Department 07) required to service the occupancy that generates this revenue will be 52,296 man-hours. Sales per man-hour then becomes $6,138,031 ÷ 52,296 = $117.37. Upon acceptance of this statistic, revenue may be compared each period with section housekeeper hours to determine whether the statistic is achieved or is more or less than budgeted. If the current year sales per man-hour figure is more than what is budgeted for the upcoming year, it indicates improved efficiencies for the department.

Budgeting Supplies and Other Controllables

The budgeting of other **controllable items**, although not as detailed as man-hours, will require

BUDGET JUSTIFICATION
FOR
MAN-HOUR UTILIZATION

Department ___*Rooms*___   Cost center *Housekeeping* Wage dept. ___*07*___

Staffing rationale   Position Title *Section Housekeepers*

Hours of operation ___*1st Shift 8:00AM to 4:30 PM*___
___*2nd Shift 3:30 PM to MIDNIGHT*___

Shifts per day __*2*__   Managers assigned __*2*__   Hourly supervisors __*6*__

Explanation of operation

Section Housekeepers to be scheduled in accordance with Table of Personnel Requirements (attached). Each Section Housekeeper is expected to service 18 rooms/day. Hours are based on 7 days/week operations. Department is staffed by "Swing team" personnel to cover days off for regular teams.

Summary

Per	OCC	Avg pers day/night	Hrs/day	Days/wk	Hrs/wk total	Hrs/prd total	Avg rate	Cost
1	75	15/1	128	7	880	3520	5.14	18,092
2	78	16/1	136		936	3744	5.16	19,319
3	86	17/1	144		992	3968	5.18	20,554
4	86	17/1	144		992	3968	5.20	20,633
5	88	18/1	152		1048	4192	5.21	21,840
6	92	19/1	160		1104	4416	5.22	23,051
7	93	19/1	160		1104	4416	5.23	23,095
8	93	19/1	160		1104	4416	5.25	23,184
9	92	19/1	160		1104	4416	5.27	23,272
10	89	18/1	152		1048	4192	5.29	22,176
11	89	18/1	152		1048	4192	5.30	22,218
12	80	16/1	136		936	3744	5.31	19,881
13	63	13/1	112		778	3112	5.32	16,556
Tot yr	85	17/1	144	7	13074	52,296	5.23	273,871

Comment on wage rate increases *Expect 20¢ increment all employees spread over the year*

Training man-hours *not included* Cost ___—___

Night operations ___*2912*___ Cost _____

Total mh ___*52,296*___
Total cost ___*273,871*___
Housekeeper
(Submitted)

Figure 11.22 Budget justification for man-hour utilization is used to support requirements for man-hours in various wage categories. A specific justification document is needed for each wage category. The method of department operation is written out and then summarized in tabular form for each period of the budget year. This form becomes a part of the budget submission package.

Rooms Dept Budget Worksheet

SALARY AND WAGE SUMMARY

Manager *Resident Manager*

Column group headers: TOTALS | (02) HK SUPERV | (06) FIXED | (07) SEC HK | (08) HK AIDE

Period	% OCC	TOTALS Amount	TOTALS Rate / Man Hours	01 Amount	01 Rate / MH	02 Amount	02 Rate / MH	03 Amount	03 Rate / MH	04 Amount	04 Rate / MH	05 Amount	05 Rate / MH	06 Amount	06 Rate / MH	07 Amount	07 Rate / MH	08 Amount	08 Rate / MH	09 Amount	09 Rate / MH
1																18,092	5.14 / 3520				
2																19,319	5.16 / 3744				
3																20,554	5.18 / 3968				
4																20,633	5.20 / 3968				
5																21,840	5.21 / 4192				
6																23,051	5.22 / 4416				
7																23,095	5.23 / 4416				
8																23,184	5.25 / 4416				
9																23,272	5.27 / 4416				
10																23,176	5.29 / 4192				
11																22,218	5.30 / 4192				
12																19,881	5.31 / 3794				
13																16,556	5.32 / 3112				
Total Year		714,751	5,38 / 132,936	32,500	6.50 / 5000	112,500	6.25 / 18,000	78,056	5.50 / 14,192	14,784	550 / 2688	—	—	73,500	5.25 / 14,000	273,871	523 / 52296	94,500	5.25 / 18,000	35,040	4.00 / 8760
		Sales Per Man Hour / Average Rate														07 Sales Per MH / Avg Rate					
Budget																117.68					
Last Year																108.89					

Figure 11.23 Salary and wage summary on which total hours, wage rates, and dollar wage cost for each wage department within the room department are totaled. For simplicity, only wage department (07) and department totals are shown.

the same effort. Figure 11.24 shows the entire rooms department budget. Note the format by which current year actuals and projections through the end of the current year are compared with next year's budget.

The final budget is divided into six parts: total sales, total salaries and wages, total employee costs, total controllables, control profit, and statistics. The presentation of wage cost is by wage department, the balance of which has now been added for the entire rooms department. The total employee costs refer to costs over and above salaries and wages, including benefits averaging about 20 percent of salary and wage cost. Controllables refer to the various supply cost accounts where monies will be needed. Not all cost accounts fall under the purview of the executive housekeeper, but those that do are obvious. They include cleaning supplies, guest supplies, laundry expenses, linen costs, and parts of several other accounts, including general expense. Each controllable cost may also be expressed as a percentage of revenue. For example, cleaning supplies might approximate three-tenths of 1 percent of revenue and guest supplies approximate six-tenths of 1 percent of revenue. Such statistics have a tendency to vary with type of hotel, type of market, expectations for excellence, and other specific factors.

Budget in Operation

Once the budget has been developed, it will be critiqued as we described earlier. Once approved, the major long-range operational plan is now in place for the upcoming year. As the budgeted year progresses, period statements will be produced by the accounting department in a form almost identical to that expressed in the budget, as illustrated in Figure 11.25.

New actual costs are next to what has been budgeted. The executive housekeeper is expected to explain any serious negative deviations from the plan and how these deviations will be corrected. This type of control is one of the major challenges to expert professional housekeeping. The executive housekeeper, having been a part of the budget process, should look forward to the management challenge afforded by budget planning, analysis, and control.

ROOMS DEPT.
BUDGET

Performance Budget

Page 1

_____ Year

#	Year	Actual $	%	NEXT YEAR Budget $	%	CURRENT YEAR Projected $	%
1	Total Room Sales			6,144531		5,325498	
2	Rebate Allowance			⟨6500⟩		⟨7125⟩	
3	Net Room Sales			6,138031		5,318373	
4	Other Sales VENDING			34511		28874	
5	Cost of Sales			⟨18284⟩		⟨15150⟩	
6	TOTAL SALES			6,154258	100	5,332097	100
7	Wage Dept 01			32500		31343	
8	02			112500		111911	
9	03			78056		77021	
10	04			14784		14721	
11	06			73500		72641	
12	07			273871	4.5	249240	4.6
13	08			94500		94664	
14	09			35040		31426	
15	TOTAL WAGES			714751	11.6	682967	12.8
16	Overtime Prem			1300		1445	
17	Holiday Pay			23198		23025	
18	Management Salaries			70000		56251	
19	Bonuses			10000		6841	
20	TOTAL SALARIES AND WAGES			819249	13.3	770529	14.5
21	Vacation Management			2600		1471	
22	Vacation Hourly			5500		3455	
23	Payroll Taxes			29146		24889	
24	H & W Ins			6356		3955	
25	Employee Relations			500		708	
26	Employee Food			22529		18696	
27	TOTAL EMPLOYEE COSTS			66631	1.1	53174	1.0
28	Controllables						
29	Bad Debts Provision					491	
30	Corp Pub Relations					276	
31	Cleaning Supplies			18463	.3	21328	.4
32	Commission Exp			1300		1260	
33	Contract Services			3000		4178	
34	Decoration & Plants			1300		787	
35	Entertainment			650		921	
36	Equipment Rental			1350		1450	
37	General Expense			1300		3469	
38	Guest Supplies			36926	.6	37325	.7
39	Holidex Rental			9000		9000	
40	Laundry Expense			41685		44621	

Figure 11.24 The rooms department budget, which combines all sales budgeting that will generate revenues for the rooms department and includes related costs from the front office and housekeeping. The budget is annualized and displayed side by side with the current year in order that comparisons can be made. Certain key budget items have been compared with revenues as a percent of revenue to provide performance targets. Dollars, as well as man-hours, are budgeted. Department control profit is established, as are statistical targets generated from which performance can be measured. Other supporting data (Figures 11.20, 11.22, and 11.23) form a part of the budget package that will be presented to top management for review and approval. Once approved, the budget is spread into 13 period budgets, which will be used to compare actual happenings when they occur in each period.

To understand budgets and the related processes, carefully analyze the explanations given in Figures 11.24 and 11.25. For Figure 11.25, a period critique of questionable items directly under the control of the executive housekeeper might appear as follows:

Critique notes

(1) and (2)   Wage cost for senior housekeeper remains high in the third period and continues a trend established in the first two periods; section housekeeper wage costs appear inordinately low, considering occupancies slightly above budget (line 29, page 2).

(3)   Major purchases of all-purpose cleaner were paid in periods one and two.

(4)   These purchases will not recur for six months. Area will be under control and will be on budget by the fifth period. Completed contract with **AJAX** Exterminator Company and paid balance of contract due. A major cost reduction will accrue upon commencement of contract with GETTABUG Company.

(5)   General expense purchases over budget by $650.00 in the third period and are $1240.00 YTD. Purchases have involved the expensing of new shelving for the main linen room, as opposed to the inclusion of these items in last year's capital

	Description	Actual $	%	NEXT YEAR Budget $	%	CURRENT YEAR Projected $	%
1	Linen Expense			43080	.7	44256	.82
2	Linen Rental						
3	Office, Print and Post.			8000		9328	
4	Telephone Expense			1300		3951	
5	Uniforms			2000		4922	
6	Walked Guests			500		807	
7	Xerox Costs			2000		1712	
8	TOTAL CONTROLLABLES:			171854	2.8	190082	3.6
9							
10	CONTROL PROFIT:			5,096524	82.8	4,318312	81.0
11							
12	HOURS:						
13	Wage Department 01			5000		5141	
14	02			18000		17984	
15	03			14192		14297	
16	04			2688		2543	
17	05						
18	06			14000		13591	
19	SLS/MH = $117.68 07			52296		48969	
20	08			18000		18721	
21	09			8760		7623	
22	TOTAL HOURS			132936		128869	
23							
24	Average Wage Rate			5 ^{38}		5 ^{30}	
25	Sales/Manhour			46 ^{29}		41 ^{38}	
26	Hskpg MH/Occ. Room			48		49	
27	Wage Cost/Sales Dollar (%)			11.6		12.8	
28							
29	% Occupancy			85		77.5	
30	Room-nights			109117		99531	
31	Average Room Rate			56 ^{25}		53 ^{43}	
32–40							

Figure 11.24 (*continued*)

expenditure budget. Controller indicates that approval is forthcoming to transfer these cost items to capital expenditures. Item is already over budget for the year. If this transfer is not made, additional funds need to be budgeted in this area.

(6) Guest supplies for third period are now under control after being well over budget for periods one and two due to payment of invoices for annual supplies of guestroom stationery. Item will remain in control for the remainder of the fiscal year.

(7) Laundry expense now under control after major breakdown in second period required the use of outside laundry services.

(8) Period linen expense reflects payment of invoice for drop shipment. Expense well under control for the year.

(9) Uniform cost well over budget due to direction from top management to change senior housekeeper's uniform (not budgeted). Cost savings during the year should bring this item near control by the end of the fiscal year.

(10) Total controllables 1.3 percent over budget for the period but only .3 percent for YTD. Controls and management decisions as indicated will make annual budget attainable and on target by the fifth period.

(11) Control profit requires no comment since it is under control.

ROOMS DEPT.
Period Statement

Page 1

Monthly Income Statement
for 3rd Period

CRITIQUE NOTES	#	Description	Period Actual $	%	Period Budget $	%	YTD Budget $	%	YTD Actual $	%
	1	Total Room Sales	468166		468000		2307110		2295895	
	2	Rebate Allowance	<285>		<500>		<1500>		<1145>	
	3	Net Room Sales	467881		467500		2299210		2294750	
	4	Other Sales	2544		2655		7965		8012	
	5	Cost of Sales	<1895>		<1406>		<4218>		<4350>	
	6	TOTAL SALES	469030	100	468752	100	2302963	100	2298412	100
	7	Wage Dept. 01	2488		2800		7500		7325	
(1)	8	02	9688		8854		25961		26341	
	9	03	5994		6004		18013		17912	
	10	04	1245		1137		3412		8544	
	11	06	5602		5654		16962		16812	
(2)	12	07	19121		20554		57965		56121	
	13	08	6450		6500		19500		19121	
	14	09	2721		2695		8086		8421	
	15	TOTAL WAGES	53309	11.4	53498	11.5	157899	12.8	155757	11.9
	16	Overtime Prem.	226		100		300		514	
	17	Holiday Pay	488		1784		5353		1621	
	18	Management Salaries	5161		5885		16154		15483	
	19	Bonuses			769		2308			
	20	TOTAL SALARIES AND WAGES	59184	12.6	61736	13.2	181514	13.9	173875	13.4
	21	Vacation Management			200		600			
	22	Vacation Hourly	655		423		1269		1471	
	23	Payroll Taxes	2188		2242		6726		5921	
	24	H & W Ins.	461		488		1467		1374	
	25	Employee Relations			39		115			
	26	Employee Food	1598		1733		5199		5044	
	27	TOTAL EMPLOYEE COSTS	4902	1.0	5124	1.1	15372	1.2	13810	1.1
	28	Controllables:								
	29	Bad Debts Provision	255						641	
	30	Corp. Pub. Relations							175	
(3)	31	Cleaning Supplies	1660		1420		4261		5691	
	32	Commission Exp.	141		100		800		321	
(4)	33	Contract Services	450		231		692		1020	
	34	Decoration & Plants			100		300			
	35	Entertainment			50		150		120	
	36	Equipment Rental			104		312			
(5)	37	General Expense	750		100		300		1540	
(6)	38	Guest Supplies	2821		2840		8521		11652	
	39	Holidex Rental	692		692		2076		2076	
(7)	40	Laundry Expense	2945		3207		9619		9991	

Figure 11.25 Rooms department period statement indicating progress toward the budget for the third of thirteen periods in the fiscal year. (Statement refers to Figure 11.24, which is based on the model hotel.) Note that the third period is compared to the spread budget for the third period, and that year-to-date (YTD) comparisons (totals of periods one, two, and three) are also made. Look closely to see if performance for the third period reflects improvement toward the overall year or a deterioration of performance.

(12) and (13) The trend noted (1 and 2) is also reflected in senior housekeeper and section housekeeper hour use. [What appears to be happening is that senior housekeepers are cleaning guestrooms in the absence of sufficient section housekeepers on daily staff. This problem will persist if (07) staffing remains low or if there is an attendance problem with section housekeepers.] Management attention to this area of personnel administration will be forthcoming. Staffing and call-off problems will be resolved and under control by the beginning of the fifth period.

(14) Average wage rate being high may be a reflection from another department. In addition, low turnover can keep a wage rate high.

(15) Rooms department sales per manhour is in excellent condition.

(16) Section housekeeper hours per occupied room is too low (.42 as opposed to .48 budgeted—and getting worse). This is another indication that rooms are being cleaned by supervisors at a higher wage rate.

The use of supervisors to clean guest rooms is the most glaring problem revealed when analyzing

ROOMS DEPT.
Period Statement

Page 2

Monthly Income Statement
for 3rd Period _____

CRITIQUE NOTES		Description	Period Actual $	%	Period Budget $	%	YTD Budget $	%	YTD Actual $	%
(8)	1	Linen Expense	4521		3814		9942		4521	
	2	Linen Rental								
	3	Office, Print and Post	602		815		1840		1735	
	4	Telephone Expense	148		100		300		626	
(9)	5	Uniforms	2421		154		461		2421	
	6	Walked Guests	88		38		115		295	
	7	Zerox Costs	88		154		461		375	
(10)	8	TOTAL CONTROLLABLES	17582	3.7	13219	2.8	40050	3.1	43200	3.3
	9									
(11)	10	CONTROL PROFIT	387362	82.4	388673	82.0	1065927	81.9	1068027	82.3
	11									
	12	HOURS								
	13	Wage Department 01	379		385		1155		1131	
(12)	14	02	1532		1385		4154		4280	
	15	03	1088		1092		3275		3198	
	16	04	214		207		621		626	
	17	05								
	18	06	1045		1077		3231		3166	
(13)	19	07	3641		3468		11232		10431	
	20	08	1839		1885		4154		3594	
	21	09	698		674		2022		1554	
	22	TOTAL HOURS	9936		10173		29844		27980	
	23									
(14)	24	Average Wage Rate		5 36		5 28		5 27		5 56
(15)	25	Sales/Manhour		47 20		46 29		46 29		46 40
(16)	26	Hskpg MH/Occ. Room		.42		.48		.49		.44
	27	Wage Cost/Sales Dollar (%)		11.4		11.5		12.1		11.8
	28									
	29	% Occupancy		86 6		85 9		80 5		79 6
	30	Room-nights	8563		8500		23883		23622	
	31	Average Room Rate		54 64		55 00		54 39		54 81
	32									
	33									
	34									
	35									
	36									
	37									
	38									
	39									
	40									

Figure 11.25 (*continued*)

the period statement. Immediate attention is needed here. Other areas out of control have been recognized and intentions for corrective measures have been given. Analyze other portions of the statement to ensure understanding.

Summary

Subroutines are as much a part of the executive housekeeper's daily concerns as is the housekeeping daily routine. Although the subroutines mentioned in this chapter do not directly relate to one another, the tie between them is the need to make each one a *routine* rather than an exception to the daily routine.

Because all routines recur periodically, they are subject to standardization and procedural specification through the use of forms. Numerous forms were introduced, all of which could be modified to fit any hotel, hospital, or health-care operation of any size or complexity.

Participation in the subroutines by junior managers and supervisors serves two important functions: It adds to personnel development and it frees the executive housekeeper to become more involved in solving unique problems and in thinking creatively. Although many subroutines are handed down by top management, a well-informed and progressive executive housekeeper can be very influential in presenting and fostering the development of subroutine ideas that could become company-wide standards of practice.

For organizational purposes, subroutines were presented under five major headings: cleaning and maintenance, operational controls, personnel administration, communication and training, and long-range planning.

KEY TERMS AND CONCEPTS

Subroutines
Public areas
Cleaning and maintenance circuits (rounds)
General cleaning
Deep cleaning
Projects
Repair and physical maintenance
Maintenance Work-Request form
Second request
Maintenance inspection
Maintenance checklist
Room inspections
Inspector/Inspectress
Spot check
Inspection day
Inspection programs
Property inspection program
Fresh look
Zone inspection program
Zones
Documented
Weekly maintenance inspection
Inventories
Control information
Cleaning and guest supply inventory
Count sheet
Inventory record log
Controller
Forecasting man-hour requirements
Weekly Wage Forecast
Forecast occupancy
Wage department
Target statistics
In control
Weekly Wage Analysis

Actual expenditures
Period Statements
Critiqued
Purchasing
Purchasing agent
Competitive shopping form
Physical linen inventory
Linen Count Sheet
Period linen inventory count record
Total linen in use
Total new linen on hand
Linen valuation
Linen brokers
Linen mills
Annual linen reorder plan
Time card control
Time sheets
Time in the hole
Leaves of Absence (LOA)
Time sheet preparation
Performance appraisal
Probationary period of employment
Pay increases
Pay scale
Leveling technique
Departmental meetings
Operational budget for housekeeping department
Operational budget cycle
Periods
Consolidated room sales summary
Wage departments
Man-hour justification
Sales per man-hour
Controllable items

DISCUSSION AND REVIEW QUESTIONS

1. What are the differences and similarities between subroutines and daily routines in housekeeping departments?
2. Name three subroutines not mentioned in this chapter. In a new operation, why is it so important to identify as many routines as possible and to prepare SOPs as quickly as possible? What major role do SOPs play in the operation of a department?
3. Describe the concept of zone inspection. How is it related to the Division of Work Document and the Area Responsibility Plan? In what way does a zone inspection program facilitate the development of junior managers?

4. Explain a maintenance work request system. Describe the flow of information required to ensure proper control.
5. Who should inspect guestrooms? Develop a plan around each person listed, indicating how many rooms should be inspected by each person, how often, and why.
6. Prepare a department meeting agenda. How would you go about gaining maximum participation from attendees?
7. Explain what is meant by the 13-period system. What are advantages and disadvantages of using this system for operational reporting? for financial reporting?
8. List the parts of a budget submission package. Explain the use of each part. How would you justify expenditures for additional section housekeeper man-hours during the evening shift after being told that room rates would be increasing?

NOTES

1. Based on an interview with Clarence R. Johnson, MELCOR. Reprinted from Stan Gottlieb, "Maintenance: A Workable Program for the Smaller Property," *Lodging*, May 1984. Copyright © 1984, American Hotel Association Directory Corporation.

PART FOUR

Special Topics: Environmental Services, Safeguarding of Assets, In-House Laundries, & the Full Circle of Management

I n Part Three the management functions of Direction and Control were applied to the "Daily Routine of Housekeeping" and to various "Subroutines" that may be encountered by members of a housekeeping team during daily operations. In this final Part, the specific topics of Environmental Services (housekeeping for hospitals and nursing homes), concerns for the safeguarding of assets (security and safety), and on-premise laundries will be covered. In conclusion, problem solving, management styles, and the future of housekeeping as a management profession will also be discussed.

12

Environmental Services— the Hospital and Nursing Home Look at Housekeeping

CHAPTER OBJECTIVES

1. To learn new terms and definitions related to hospital and nursing home housekeeping.
2. To learn about microbiology, types of soil, the chemistry of cleaning, contamination, disinfection, the precautionary handling of linen and soiled articles, and the requirements for disposal of infectious waste.
3. To visualize the all-encompassing concerns of environmental services, including pest control and the control and disposal of garbage and infectious waste.
4. To become acquainted with the Joint Commission on the Accreditation of Health Care Organizations and its role in the establishment of quality standards for environmental control.

5. To understand the nature of our planet, ecology, and the significance of our responsibilities regarding pollution of the earth and its atmosphere.

Environmental Services: Nature of the Profession

The National Executive Housekeeper's Association (N.E.H.A.) has long recognized the similarity in responsibilities of persons performing housekeeping functions in hospitals, hotels, and nursing homes. The Association draws its membership not only from hotels, retirement centers, and contract cleaning establishments, but also from hospitals and nursing homes. Also, the movement of management personnel between these fields is well documented.

When asked how difficult it is for a manager to make the transition in either direction, Don Richie, **Director of Environmental Services**, University Medical Center, Las Vegas, Nevada, stated that "the main function of housekeeping in both areas is to clean rooms and public areas, and to dispose of trash and rubbish. There is only one major difference, however, and that is in hospitals we know exactly what we are walking into, and in hotels, you don't know what you may be dealing with." Herein lies the primary difference in technical training between the executive housekeeper and the environmental services director of a hospital or nursing home.

Although the environmental services director may benefit equally with the hotel executive housekeeper by understanding the principles of planning, organizing, staffing, directing, and controlling set forth in the earlier chapters of this book, the **Joint Commission on Accreditation of Health Care Organizations (JCAHO)** has stringent requirements that must be met in the fields of environmental services for hospitals and nursing homes. This chapter is devoted to the terminology and definitions encountered in this unique environment and to the requirements as set forth by the various agencies that control these issues.

Grateful appreciation is extended to Ms. Janice M. Kurth, Vice President of Operations, Metropolitan Hospital, New York City, N.Y. and to Aspen Publications for allowing the use of their publication "Hospital Environmental Services Policy and Procedure Manual" as a framework for this chapter. Also, to the Desert Springs Hospital of Las Vegas, Nevada for their assistance and access to their procedural manuals.

Hospitals and Hotels Require Similar Professional Skills

In most cases, the action required of persons working in hospital environmental service departments is very much the same as the actions required of persons working in hotel housekeeping. After studies are made of the work that must be performed, Job Descriptions are prepared indicating the proper divisions of work; then step-by-step guidelines are prepared in the form of *Standard Operating Procedures (SOPs)*. These documents *formalize* procedures that must be performed by workers assigned to specific routines. In Appendix A the reader will find two complete sets of Job Descriptions for both hotels and hospitals.

The uniqueness of hospitals and health care institutions becomes evident, however, when one investigates the special care and consideration that must be taken when dealing with the following:

- The daily and terminal **disinfection** of patient rooms
- The **terminal cleaning** of hospital surgical suites (operating rooms)
- The disposition of used **needles, syringes, and sharps**
- The disposal of infectious waste

Each of these procedural tasks will be dealt with in detail; but first, a proper groundwork must be laid regarding basic knowledge of **microbiology** and the **chemistry of cleaning and disinfecting**.

Basic Microbiology*

Microbiology is a natural science that began with the discovery of the microscope, which led, in the seventeenth century, to the dramatic realization that living forms exist that are invisible to the naked eye. It had been suggested as early as the thirteenth century that "invisible" organisms were responsible for decay and disease. The word *microbe* was coined in the last quarter of the nineteenth century to describe these organisms, all of which were thought to be related. As microbiology eventually developed into a separate science, microbes (small living things) were found to comprise a very large group of extremely diverse organisms—thus the subdivision of the discipline into three parts, known today as bacteriology, protozoology, and virology.

Microbiology, therefore, is the study and identification of **microorganisms**. Such study encompasses the study of bacteria, rickettsiae, small fungi (such as yeasts and molds), algae, and protozoans, as well as problematical forms of life such as viruses. Because of the difficulty in assigning plant or animal status to microorganisms—some are plant-like, others animal-like—they are sometimes considered to be a separate group called **protists**. Microbes can also be divided into prokaryotes, which have a primitive and dispersed kind of nuclear material—such as the blue-green algae, bacteria, and rickettsiae—and eukaryotes, which display a distinct nucleus bounded by a membrane. These are the small algae other than the blue-greens, yeasts and molds, and protozoans. (All higher organisms are eukaryotes.)

*Adapted with permission from the introduction to "Microbiology", *Encyclopaedia Britannica*, 15th Edition, © 1979, by Encyclopaedia Britannica, Inc.

Man's daily life is interwoven with microorganisms. They are found in the soil, in the sea, and in the air. Although unnoticed, they are abundant everywhere and provide ample evidence of their presence, sometimes unfavorably, as when they cause decay in objects valued by humans, or generate disease; and sometimes favorably, as when they ferment alcohol to wine and beer, raise bread, flavor cheeses, and create other dairy products. Microorganisms are of incalculable value in nature, causing the disintegration of animal and plant remains and converting them into gases and minerals that can be recycled in other organisms.

It might be said that approximately 90 percent of all microorganisms are good and essential to nature and mankind. Our concern in this text, however, are the 10 percent that are not.

Terminology Appropriate to the Subject of Microbiology

What follows is a list of specific microorganisms worthy of our concern. Some are represented below as if they were properly stained and seen under a microscope at 500 × magnification.

Bacteria	Used to refer to microorganisms in general, also the same as germs and/or microbes
Bacillus	Bacteria that is rod shaped

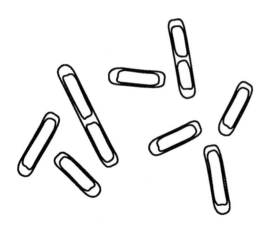

Coccus	Bacteria that is round shaped

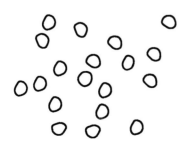

Fungus	Simple plants lacking chlorophyll, bread mold is an example
Spirochete	Cocrkscrew-shaped microorganisms

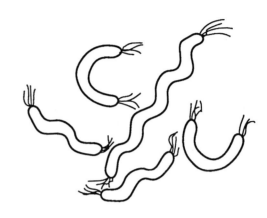

Spore	Microorganisms that are in a restive, protective shell
Staphylococcus	A grape-like cluster organism which can cause boils, skin infections, purulent discharge and/or peritonitis

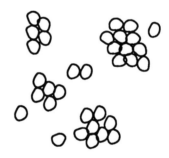

Streptococcus	Chain-like round organism which causes the strep throat infection

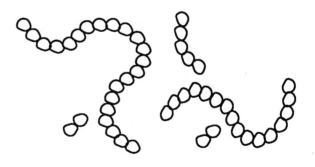

Virus	The smallest of all microorganisms

Other words significant to the study of microbiology include the following:

Aerobic	A bacteria that must be exposed to, and requires, air (oxygen) to survive and grow.
Anaerobic	A bacteria that can live without exposure to air (oxygen).
Antisepsis	A process whereby chemicals are used on the skin for bacteriostatic and germicidal purposes.
Asepsis	To be free from germs and infection.
Asepsis (medical)	A method used to prevent the spread of a communicable disease. Handwashing and isolation are examples.
Asepsis (surgical)	A method using sterile equipment, supplies, and procedures when entering the "sterile" interior of the body.
Autoclave	An oven-like machine, using steam under pressure, in which supplies are subjected to intense heat for a specified period of time. It is also called a sterilizer.
Chemical agent	A chemical added to a solution in the correct dosage that will kill bacteria, or at least stop its growth.
Disinfection	Process whereby chemicals are used on floors and equipment for bacteriostatic and germicidal purposes.
Disinfection (concurrent)	Process used while disease is still in progress.
Disinfection (terminal)	Process used when disease is ended.
Gram (positive/negative)	Refers to the color staining of test samples for certain bacteria. *Gram positive* is a "blue" test result when certain bacteria are treated with testing reagents. *Gram negative* is a "red" test indication.
Intermediate host	One who transmits a disease but is not affected by it. Also known as an "immune carrier." An example would be the anopheles mosquito, which would bite a person infected with malaria, then bite another person, thus transmitting the disease.
Micron	A unit of measure — 1/25,000 of 1 inch. (Bacteria usually found in the range of 1 to 300 microns.)
Pathogenic	Disease causing or disease producing.
Physical agents	Nonchemical agents that will affect the growth of bacteria or will destroy it. Examples of nonchemical agents are sunlight, temperature, heat, moisture, or pressure.
Reagents	A group of testing solutions used to identify certain bacteria and their properties. Such tests can help determine what chemicals should be used to kill certain bacteria.
Sterilization	A process whereby all bacteria are killed by heat.

Several Specific Microorganisms and their Characteristics

The following is a list of eleven common microorganisms that one might come in contact with whether working in a hospital nursing home or hotel. The phonetic pronunciation of the name and several characteristics will also be given.

Staphylococcus Aureus (staff-ill-i-COCK-us OAR-ea-us). Gram positive (blue stain). Major cause of infections (boils, carbuncles, ear infections), food poisoning. Size: .8 to 1 micron. Is resistant to antibiotics. Best cure is heat.

Mycobacterium Tuberculosis (my-co-back-TEER-ee-um too-BER-cue-LOW-sis). Gram negative (red stain). Acid fast (cannot be killed with acid).

Salmonella Choleraesuis (sal-moe-NELL-a coller-ah-SUE-iss). Gram negative. A form of food poisoning. Body can usually tolerate and throw off. The bacteria is used to test germicides.

Pseudomonas Aeruginosa (sue-doe-MOAN-us air-o-gin-O-sa). Gram negative. Very resistant to disinfectants. Major problems are public restrooms. Disease is more prevalent in women. Bacteria will grow in standing water.

Streptococcus Pyogenes (strep-tow-COCK-us pie-O-jeans). Gram positive. Bacteria found in public places; wound and throat infections.

Also associated with scarlet fever and rheumatic fever.

Diplococcus Pneumoniae (dip-lo-COCK-us new-MOAN-ee-a). Gram Positive. Lobar (lung) pneumonia. Also walking pneumonia. Treatable with antibiotics.

Mycobacterium Diptheria (my-co-back-TEER-ee-um dip-THE-ree-ah). Gram positive. Transmitted in milk. Not too prevalent due to vaccination.

Escherichia Coli (ee-shear-EEK-ee-ah COAL-i). Gram negative. Can grow in soap. Never use bar soap in a public washroom. Bacteria can be spread through animal droppings.

Clostridium Perfringens (clos-TRID-ee-um per-FRIN-gins). No gram stain. An anaerobic spore. "Botulism." Found in feces, sewers, improperly sterilized milk, or sealed foods. Also found in untreated wounds (gaseous gangrene).

Tricophyton Interdigitale (tri-CO-fi-ton inter-digit-ALL-ee). No gram stain. A fungus (Athlete's Foot). The fungus can be used to evaluate a germicidal.

Virus A part of the protist kingdom. Includes influenza, A (flue virus), herpes simplex, Vaccinia (cowpox), adenovirus type 2, and AIDS.

The Five Types of Soil

There are five types of soil that present the environmental service manager, or anyone with the responsibility to "clean," with a challenge. Not all soils are directly and solely bacteria-related, but we shall keep bacteria on the list. Each soil, regardless of whether it is organic or inorganic, is a compound capable of being altered by chemical reaction.

The following are the five types of soil:

1. *Mineral* A solid homogeneous crystalline chemical element or compound, having a specific chemical composition, that results from the inorganic processes of nature.
2. *Organic* A substance consisting only of matter or products of plant or animal origin. Chemically they are compounds containing strings of carbon molecules attached to one or more hydrogen molecules.
3. *Osmological* Relating to soils of organic or inorganic matter that emit an (unpleasant) odor.
4. *Bacterial* Soils or compounds containing active (live) bacteria.

5. *Entomological* Soils involving insects, especially those that can cause or carry diseases.

The Chemistry of Cleaning

To understand the chemistry of cleaning, the student must first accept the fact that he or she need *not* become a chemist to do their jobs. Having a layperson's understanding of what is happening as we apply a disinfectant or detergent can give us respect for the value of using products for whatever purpose they are designed. Too often, employees will "assume" that something *red* will clean better than something *blue*, that a *thick* solution must be better than a *watery* one, or most often, that *more* is *better*. This section, while presenting no **chemical formulas**, does require the student to master a new group of terms and hopefully, to develop a respect for what has gone into the several products currently in use in the world of cleaning and disinfecting. The chemistry of cleaning is most appropriate in this section since we are not only cleaning, we are also killing bacteria (disinfecting).

What follows is a small amount of lay chemistry for the professional who might then better understand the history and significance of product development:

Atom. According to the "Periodic Table of Elements," the smallest combination of nucleus (center core of protons and neutrons) and surrounding electrons associated with a given named **Element**. For example, an atom of sulfur (S) or oxygen (O) or hydrogen (H) or carbon (C) is the smallest particle that is recognizable by that name. These all have different "weights," hydrogen being the lightest and uranium one of the heaviest, because of their respective atomic structures. Over 106 elements have been discovered in the universe. Some of them do not even occur naturally but have been created by man in only the last century.

Molecule. a compound created by combining a certain group of atoms. Many of the atoms described above *when found in nature* are seen as molecules that will combine with other molecules to form more complex chemical compounds. For example: Chemically speaking, atoms of hydrogen (H) or oxygen (O) in nature are found as gaseous molecules of hydrogen (H_2) or oxygen (O_2). The associated suffix number describes certain characteristics as to how they react chemically when combined with each other or with other elements. Their "chemical" reactions are based on many different phenomena, but primarily on how many free electrons are found in their outer ring of electrons. A molecule having the same number of protons in its nucleus as it has electrons in orbit around the nucleus would have an electrical charge of 0 (zero **valence**). If there is an excess of protons in the nucleus, a positive charge of +1 or +2 exists (positive valence); if there are more electrons than protons, then the charge would be negative (−1 or −2, negative valence). The combination of valence plus the "type" of atom being considered determines how difficult, easy, violent, or modest the reaction will be as we try to combine molecules of atoms with other molecules to form more elaborate compounds. Each single molecule of *water* is made up of two atoms of *hydrogen* and one atom of *oxygen*. The smallest atom of hydrogen found in nature is a gaseous molecule of hydrogen (H_2). The smallest molecule of oxygen found in nature is gaseous oxygen (O_2). Under certain conditions, igniting hydrogen in the presence of oxygen causes a violent explosion with the by-product of water. To keep the accounting correct, one molecular formula is mentioned to show that things do balance. For example: Two molecules of gaseous hydrogen, $2H_2(g)$, will chemically combine with one molecule of gaseous oxygen, $O_2(g)$, to form two molecules of liquid water, $2H_2O(l)$.

Some molecules, particularly those in biological systems and plastics, are very large and contain thousands of atoms.

Chemical Compounds

Chemical reactions are also called chemical transformations. They entail the conversion of one or more substances into one or more different substances called **compounds**. The substances that react are called **reactants**, and the results of the reaction are called **products**.

In a chemical reaction atoms are regrouped to form different substances; atoms are not destroyed or converted into atoms of other elements (as one might find in **atomic reactions**). Cleaning chemicals are designed to chemically combine with specific types of soil. The chemical products are then removed chemically, clinging to the soil to be removed.

The following is a list of some basic terms relevant to chemical reactions:

Radical: a group of atoms that do not dissociate during a chemical reaction but stay together. The following are common radicals.

(OH) Hydroxide	(NO_3) Nitrate
(SO_4) Sulfate	(PO_4) Phosphate
(NH_4) Ammonium	(CO_3) Carbonate

Organic compounds: compounds made up of carbon, hydrogen, and oxygen.

Ion: an atom or group of atoms that has acquired an electrical charge by a gain or loss of electrons.

Anion: an atom containing a negative electrical charge.

Cation: an atom containing a positive electrical charge.

Acid: a compound in which a majority of anions, either atoms or radicals, are combined with the cation hydrogen (H^+).

Alkali: a cationic metal combined with the anionic hydroxyl (OH) radical known chemically as a hydroxide of the metal. Alkalis combine with acids to form *water* and *salts*.

Salts: result when the hydrogen ion of an acid is replaced with a metal.

Water: the **Universal Solvent** (usually the first liquid tried when testing a substance to see if it can be dissolved into a solution).

pH (Specific gravity): a measure of the acidity or alkalinity of a substance. A scale from 0 to 14 is used. The number 7 is the neutral point. All substances with a measured (pH) more than 7 are **alkaline**; less than 7 and the product is **acidic**.

R: the letter used to identify a long carbon group of some known chain length or configuration of a chemical compound.

Disinfectant: compound that kills bacteria.

Quaternary Ammonium Compounds: A class of disinfectants that are cationic surface active agents containing nitrogen, long carbon chains (Rs), and an anion, usually chlorine.

Phenol: carbolic acid.

Phenolic: derivations of phenol widely used as disinfectants. Long carbon chains are attached to a precise position on the phenol molecule. One thousand times more active than pure phenol.

Iodine: a highly reactive element, which makes it a highly effective disinfectant with a broad spectrum of efficiency.

Alcohols: methanol, ethanol, isopropanol; function similarly to Quaternary Ammonium Compounds in method of action.

Detergent: a synthetic organic soap, either oil or water soluble, derived from hydrocarbons, petroleum, alcohols, amines, sulfonates, or other organic compounds.

Most chemical agents that have been created for use in cleaning *and* disinfecting fall into the *Quaternary Ammonium* or the *Phenolic* category. They both destroy pathogenic bacteria.

Antiseptics: substances that slow bacterial growth; includes both iodine and alcohols.

Bacteriostat: prevents bacteria from multiplying. An antibiotic (not for consumption, but for use in such places as laundries).

Sanitizer: normally used in food areas and to chemically treat filters in air-handling units.

Preservatives: used in foods to inhibit bacterial growth.

Familiarization with the various aspects of chemical usage in both health care institutions and hotels requires a basic understanding of not only chemicals but also the chemical process. The wise director of environmental service knows and understands the chemical products being used at his or her facility and how to use them.

Product Testing

There are several tests that can determine the efficiency and effectiveness of a product. The Association of Analytical Chemists (AOAC) can also test products both for the manufacturer and the user.

A typical test would be to prepare several *petri test dishes* (small flat round dishes with a nourishing gelatin [host]), which can be daubed with a swab containing the bacteria to be tested. First the bacteria is given a period of time to grow. Then the bacteria is treated with differing dilutions of a germicidal product. The goal of the test is to determine at what **dilution ratio** the product kills a bacteria. Further tests might be done to determine how long it takes for a given germicidal to kill bacteria at a set dilution, or to determine the effects of adding certain products to increase the efficiency of a certain germicidal.

The Product Manufacturer and the Chemical Challenge

After having been exposed to a layman's microbiology and chemistry, the challenge to the product manufacturer becomes more obvious: to determine what product can first clean, then disinfect. Inorganic cleaning can be as simple as sweeping dust from the floor, picking it up and disposing of it in such a way that it will not find its way back into a space. The products available in supermarkets most often exploit certain chemicals that will loosen "soil," hold it in **chemical suspension**, and then pick the suspension up by a number of different means and dispose of it.

The disinfectant, however, adds an addition challenge: Not only to clean, but to enter the membrane of the bacterial cell and kill the bacteria nucleus.

Carbolic Acid (Phenol)

Carbolic Acid (Phenol) was, for years, the best killer of bacteria available for disinfecting an area. However, the compound required extended periods of contact with the area to be disinfected. Additionally, where phenol would kill bacteria, it was not a good cleaning agent.

With the development of **phenolic** (a derivative of phenol), the disinfectant became 1000 times more effective at entering the protective membrane of bacteria and killing them. However, it continues to be a poor cleaning agent, and it is a highly **toxic** material. The normal dilution ratio for this product is 256 to 1 (1/2 ounce in one gallon of water).

Quaternary Ammonium Compounds

In addition to being effective antibacterial agents, quaternary ammonium compounds are also good cleaning agents. They are also highly toxic, however, and for years these compounds had one additional drawback as a disinfectant: they were ineffective against the tuberculosis bacteria. Recent progress in the development of quaternaries, however, has conquered the tuberculosis problem, and these compounds have since become the disinfectant of choice in hospitals.

Nonchemical Agents That Kill or Slow Bacterial Growth

Light is an excellent killer of bacteria as long as it is on the surface of an object or on the skin. Sunlight and ultra violet light are excellent sanitizers but do not penetrate beyond the surface of an object or the skin.

Cold does not kill but slows and inhibits growth; in some cases bacteria will go dormant due to cold.

Heat kills bacteria. A steam sterilizer is vital sterilizing equipment. In cases where human tissue is involved, contact time of heat is important.

Physical removal. Use of air filters and electrostatic filters is significant. Also, vacuuming and simply wiping can remove bacteria.

A Controlled Bacterial Environment

A controlled bacterial environment is an environment that is kept clean and bug-free, and has garbage properly disposed of. In addition, covered storage is needed, garbage handlers should wear gloves, and steps should be taken to prevent all forms of pollution.

To *prevent the spread of infection*, facilities must be kept clean and healthy. Disease is spread through **bacteria trails**. The following chain of events is seen as the bacteria trail. The **chain of infection** starts with a *Pathogenic Causative Agent*. Next is the *Reservoir* or place for the **pathogen** to live, followed by the *Mode of Escape, Method of Transmission, and Mode of Entry into the Host*. The person is the Host who passes the pathogen and the chain continues. Break the chain of events at any point and the infection is stopped.

The Isolation Unit

Figure 12.1 shows the layout of an **"Isolation Unit"** in a major hospital. Note how the isolation cart contains a supply of gowns, gloves, masks, plastic bags, meltaway bags, and laundry bags. Inside the unit are various methods and locations to dispose of isolation clothing prior to coming out of the room.

Contaminated Articles and Excreta

For some patients in isolation, it is necessary to take special precautions with articles contaminated by urine or feces. For example, it may be necessary to disinfect (or discard) a bedpan with the excreta.

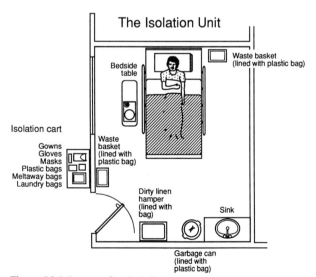

Figure 12.1 Layout of an isolation unit.

Terminal Cleaning and Disinfecting the Surgical Suite

The purpose of cleaning and disinfecting a surgical suite is to reduce the number of microorganisms present and thereby maintain a clean, safe environment for patients, staff, and visitors.

The necessary equipment must first be assembled. Items needed would be:

A 10-quart plastic bucket for washing furniture

Cloths for damp wiping, wet and dry

Disinfectant/detergent

Spray tanks for applying solution to floors

Water vacuums to pick up solution

Floor machine with scrub pad

Wall-washing suit (includes bucket, wringer, mop handle, and mop heads)

The suite-cleaning procedure would then include the following:

1. Prepare, clean, and check all equipment.
2. Prepare disinfectant solution and place in the spray tank, wall-washing unit, and 10-quart bucket.
3. Proceed to the first assigned surgical suite; clean and disinfect the bed/table and damp wipe every surface with the disinfecting/cleaning agent.
4. Using a similar technique, disinfect all furniture (ring stands, kick buckets, tables, or other pieces of rolling equipment), moving them to the middle of the room around the table/bed. Rinse each item with a hand cloth after damp wiping.
5. Disinfect all wall hanging fixtures, being careful not to get solution inside or behind humistats, thermostats, x-ray screens, sterile cabinet doors, or electrical outlets.
6. Spray disinfectant solution on the floor; use a water vacuum to pick up solution. Leave a 12-inch wet strip close to and around the furniture that is still in the middle of the room.
7. Replace the furniture, being sure to roll the wheels through the 12-inch wet strip to disinfect them. Then roll the bed/table through the solution to one side of the room.
8. Clean the light fixture in the same way the furniture was cleaned.
9. Spray solution on the floor in the middle of the suite. Use the wet vacuum to pick up all remaining solution.

10. Return the table/bed to its proper place.
11. Retire from the suite and thoroughly clean all equipment with disinfectant/detergent. Store equipment properly or proceed to the next surgical suite and repeat the procedure.

Special Concerns

1. There should be no spraying of solutions close to sterile carts.
2. Corridors, ceilings, and walls should be disinfected monthly. Spot wash as needed.
3. Cubicle curtains in the recovery area or elsewhere in the surgical theater should be changed monthly, or sooner as needed.

Disposition of Used Needles, Syringes, and "Sharps"

The purpose of this procedure is to ensure that used sharp objects such as needles, syringes, and sharps (sharp plastic cases in which needles and disposable scalpels are placed for disposal) are carefully and safely removed from the hospital and safely disposed of in such a manner that unsuspecting persons coming in contact with such items run little risk of becoming contaminated. The hospital nursing service has primary responsibility in preparing such objects for disposal.

The following procedures should be used:

1. Nursing service personnel—place used syringes found in patient floor care areas into the plastic disposal containers designated by Nursing Service as "for sharps disposal."
2. Sterilize all sharps containers from patient floor care areas and send to Central Service for collection and disposal.
3. Sterilize containers from Surgery, Emergency Room, Isolations, Respiratory Care, Pulmonary Function, and Nuclear Medicine and send to Central Service for collection and disposal.
4. Central service personnel—send all sterilized sharps to the laboratory for final disposition.
5. Laboratory personnel—place all needles and syringes into the proper containers; seal them, place in a red plastic bag, and sterilize before final disposal.
6. The laboratory must then ensure that Environmental Service personnel pick up the sterilized sharps and dispose of them with normal refuse.

Disposal of Refuse From Antineoplastic Agents

The purpose of safe removal and disposal of waste associated with the preparation and disposal of antineoplastic agents is to ensure that unauthorized or unsuspecting personnel will not become contaminated by coming in contact with such agents.

The following procedure should be used:

1. Environmental Services will be responsible for the removal of the sealed trash receptacles marked with a green label as **chemotherapy drugs**. These containers are usually found in the soiled utility rooms on floors where antineoplastic agents are administered.
2. The environmental technician, aide, nurse, or unit secretary will notify Environmental Services when containers are full.
3. The full container will be sealed before it is removed from the soiled utility room by the assigned environmental service technician, who will replace it with an empty container.
4. The full container will be taken to the temporary storage area designated for antineoplastic agents refuse.
5. Containers will be removed periodically by a properly licensed firm authorized to remove such waste.

The above procedures are subject to review and periodic inspection by an agent of the Joint Commission. Unsatisfactory results of such inspections could form the basis of a "Warning" with notification of action required to maintain "Certification." Unheeded warnings or lack of action to correct could ultimately lead to the suspension of certification.

Pest Control

Insects have been on this earth for millions of years and most have "weathered the storm" better than any other species. Most have short life spans; they propagate over short spans of time and die, yet the species lives on and on.

The plates that follow (Figure 12.2) show 12 of the "garden variety" pests that should be kept under control as best as possible and not all necessarily for the same reasons. Some insects sting, others either live in damp contaminated areas or in human and food waste and can contaminate the human environment. All insects are capable of transmitting bacteria by picking it up on their bodies and legs and then traveling through their domain and infecting everything they touch, whether human or otherwise.

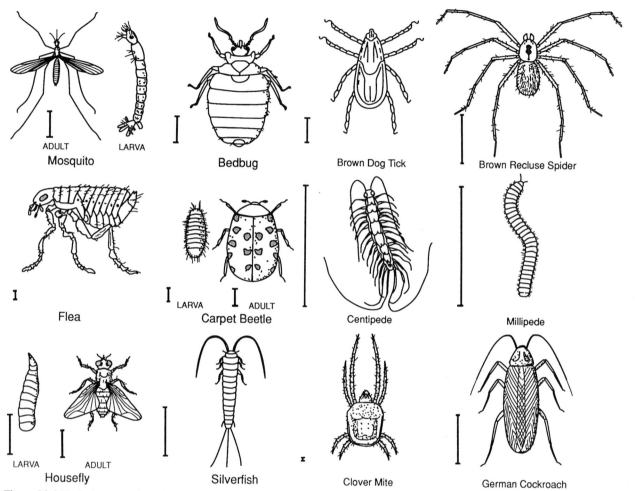

Figure 12.2 Twelve common household pests. The line adjacent to each illustration indicates approximate sizes.

A True Scenario

The ordinary "wood tick" provides a good example of all the elements of the chain of infection. The tick normally originates (propagates) in damp heavily wooded or vegetated areas. It lies in wait for a warm-blooded animal to pass close enough for it to sense body heat. It then hops (and/ or flies) 10 to 15 feet and firmly attaches itself to the animal and begins to siphon blood. This activity continues over a period of several days, during which time the host animal may travel long distances. While a passenger, the tick will be exposed to areas heavily contaminated with bacteria through contact with feces and other decomposing tissue **(causative agent)**. After several days the tick will grow to the size of a human thumb-nail (the **reservoir**). The wound area created by the tick's attachment now grows purulent and weak, allowing the weight of the tick to cause it to drop to the ground **(mode of escape)**, possibly thousands of miles from its initial location. It winds up carrying not only its supply of blood, which it digests over a period of several days, but also a plethora of bacteria on its body shell **(immune carrier)**. Eventually the tick returns to its original size and again takes up the stalk, lying in wait for the next exposure to the heat of animal warmth **(method of transmission)**. This time it is a human who becomes the target for the bite of the long-jumping tick (mode of entry into the new **host**). Ten days to two weeks later, the human notices a rash developing on the extremities and commencing to radiate inwards to the torso, giving the appearance of measles. What appeared to be measles, however, was not, since the recovery time for measles is within ten days from the onset of the rash. Upon close examination, a tick is discovered in the hair of the human and the diagnosis is changed to "Rocky Mountain Spotted Fever" (tick fever). One day later, the young girl dies in her home . . . in Florida. This true scenario clearly demonstrates how the first animal and the tick may both be immune carriers, and the **chain of infection** may be discovered thousands of miles from where the sickness is readily suspected—discovered too late for effective treatment.

Keeping Pests Under Control Means Manipulating the Environment

Persons working in environmental services must set goals regarding tasks related to pest control:

1. Keep the area clean.
2. Remove and dispose of all trash frequently and completely.
3. Use screens in areas where insects are prevalent.
4. Keep facilities in a good state of repair.
5. Have a program of chemical pest control to rid *all* the property of all insects.

Application of Pesticides

The application of pesticides must be closely monitored and controlled. Only those personnel properly trained in the storage, dilution, and application of pesticides and properly licensed by the appropriate state agency should be authorized to apply pesticides. Records should be maintained as to the licensing of specific personnel.

When outside agencies are contracted to do pest control work, credentials should be checked and contracts let for no more than a one year time period. This will allow the facility manager to have quick access to a new outside contractor if pests are not being kept under control.

Types of Pesticides

Pesticides may be classified in a number of ways:

1. By their effectiveness against certain kinds of pests:

   insecticides versus insects

   herbicides versus weeds

2. By how they are formulated and applied:

   dusts

   fogging oils

   granular powders

   wettable powders

3. By the chemistry of the pesticide:

   chlorinated hydrocarbons (Chlordane)

   organic phosphates (Malathion)

   natural organic insecticides (Pyrethmun)

Effectiveness against a particular pest species, safety, clinical hazard to property, type of formulations available, equipment required, and cost of ma-

terial must all be taken into account when choosing a pesticide for a particular job. Recommendations change with experience, the development of new materials, and new governmental regulations. However, there is a degree of stability, and most recommendations last over a period of years. The pesticides recommended in this chapter are likely to be in use for many years. It should be kept in mind, however, that these are not the only materials that will work, but they are standard products that will work if properly used.

Chlordane is a chlorinated hydrocarbon. It is a wide-spectrum, long-residual insecticide widely used against household pests, termites, and turf pests. It is regarded as moderately toxic; however, certain formulations commonly used for termite control have a high percentage of the active compound and should be regarded as quite hazardous to nonprofessionals. Preformulated 2 to 3 percent chlordane oil solutions are available to the nonprofessional for cockroach control. Generally, the nonprofessional lacks the equipment and knowledge to do a satisfactory job of controlling cockroaches.

Diazinon (spectracide) is an organophosphate type, broad-spectrum insecticide that has a rather long residual and is fairly toxic. It is widely used to control cockroaches, ticks, ants, silverfish, spiders, and many other household pests. Diazinon is formulated as a 50 percent wettable powder or 25 percent emulsion. If used by a nonprofessional, considerable care should be exercised and directions followed precisely.

DDVP (vapona, dichlorous) is an organophosphate, volatile insecticide-acaricide which is used under special conditions. Although it is quite toxic, DDVP breaks down rapidly. It is used in cockroach control programs by professional pest control operators and is widely used against flies. It is formulated as a resin strip which is hung from the ceiling. In many cases, however, these resin strips are used in an ineffective manner. One or two strips cannot possibly protect a huge room that has a constant source of fresh air entering from the outside. Follow the formulator's recommendations when using this device.

Kelthane (dicofol) is a chlorinated hydrocarbon-type miticide that is relatively safe when used according to directions. It is widely employed for the control of mites, including both the clover mite and the two-spotted or red spider mite. It is available as a 35 percent wettable powder and is recommended for use by nonprofessionals.

Malathion is an organophosphate-type, broad-spectrum insecticide that has a very low hazard threshold when used according to directions. Although only slightly toxic to man and other mammals, it is highly toxic to fish and birds. It is effective against the two-spotted spider mite. Premium grade, 2 to 3 percent Malathion residual sprays can be used against most household pests; there is less chance of an odor problem with the premium rather than the regular grade. Malathion may be purchased as a 57 percent emulsion concentrate or a 25 percent wettable powder. It *is* recommended for use by nonprofessionals.

Methoxychlor (marlate) is a chlorinated hydrocarbon type, slightly toxic insecticide that is being used as a replacement for DDT. Methoxychlor is not accumulated in human body fat and does not contaminate the environment as does DDT. It is available as a 50 percent wettable powder and is commonly sold as marlate. It is safe for use by nonprofessionals.

DDT is a chlorinated hydrocarbon type, broad-spectrum insecticide that is very stable and persistent. It is only moderately toxic to man. However, because of its cumulative and persistent qualities it is no longer widely used in areas where there is any hazard of environmental contamination. In some states, it is no longer legal to use DDT. However, where legal, under some circumstances (such as the control of lice, fleas, and bedbugs), pest control operators and other environmental service workers still use DDT because it gives the best results and is the safest material available. It *is not* recommended for use by nonprofessionals.

Dimethoate (eygon) is a moderately toxic, organophosphate type insecticide used for fly control. It *is not* recommended for use by nonprofessionals.

Other pesticides. There are many other pesticides available. In commercial, hospital, or nursing home settings, however, pest control is best left to competent experts in the field, properly licensed and experienced to do the job of pest control. Contracting out pest control also removes the necessity of storing pest control products and equipment.

The environmental concern with insect (pests) is primarily **preventive** in nature. Clean-out and clean-up will probably do more to control insects in areas where they are not wanted than any other prevention that can be adopted.

Waste Disposal and Control

There are nine classifications of **waste**, each presenting a slightly different disposal requirement. The term waste is associated with that which is useless, unused, unwanted, or discarded. Classifications are as follows:

Type 0—Trash. Primarily paper. After incineration there is less than 5% residual solid remaining.

Type 1—Rubbish. 80% Type 0, 20% Restaurant waste; 10% will be incombustible. This term includes all nonputrescible refuse except ashes; there are two categories of rubbish, combustible and noncombustible.

   A. *Combustible:* This material is primarily organic—it includes items such as paper, plastics, cardboard, wood, rubber, and bedding

   B. *Noncombustible:* This material is primarily inorganic and includes tin cans, metals, glass, ceramics, and other mineral refuse.

Type 2—Refuse. 50% type 0, 50% type 1. Has a residual moisture content of 50. Requires firing at a higher heat. Leaves 10% solids after firing.

Type 3—Garbage. All food waste. 70% water. Designates putrescible wastes resulting from handling, preparing cooking, and serving food.

Type 4—Residue. Includes all solid wastes. In practice this category includes garbage, rubbish, ashes, and dead animals.

Type 5—Ashes. Residue from fires used for cooking, heating, and on-site incineration.

Type 6—Biologic wastes (includes human and animal remains). Wastes resulting directly from patient diagnosis and treatment procedures; includes materials of medical, surgical, autopsy, and laboratory origin.

   A. *Medical Wastes:* These wastes are usually produced in patient rooms, treatment rooms, and nursing stations. The operating room may also be a contributor. Items include soiled dressings, bandages, catheters, swabs, plaster casts, receptacles, and masks.

   B. *Surgical and Autopsy Wastes* (pathologic wastes): These wastes may be produced in surgical suites or autopsy rooms. Items that may be included are placentas, tissues and organs, amputated limbs, and similar material.

   C. *Laboratory Wastes:* These wastes are produced in diagnostic or research laboratories. Items that may be included are cultures, spinal fluid samples, dead animals, and animal bedding. Eighty-five percent of this type of waste is released to morticians for incineration.

Type 7—Liquid by-product wastes. Usually toxic and hazardous. Must be treated with germicidal/disinfectant prior to disposal in sanitary sewers.

Type 8—Solid by-product wastes. Toxic, hazardous, capable of being sterilized, packaged, and discarded with normal trash.

Any of the above categories can produce **infectious waste**. It is the method of handling, however, that allows for safe disposal. Each environmental service center will develop its own procedures for disposal of all types of waste. (See procedures previously mentioned for disposal of "Needles, Syringes and Sharps", and "Antineoplastic Agents.")

The Joint Commission (JCAHO)

The Joint Commission on Accreditation of Health Care Organizations (JCAHO) is the prime **certifying authority** for hospitals and nursing homes in this country. This organization sets the standards for not only hospital and health care administration but also housekeeping standards within the institutions.

Each institution is initially and annually surveyed to ensure that departments are organized to carry out their functions properly and that standards of operations and cleanliness are being maintained.

The Facility Survey in Housekeeping

The JCAHO usually begins with a review of all written policies and procedures. Documentation of a continuing education program for housekeeping personnel is required. Contracts or written agreements with any outside sources providing such documentation are also required.

The individual who has primary responsibility for the environmental services department as designated by the chief facility administrator must complete certain sections of a written facility survey questionnaire.

The following conditions must be met in the survey:

1. The director's responsibilities must include participation in the development of department procedures, training and supervising personnel, scheduling and assigning personnel, and maintaining communications with other department heads.
2. Written departmental procedures must relate to the use, cleaning, and care of equipment; the cleaning of specialized areas; the selection, measurement, and proper use of housekeeping and cleaning supplies; the maintenance of cleaning schedules; infection control; and personal hygiene.
3. Participation of housekeeping personnel in a relevant continuing education program must be documented.
4. The extent to which outside housekeeping services are used must be documented. (If housekeeping services are provided by outside sources, a written agreement must require that the company meet JCAHO standards of such services. If such services have been terminated in the past year, the reasons for such termination must be stated.)

Linen and Laundry

There are also strict controls and procedures associated with collection, processing, and distribution of linen and laundry. The **JCAHO standards** in this regard require that:

1. A statement is made as to what organization (internal or external) is responsible for linen and laundry.
2. There is an adequate supply of clean linen.
3. Clean linen is handled and stored so that the possibility of its contamination is minimized.
4. Soiled linen is placed in bags or containers of sufficient quality to functionally contain wet/soiled linen during the time required to collect it and remove it from the patient-care area.
5. Linen is placed in bags or containers that, when filled, are properly closed prior to further transport.
6. Linen is identified when originating from isolation and septic surgical cases.
7. Soiled linen is kept separated from clean linen.
8. Functionally separate containers are used for the transportation of clean and soiled linen.
9. The hospital laundry is functionally separate from the patient-care facility.
10. The laundry ventilation system has an adequate intake, filtration, exchange, and exhaust system.
11. Quality assurance procedures are in effect for both outside services and in-house laundries.
12. The participation of linen and laundry personnel in relevant continuing education programs is documented.

Environmental Pollution

It would be improper to dissociate the topic of environmental services from discussion of the topic of pollution; it is a major concern of all mankind, especially for those of us in the profession where so much pollution is generated. First, here is a layman's look at the environment.

Elements of the Environment

The *earth's crust* is composed of **oxides** of the following elements:

Silicon	SiO_2	66.4 %
Aluminum	Al_2O_2	15.5 %
Calcium	CaO	3.8 %
Sodium	Na_2O	3.5 %
Potassium	K_2O	3.3 %
Iron	FeO	2.8 %
Magnesium	MgO	2.0 %
Iron	Fe_2O_3	1.8 %
Manganese	MnO	0.1 %
Phosphorus	P_2O_3	.3 %
All other elements (rare earth)		.5 %

Water (oceanic) is composed of the combination of hydrogen and oxygen (H_2O), sodium chloride ($NaCl$) [common table salt], and numerous trace minerals. The *fresh water element* of total water is derived from seawater evaporating and condensing into clouds and precipitation and thereafter finding its way into underground water tables, lakes, and rivers.

The *earth's atmosphere*, commonly called air, consists of layers of gases, mixtures of gases, water vapor, and solid and liquid particles.

The air near the earth's surface (0 to 15 kilometers [km]) is known as the troposphere. This is an area of well-defined gases of two different groups, as follows:

Principal		
Nitrogen	N_2	78%
Oxygen	O_2	21%
Argon	Ar	1%
Minor		
Carbon dioxide	CO_2	
Nitrous oxide	N_2O	
Carbon monoxide	CO	
Ozone	O_3	
Methane	CH_4	
Nitrogen monoxide	NO_2	
Hydrogen	H_2	
Helium	He	

The *middle layer* (15 to 500 km) is known as the stratosphere. This is where a mixing of atomic gases is taking place, forming the molecular gases.

The *ionosphere* (greater than 500 km) is a part of the atmosphere where free atoms of oxygen (O),

helium (He), and hydrogen (H) exist in a free state, hydrogen (H) being the lightest and most distant layer of gas in the atmosphere.

The Earth's Protective Shield

The earth is constantly being bombarded by **ultraviolet radiation** from the sun. Molecular oxygen (O_2) is being photodissociated into atoms of oxygen (O), immediately leading to the production of ozone ($O + O_2 = O_3$). Ozone (O_3) becomes a barrier that restricts the amount of ultraviolet radiation reaching the earth's surface. This barrier protects land and plant, and animal life from ultraviolet destruction. Since ultraviolet radiation has little penetrating effect, plant and animal life in the oceans is readily protected; this explains why such life was the first to occur on earth. Life on land, however, could not occur until oxygen that was created from the sea ultimately became a part of the creation of ozone in the atmosphere, which was then to protect life on the land.

Ecology

Ecology, as a branch of biology, is a study that is concerned with the relationship of plants and animals to their environment and to each other. It is our interest in ecology which hopefully will bring about a major concern for what we are doing to ourselves by abusing our environment. The pollution we are generating today must be recognized and aborted if life as we know it on this planet is to continue. The time of life of humankind on earth in relation to the time of life of the earth is so infinitesimally small, it is difficult to realize how foreshortened the human life span can become unless we realize in the very near future what we are doing to our planet.

Air Pollution

Air Pollution occurs both naturally and unnaturally. Natural air pollution includes volcanic ash, blowing dust, and smoke from forest fires. These forms of air pollution have existed for millions of years and are not a major concern.

Unnatural air pollution, however, consists of packing the natural air currents with carbon monoxide, hydrocarbons containing sulfurs, nitrous oxide causing **smog**, and the components which are picked up in water vapor and return to the land in the form of **acid rain**.

Of even greater long-range concern, however, is the release of refrigerant-type aerosols into the atmosphere, which contain the hydrocarbon known as **ChloroFluoroCarbon**. As these gases drift up into the ionosphere, they react with the ozone in such a way that the ozone is destroyed. Unexplained **holes in the ozone layer** at the poles of the earth have not only developed but are now expanding.

There is also the air pollution caused by the burning of the world's forested areas. An excessive release of carbon dioxide to the atmosphere causes an undue blanketing of heat that cannot be normally radiated from the earth's surface. This is known as the **greenhouse effect** and can bring about changes in the earth's weather patterns. Such changes can begin to shift rain areas, creating deserts where heretofore temperate areas of high vegetation had existed.

The burning of some wastes can add toxic hydrocarbons into both air and water.

Water Pollution

Water Pollution is another concern that presents the environmentalist with challenges. Garbage, and industrial waste that will not readily decompose, can cause toxic pollution of water supplies. Such activity can bring about acid soils; alkaline detergents can prevent decomposition of wastes.

Other Forms of Pollution

Other forms of pollution include that caused by radioactive waste, pesticides, noise, and solid waste landfills, which do not decompose.

The Housekeeper's Role In Environmental Control

A sound program of **pollution, waste control, waste disposal**, and **recycling** must become one of the major goals for all persons involved with housekeeping operations. Regardless of the type of facility—hospitals; nursing, convalescent or retirement homes; or service establishments such as hotels and restaurants—all must make the environment a part of their professional concern.

Governmental regulation has already entered the ecological scene and will continue to grow and influence our daily operations if responsible management does not *take charge* of the problem of environmental pollution.

Summary

The work of those involved in environmental services in hospitals and health care institutions is not unlike that of the hotel housekeeping employee. Both have policies and procedures that are documented. Both have job descriptions capable of setting forth the various jobs that must be done, and there is a hierarchy of supervision similar to that found in hotel housekeeping. The knowledge, however, of "what one might be dealing with" is far more detailed for the environmental service worker. It would therefore be well for the hotel housekeeper to be aware of the hidden dangers that could abound in hotel housekeeping.

Diseases are caused by microorganisms. The spread of pathogens is reduced by keeping everything clean. Being extra careful to avoid contamination is a way of keeping the hospital (and hotel) environment safe.

Isolation techniques in hospitals are especially important. Each step in every isolation procedure must be done carefully and completely.

Pest control was addressed, and examples were given of the various types of pest that can create a contamination problem. Also, types of insecticides were presented along with recommendations for their use. There was a strong recommendation to use qualified contract people to perform pest control work.

Different types of wastes were identified and categorized, and information was presented on how to dispose of the several classifications of waste.

The Joint Commission on the Accreditation of Health Care Organizations is the agency that establishes the standards whereby such institutions are maintained and operated.

The **washing of hands** before and after contact with patients is probably the most important item to remember that will serve to protect the people—personnel as well as patients.

Finally the subject of pollution was developed, indicating the challenges to all housekeeping-oriented operations to *deal with the problem* before government regulation descends upon the profession, leaving no chance for the profession to solve these problems through sound management. Both hospitals and hotels have much in common on this issue.

KEY TERMS AND CONCEPTS

National Executive Housekeepers Association
Director of Environmental Services

Joint Commission on Accreditation of Health Care Organizations (JCAHO)
Disinfection

Terminal cleaning
Needles
Syringes
Sharps
Microbiology
Chemistry of cleaning and
  disinfecting
Microorganisms
Protist
Bacteria
Bacillus
Coccus
Fungus
Spirochete
Spore
Staphylococcus
Streptococcus
Virus
Aerobic
Anaerobic
Antisepsis
Asepsis
Asepsis (Medical)
Asepsis (Surgical)
Autoclave
Chemical agent
Disinfection
Disinfection (Concurrent)
Disinfection (Terminal)
Gram (positive/negative)
Intermediate host
Micron
Pathogenic
Physical agents
Reagents
Sterilization
Mineral
Organic
Osmological
Bacterial
Entomological
Chemical formulas
Atom
Element
Molecule
Valence
Compounds
Reactants
Products
Atomic reactions
Radical
Organic compounds
Ion
Anion
Salts

Universal Solvent
Cation
Acid
Alkali
pH
alkaline
acidic
R
Disinfectant
Quaternary ammonium
  compounds
Phenol
Phenolic
Iodine
Alcohols
Detergent
Disinfectant (Germicides)
Antiseptics
Bacteriostat
Sanitizer
Preservatives
Petri test dishes
Dilution ratio
Chemical suspension
Carbolic acid (Phenol)
Phenolic
Toxic
Bacteria trails
Pathogen
Isolation unit
Needles
Syringes
Sharps
Refuse from antineoplastic agents
Chemotherapy drugs
Causative agent
Reservoir
Mode of escape
Immune carrier
Method of transmission
Host
Chain of infection
Preventive in nature
Waste disposal and control
Waste
Infectious waste
Joint Commission (JCAHO)
Certifying authority
JCAHO standards
Environmental pollution
Oxides
Ultraviolet radiation
Ecology
Smog
Acid rain

ChloroFluoroCarbon
Holes in the ozone layer
Greenhouse effect
Pollution

Waste control
Waste disposal
Recycling
Washing of hands

DISCUSSION AND REVIEW QUESTIONS

1. Mr. James from Houston, Texas, checked into the University Inn in late afternoon. He was feeling feverish and nauseated after his flight from Los Angeles. He called the front desk and asked for some ice, drank a glass of water and went directly to bed. He noticed a red swelling on the back of his neck, which had been draining on to his shirt collar. He used a wash rag to rinse it off.

   When Mildred, the housekeeper, came to turn down the bed, she found Mr. James very ill. She gave him some water from his glass at the bedside and asked Mr. James, "Do you want me to call you a doctor?" to which he answered, "Yes."

   A. What kind of policy should be written that would help Mildred know what to do in this situation?
   B. What specific items in the room are contaminated?
   C. When the doctor arrives, he has Mr. James transported to the hospital. What kind of step-by-step procedure should Mildred use to clean up this room?

2. Upon admission to the hospital Mr. James' temperature was 102°, the red swollen spot on his neck was draining, and he was having difficulty breathing.

   A. What type of isolation would be best for him?
   B. What specific steps should the housekeeper take in the isolation unit?
      a. For handling trash?
      b. For handling laundry?
   C. What articles must be cleaned, removed, or sterilized in the unit when Mr. James leaves?

13

The Safeguarding of Assets: Concerns for Safety and Security in Housekeeping Operations

CHAPTER OBJECTIVES

1. To learn about the concepts of Risk Management and the safeguarding of assets.
2. To understand the underlying problems regarding security and safety within hotels and hospitals.
3. To know how to reduce theft in housekeeping departments.
4. To know how to make guestrooms and guests secure.
5. To understand the nature of emergencies that can occur in a hotel or hospital operation.
6. To learn about "Emergency Planning" and how to safeguard against potential disasters and what to do in case of emergencies.

There is a new **body of knowledge** that is of major concern to those involved in management of the service professions. This concern is about **safeguard-**

ing assets of an organization, the responsibility for which is now being assigned to all who work within such organizations.

The **American Society of Industrial Security (ASIS**—the national association for Directors of Security) has now cataloged this body of knowledge into one which forms the basis for educating, certifying, and training not only directors of security groups but also those in charge of other organizational departments.

It is to this end that environmental service directors and hotel executive housekeepers must become involved in the analysis of risks being taken daily by their companies (**risk analysis**) and with the management of such risks (**risk management**) in such a way as to reduce the threat to a company's assets.

The Concept of Safeguarding Assets

It is first necessary to understand what might be recognized as "the assets" of a hospitality or health care organization.

HUMAN	PHYSICAL	INTRINSIC
Guests	Land	Good will
Patients	The facility	Reputation
Employees	Equipment	
	Inventory	
	Cash	
	Accounts receivable	

Fifty years ago it was normal to recognize one member of the hotel staff as the **house detective**. His primary job was to sit in the lobby and await the hand-beckoning of the front desk clerk. Such was the case when either a guest was complaining or was being complained about, at which time the house detective would proceed to the room and "handle the problem."

The assets listed above at today's prices can, however, quickly bring into focus the cost of losses that are faced today, if we would care to total them up. Imagine:

1. Negligence suits due to carelessness of the staff, or for lack of **foreseeability**, allowing a guest, patient, or employee to be injured or killed
2. The theft, pilferage, or negligent loss or destruction of the physical assets of a company
3. The loss of future and potential revenues that can result from an incident that can damage a company's reputation

Is it no wonder that we now have corporations of both hotels and health institutions with "Vice Presidents of Loss Prevention" overseeing security forces, the sizes of which are in three digits. And the network is still not large enough to do an adequate job of foreseeing potential problems that, if not discovered and planned for, can lead to disaster.

It is now well recognized that housekeeping departments and other staff members must become the "eyes of the security organization" in the guestrooms and patient wings of our facilities. Additionally, everyone in the organization must be trained and drilled in **foreseeable events**.

Safety and Security

The subjects of security and safety are usually addressed in tandem even though they are somewhat different in nature. The trend today is to use the term **safety** when discussing disasters, fire prevention and protection; protection devices; and conditions that provide for freedom from injury and damage to property. **Security** refers to the freedom from fear, anxiety, and doubt involving ourselves, as well as to the protection and defense against the loss or theft of guest, patient, employee, and company property. Property owners and managers are responsible for both the safety and security of guests, patients, employees, property, and company assets. Many articles have been and are being written about safety and security with regard to the hotel, hospital, and health care industry, most of which relate to facility improvements, card entry systems, in-room safes, fire protection systems, TV surveillance, and innovative hardware affecting safety and security. In this chapter we will discuss each of these subjects, with an emphasis on the personnel and training aspects of safety and security as they apply to the administration and management of a housekeeping department.

Security from Theft in the Housekeeping Department

Employee Theft—Nature of the Problem

No other hotel employees have as much access to hotel assets and guest property as do members of the housekeeping department. Omer Henry [1] outlined the depth of the problem in his article "Our Employees are Stealing Us Blind" when he stated:

> Joanie makes $3.00 an hour as a motel maid. She takes home $20,000 a year. She steals most of it from the motel. Joanie is not alone in this larcenous operation. It is estimated that 50% of all employees steal from their employers—5 to 8% steal in volume. And the situation is growing more critical every day.
>
> Dale Systems, Inc., nationwide business-security and research organization, reports that clever employees steal more than $2 billion a year from their employers. Other estimates run even higher.

I recall being shown a photograph taken by an employee of her children at home. In the background were drapes, bedspread, and a lamp from the hotel in which she was employed.

Management's attitude about employee honesty runs to the extremes, as illustrated by the following commonly heard statements: "My employees would never steal" or "I don't trust any of my employees; they will all steal if given a chance." Both statements tell a story: Either management is naive about people in general, or the only way to manage people is by Theory X techniques using scare tactics.

Dr. Harold Gluck,[2] a registered criminologist and a member of the American Association of Criminology, quoted reports stating that "30% of your employees will steal from you; 30% of them are honest and the remaining 40% go with the tide and the opportunity." Dr. Gluck's conclusion provides hope that there is an unemotional and objective point from which to depart in establishing a sound program for **employee theft prevention**.

Employee Contamination—A Real and Present Danger

Bob Curtis[3] talks about **contamination of employees**, stating that it may come from several causes:

1. When one employee is known to be stealing, others will tend to follow.
2. Employees who are frustrated and angry at the way they are being treated by management think nothing of talking with each other about how easy it is to rip off the firm. These employees receive the plaudits of peers for their ability to beat the system. Once an employee starts to beat the system, he or she will brag about it to companions or will even put himself or herself in a place in which companions can view the theft. When word gets around that management cannot uncover the stealing, others join in.
3. Borderline honest employees do not think it dishonest to "get even" with a greedy, impersonal, giant company that is indifferent to employee needs for recognition and support.
4. Low morale is a sickness sign that forewarns of contamination of employees regarding theft.
5. The problem of contamination is considerable in firms with a highly authoritarian management style, because authoritarian management is only successful where punishment and threats of punishment are primary controls.

The Section Housekeeper and Room Theft

No one is more sensitive to the problems of theft from hotel guestrooms than the honest section housekeeper who is known to possess a floor master key to a guestroom that has just been robbed. There is the unfortunate assumption that, because the section housekeeper has a key to the room, if anything is missing she or he is automatically the culprit. Seldom does the guest realize that the floor supervisor, bellperson, room clerk, engineer, room service waiter, executive housekeeper, and general manager also have keys, as does possibly the last guest to

check out of the room, to say nothing of the professional hotel thief who may have just purchased a key to the room from some pawn shop.

In such cases, if section housekeepers are part of Gluck's 30 percent honest people, they may lose heart and resign. If part of the 40 percent who go with the tide, they may become a part of the Curtis sample and conclude, "Why not steal—I am going to be accused anyway, and no one will support me if I don't do it."

Even though Gluck and Curtis both present convincing arguments, an objective and professional approach to theft control can be established and maintained, provided that personnel within the department are enlisted into a practical and positive program of theft prevention similar to that which follows.

A Fourteen-Point Program for Employee Theft Prevention

Let us begin by assuming that applications will be made for positions within the department by people who are symbolic of Gluck's 30–40–30 percent sample distribution. The following **14-point theft prevention program** is a reasonable attack on the 30 percent who will steal at any price and a positive program to keep the questionable 40 percent on the honest side of the equation.

1. *Institute and ensure professional hiring practices.* Ensure that proper screening methods are used during hiring operations. Complete applications, including follow-up of questionable information and gaps, are vital to good hiring practices. Gaps in **employment history** on applications may hide significant information.

   Every employee should understand that references will be checked before any hiring decision will be made. When making reference checks, phone calls are often better than requests in writing. It is of maximum benefit during a reference check to get as close to the truth as possible, even to the point of asking pointed questions such as whether or not the person giving the reference would take the applicant back if given the chance. A hesitation in an answer may be all that is needed to indicate the right-go or no-go decision.

   In places in which **polygraph (lie detector) examinations** are not prohibited by law or union contract, they maybe considered, especially for people who will handle company funds. Every employee, however, should understand as a condition of employment that, should a situation arise where suspicion is cast over an over an employee, that person may be given the opportunity to establish innocence by voluntarily undergoing a polygraph examination. In such cases, the polygraph examination is not being used to prove guilt in a court of law but to establish innocence by creating reasonable doubt as to the guilt of an employee in a given set of circumstances.

Employees who are hired after exposure to thorough reference checks and indoctrination are usually better employees because they know that management is aware of their backgrounds, recognizes their application statements to be honest, and is less likely to tolerate dishonesty. Applicants should also be made aware of controls such as package checks and periodic locker inspections in order that they understand that management does exert reasonable theft control over employees as a routine course of doing business.

2. *Establish positive identification techniques for employees.* Large properties require identification of all employees, usually by a **badge system** that contains photograph, signature, and a color code indicating the department or work area of the employee. Such identification systems discourage people bent on thievery from trying to pass as employees.

Color identification of badges or even name tags identify the work areas of employees and expose employees who are out of work areas without good explanations. Special uniforms also identify an employee as to work area, provided such uniforms are not off-the-rack uniforms that may be purchased by anyone. Photo name badges are the best means of identification, provided security personnel and supervisors are trained to observe them as a routine course of business. Close observation will not be necessary after the employee becomes known to management and security personnel. But most hotels have a few new employees every day or at least every week. Management and security personnel also change over periods of time. Therefore, constant checking of photo identification badges is necessary and in the long run will have an effect on company profits and, ultimately, costs to guests.

3. *Conduct theft orientation and attitude training.* During employee training it is important to remind trainees that even though the vast majority of employees are completely honest, one dishonest housekeeper with a pass key can be devastating to an operation. One such

person in the midst of other honest employees can cast shadows and mistrust over the entire organization. Discuss the **scenario** in which the honest section housekeeper is confronted by an irate guest who thinks the housekeeper has stolen property from the guestroom. Therefore, it is each person's duty not only to encourage honesty among fellow workers but also to confront and bring forth those who would cause each employee to fall under suspicion for dishonesty.

Employees should be taught that many guests will misplace items brought with them to the hotel and for an instant will assume the "simplest" explanation—that the item has been taken, and that the housekeeper is the guilty person. Employees should be taught that during such a moment, their attitude, composure, and behavior will tend to foretell future actions on the part of the guest and even management. The employee who becomes emotional, denies with force, or cannot seem to be found at that moment engenders deeper suspicion, whereas the employee who is composed, calls management or security to the scene immediately, then offers to help search for the missing item is much less likely to be suspected in the long run. Honest employees need not be thin-skinned in such a moment but should try to put themselves in the guest's place and ask themselves, "What kind of reaction would be expected from a hotel employee if situations were reversed?" Possibilities other than theft by the housekeeper are best explained to the guest by a member of management or by security personnel. Employees' actions should be those of being helpful and cooperative.

It should be explained during training that employees are not handed over by management to accusing guests, but the name of the housekeeper who cleaned a room from which items have been found missing will be made available to the police should the guest actually make a formal charge against an employee, as will the record of the employee, which hopefully will indicate no prior suspicious behavior. Employees should also be informed that records involving items missing from rooms cleaned by section housekeepers will be maintained in employee personnel files. Several such unexplained or unresolved occurrences will most certainly cast suspicion on an employee, who should then be given an opportunity to remove such suspicion by voluntarily participating in a polygraph examination.

Other important matters that should be covered in training regarding theft prevention are procedures involving the lost-and-found, what to do if illegal acts are observed while working, procedures to use regarding the use of locker rooms, and rules about handbags not being permitted in hotel guestrooms and satellite linen room areas. The fact that these procedures and rules are mentioned during training indicates to employees that the company is conscious of the ramifications of theft, that it intends to exercise reasonable controls and institute procedures that will assist people in maintaining integrity, and that the presence of temptations is recognized but needs not be compelling. Finally, it shows employees that most procedures enacted to prevent theft are also inclined to prevent suspicion against employees if they are followed.

4. *Supervisors should closely monitor behavior and adherence to company policies and procedures during employee training and probationary periods.* Too often **probationary periods** are perfunctory and taken for granted. Probationary periods should be understood as trial periods in which the employee is to demonstrate not only worker skills, but also attitudes and perceptions about compliance with company policies.

Probationary periods are also trial periods for the company. Management and supervisors should demonstrate the type of attitudes that are held about employees and the manner in which

employees are to be treated, thus giving the employee an opportunity to learn about the company before employment becomes permanent.

Attitude observations are very important at this crucial time of employment, and employees should not be passed into permanent full-time employment without some evaluation of their attitudes toward guests, other employees, property, and company assets. All too often, an employee is allowed to pass into full-time permanent status with questionable attitudes about the company and its guests, which may later prove to be grounds for termination, when all during probationary employment the evidence was present but not challenged.

5. *Inaugurate and closely administer a program of key control.* The large number of multipurpose keys maintained within the housekeeping department makes it necessary for a **key-control program** to be all-encompassing and strictly enforced. Each day keys should be subcustodied to employees who have a need for them by an acknowledging signature; they should be properly receipted for when turned in at the end of each workday. Keys must be properly accounted for at all times, either as inventory in a key locker or properly logged out.

Workers should be provided with a way to attach keys to their person so that they need not be unattached while being used. Figure 13.1 shows such a method, which allows section housekeepers and senior housekeepers to attach master keys to their person. The master keys are on a lanyard with a slip O ring that is attached to

Figure 13.1 Guestroom master keys attached to a lanyard with storage pouch. When not being used, keys can be put in the pouch and the lanyard wrapped around the pouch.

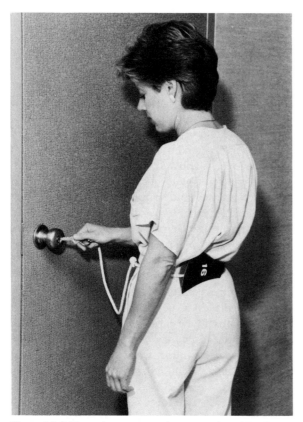

Figure 13.2 Master keys are worn by an attendant. Note how the key pouch is located in the back of the attendant. Sufficient lanyard is available for easy use of the keys. When not in use, the keys can fit into the pocket.

a **key pouch**. The key can be stored in the pouch when not in use. The pouch can be appropriately marked by section number and inventoried in a like manner. When the key is worn, as shown in Figure 13.2, the lanyard is placed around the waist with pouch in back, out of the way. A pelican hook is attached to the slip O ring, allowing the keys to be carried in the pocket until they are needed. The strap length is sufficient to allow freedom of movement.

The entire issue of department keys should be sight inventoried at the end of each day and management notified immediately should any irregularities be noticed in the key inventory. All employees must be strongly impressed with the necessity to safeguard master keys entrusted to them. The loss or misplacement of a master key must be immediately reported to management, and location of the key must take precedence over further work. Therefore, several people must become involved in finding a misplaced key. Finally, employees should be made to understand that the loss of a master key may be grounds for termination, especially if negligence is determined.

Guestroom keys left by departing guests and subsequently found by section housekeepers who are cleaning the rooms must be safeguarded by the section housekeeper and not left on the top of section housekeepers' carts. Many hotels provide lock boxes on the top of carts that can be used for depositing room keys. The hotel should have someone regularly pass among the working section housekeepers to retrieve and return such keys to the front desk. Professional hotel thieves are known to search for room keys left in sight on the top of carts.

6. *Have a red tag program.* There are legitimate reasons why an employee may be allowed to remove property from the premise. Property given to an employee or awarded from the lost-and-found can be removed under the protection of a **red tag system**.

   Red tags, shown in Figure 13.3, are issued by management to employees after the manager has sighted the item to be removed. The red tag contains granted authority for the removal of property and in some cases will cover the loan of company property, such as a vacuum cleaner or a roll-away bed. For such red tag programs to work, they must have the support and compliance of employees.

   Tags should be attached to parcels and collected by security personnel as the parcel is removed from the premise. As a form of control, red tags collected by employee gate security guards should be subsequently returned to the manager who signed the tag in order that the manager may know what went out of the building over his or her signature.

7. *Have regular locker inspections.* Although regular and routine locker inspections (even though unannounced) are conducted primarily to ensure that items such as company property, drugs, alcohol, and soiled uniforms are not being allowed to accumulate in lockers, the knowledge that a locker inspection could occur at any time tacitly disqualifies the locker as a place for temporarily storing contraband or stolen items. Employees should be made aware at hiring that locker inspections will be conducted periodically by a member of management and the hourly work force. Employees should also be informed as to the purpose of locker inspections.

8. *Inventory control programs should be established and physical inventories regularly conducted with results (and implications) published to the entire department.* Guest supplies, cleaning supplies, linens, and other capital items should be in-

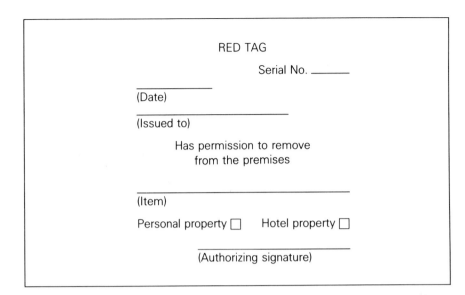

```
                        RED TAG
                                Serial No. _____

    _____
    (Date)

    _____
    (Issued to)

            Has permission to remove
                from the premises

    _____
    (Item)

    Personal property ☐    Hotel property ☐

                    _____
                    (Authorizing signature)
```

Figure 13.3 Red tag used to authorize removal of personal or hotel property from the premises. All red tags should be serially numbered, issued by a manager, and surrendered to a security officer at the employee entrance when leaving the premises. Red tags should be returned to the issuing manager in order that authenticity can be assured.

ventoried regularly and the results and implications presented to all employees. Employees who have been counseled to be frugal with supplies need to be told when their efforts have brought about cost reductions. Special recognition should be made in front of the entire department. On the other hand, employees must understand that situations in which inventory usage is high and out of control will have the immediate attention of management.

Admittance to storerooms and issuance of supplies should be limited to a few employees; policies that allow help-yourself access to supplies by employees are not recommended. The issuance of supplies should not be so restrictive as to prevent efficient work procedures; a proper balance between restrictive and loose procedures should be maintained. Any sudden affluence on the part of an employee warrants concern.

9. *Keep records of missing items of guests and of the hotel.* When items are reported or found to be missing, make cross-reference files of the item by type and of the employee who could have been involved. Sometimes patterns develop that are valuable in uncovering causes for disappearance of items.

10. *Employee parking should not be adjacent to the building.* Employee parking areas should be sufficiently far away from buildings and structures so as to make it difficult to slip in and out of an entrance several times a day and into a parked car. Areas to and from employee parking should be well lighted.

11. *Trash handling requires special consideration.* The handling and disposal of trash is a significant part of most housekeeping department jobs.

Trash collection and disposal should be monitored by different supervisors on a rotating basis. Because of the possibility that trash might be used to hide contraband, it should not be allowed to accumulate near incoming supplies and equipment.

Employees' automobiles should be periodically observed, and any employee cars that are parked near a trash disposal site should be carefully checked.

There are classic cases in which one or more employees have been in collusion with trash pickup personnel. Should the housekeeping department have its own loading dock, only allow a truck to park at the dock to unload; it should be moved as soon as it is unloaded. Many hotel television sets disappear in delivery trucks that are allowed to remain at the loading dock for more time than is necessary.

12. *Enlist employees as part of the security team.* Security is not a one-person job. Section housekeepers and supervisors can be valuable in theft prevention and security by reporting suspicious behavior on the part of guests, damage to rooms, items noted as missing from rooms, and special or unique types of belongings noted in opened luggage in guestrooms. Several large suitcases with few articles of clothing hanging in a closet may be an indication of things to come—or possibly go—such as linens, bedspreads, and towels.

All housekeeping personnel should know on sight all engineering personnel. The TV repair person, especially, should be well known. A TV removed from a room should be accompanied by an immediate replacement, or else suspicion should be aroused.

Satellite linen rooms and other storage areas should always be kept locked unless attended. Satellite linen rooms should be kept clean and free of litter, and every item in the linen room should be recognized.

Strange items or packages found adrift or in hallway corridors could spell trouble and can even be worthy of an immediate phone call to the security department.

13. *When problems are suspected, bring in an expert.* Many times inventory losses or reported thefts indicate a problem that may not easily reveal itself. When such is the case, hire an expert **snoop.** **Snoops** are security specialists who pass as employees, gather the evidence needed to resolve theft problems, then quietly fade out of the employee workforce.

I once hired a snoop when a department was plagued with the disappearance of linens from section housekeepers' carts during the daytime. The snoop applied for work as a section housekeeping aide, giving the appearance that he could neither read nor write. The actual identity of the snoop was limited only to the executive housekeeper and resident manager. The snoop (for want of a name, John) worked as a utility employee, which allowed him presence in all areas of the property.

John was known as a talker, was well liked by all who met him, and was seen to lean on his broom and gossip quite often. In about three weeks, John came to work intoxicated and unfortunately had to be terminated. Three days later a detailed, comprehensive, and very professional report was received from the security specialist (who had been John), naming three employees who had been in collusion and had tried to enlist John into their organization. John's statement was sufficient to convict all three employees on grand larceny charges, as well as to recover about 25 percent of the stolen inventory. What was most surprising was that one of the three employees uncovered in the theft ring was a junior manager.

14. *Set the example.* The first 13 steps of this theft prevention program require positive planning and follow-through. Aside from those measures used in hiring employees and the systems used to identify employees, all other steps may appear overly oppressive and authoritarian. To the contrary, each step is designed to help honest employees remain honest by removing temptation through known and publicized controls and by emphasizing the fact that honest employees have no problem coping. Dishonest employees, however, will find that dishonest acts meet with equal and opposite vigor.

No one step has as much effect as does management, from the top down, setting the proper example. In the case of the housekeeping department, the executive housekeeper must demonstrate that the rules and controls outlined apply to management, as well as to the most junior employee, to the fullest extent. No exceptions—not even a pencil or sheet of paper for the children to do their homework—can be tolerated. Many times it is being completely trustworthy about these small items that sets the tone for what management expects or, better yet, has a right to expect. And there is nothing more tempting to an honest employee than to see the boss taking something.

Usefulness of Employee Profiles

Barbara Powers, general manager of the Branford Motor Inn, Branford, Connecticut, and officer of the Connecticut AH & MA, suggests that there is an **employee profile** by which a prospective thief among employees might be identified.[4]

Such profiles are developed on the basis of experience with people who have been proved guilty of pilferage or theft. Understand, the profile might apply to honest people. That said—here are the characteristics employees likely to be dishonest often have in common:

- They wear an air of dissatisfaction with someone or something.
- They don't identify with the hotel. The hotel is "they" rather than "we."
- They lack respect for people or property; don't tend to accept responsibility; and are self-centered.
- They resent criticism.
- They have financial difficulties.

An additional point might be added to an effective theft-prevention program by maintaining profiles on employees who display the characteristics enumerated by Powers. Such profiles might prove useful in establishing a likely list of suspects when things start to disappear and no further indications or evidence is immediately at hand, if only to know who to watch more closely in the future.

Theft by Guests and Others

There is some question as to who might be more to blame for theft losses: employees, guests, or other people bent on dishonesty. The degree of loss from each source seems to depend more on the attention paid by management to each of the sources than any other factor. Management cannot assume that theft losses will come more from one source than any other source. Guests bent on stealing linens can bring as much havoc to inventory cost as can employees or outsiders who have targeted the hotel as a source for contraband.

As mentioned above, employees should be enlisted into a network of security-conscious people trained to react when they observe suspicious activities. Section housekeepers, especially, should be trained to sight each item of furniture and software as they enter a guestroom. Missing items should be immediately reported to management in order that positive action may be taken.

If section housekeepers report seeing a guest's suitcase loaded with towels, the executive housekeeper should notify the front desk manager to discreetly but with certainty add a specified amount to the guest's account in the form of a **miscellaneous charge**. If questioned by the guest, the clerk can say that it was assumed that the guest intended to pay for the souvenirs being removed from the hotel, and that it was customary to add appropriate charges to the guest account to cover the cost of such souvenirs when they happen to be linens. In most such cases, the guest does not press the matter further but pays the account in full. Revenues received as a result of such charges are transferred to inventory accounts so that the housekeeping department costs are kept in control.

Television as a Problem

The most expensive item that attracts the attention of thieves in hotels is the television set. This is especially true of television sets in rooms that are first-floor drive-up rooms, which have sliding glass doors that open directly into parking areas. There is only one thing that can improve on this setup as far as the thief is concerned—not to have to unbolt the television to remove it.

First and foremost, all televisions *should be bolted down*, either on a pedestal or on a chest top, so that without a key or the proper tool, removing the television is a major undertaking. Many hotels have security systems on televisions that initiate an alarm at the front desk if the antenna is disconnected. Such systems have greatly reduced the clandestine removal of televisions, especially where security personnel have been trained to respond quickly to such alarms.

The modus operandi of many television thieves is to cruise a hotel parking lot during the daytime and observe first-floor rooms that are unoccupied.

After selecting several such rooms, the thief enters the hotel and, under pretense of having just checked out and inadvertently leaving an article in the room, prompts the section housekeeper to let him or her into the room. Once in the room, the thief chains the door so as not to be immediately interrupted. The thief then goes about the business of separating the television from the premises, removing it through the sliding glass door, and putting it into a van that a partner has waiting outside the room.

Housekeepers must be trained never to open a door of a guestroom for anyone claiming to be a guest unless she or he has personally observed the person to be a guest on several prior occasions; then the housekeeper is best advised to call a supervisor. If you open a door for a guest not in possession of a key, do not allow the guest to enter the room until a phone call is made to the front desk to verify the name of the party registered in the room. Legitimate guests are impressed with this type of precaution taken in their behalf.

Visibility into first-floor rooms from the outside during daylight hours must be restricted. This is easily accomplished by using a glass casement curtain in all first-floor rooms. During daylight, if there is no lamp or other light on the inside of a guestroom, it is impossible to see inside a room with a drawn glass curtain and to determine if the room is in fact vacant.

All employees must be trained to be suspicious of unusual happenings and report them to the proper authority. I heard of a bizarre incident in which a general manager was touring a first-floor corridor of a hotel. The general manager was confronted with a guest struggling with a television that seemed to be quite heavy; the general manager promptly offered to help the guest with his heavy load. After helping the guest load the television into a waiting automobile and wishing him a safe journey and speedy return, he overheard a section housekeeper exclaim that a television had just been stolen from one of the guestrooms. Everyone needs training.

Security within Hotel Guestrooms

Innkeepers have a common-law responsibility to provide secure premises within which guests may abide. Security is defined as the measures that are required to promote a state of well-being relative to an establishment to protect life and property, and to minimize risks of natural disasters or crime. The protection of guests within their rooms must be paramount.

Several states have become quite specific in what constitutes adequate security for hotel guestrooms.

In addition, most major hotel companies have set minimum standards relating to locking devices for guestroom doors. Holiday Inns, Inc., specifies about 16 criteria that door locks must meet or exceed before they may be used in Holiday Inns.

Reasonable security for guestrooms includes the following:

- Automatic closing doors
- Automatic latching devices on latch bolts that require a key or other specialized device to open or unlock the door from the outside
- Dead-bolts that are an integral part of latch bolts; set from inside the room; must be capable of being opened from outside the room with an emergency pass key
- A door chain or other mechanical locking device that may be set from inside the room such as the mechanical locking device in Figure 13.4 that has replaced door chains in the Los Angeles Airport/Marriott Hotel
- A peep hole installed in the room door whereby the guestroom occupant may see who is on the outside of the door before opening it
- Drapes that fully close and are capable of blacking out the room in bright sunlight
- Locking latches and chain locks on all sliding glass doors

Card Entry Systems

The greatest change to have come about in many years for guestroom security is the **card entry sys-** **tem**. The large numbers of manufacturers that are now involved in producing such systems is a testament to the need for some technique that will replace the antiquated systems of guestroom door keys.

The difficulty in making a system of guestroom keys secure, especially in hotels that have lavish key tags hanging from keys, is well known. The replacement cost for lost, misplaced, stolen, or simply carried-away keys as souvenirs is in itself a major cost problem, to say nothing of the lack of control resulting from such practices. Hotel maintenance departments usually have to establish a routine **lock cylinder** change program, whereby cylinders from locks on one floor are swapped with cylinders from locks on other floors and new keys are manufactured and stamped with new room numbers if any control is to be maintained at all.

Card entry systems have simplified and greatly improved the security capability of locking systems in hotel guestrooms. Most of the systems are designed around the premise that when a guest checks into the hotel, a plastic card of some type, which has an electrical or electronic signature impressed thereon, is presented to the guest. The card operates the assigned room door with a combination that has been set just for the new occupant. When the guest checks out, all prior memory of the card signature is wiped out of the door combination and the system to await the arrival of the new guest.

Housekeeping and other master card systems may be set or reset in an instant as the need arises, and the fear of a lost master key can be short lived.

Figure 13.4 Locking device that replaces door chains at the Los Angeles Airport Marriott Hotel. Notice the lock in the unlocked position. When the lever attached to the door frame (right) is thrown across the ball attached to the door (left), opening the door will catch the ball up in the track slot, allowing the door to be opened only three inches. (Photo courtesy of the Los Angeles Airport Marriott Hotel.)

State of the art is such that retrofits for hotels still using regular key systems are available and warrant immediate investigation and possible conversion.

Security Consciousness for Guests

Today's seasoned hotel traveler is much more security conscious than travelers in past years. The guest who frequently travels has been forewarned and is therefore forearmed to use all locks provided on guestroom doors when retiring for the night. All too often robberies involving guests in hotel rooms can be traced to the guest who failed to lock and chain the door properly before retiring, to say nothing of the guest who indiscriminantly opened the door without looking through the peephole to see who was in the hall.

Day or night, the executive housekeeper and all members of the housekeeping staff should be trained to close every door found open within the hotel. This practice is a measure of protection for guests who may or may not be in their rooms, as well as a means of protection for hotel property.

The Los Angeles Airport/Marriott Hotel has provided a reassuring touch with their table card shown in Figure 13.5. The sign provides a phone number that guests may call if there is reason to believe that they need extra security attention.

Dual Responsibility

Although it is the duty of all innkeepers to provide a secure area within which guests might abide in relaxing comfort, free from usual threats from the street, guests should never be lulled into a false sense of security so as to abdicate responsibility for their own security. Guests must be prudent and cautious. Housekeeping personnel should therefore never infer that there is nothing to worry about when staying in the hotel. To the contrary, housekeeping personnel should gently and appropriately remind guests to be cautious about leaving doors unlocked and about reasonable rules of security.

The Do-Not-Disturb Sign Competes with the "Need to Foresee"

The Guest's Absolute Right to Privacy

Most common laws affecting hotels in America stem from the English Common Laws of Innkeepers, which originated in the seventeenth century. One such law deals with the guest's right to privacy and is quoted frequently even to this day. On occasion, guests, and more to our surprise, many hotel operators, presume that the guest has an **absolute right to privacy** and when in his or her room, should *never* be disturbed. Actually, research indicates that the English Common Law was not constructed to guarantee that the guest would never be disturbed; only that he or she would be guaranteed sole occupancy of the assigned quarters. Prior to the law being enacted, it was common practice for the innkeeper to **dormitory** his guests; all men in one sleeping room and women in another room. The law later provided

Figure 13.5 Desk-top display used in guestrooms at the Los Angeles Airport Marriott Hotel. Such messages caution guests about security for valuables and provide a phone number for security if assistance is needed without causing undue alarm to guests. (Used with permission of the Los Angeles Airport Marriott Hotel.)

that upon issuance of the key, the guest who paid for *private* quarters had sole use of the assigned room and no one else would be moved into the room; hence, the "absolute" right to privacy. It was not meant to be a guarantee that the guest would never under any circumstances be disturbed.

Management's Responsibility to Ownership, the Laws of the Land, and the Guest

With due and proper regard for the guest's privacy, management has an important responsibility, to the owner of the hotel (which happens to be private property), to state and federal laws that must be enforced on the property, and to the guest whose safety should always be paramount to the hotel staff.

In light of this management responsibility, and with due respect for the guest's right to privacy, there must be a **reasonable time** each day that management, or its representative, enters the room to service the room, and to ensure that (1) the room has not been vandalized or furniture and fixtures destroyed, (2) the law is not being broken in the room, and (3) there is no guest in distress in the room.

Without specific information to the contrary respecting the guest's right to privacy, it is considered reasonable to enter the guest's room between the hours of 8:00 A.M. and 4:00 P.M. daily to service the room. Should the guest display the Do-Not-Disturb sign, or have the door **dead-bolted** from the inside, every attempt should be made to avoid disturbing the guest, at least until normal check-out time. Also, should the guest leave a specific request for late service, this too should be honored.

A Matter of Foreseeability

Imagine the following scenario: You are the executive housekeeper in a suburban hotel catering heavily to the individual traveling business person. It is one hour after check-out time and you receive a call from the guestroom attendant on the third floor who says that room 3019 has had a DND sign on the door all morning. When she checked with housekeeping and the front desk there had been no instructions given to *not* disturb the guest until some later appointed hour. The front desk has no record of a check-out due today from room 3019. The GRA has called the room to find out what time the guest would like to have the room serviced, but no one answered the phone. The GRA tried to enter the room with her pass key but found the room dead-bolted from the inside. End of scenario.

At that moment, what becomes the most foreseeable probability regarding room 3019? Would this be a proper time to respect, above all else, the guest's absolute right to privacy?

Another scenario; one that actually occurred. In November 1990, this author was certified as an expert in hotel operations in a federal court in Maryland and did testify in behalf of a plaintiff who was suing a major hotel for gross negligence. This negligence was alleged to have resulted from the hotel not taking reasonable precaution regarding a prior visit by her husband to the hotel during which he had suffered a diabetic coma in his guestroom. He was not discovered for a period of over 50 hours. Once discovered, he was hospitalized but died five days later. A medical doctor testified that had the victim been discovered 10 hours sooner, he would have survived.

The chronology of events was reconstructed as follows: The victim had been at the hotel for several days. His room had been last serviced on Tuesday morning about 9:00 A.M. while he was not in the room. He had returned to his room sometime before midnight on Tuesday, and chained and dead-bolted his door prior to retiring. On Wednesday, the GRA had noticed the dead-bolt and had honored it until about 3:00 P.M. on Wednesday afternoon, at which time she knocked on the door but got no response. She then used her key but was stopped by the chain on the door. She followed her departmental instructions and summoned a security officer to the room. The security officer noticed that a TV was on in the room and then commented that "the guest just does not want to be disturbed," even though there had been no *coherent response* to the security officer's knock on the door.

No further check was made on the guest or the room until the following day when, at 4:00 P.M. on Thursday, the GRA again called Security to report that she still had not been able to gain entry into the room. At this time the same security officer came to the room, knocked on the door, got no response, and said he would report the incident to the Security office.

Finally, at about 6:00 P.M., another manager foresaw the potential possibilities, called for an engineer to cut the chain on the door, and entered the room to find the guest unconscious in the bathroom; 56 hours having lapsed since the room was last entered by a member of the hotel staff.

The hotel's insurance company, after hearing the testimony of the case, offered a settlement out of court to the plaintiff which she accepted—in excess of $1 million.

In this case, negligence occurred because the hotel failed to follow a **reasonable procedure** whereby the guestrooms would be checked at least once each day. Respect for the guest's right to privacy was allowed to overshadow the need to ensure the guest's safety at a reasonable time during the day, at least once every 24 hours.

Not only did staff negligence contribute to the demise of the guest, the same negligence contributed to a failure to protect the assets of the hotel company, namely, cash and reputation.

Safety

Nature of Emergencies

The two most important aspects of **emergencies** are that they are *unforeseeable* and *uncontrollable*. Both of these factors produce unwanted and unanticipated side effects, since reactions to emergencies by guests and, at times, employees are equally unanticipated and (sometimes) unwanted. It is therefore imperative that there be advance planning and that training and drills be held in combatting all types of emergencies.

In order to maintain safe premises, management must be ready to cope with four types of emergencies:

Fire

Bomb threats and bombings

Natural disasters

Riots and civil disturbances

Since property is replaceable but life is not, it is obvious where most concern must rest. The burden is to first *prevent* any occurrence that may bring about one of the emergencies listed above. If prevention is impossible, the burden shifts to minimizing:

Risk of death or injury

Property damage

Because housekeeping employees are usually in the vicinity of a large number of guests during daytime hours, it is imperative that they be well-trained in procedures that command confidence in order that they set the best possible example for guests who may be caught in an emergency. For example, some housekeeping personnel are afraid of using handheld extinguishers because of the noise generated and the cloud of white smoke created when activated. Such fears require training and drill to quell. Drills should be regular and should not be concealed from guests. Rather, guests should be informed when drills are to take place in order that those present can see what precautions are taken to deal with emergencies.

Fire Protection and the Hotel Guest

Timothy Harper,[5] in the *San Francisco Chronicle*, wrote the following:

> Until recently, hoteliers were about as eager to talk about fire as they were to jump off the 13th floor. But with 118 people killed and hundreds injured in three disastrous hotel fires this winter [1980, when 84 were killed at the MGM Grand, Las Vegas; 26 were killed at Stouffer's Inn in White Plains, New York; and 8 were killed at the Las Vegas Hilton], it is obviously on their minds....
>
> It's no longer bad business to give guests the idea there may be a fire in their hotel. Indeed, the 14-story Red Lion Inn SEATAC near Seattle-Tacoma International Airport in Washington State, gives every guest a copy of a letter from the local fire chief, saying that the motel is one of the safest hotel-convention centers in the country.

Harper continues by quoting Michael Scherkman of the Fire Protection Association as saying,

> Despite all the improvements in hotel fire safety, people should remember two things. First, people are usually safer in hotels than in their own homes, which is where 75 percent of all fire deaths occur. Secondly, people have to be responsible for their own safety wherever they go, whether in hotels or in their own homes.

Recently, hotel guests have been bombarded with information about how safe hotels have become. Although fire protection and prevention and training have been highly upgraded, the manner in which some guests will receive and accept the information can be dangerous. Guests are inclined to let their guards down if or when someone else infers that there is nothing to worry about. It is not necessary to scare hotel guests into an early departure, but there is excellent reason to counsel guests gently about what to do in what-if situations.

An excellent **"what if" publication** was recently created and published by the James H. Barry Company, San Francisco. This publication may be customized and made available for hotels to place in guestrooms. It is a simple, yet appropriate, publication that subtly reminds guests that fire can happen and, it if does, what they should do. Appendix F contains a copy of this publication.

A great concern for training in the housekeeping department is an understanding of the **panic emotion**. Panic is defined as follows by the National Fire Protection Association:

> A sudden overpowering terror, often affecting many people at once. Panic is the product of one's

imagination running wild, and panic will set in as soon as it dawns on a person that they are lost, disoriented, or without knowledge of what to do in an emergency situation. Panic is also contagious and can spread to anyone and everyone. Panic is also irreversible, and once set in, seems to grow. Panic can make a person do things that can kill. People in a state of panic are rarely able to save themselves.

Training employees and drilling them in various situations is a most effective tool to reduce the possibility of panic in a fire situation.

I have been associated with five hotels in which fires have occurred; four of them were directly associated with the rooms department. The situations causing the fires and related hotel rule violations follow.

1. *An intoxicated smoker in bed set a mattress on fire.* No one was injured. The smoker, however, was extremely lucky that he was not overcome, because the smoke was heavy enough to fill the entire rooms department on three floors and was dense enough to prevent visibility beyond 10 feet. *Rule violation:* Renting a room to an intoxicated guest without taking away all smoking materials.

2. *Late night fire in a satellite linen room.* The direct cause of this fire was trash and rubbish left on a housekeeper's cart overnight in a satellite linen room in which the door had been left not only unlocked but also ajar. Had it not been for an alert security patrol at 2:00 A.M., this situation could have been disastrous. The fire was noticed because of a hallway filled with smoke and was found in a smoldering stage within the trash hamper. *Rule violation:* Failing to dispose of trash properly at the end of the workday and leaving a service door unlocked.

3. *Late-night fire deliberately set in an elevator.* Because of the hour, few people were up and about. The entire rooms department of the hotel became completely filled with smoke without being noticed. On this particular night the hotel was full and a large number of elderly people in a tour group were in occupancy. Outside temperatures were below freezing. The fire itself was completely contained within the elevator and burned a section of the carpet less than three square feet. Yet because of the shaft of the elevator, smoke completely filled the hallways on all three floors. There had been no smoke in any guestroom until one panicking guest ran blindly through the hallway shouting "fire" and banging on doors. As guests became aroused, they entered the smoke-filled hallways, in many cases leaving their rooms without their keys, thus preventing their return to a safe environment. Many of the guests quickly evacuated the building, only to become exposed to the elements in unsuitable clothing. *Rule violation:* Leaving a known safe environment when a fire is reported without protecting your ability to retrace your path.

4. *A television exploded within a guestroom.* This is a rare happening, but if it occurs, it is usually in a vacant room where the television has been left in operation. In this particular fire, maximum damage occurred within the guestroom in a very short time. The guest was at dinner and upon returning to his room was surprised to find that all the commotion and fire apparatus had been called because of the fire in *his* room. *Rule violation:* Leaving a television in operation in a vacant room.

Knowledge about Smoke and Fire as a Foundation for Training Programs

Contrary to what has been seen on television or in the movies, **fire** is not likely to chase people down and burn them to death. It is almost always the **by-products of fire** that kill. Smoke and panic will more likely be the cause of death long before a fire arrives, if it ever does. It is most important that all employees, especially housekeeping employees, be drilled about the effects of smoke and be taught how to avoid smoke and panic in order that they might set a proper example for guests.

Where there is smoke there is not necessarily a fire out of control. A smoldering mattress will produce great amounts of smoke that may be picked up in air-conditioning systems and transported over vast areas of the hotel. Since smoke is warmer than air, it will start accumulating in ceiling areas and work its way down. When a hotel hallway fills with smoke, it is too late to start looking for exit signs, since they are *always* mounted in ceilings and become obscured by the smoke, which rises to the top of the hallway. (We hope that someday building codes will require the placement of indestructible emergency exit signs near baseboards where they can be seen in a fire emergency.)

Smoke will, in the long run, affect your eyes. Eyes can take only so much smoke, and then they will close by reflex. As hard as you try, once your eyes are closed they will not reopen in a smoke-filled area. Lastly, the only fresh air that will be available will be at or near the floor. Employees must be taught to get on their hands and knees to take advantage of what fresh air might be available.

There are articles about fire prevention and safety available through the National Fire Protection Association in Washington, D.C. This agency can provide the latest state-of-the-art information to support training programs in fire protection in hotels.

Fire drills should be conducted and should include, but not be limited to, the following:

1. Demonstration of blindfolded employee leaving a hotel from any known point within the hotel
2. Demonstration of proper action when there is reduced visibility in a hotel hallway due to smoke
3. Under the supervision of local fire department personnel, demonstration of the use of handheld extinguishers to put out an actual preset fire (Fires set in a trash can in the hotel parking lot can usually provide insights as to employee behavior when using these extinguishers.)
4. Showing any of the numerous films available from local fire prevention agencies for housekeeping employees
5. Making demonstrated knowledge about fire protection and the use of fire equipment a part of performance appraisal

Bomb Threats

The hotel personnel who will be involved during a **bomb threat** will probably be the PBX department, hotel management, and the fire or police department. Whether or not a hotel should be evacuated is the decision of the **on-scene commander**, who is usually a member of the local police or fire department. The decision as to who will order an evacuation is not made on the spur of the moment. It is usually prearranged that the on-scene commander will order any evacuation that is considered necessary.

In most cases, selected personnel who thoroughly know the hotel will be a part of search teams; the executive housekeeper, chief engineer, resident manager, and other such management personnel might become involved with property searches.

The hotel facility must always be kept clean and free of debris and unnecessary equipment and supplies. If everything is neatly stored in its proper place, suspicious looking articles are much easier to spot and housekeeping personnel are better able to participate in searches and make observations faster.

Housekeeping department personnel should be trained not to touch strange items when a property search for a possible explosive device is in progress; they should be trained to notice strange objects and report them to the proper authority.

Natural Disasters

Floods, hurricanes, earthquakes, and sometimes freezing temperatures and snowstorms are **natural disasters**. Each has its own set of rules. When such occurrences happen, some hotels tend to empty, whereas others fill up, depending on the location and type of problem.

Hotels on major arteries and interstate highways fill when weather conditions prevent traffic from moving. Such unexpected heavy occupancy can cause hotels to find themselves in unpredicted circumstances. In most cases, the first conclusion of management would be to send their employees home thinking that business would become extremely slow. Then as emergency conditions start to compound, the hotel might start to fill, and 100 percent occupancy could be reached. Real problems set in when the hotel does fill and there is no one who can come to work because of the disaster.

Planning is the answer to such occurrences. At any time the hotel might fill due to a natural disaster or extreme weather, provision should be made for employees who can stay without creating additional personal hardship to remain at the hotel; there are always sufficient numbers of such employees. An adequate number of guestrooms should be set aside for food and beverage and housekeeping personnel to ensure that by having employees work in relays, all guests will be accommodated in a reasonable fashion.

Riots and Civil Disturbances

Civil disturbances may originate in the hotel or may start miles away and drift into the hotel. People in an unruly crowd at a football game may return to their accommodations and continue their unruliness. Housekeeping personnel should be exposed to the possibilities that such events could take place and should be trained in techniques that will calm unruly people.

Employees can learn the principles of transactional analysis and be exposed to *Games People Play*.[6] Transactional analysis (TA) is the study of communications (transactions) between people based on theories presented in the mid-1960s. Of primary concern is for employees to treat guests properly and avoid injuries to guests. The hotel is liable for any injury that might beset a guest because of a short-tempered employee. This is another reason for close observation of the temperament of employees during probationary periods of employment.

Loss Prevention Programs and The Emergency Action Plan

Holiday Inns, Inc., as part of its **loss prevention program**, provides excellent training and training outlines for its property management in order that a proper and professional emphasis may be applied in the areas of safety and security. Excerpts from its Emergency Action Plan are outlined on the next page; the plan is presented in detail in Appendix G.

Housekeeping	Key controls
	Safety and security procedures
	How to handle Do Not Disturb signs
Total hotel	Key control
	Emergency fire fighting procedures
	Bomb threats
	Bomb searches
	Evacuation procedures
	Floods
	Hurricanes
	Tornadoes
	Winter storms
	Death of a guest
	Death of an employee

Summary

In this chapter we introduced the concept of the safeguarding of assets and explored the subjects of security and safety, emphasizing that each requires special and separate attention. We discussed how to maintain a secure housekeeping department and presented a 14-point program for employee theft prevention. We also talked about security within hotel guestrooms, specifically card entry systems and dual responsibility.

After a general discussion of the nature of emergencies in a hotel situation, we gave specific procedures for dealing with fires, bomb threats, natural disasters, and civil disturbances. The emphasis was on safety in all situations.

Management's responsibility in the areas of security and safety is clear and must not under any circumstances be abdicated in favor of the belief that nothing of an emergency nature could ever happen to this hotel or health care facility or to our guests, patients, or employees. Wariness, training, objectivity, and study are the keys to protection from the perils brought by lax attitudes toward security and safety within the housekeeping department of either hotel or health care institution. All planning should culminate in the creation of an emergency action plan that foresees potential problem areas and catalogs plans for swift, effective action to prevent the loss or destruction of assets. Emergency action plans should also have as their objective a quick recovery and return to a "business as usual" status as soon as possible.

KEY TERMS AND CONCEPTS

Body of knowledge
Safeguarding assets
American Society of Industrial
  Security (ASIS)
Risk analysis
Risk management
House detective
Foreseeability
Foreseeable events
Safety
Security
Employee theft prevention
Contamination of employees
Fourteen-point theft prevention
  program
Employment history
Polygraph examination
Badge system
Scenario
Probationary period
Key-control program
Key pouch
Red tag system

Snoop
Employee profile
Miscellaneous charge
Reasonable security for
  guestrooms
Card entry system
Lock cylinder
Absolute right to privacy
Dormitory
Reasonable time
Dead-bolted
Reasonable procedure
Emergencies
"What if" publication
Panic emotion
Fire
By-products of fire
Bomb threats
On-scene commander
Natural disaster
Civil disturbances
Loss prevention program

DISCUSSION AND REVIEW QUESTIONS

1. Explain the difference between safety and security.
2. What is employee contamination? List several reasons for it.
3. What is an employee profile? How and when is it used? What are the characteristics of it that should cause concern?
4. How would you use employees to reduce theft by employees? by guests? What points would you make during employee orientation to gain participation in a theft prevention program?
5. Explain the benefits of a card entry system over the hard key method of entry for guestrooms.
6. Explain the panic emotion. Give several characteristics of people acting in panic. How can panic be avoided in an emergency? How can guest panic be controlled?
7. In what ways can the National Fire Protection Agency assist in a program of fire prevention and protection for department managers?
8. What preventive measures can be taken by housekeeping department personnel to minimize the disruption of routines during bomb threats and to facilitate rapid inspections for explosive devices?

NOTES

1. Omer Henry, "Our Employees Are Stealing Us Blind," *Motel/Motor Inn Journal*, 1979, p. 2.
2. Harold Gluck, "How To Reduce Loss Potential During The Hiring Process," *Motel/Motor Inn Journal*, 1979, p. 5.
3. Bob Curtis, "Tips On Keeping Employees Honest," NRN Book Excerpt, *Nation's Restaurant News*, September 1979, p. 1.
4. Barbara Powers, "Crime Shouldn't Pay; Curbing Employee Theft." From an interview conducted by *Lodging*, May 1983, p. 31.
5. Timothy Harper, "U. S. Hotels Find Guest Keen On Fire Protection," *San Francisco Chronicle*, 1981.
6. Eric Berne, *Games People Play: The Psychology of Human Relationships* (New York: Grove Press, 1961). For an excellent and more direct application of the subject to the hospitality and service industries, see Maurice F. Villere, Thomas S. O'Connor, and William J. Quain, "Games Nobody Wins," *The Cornell HRA Quarterly*, November vol. 24, No. 3, 1983, pp. 72–79.

14

The On-Premises Laundry: An Understanding of Basic Engineering and Operational Considerations Before Installation

CHAPTER OBJECTIVES

1. To find out how to justify the need for an on-premise laundry
2. To learn how to plan for an on-premise laundry, using consultants when necessary
3. To learn how to size a laundry
4. To understand the importance of proper electrical, mechanical, plumbing, and airflow engineering when planning an on-premise laundry

Most of the material written about **on-premises laundries** addresses the issue of whether or not to have such a facility. Numerous trade publications have dealt both analytically and subjectively with cost-saving considerations and with quality and inventory control, efficiency of operation, dependability of outside contracts, and linen investment costs.

This chapter has a different purpose: It provides the reasons for having an on-premise laundry and discusses criteria that small property owners may use when considering the installation of on-premises laundries.

A Statement in Favor of On-Premises Laundry Operations

Jack E. Scott, president of Baker Linen Company of California,[1] believes that one should strongly consider installing an on-premises laundry if outside laundry costs are in excess of $900 per month. The latest research report by the American Hotel and Motel Association (AHMA), cited and updated by Scott, indicates the following comparisons for in-house service, outside service, and rental service for a typical 120 room unit:

Weekly in-house laundry costs	$324.00
Allowance for weekly linen depreciation	133.91
Total in-house laundry costs	$457.91
Weekly outside service costs	
Using owned linens—8806 pounds at 10 cents per pound	$880.60
Allowance for weekly linen depreciation	133.91
Total outside laundry costs	$1014.51
Weekly linen rental service	$1782.17

Old Concerns Resolved

Maintaining the quality of linens has always been a deterrent to in-house laundries, but the primary problem has been resolved. Modern **no-iron linens** (50/50 polyester blends) now undergo a dual finish process that improves the molecular structure of the polyester fiber, resulting in a linen that retains its no-iron properties throughout its normal life expectancy. Refined blend sheets now last three times as long as their cotton predecessors. In fact, the polyester fiber in new-generation no-iron linens tends to relax and actually increases in elasticity with use.

The no-iron linen industry has also perfected the equipment that processes the new-generation linens. The timing of wash-and-rinse cycles, temperature control, and the automatic adding of detergents, bleaches, and softeners have eliminated the problems of human error, need for extensive employee training, and operator inattention.

In summary, the reasons for having economical in-house operations, now more than ever before, far outweigh the need to abdicate this important operation to the province of others.

Planning and Pre-Engineering

Some architects of small laundry facilities suggest that an on-premise laundry is nothing more than installing a few washers and dryers in some remote space in the facility. Such inadequate planning usually results in laundries that must be re-engineered by qualified designers and laundry equipment contractors resulting in costly modifications. For example, let's consider one of Canada's newest hotels, described as a magnificent creation[2]: The location was inspiring, the architectural design was impressive, the accommodations were outstanding, and the quality and comfort standards were exemplary. It was perceived as exceptional in every respect except one. In spite of detailed planning, the laundry was poorly engineered and had less than half the space required to be efficient. What area it did have was poorly designed. The problem was more than mere engineering and design; machinery was not of the industrial caliber demanded by millions of pounds of laundry each year. In an attempt to keep up with volume, 11 shifts per week were required.

Large laundries are not the only ones that receive improper planning and initial engineering attention. Often it is the owners of small properties who, after having made the decision to have an on-premise laundry, fail to give the consideration and planning that laundry operations warrant.

For example, here is a description of what one small property owner built as an in-house laundry in the basement of a new 80-room hotel. The amount and size of equipment were basically correct, but decisions had not been based on an understanding of efficient laundry operation and mechanical requirements. There was *one* 4-inch floor drain provided to receive the effluent water from two, or possibly three, washer/extractors draining under pressure, each having a 3-inch diameter drain line. No complimentary drain trough was provided with the floor drain to handle the effluent overflow temporarily. Instant floods would occur every time two or possibly three washers discharged effluent into the undersized drain system. In addition, three 100-pound dryers each exhausted 800 cubic feet of air per minute into the laundry room, which had a low ceiling. No provision had been made to exhaust this heavily heated and moisture-laden air. Unbearable working conditions and moisture condensing on every pipe in the basement were certain to occur. In addition, a supplemental lint disposal system was not provided. The only lint removal was provided by the lint traps of each individual dryer. Lint can be a serious fire hazard in laundry operations and must be dealt with accordingly.

Small properties may not require the detailed planning needed in larger properties (between 300 and 2500 rooms); however, planning variables apply equally to small and large hotel laundries. The AHMA can supply the names of reputable and knowledgeable **laundry consultants**, engineers, and equipment manufacturers, most of whom will engineer laundries and specify equipment within certain budgetary constraints. In addition, they oversee installation and provide management and worker training during startup operations. One of the many companies that provides this type of service, Baring Industries,[3] has coined the term **systemeering** to represent the following 10 services it specifies in all of their contracts. These steps may be followed regardless of the specific laundry consultant used.

1. *Determination of needs* This step involves meeting with owners, architects, interior designers, engineers, and other project consultants to obtain all the data pertinent to **sizing laundries** in housekeeping systems. Data include the number of rooms, number of beds, expected occupancy, variety of services, areas of services, and budgetary restrictions. From this data a report containing information about size, type, and location of facilities is composed. This report describes the basic integration and development of the laundry in the overall hotel concept and design.

2. *System definition and space allocation* Once needs are defined, specialists concentrate on selecting systems and components most able to handle the project requirements. Interrelationships of those allocated spaces are analyzed from a human engineering standpoint to eliminate costly extra steps or crossed traffic patterns. Many different approaches are considered in designing a system that optimizes efficiency and, therefore, economy of operations.

3. *Equipment layouts* Labor-saving ideas are meshed with the most efficient work-flow patterns that can be designed within the given space. Alternate system components and layouts are investigated to ensure selection of the best possible system.

4. *Equipment selection, specifications, and budgets* The selection of quality options for equipment are presented. Costs are studied, including equipment installation and rigging equipment costs. Follow-up maintenance considerations are included, along with the expected life of the equipment. Budgets are finalized using standard specifications that allow for fast tracking to early completion of the project.

5. *Detailed drawing and specification* Equipment connection schedules and mechanical, electrical, and ventilation details are defined, showing exact locations of all rough-in points. Such drawings enable the contractor to rough-in utilities properly before equipment arrives.

These steps expedite connection and installation of equipment. Detailed specifications for each piece of equipment are provided, reflecting every option selected. All mechanical and electrical requirements must be coordinated with architects, engineers, and contractors throughout this phase.

The next five steps in Baring's service are

6. *Equipment procurement and shipment coordination*
7. *Installation scheduling and supervision*
8. *Start-up, test, and demonstration*
9. *Operator training, maintenance*
10. *After-sale service*

Regardless of the size of the laundry facility, all steps in the systemeering plan should be carried out to ensure the best possible laundry facilities.

Basic Knowledge for the Owner

It may not be economically advantageous for small property owners to use the services of a laundry consultant. In such cases, owners need to know the basic considerations in the development of a small on-premise laundry operation.

The most commonly used and technically correct way of deciding the size and composition of equipment is by analyzing **linen poundage requirements.** It is usual for laundry equipment manufacturers to design and specify equipment using this criteria. Thus, washers and/or dryers are available with load capabilities ranging from 25 to 600 pounds, allowing for the selection of the most reasonably sized equipment for a given set of requirements. Most washers extract their own wash and rinse water; therefore, separate extractors are not necessary. Recognizing that labor costs will normally be the highest of all operating costs, it is desirable to specify the optimum-sized equipment that will minimize these costs.

Another consideration is that either **washing capacity, drying capacity,** or **handling capacity** can provide the primary constraint for the laundry, and therefore these three constraints should be balanced. For example, a laundry with 400 pounds of washing capacity operating on a 30-minute cycle, 150 pounds of drying capacity operating on a 50-minute cycle, with adequate space for handling, storing, and folding linen, would be dryer limited. On the other hand, a laundry with one 50-pound washing machine operating on a 30-minute cycle and one 100-pound dryer operating on a 1-hour cycle with adequate handling capacity would be properly sized.

In small operations, the number of dryers is normally related to the number of washers in a 2 to 1 ratio; for example, two 50-pound dryers to one 50-pound washer. This rule is based on the fact that a standard drying cycle is likely to be twice as long as a standard washing cycle.

Laundries equipped with **ironers** do not require that sheets and pillow-cases pass through dryers. In such operations, dryers are used only for terry linen. All of these factors enter into the planning of how much and what type of equipment needs to be installed.

Major Equipment Requirements

Washers

Let us consider a hotel with 100 guestrooms and linen requirements as shown in Table 14.1. The approximately 1000 pounds of daily laundered linen in this 100-room hotel will be used as a guide for determining equipment requirements. (Also see Figure 14.1.)

Washer/extractor selection should be the best balance of machine capability and labor require-

Table 14.1   Linen Par and Weight Determination

Sheet Count

NO. ROOMS	TYPE	NO. BEDS/ROOM	TOTAL BEDS	TOTAL SHEETS	WT/UNIT ITEM IN POUNDS	TOTAL WEIGHT IN POUNDS
10	King Single	1	10	20	2.20	44.0
70	Queen Double	2	140	280	1.45	406.0
20	Queen Single	1	20	40	1.45	58.0
Totals						
100	All types		170	340		508.0

Pillowcases

TYPE BED	NO. PILLOWCASES PER BED	TOTAL NO. PER BED TYPE
King	3	$3 \times 10 = 30$
Queen	2	$2 \times 160 = 320$
Total no. pillowcases		350

350 cases at 0.25 pound/pillowcase = 87.5 pounds

Terry Linen[a]

ITEM	QUANTITY	WEIGHT/ITEM (POUNDS)	TOTAL WEIGHT
BT	350	0.714	249.9
HT	350	0.231	80.85
WC	350	0.053	18.55
BM	100	0.437	43.70
Totals	1150		393.00

One Par Total Weight

Sheets	508.00 pounds
Pillowcases	87.5
Terry linen	393.0
Total	988.5
Approximately	1000.00 pounds

[a] Assume one bath towel (BT), one hand towel (HT), one washcloth (WC), per pillow and one bath mat (BM) per room.

ments; the best balance is the least machinery that allows for the smallest labor force (one person working an eight-hour shift is optimum). After setting a constraint that requires the production of **1 par linen** (the total amount of linen required to cover every bed and supply every bathroom once) in one shift, we now select a mix of washing machine capacity that is most practical.

One 500-pound washer, washing two loads, which can be completed in about one hour washing time, can handle the 1000-pound requirement, but then the washer would be idle for seven hours.

The opposite extreme, one 50-pound washer working slightly less than a half-hour cycle, can produce the same amount of linen in 10 hours of operation. Neither of these is the best choice. Two 50-pound washers can produce the 1000-pound requirement in about five hours, and two 50-pound capacity machines cost considerably less than one 500-pound machine and require less energy and mechanical support.

There is another consideration, which is that all linens will not be washed using the same **wash formula**. Linens must be separated by linen types and

Figure 14.1 A bank of four 50-lb. washers plumbed for automatic chemical and water intake. (Photo taken with permission.)

degree of soiling. Wash formula refers to the combination of washing time, rinsing time, temperature control, and automatic addition of chemical detergents, bleaches, and softeners.

Linens must also be weighed for proper washing. By analyzing the weights of each type of linen noted in Table 14.1, we can find the most practical loading combination for a 50-pound washer. Table 14.2 shows that two 50-pound washers, working one cycle of approximately 30 minutes, can complete all wash operations in about five and one-half hours.

Dryers

As we mentioned earlier, in a no-iron laundry the number of dryers relates to the number of washers in the ratio of 2 to 1. At 100 percent occupancy, the production of up to 1000 pounds of washed linen (21 loads of wash) can be accommodated by three 100-pound dryers in a six and one-half hour period (Figure 14.2).

Less than 100 Percent Occupancy

We have been assuming 100 percent occupancy in determining our washing and drying equipment requirements. As we know, hotel operations are not always full. How, then, do we determine the hours of laundry production as related to hotel occupancy?

Figure 14.3 equates the washing capability of the two 50-pound washers to 100 percent occupancy of the 100-room hotel example on a linear basis, thereby indicating the number of hours a laundry must operate for any given occupancy. We see that two 50-pound washers can generate the linen required for 100 percent occupancy in slightly more than five and one-half hours; 70 percent occupancy would require

Table 14.2 Load Schedules for One 50-Pound Washer

ITEM[a]	QUANTITY	TOTAL WEIGHT (POUNDS)	ITEMS/LOAD	TOTAL LOADS
Sheets (King)	20	44	20	1
Sheets (Queen)	320	464	32	10
PC	350	88	175	2
BT	350	250	70	5
HT	350	81	175	2
WC	350	19	350	1

[a] PC, pillowcase; BT, bath towel; HT, hand towel; WC, washcloth.

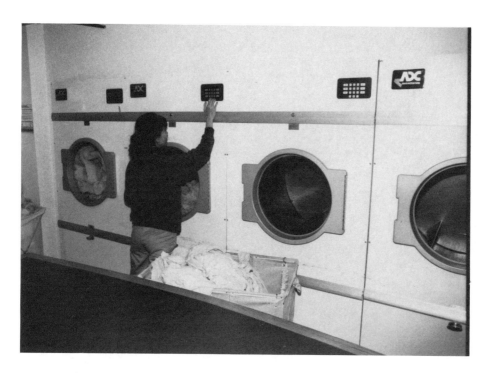

Figure 14.2 Four 100-pound dryers make a compatible arrangement with four 50-lb. washers. (Photo taken with permission.)

4 hours of operation; lesser occupancies would require less wash-hour requirements.

Additional Equipment

Having specified two washer/extractors and three dryers as basic machinery required for our 100-room example property, what other equipment may be

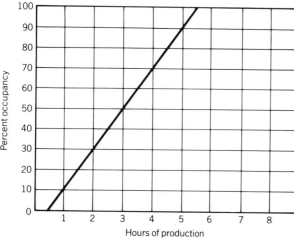

Figure 14.3 Washer productivity versus occupancy graph developed for a 100-room example property. At optimum efficiency and with no breakdowns, two 50-pound washers on a 30-minute cycle can generate 1000 pounds of wash in about $5\frac{1}{2}$ hours. Loading time and requirements due to different wash formulas for sheets and terry linen were also considered when the graph was developed. The two 50-pound washers require only 4 hours of operating time to produce the load requirement generated by a 70 percent occupancy of the 100-room example hotel.

considered essential? Mary Chew[4] recommends the following ancillary equipment:

- *1 Soak sink:* Double basin, plastic formed, for soaking stained linens in special wash formulas for spot and stain removal (Figure 14.4).
- *1 Folding table* (4 by 6 feet): Centrally located between dryers and storage shelving. It is used primarily for folding terry linens.
- *5 Laundry hampers:* Either vinyl-coated canvas or plastic-molded hamper. Two hampers are used for soiled separated linen: One is to receive washed-wet linen, and two are for washed-dry linen. These hampers should not be used outside the laundry.

In addition to Chew's recommendations, the following equipment is also recommended:

- *6 Convertible/mobile linen storage carts:* Three convertible/mobile storage carts should be in the laundry and receive clean linen throughout the day. These three carts are moved to satellite linen rooms for the next day's operation. As linen is moved from the mobile carts to the maids' carts, the shelving is repositioned so as to create soiled linen hampers for the next day's housekeeping.

Three mobile linen carts should be in the satellite linen rooms to accommodate soiled linen during the day. At day's end they are ready to be moved to the laundry for washing the following day. After soiled linen has been removed and sorted, shelving on the convertible mobile carts are repositioned to accept clean linen. The cycle

Figure 14.4 Soak sink and chemical mixing center. Note detergent lines leading to washing machines. Other chemicals are arranged for proper dispensing. Soak sink is an important item on laundry small equipment list. (Photo taken with permission.)

will then be repeated. (AHMA can provide the names of several manufacturers of this type of convertible mobile cart.) Figures 14.5 and 14.6 are examples of a convertible/mobile cart with shelves in the positions for clean and soiled linen, respectively.

Mobile shelving does not preclude the need for some permanent shelving, but it does remove the requirement for most and it does allow for transporting linen. The total need for mobile linen carts is determined by the number of satellite linen rooms; two are needed for each linen storage area, one of which would be positioned in the laundry each day.

• *1 Extra Hand sheet/spread folder*[5]: There are several ways to fold sheets. The one used is normally determined by the size of the laundry workload. When workloads are low, capital expenditures for sheet folders would usually not be warranted or recommended, since two attendants working together can fold about 90 to 100 sheets per hour. For example, a small laundry load (50 percent average occupancy) in our 100-room example hotel yields a workload of about 150 sheets and requires two people to fold sheets for about one and one-half hours.

If the workload permanently increases, it then becomes appropriate to consider purchasing an **Extra Hand** folder. The Extra Hand gives one employee about the same production capability as two employees folding sheets by hand. Figure 14.7 illustrates an Extra Hand device in use; one employee is performing six basic steps and folding approximately 120 sheets an hour.

Figure 14.5 Convertible Mobile Linen Cart with shelving positioned to receive fresh linen. (Photo courtesy of Inter Metro Industries Corp.)

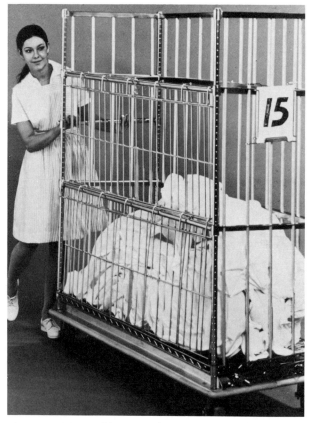

Figure 14.6 Convertible Cart with shelving positioned to receive soiled linen. (Photo courtesy of Inter Metro Industries Corp.)

General Nonequipment Factors and Requirements

Linen Supply

As mentioned in Chapter 7, about $3\frac{1}{2}$ par of linen is required for efficient housekeeping operations: One par of linen is found on the beds and in bathrooms of all guestrooms; one par is clean and is either on maid's carts or on shelves for tomorrow's cleaning operations (Figure 14.8); and one par is soiled, awaiting the next day's laundry operations. The remaining half par is related to new linen in storage. (If linens were owned and had to be sent off the property to a commercial laundry each day, add one additional par to total requirements because of the time required to transport linen back and forth to a commercial laundry.)

Floorplan Layout and Size

About 4 square feet of space for each guestroom is required for the laundry facility itself, and an additional 4 square feet per guestroom is needed for linen handling and storage throughout the property. Figure 14.9 shows a typical **floorplan layout** for a small laundry with only two washers. Figure 14.10 shows the actual layout of a four washer/dryer laundry.

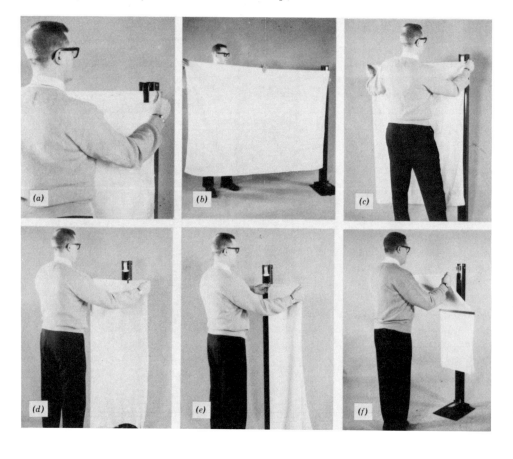

Figure 14.7 An Extra Hand sheet folder in operation. One operator performs six basic steps, as illustrated in the folding process. The same procedure can be followed for spreads, blankets, bed pads, shower curtains, and so on. (Photo courtesy of S & S Products.)

Figure 14.8 Fresh linen supply awaiting pickup for future use. (Photo take with permission.)

Soiled linens are first moved to a sorting and wash area. After washing and drying, linen is moved to the folding area. Both folded sheets and folded terry linen are then moved to convertible/mobile storage carts for passage out of the laundry.

A third washer could be added to accommodate expansion. Dryers should be installed as shown and are part of the original equipment. (Note the venting capability.)

If a hot water system is not sufficient to accommodate two washers, a fast-generating hot water heater will be necessary. Gas hot water heaters must be properly vented when installed.

Two soak sinks provide capability for soaking stained and spotted linen rather than using valuable washing time.

A 4 foot × 6 foot folding table positioned as indicated is recommended.

Staffing Considerations

Staffing for the 100-room hotel example laundry in this chapter (no food and beverage linen or uniforms considered) is

1 wash person

1 laundry attendant

The wash person handles the loading and unloading of washers and the loading of dryers. The laundry attendant unloads the dryers, folds sheets, and stacks terry linen and pillowcases in flat stacks of appropriate numbers (Figure 14.11). Folding rates for the Extra Hand sheet folder are approximately one and one-half sheets per minute. A full par of sheets (242) can therefore be folded in two hours by the laundry attendant.

The laundry attendant spends the balance of the shift stacking terry linen and pillowcases in counted stacks to be passed to the satellite linen rooms at the end of the day via the mobile linen carts.

For the model hotel (353 rooms) laundry staffing is approximately seven people (one wash person supervisor, one utility helper and five laundry attendants). Since this is the same number of people as in a housekeeping team (see Chapter 2), the laundry crew, with proper cross-training, working a five-day week, can be relieved on the sixth and seventh day by the swing teams.

Laundry Floors

Even with proper drainage, washer spills and overflows will occur. It is therefore essential that the laundry floor be waterproofed (sealed).

Soiled sorted linen and even clean linen may be found trailing on the floor occasionally, and as a result, the laundry floor must be damp-mopped daily. Linen on the floor is of no consequence provided the floor has been sealed and is kept clean.

Mechanical Engineering Requirements

When small facility equipment has been installed with no attention to engineering considerations

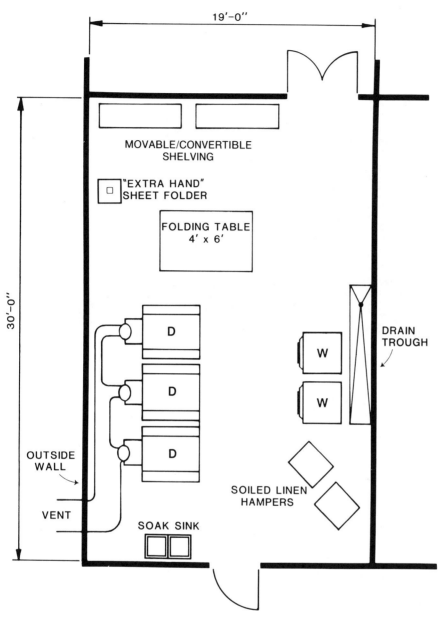

Figure 14.9 Small laundry floorplan layout suitable for supporting rooms operations of a 60-to 100-room hotel.

such as electrical wiring, water supply and drainage plumbing, and ventilation, it can create a shutdown. The greatest of these "unrecognized problems" is inadequate water disposal drainage caused by extraction cycles of several washing machines draining simultaneously. For example, can a 4-inch floor drain accommodate the drainage from three washers, each with a 3-inch discharge line? According to most specifications, the answer is no. A drain trough or holding basin that can hold 100 gallons of water can allow for the overload of effluent water under pressure and will allow time for the drain water to pass into the 4-inch floor drain over a period of several minutes. (Refer to Figure 14.9 and note the specified drain trough associated with the two washers. There is also a provision for drainage of a third washer.)

Ventilation Requirements

Another requirement is the necessity to exhaust moisture-laden air from the three dryers out of the laundry room. Small properties usually have laundries with low ceilings, which compound the problem of dryer effluent exhaust. Most 100-pound dryers each exhaust about 800 cubic feet per minute (cfm) of air. Operating three dryers together results in 2400 cfm of this moist hot air.

Laundry rooms also require adequate space through regular doors to intake or supply an equal amount of fresh dry air. Without ample intake through regular doors or a separate forced dry air supply, dryers will not operate at specified efficiencies. Some modern dryers now provide for heat

Figure 14.10 Laundry layout indicating how linen flows from washer to dryer to folding tables. Laundry hampers are rolled under folding table with cleaned and dried linen to be folded. (Photo taken with permission.)

recovery equipment, which will reduce laundry energy requirements *if* provision is made for this type of accessory in advance.

Provision for Lint Removal

It is absolutely essential that the laundry room and adjacent areas be kept clean and free of lint. Lint is a major fire hazard in laundry operations and must be dealt with accordingly. Not only must lint be removed from dryer air ventilation, but lint must be dusted away from overhead pipes and hard-to-reach areas. A regular campaign must be maintained to keep lint accumulation to a minimum.

Summary

The determination of whether or not to have an on-premise laundry is based upon cost considerations. If it is appropriate, the need for accurate planning arises. Decisions must be made concerning the

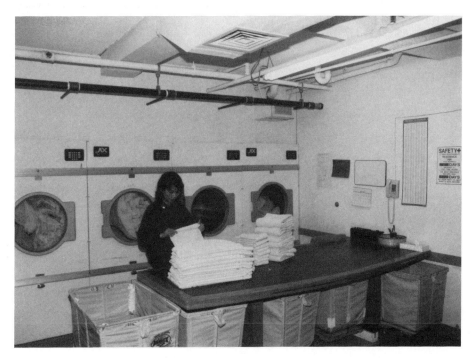

Figure 14.11 Laundry attendant folds terry linen and places it in stacks of appropriate size. (Photo taken with permission.)

proper size of equipment, facility layout, ancillary equipment, staffing considerations, work-flow patterns, and floor treatment. A critical factor in preliminary planning is a necessary concern for mechanical, electrical, plumbing, and airflow engineering to ensure proper equipment operation after construction and installation.

Frequently, once the decision is made to have an on-premise laundry, facility architects unfamiliar with hotel operational design and the need to trim capital costs ignore the necessity of seeking and obtaining professional laundry facility advice. Shortcuts in this area create problems that haunt the operator during startup operations and for some time thereafter until they are identified and corrected. The decision to have an on-premise laundry facility should therefore include the decision to contact a nationally recognized laundry consulting firm. Small operators should not become overly concerned about the costs of such consulting services. The payback in months and in future years of trouble-free operations far outweigh the initial cost of proper planning and foresight.

KEY TERMS AND CONCEPTS

On-premise laundry	Drying capacity
No-iron linens	Handling capacity
Laundry consultant	Ironers
Systemeering	1 par linen
Sizing laundries	Wash formula
Linen poundage requirements	Extra Hand
Washing capacity	Floorplan layout

DISCUSSION AND REVIEW QUESTIONS

1. List several advantages of having an on-premise laundry.
2. Discuss the characteristics of no-iron linens. Indicate why no-iron linens have made on-premise laundries more practical today than they were in the past.
3. When on-premise laundries are being considered, why are the services of a qualified laundry consultant so important? List several of the factors that are often overlooked when inexperienced people are involved in planning small laundry operations.
4. What does the term "sizing a laundry" mean? What are the constraints that must be considered when a laundry is being sized? How is the productivity of a laundry measured?
5. Aside from washing and drying equipment, what equipment is needed in a small on-premise laundry?
6. Explain the value of using convertible mobile linen storage carts. How do you determine the proper quantity of these carts for linen handling operations?
7. When developing the requirements for an on-premise laundry, what are the nonequipment factors that should be considered? What are the mechanical equipment factors that must be considered?

NOTES

1. Jack E. Scott, Why You Should Install Your Own Laundry, *Lodging*, November 1976, pp. 38–39.
2. Paul Schweid, "A Laundry in Your Plans, Don't Underestimate Its Importance," *Cornell Quarterly*, vol. 17, November 1976, pp. 40–46.
3. "Baring Laundry-Valet Profile," Baring Industries, 655 NW 122 Street, Miami, Florida, 33268, undated brochure.
4. Mary Chew, "Those Indispensable Laundry Accessories," *The Executive Housekeeper*, March 1977, p. 46.
5. *The Extra Hand*, S & S Products, 8377 Neiman Road, Lenexa, Kansas, 66214, undated brochure.

15

The Full Circle of Management

CHAPTER OBJECTIVES

1. To understand what is meant by the full circle of management.
2. To learn what it means for executive housekeepers to be problem solvers, including several of the specific problems with which they become involved.
3. To see what it means for the executive housekeeper to be a leader as well as a manager.
4. To understand the executive housekeeper's role in the development of subordinates.
5. To understand the importance of on-going personal development for managers.

Thus far, we have discussed the theoretical aspects of scientific management and how they are applied to the tasks of the executive housekeeper; that is, opening a hotel and operating a housekeeping department. We have seen that the executive housekeeper has to be systematic in the development of procedures, whereby most housekeeping tasks are delegated to department personnel and controls are in-

augurated so that the technique of management by exception can be used. Additionally, we discussed the special topics of safety and security and on-premises laundries.

Once these procedures and tasks are mastered, what is left for the manager to do? Nothing—provided all systems work perfectly; no problems arise; employees do not need any caring, human understanding, attention, guidance, and inspiration; morale is not an issue; and no progress is expected. Of course, such situations never exist, and we thus see that it is the manager who deals with these issues and brings the art and science of management full circle.

The integration of the art and science of management is especially apparent for managers of hotel or hospital housekeeping departments. This is so because of the large numbers of personnel employed, requiring orientation, training, development, guidance, and supervision, and the day-to-day problems that arise as a result of the unexpected human dynamics and interactions among personnel. There are also the needs for flexibility, for recognition of occasional change in operational direction, and for application of new techniques.

In this chapter we will thus present topics related to the special on-going responsibilities of managers: problem solving, managerial styles, employee development, and personal professional growth.

Problem Solving

At one particular time I was assigned responsibilities as regional director of technical services for the Midwest region of Marriott Hotels, Inc. Upon reporting for duty, I was introduced to many members of top management, including other regional directors in an office complex in which all directors were housed. The directors' offices gave the impression of heavy and complex activity. Desks were covered with work in progress; bookshelves were full of references; walls were covered with charts and graphs; and most telephones were either being used, ringing, or had lights flashing.

All offices except one were like this—the one that had just been assigned to the new regional director of the Midwest region. In my office were a clean desk, empty drawers, clean walls, empty bookshelf, credenza, and quiet telephone. The appearance of the office gave no clue as to the work content of this new staff position. This uncertainty lasted only momentarily, however.

The phone rang—it was the executive housekeeper of the Houston Marriott indicating that there was a problem with their recently installed laundry. From that moment on, there was never any doubt as to the responsibilities involved in the new assignment. The incumbent was to become a problem solver, and within one month the office of the Midwest regional director provided the same evidence of activity as did the other offices.

Problem solving can be one of the greatest challenges faced each day by the executive housekeeper. Few if any days will pass that someone in the organization will not utter the infamous phrase: "I've got a problem." Most problems are best resolved by ensuring that the supervisor in whose area the problem lies is not allowed to shift the problem upward. Solutions must come from the person rather than from higher authority. The characteristic of human nature, whereby people tend to push their problems onto anyone who will accept them rather than solve the problem themselves, must be avoided. In addition, the tendency for overzealous managers to take on the problems of others as their own must be overcome.

Many employees are afraid to solve problems for fear of making mistakes. Mistakes are a great teaching device, provided they are used for objective counseling as opposed to unsatisfactory performance evaluations. Most mistakes made in a housekeeping department are not costly to overcome, and the development that can occur from making and learning from a mistake far outweighs the cost of managerial and supervisory training that may be required to have prevented the mistake from happening in the first place. Executive housekeepers should therefore guard carefully against solving problems in areas in which junior managers and supervisors have simply failed to act.

Not all problems can be referred back to junior managers for solution without some form of guidance, however. There are those problems that must have the direct involvement of the executive housekeeper or they will grow in complexity and intensity. A review of some of the more common problems that require the executive housekeeper's attention is therefore in order.

Employee Absenteeism

The reasons why most employees do not report for work as scheduled are usually predictable and therefore preventable. When questioned as to the reasons for an absence pattern, most employees indicate "a personal problem," when in fact the roots to such problems may be found in management's insensitivity to some critical issue: poor orientation, lack of understanding of self-worth to the housekeeping operation, lack of proper observation during probationary periods of training, poor supervision or difficulties with supervisory personnel, and management's insensitivity to the personal needs of employees are among the prime causes of **employee absenteeism**.

Poor Orientation

During orientation meetings, it is essential that management convey the notion that employees are hired because they are needed and that management does not hire employees with a view toward terminating them. It should be made clear that employees are hired to perform tasks that are vital to the success of the operation and that the cost of hiring and training employees is not to be taken lightly.

Such comments made during employee orientation meetings are crucial to the initiation of morale-building environments, whereby employees can begin to motivate themselves to come to work when scheduled. In so doing, employees are allowed to consider themselves *valuable* to the success or failure of the operation. In addition, it shows employees that they are working for a company that is successful. It is thus reasonable to assume that working for a successful organization requires every employee's contribution, commitment, and dedication to that success.

Lack of Appreciation of Self-Worth

Although tasks may be different, employees who understand that their contributions are just as valuable as those of executive housekeepers and general managers will more than likely sense their own self-worth and role in the success of the operation. They will look forward to participation each day in that success rather than find excuses to avoid coming to work.

Improper Observation During Probation

Only employees who demonstrate technical competence and attitudes that support company objectives should be allowed to complete probationary periods of employment successfully and become permanent employees. Too often employees are allowed to slide through probationary periods when it should have been obvious that certain trainees were not in tune with company objectives and goals. In the truest sense, a company's goals include the objectives of every full-time, permanent employee who has successfully demonstrated a desire to be a part of the organization. In fact, a disservice may be done to good employees who must work with others of questionable loyalty to those ideals pledged by regular employees.

Poor Supervision

Poor or inept supervision may be another common reason for employee absenteeism. The positive measures enumerated above are actually put into practice by supervisory personnel, and becoming a competent supervisor requires training in personnel relationships, leadership, responsible action, and human dynamics.

How often is outstanding performance in a housekeeping department rewarded with promotion to supervisor? How seldom, however, is the new supervisor adequately trained for these new and different types of responsibilities? Sustained superior performance by a section housekeeper or section housekeeping aide should be rewarded with public recognition and incentive pay, not by promotion into positions in which potential in dealing with personnel problems has not been demonstrated or development has yet to take place.

This is not to say that some employees are unpromotable; it only means that promotion should be based on demonstrated professional development, not be a reward for outstanding performance of technical skills already learned. Newly promoted supervisors should themselves be placed in supervisory training classes in which they will be exposed to new skills. Role playing should be used to familiarize the new supervisor with personnel relationship situations *before* they happen, rather than requiring the new supervisor to stumble and fall—*after* an encounter.

Chances are that 95 percent of all problems encountered by a supervisor have been encountered before; mistakes have been made and solutions have been found. Failure to take advantage of the learning available from the resolution of past mistakes of others is equivalent to reinventing the wheel. Confidence will be gained when the new supervisor is exposed to situation dynamics that have been experienced by others to the extent that the remaining 5 percent of problems yet to be faced will be tolerated well and will form the basis for new problem-solving opportunities. Temperament, attitudes about people in general, and a willingness to apply an old yet valuable management technique—the Golden Rule—should also be a part of supervisory training.

Management Insensitivity

Management must remain sensitive to the personal needs of employees. Such a premise does not require that managers become involved with the personal problems of employees, only that they recognize that different things matter more or less to different people. To understand this is to recognize that employees work for different reasons. Some employees work to support themselves, whereas others work to augment family incomes. Working mothers see their priorities differently from women who have no children. Some employees see their employment secondary to the demands placed on them by school, whereas others work to conquer boredom.

Each of these reasons for working results in a motivation from a different source, each of which should be discovered during preemployment interviews. The executive housekeeper who visits the floors with employees regularly stays in tune with individual employee concerns, is better informed as to what counts in the lives of employees, and may therefore be forewarned of impending problems. For example, it would be expected that a working mother whose child becomes ill would readjust her priorities accordingly, and as a result may need to be absent. Of major concern would not be that the working mother failed to show up for work, but whether or not she notified the department in sufficient time to allow for her temporary replacement.

It has been well-documented that managers who demonstrate genuine respect, feeling, and caring for employees create maximum employee loyalty and productivity. Feelings must be genuine, however, since patronization can be quickly sensed and can cause the reverse effect.

William T. Scherer takes such caring a step further and cites "love" of employees as necessary to convey caring. Scherer states

> Some...will argue that "love" is too strong a word to use when describing the attitude managers should have for their people. Some will even laugh at the idea. If you happen to be such a person stop and think for a moment. The late Vince Lombardi of the Green Bay Packers was a great football coach and leader of men. Many might think that "love" is too delicate a term to describe the feelings between a coach and his players. But listen to the men who played and won for Vince Lombardi. They aren't ashamed to say that they loved him and gave their all for him, because, to a man, they knew he loved each of them.[1]

Scherer continues by reminding us that love is usually a reciprocal emotion. When love and caring are in evidence between the manager and employees, team spirit flowers and loyalty, compassion, and understanding are returned to the manager in the form of increased openness and successful performance.

Management's sensitivity to the needs of employees culminates with an accurate understanding of what motivates employees to take a desired action. Motivation comes from within. Motivation is a complex reaction between an individual and his or her environment.

The executive housekeepers or supervisors who feel that they can motivate their employees are allowing the shift of responsibility for motivation from the worker to the supervisor, which in itself is a poor technique. Although the supervisor may assist in motivational development by creating an atmosphere wherein the employees can motivate themselves, techniques that infer an "I am going to motivate you" mentality are highly suspect.

Solutions lie in those activities over which the supervisor does have control: open communication, caring, sensitivity to personal needs, and ensuring that employees understand their personal worth to the overall operation all help to create a self-motivating atmosphere.

Employee absenteeism as indicated is both predictable and preventable, provided the executive housekeeper looks in the right places. Poor orientation, lack of understanding of worth, little or no observation of attitudes during periods of probationary employment, inept supervision, and insensitive management can be found at the roots of most absenteeism. Section housekeepers who leave work each day with quiet hearts because they know their contributions were necessary and valuable to an overall worthwhile and successful operation look forward to the next workday with great expectation, not for a way to prevent coming to work.

Employee Turnover

Another problem with which executive housekeepers must become involved is **employee turnover**. The problem is an extension of employee absenteeism in that when failure to come to work becomes excessive, there is the cost of having to hire and train a new employee.

Employee turnover in housekeeping departments may range from 2 to 15 percent per month, which at a minimum represents one-fourth of the staff each year. Although it is true that 90 percent of all turnover occurs in less than 10 percent of the housekeeping jobs, an analysis of causes *is* important. To hire and induct an employee into the department on Monday only to have him or her fail to report for work on Tuesday is an indication that hiring practices should be highly suspect. All too often, the press of business tends to force the manager to skip important matters, such as a thorough and professional look at past work history, when reviewing an applicant's background in hopes that everything will work out. Obviously, care and attention should go into selecting employees.

After a person is hired, there are several things that executive housekeepers and managers in general can do to ensure the success and long-term commitment of the employee. First, staff members who will train others should be carefully considered. More than one potentially good employee has been discouraged by the techniques of the person assigned to do the training, causing an early and unnecessary departure. Second, job enrichment is a technique whereby the employee may see the job as important and necessary to proper functioning of the organization. Third, participative management, whereby employees are involved in discussions as to why some employees choose to leave the company, often reveals motives not readily shared or even understood by people working at the management level. Employees themselves may be able to point out matters of importance in reducing turnover.

Fourth, being looked down upon by outsiders because of the nature of the work being performed is a major cause of employee dissatisfaction, which can lead to employee turnover. This unrest usually stems from new and unenlightened junior management who openly profess distaste for the housekeeping function and would therefore not perform such duties. Junior managers' training programs that include orientation in the housekeeping department result in a much keener awareness of the value of those performing such functions.[2] For example, the close personal relationships that can develop between an expert section housekeeper and a young sales trainee who is being taught how to service a guestroom can prove invaluable in developing mutual respect for each function. Executive housekeepers should therefore push for junior management development programs that cycle the young manager through the housekeeping department.

The underlying causes of absenteeism are at work in causing high turnover rates and should therefore be considered when looking for solutions. The executive housekeeper should first assess the level of turnover and then set goals for reduction of turnover rate. When properly addressed, most turnover rates can be reduced by one-half over the period of a year.

Employee Problems

Employee problems involving difficulties in working with supervisors or with each other necessitate constant attention. It is not necessary that employees like each other, provided they respect each other at work.

Employees should be counseled at the onset that personal problems involving the family are best left at home and not be aired in public at work. This is not to diminish the manager's concern for each employee; it is only to reinforce the fact that those people who expose their personal family problems at work create gossip that usually returns to haunt them.

Counseling is best used as a preventive measure rather than waiting until problems arise. Employees should be counseled to keep their professional and personal lives separate. Even though management should remain aloof and objective about personal relationships that emanate from working relationships, personal relationships should not be allowed to interfere with the working environment.

Poor Appearance and Hygiene

An **employee's appearance** and manner of dress will never be better than when applying for employment. It is surprising how many employees, once hired, assume that having their hair in curlers or under a bandana or working in a soiled uniform is normal and perfectly acceptable. This problem must be addressed during orientation in order that every employee understand that appearance goes hand in hand with the overall quality and look of the property.

Housekeeping work is not like secretarial work in that much physical energy is expended during the workday. Employees must therefore be counseled that regardless of the type of work to be done in a hotel, they must keep themselves as neat as possible; otherwise they will look out of place with their surroundings. A sturdy, comfortable uniform that allows freedom of movement should be provided. In addition, a prescribed sweater or foul-weather jacket should be specified rather than having employees wear odd colors over their uniforms.

To gain acceptance of such concepts of dress requires that employees themselves become involved in the selection of uniforms. Colors might be specified by hotel decor, but type and quality should be left up to employee since appearance has an important effect on morale and personal pride. A panel of employees could be used to review uniform catalogs and make recommendation as to what uniform it feels would be enjoyed by the most workers.

The care and overall treatment of uniforms should be monitored, and those not familiar with proper laundering techniques should be taught how to care for their uniforms. Some hotels require that uniforms be serviced and issued on a daily basis. Such service is costly, however, and it rules out the possibility of allowing the employee to become involved in the uniform maintenance and selection process.

Employee hygiene is another matter that must not be ignored. When employees consistently have a problem with personal hygiene, the manager should first consider that the employee may have never been counseled in how to prevent heavy body orders when doing heavy physical work. The axiom that "only your best friends will tell you" is more true than we might expect—provided counsel is discreet and professional. The cost of holding professional classes in how to dress for success, how to wear you hair, and how to apply makeup is far outweighed by the benefit in overall appearance of each employee and in morale. Regardless of how personal a matter might be, problems in appearance and hygiene should not be ignored and must be dealt with in a personal and professional way.

Employee Claims of Unfairness

One of the greatest causes of **employee claims regarding unfairness** is associated with a desire for information—asking questions and not receiving answers, not knowing what is happening, and going away with a feeling that "no one cares about me or what I think." Employees who ask questions deserve answers. If the answer is not currently known, then a genuine attempt must be made to obtain the answer; the employee should be informed in a reasonable period of time. Questions asked of management that go unanswered will be answered by someone else—and most often incorrectly.

Every question asked is a management opportunity to demonstrate concern for employees. Also remember that employees who feel they cannot receive answers as individuals usually seek someone to represent them: the result is that of opening the door to unionism. Employees who ask questions and receive answers may not like the answer, but they are much more likely to accept them when explanations are forthcoming.

Poor Performance

Employees who satisfactorily complete probationary periods of employment would have demonstrated their capability to perform all tasks required for the job satisfactorily. **Poor performance** after probationary periods thus indicates some reason that had been nonexistent previously.

There are many factors relating to employee behavior that end in unsatisfactory performance that have little to do with the employee's ability to do a job properly. Problems at home, poor relationships with supervisors, changes in priorities, illness, and poor morale can cause a deterioration in performance.

The executive housekeeper's challenge in each case is to find the underlying cause of stress leading to substandard performance and deal with the causes before the situation becomes irreversible. The leveling technique discussed in Chapter 11 is most effective in working with employees whose performances have become substandard, especially when managers send "I" messages. "I" messages (rather than "you" messages) infer the manager's concern for how operations may be suffering as a result of poor performance as opposed to inferring that the employee is a bad person. "I am troubled because your performance is not what it used to be" as opposed to "You are not performing up to standards" hits the core of the problem without inferring that the employee has a serious personality defect. Actually, the employee whose performance starts to diminish may not even be aware of such deterioration because no one *until now* has given him or her an objective evaluation of what was becoming obvious over a several week period.

The Problem-Solving Temperament

Housekeeping managers need to develop a **temperament for problem solving**. Seeing a problem as an occurrence to be dreaded as opposed to an opportunity requiring a solution can seriously hinder the manager's development for greater responsibilities. Such feelings need to be addressed before negative attitudes begin to bring about the head-in-sand phenomenon.

I recall a junior manager who possessed excellent problem-solving abilities and was selected for promotion to executive housekeeper, resulting in a transfer to a smaller property. The young manager at first refused the promotion, which amazed many people since it appeared that he was on the fast track to rapid growth within the company. When questioned, the junior manager indicated a major concern for being assigned to a smaller property: "I would miss the hassle" was his reply, referring to the fact that the day-to-day problem-solving challenges presented by the larger property provided the major source of enjoyment in his current position. He feared that losing that challenge could prove boring. It was pointed out that promotion has seldom been the cause of a lessening of problem-solving opportunities, only a change in the type of problems that may be encountered. The young manager was encouraged to reconsider his decision, which he did, and today he is one of the company's general managers. Solving problems must be a challenge that the manager welcomes.

Managerial Styles
Changing Philosophies

Managerial styles run the gamut from highly authoritarian to total abdication. Western philosophy about how to manage has for years concerned itself with the axiom that managers tell workers what to do, and workers do what they are told. Such philosophy has been behind the development of the entrepreneurial spirit in America, which has glorified the self-made person for being in the forefront of American industrial progress. Such people succeeded through directive leadership and in many cases became board chairmen and chief operating officers of many successful companies—50 years ago.

It is no wonder that to succeed in such companies junior managers had to model their own management styles after these leaders; failing to do so would surely bring about mediocrity in personal development and prevent success beyond the midrange point of management.

There have been those entrepreneurs, however, who have dared to question their own employees on how their organizations might be improved and then had the courage to accept the fact that they themselves might be a part of the problem of creeping mediocrity. Let us consider four different attitudes toward power as illustrated in material gathered from managers at different companies by management experts Robert Tanenbaum and Warren Schmidt.[3]

1. I believe in getting things done. I can't waste time calling meetings. Someone has to call

the shots around here, and I think it should be me.

2. I'm being paid to lead. If I let a lot of the other people make the decisions I should be making, then I'm not worth my salt.
3. Once I have decided on a course of action, I do my best to sell my ideas to my employees.
4. It is foolish to make decisions oneself on matters that affect [other] people. I always talk things over with my subordinates, but I make it clear to them that I'm the one who has the final say.

The first two statements are symbolic of military-type leadership, which may produce an instantaneous response but may not necessarily produce the best decision. Emergency situations involving life-and-death situations may require highly directive leadership, but the majority of decisions made by managers do not involve life and death and do not require the indispensability of the manager.

The second two statements are more symbolic of the manager who has chosen to share power with those who will be affected by decisions that must be made and as a result are more likely to encourage participation by subordinates who in turn will commit themselves to the decisions.

The democratic principles advocated in the latter two positions are today called by terms such as "participative management," "industrial democracy," and "quality circles." The sharing of power does not mean the abdication of responsibility; it means a recognition that greater employee commitment is attained by involving those who have a stake in the outcome of decisions.

The Executive Housekeeper and Participative Management

The surest way for the executive housekeeper to establish a style of patronizing benevolence is to assume that housekeeping employees, lacking in experience and education, are short on common sense or could never care about the overall success or failure of the housekeeping operation. Unfortunately, such executive housekeepers remain in evidence today. Employees are sometimes treated like children; they are stroked affectionately when their performance is above average and scolded when the quality of their work is less than desired. Assumptions are made that employees do not have the concern or inclination to get involved.

The actuality is that when employees, regardless of their level of education, are involved in decision-making discussions, they become highly contributive to successful decisions of major consequence. They are then not only committed to the outcome of these decisions, they are involved in the success or failure of such decisions and are thereby motivated to continue their participation and personal growth.

For example, consider a case in which guest-room cleaning was being considerably slowed when beater-bar belts would break on vacuum cleaners. Engineering priorities could cause several days to pass before the broken belt would be replaced and the machine returned to the appropriate section housekeeper. It was a section housekeeper who pointed out that time could be saved if belts could be changed by users rather than involving engineering in such a small mechanical task. "No one changed her belt for her at home, and she never used a screwdriver, just a dime." As a result of the section housekeeper's participation in the resolution of this common work-slowing problem, all section housekeepers were thereafter provided with a spare belt with a dime taped to it and were given the technical training required to make the belt change. Those employees who had complained about the breaking belt and about how long it took to receive the vacuum back in a repaired condition became involved in a contest to see who could change a belt in the shortest time. The winner received simple but public recognition, which further encouraged participation in implementing the change in this work practice.

Successful executive housekeepers who allow participation in decision making affirm that delegation does not leave people with the feeling of being stripped of power. Actually, power is held only if we can empower others. Nothing in participative decision making can remove the responsibility created for the executive housekeeper; decisions are just made with greater input.

The Executive Housekeeper— Manager or Leader

For the executive housekeeper to become a manager requires only the decree from higher authority that such is the case. Such a decree empowers the manager to carry out the sequential and continuous functions of management within the department: analyzing problems, making decisions, and communicating direction regarding plans, organization, staffing, and control of housekeeping operations.

Decrees of management appointment, however, do not certify the **manager as a leader**. Such certification lies in the purview of those being led. It is difficult to assess our own leadership abilities, since proof of such attributes may remain smoldering in the feelings and attitudes of those being led. However, the following questions can be used for candid self-evaluation as to what kind of leader you might be. For each one, determine which option is better:

1. To drive employees or to coach them?
2. To take credit or give credit?
3. To be concerned with things or with people?
4. To tell employees to be at work on time or to be at work ahead of time personally?
5. To think "I" or to think "we"?
6. To inspire fear or enthusiasm?
7. To see today or look at tomorrow?
8. To know how the job is done or to show employees how to do the job?
9. To depend on authority or good-will?
10. To work hard to produce or work hard to help employees produce?
11. To let employees know where you (the leader) stand or where they stand?
12. To never have enough time or to make time for things that matter?
13. To say "go" or "let's go"?
14. To fix blame for breakdowns or show how to fix the breakdown?
15. To use employees or to develop them?
16. To command or to ask?

Should you dare to ask *your employees* for such an objective evaluation of your leadership attributes? Courageous managers do.

Development of Others

It is unfortunate that some managers erect barriers to the **development of subordinates**. In most cases, fear of being outperformed by subordinates is the cause of such behavior. Successful managers welcome the development of supervisors who can ultimately serve as the manager's replacement, thus allowing for their own advancement. Consider one warning given to a group of young managers: "Opportunities may come and go, but until you have trained a replacement for your current position, I consider you indispensable to your current assignment, therefore unpromotable." A comment in the group was then overheard: "I'm going to become the most dispensable person I know."

Developing Executive Housekeepers

The challenge of opening a housekeeping department does much for developing the executive housekeeper, as well as other employees with potential. Department openings require long hours and few days off since, at first, the abilities of subordinates are limited. Thus, the executive housekeeper's primary concern

is to identify those people who welcome responsibility and then to develop them to the greatest possible extent.

There are many section housekeepers and section housekeeping aides who will do an outstanding job in their current position, but will resist additional responsibility. Some excellent performers in current assignments balk at accountability for greater challenge. Others may welcome the recognition that promotion may bring but a week later will begin to show signs that they did not know how different a new set of responsibilities can be; the skills needed to deal with subordinates are different from those needed to make beds. As a result, performance may decline, and signs of greater deterioration may become evident.

Being promoted to supervisor in housekeeping is as close to being on the first rung of the supervisory growth ladder as you can find; and this first step is the largest step that will ever be encountered. The key, therefore, is to identify the employee who demonstrates a desire for greater responsibility. Jasper Dorsey comments on two important factors:[4] the willingness to take risks and the ability to discover a person's capabilities.

Risk taking implies that no manager can develop others without being willing to allow people to make mistakes and learn from them. Effective risk taking allows for the opportunity to fail. Unfortunately, some employees may fail completely, but failing at a task does not mean that a person is a failure. It is what happens after failing at the task that counts.

Dorsey indicates that a person's potential is "discovered by placing them in a position requiring a 100 percent effort. Once the person feels comfortable at that level of achievement, add to the load. Growth comes to those who welcome responsibility." Dorsey recalls these methods as "placing someone in water up to his neck and, when he becomes comfortable there, placing him in water over his head. After he becomes a good swimmer, start making waves."

Training and Evaluating Supervisors and Managers

The development of management and supervisory personnel requires planning and systematic, periodic evaluation. Some companies use a system of self-development for fast-track employees. The Marriott Corporation, for example, uses a system known as the **Individual Development (ID) Program**, whereby employees identified for advancement become responsible for their own development at a pace suitable to individual learning. The Marriott system involves the assignment of predetermined tasks (possibly as many as 100) to be performed. Many of these tasks involve hands-on work regularly performed by personnel who might later be supervised. (The trainers in the task are usually the regular performers of the function to be learned.) Some tasks involve administrative work and the study of systems and procedures, and some involve the trainee moving into other departments in which knowledge outside of the primary department may be imperative for proper understanding of the primary training area (for example, how front desk operations relate to housekeeping).

After tasks are performed, self-critique in training performance is required through analysis of certain key points and questions regarding the tasks. In each task area, the trainee has an advisor who coaches and counsels him or her. Periodically, the trainee meets with a counselor (usually a senior manager in the hotel) to review training performance and phase progress and to map out future training functions and goals.

Several other major hotel organizations recruit management trainees directly from university campuses and place them into formalized development programs that guide the trainee through all departments of the hotel. Some companies hire trainees into specific departments. In chain operations, successful development normally heralds transfer to another property, since a supervisor elevated from the ranks of a group of employees may have difficulty forming a supervisory relationship with that same group. In most cases transfer makes it easier to end old working relationships and begin new ones.

Often, the executive housekeeper will become involved with formal training programs created by other entities (corporate training offices) within the company. When this happens, the executive housekeeper must contribute time and effort to the development of trainees and guard against using them for personal advantage. Since one of the primary responsibilities of the manager is to develop other employees, no housekeeper should ever be too busy to devote adequate time to this important responsibility.

In small operations in which such development programs are not in evidence, the executive housekeeper would do well to establish such a program in his or her own department, regardless of what might be done in other parts of the organization. The executive housekeeper being considered for promotion has done well if, when asked for the name of a person qualified to replace him or herself, the executive housekeeper can provide a *list* of such people.

Personal Development

Training an individual to perform the technical functions of a housekeeping department can take weeks of hard work. The **personal development of a manager**, however, never ends, and progress is recognized only with the assumption of greater management responsibility. It is for this reason that executive housekeepers should take advantage of every opportunity to improve their technical knowledge of the profession and their management skills.

The executive housekeeper should keep up with new techniques, systems, and procedures being used in the housekeeping profession. Periodicals such as *Executive Housekeeping Today, Lodging, Hospitality Management*, and *Lodging Hospitality* are only some of the publications that offer information regarding technical aspects of housekeeping operations. There is also a wealth of information available regarding the subject of management in general. Many hotels subscribe to management publications such as the *Journal of the American Management Association*. Sharing these publications increases tenfold the amount of information available to each manager. In addition, there are associations that cater to the needs of the professional housekeeper. Membership in the National Executive Housekeeper's Association (NEHA) as well as in local organizations can be beneficial not only in personal development through certification programs but also in the sharing of information about products, systems, procedures, personnel availability, and general knowledge about labor markets and personnel recruitment.

Advertisements pertaining to management seminars and forthcoming conventions in the housekeeping and management disciplines should be researched and the conventions attended when appropriate. Most hotel companies are interested in assisting the development of their managers who show interest in developing themselves and will gladly pay for the managers' attendance at such functions.

The Personal Plan

It is not sufficient that the executive housekeeper leave personal development to chance. A written **personal plan** should be prepared by every manager, critiqued by the manager's supervisor, and progressed over a specified period of time.

An example of such a plan, whereby the manager indicates in detail what is intended to be accomplished over a given time period, is presented in Appendix H. Appendix H relates specifically to an executive housekeeper and deals with technical expertise and accomplishments for the areas of administration, managerial skills, and personal development. It offers specific goals to be attained in a given time frame. The personal plan cites how the manager intends to carry out primary responsibilities and serves as an instrument for monitoring personal development. Thoroughly review this document and use it as a model for writing your own personal plan.

Housekeeping Managers of the Future

The recession year of 1982 provided some interesting observations regarding on-campus recruitment. Whereas in the past most students received several job offers, in 1982 only a few students were lucky enough to receive even one offer.

Since students were interested in management-training positions, they were told to consider what needs recruiters might have in the housekeeping field. To their surprise, three students were offered and did accept positions as housekeeping manager trainees with major hotel organizations. Not only were these students surprised to find such openings available, but some recruiters were surprised to find students with goals in top management who were willing to enter through the housekeeping door.

Communications from these students verify three important conditions: (1) The housekeeping door was a viable career entry level opportunity that allowed progression to higher management within the hotel organization, (2) the opportunity to supervise large numbers of people and, as a result, to develop supervisory skills was much greater than had been expected or was greater than noted in other departments, and (3) opportunities for men and women were equal.

The idea that the position of executive housekeeper is a dead-end situation is a condition of the past or of the mind. Most certainly, there are executive housekeepers who see their roles as one that they favor to keep as a goal, since satisfaction in the position is reward in itself. For the executive housekeeper who wishes to advance, however, the opportunity is there more than ever because they can demonstrate management skills and ability, as well as technical housekeeping skills.

The position of executive housekeeper can be agonizing or inspiring, fraught with pitfalls or opportunities, tiring or refreshing, guarded or benevolent, interesting or boring, meaningful or pointless. Whatever it is to be will depend upon the input of the person who is to aspire to, hold, and possibly progress from the executive housekeeping position.

To those who wish to be the best possible executive housekeeper, I hope that this text inspires you to improve systems and techniques, that it indicates the excitement that awaits the manager who chooses to progress and become a better manager, and that it presents housekeeping as an avenue to career development to top management.

Summary

A large part of the executive housekeeper's responsibilities involve the creation of tasks that may be performed by other members of the housekeeping department. This text has strongly emphasized the delegation of such tasks to people within the department whenever possible. What is then left for the executive housekeeper's personal accomplishment revolves around those continuous functions of management enumerated in Chapter 1: analyzing problems, making decisions, and communicating. A major emphasis for personal involvement must therefore rest within the area of problem solving.

Problem solving does not mean taking on subordinates' responsibilities but is the guidance of thought so as to help them arrive at solutions to problems for which they are responsible. In addition, there are specific problem areas that are the direct responsibility of the executive housekeeper and therefore give meaning to the term *full circle of management*.

Employee absenteeism, poor employee orientation, lack of employee appreciation of self-worth, inadequate employee observation during probationary periods, poor supervision, and the insensitivity of management to employee needs are the causes of most problems that regularly face the executive housekeeper. These problems must be dealt with professionally when they occur and must not be allowed to grow through neglect.

Problem solving requires the development of a unique temperament that recognizes problems as opportunities for solutions rather than as bothersome chores. It is this fact that should cause the astute manager to investigate his or her own management style and leadership qualities. The executive housekeeper may be designated as a manager by higher management, but it will be those who work for the executive housekeeper who will determine whether or not such a person is a good leader.

The full circle of management does not end with the manager's ability to solve problems; it continues into the realm of developing others for higher responsibilities and for self-development. The development of potential in others assures the executive housekeeper's availability when higher positions of responsibility become available. An aggressive program of self-development not only signals the desire for advancement but also helps qualify the manager for greater responsibility.

Executive housekeepers of the future will be seeing their positions not only from a more professional standpoint but also as meaningful entry-level positions into the field of hospitality and hospital operations that lead to top administrative positions.

KEY TERMS AND CONCEPTS

Problem solving
Employee absenteeism
Employee turnover
Employee problems
Employee's appearance
Employee hygiene
Employee claims of unfairness
Poor performance

Problem-solving temperament
Managerial styles
Manager as a leader
Development of subordinates
Individual Development (ID) Program
Personal development of managers
Personal plan

DISCUSSION AND REVIEW QUESTIONS

1. The full circle of management requires that the executive housekeeper be a problem solver. How can this be done without assuming the responsibilities of subordinates to solve their own problems?
2. The success or failure of a manager as an effective problem solver may rest with the manager's style. Identify several management styles and assess their worth in dealing with various types of problems and different types of people.
3. Explain the difference between a manager and a leader.
4. Assume that as executive housekeeper you observe one of your junior managers about to make a mistake. Recognizing that most people learn greatly from their mistakes, under what conditions, if any, would you step in and prevent the subordinate from making the mistake? If the mistake were to cost money, how would you justify the mistake to your own manager after you allowed it to be made?
5. Recognizing that personal plans are written as guides to achievement, why should they be negotiated with your supervisor? As your performance year unfolds and you see that you will not be achieving your specific objectives as set forth in your personal plan, what would your actions be?
6. Some managers aspire to the position of executive housekeeper as an end; others see the position as a stepping stone to higher administrative responsibility. Which condition is more likely to cause a leadership style that is conducive to subordinate growth? Why?

NOTES

1. William T. Scherer, "Is Caring about People a Lot of Hogwash?" *Chemical Engineering*, February 14, 1977, pp. 93–94.
2. Robert J. Martin, "Recognition of Employee Worth vs. Turnover," *Executive Housekeeping Today*, March 1983, pp. 18–20.
3. John Simmons and William Mares, "Return of the Pied Piper," *Savvy*, October 1982, pp. 40–44. Adapted from *Working Together* by John Simmons and William J. Mares, to be published by Alfred A. Knopf. Copyright ©1983 by John Simmons and William J. Mares.
4. Jasper Dorsey, "Are You a Good Manager?" *The Saturday Evening Post*, January/February, 1981, pp. 46–47.

Appendices

Job Descriptions

This appendix contains several examples of job descriptions. They may be written for unskilled, semiskilled, and skilled employees. They may also be written for supervisors, managers, and executives. The techniques of presentation may vary considerably. Simply stated, however, they are designed to set forth a group of tasks combined into one job, indicate a person's responsibility to do the tasks, provide the necessary authority to that person to do the work, and indicate to whom the worker filling the job will be accountable to for the proper performance of the work.

There are two styles presented herein; an informal or soft style and a formal style. The informal style has been further differentiated between a *Job* Description for the hourly worker and a *Position* Description for persons classified as part of management.

Housekeeping positions have been used to demonstrate the informal style, and environmental service positions have been used to demonstrate the more formal style. (Note the standard form. Many organizations prefer that all Job Descriptions, whether management or hourly, be represented on a standard form.)

Position Descriptions for the Housekeeping Department

EXECUTIVE HOUSEKEEPER

Basic Function

Assume complete direction, operational control, and supervision of the housekeeping and laundry departments and pool areas.

Scope

Operate the departments under his or her control in the most efficient manner possible through effective application and enforcement of company policies, the use of methods described in standard operating procedures, and the use of sound management principles. The incumbent is primarily responsible for the cleanliness of guestrooms and public areas assigned to the housekeeping department. Accomplish assigned tasks through proper training, motivation, and supervision of all personnel assigned to the housekeeping and laundry departments.

Specific Responsibilities

1. Coordinate with the personnel department regarding prescreening of employees, indicating staffing needs and qualifications desired of personnel necessary to staff the housekeeping and laundry departments. Coordinate with resident manager on hiring of immediate subordinates.
2. Develop plans, actions, and standard operating procedures for the operation and administration of assigned departments. Establish and maintain housekeeping and laundry scheduling procedures, taking into consideration percent occupancy, time and use of facilities, and related public specialty areas and events.
3. Organize the housekeeping department using the **housekeeping team concept**, with each housekeeper cleaning room sections.
4. Develop an inspection program for all public areas and guestrooms to ensure that proper maintenance and standards are achieved and sustained.
5. Coordinate the operation of the housekeeping and laundry departments in the hotel to guarantee minimum disruption in the overall operation of the hotel.
6. With assistance from the resident manager, develop budgets for housekeeping, laundry, and recreation departments to ensure that each operates within established costs while providing maximum service.
7. Establish a training program within assigned departments which will enable positions of increased responsibility to be filled from within the department.
8. Be constantly alert for newer methods, techniques, equipment, and materials that will improve the overall operation of the departments and will provide a more efficient operation at reduced costs.
9. Stimulate within all employees a friendly and cheerful attitude, giving proper emphasis to courtesy in contacts with guests and other employees.
10. Administer time card control over all assigned hourly employees.
11. Maintain strict inventory and purchase control over all controllable items.
12. Develop job descriptions for all members of assigned staff.
13. Serve as expeditor on special projects assigned by the resident manager or the general manager.
14. Communicate freely and effectively with assigned personnel, continuously passing on to assistants and subordinates any information necessary to make them feel included in the overall operation of the hotel. Reassure, if necessary, the objectives toward which hotel employees are striving.
15. Conduct employee performance appraisals on time, showing objectivity and sincerity. Employees should be personally counseled toward improvement.

16. Coordinate with the resident manager concerning the termination of any employee.
17. Maintain control of linen rooms, storerooms, new linen, and cleaning supplies, ensuring adequate security and supply.
18. Be responsible for the proper scheduling of the department, keeping in mind the forecast of daily occupancy.
19. Develop a personal plan to carry out responsibilities.

Relationships to Responsibility

1. Reports directly to the resident manager.
2. Has access to the general manager.

3. Coordinates functions of housekeeping, laundry, and recreation departments with all other departments.
4. Supervises and coordinates the activities of assigned assistants.

Work Emphasis

Time allocation for performance of position responsibilities:

50 percent administrative

30 percent operations, inspections, and training

20 percent coordination and follow-up

Job Descriptions for a Hotel Hourly Worker

Here is an example of a job description for a hotel housekeeping department hourly worker.

Once an organization has been designed, it becomes necessary to set forth exactly what is expected of each member of the organization. Job descriptions ensure that every operation that needs to be performed is covered by assignment and that the operations are not assigned to more than one specific classification of individual.

Job descriptions will normally specify the **job title**, **working hours**, and position or job title of the incumbent's **immediate supervisor**, whether they be hourly supervisors or members of management. **Responsibilities** and specific **duties** are then spelled out in detail. Whether or not the incumbent is to wear a uniform and punch a time clock and the pay scale standard for a particular job may also be shown.

Job descriptions are excellent tools for training, and a copy can be given to the incumbent as training begins. They are also excellent documents to use for periodic reviews at departmental meetings. They should not necessarily be used to evaluate performance, since they are by nature rather inflexible and are inclined to foster the concept of limiting development. Performance appraisals, discussed later in this text, should be based on *meeting established* **standards**.

Several Job Descriptions for a Hotel Housekeeping Department

SENIOR HOUSEKEEPER (SUPERVISOR)

Title

Senior housekeeper

Immediate Supervisor

Housekeeping manager

Hours

8:00 A.M.–4:30 P.M.
Weekdays and Saturdays
9:00 A.M.–5:30 P.M.
Sundays and holidays

Responsibilities

To follow the instructions of the executive housekeeper and/or housekeeping manager in order to maintain company standards of cleanliness throughout the rooms section of the hotel. To supervise the section housekeepers and section housekeeping aides assigned to the housekeeping team. To relay information concerning the status of rooms to and from the housekeeping office.

Duties

1. Report to housekeeping at 8:00 A.M. in uniform and clock in.
2. Secure keys and worksheet for assigned area.
3. Note all **ready rooms** and **checkouts** on the worksheet.
4. Proceed to assigned area and check all ready rooms to make sure they are up to standard for early morning check-ins. Should a **tidy** be necessary, tidy the room. If a room needs extensive cleaning, it should be reported to the housekeeping manager and noted on the discrepancy report.
5. Report all checkouts and other information such as **early makeups** and **A.S.A.P.** (as soon as possible) **rooms** to section housekeepers.
6. Make a round of entire assigned area, checking for items in need of immediate attention such as burned-out lights, spots on hall carpets or walls, trash in stairwells, and spills in ice machine areas.
7. Check all section housekeeper's supplies and equipment to be sure they are in working condition. (All section housekeeping supervisors should know the prescribed use of all authorized cleaning equipment and chemicals.)
8. Spot-check (inspect) rooms completed by the section housekeepers in the section. Make sure that standards have been properly met in rooms being cleaned and that rooms are ready to be sold for occupancy to a guest before releasing the room to the housekeeping office.
9. Keep a record of all rooms **deep-cleaned** in each section so that rooms are periodically deep-cleaned on a rotating basis.
10. Report any damage to guestrooms, corridors, or equipment seen or reported by a section housekeeper. Such information should be reported to the housekeeping manager or executive housekeeper.
11. Report to the engineering department, using a **Maintenance Work Request Form**, any defect or equipment failure that cannot be corrected by the housekeeping department.
12. Throughout the day, periodically telephone the housekeeping office to advise them of all **ready** rooms and to receive **checkout** rooms.
13. Inspect linen and storerooms in assigned areas for cleanliness and for adequate supplies used by the section housekeepers. Be sure linen rooms are secured and locked when not in use.
14. At 3:00 P.M. the **evening room check** will be collected from the section housekeepers. Room checks on any open section (pickups) will be taken by the section supervisor. The room check reports will

be delivered to the housekeeping office promptly in order to make up the housekeeping report for the front desk. Any room not serviced that day, refused service, or requesting late service by the night staff will be reported to the night supervisor.

15. Report persistent complaints or remarks by the employees about working conditions, wages, or any other matter to the housekeeping manager.

16. Periodically report to the housekeeping manager on the quality of the performance of each person she or he supervises, offering remarks about which employees are performing above average, average, or below average.

17. Complete any special assignments as directed by the executive housekeeper promptly.

18. At 4:30 P.M. turn in the keys and clock out.

SECTION HOUSEKEEPER
GUESTROOM ATTENDANT (GRA)

Title

Section Housekeeper (or GRA)

Immediate Supervisor

Senior housekeeper (supervisor) assigned section

Hours

8:00 A.M.–4:30 P.M.
Weekdays
9:00 A.M.–5:30 P.M.
Sundays and holidays

Responsibilities

1. Report to the housekeeping department at 8:00 A.M. in uniform and clock in.
2. Pick up keys and **Section Housekeeper's Daily Report** for cleaning assignment. Note any special instructions.
3. Remove assigned cart from satellite linen room and begin cleaning assignment. Special guest requests, checkouts, and early makeups should be cleaned first.

Entering a Guestroom

4. *Procedure for entering a guestroom.* If there is no "Do Not Disturb" sign and if the **hard lock** is not on, knock softly with your knuckles and softly announce "Housekeeper." Wait a few moments and enter the room. Leave the door wide open. Pull cart across the doorway, with the clean linen facing the room.
5. Open the drapes for maximum light and turn out unnecessary lights.
6. Look at the condition of the room. If linens, wastebaskets, TV, and so on are missing or furniture is damaged or broken, report it to the main linen room and senior housekeeper immediately.
7. In occupied rooms, pick up newspapers and periodicals, fold them neatly,

and place them on the desk. *Never* throw away newspapers unless they are in the wastebasket.

Bedroom

8. Strip the bed linen, shaking it carefully off the bed. Pillow cases are favorite hiding places for valuables. All lost articles should be turned in to the main linen room to be labeled, logged, and locked up. Notify senior housekeeper if foam pillows, bed boards, and so on are found in the room.
9. Mattresses and box springs should be straight on top of each other and against the headboard. Bed pad should be clean and in place. Check between mattress and box spring for magazines and other articles.
10. Make the beds using the **once-around method**. Do not use torn or dirty linen. Replace soiled or burned blankets and spreads. The bed is the focal point of the room. It should not have wrinkles or lumps. Pillows should be smooth. Blanket and top sheet should be six inches from top of bed.
11. Roll-away beds are to be made up with clean linen. If the room is a checkout, make up roll-away bed and close it. A section housekeeping aide will take it from the guestroom to the proper satellite linen room for storage.
12. Dust bed area. Wipe vinyl headboard, and dust all pictures, baseboards, corners, and ledges where cobwebs gather. Dust the nightstand and telephone book. Clean the ashtray; replace memo pad, matches, and any literature as instructed. Place your own name card on nightstand.
13. Clean the telephone and plastic phone card with a clean cloth and the **one-stroke solution**.
14. Dust chairs and table near window. Remember the legs, backs, and under the cushions. Dust floor lamp, placing lamp shade seam to the wall.

15. Dust the TV—screen, stand, back, and underneath the set. No liquid should be sprayed on the screen since it may damage the inside of the set.

16. Dust the desk area, including lamp, chair, and all furniture surfaces. Remove desk chair and clean sides of furniture. Dust lamp shade, and be sure seam is to the wall. Clean tray and ashtray. Arrange pitcher, glasses, and matches properly. Literature on desk top and in drawer should be arranged correctly and replaced as needed.

17. In checkout rooms, drawers should be inspected for cleanliness and lost items. In occupied rooms, *do not* go into drawers.

18. Dust the coat rack. In checkout rooms, remove wire and wooden hangers not belonging to the company. Replace missing hangers. There should be eight in each room. Place two laundry bags with slips on coat rack shelf. The company logo should face the front. Dust overhead light.

19. Check that all light bulbs are working.

20. Vacuum carpet as necessary. Push the vacuum slowly and steadily over the whole area. Watch for pins, bits of string, coins, and the like, and pick them up by hand because they can damage the vacuum cleaner. Occasionally the carpet edges will need to be swept with a broom or wiped with a damp cloth.

21. Adjust the drapes and sheer panels as instructed. Be sure all hooks are in place, pulleys are working, and wands are attached. Report anything not working to senior housekeeper who will make out a maintenance work request form.

22. Adjust heater and air conditioner controls as instructed.

Bathroom

23. Turn on heat lamp and vanity lamp for maximum light. Wipe off light switch plate and soiled area on wall around switch. Report needed light bulbs to senior housekeeper.

24. Flush toilet. When water level has returned to normal, place one-stroke solution from stock solution bottle in the toilet bowl. Let it work while cleaning the rest of the bathroom.

25. Use the one-stroke solution to clean the mirror.

26. Dust the vanity light. Check that the bulbs work.

27. Wipe bathroom door and door knob.

28. Clean and polish chrome plumbing fixture under the sink.

29. Pull sink stopper and clean it thoroughly. Use the **three-stroke solution** to scrub the sink. Dry it and polish the chrome faucet. Replace the stopper.

30. Empty and wipe out the wastebasket. Be careful of glass and razor blades. Check supplies. Replace toilet paper if roll is less than half full or if it is dirty. Paper should roll outside from the top. Facial tissue may need to be replaced. Fold ends of both toilet paper and facial tissue into a "V". Each bathroom should have one ashtray with matches and two bars of soap. Place clean towels in their proper places.

31. Wash and dry the vanity top using the three-stroke solution.

32. Using the three-stroke solution, scrub tub walls, soap dish, and tub. Clean tub stopper. Wipe tub dry. Polish chrome fixtures, including shower head. Place bath mat so the name of the hotel can be read.

33. Spray three-stroke solution on shower curtains and wipe both sides dry. Position curtain neatly against the wall near the toilet.

34. Clean toilet lid, seat, and base with three-stroke solution. Clean inside of bowl using the solution that is already in it. Toilet should be dried thoroughly and a sanitary strip put in place across the seat.

35. Sweep hair from bathroom floor. Mop the floor starting at the far corner. Mop behind the toilet and the door.

36. Check the bathroom before turning out the lights.

37. Wipe off bedroom door and door frame.

38. Hook the chain lock and turn out the light.

39. Check the guestroom and close the door.

3 P.M. Check

40. At 3:00 P.M., the housekeeper begins her 3 P.M. check on the section housekeeper's daily report, which is designated "P.M." Every room on the report must be entered and the status checked. The status will be **C/O** (the room needs cleaning or tidying), **OCC** (occupied), or **R** (ready to rent). The P.M. reports are collected and used by the night housekeeping supervisor or the P.M. housekeeper to complete the Daily Housekeeping Report for the front desk. On weekends and holidays, the 3 P.M. check is made at 4:00 P.M.

41. At 4:00 P.M. weekdays or 5:00 P.M. Sundays and holidays, the house keeper should take the cart to the floor linen room to clean and stock the cart for the next day's work. Sufficient time has been allotted so that a good job can be done, thus making any time spent the following morning stocking the cart unnecessary.

42. Notify section supervisor if there is anything wrong with a housekeeper's cart or vacuum.

43. At 4:25 P.M. weekdays, 5:25 P.M. Sundays and holidays, return to the main linen room, turn in keys, and clock out.

44. On occasion, a section housekeeper may be required to function as a laundry attendant. When this happens, the job description for laundry attendant will apply.

SECTION HOUSEKEEPING AIDE

Title

Section Housekeeping aide

Immediate Supervisor

Senior housekeeper (supervisor)
Assigned section

Hours

8:00 A.M.–4:30 P.M.
Weekdays
9:00 A.M.–5:30 P.M.
Sundays and holidays—less 30 minutes for lunch

Responsibilities

To work as a member of a team in conjunction with the senior housekeeper and section housekeepers, maintaining a high standard of cleanliness in the guest sleeping room area of the hotel and in the public areas of that section of the hotel assigned to the team.

Duties

1. Report to the housekeeping department in uniform at the time the shift begins and clock in.
2. Receive keys necessary to perform functions for that day.
3. Check with the senior housekeeper for any special instructions.
4. Proceed to assigned area, satellite linen rooms, and determine if any supplies are needed in the room for that day (general-purpose soap, clean glasses, etc.).
5. Tour and inspect the entire area assigned, looking for items requiring immediate attention.
6. Proceed with usual cleaning program in rooms department public areas.

   a. Elevators—daily
   b. Corridors—twice weekly
   c. Ice and vending areas—twice weekly
   d. Stairwells—once weekly
   e. Any specific task assigned by the senior housekeeper

7. At least four times a day (more often if necessary), remove all trash from section housekeeper's linen carts. Remove trash to dumpster area and discard.
8. At least three times a day (more often if necessary), remove all soiled linen from team section housekeeper's linen carts. Deliver and deposit into laundry.
9. At approximately 3:00 P.M. each day, restock satellite linen rooms with bed linens needed by section housekeepers to load carts for the next day's work. (This linen should be picked up in the laundry and moved to the satellite linen rooms.)
10. There will be at least two rooms in each section of the hotel that will be **general cleaned** each day. Your senior housekeeper will tell you which rooms are to be general cleaned. The section housekeeping aide helps the deep cleaner or person assigned the responsibility for general cleaning move and replace any furniture necessary during cleaning.
11. As a member of your team, recognize and assist any team section housekeeper when it is obvious that a particular room presents an unusual problem in trash removal. Assist as necessary.
12. Take care of equipment; ensure that all mops are clean, vacuum cleaners are properly cleaned out, and all equipment is properly put away and locked up at the end of each day. It is especially important to ensure that there is no trash stored in any satellite linen room overnight. *This is an extreme fire hazard.*
13. When requested or required by housekeeping, take items such as roll-away beds and cribs that have been requested by the guest to the guestroom.

14. Return all special-use items such as roll-aways and cribs to the satellite linen rooms after they have been properly made up by the section housekeepers.

15. Make special setups in guestrooms (e.g., tables and chairs) when requested.

16. Remove same and return to storage upon completion of use.

17. Perform other functions assigned by your senior housekeeper.

What now follows is the more formalized Job Description. Whether manager, administrator, supervisor, or worker, all Job Descriptions are prepared using a standard form.

JOB TITLE: __Director_____ POSITION CODE:_____

DEPARTMENT: __Environmental Services_____

DEPARTMENT HEAD APPROVAL:_____ DATE:_____

ADMINISTRATIVE APPROVAL:_____ DATE:_____

DATE OF LAST UPDATE:_____ DATE OF NEXT UPDATE:_____

Job Summary

To plan, organize, execute, and control work activities of Environmental Services personnel so as to maintain the highest possible sanitary standards and good public relations, by creating a clean, attractive, safe environment.

Principal Duties and Responsibilities

1. Responsible for all personnel actions as they affect department personnel including:
   a. evaluating employee work performance annually
   b. ensuring that work environment is conducive to a high level of productivity, free of barriers that would inhibit work flow
   c. orienting employees to their work so that they know what is expected of them
   d. training and educating employees so as to ensure high levels of quality and productivity
   e. ensuring that employee needs are met in terms of fair pay and fair administration of personal policies and promotions, and that all employees are treated with dignity and respect.
2. Responsible for departmental fiscal actions and the careful use of hospital resources. This responsibility includes:
   a. preparation of an annual department budget addressing capital equipment, personnel, institutes, supplies, and other department costs
   b. participation in volume and revenue projections when applicable; this involves continual monitoring of statistics to seek out trends and variations in departmental volumes; assisting in the determination of departmental costs
   c. completion of the Departmental Productivity Analysis form on an annual basis to ensure adequate staffing
   d. active involvement in hospital cost reduction and/or control that includes seeking alternative, less expensive methods of providing service; eliminating wasteful or unnecessary procedures or activities; evaluating new programs or services in terms of cost effectiveness and critical need for the services; and in general being aware of and sensitive to relevant hospital practices.
3. Responsible for providing periodic written reports as requested by Administration to describe or otherwise provide information related to the activities of the department, such as monthly statistical reports, overtime authorization forms, etc.
4. Responsible for attending meetings so as to receive and disseminate hospital information and direction; equally as important is the scheduling of periodic departmental meetings so that all employees have opportunities to receive hospital information and to express them selves.
5. Responsible for marketing the services and programs of the department; specifically, development of programs for Channel 3 of the hospital speakers' bureau.
6. Responsible for the formal development, implementation, and publication of departmental quality control/assurance programs.

7. Responsible for the preparation of efficient yet fair work schedules.
8. Responsible for interpreting and executing personnel and Hospital policies.
9. Responsible for assuring that each patient, visitor, and employee is treated with compassion and courtesy.
10. Responsible for assisting in design renovation and maintenance of interior building space to ensure an aesthetically pleasing and safe environment.

Specific Principal Duties and Responsibilities

1. Maintains the highest possible quality standards to ensure a clean, attractive, and safe environment.
2. Participates in programs and activities that will develop self and/or employees.
3. Monitors quality control and inspection reports from Area Managers.
4. Monitors and controls cost and usage of labor hours and supplies.
5. Recommends new procedures, products, and equipment for better efficiency, cost, and quality.
6. Develops systems and procedures for planning the functioning of the department.
7. Evaluates workloads and arranges job structure, job assignments, and procedures used.
8. Inspects and surveys hospital and departmental facilities and equipment for compliance with departmental standards.

Knowledge, Skills, and Abilities Required

Minimum Education/Training:

Bachelor's degree in management.

Minimum Work Experience:

Three to five years' previous experience, training, and job knowledge in technical as well as management theory.

Physical Effort Required:

Ability to walk or stand for long periods of time.

License/Registration/Certification:

None

Analytical Skills:

Ability to plan and project for the needs of the department; problem-solving skills; good communication within department and across departments.

Level of Supervision

Reports to:

Senior Associate Executive Director

Supervises:

Area Managers, office personnel, environmental technicians

Working Conditions

Job Hazards:

May require handling of biologically unclean or infectious material. May require contact with water and strong cleaning and disinfecting solutions.

Physical Working Environment:

Normally works in a well-lighted, well-ventilated area; must be able to work under stress and under the conditions that normally exist in a hospital.

(These statements describe the general level and nature of work performed by individuals assigned to this job. The description is not an exhaustive listing, and additional job-related duties/responsibilities of the nature and level described may be required of persons so classified.)

JOB TITLE:__Area Manager_____POSITION CODE:_____
DEPARTMENT:__Environmental Services_____
DEPARTMENT HEAD APPROVAL:_____DATE:_____
ADMINISTRATIVE APPROVAL:_____DATE:_____
DATE OF LAST UPDATE:_____DATE OF NEXT UPDATE:_____

Job Summary

To plan, organize, execute, and control work activities of Environmental Services personnel to maintain the highest possible sanitary standards and good public relations. This will ensure the safety, health, and morale of patients, visitors, and employees, and of patients' recovery, by providing a clean, attractive, safe environment.

Principal Duties and Responsibilities

1. Maintains the highest possible quality standards in the hospital.
2. Ensures that all equipment is clean and in good repair.
3. Trains Environmental Technicians in hospital housekeeping techniques and use of equipment.
4. Inspects and surveys for compliance with departmental standards.
5. Interviews, hires, and terminates with approval of Director.
6. Conducts performance evaluations, counsels, and disciplines in accordance with personnel policy.
7. Assigns and directs duties of Environmental Technicians.
8. Delegates authority to appropriate employees.
9. Controls labor hours and supplies usage.
10. Participates in self-development programs and activities.
11. Tests new procedures, products, and equipment and uses those that are approved.
12. Verifies and approves timecards of employees.
13. Prepares daily and monthly reports.
14. Develops schedules to provide adequate work coverage.
15. Requests maintenance for buildings, furnishings, and equipment as necessary.
16. Treats each patient, visitor, and employee with compassion and courtesy.

Knowledge, Skill, and Abilities Required

Minimum Education/Training:

High school diploma or equivalent. Some college preferred, but not mandatory.

Minimum Work Experience:

Previous experience, training, and job knowledge in management theory and environmental duties.

Physical Effort Required:

Ability to walk and stand for long periods of time.

License/Registration/Certification:

None.

Analytical Skills:

Ability to evaluate needs and implement.

Level of Supervision

Reports to:

Director of Environmental Services

Supervises:

Environmental Technicians

Working Conditions

Job Hazards:

Requires some handling of infectious materials. Requires handling of biologically unclean materials.

Physical Working Environment:

Normally works in a well-lighted, well-ventilated area.

(These statements describe the general level and nature of work performed by individuals assigned to this job. The description is not an exhaustive listing, and additional job-related duties/responsibilities of the nature and level described may be required of persons so classified.)

JOB TITLE: **Lead Technician,** _____ POSITION CODE: _____
DEPARTMENT: **Environmental Services** _____
DEPARTMENT HEAD APPROVAL: _____
ADMINISTRATIVE APPROVAL: _____ DATE: _____
DATE OF LAST UPDATE: _____ DATE OF NEXT UPDATE: _____

Job Summary

To assist the Area Manager with the daily operations of the Environmental Services Department. To fill in for the Area Manager in that person's absence. Also performs duties of Environmental Technician.

Principal Duties and Responsibilities

1. Acts as liaison for Area Manager and Environmental Technicians.
2. Inspects and surveys for compliance with departmental standards.
3. Assists Area Manager with scheduling, auditing of timecards, and work assignments.
4. Provides input for employee evaluations.
5. Performs duties of Environmental Technicians as assigned by Area Manager.
6. Participates in self-development programs and activities.
7. Monitors equipment and supply usage.
8. Trains new employees in housekeeping techniques and use of equipment.
9. Requests maintenance of building, furnishings, and equipment as necessary.
10. Treats each patient, visitor, and employee with compassion and courtesy.

Knowledge, Skills, and Abilities Required

Minimum Education/Training.

High school diploma or equivalent (can be completed after six months in position).

Minimum Work Experience.

Previous experience in housekeeping and/or management techniques.

Physical Effort Required.

Excellent physical stamina; ability to walk or stand for long periods of time.

License/Registration/Certification.

None required.

Analytical Skills.

Ability to schedule and discipline when necessary.

Level of Supervision

Reports to.

Area manager; Director of Environmental Services

Supervises.

Environmental Technicians

Working Conditions

Job Hazards.

Requires some handling of infectious materials. Requires handling of biologically unclean materials. May be in frequent contact with water and strong cleaning and disinfecting solutions.

Physical Working Environment.

Normally works in a well-lighted, well-ventilated area.

(These statements describe the general level and nature of work performed by individuals assigned to this job. The description is not an exhaustive listing and additional job-related duties/responsibilities of the nature and level described may be required of persons so classified.)

JOB TITLE: **Environmental Services Technician**   POSITION CODE:_____
DEPARTMENT:_____
DEPARTMENT HEAD APPROVAL:_____DATE_____
ADMINISTRATIVE APPROVAL:_____DATE:_____
DATE OF LAST UPDATE:_____DATE OF NEXT UPDATE:_____

Job Summary

Cleans and services hospital areas to ensure the safety, health, and morale of patients, visitors, and employees, and of patients' recovery, by helping provide a clean, attractive, safe environment with minimal interference to others.

Principal Duties and Responsibilities

1. Sweeps, mops, and wet-washes floors. Periodically cleans and/or polishes floors using buffing machines.
2. Strips or scrubs and refinishes floors when assigned.
3. Vacuums, spot cleans, or shampoos carpets when assigned.
4. Polishes metal or other bright surfaces. Scours glass or enamel fixtures.
5. Cleans vertical and horizontal surfaces that collect dust.
6. Collects and transports refuse, cleans and relines refuse containers with plastic bags.
7. Cleans tops of windows, door frames, and other high places, using ladder when necessary.
8. Washes sinks and other plumbing fixtures and replaces disposables such as paper towels, soap, and toilet paper.
9. Dust, cleans, and polishes furniture, including beds.
10. Completes all cleaning and preparation of discharge units.
11. Utilizes detergents, disinfectants, polishes, finishes, etc.
12. Joins a labor pool in case of fire, disaster, or special projects.
13. Uses floor machines, automatic scrubbers, wall-washing equipment, waste collection equipment, etc.
14. Changes cubicle curtains and drapes.
15. Loads, operates, and cleans the incinerator and incinerator machine.
16. Washes walls and ceiling using wall-washing machine.
17. Moves furniture, beds, supplies, etc.
18. Treats each patient, visitor, and employee with compassion and courtesy.

Knowledge, Skills, and Abilities Required

Minimum Education/Training:

Able to read written instruction and comprehend verbal instructions given in English.

Minimum Work Experience:

None required.

Physical Effort Required:

Able to use 16- or 24-ounce mop, lift and carry three-gallon or five-gallon buckets of water for short distances and lesser weights for longer distances.

License/Registration/Certification:

None required.

Analytical Skills:

Ability to take and understand directions.

Level of Supervision

Reports to:

Director; Area Manager; Lead Technician.

Supervises:

No one.

Working conditions

Job Hazards:

Requires some handling of infectious materials. Requires handling of biologically unclean materials. May be in frequent contact with water and strong cleaning and disinfecting solutions.

Physical Working Environment:

Normally works in a well-lighted, well-ventilated area.

(These statements describe the general level and nature of work performed by individuals assigned to this job. The description is not an exhaustive listing and additional job-related duties/responsibilities of the nature and level described may be required of persons so classified.)

APPENDIX B

Employee Hotel Handbook

Every organization that employs service personnel should have an employee orientation manual or *handbook* so that common questions asked by employees may be answered as soon as possible. Various rules, regulations, and procedures that are specified should apply to all members of the hotel staff.

This appendix presents a generic **employee handbook** typical of those used in many hotels. On the last page of the handbook, the employee is provided with the name of his or her supervisor and/or manager, the name of the job, the pay scale, when he or she is to receive a first check, and working hours. The employee signs a receipt for this information, which is kept in the personnel file of the new employee.

WELCOME ABOARD!

Congratulations, and welcome to one of the fastest growing companies and the most exciting of all industries—the hospitality industry.

We appreciate your desire to join us, and we wish you every success with your new career—a career loaded with opportunity to say to your fellowman, "Welcome! May I be of service? I'm glad you're here and I am concerned about you while you are our guest." If you have that feeling toward people in general, then you will have it toward our guests, and you will soon learn that what you are about to do in your new job can bring happiness and self-satisfaction—regardless of whether your job has you performing directly in front of the public or in support of those who do.

The hospitality industry probably has more different kinds of jobs than any other industry you can think of; but I can assure you that no one job is any more important than another. What you will be doing is just as important as what I do every day. (We just do different things, that's all!) And that applies to every job and every person equally.

Few, if any, of us started anywhere except "at the bottom"—so you will find your supervisors and managers understanding of your need to be properly trained, and ready to help you if and when you need their help. We were all beginners ourselves at one time; we know you will have many questions about your job, company policies, the do's and don'ts, promotional opportunities, and your own opportunities to grow. Don't be afraid to ask questions, because to you the answers to those questions will be important. And don't be afraid of making a mistake. It is from our mistakes that we learn our best lessons.

A well-informed employee who knows what is expected of him or her and who knows the rules and recognizes his or her contribution to the overall effort is usually an employee who is content with his or her job and looks forward to coming to work every day.

It is our hope that this booklet will help you learn more about us, helping you to keep informed and to know what you can expect from us.

AGAIN, WELCOME ABOARD!
General Manager

It is our policy to implement affirmatively equal opportunity to all qualified employees and applicants for employment without regard to race, creed, color, sex, national origin, or religion.

The hiring objective of the company is to obtain individuals qualified and/or trainable for any position by virtue of job-related standards of education, training, experience and personal qualifications, who can carry on our work competently, who have capacity for growth, and who will become a living part of our organization. We will use every reasonable means available to select the best employee for the position to be filled.

New Employees

Every newly hired employee must complete a set of employment papers in the Personnel Department prior to beginning work. Your address, telephone number, and information about family status must be on record. Any changes in this information must be reported immediately, as it is very important for us to have it in the event of an emergency and in connection with Social Security and withholding taxes.

Please notify the Personnel Department in the event of any change in the following:

- Address or telephone number
- Marriage, divorce, or legal separation
- Birth or death in immediate family
- Legal change of name

Your personnel records are maintained in a secured place and locked when not in use. Only certain authorized personnel have access to these records. They are confidential and as such will not be used outside the company for any purpose, including Christmas card mailing lists, city directories, or for any other purposes.

After completing your employment papers, a copy of our Employee's Handbook will be given to you. This handbook is for your benefit, to inform you of what is expected of you and to help you perform satisfactorily on the job. It is to your advantage to read it carefully and keep it as a reference.

Employment Status

The following list of employment statuses, with definitions, represents the four categories of employees in our company.

1. *Full-Time Employee*
   An employee who may be expected to be and is normally scheduled to work a minimum of thirty (30) hours per week. Such persons will be classified as full-time. An employee classified as full-time may on occasion be scheduled to work less than thirty (30) hours a week. This does not change the employee's status from full-time unless the average hours worked per week, over a six-(6-) week period of time, fall below 30 hours. If this occurs for a period of six weeks, the employee's status may be changed from full-time to part-time.

2. *Part-Time Employee*
   An employee who is expected to be and is regularly scheduled to work twenty-nine (29) hours a week or less. Such an employee would be classified as part-time. Part-time employees may on occasion be scheduled more than twenty-nine (29) hours. If scheduling of more than twenty-nine (29) hours a week occurs more than three weeks in a row, employees will be given the opportunity to have their status changed to full-time.

3. *Temporary Employee*
   An employee who is hired to work for a specified period of time. In the case of a temporary employee, the termination of employment may be predetermined at the time of

employment. The number of hours worked per week is insignificant to the definition of temporary employee.

4. *Pool Employee*

An employee who is on call on an as-needed basis. The number of hours worked is irrelevant to the definition of a pool employee.

Probationary Period

Every new employee and current employees transferred or promoted into a new position will be placed on a ninety- (90-) day probationary period. During this time, both the employee and the company will pass through a "breaking-in period." You will want to know how the company operates and what our methods are, and we will want to know if you can report to work regularly, follow instructions, and get along with guests, managers, and fellow employees. Therefore, your performance and suitability for the job will be carefully evaluated during these first 90 days.

Guarantee of Fair Treatment

As an employee of this company, you as an individual have the right to appeal any decision or voice any complaint you may have concerning your treatment or working conditions to your immediate supervisor. Should you fail to receive what you consider to be a fair response, you have the right to appeal through channels to the president of the company.

Bulletin Boards

We have mounted several bulletin boards throughout the hotel. These boards are intended to keep you informed on important announcements concerning company policy, procedures, organization, and changes. By making it a habit to regularly check these boards, you will be kept well informed and up to date.

Employee Referrals

If you desire to recommend a qualified friend or relative for employment, we will be glad to interview that person.

We will consider any of your relatives for employment; however, they will not be employed in the same department where you work because of conflict-of-interest situations such as transportation, scheduling, etc.

Job Security

One of our objectives is to provide job security and steady work to our employees insofar as careful planning and sound management can afford. You have the assurance that we will do everything possible to provide continued employment for you as long as you perform your job satisfactorily and follow our policies and rules.

Job Abolishment

From time to time as we grow, changes will occur. New jobs may be created, and some jobs may be abolished. Any employee who is filling a job that is to be abolished will be given two weeks' notice of job termination or two weeks' pay in lieu thereof. In addition, every attempt will be made to relocate the employee in a new job, provided the employee is qualified.

WAGE AND PAYROLL INFORMATION

Pay Rates

It is company policy to pay the highest wages possible consistent with good business practices and in comparison with companies in the same business.

Pay rates for each position are determined by degree of difficulty and responsibility. Pay rates are reviewed annually to ensure our competitiveness within the industry and local area.

Pay Scales

Employees will be shown the pay scale for the job they are performing. The pay scale will show the *start rate, job rate* (3-month rate), *one-year rate, raise increment,* and *maximum rate.*

Time Clocks and Time Cards

Every employee is provided with a weekly time card. You are required to punch in when you report to work and punch out when you leave. Since time cards are the basis for computing your pay, it is your responsibility to make sure that the time reported on your cards is accurate. You must punch your own time card and only your card. You are paid for your *scheduled time,* so make sure you obtain your supervisor's signature on your time card when you begin work early or work late.

Work Schedules

Your work schedule will be prepared and posted in advance of each workweek. Since our hotel is a seven-day operation, we cannot always account for last-minute changes or unforeseeable circumstances. Therefore, a regular shift or regular day off cannot always be granted, as last-minute changes in schedules will sometimes occur.

Paydays

Your paycheck will be issued every other Friday and distributed after 3:00 P.M. twenty-six (26) times a year. Our legal workweek begins each Saturday and ends the following Friday. In order to process time cards, complete payrolls, and issue checks, the pay period closes seven days prior to your Friday payday.

Employees are not permitted to borrow on their earnings in advance of payday. Certain emergency situations may be exceptions with prior approval of the General Manager.

Payroll Deductions

Certain deductions that we are required by law to deduct will be made from your pay. The major portion of deductions is generally for taxes such as federal income tax, state income tax, and social security taxes. If you are a tipped employee and receive tips amounting to more than $20.00 per month, you must report the amount you receive to the Personnel Department each week. A tip report has been stamped on the back of your time card for your convenience. Your check cannot be issued until you have completed this information so that the appropriate tax deductions can be made.

Other deductions are allowed if you request; however, we reserve the right of deciding what other deductions will be allowed. All deductions made on your pay will be itemized on your paycheck stub.

At the end of the year you will be furnished a statement of your earnings and the amount of taxes withheld so that you can furnish this information to the government when you file your own tax report.

EMPLOYEE CONDUCT

Every well-run company must have rules and regulations governing the conduct of its employees in order to achieve the company's objectives. You should read this section carefully so that you have an understanding of the rules by which you and every other employee must abide.

The following is a list of important work rules. Your supervisor may have certain departmental rules to add to these.

Attendance	Prompt attendance on the job is an important part of your performance record. Failure to be on the job not only disturbs the smooth operations of your department, but also affects the jobs of your co-workers.
Alcohol and Drugs	Employees will not report to work under the influence of alcohol or drugs.
Absence	Absence without good and sufficient cause cannot be tolerated. When you are sick and unable to work, notify your supervisor immediately.

If illness is given as a cause of absence, we have the right to require a written statement from your doctor. When you return to work after a serious illness, injury, surgical operation, maternity leave, or other physical reason(s), you must submit a doctor's release to work prior to your return in order to safeguard your health.

An employee who is absent for three consecutive work days without notifying his or her supervisor will be considered to have voluntarily resigned and will be automatically terminated.

Breaks — Employees are entitled to a 15-minute break for every four hours worked.

Deadly weapons — Employees cannot carry a firearm or any other deadly weapon on company premises or in company vehicles at any time for any reason.

Following instructions — All employees are expected to follow the instructions of their supervisors. Refusal or failure to do so is considered insubordination. You are also expected to perform your work or job assignments in a satisfactorily and effective manner.

Fraternization — Employees will not fraternize with any inn guest on or off duty. In simple terms, you should not use your job as an opportunity to build personal relationships with guests.

Hotel facilities — The lounge and pool areas and guest areas are for the guests of our hotel only. Employees will not be allowed to use these facilities but may obtain special permission to eat in the dining room for a special occasion with prior approval of the General Manager.

Leaving work during working hours — Employees are not allowed to leave the company premises during working hours.

If an emergency situation necessitates your leaving, obtain the permission of your supervisor prior to your leaving. Meal periods are not considered working hours.

Lost and found — All articles found should be turned in to your supervisor for your own protection. When articles are properly identified, they will be returned to their owner.

Name tags — All employees will be issued a name tag, which is to be worn during each working shift.

Meals — All employees are entitled to one meal period (one-half hour) for each shift of work, with a minimum of a four-hour shift. All employees working a shift of nine or more hours are entitled to two meal periods. Employees' meal periods will be taken in the employees' cafeteria.

Nonsolicitation rule — For your protection and to avoid disruption of work, outside solicitors will not be permitted to solicit employees on the company's premises. The solicitation of employees by other employees will not be permitted during working hours. The distribution or circulation of leaflets, pamphlets, literature, or other materials among employees dur-

	ing working time or in working areas of the company is not permitted.
Off-duty employees	Upon completion of the work shift, employees are to clock out, depart the property, and not return in an off-duty status without prior approval from their supervisor.
Packages	We reserve the right to check all packages being taken off the property, personal or otherwise. No company property will be removed from the hotel without written authorization of your supervisor.
Parking	All employees are to park in the northern gravel lot adjacent to the hotel.
Personal deportment	Employees are expected to: (1) get along with managers, supervisors, and fellow employees and guests; (2) not discuss personal or unauthorized company matters in public areas where a guest could overhear these conversations and either be offended or made to feel ill at ease; and (3) not engage in actions on or off the property which could bring discredit to the company or its employees.
Restrooms	Employees are to use the restroom facilities upstairs by our employee cafeteria.
Standards of appearance	Every employee is expected to maintain a high standard of personal cleanliness and appearance.
Standards of cleanliness	We provide comfortable and clean working conditions in an effort to provide safe areas and promote productivity. We take pride in the general neat appearance of our facilities and equipment. In order

	to maintain good housekeeping, you must keep your work area neat, clean, and free of articles not being used. This includes keeping equipment in the proper place, disposing of waste in proper containers, and storing materials and equipment and supplies in an orderly manner and in their designated place.
Smoking	Uniformed employees will not smoke in public areas. No employee will be allowed to smoke in the kitchen because of health regulations.
Telephone usage	Employees will be called to the telephone only in emergency situations. Employees are to use the pay telephone located in the housekeeping department when they need to make an outgoing call.
Uniforms	Uniforms will be furnished by the company where required and must be worn for each scheduled shift.
Working areas	Employees are expected to refrain from being in areas in which their job does not require them to be.

DISCIPLINE

In order to deliver a consistently fair application of company rules and equitable treatment to all employees, a system of violation notices, called *written warnings,* will be administered to offer constructive criticism and provide an opportunity for you to improve or correct a problem, or to help you perform your job better.

A written warning will be issued for any violation of a company rule or regulation or for substandard work. Should you receive a written warning, it will be issued in writing and signed by you and your manager. Your signature on the warning only indicates that you have been informed of the violation or problem and that you understand what your supervisor is telling you in the warning. It does not necessarily mean that you agree with what is being said.

During an employee's probationary period, if the facts indicate unsatisfactory progress in his or her position, an employee may be terminated without notice for any justifiable reason, including reduction in force.

After the probationary period, an employee may be discharged if he or she has been given three (3) written warnings for the same or different offenses in the last twelve (12) months (except for those reasons listed under just cause).

TERMINATIONS

Our employment procedures are aimed at hiring people who will become reliable and satisfied employees. Nevertheless, employees may resign or be dismissed for various reasons. Some of these terminations will be within our control; others will be beyond it.

Voluntary Terminations

Any employee who decides to terminate his or her employment is expected to give a proper notice of at least one week and preferably two weeks. Supervisory personnel should give a notice of one month or more.

When an employee resigns, continuous service is ended. If, at some point in the future, a previous employee is hired, he or she starts as a new employee. Employees who terminate without proper notice will not be considered for reemployment.

Company Terminations

If it becomes necessary to dismiss an employee (barring reduction in force), this will be a result of the employee's own actions. An employee who has completed his or her probationary period shall not be discharged without

first having been given three (3) written warnings. This protects an employee from losing his or her job unfairly and provides him or her an opportunity to improve performance or correct the problem.

Termination for Just Cause

Additionally, an employee may be terminated immediately for certain specific offenses. The following violations may justify discharge without warning or advance notice:

- Willful damage to company property or misappropriation thereof
- Theft of company, employee, or guest property or unauthorized removal of the above, including lost and found items
- Consuming alcohol or drugs on employer premises during working hours, or possession of alcohol or drugs during working hours without authorization
- Willful falsification of company records (i.e., employment applications, payroll, financial, etc.)
- Conduct that could endanger the safety of the employee, coworkers, or a guest
- Incarceration in jail following conviction of a misdemeanor or felony by a court of competent jurisdiction
- Refusing to obey an order of a supervisor and/or insubordinate conduct towards a guest, supervisor, or manager
- Immoral or indecent conduct, soliciting persons for immoral reasons, or the aiding and/or abetting of the above
- Being absent for three consecutive scheduled work days without notification to the supervisor
- Unauthorized entry into a guestroom
- Unauthorized removal of guest property from the guestroom or the hotel

HEALTH AND SAFETY

We are interested in your safety and well-being. We can all do much to prevent accidents and injuries by working safely and carefully on our jobs. Always remain alert and report any working condition that you feel may cause an accident or injury.

Any accident occurring at work, no matter how small it may seem, must be reported to your supervisor. If necessary, an injured employee will be sent to an available doctor.

EMPLOYEE BENEFITS

Paid Holidays

There are six (6) paid holidays annually: New Year's Day, Memorial Day, Independence Day, Labor Day, Thanksgiving Day, and Christmas Day.

After thirty (30) days of employment, all full-time employees will receive eight (8) hours of holiday pay at their regular hourly rate. Temporary and Pool Status employees will not be eligible for holiday pay.

Since the hotel never closes, you may be asked to work any of these six holidays. If you do work on any one of these holidays, you will receive pay for the hours you work plus your eight hours holiday pay.

If you are scheduled to work the day before the holiday, the holiday, or the day after the holiday, then you must work your schedule in order to receive your holiday pay.

Paid Vacations

After the completion of one year of service, full-time employees will have earned the right to take a paid vacation: one full week of vacation time with pay, assuming an average of forty (40) hours per week were worked. After two (2) years of service, you will receive two full weeks of vacation each year. Thereafter, you will receive two full weeks of vacation each year. The amount of vacation pay to be received is determined by the number of average hours worked per week for that year.

Vacations cannot be saved up—you must take your vacation time each year. Every employee should take advantage of vacation time for rest and relaxation. Cash payment rather than time off will not be authorized.

If you are a part-time employee and your employment status is changed to full-time, then you will have earned one full week of vacation time with pay after one year of full-time service.

Meal Provision

Meals are provided for your convenience in the employees' cafeteria. Employees may have one meal after (4) hours of work, and a second meal if working more than nine (9) hours.

Leave of Absence

After you have completed six months of employment, you may, in the event of illness, maternity, or military duty, be granted a leave of absence without pay, at the discretion of the company.

With the exception of military and maternity leaves, an employee may take a minimum of thirty (30) days and a maximum of ninety (90) days for leave of absence.

Vacations and holidays will not accrue or be paid during a leave of absence. Length of service will be retained at the time of the leave but will not accrue during the leave. The company cannot hold your job open for the duration of the leave. However, upon return from leave the employee will be given the first open position of like classification and pay for which he or she is qualified, if the original job is not open.

Military Service Leave

It is a policy of the company to re-employ personnel after any required military service. Personnel entering military service will be placed on military leave of absence. Upon honorable discharge and being physically able, and within ninety (90) days of date of discharge, the employee will be reinstated in the same position and at the same rate of pay, if vacancies permit; otherwise, the employee will be given the option to accept another job for which there is a vacancy or be placed on a preferred waiting list for the next vacancy.

Military Training Leave

If you are serving an obligated period of duty with the National Guard or a reserve unit, you will be granted military leave for not more than two (2) weeks for the purpose of attending summer camp and or training. When you are absent from work because of required National Guard or reserve training, you will be paid the difference between your military pay and your company pay for not more than two weeks in any one calendar year. If a paid company holiday falls during the training time, you will receive an extra day's pay.

Maternity Leave

The hotel will grant leave of absence without pay to any expecting employee. To protect your health, we ask that you begin your leave not less than two (2) months before the baby is expected. Pregnant employees may, however, work as long as they like with the written approval of a doctor, but the company reserves the right to place such employee in a temporary position commensurate with our customer's expectations.

When it is confirmed that you are pregnant, you must give a release in writing from your doctor to the Personnel Department assuring that you are able to continue in your position. Without this release, you will not be allowed to continue working.

Funeral Leave

In the event of a death in your immediate family, three (3) days off with pay is permitted. Immediate family includes husband, wife, children, father, mother, brother, or sister.

Unemployment Compensation

Under the State Unemployment Act, you are insured against unemployment. The company pays the entire cost of this insurance.

If you become unemployed through no fault of your own, you are eligible for unemployment compensation for a limited period under provisions and law of the State. This law is administered by the State Unemployment Compensation Commission. You must apply for this compensation from the Commission.

Workmen's Compensation

Under state laws in the United States you are covered by Workmen's Compensation for injuries sustained in the course of your work. Be sure to report any such injury promptly to your department head. The cost of this insurance is paid entirely by the company.

Workmen's Compensation

Under state laws in the United States you are covered by Workmen's Compensation for injuries sustained in the course of your work. Be sure to report any such injury promptly to your department head. The cost of this insurance is paid entirely by your company.

FOR YOUR INFORMATION

Your employment status   _____ Full-time   _____ Part-time

                                _____ Pool   _____ Temporary

Your position title   _____

Your supervisor's name   _____

Your manager's name   _____

Your executive's name   _____

Your starting date   _____

Your starting pay rate   _____

Your first pay day   _____

I acknowledge receipt of and will read the Hotel Employment Handbook, which outlines my benefits and obligations as an employee of the company.

Date _____   Signed _____

All employment papers completed on _____

Company orientation lecture completed on _____
at which time employee was briefed on rules, regulations, benefits, policies, and procedures.

Date _____   Signed _____
                                       Director of Personnel

Bally's Casino Resort Housekeeping Department Rules and Regulations

The Bally's Casino Resort is a luxury casino and resort hotel located in Las Vegas, Nevada. The resort has 2832 rooms and employs approximately 560 unionized housekeeping employees when operating at 100 percent occupancy. This document provides explicit details on the housekeeping department's regulations.*

*Reprinted with permission of Bally's Casino Resort, Las Vegas, NV.

What follows is a set of **departmental instructions.** In most service organizations, a proper orientation for a new employee will include a complete acquisition program by the human resources department, property tour, and presentation of a company handbook. Many organizations go further by presenting a set of hotel housekeeping **departmental guidelines.**

Appreciation is extended to the Bally's Casino Resort Hotel of Las Vegas, Nevada for allowing the presentation of their Housekeeping Department Handbook.

BALLY'S
CASINO RESORT · LAS VEGAS

WELCOME TO BALLY'S CASINO RESORT

You have been selected to work for Bally's Casino Resort in the Housekeeping Department. We're very pleased to have you join our team.

Prior to working in your assigned area you will go through an eight day orientation program. During this time you will be placed in the care of our Training Specialist/ Supervisor and receive instructions on what we expect.

You will be taken on a tour of the Hotel and will be shown the front desk, casino areas, shopping mall, the employee cafeteria, etc. You shall be advised of Hotel polices and procedures, days off, break periods and lunch schedules.

I have an open door policy and am here to help you in any way possible. We want you to feel comfortable working with us. Our guests should see in you a friendly, competent, and caring employee. Good work and a positive attitude will please them and that's our goal. Again, Welcome.

Sincerely,

Kay Weirick

Kay Weirick, R.E.H.
Director of Housekeeping
Services

KW/bn

HOUSEKEEPING RULES/REGULATIONS

I. Guest Room Attendants

   A. General

   1. Please speak softly in all guest areas. Do not call down the hallway.

   2. Contact the Inspectress for further instructions regarding ALL liquor left in check-out rooms. DO NOT leave any liquor unattended in the hallway which has been removed from a guest room.

   3. Sleeping on the job is grounds for immediate dismissal.

   4. Linen lockers and storage areas may not be used for rest areas, except as indicated in item #6 below.

   5. Profane language is strictly forbidden.

   6. Smoking is prohibited in guestrooms, hallways, storage rooms, exit landings, foyers, etc. GRA's will be permitted to smoke in the following areas.

      a. Employee cafeteria

      b. Dressing rooms

      c. All employee restrooms

      d. Designated area in linen locker (on break period only)

   7. Purses will remain in the dressing room locker.

   8. DO NOT remove shoes at any time during working hours. Continued abuse will result in disciplinary action.

   9. Uniforms will NOT be removed from the hotel building.

   10. Identification badges will be worn at all times during working hours, (FACE SHOWING WITHOUT ANY DECORATION).

   11. Report for work well-groomed and neat in appearance at all times.

   12. Park vehicles ONLY in enclosed employee parking areas.

   13. DO NOT offer or accept offers from guests for baby-sitting, ironing, dry cleaning, or washing.

   14. It is NOT permitted to solicit funds, sell tickets or articles for personal use, churches, clubs or social events while on the premises of the hotel.

   15. DO NOT use the Bally's Casino Resort as a mailing address. All personal mail will be returned to sender.

   16. Friends or family members of GRA's are not to visit employees at any time during a shift. All personal calls and messages, of an emergency nature only, should be made through the Housekeeping Office.

   17. Do not discuss or volunteer information to any individual—guests, investigators, or any other persons—relative to accident or damage claims which have emanated from the Bally's Casino Resort. All inquiries of this nature shall be directed immediately to the Director of Housekeeping.

   18. Guest complaints will be logged and the personnel involved will be notified. Warning Notices will be issued if it is established that the employee was negligent in performing his/her duties or was discourteous to a guest.

19. No items of any kind will be removed from the hotel except personal items, and these must be identified by the Director of Housekeeping or her assistants, and then removed only with a written pass, duly signed.

20. Personal use of Hotel linen is prohibited.

21. Linen lockers and storage rooms must be kept closed and locked at all times.

22. Pick up guestroom keys and turn them over to the Inspectress at the end of the shift.

23. Do not enter a guestroom without first knocking on the door. The word "HOUSEKEEPING" must be repeated at least twice before opening the door. After the door is opened, the word "HOUSEKEEPING" must be repeated again loud and clear before entering.

24. Other than for performing your normal duties, guestrooms will not be opened for anyone without proper authorization from Housekeeping or the Hotel Manager's Office. GRA's will push soiled Room Service tables into the hallway, with the warming unit furthest from them.

25. The linen cart will be placed in the hallway, blocking the entrance of the guestroom while room is being serviced.

26. Keep linen carts neat at all times.

27. Vacuums are to be inside the room you are servicing. When standing in the hall waiting to service a room, the vacuum must be next to you on your linen cart.

28. Room and public area toilet bowls will not be used as trash receptacles, except for cigarette butts that may not be completely extinguished.

29. Two or more GRAs or Housepersons are not to be present in any one room at the same time, except when Supervisor specifically states differently.

30. Roll-away beds or cribs will not be delivered to a guestroom without direct order from the Housekeeping Office.

31. Playing of television sets in guest-rooms will not be permitted at any time. You may listen to the radio quietly. If guests are in room, do NOT turn off radio or television, or change the station.

32. Under no circumstances will GRAs be permitted to write and leave letters or notes in rooms for guests to read.

33. GRAs will not escort guests to their rooms. They may only direct them.

34. DO NOT inform guests of rooms already cleaned or located in a better area.

35. GRAs will report immediately to the Housekeeping Office the following:

    a. Keys found in hallways
    b. Open room doors
    c. Keys left in room door locks
    d. Excessive noises in rooms and hallways
    e. Smoke or burning odors

f. Water leaks

g. Floods

h. Sick or intoxicated guests sleeping in hallways

i. Lost children

j. Especially suspicious-looking individuals

k. Pets, dogs, cats, etc.

l. Hot plates, etc., found in guest-rooms

m. Report room number where they find a guest who is ill and alone.

n. Report to Housekeeping IMMEDIATELY any time you find a suitcase, box, carton, or container, in the hallways, foyers, or elevator area.

36. Abuse or loss of Bally's equipment and/or property including keys will be cause for disciplinary action. Continued abuse or loss may result in termination. Loss of MASTER KEYS may result in immediate TERMINATION!!!

37. Report immediately to Housekeeping any accident that occurs during a shift. Complete an Accident Report (See Safety Regulation) as soon as possible.

38. Room telephones must be used to enter your code and disposition of room. Room telephones will NOT be used for personal calls at any time. Use of a Guestroom telephone for personal calls is cause for disciplinary action.

39. All Lost and Found items found in Guestrooms or Hallways are to be reported and turned over to your Inspectress with your name, room num-ber, and description of item. The Inspectress will pick up item, complete a Lost and Found (3-part) form giving a copy to the GRA, and see that it is turned in to the Housekeeping Office. There it will be logged into the "LOST AND FOUND LEDGER," and the item is turned over to Security.

40. Report immediately any money or jewelry left visible in a make-up room.

41. Guest articles left on a bed in an occupied room will be immediately reported to the Housekeeping Office, or to your Inspectress. DO NOT REMOVE THE ARTICLES, ESPECIALLY PURSES/WALLETS, MONEY, JEWELRY, AND OTHER EXPENSIVE ITEMS. Place a card on the bed which states:

> Dear Guest,
> We are hesitant to remove articles from your bed. Please touch Housekeeping on your telephone for service.
> Thank you.

42. Guest articles will not be used or removed from an occupied room at any time.

43. GRAs will double check entrance doors to rooms they are servicing to see that they are closed and locked when leaving. Report any door you find hard to lock, close, or unlock.

44. GUEST ELEVATORS WILL NOT BE USED, except in emergencies. Permission is given by the Director of Housekeeping.

45. "Do Not Disturb" rooms shall be called by 12 Noon and request of the guest reported to the Inspectress.

46. All work accomplished during a shift must be thorough and to the satisfaction of the supervisor, (Inspectress). GRAs not servicing rooms according to Housekeeping procedures will be subject to disciplinary action.

47. Failure to follow a Supervisor's instructions constitutes insubordination, which is grounds for immediate dismissal.

48. Moccasins, tennis shoes, open-toed shoes, any soft shoes, or shoes with high heels are NOT permitted. Hose must be worn with the uniform. No socks may be worn.

B. Shift Schedules/Breaks/Absenteeism

1. Report to assigned station ONLY. DO NOT go to another floor for any reason, unless sent by a Supervisor.

2. All employees must sign in at the Housekeeping Office five minutes before shift begins in uniform ready to work. If you are more than 5 minutes late, you will be docked 15 minutes.

3. Excessive absenteeism/tardiness will result in disciplinary action. Excused sick calls may require a doctor's statement.

4. To leave the hotel during a shift, proper permission must be obtained. After permission is granted, turn in all station keys to your Inspector prior to leaving.

C. Guestroom Attendant Procedures

1. Sign in at the Housekeeping Office.

2. Check "Work Board" posted outside of Housekeeping Of-

fice to verify work station and report to assigned floor.

3. Obtain work sheet and station assignment from Inspectress and sign Pass Key Control Sheet for station key issued to you. At this time a room check of your assigned station is taken and room status is reported to the Inspectress.

4. Complete your own work sheet report as you make up the rooms.

5. Rooms are made up in the following priority sequence whenever possible:
   1) RUSH
   2) V.I.P.
   3) CHECK-OUT
   4) EARLY MAKE-UP
   5) STAY-OVER

6. Responsible for servicing all rooms assigned to you.

7. At the end of the shift, return the GRA work sheet report and your station keys to your Inspectress.

D. Turn Down Service

1. Close the drapes.

2. Clean ashtrays.

3. Replace soiled bath linens.

4. Empty waste paper baskets.

5. When turning spreads back, fold three times, leaving the spread at the foot of the bed. Fold sheet and place Sweet Dream card and mint on the pillow.

6. If the room is not a make-up, and the bed has been slept in, change the sheets, and turn down as usual.

7. Notify your Inspectress IMMEDIATELY if you find a wallet, pocket book, money, or jewelry on the bed. Other garments or

items may be removed from the bed for turn down service. If there are too many articles, leave the card noted in the General Rules, item #41.

8. Leave light on by nightstand.

9. If the guest has a "Do Not Disturb" sign on the door knob, slip this card underneath the door.

Respecting your privacy we were unable to turn down your bed.

You may request this service by touching Housekeeping on your telephone before 10:00 P.M.

Thank you.

II. Safety

Your Safety is very important to the Housekeeping Department and to Bally's Casino Resort. Please follow these safety procedures to the letter.

1. No matter how slight an accident may seem, it must be reported to your Supervisor.

2. a. The Supervisor shall send you to the Housekeeping office to report the accident to the Department Safety Coordinator. You will fill out an "Employee Accident Report."

   b. If the accident disables you, your Supervisor will call Security, who will immediately investigate. Housekeeping will then be notified. If the accident is serious, Paramedics shall be called by security.

3. If you are unable to fill out an accident report at the time of in-jury, it will be completed at your first opportunity.

4. Accident reports will be sent to the Personnel Department for follow-up.

5. You may be requested to attend a "Safety Class" explaining how future accidents may be prevented.

6. Remember—never use an unlabeled spray bottle. Do not mix cleaning solutions for any reason. Spray cleaning solutions only in ventilated areas.

7. Material Safety Data Sheets are located in the Housekeeping Office and are available to you. You have the right to know what it is you are using.

8. Always wear rubber gloves while using cleaning solutions.

9. When bending, use your knees correctly.

10. Never use machinery with naked wires showing. Never yank electrical cords from outlets.

11. Report all odors, smoke, etc. immediately to #4911 and then to the Housekeeping Department.

12. Matches must be stored in a closed container.

13. Know where all exits are on the guest floors.

14. Keep all rules and regulations given to you in the Orientation Safety Briefing.

15. Call Security #4911 for emergencies, and the Housekeeping Office #4766, immediately after reporting the emergency to Security.

BE CAREFUL—BE SAFE.

APPENDIX D

Hospital Standard Operating Procedures (SOPs)

The following group of SOPs have been extracted from *Environmental Services Policy and Procedure Manual* authored by Janice Kurth and published by Aspen Publishers. Grateful appreciation is extended to both author and publisher for their extending permission to have this work reprinted.

SUBJECT: __Standard Cleaning__

DEPARTMENT: __Environmental Services__   DATE ISSUED:_____

APPROVED BY:_____ DATE EFFECTIVE:_____

ORIGINATED BY:_____ SUPERSEDES DATE:_____

Page 1 of 1

Purpose: To maintain a clean, safe, and aesthetically pleasant environment for patients, staff, and visitors.

Procedure: The following procedure is to be used in cleaning all areas of the hospital, including patient rooms, offices, and public areas. Technicians should:

1. Pull trash and empty ashtrays in entire room, leaving clean liners out until the container has been damp-wiped inside and out.

2. Begin at the door of the room, moving clockwise (or counterclockwise) around the room, dusting everything above shoulder height, finishing back at the door of the room.

3. Dust mop hard surface floor or vacuum carpeting, beginning at the farthest corner and working around to the door.

4. Damp-wipe all surfaces below shoulder level (including waste containers) beginning at the door and moving clockwise (or counterclockwise) around the room, finishing at the door. This step includes spot-washing of walls around light switches, door knobs, and other obviously dirty areas.

5. Clean bathroom according to departmental procedure for bathroom cleaning.

6. Disinfect the floor (damp mop), starting at the far corner and working out the door.

All damp wiping, bathroom cleaning, and floor disinfecting must be done with an approved detergent disinfectant mixed at the correct dilution ratio.

Solutions must be changed after three rooms; heavily soiled rooms may require more frequent solution changes.

SUBJECT:__Restroom Cleaning__

DEPARTMENT:__Environmental Services_____DATE ISSUED:_____

APPROVED BY:_____DATE EFFECTIVE: _____

ORIGINATED BY:_____SUPERSEDES DATE: _____

Page 1 of 1

Purpose: To ensure the cleanliness and safety of all bathrooms in the hospital for use by patients, staff, and visitors.

Trash removal, high dusting, and floor dusting are to be accomplished before beginning to clean the fixtures according to the standard cleaning procedure.

Procedure:

1. Spray all fixtures including pipes and faucets with an approved detergent disinfectant, mixed at the correct dilution ratio. If mineral deposits are visible, squirt a toilet bowl cleaner around the inner edge of the bowl and use a bowl brush to clean the inside of the bowl. Be sure to flush after cleaning. Toilet bowl cleaners are acid-based compounds and should be used with caution and only inside the toilet bowl.

When no mineral deposit is visible, do not use a toilet bowl cleaner. Be sure to spray inside of toilet bowl with disinfectant solution.

2. Use a damp rag to thoroughly wipe fixtures, including pipes and faucets. If the sink or shower is heavily soiled, use the liquid cleanser in addition to the detergent disinfectant and rinse thoroughly.

3. Be sure to clean both sides of the toilet seat as well as around the hinges and all brightwork. Be sure to clean the underside of the sink and the pipes below.

4. Damp-wipe the cover of the light fixture over the sink, paper towel dispenser, and other wall-mounted fixtures; wipe dry if needed.

5. Clean mirror and dry with paper towel or dry cloth.

SUBJECT: **Use and Care of Standard Upright Vacuum**

DEPARTMENT: **Environmental Services** DATE ISSUED:

APPROVED BY: DATE EFFECTIVE:

ORIGINATED BY: SUPERSEDES DATE:

Page 1 of 1

Purpose: To maintain all upright vacuum cleaners through proper daily and periodic measures.

Procedure:

Vacuum bag replacement:

1. Open the cloth outside liner by unzipping bag all the way down to the bottom.

2. Remove the top half of disposable paper bag from within the cloth cover.

3. Roll the coil spring on the inside bottom of the vacuum down around the throat of the bag until the throat is free.

4. Remove bag carefully and dispose of it.

5. Start replacement by noting that each bag has TOP and BOTTOM printed on the front.

6. Hold the bag so the word TOP is at the top and the throat is next to the machine.

7. Slide the throat of the bag onto the sleeve fold or wrap the throat so that it is fixed tightly around the sleeve.

8. Roll the spring back over the throat of the bag all the way to the groove of the sleeve.

9. Tuck the remainder of the bag in and zip cloth cover closed, taking care not to catch the cloth bag.

Daily maintenance:

1. Each time a vacuum is used, the cord and motor housing should be damp-wiped—without exception.

2. Make a visual check to ensure that the rubber bumper is fitted properly around the vacuum.

3. Change the bag as frequently as necessary; the fuller the bag becomes, the less effectively the machine will work. A good rule of thumb is to change the bag when it is half full.

4. Check belt for wear.

5. Check brushes for wear and soil.

6. Report any problems such as worn belts or brushes or frayed or damaged cords to your Area Manager for immediate repair.

SUBJECT: **Wet Mopping**

DEPARTMENT: **Environmental Services**   DATE ISSUED:_____

APPROVED BY:_____   DATE EFFECTIVE: _____

ORIGINATED BY:_____   SUPERSEDES DATE: _____

Page 1 of 1

Purpose: To clean and/or disinfect hard-surface flooring using the physically correct procedure.

The equipment necessary for wet mopping will vary, depending on the area and the cleaning procedure, but in general the following equipment will be needed:

Dust mop head and handle

Bucket for cleaning solution

Wringer

Wet mop handle

Wet mop heads

"Wet Floor" signs

Scraper

Procedure:

1. Dust mop area prior to wet mopping (do not omit this step).

2. Place "Wet Floor" signs in such a way as to clearly mark the area that is to be mopped.

3. Place the mop into the cleaning solution and allow solution to be absorbed; carefully lift mop out of bucket and place in the wringer. How dry the mop is wrung will depend on the procedure, i.e., stripping floors, etc.

4. Begin at the farthest point in the room or area and work down the hall or out of the room to avoid mopping yourself into a corner.

5. Place right hand on top, knuckles facing forward; left hand below, also with knuckles facing forward. Right hand should be near the top of the handle. (Reverse procedure for left-handers.)

6. Place mop onto floor close to the baseboard and gently pull mop along edge for several feet. All edges should be cleaned in this manner.

7. Return to the beginning and place the mop onto the floor at the halfway point (in a corridor or stairwell) or approximately four feet from the starting edge. Make a series of small overlapping S's on the floor. It won't be necessary to bring the wet mop close to the wall, as this area has been mopped already.

8. Continue to wet mop the area in sections of about four feet, being sure to cover area adjacent to walls, as noted above.

9. Rewet mop as necessary for equal coverage.

10. Reposition "Wet Floor" signs as needed; do not remove signs until area is completely dry.

11. Change cleaning solution and mop heads frequently for best results. (As a general rule: change every three patient rooms or their equivalent.)

12. Clean equipment and store properly.

SUBJECT: __Finish Application__

DEPARTMENT: __Environmental Services__ DATE ISSUED:_____

APPROVED BY:_____ DATE EFFECTIVE: _____

ORIGINATED BY:_____ SUPERSEDES DATE: _____

Page 1 of 1

Purpose: To enhance the appearance of, and to protect, hard-surface and/or resilient flooring by applying products specially formulated for that purpose.

Assemble needed equipment:

Bucket with wringer

Mop handle

Clean mop heads

Plastic bags

Damp rag

"Wet Floor" signs

Floor finish

Procedure:

1. Line bucket with plastic bag.

2. Moisten mop head with clear, cool water.

3. Pour estimated amount of finish into lined bucket.

4. Place dampened wet mop into finish and allow product to be absorbed before wringing lightly.

5. Apply finish, beginning at the farthest point of area by outlining the top and sides of an area approximately 4 feet square.

6. Fill in outlined area using an S stroke (be sure that passes overlap for even coverage).

7. Repeat process until entire area has been completed.

8. Allow product to dry according to label directions.

9. Apply succeeding coats of finish following this procedure and following recommended drying time between coats.

10. Begin succeeding coats of finish at least six inches from the baseboard to avoid unnecessary build-up at edges and in corners.

11. Clean and store equipment properly.

Failure to allow finish to cure according to label directions may result in powdering and/or poor appearance.

Any remaining floor finish should be disposed of. Do not save or reuse.

SUBJECT: <u>**Cleaning Corridors**</u>

DEPARTMENT: <u>**Environmental Services**</u>   DATE ISSUED:_____

APPROVED BY:_____DATE EFFECTIVE: _____

ORIGINATED BY:_____SUPERSEDES DATE: _____

Page 1 of 1

Purpose: To clean corridors within the facility safely and with as little interference as possible with daily activities, and to minimize the potential risk associated with wet floors.

Several situations separate the routine cleaning of corridors from the routine cleaning of other areas. It essentially is accomplished using the Standard Cleaning Procedure, with the following additions.

Procedure:

1. Place "Wet Floor" caution signs at both ends of corridor to alert staff and visitors to a potential hazard.

2. Wet mop all corridors, covering only half of the width at a time. This allows safe foot traffic at all times in any given corridor.

3. Wet mop the remaining half of the corridor only when the first half has dried completely.

4. React to an emergency code in the area being cleaned by moving all equipment and supplies (except "Wet Floor" signs, which should remain in place to mark potentially slippery areas) out of the main traffic area to avoid interfering with emergency personnel.

SUBJECT: **Elevator Cleaning**

DEPARTMENT: **Environmental Services**   DATE ISSUED:_____

APPROVED BY:_____DATE EFFECTIVE: _____

ORIGINATED BY:_____SUPERSEDES DATE: _____

Page 1 of 1

Purpose: To clean elevator cars, tracks, and interior and exterior of doors safely with as little inconvenience as possible to the passengers.

Assemble needed equipment:

Step ladder

10-quart plastic pail

Rags

Dust mop

Bucket with wringer

Wet mop

Liquid cleanser

Disinfectant detergent

Hand vacuum

Stainless steel cleaner (if needed)

Small brush

Rubber gloves

Procedure:

1. Take the elevator to a nonpatient, nonpublic floor for cleaning and turn off with key.

2. Mix disinfectant detergent according to label directions in pail and bucket.

3. Remove the light diffusers carefully and clean with damp cloth soaked in disinfectant detergent. Wipe dry to prevent streaking and replace.

4. Dust mop the floor.

5. Vacuum the tracks with vacuum equipped with crevice tool.

6. Wash the walls. Use stainless steel cleaner, sparingly, if walls are stainless, rinsing thoroughly with warm water; then apply very thin coat of baby oil and buff it in. Use damp rags if walls are painted. Use vacuum if walls are carpeted. Use liquid cleanser to remove graffiti or stubborn spots if necessary. Rinse well before continuing.

7. Clean tracks thoroughly, using small brush dipped in disinfectant detergent. Dry tracks with absorbent cloths.

8. Wash the inside of the doors with appropriate product.

9. Wet mop floor.

10. Return elevator to service when floor has dried completely.

11. Wash outside of doors with appropriate product.

12. Clean equipment and store properly.

SUBJECT: __Spray Buffing__

DEPARTMENT: __Environmental Services__   DATE ISSUED:_____

APPROVED BY:_____ DATE EFFECTIVE: _____

ORIGINATED BY:_____ SUPERSEDES DATE: _____

Page 1 of 1

Purpose: To restore hard-surface and/or resilient flooring, i.e., terrazzo, vinyl, or vinyl asbestos tile to a clean, shiny but nonskid finish.

Assemble needed equipment:

Rotary floor machine with pad holder (drive block)

Red floor pad

Plastic bottle with trigger sprayer

Spray buff solution

Procedure: (consider 3 rows; a, b, & c)

1. Dust mop and wet mop floor.

2. Spray solution across row B.

3. Run buffer once across line between row A and row B, then once across line between row B and row C. This will spread spray buff across entire area.

4. Run buffer across row A two or three times; finish will get dull; buff to an even shine. If no shine appears, repeat process.

5. Repeat the sequence for rows B and C.

6. Repeat sequence on the next three tows of tile, etc.

7. Change pads when they begin to build up or become damp. The buffer will start to "grab" when the pad is dirty or wet. Dirty pads do not absorb the dirt from the floor and may leave burn marks.

8. Remove black heel marks by spraying solution on them, and heeling the buffer sightly. Stubborn marks can be removed with a hand pad. Heeling with a dirty pad will leave marks that must be scraped off the floor. It is important not to let buffer run in one spot too long as this also may leave burn marks.

9. Dust mop or vacuum again after each buffing to pick up buffing dust and to prevent floors from becoming slippery.

It may take several days of spray buffing to get best results. Spray buffing accomplishes three things: It removes black marks, levels the finish, and buffs. The amount of additional finish added is so negligible that it cannot be measured.

The floor must be vacuumed or dust mopped and damp mopped thoroughly before spray buffing. Small grains of sand, dirt, etc., will cause great damage if whirled around by the buffer. Spray buffing removes some dirt and spreads the rest evenly over the floor. Therefore, the cleaner the floor is to start, the less dirt is spread out and the fewer times you will have to change or clean pads.

SUBJECT: **Ceramic and Quarry Tile Cleaning with Roto Wash**

DEPARTMENT: **Environmental Services**   DATE ISSUED:_____

APPROVED BY:_____DATE EFFECTIVE: _____

ORIGINATED BY:_____SUPERSEDES DATE: _____

Page 1 of 1.

Purpose: To thoroughly clean and scrub ceramic and quarry tile and its grout.

Assemble needed equipment:

Dust mop

Disinfectant/detergent or other appropriate cleaning chemical

Roto Wash equipped with Nylo Grit brushes (grit brushes are very abrasive and should be used only on hard surfaces—never on carpet—and with lots of water.)

Bucket for cleaning solution

Bucket for retrieved solution

Pressure sprayer (if necessary)

Procedure:

1. Mix cleaning chemical according to label directions; use a degreaser or other heavy-duty cleaner for kitchen areas if necessary.

2. Pour solution into solution tank.

3. Spray heavily soiled areas with cleaning chemical and allow them to soak for five minutes to loosen soil.

4. Start machine by pulling back on handle to retract the wheels automatically.

5. Put stop handle briefly in neutral (straight up) to allow brushes to run for a moment.

6. Lift solution control handle to release the cleaning solution.

7. Operate the machine in overlapping passes to ensure complete coverage; machine also may be operated forward and backward.

8. Empty waste water tray as necessary.

9. Clean equipment and store properly.

The Roto Wash is a machine designed to clean most floor surfaces and using two cylindrical counterrotating brushes.

SUBJECT: <u>**Window Cleaning**</u>

DEPARTMENT: <u>**Environmental Services**</u>   DATE ISSUED:_____

APPROVED BY:_____ DATE EFFECTIVE: _____

ORIGINATED BY:_____SUPERSEDES DATE: _____

Page 1 of 1

Purpose: To maintain a clean and smudge-free surface on interior and exterior window glass.

Assemble needed equipment:

    Squeegee with handle

    Window cleaner

    Small plastic bucket

    Clean rags

    Sponge

    Glass scraper

    Window brush

Procedure:

1. Prepare window-cleaning solution according to label directions.

2. Place window brush into solution.

3. Apply solution to window surface using S strokes.

4. Use squeegee, starting at bottom corner and working upward along outside edge, across top, then downward using S stroke.

5. Dry squeegee blade as needed with clean dry cloth.

6. Remove any solution remaining on window frames or ledges with clean cloth.

7. Clean equipment and store properly.

Some areas may require the use of a glass scraper to remove stubborn material.

Some window cleaners may have an unpleasant odor and should be used with caution.

SUBJECT: **Carpet Spotting for Water-Based Stains**

DEPARTMENT: **Environmental Services**   DATE ISSUED:

APPROVED BY: DATE EFFECTIVE:

ORIGINATED BY: SUPERSEDES DATE:

Page 1 of 1

Purpose: To preserve the appearance of carpeted surfaces through the timely and appropriate removal of spots and stains.

Assemble needed equipment:

Clean white rags

Premixed water-based carpet spotting chemical or concentrated prespotting chemical

Plastic bottle with trigger sprayer or bucket for mixing spotting chemical

Scraper (optional)

Soft brush

Procedure:

1. Remove excess substance: remove liquids with a wet vacuum; solids or semisolids with scraper, your finger, or other handy blunt object.

2. Mix spotting chemical according to label directions.

3. Apply solution to spot with trigger sprayer, working it in with cloth, soft brush, or fingers.

4. Blot (do not rub) the area, using downward pressure.

5. Absorb excess solution by applying pressure to area with soft, clean, white cloth.

6. Repeat process until spot has been removed.

7. Use clear water to avoid unnecessary chemical build-up if more than three applications are needed.

8. Absorb excess moisture by applying pressure, using clean, white cloths weighted down with a heavy object such as a five-gallon container of floor finish.

9. Clean equipment and store properly.

SUBJECT: **Carpet Cleaning-Extraction**

DEPARTMENT: **Environmental Services**   DATE ISSUED:_____

APPROVED BY:_____ DATE EFFECTIVE: _____

ORIGINATED BY:_____ SUPERSEDES DATE: _____

Page 1 of 1

Purpose: To clean carpeted surfaces thoroughly, using high-pressure injection of cleaning solution and vacuum retrieval.

Assemble needed equipment:

Vacuum cleaner

Extractor

Dry cleaning solvent

Prespotter in trigger sprayer

White cloths for spotting

Carpet shampoo for use in extractors

Antifoam emulsion

Procedure:

To Prespot:

1. Vacuum area to be cleaned thoroughly, first widthwise across the room, then lengthwise. This is a crucial step. DO NOT OMIT! The more soil that is removed prior to wetting, the cleaner the carpet will be when completed.

2. Treat any visible spots or stains before extraction is begun.

3. Use the appropriate chemical, depending on the origin of the stain. If the origin is unknown, use the dry cleaning solvent. The solvent must always be used according to label directions, with proper ventilation. Always use extreme care with this product.

To Shampoo:

1. Make sketch of furniture as it is arranged in the room, then remove it.

2. Fill the extractor with hot water, add shampoo and mix thoroughly. (Shampoo may be eliminated in situations where the carpet has been cleaned many times; extracting solely with hot water may be satisfactory.) Read label directions carefully to determine proper dilution ratios.

3. Pour the suggested amount of antifoam emulsion into the recovery tank. (If large amounts of foam are generated, more emulsion may be necessary. Vinegar may be substituted for the antifoam emulsion.)

4. Work in three-foot overlapping strokes, beginning in the corner of the room. As the head is pulled slowly toward you, apply solution.

5. Make a second pass over the area, but do not apply solution.

6. Work slowly to allow the solution to penetrate and to allow the vacuum to remove the maximum amount of soil and solution.

7. Continue in this manner until the entire area has been completed. (Heavily soiled carpet may require cleaning using the bonnet method or the rotary brush method before extraction.)

8. Clean and store equipment properly.

9. Allow carpet to dry completely and replace furniture according to sketch.

SUBJECT: **Mercury Spill**

DEPARTMENT: **Environmental Services**   DATE ISSUED:_____

APPROVED BY:_____DATE EFFECTIVE: _____

ORIGINATED BY:_____SUPERSEDES DATE: _____

Page 1 of 1

Purpose: To retrieve and contain any mercury spilled or dropped within the facility (from a broken thermometer, blood pressure gauge, etc.) and return it to Central Service.

Procedure:

1. Locate the mercury before beginning the cleanup process.

2. Use a piece of heavy paper or cardboard to pick up the mercury or a large syringe to "vacuum" or suck it up.

3. Place the mercury in a plastic cup or other container and put it in a safe place while the rest of the cleanup is being done.

4. Sweep up and remove any broken glass and debris.

5. Wet mop the area with an approved disinfectant detergent.

6. Take the recovered mercury to Central Service.

Property Zone Inspection Form*

The following property zone inspection program is used by the Tropicana Hotel in Las Vegas, Nevada. The program is presented in the form of a Standard Operating Procedure (SOP), a copy of which is given to a "chief inspector" for each zone before inspection.

To understand how it works, consider the inspector for Zone 1, who will inspect 14 rooms in addition to the general public areas associated with the rooms to be inspected. The inspection packet will include 14 room inspection report forms, one for each room to be inspected. (For brevity, the duplication of guestroom inspection reports of the several guestrooms in each building has been omitted.)

Pay particular attention to the techniques of control used *after* the inspection has been completed.

*Provided courtesy of Ramada's Tropicana Hotel, Las Vegas, Nevada, 1984. Reprinted with permission.

Standard Operating Procedure

Property Zone Inspection Program

Concept

It is not enough that advertising proclaims the excellence of the "new" Tropicana facility. The property must speak for itself in such a way that our guests recognize this quality as it is, and that there is in fact "none superior" in the City of Las Vegas. It is imperative, therefore, that the highest standards of property maintenance, cleanliness, and upkeep be attained. In order to accomplish this task, an inspection system involving "fresh looks" on a periodic basis, coupled with an adequate system of controlled follow-up, is essential so that standards can be maintained and improved upon.

Policy

It will be policy that the entire Tropicana facility be inspected every other week by zone. The general manager may, on occasion, waive a particular zone from inspection, should past and repeated high-quality zone inspection results regularly occur. ZONE inspection will not be a substitute for departmental supervisory inspections on an as-needed basis.

Zone Designation

The following zones are hereby established, defined, and assigned to the person filling the position indicated for accountability.

Zone 1: Housekeeping and guestroom area (see inspection form)

Accountable manager: executive housekeeper

Zone 1 includes the inspection of 14 guestrooms (3 rooms in the 3000 building, 3 rooms in the 4000 building, 3 rooms in the 5000 building, and 5 rooms in the tower), all public areas within the garden buildings and the tower above the mezzanine, and all service areas contiguous thereto; all guest and service elevators and elevator landings (landings on tower lobby and mezzanine floor excluded). Also included in this zone will be the housekeeping office, linen room, and uniform storage.

Prior to inspecting this zone, the inspector will obtain keys to rooms to be inspected from the front desk. Zone 1 will be a guided inspection tour conducted by the executive housekeeper or his/her assistant.

Zone 2: General public areas (see inspection form) Accountable manager: director of housekeeping

Zone 2 includes all public areas and public restrooms on the first floor and mezzanine (exclusive of the pool and garden buildings). Zone 2 also includes the Plaza and Monte Carlo rooms, executive offices, all brown carpeted area associated therewith, and the sports pavilion.

Zone 3: Kitchens, food prep, receiving, service, and disposal areas (see inspection form)

Accountable manager: executive steward

Zone 3 includes all kitchens, food service areas (unless associated with restaurant service), food storerooms, refrigerators, freezers, butcher shop, baker shop, dishrooms, back dock receiving, trash removal areas, trash compactor, garbage disposal, and the outside areas immediately adjacent thereto.

Zone 4: Restaurants and lounges (see inspection form)

Accountable manager: director of food and beverage/public space manager

This zone includes all food and beverage outlets as observed by the public, and all service areas immediately adjacent thereto, exclusive of kitchens. Includes food and beverage areas at the Country Club, and the employees' cafeteria.

Zone 5: Building exterior and grounds (see inspection form)

Accountable manager: grounds superintendent/Country Club manager/chief engineer, as appropriate

This zone includes an appraisal of the exterior surfaces of all structures, signage, graphics, parking lots, lawn areas, swimming pool and associated decking, front entrance (exterior), exterior lighting, and the exterior of the Country Club facility.

Zone 6: Maintenance and general service areas (see inspection form)

Accountable manager: director of facilities This zone includes all basement spaces not heretofore mentioned, such as maintenance shops.

Zone Inspectors

There will be eight Chief Inspectors and as many Assistant Inspectors as are assigned in this procedure.

Incumbents to positions will conduct inspections when assigned by Chief Inspectors. Chief Inspectors are responsible for ensuring that weekly inspections are conducted, and will review inspection reports prior to their submission to the Executive Office. For the purposes of zone inspections, persons listed as Assistant Inspectors are accountable to the Chief Inspector under whose name they appear. As a rule, Assistant Inspectors have been assigned along organizational lines as much as possible. Exceptions to the above rule have been made to balance inspection units so that one group of assistant inspectors is not taxed more than another. Chief Inspectors will ensure that a fair and even rotation of inspectors is conducted and will periodically conduct inspections themselves. In addition, they should on occasion accompany their Assistant Inspectors for training purposes.

Chief Inspectors	*Assistant Inspectors*
Vice President, Hotel Operations	Hotel Manager
	Rooms Division Manager
	Executive Assistant Hotel Manager
	Executive Housekeeper
	Room Reservations Manager
	All Assistant Managers
	Hotel Credit Manager
	Guest Services Manager
Director of Food and Beverage	Executive Chef
	Buffet Manager
	Banquet Manager
	Assistant Executive Chef
	Executive Kitchen Steward
	Tiffany Theater Manager
	Room Service Manager
	Summerfield's Manager
	Gourmet Room Manager
	Head Cashier/Checker
	Lord Byron Manager
	Food & Beverage Supervisors
Vice President, Marketing	Director of Sales
	Public Relations Director
	Entertainment Director
	All Sales Managers
	Director of Advertising and Promotions
	Director of Marketing Analysis
Vice President, Casino Operations	Assistant Casino Manager
	Shift Managers
	Baccarat Manager
	Baccarat Shift Managers
	"21" Pit Bosses
	Baccarat Pit Bosses
	Dice Pit Bosses
Vice President, Slot Operations	Assistant Slot Manager
	Shift Managers
	Keno Manager
	Assistant Keno Manager
	Card Room Manager
	Director of Casino Marketing
Vice President, Finance	Controller
	Assistant Controller, Casino

Assistant Controller, Hotel
Financial Analyst
Data Processing Manager
Casino Cage Manager
Casino Credit Manager
Vice President, Chief of Surveillance
Loss Chief of Security
Prevention Personnel Director
Assistant Personnel Director
Purchasing Director
Country Club Manager
Administrative Assistant to
  the GM
Director of Public Space Manager
Facilities Chief Engineer
Assistant Chief Engineers
Convention Services
  Manager
Director of Catering and
  Convention Services
Chief PBX Operator

Scheduling

A rotating schedule of the eight Principal Inspectors among the 6 zones on a weekly basis will be maintained by the Executive Secretary (see Appendix H for scheduling form). After the Principal Inspector has been assigned by the Schedule, the Principal Inspector may then delegate to one of the appropriate Assistant Inspectors the task of actually performing the inspection. However, the Principal Inspector is responsible for ensuring that the inspection is properly conducted and will review the inspection report prior to its being turned in.

Procedures (administration and follow-up)

1. The Executive Secretary will provide each Chief Inspector with a folder for the appropriate zone at staff meetings on Wednesdays. The zone folder will contain a blank inspection form for the appropriate zone and a copy of the prior week's completed inspection.

2. Zone inspection may then be conducted any time after the staff meeting but prior to Thursday at 4:00 P.M.
3. Chief Inspectors will review results as necessary and make two copies of the completed inspection form.
4. Inspectors should not hesitate to make suggestions for the improvement of safety, service, and appearance, and should not be held to the Inspection Guide only. Imagination and creativity will become the basis for even greater improvement and future planning.
5. Zone 1 inspections will be conducted by escort.
6. Any guestroom in Zone 1 marked unsatisfactory must be placed out of service until such time as the unsatisfactory condition is corrected.

Accountable Managers Procedure

Upon receiving a copy of the inspection report for their zone from the Chief Inspector, Accountable Managers will initiate or take action and report that action in accordance with the following codes. Note the action taken against the deficient item reported on the inspection form in the space provided using these codes.

CORR	Corrected
CLND	Cleaned—now meets Tropicana standards
WO(_____)	Work Order (number) prepared and submitted completion date (_____)
PWO(_____)	Previous work order (number), expected completion date (_____)
REP(_____)	Repaired (date____) now meets Tropicana standards.
CI	Capital item submitted for budget approval
CIA(_____)	Capital item approved scheduled (date____) for completion

X(_____) Item not corrected (low priority); expected completion by (date____)

1. Guestrooms marked UNSAT must be removed from service until the reported unsatisfactory condition has been corrected.
2. Accountable Manager must forward follow-up to the executive office prior to noon the following Tuesday.
3. Chief Inspectors will turn in the original and one copy of the inspection form to the Executive Secretary.
4. Inspectors will hand-deliver to, and personally review as necessary, the second copy of the inspection results with the Manager accountable for the zone inspected prior to noon on Fridays.
5. The Executive Secretary will deliver the original inspection form to the General Manager, who will comment as necessary and forward the original to the Vice President of Operations. The Vice President of Operations will also comment and forward the original to the Hotel Manager.
6. The Executive Secretary will place the other copy of the Inspection Report in the zone folder with a new inspection form for the next inspection.
7. The Accountable Manager will take action and comment as necessary on the copy of the inspection he or she received from the Chief Inspector. This copy of the inspection will be forwarded to the Executive Office no later than Tuesday of the following week. It will be reviewed by the Hotel Manager, who will prepare monthly critiques on those items not being corrected in a timely fashion, indicating any reasons.
8. Inspection results and critiques will form a partial basis for performance appraisals.

Inspection Procedures

Inspectors

1. Inspectors randomly selected on a biweekly basis help give a "fresh look" at areas where the same eyes, week after week, can allow standards to deteriorate. What can be minor one week may become major at a later time, but many go unnoticed because of its familiarity.
2. Inspectors must therefore take note of deficiencies on prior weeks' reports and must personally note whether such deficiencies have been corrected. If they have not, they are recorded again and noted on the repeat discrepancy form.

Conclusion

Objective Inspectors and Accountable Managers are the key to the entire inspection program. The zone inspection program is only a management tool that can simplify procedures if it becomes a strictly adhered-to routine. Working as a team, the Inspector and the Accountable Manager can jointly produce results and, as a result, will both deserve the credit when the zone inspection system is working smoothly.

Cancellation

All instructions and memoranda previously issued having reference to general property inspections are hereby cancelled. Nothing in this instruction is designed to prevent the individual manager from inspecting his or her areas of responsibility and from taking appropriate action to correct deficiencies.

TROPICANA

ZONE INSPECTION REPORT

Zone 1

HOUSEKEEPING AND GUEST ROOM AREA

Accountable Manager <u>EXECUTIVE HOUSEKEEPER</u>

Inspected by _____ Date/time _____

Inspection to be completed no later than Thursday (4:00 P.M.) on weeks scheduled. Make two copies. Original and one copy is to be forwarded to the Executive Secretary by 4:00 P.M. on Thursday. Second copy to be delivered to the Accountable Manager for this zone. Discuss as necessary. The Accountable Manager will indicate corrective action taken in accordance with corrective code (see basic procedure). Follow-up copy to be forwarded to the executive office no later than the following Tuesday.

Space	Sat.	NI	Unsat.	Comment	ACC. MGR. Corrective Action
Housekeeping office					
Uniform room					
Linen room					
Garden rooms (3000)					
Entrances and exits					
Doors					
Hallways					
Guest elevators					
Service elevators					
Walls					
Carpets					
Lights					
Fire exits					
Exit signs					
Smoke detectors					

Space	Sat.	NI	Unsat.	Comment	ACC. MGR. Corrective Action
Fire extinguishers					
Linen storage					
Stairwells					
Handrails					
Other					

Tropicana Hotel and Country Club *Las Vegas, Nevada*

GARDEN ROOMS
(3000)

ROOM INSPECTION REPORT

INSPECTED BY:	ROOM NO.:
MAID:	TYPE:
INSPECTRESS:	DATE INSPECTED:

CONDITION: ☐ ACCEPTABLE ☐ ACCEPTABLE WITH FOLLOW UP ☐ NOT ACCEPTABLE

OK	ROOM	DETAILS	OK	BATH ROOM	DETAILS
	ELECTRICAL: THERMOSTAT CONTROL			LIGHTS, BULBS, SWITCHES & PLATES	
	WALL SWITCHES, LIGHTS, BULBS			WASH BASIN, VANITY & STOOL	
	LAMPS, SHADES, SEAMS, BULBS			WATER FAUCETS, DRAINS & STOPPERS	
	LOCKS – STICKERS			MIRROR	
	DEAD BOLT			TUB, SHOWER ENCLOSURE, CAULKING, GRAB BAR	
	DOORS, HARDWARE, STOPS			TILE FLOOR & WALLS	
	CEILING & A/C VENTS			TOWELS – WASH CLOTHS	
	WALLS, PAINT, WALLPAPER, VINYL, MURALS, ETC.			RUBBER MAT – RUGS	
	CURTAINS – DRAPES			TOWEL RACK CHROME	
	DRAPERY: PINS, CORDS, SPRINGS, PULLS			TOILET BOWL & SEAT, FLUSH	
	MIRRORS & PICTURES			TOILET TISSUE – HOLDER	
	WOODWORK & TRIM			SHOWER HEAD	
	CARPET			SOAP & HOLDER	
	WINDOWS, LOCKS & LEDGES			BOTTLE OPENER	
	FURNITURE: DRESSER, NITE STAND(S)			DOOR HOOK	
	CHAIRS & COUCHES			GLASSES	
	HEADBOARDS, BEDS			SHOE SHINE CLOTHS	
	SPREADS, PILLOWS, BLANKETS			KLEENEX – HOLDER	
	T. V., RADIO, CLOCK			BATHROOM BENCH (NOT IN ALL ROOMS)	
	(2) FOLDING CHAIRS			PIPE UNDER SINK	
	WASTE BASKET			WASTE BASKET	
	D D CARD / EARLY MAKEUP			WALLS, VINYL & PAINT	
	TELEPHONE BOOK, TELEGRAM BLANKS			CEILING – EXHAUST FAN	
	PHONE SCRATCH PAD, STATIONERY, PEN				
	LAUNDRY LIST				
	PLASTIC BAGS & SEWING KITS				
	MENUS, POSTCARDS, ETC.		**OK**	**CLOSET**	**DETAILS**
	ASH TRAYS – MATCHES			HANGERS – PLASTIC, WOOD	
				LIGHT	
				LAUNDRY BAGS	
				SHELVES	
GENERAL CLEANING				POLE	
	DUSTING			LUGGAGE RACKS	
				CEILING, WALLS, BASEBOARDS	
				DOOR LOUVRES	
				DOORS – STOPS & HARDWARE	

REMARKS AND MISCELLANEOUS: _____

APPENDIX F

What If

"What If" is a booklet that is available to hotels to place in each guestroom. It presents an excellent technique for educating guests about what to do in case of fire.

(This material is reprinted with permission of the copyright owner: the James H. Barry Co. of San Francisco, California. It may not be reprinted without written permission. (Booklets may be ordered by writing the James H. Barry Co., 170 S. Van Ness Ave., San Francisco, CA 94103.)

What if...?

Your Hotel Name
City

What if...?

What if...
you're in a fire?

Probably it won't happen. You are in a building which was constructed to meet modern fire codes and which offers reasonable protection against such an occurrence. Your chances of being involved in a fire here may be thousands to one.

But your chances are even better if you understand, in advance, what to do in case of fire. Countless people are needlessly harmed by fires because they did *not* understand what to do.

This little booklet will tell you what to do, and it takes only three minutes to read. Increase your chances: please read it.

Andrew C. Casper

Andrew C. Casper
Chairman of Board of Visitors,
National Fire Academy,
U.S. Fire Administration

What if ... you've just arrived?

Learn Where The Exits Are ... before you first enter your room, look to the right and left of the door and locate at least *two* exits.

Walk To Each Exit ... to help you remember their locations, walk to each exit from your room.

Count Doors On The Way ... Choose a wall and, as you walk to each exit, count the doors along that wall between the exit and your room. This helps you remember the distance and location of exits—and may also help in case you have to find an exit when it's dark or smoky.

Find Alarms & Extinguishers ... locate and walk to the Fire Alarm and Fire Extinguisher on your floor.

Find The "Off-switch" On Your Air Conditioner ... in your own room, learn how to turn off your air conditioning system. This way, in case of fire, you can prevent smoke from being sucked into your room.

What if...
you find
a fire?

Pull The Nearest Fire Alarm . . . if you find a
fire in your room or somewhere else, sound the alarm.

Close Doors Against The Fire . . . if possible, close the
doors around the fire area, to keep the fire from
spreading.

Phone Management For Help . . . immediately telephone the front desk or building management to report the fire. If you cannot reach them, don't hesitate
to call the local fire department—its number is on the
inside front page of all phonebooks.

Fight Only Tiny Fires . . . use a fire extinguisher—*if* it
is a small fire.

Flee Larger Fires . . . if possible, exit from the building
if the fire is not small.

Always Take Your Room Key . . . before trying to
exit, be sure to take your room key. A tip—if possible,
loop the key to your wrist with a rubber band.

Stay Calm . . . don't hurry, keep relaxed, and *think*.
Your danger is almost always less than you imagine it
to be.

What if...
you hear an alarm
from your room?

Take Your Room Key . . . if you're in your room, find your key. Again, if possible, loop it around your wrist with a rubber band.

Test Doors For Heat Before You Open Them . . . with your hand test the door to the hallway to see if it is hot or cool.

Inch the Door Open if It's Cool . . . if the door to the hall is cool, open it carefully, looking out for smoke. Slam it shut fast if there is thick smoke outside, and stay in your room.

Exit If There's No Smoke Outside . . . if the hallway contains little or no smoke, head for the nearest exit.

Hug Walls While Exiting . . . while moving to the nearest exit, keep close to the walls. If it's dark or smoky, count the number of doors to the exit, and feel along the walls as you go.

Exit With Caution . . . test the exit door for heat before opening it—and, again, watch out for thick smoke in the stairwell. If the stairwell is safe, exit down to the street.

Avoid Elevators . . . in case of fire, never use elevators for emergency exits.

Stay Calm . . . don't hurry, keep relaxed, and *think*. Your danger is almost always less than you imagine it to be.

What if...
your exit's
blocked?

Go Back To Your Room . . . should the stairwell start filling with thick smoke, and your exit turns out to be unsafe, if possible return to your room—it's the safest place for you.

Or Otherwise Go To The Roof . . . if you can't return to your room from the stairwell, go up to the roof. There you can wait out the fire or be in position for a possible helicopter rescue.

Stay Calm . . . don't hurry, keep relaxed, and *think*. Your danger is almost always less than you imagine it to be.

What if...
you can't leave
your room?

Stay There...if you can't exit, your room is the safest place to be.

Shut Off The Air Conditioner...to prevent smoke from being sucked into your room, flip the "off-switch" on your air conditioning system.

Stuff Wet Cloth Under The Door...wet towels, sheets or blankets can keep smoke from entering through the crack under your door

Stuff Air Vents With Wet Cloth...this will also keep out smoke.

Remove All Drapes From The Windows...in case fire should enter a window, no fabric will be nearby.

Fill Your Bathtub...keep plenty of water in the tub, and have wastebaskets or icebuckets nearby for carrying water. This way, you can quickly re-moisten the wet cloths that are keeping smoke out.

Phone Your Location...telephone the front desk or building management and tell them your location. If you can't reach them, don't hesitate to call the local fire department—its number is on the inside front page of all phonebooks.

Stay Calm...don't hurry, keep relaxed, and *think*. Your danger is almost always less than you imagine it to be.

What if...
nothing ever
happens to you?

As Chief Andrew C. Casper said at the beginning, probably nothing will.

If you never have a bad experience with fire, there could be several reasons why. Maybe it's because this building is unusually well-constructed to guard against the outbreak of fire. Or maybe you and all its other occupants have been careful not to smoke in bed or to empty ashtrays into wastebaskets.

Or maybe it's because you've understood this booklet. We sincerely hope you have.

Thomas T. Nyhan

Thomas T. Nyhan
Public Fire Educator
Bureau of Fire Prevention
San Francisco Fire Department

Holiday Inns, Inc. Loss Prevention Training Outlines and Instructions: Excerpts from the Loss Control Manual and the Emergency Action Plan

Holiday Inns, Inc., as part of its concern for safety and loss prevention, provides excellent training and training outlines for its corporate property managers in order that a proper professional emphasis may be applied in areas of safety and security. These training aids are also made available to franchise holders who may either use them outright or use them as guides to write their own policies and guidelines. The Appendix has three parts.

Part 1 contains specific instructions for the **training of housekeeping personnel** in matters relating to key controls, safety and security procedures, and the handling of do-not-disturb signs.

Part 2 is an excerpt from a loss control policy manual regarding **Key Controls**.

Part 3 presents representative segments of Holiday Inns **Emergency Action Plan**. This plan also contains guidelines regarding Fire Prevention and Protection. The Plan is used in company inns and is made available to franchise holders as a guideline for the safety and security management of the owner's property. The Plan is also used in the training of Innkeepers at the Holiday Inn University in Olive Branch, Mississippi. Note the degree of detail and formalization in these procedures. Space does not permit reprinting the entire emergency action plan. Other topics covered by the plan but not covered here include: death of a guest, death of an employee, floods, hurricanes/typhoons, tornadoes, winter storms, and civil disturbances.

The appendix concludes with a guest information card that should be placed in each guestroom. The card reminds the guests to be cautious about their own safety. (The guests should never be lulled into a false sense of security whereby they might *abdicate* responsibility for their own safety.)

Appreciation is extended to Holiday Inns, Inc., for allowing the inclusion of these training materials. Procedures are copyrighted (1991) and may not be reproduced without prior permission from Holiday Inns, Inc.

Part One

HOUSEKEEPING PROCEDURES			
SUBJECT		DATE	NUMBER
SECURITY		9.1.81	200.00

TABLE OF CONTENTS

HOUSEKEEPING PROCEDURES

SUBJECT	DATE	NUMBER
KEY CONTROLS	9.1.81	200.01

Key security is of critical importance to the hotel's guests and employees. Severe penalties can be paid by the hotel responsible for thefts or assaults directly related to poor key controls. Access to guest rooms can be gained by taking advantage of careless supervision of master and submaster keys. Therefore, to protect guests and employees from criminal actions, careful attention must be paid to preventing the loss or theft of master and submaster keys.

Coding

o   Code all master and submaster keys.

Issuing Keys

o   Make sure all keys are issued by and turned in to the housekeeping office.

o   Make sure the following information is recorded on a key control sheet:

1) Current date

2) Key code

3) Name of person to whom key will be issued

4) Signature of person to whom key is issued

5) Time that the key is issued

6) Initials of person issuing keys

Custody of Keys

o   Do not allow employees to loan their assigned keys to one another. Such loans increase the chances of keys being lost or stolen and make it harder to trace missing keys.

o   Make sure that room attendants keep their keys with them at all times. Keys must never be left on a cart or laid down in a room; room attendants should keep keys affixed to their person by a leather strap or some other means.

o   Whenever employees leave the property, even for meal breaks, have them sign the keys in on the key control sheet.

| | | | | | | | KEY CONTROL SHEET | | |

KEY CONTROL SHEET

Date 11-18-81   Page 1 of 1

Key Code	Name	Signature	Time Out	Issued By	Time In	Signature	Received By
A-3	Jean Simmons	Jean Simmons	7:30 a.m.	A.D.	3:30 p.m.	Jean Simmons	A.D.
A-4	Joanne Black	Joanne Black	7:30 a.m.	A.D.	3:30 p.m.	Joanne Black	A.D.
A-5	Lisa Schmidt	Lisa Schmidt	7:30 a.m.	A.D.	3:30 p.m.	Lisa Schmidt	A.D.
A-6	Ellen Hardy	Ellen Hardy	7:30 a.m.	A.D.	3:30 p.m.	Ellen Hardy	A.D.

HOUSEKEEPING PROCEDURES

SUBJECT	DATE	NUMBER
KEY CONTROLS	9.1.81	200.01

Returning Assigned Keys

o Check each key turned in against the key record, verifying the key code.

o Make sure the key control sheet is completed with the following entries:

1) Time that the key is turned in

2) Signature of employee returning key

3) Initials of person receiving the keys

Key Storage

o At night, store the floor submasters and storeroom keys in a sturdy, locked key cabinet anchored to the wall in the house-keeping department, or in the assigned house-keeping safe deposit box at the front desk.

o Keep the housekeeping office locked at night.

o During the day, the housekeeper's master key and the keys to the housekeeping office and key storage cabinet should be kept on the executive housekeeper's person.

o At night, log these keys in the key log book maintained at the front desk, and place them in the housekeeping safe deposit box.

Guest Room Keys

o Obtain guest room keys found in check-out rooms from the room attendants and return them to the front desk within an hour after the posted check-out time. These keys should be held in a locked key box on the cart or kept on the room attendant's person until they are picked up by the housekeeper.

HOUSEKEEPING PROCEDURES		
SUBJECT SAFETY AND SECURITY PROCEDURES	DATE 10.1.82	NUMBER 200.02

The housekeeping department makes an important contribution to guest satisfaction by preparing and maintaining clean and orderly guest rooms. Housekeeping personnel can further ensure guest satisfaction by following precautions designed to reduce safety hazards and reinforce security. In addition to protecting guests and their property, employees can help protect themselves from injury and the hotel from serious losses.

Safety

o   All employees should know what actions to take in case of emergencies. The hotel's emergency plan should be discussed with all new employees during orientation, and the procedures should be reviewed periodically at department staff meetings.

o   When an emergency occurs, room attendants should pull their carts into the rooms they are cleaning to avoid blocking the hallways. They should be sure that no one is in the room that they are using. The doors must be <u>closed</u> when they leave to prevent the spread of fire.

Fire Hazards:

o   Housekeeping employees should never smoke in guest rooms or keep lighted cigarettes on room attendant carts.

o   If carts must be stored near electrical equipment, they should be placed far enough away from the equipment to allow air circulation and reduce the risk of fire.

o   At the end of the day, all corridors should be free of linen, trash or any other combustible material.

o   Laundry chutes should be kept shut and locked.

o   Lint filters on dryers should be cleaned at least twice a day. The area under the filters should be cleaned as often as necessary to remove excess lint.

HOUSEKEEPING PROCEDURES

SUBJECT	DATE	NUMBER
SAFETY AND SECURITY PROCEDURES	10.1.82	200.02

Bodily Injury:

o   When mixing chemicals, housekeeping or maintenance employees should always wear gloves and goggles.

o   Housekeeping chemicals must not be given to guests under any circumstances, even though they may request such products. Guests may not follow correct procedures or cautions in the use of these chemicals, and could be injured as a result.

o   Room service trays left in halls should be removed or reported to the appropriate person for pick-up as soon as possible.

o   All cribs should be checked for stability after being set up for guests.

o   Headboards and nightstands attached to the wall should be checked regularly for stability.

o   All nonskid strips in the bathtub should be checked regularly.

o   Light bulbs should be dusted with DRY cloths only.

o   Housekeeping personnel should avoid using excessively long extension cords. When guest room lamps have longer cords than necessary to reach the electrical outlet, the cord should be shortened or tucked under the base of the lamp.

Security

While Cleaning Rooms:

o   All connecting doors, windows and sliding doors must be locked. The guest room door should be checked to be sure it is locked when the room attendant has finished cleaning.

HOUSEKEEPING PROCEDURES

SUBJECT		DATE	NUMBER
SAFETY AND SECURITY PROCEDURES		10.1.82	200.02

o   Room attendants must not permit anyone to enter the rooms they are cleaning unless the person can produce the key to that room.

Personal and Property Protection:

o   Employees should notify management <u>immediately</u> of any persons loitering on the property or otherwise behaving in a questionable manner.

o   Guest rooms should never be left with the door open (including on change or vacant rooms).

o   Rooms must never be opened for guests who claim they are locked out; guests should be referred to the front desk for admittance to the rooms with an explanation that it is for their own protection.

o   All storage rooms should be locked at all times.

o   Room attendant carts should not be left unattended in hallways; when not being used, they should be placed in a vacant guest room or in a storeroom.

HOUSEKEEPING PROCEDURES		
SUBJECT DO NOT DISTURB SIGNS	DATE 12.1.82	NUMBER 200.03

Rooms with "Do Not Disturb" signs left on the door must be investigated by management if the sign is on the door two hours after the posted check-out time. The sign should be reported to the executive housekeeper by the room attendant to whom the room was assigned for cleaning. It should be noted on the Housekeeping Assignment Sheet.

This practice is not meant as a violation of the guest's privacy. It is established for the protection of the guest who may be ill or otherwise unable to contact the front desk when in need of help.

Procedures: NOTE: If at any time during the check of the room you are able to contact the guest, apologize for disturbing the guest. Explain that the hotel was concerned for the guest's welfare. Ask if the guest would like to have the room cleaned.

1) Check with the front desk to make sure that the guest is not a late arrival from the previous night, or has checked in during the morning.

A guest who is a late arrival or an early check-in could still be resting and should not be disturbed. Special arrangements may have to be made for cleaning these rooms later in the day.

2) Try to contact the guest by phone.

3) If there is no answer, go to the guest room. Take another employee with you in case you should need help.

4) Knock on the guest room door and call out "Housekeeping."

5) If there is no response, check to see if the deadbolt on the door has been thrown.

6) When the door is not bolted, open the door and identify yourself before entering.

o If no one is in the room, and there are no unusual conditions requiring further attention, leave the room as it is. Close the door, and leave the "Do Not Disturb" sign on the knob.

o If you should find a guest who is ill or unconscious in the room, summon help immediately.

HOUSEKEEPING PROCEDURES		
SUBJECT DO NOT DISTURB SIGNS	DATE 12.1.82	NUMBER 200.03

7) When the door is <u>bolted</u>, and the room cannot be entered through a connecting door or a sliding glass door, report the room to the manager on duty for further investigation.

Part Two

Key Controls

It is essential for each facility to establish sound key control procedures. These procedures should include regular inventories, secure storage, and replacement of locks when necessary.

Key Inventories

Departmental Keys - Department heads should inventory and list all keys within their departments in order to account for them at any given time.

Guest Room Duplicating Keys, Key Blanks, and Key Cutting Machines - Accountability for and custody of all guest room duplicating keys, key blanks, and key cutting machines should be the responsibility of the chief engineer/maintenance chief of each property. Inventories of the guest room duplicating keys should be conducted every three months, and the results furnished to the general manager. In the event that any of the keys are missing, the appropriate room locks should be changed immediately.

Safe Deposit Box Keys - All safe deposit box keys should be inventoried every three months.

Guest Room Keys - It is suggested that hotels have an inventory at least six keys for *each* guest room. Three of the six keys remain at the desk for guest use. The other three keys are kept in a locked, metal cabinet in the front office area. The key to this cabinet is locked in a separate cabinet under the control of a person designated by the general manager.

Keep a list of room numbers in the front office storage cabinet. As keys are taken out, the number of keys removed, the date, and the initials of the person removing the keys are written next to the room number on the list. When three keys to a particular room are lost, a maintenance request should be written to change the lock before the remaining three room keys are lost. No guest room keys should be duplicated without changing the cylinder or core. Only the maintenance engineer and/or designee are authorized to duplicate keys.

Keys, if attached to a tag, should have no identification on the key itself. The attached tag should have minimal identification, at most the Holiday Inn logo or the words "Holiday Inn" and the room number. for security purposes the particular hotel should not be identified by name and address.

Keys without tags may be stamped with a room number. In this case, it would still not be possible to identify a particular hotel with a key.

When a guest requests a second room key due to a lock out or some other reason, ask for his/her name, room number and identification such as a driver's license. When no identification can be provided at the time, the guest should sign his/her name for signature comparison with the registration card. If the person claims to be another registered occupant of the room (such as a family member) the room should be called. If there is no answer, the guest should be accompanied to the room by the MOD or front desk employee. The guest should *not* be given the key until some identification has been established. At no time should this person be permitted in the room alone. Note on the appropriate folio or registration card any additional room keys issued.

At check out time, front desk personnel should tactfully ask departing guests if all keys have been turned in. A locked drop box, identified as a depository for keys, may be installed near the front door as an additional reminder to guests. Empty the drop box periodically, and return the keys recovered to the front desk.

When a room attendant finds a key in the room of a departed guest, that key should be kept with the room attendant if a lock box is not provided on the housekeeping cart. These keys should be given to the housekeeper who returns them to the front desk. Keys found in a guest room door by hotel personnel should be removed from the door lock and returned to the front desk.

Security of Keys

Emergency Keys - The emergency "E" key should be kept by the general manager or locked in his office safe. A second "E" key should be kept at the front desk for use in emergencies. It should be kept in a secure place, such as a safe deposit box or a glass-fronted key box mounted on the wall. This key can be released when the key control log is signed, and is for use by the assistant general manager or designated management person.

Duplicating Master Keys - Keys used for duplication of storeroom, submaster, and master keys, as well as spare in-house administrative safe deposit keys, are to be retained in the general manager's locked office safe.

Guest Room Duplicating Keys - The guest room duplicating keys and the key blanks should be kept inside a locked metal key cabinet on the wall and made with hinges that cannot be removed. The cabinet should remain locked when not in use, and the key should be removed from the lock. Both the key cabinet and the key cutting machine should be in a secured part of the maintenance department.

If removable cores are used, the spare cores with their respective keys should also be kept in the same key cabinet. Only the general manager, the chief engineer, and the designated assistant chief engineer should have the keys to the cabinet.

Unassigned Safe Deposit Box Keys - These keys can be kept in a key tray in a designated safe deposit box to which front desk personnel have access for issuing keys to guests. The hotel's safe deposit control key is not to be left in any safe deposit key slot. Instead, it should be kept in a secure location that is under the control of the guest service shift leader and inaccessible to unauthorized personnel.

Removable Core Sections and Control Keys - A spare submastered section of lock cores with their keys should be stored in the general manager's safe. The spare core section should be used to immediately replace any guest room section for which a submaster key has been lost, stolen, or compromised.

> NOTE: If a master, grand master, control, or emergency key is lost, stolen, or compromised, telephone the Loss Prevention Department and increase the frequency of security patrols.

Spare control keys should also be stored in the general manager's safe. The keys should be placed in a sealed envelope, and the general manager should initial the flap of the envelope before it is placed in the safe.

One control key should be maintained by the general manager in a locked key cabinet or under the same locked security as other critical keys in his custody. The control key may be issued to the chief engineer as needed to change door locks. This key should be signed out and its return recorded in a key log. When not in use, it should be retained under the control of the general manager.

Individual Key Controls

General Manager's Keys - These keys are kept on the general manager's person and locked in the office safe when he/she leaves the premises.

Assistant General Manager/Food and Beverage Manager Keys - These keys are to be kept by the assistant general manager.

When the assistant general manager leaves the property, the keys should be locked in the key cabinet in the food and beverage department's office, and the office should also be locked.

If no key cabinet is available in the food and beverage department's office, the keys should be locked in a safe deposit box, and the key to the box should be kept by the food and beverage manager. The general manager should also have a key to the box so it can be opened in case of an emergency.

Assistant Food and Beverage Manager Keys - These keys are to be maintained in a locked key cabinet in the food and beverage department's office under the supervision of the food and beverage manager. If no office key cabinet is available, the keys should be stored in a separate safe deposit box at the front desk.

Housekeeper/Room Attendant Keys - The housekeeping department keys should be kept in a metal key cabinet mounted on a wall in the department's office. The cabinet should be locked when not in use. After regular working hours, both the cabinet and the office should be locked. Keys to the office and the key cabinet should be maintained by the executive housekeeper and the assistant housekeeper. An emergency set of keys should be kept in the general manager's safe.

Submaster keys are issued daily to housekeeping personnel and their custody recorded by the executive housekeeper. Each key should be coded and the code recorded in the housekeeping key control log. A sample of this form is shown as Exhibit 1, "Key Control Sheet", on page 389.

Housekeeping employees should carry assigned room pass keys attached to their uniforms by lanyard, key chain, ribbon or by other acceptable means to prevent loss or theft. These keys are turned in daily to the housekeeper for storage in an approved double-locked area within the housekeeping department or locked in a private safe deposit box at the front desk. The housekeeper and assistant housekeeper should each retain an access key.

Any keys to be kept past regular working hours should be placed in an envelope that is sealed and initialed by the person returning the keys. The initials should be written across the seal so it cannot be broken without detection. The envelope is then signed in on the key log at the front desk and placed in the drop box.

Maintenance Personnel Keys - The chief engineer should keep the maintenance department keys in a locked metal cabinet mounted on a wall in the department's office. The cabinet should be locked when not in use. After regular working hours both the cabinet and the office should be locked. Keys to the office

and the key cabinet should be maintained by the chief engineer and the assistant chief engineer. An emergency set of keys should be kept in the general manager's safe.

All maintenance master keys are issued daily by the chief engineer to designated members of the maintenance staff. These keys are to be attached to their uniforms or belts in a suitable and secure manner. At the end of the day, the keys are to be returned to a safe deposit box, or to the approved, double-locked area within the maintenance department.

Any keys to be kept past regular working hours should be placed in an envelope that is sealed and initialed by the person returning the keys. The initials should be written across the seal so it cannot be broken without detection. The envelope is then signed in on the key log at the front desk and placed in the drop box.

Bar Keys - One onset of bar keys is to be signed for and issued to the senior bartender of the first shift to allow the lounge to be opened and to give access to the par stock of liquor, cooled beer, and wine. Keys are to be passed to the senior bar attendant of each shift, with the closing shift signing the keys back in and placing them in a safe deposit "drop-slot" box.

Kitchen Staff Keys - One set of daily provision work box keys is signed out at the front desk by the chef on the first shift. Afterwards it is passed from chef to chef, and, when the kitchen closes, is dropped in the safe deposit box and signed in. This procedure applies only to daily provision work boxes, and not to freezers or storage lockers containing valuable goods (controlled by the food and beverage manager).

Security of Banks and Cashier Keys - Each bank should be stored in a safe deposit box that must be opened with two keys.

One key to the safe deposit box is issued to every cashier for their respective shift banks. A receipt for the key should be signed by each cashier and placed in the personnel files. The key must be returned at the time of the employee's resignation.

The hotel's safe deposit master key is controlled by the guest service shift leader. Whenever the bank is removed from or returned to the box, both the cashier's key and the master key must be used together to open and close the box.

A record should be kept by the guest service shift leader each time that the safe deposit box is opened. The record should show the following:

- Date and time the box was opened
- Signature of the cashier
- Signature of the guest service shift leader

Assigned Safe Deposit Box Keys - These keys are kept by each box holder with the office control key held at the desk. There are to be no duplicate safe deposit box keys for boxes assigned to guests. Access keys to unassigned safe deposit boxes should be stored in a locked safe deposit box with access restricted to the guest service representatives on duty.

Security Keys - One set of essential submaster keys is signed out at the front desk by the senior guard of the first shift and is passed on to the next shift as appropriate. These keys are to be returned to the front desk and signed in. In cases of continuous security, appropriate submaster keys should be signed out to the head of security and retained in the security department on a continuing basis. They should be inventoried monthly to insure integrity of the key control system.

No hotel keys should leave the property with the exception of an office entrance key or the access key to a private lock box at the front desk.

Duplication of Keys

Any request for the duplication of storeroom, submaster, or master keys must be submitted in writing to the general manager who thoroughly reviews the request before granting approval. Approval must be in writing. If the key was broken, the broken parts should be given to the general manager for comparison with the master duplicator. If the key was lost, the circumstances under which it was lost (how, where, and when) should be discussed to determine the need for changing the locks that could be opened by the lost key.

When three spare room keys from the front office key cabinet have been placed in use, a request should be made for the room lock to be changed before all remaining keys are missing. When the lock is changed, six keys for the replacing lock are to be made available. The remaining keys to the original lock will be retrieved by maintenance from the front desk. No additional keys are to be duplicated which will allow a delay in changing the lock in the guest room door.

If the room lock is changed while the room occupants are absent, a notice indicating the change should be placed over the lock on the corridor side of the door. This notice may be worded as follows: "Room lock changed as a routine security procedure. Please obtain a key at the front desk." Guests in affected rooms may exchange on a key-for-key basis at the front desk after their identity as a registered room guest has been verified. Guests who are in their rooms at the time the lock change occurs may exchange keys with the maintenance representative on a key-for-key exchange basis.

The maintenance engineer and/or designee are the only persons authorized to duplicate keys. If an unauthorized person enters the room, rotate the core.

Two key control records should be maintained by the chief engineer: a guest room key duplication record and a core or cylinder rotation log. These records are to be kept in accordance with key control procedures.

All key records, including those showing keys issued after hours, should be reviewed monthly by the general manager. This check should reveal any patterns of access by personnel, or a weakness in the hotel's key control program which needs attention. Key control records should be retained for the same length of time as the statute of limitations for a civil law suit.

Exhibit 1

KEY CONTROL SHEET

Date _____

Page _____ of _____

Key Code	Name	Signature	Time Out	Issued By	Time In	Signature	Received By

Part Three: Segments of Holiday Inns' Emerging Action Plan

Handling of Do Not Disturb Signs

Guest rooms with "DO NOT DISTURB" signs left on the door two hours after posted check-out time must be investigated by management in accordance with existing procedures. This practice is not to violate a guest's privacy, but is for the protection of the guest who may be ill or otherwise unable to contact the front desk. Prior to taking any action, front desk records should be checked to verify that the guest was not an early morning arrival. These persons could still be resting and should not be disturbed.

The housekeeper or the housekeeper's assistant will try to contact the guest by telephone. If there is no answer, either of these two management personnel accompanied by another employee should go to the guest room. They will knock on the door several times and announce, "Housekeeping." If there is still no answer, the room should be entered by both employees using their access key.

The room and bath should be checked to determine that the guest is not incapacitated. After determining there is no ill or incapacitated guest in the room, the employees should leave, making sure the door is properly closed and locked. A message should be left for the guest at the front desk noting the room was not serviced because of the guest's expressed wishes. The room telephone message light should be activated to advise the guest to contact the front desk for this message. The guest should be informed that clean towels are available if desired.

Accidents

When a guest has an accident at your hotel, these important procedures should be used.

- Be courteous and do not argue.

- When the injury is slight, render first-aid, if practical. If further attention is necessary, have the guest taken to the nearest doctor or hospital emergency room by taxi.

- When the injury is serious, an ambulance should be called and the individual should be taken to the nearest hospital emergency room at once.

- Do not discuss the cause of the accident or offer any opinions about the accident.

- Correct any problems on the premises as soon as possible.

- Do not discuss insurance or claim settlements with the guest.

- If necessary, contact the claims adjustment organization by telephone.

- If the guest is admitted to the hospital, make an inventory in the presence of witnesses, of the personal effects left in the room. Relatives claiming these items should sign the inventory list as the receipt for the items.

- Make detailed notes concerning the cause of the accident and the condition of the guest (thick glasses, slurred speech, smell of alcohol, and other noticeable details). At the discretion of hotel management, photographs of the area where the accident occurred may be taken.

- Obtain all pertinent information and submit a Loss and Incident Report.

Fire Prevention

The Emergency Fire-Fighting Organization

Fire Extinguishers

Fire Protection Equipment

Fire Prevention Tips

The Emergency Fire-Fighting Organization

Each hotel should have an emergency organization which can respond to a fire. The emergency organization uses in-house equipment to fight the fire until relieved by the local fire department. The following diagram shows the positions to be filled in the emergency organization.

HOLIDAY INNS

EMERGENCY ORGANIZATION

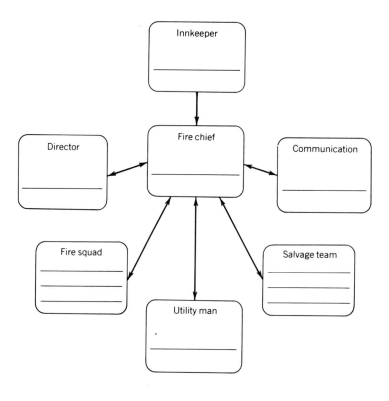

- The communications member of the committee calls the fire department, notifies the emergency organization, and coordinates evacuation of the building if told to do so by the general manager, public fire official, or in-house fire chief.

Director:
- This individual will direct fire fighters to the scene of the fire.
- He will then keep driveways open until relieved by public authorities.

Salvage Team:
- The salvage team should consist of three to six people who are responsible for minimizing water and smoke damage during and after the fire.
- The team should have mops, squeegees, rags, and other cleaning equipment ready, and have rolls of plastic available to cover exposed carpet and furniture.

The emergency organization should conduct a fire drill monthly on each shift. The local fire department should be invited to witness and participate in at least one fire drill annually. The drill results should be recorded on a form. These reports should be maintained on file at the hotel for one year.

EMERGENCY ORGANIZATION FIRE DRILL

Hotel:

Shift on which the drill was conducted:

Fire Chief:

Date drill was conducted:

Emergency Organization members present:

Location of mock fire: Type of fire:

Type of fire equipment available in area of use:

List deviations from normal procedure:

Corrective actions necessary:

_____

Emergency Organization Chief

Fire Extinguishers

A fire extinguisher can only be as effective as its operator. All employees should be familiar with the use and operation of the various types of fire extinguishers on the property.

When To Use A Fire Extinguisher

A fire extinguisher should *not* be used to fight a fire when:

- The fire is spreading rapidly beyond the point of origin.
- The fire could block the user's exit.
- The user is not sure how to operate the extinguisher.

An extinguisher should be used to fight a fire when:

- The fire department has been called.
- The fire is small (confined to its origin, as in a mattress, waste basket, cushion or small appliance).
- The person using the extinguisher can fight the fire with his back to an exit.
- The extinguisher is in working order and the individual knows how to use it.

Guidelines for Extinguisher Placement and Service

Follow these basic guidelines in placing and servicing extinguishers in your hotel:

- One class 2A fire extinguisher can serve approximately 3,000 square feet of floor area.
- The maximum distance between class A extinguishers should be 75 ft.
- Extinguishers should be selected and located to fit the hazards in the area.
- Extinguishers should be hung with operating instructions facing out.
- Number each extinguisher and record its location for easy maintenance and inspection.
- Maintain all extinguishers in a fully charged and operative condition at all times.
- Replace immediately any extinguisher that is removed from its proper location.

- Extinguishers should be checked monthly and serviced annually.

NOTE: Inverting types of extinguishers and pyrene extinguishers are no longer approved and should be phased out.

Categories of Fires

There are four classes of fires, based upon the different types of combustible materials:

Class A - Common Combustibles: Paper, cloth, wood and most plastics.

Class B - Flammable Liquids: Grease, paint, oil, solvents, gasoline, etc.

Class C - Electrical: Wiring, appliances, motors. Any energized electrical equipment.

Class D - Combustible Metals: Magnesium titanium, sodium (because of the infrequent occurrence of Class D fires in hotels, no further reference will be made to this type fire.)

The chart shown as Exhibit 2 on page 396 illustrates the types of extinguishers required for use on the three types of fires that can occur in hotels.

Alarm Systems

If the fire alarm system becomes inoperative, immediately notify the general manager, the fire department, the Holiday Inn Loss Prevention Department, and the hotel's insurance carrier. The repair company should be contacted and asked for expedited service. One or more persons should be given the responsibility for a fire watch that patrols the affected area, and necessary precautions should be taken to maintain the safety of employees and guests.

When the repairs are completed and have been satisfactorily tested, obtain written certification from the servicing company of the repairs that were made and of the fact that the system was made fully operational. File the certification.

All aforementioned persons and organizations should be informed of the return to normal operations.

Exhibit 2

TYPE OF EXTINGUISHER	WATER		LOADED STREAM	CARBON-DIOXIDE	DRY CHEMICAL									
					REGULAR OR ORDINARY		POTASSIUM BICARBONATE "PURPLE K"		POTASSIUM CHLORIDE KCL		MULTI-PURPOSE "ABC"		POTASSIUM BICARBONATE/UREA	
	STORED PRESSURE	PUMP TANK	STORED PRESSURE		STORED PRESSURE*	CARTRIDGE OPERATED	STORED PRESSURE*	CARTRIDGE OPERATED	STORED PRESSURE*	CARTRIDGE OPERATED	STORED PRESSURE*	CARTRIDGE OPERATED	STORED PRESSURE	CARTRIDGE OPERATED
SIZES COMMONLY IN USE (NOMINAL CAPACITY)	2½ Gal.	2½ and 5 Gal.	2½ Gal.*	2½ to 20 lbs.*	2 to 30 lbs.*	4 to 30 lbs.*	2 to 30 lbs.*	4 to 30 lbs.*	2 to 30 lbs.*	4 to 30 lbs.*	2 to 30 lbs.*	4 to 30 lbs.*	11 to 23 lbs.*	11 to 23 lbs.*
CLASSIFICATION OF FIRES (See explanation at bottom of table) — A	Yes	Yes	Yes	No	No	No	No	No	No	No	Yes	Yes	No	No
B	No	No	Yes	Yes	Yes	Yes	Yes	Yes	Yes	Yes	Yes	Yes	Yes	Yes
C	No	No	No	Yes	Yes	Yes	Yes	Yes	Yes	Yes	Yes	Yes	Yes	Yes
D	No	No	No	No	No	No	No	No	No	No	No	No	No	No
EXTINGUISHING AGENT	Water	Water	Alkali-Metal Salt Solution	Carbon Dioxide	Sodium Bicarbonate Base		Potassium Bicarbonate Base		Potassium Chloride Base		Ammonium Phosphate Base		Potassium Bicarbonate/Urea Base	
APPROXIMATE HORIZONTAL RANGE	30-40 ft.	30-40 ft.	30-40 ft.	3 to 8 ft.*	5 to 20 ft.*	5 to 20 ft.*	5 to 20 ft.*	5 to 20 ft.*	5 to 20 ft.*	5 to 20 ft.*	5 to 20 ft.*	5 to 20 ft.*	5 to 30 ft.*	5 to 30 ft.*
APPROXIMATE DISCHARGE TIME	1 Minute	1 to 2 Minutes	1 Minute*	8 to 30 Sec.*	8 to 25 Sec.*	8 to 25 Sec.*	8 to 25 Sec.*	8 to 25 Sec.*	8 to 25 Sec.*	8 to 25 Sec.*	8 to 25 Sec.*	8 to 25 Sec.*	20 to 31 Sec.*	20 to 31 Sec.*
MINIMUM INSPECTION & MAINTENANCE	*MONTHLY:* Inspection — *SEMI-ANNUALLY:* Complete maintenance which may include recharging. In certain locations more frequent inspections may be required.													
HYDROSTATIC MINIMUM TEST INTERVAL▲	5 Yrs.		5 Yrs.	5 Yrs.	5 Years on Stainless Steel, or Soldered-Brass Shells. 12 Years on Aluminum, Brazed-Brass or Mild-Steel Shells. (See Para. 1330 on reverse).									
PROTECTION REQUIRED BELOW 40° FAHRENHEIT, No extinguisher can be stored above 120° Farenheit	Yes	Yes	No	No	No	No	No	No	No	No	No	No	No	No

Smoke Detectors

Many hotels have been provided with smoke detection equipment. There are two basic types of detectors in use.

The photoelectric detector operates on a simple mechanism which transmits a beam of light from one cell to another. As the smoke enters the light chamber, the intensity of the light beam is reduced. This reduction of light causes the detector to alarm.

The ionization detector operates by ionizing the air in a special chamber. Smoke particles entering the chamber upset the normal ionization which results in an alarm condition.

Smoke detectors, once installed, cannot be forgotten. To maximize proper operation, test the detectors according to the manufacturer's instructions, or as specified by the governmental authority having jurisdiction. Record the test dates and response times. A detector which has a very slow response time, or one that fails, should be replaced immediately.

The Preventive Maintenance Manual and the instructions left by the company that installs the alarm system should be followed for routine maintenance of the hotel's system. (Obtain instructions from the installation company if they cannot be found on the property.) Problems which develop and cannot be corrected by the hotel's maintenance personnel should be brought to the attention of the installation company immediately.

If local officials of the fire marshal's office inspect the hotel and indicate that additional fire protection equipment is necessary to comply with the local fire code, please contact the Loss Prevention Department for assistance in complying with the code.

Procedures for maintaining and testing other fire protection equipment can be found in the Property Operations Maintenance Manual.

Fire Prevention Tips

Public Areas

- Provide receptacles for smoking materials.
- Keep all storage out of stairways.
- Keep laundry and trash chute doors closed and locked when not in use.

Maintenance and Engineering

- Flammable liquids should be stored in flammable liquid cabinets.
- Oily rags should be stored in covered metal containers.
- Welding and cutting areas should be free of all combustibles.

Laundry and Housekeeping

- Dryer lint screens should be cleaned at least daily.

- Fusible links should be installed at the bottom of all linen and trash chutes.
- Combustibles should be kept at least three (3) feet from all heaters and dryer flames.

Kitchen

- Clean kitchen hood filters and ducts regularly. Kitchen hood filters should be cleaned daily.
- Install an eight (8) inch baffle between the deep fryer and the open top flames of the stove, unless there is at least an eighteen (18) inch separation between these two appliances.
- Turn all stoves and appliances off when the kitchen closes.

Front Desk and Office Equipment

- Keep electrical space heaters at least three (3) feet from combustibles.
- Do not overload electrical circuits by using multi-plug adapters.

Bomb Threats

When there has been organized, advance planning to handle bomb threats, the actual threat can be handled without panic. No two incidents will be alike, but the following guidelines are set forth to assist you.

Written Bomb Threat

Rarely will the hotel receive a bomb threat in the form of a letter, note, or telegram. However, should this occur, the message and envelope should be handled carefully and at the corners to preserve fingerprints and other available evidence. Protect the document and the envelope and give it to the general manager, or the individual acting in his absence. Inform the police and FBI of the contents of the note.

If the letter is delivered by a messenger, detain the messenger for police questioning, if possible. If the messenger has left the area, the employee accepting the note should immediately prepare a memorandum listing the circumstances, the time that the message was received, any known witnesses, and a detailed description of the messenger.

Oral Bomb Threat

Any employee who becomes aware of a bomb threat through personal contact or by overhearing someone make such a threat, should advise the general manager quickly and quietly, making every effort not to alarm the guests. The police should be called promptly.

The person issuing the threat should be kept under observation, if possible, and the person's physical characteristics noted. These include race, sex, age, height, weight and build, color of hair and eyes, a description of clothes and jewelry, and any other identifying features like a beard, scars, or limp.

If this person leaves the hotel before he can be stopped to determine his identity, record the mode of transportation and the direction. This would include a bus number, the car company and number, an automobile description (make and model, license plate number and state), and the number of persons in the car.

These facts should be furnished to the general manager immediately for communication to security and the police.

Telephone Bomb Threat

A person normally calls to report that a bomb is set to explode in your hotel because:

- The caller placed the bomb, or has learned of the placement of the bomb, and wants to reduce personal injury or property damage, or
- The caller wants to disrupt normal business activity by creating an atmosphere of panic and anxiety at your facility.

Bomb threats are most often received at the switchboard on the publicly listed telephone number. The call is usually brief so that there is no chance to trace the number. Therefore, it is imperative that all information be recorded accurately by the operator in order to provide security and the police with documented information. A Telephone Procedures Bomb Threat Checklist, included in this section as Exhibit 3 on page 401, should be used to make a detailed record of the call. In the event of a bomb threat, responsibilities should be delegated as follows:

Operator Instructions:

When a bomb threat is received by phone, the operator should remain calm and respond in the following manner:

- Note the exact time that the call was received.
- Try to have another employee monitor the call to duplicate any information obtained through the call.
- Listen to every word spoken and pay attention to background noises.
- Ask the caller to repeat the message to keep him on the line as long as possible.

- Engage him in conversation through brief questions to determine the following:
- Expected explosion time
- The location of the bomb
- What type of explosives are being used
- How the bomb can be recognized
- What would set it off
- The caller's motive for setting the bomb
- What would influence him to change his tactics

(See the Telephone Procedures Bomb Threat Checklist included in this section as Exhibit 3.)

- Tell the caller of the large number of guests registered at the hotel, and describe the many innocent adults and children who may be killed or injured.

- When the caller hangs up, be sure the general manager or assistant has all the details so one of them can inform the police. This incident should not be discussed with unauthorized personnel in order to avoid rumors or unnecessary panic.

General Manager Instructions:

- Notify the police and the fire department; hotel security and maintenance; Alcohol, Tobacco and Firearms (ATF); and the Federal Bureau of Investigation (FBI) as soon as possible.

- Start a chronological record of actions and events. Carefully review all the facts obtained, evaluating the validity of the information furnished by the caller. Discuss the call with police to determine whether a partial or complete evacuation of the building should be ordered. Police may have advice to offer based upon any recent information they have. (For more details, see the article entitled "Evacuation Procedures" in this section.)

- As soon as possible, complete the telephone bomb threat checklist with the employee who took the call while the events are still fresh in his or her mind.

- Based on the amount of information received about the bomb location, decide whether to make a localized or general search. (For more details, see the article entitled "Search Procedures" in this section.)

- If the caller indicated that he would call back, the telephone company security office should be advised.

- Notify appropriate personnel to institute a search.

- Set up a command post at the best communications center, which is usually the switchboard.

Security Manager Instructions:

- Assist the general manager in evaluating the operator's information received from the caller.

- Be sure that emergency organizations have been notified by the general manager.

- Alert security staff to stand-by (including off-duty men).

Exhibit 3

TELEPHONE PROCEDURES BOMB THREAT CHECKLIST

INSTRUCTIONS: BE CALM, BE COURTEOUS, LISTEN, DO NOT INTERRUPT THE CALLER, NOTIFY SUPERVISOR/SECURITY OFFICER BY A PREARRANGED SIGNAL WHILE THE CALLER IS ON LINE.

NAME OF OPERATOR_____ TIME_____ DATE_____

CALLER'S IDENTITY:

____Male ____Female ____Adult ____Juvenile ____Approximate Age

ORIGIN OF CALL:

____Local ____Long Distance ____Booth ____Internal

TIME CALL ENDED_____ HOTEL_____

BOMB FACTS

KEEP CALLER TALKING—IF CALLER SEEMS AGREEABLE TO FURTHER CONVERSATION, ASK QUESTIONS SUCH AS:

When will it go off? Certain Hour_____ Time Remaining_____

Where is it located? Building_____ Floor____ Room____

What kind of bomb?_____ What is the explosive?_____

How do you know so much about the bomb?_____

What is your name and address?_____

If building is occupied, inform caller that detonation could cause injury or death.

Did caller appear familiar with building by his or her description of the bomb location?

Write out the message in its entirety and any other comments on a separate sheet of paper and attach to this checklist.

VOICE FEATURES
____LOUD   ____SOFT
____HIGH PITCH   ____DEEP
____DISGUSTED   ____GRUFF

SPEECH
____FAST   ____SLOW
____DISTINCT   ____GARBLED
____SLURRED   ____LISP

LANGUAGE
____EXCELLENT   ____POOR
____FOUL   ____OTHER

ACCENT
____LOCAL   ____FOREIGN
____RACE   ____REGIONAL

ATTITUDE
____CALM   ____DEMANDING
____RATIONAL   ____ANGRY
____COHERENT   ____IRRATIONAL
____DELIBERATE   ____INCOHERENT
____LAUGHING   ____EXCITED

BACKGROUND NOISE
____ANIMALS   ____TRAINS
____MUSIC   ____QUIET
____CONFUSION   ____VOICES
____AIRPLANES   ____GAIETY
____OFFICE   ____FACTORY
MACHINES   MACHINES
____STREET
TRAFFIC

NOTIFY PROPER MANAGEMENT EMPLOYEE/AUTHORITIES IMMEDIATELY AFTER CALL.

Evacuation Procedures

These procedural guidelines can be used when the decision is made to evacuate any part of a building for any reason. At all times, the personal safety of the guests and employees should have priority.

In a large building that is structurally sound, authorities may not wish to evacuate all floors even if a bomb is found, because of the risk of panic. Normally initial evacuation would include the floor on which the bomb is found, and the two floors above and below that floor.

A record of chronological activity should be established.

Before an evacuation is put into effect, personnel should be dispatched to the stairwell entrances on each floor to direct and reassure the guests. Elevators, initially, may not be used, and should be returned to the main floor.

In a calm voice, the general manager should make an announcement over the public address system, similar to the following example, and repeat the message at least once:

"Attention please – Attention please – the management requests that all guests and visitors evacuate the hotel (or evacuate specific floors) as a precaution. Please leave the building by the nearest exit. Walk, do not run, please."

In fire evacuation the message should instruct guests to close room windows and doors. In bomb threat evacuation, the message should instruct guests to leave windows open. DO NOT MENTION THE REASON FOR EVACUATION.

When directed by the general manager, the switchboard operator should systematically begin to ring the rooms, indicating to the guests the following:

"I am sorry to disturb you, but the management has asked that all guests in your area vacate their rooms, immediately, for security reasons. Please use the stairwell at the ends of the corridor to leave the floor." (In fire evacuation), "Please close all windows and doors behind you." (In bomb evacuation), "Please leave your windows open."

The switchboard rack should be checked to determine if any cards are marked with a colored "flag" to indicate that handicapped guests are registered at the hotel. When there are handicapped guests staying in the hotel, employees should be sent to the rooms occupied by these guests to assist them in evacuating the hotel. When the guest is deaf, but is accompanied by someone who can hear, the switchboard operator should call the room to inform both guests that someone is coming to assist them.

Many telephone companies provide switchboards capable of simultaneous calling to a group of rooms. If this is available at your hotel, it should be used.

List rooms not responding to the switchboard's call. Contact room occupants personally for their safety.

Highrise Buildings

Due to the structural make-up of highrise buildings, initial and immediate evacuation should be carried out on the two floors above the fire, the fire floor, and at least one floor below.

Doors to stair towers should be kept closed, but floor monitors should remain in the vicinity of these doors to let people out of their stair tower. Elevators should be returned to the main floor and locked at that location.

If it is necessary to evacuate the entire building, have the fire department determine what elevators, if any, may be released for evacuation. Direct occupants of floors which can be evacuated to these elevator banks. However, under no circumstances are elevators to be used by anyone on the floor where the fire is located. On the floor where the fire is contained, evacuation should be made by using the nearest available exit which can be reached safely.

To regulate the flow of persons in the stairwells, alternate floors may be assigned different stairwells, thus providing an interval of two full flights between evacuating floors.

Security personnel should be at each entrance to the building to oversee the evacuation and to prevent anyone from entering.

Emergency equipment arriving at the hotel should be directed by security or a member of management to the scene of the emergency. All personnel should calmly reassure the guests of their safety to make an orderly departure from the area easier.

On the ground level, guests from the stairwells should be directed by hotel personnel to an assembly area two hundred feet or more from the emergency vehicle routes and should be behind solid cover in bomb threats as protection from possible blast effects.

If the location of the bomb, in bomb threat emergencies, is known, at least the floor on which the bomb is found, and the floors above and below it, should be evacuated, or if responsible officials request this action, do not hesitate to comply. In multi-story buildings, persons on the floors above the location should be evacuated first.

Personnel on each floor should have a pass key to check every guest room to be sure that all guests have received, understood, and complied with the evacuation instructions. The elderly and the handicapped will require special assistance.

As the evacuation begins, shut down the air-conditioning and ventilation system and, in fire emergencies, start the smoke exhaust fans in the stairwells.

Turn off all gas and fuel lines at the main connection. This should be accomplished by knowledgeable personnel who are familiar with equipment shut-down procedures and, when it is safe, will be able to place back in safe operation, the boilers, furnaces, pumps, and appliances.

Cashiers must close and lock registers, or if time allows, place their cash in the safe, which is then locked by the senior management person.

Guests can be assisted further if a diagram of the floor is posted at each elevator entrance and in each room, identifying the location of the emergency stairwells.

Provisions should be made to have first-aid and other emergency equipment available.

Search Procedures

The security manager or the person appointed by the general manager to handle emergencies is the coordinator of all searches. He ensures that specific areas are completely searched. The coordinator establishes a search center (usually in the lobby) where floor plans are made available as aids in setting up search areas.

A search of the hotel is made easier if all utility closets and housekeeping storerooms are kept locked routinely except when actually in use.

Operational personnel and department heads with master keys should assemble at the search center. All search personnel are given a description of the object of the search at this central location. If the item is a bomb, instruct everyone not to touch or disturb any suspicious objects, but to report them to the search center.

Give professional personnel complete authority when they arrive. Hotel personnel, who know the layout of the hotel buildings well, can give special assistance.

General Search Procedures

Divide the building into sections using the floor plan diagram.

- The search is made easier if personnel are assigned areas with which they are most familiar, and department heads search their respective areas of responsibility.

- Appoint a warden or overseer for each floor. If the floor area is quite large, it should be divided into several sections with an overseer for each section. Each overseer reports his results to search control as the search progresses. Search control clearly marks, on the plans, those areas cleared and those still questionable, to keep up with the progress of the search.

- Never use a larger search force than is absolutely necessary.

- Do not assume that only one explosive device has been planted. If one is found, con-

tinue searching operations until the whole area is checked.

- Experience has shown that stairwells and restrooms are the areas where most explosive devices are found in public buildings. These areas should be searched immediately.

Search Procedures for Explosive Devices

A search for an explosive device requires additional safety precautions. The following is a list of steps to take. An asterisk (*) is placed before those applying primarily to bomb searches.

- Before entering a room or area, divide the site into two sections, drawing an imaginary line between two objects in the room. Starting at floor level, searchers progress into the room, working away from each other and checking every item in the room up to a height of eye level.

- If the search to eye level height reveals nothing of significance, the area up to the ceiling should be checked in the respective section. Continue upward to inspect areas above false or dropped ceilings, behind ceiling light fixtures, and behind pictures.

- After the area or room search is completed, the team should report to the overseer and move to the next assigned space.

- Include the following areas in the search:

Bar
Boiler Rooms
Electrical Rooms
Elevator Shaft and Machinery Rooms
Employee Locker Rooms
Employee Coffee Rooms
Guest Rooms
Fire Hose Racks
Janitorial/Maid Closets
Loading/Receiving Areas
Lobby
Meeting Rooms
Restaurant
Rest Rooms
Rooftop

Stage, and areas above and below it
Stairwells
Storage Areas
Trash Receptacles
Any place that has quick access to the
outside with minimal detection

- Use emergency lighting to assist in the search.

- Elevator wells are usually one to three feet deep with grease, dirt, and trash, and must be probed by hand. To check elevator shafts, get on top of the car with a battery-powered lantern and move the car up, a floor or less at a time. Look around the shaft and the elevator door openings. Be careful, because as you ascend on the elevator, the counter weights will be moving downward. Check these also. Do not stand near the edge of the car, and be alert for strong winds in the elevator shaft. Elevator machinery, normally located on the roof, should be checked also.

- Meeting room searches require that all seats, if permanently fixed, be checked on hands and knees. Look for cuts in the upholstery where an item may be hidden.

- *Alternate rooms or areas should be checked by teams so that a blast affecting one team has a smaller chance of reaching the second team.

- *Elevators cannot be used with any degree of safety.

- *Flashlights or battery-powered lanterns are essential. For example, searchers entering darkened areas should *not* turn on lights until after the wall switch and connected lighting fixtures have been examined. The switches may be wired to trigger an explosion.

- *Do not use two-way portable radio communication at this time.

- *The discovery of unidentified pieces of wire, any materials that could be used to prepare a bomb, paint chips, or heavy dust apparently caused by recent removal of a vent are reason enough to call for experienced bomb personnel.

*If a bomb or suspicious object is found, DO NOT MOVE, JAR, OR TOUCH IT!! Professionals in explosive ordnance disposal should be called. Mattresses and pillows should be placed around, *but not on*, the object. No metal shield plates or fragmentary items are to be used. Establish a sterile area or danger zone of about 300 feet vertically and horizontally around the object. Evacuate that area. Check to see that all doors and windows are open.

SAFETY AND SECURITY PROCEDURES

Your safety and the security of your personal property are of the upmost concern to those of us who welcome you as our guest. We urge you to take advantage of the following suggestions.

SAFE DEPOSIT BOXES

DO NOT LEAVE MONEY OR VALUABLES IN YOUR ROOM. We provide safe deposit boxes for your use in our front office at no charge. Under state law, the hotel is not responsible for loss unless articles have been secured properly in these boxes.

DOUBLE LOCKS & CHAINS

For additional security utilize the deadbolt provided on your door upon entering. This will prevent the door from being opened by a regular room key. As an additional precaution, please secure the safety chain lock.

ADMITTANCE

Do not admit persons to your room without first making identification. A "peep hole" is provided in your door for your convenience. If there is any doubt about the person's true identity, please contact the front desk.

KEYS

Do safeguard your key. Be sure to leave it with the cashier upon departure. Do not leave it in your room or in the door. Do not give your key to others.

FIRE

Please familiarize yourself with the location of the nearest fire exit stairway. In the unlikely event of a fire, please move quickly but calmly to the stairs. Avoid the use of elevators. Report fire or smoke to the hotel operator.

We hope that these procedures will contribute to your comfort and well-being during your stay at our hotel.

FORM NO. 3-1403   A•S GRAPHICS

APPENDIX H

The Personal Plan

The **Personal Plan** is a document prepared by an individual manager, indicating how he or she intends to fulfill assigned management responsibilities over a given period of time. The Personal Plan is designed by the manager after consultation with an immediate supervisor. It may then be used as a guide to performance appraisal at the end of a given time period. Of even greater significance is the use of the plan as a guide to professional development.

This appendix presents the Personal Plan I developed while employed as executive housekeeper for the Los Angeles Airport Marriott Hotel during the opening year of the facility. The Plan indicates areas in which development should occur during the upcoming year of operation.

Note the last paragraph, in which specific goals were established as *results expected*. At the end of the year, the manager and supervisor use the plan to evaluate performance against these results expected; that is, what had been specified as intended action. Once the year is complete, a new plan should be developed for the next performance period.

THE EXECUTIVE HOUSEKEEPER'S PERSONAL PLAN FOR _____
(name)

I. Technical Skills
   A. Job and technical knowledge
   In order to perform the technical requirements of my position, I plan to do the following:
    1. Continue to review all media at my disposal for products, equipment, and techniques. Test and implement new ideas and equipment found worthy of consideration that might improve operational methods and standards and/or decrease costs.
    2. Periodically review job descriptions, personal staffing organization, and standard operating procedures (SOPs) to increase effectiveness of assigned employees.
    3. Improve effective communications with all members of my staff.
    4. Stimulate and effect career progression of qualified personnel. Set the right kind of example for all subordinates. Cross-train to increase potential for this property; increase cooperation and respect of employees for each other and develop skill depth within the department.

II. Administration
   A. I will consider my area of responsibility properly administered when
    1. Organization charts and job descriptions are prepared and published for all positions within my area of control.
    2. Equitable work distribution and production have been balanced to provide high morale and effective operation.
    3. Correspondence, records, reports, and training objectives have been timely and efficiently accomplished.
    4. Adequate controls affect increased productivity and decreased operational expenses to the degree that high priority standards will achieve the proper balance against profits for the rooms department.
    5. Communications are free and open.
    6. Proper creation of responsibilities and delegation of authority will create effective utilization of personnel.
    7. Production standards exceed required standards.

III. Managerial
   A. My areas of responsibility will be well managed when
    1. Administrative goals have been attained.
    2. Wages and controllable expenses are maintained at or less than authorized percent of sales.
    3. Section housekeeper hours per rooms rented is in control.
    4. Turnover rate and employee opinion reflect high morale and efficient operation.
    5. Promotion of qualified career progression employees have been made, and success in development of personnel and depth of the staff is accomplished.
    6. Standards are attained or exceeded in producing guest satisfaction with minimum guest complaints.
    7. Objectives of my Personal Plan have been attained.

IV. Personal Development
   A. I will be advancing myself in my present position when I

1. Have full knowledge of all operational aspects within the areas I control. To improve this knowledge, I intend to

   a. Learn other technical skills that relate to my present position.

   b. Obtain knowledge from technically competent personnel who have experience with items of equipment being used.

   c. Increase knowledge through formal educational opportunities.

   d. Grasp every opportunity that my spare time will allow to learn other departmental responsibilities.

   e. Seek out responsibility and critiques and learn by doing.

2. Cross-train in front desk operations to develop my knowledge in areas directly affected by actions in my department.

3. Obtain a general grounding in other areas (food and beverage) not directly related to my present operation.

4. Take advantage of every opportunity offered to enroll in training courses available through the company or educational facilities for the advancement of my managerial skills. Continue working toward certification as AH & MA hotel administrator.

5. Reach my primary goal (promotion) by (date).

V. Expected Results

   A. I expect to accomplish the following results by the dates indicated:

      1. Attain a smooth and coordinated hotel opening for all back-of-the-house operations by (completion of opening).

      2. Solidify operating targets by (date).

      3. Institute systems for scheduling, stock control, cost control, inventories, continued formal training of new personnel, linen control, and budget control by (date).

      4. Stabilize labor turnover at 8 percent or less by (date).

This plan approved and implemented: ___(date)___.
Expected performance appraisal date: ___(date)___.
Submitted by _____.
Accepted by _____.

Glossary

Italicized words identify words or phrases in each definition that are defined elsewhere in this glossary.

absenteeism Employee absence from work. A high rate of absenteeism is considered to be a reliable indicator of low employee morale.

acrylics A group of clear, tough plastic resins produced from acrylic acids.

actual expenditures Actual spending for labor and supplies to support the generation of revenue as opposed to budgeted (planned) costs or forecast (expected) costs.

administration A *management task*. Attending to the details of executive affairs.

administrative theory First introduced by Henri Fayol, it was an attempt to apply scientific principles to a business organization. A subcomponent of the *classical school*.

aerobic A bacteria that must be exposed to, and requires, air (oxygen) to survive and grow.

all-purpose cleaner A multi-purpose agent designed for several different cleaning tasks depending upon the *dilution ratio* applied.

amenity Anything that makes a guest's stay easier and more pleasant. Often pertains to items that are viewed as luxurious. An amenity is not normally categorized as a guest essential.

amortize To periodically and gradually decrease a cost or expenditure to zero over a stated period of time; for example, the preopening cost of a hotel or hospital.

A.M. room check A visual look at guestrooms that are supposed to be ready to receive guests for the purpose of verifying status. Check is made at about 8:00 A.M. Those rooms not in a ready status are called A.M. *discrepancies* and must be investigated. Some ho-

tels conduct A.M. room checks on every room to determine each room's status. Sometimes the housekeeping department schedules workers according to the results of the A.M. room check.

anaerobic A bacteria that can live without exposure to air (oxygen).

analyze problems Gather facts, ascertain causes, and develop alternative solutions.

annual linen reorder plan System of ordering linen that provides long lead times for various items of linens; allows the hotel or hospital to deal directly with a *linen mill;* allows for the mill to weave linen at a time most beneficial to the mill.

antichlors A substance used to remove excess chlorine from fabric after bleaching.

antisepsis A process where chemicals are used on the skin for bacteriostatic and germicidal purposes.

area responsibility plan A document that geographically defines physical areas of a facility and assigns responsibility for cleaning among the various departments of a hotel or hospital organization; usually developed from the *division of work document.*

asepsis To be free from germs and infection.

asepsis (medical) A method used to prevent the spread of a communicable disease. Handwashing and isolation are examples.

asepsis (surgical) A method using sterile equipment, supplies, and procedures when entering the "sterile" interior of the body.

assets Items of value. Notations on a company balance sheet in the *books of account,* which represents the book value of assets. See also *capital assets; current assets; fixed assets.*

atom   The smallest combination of nucleus (core or protons and neutrons) and surrounding electrons that is associated with a given "named element."

autoclave   An oven-like machine, using steam under pressure, in which supplies are subjected to intense heat for a specific period of time. It is also called a sterilizer.

bacillus   Bacteria that is rod-shaped.

bacteria   Used to refer to *microorganisms* in general, also the same as germs and/or microbes.

bacterial   Soils or compounds containing active (live) *bacteria*.

bacteriostat   An agent that arrests the growth of bacteria.

badge system   Method of identifying employees by their identification badges. Badges usually indicate where the employee works and identification number and may contain the employee's photograph.

bed and bath linen   Items such as sheets, pillowcases, hand towels, bath towels, washcloths, and cloth bath mats.

bedding   All bed linens, such as sheets and pillow cases, and all blankets, shams, dust ruffles, pillows, quilts, comforters, coverlets, mattress pads, and bedspreads.

behavioral school   Attempts to apply knowledge gained from the disciplines of human psychology and sociology to the management of employees. Proponents assert that organizational productivity can be enhanced by meeting the psychological needs of the employee.

bomb threats   Malicious announcements of forthcoming explosions or bombings.

books of account   Collection of all accounting ledgers, journals, and files associated with the financial accounting system established for the particular housekeeping operation.

budgeting   Act of creating a management system used for the allocation of resources over a given period of time.

buffing   The act of polishing the surface of a floor with a low-speed (175–350 rpm) floor machine.

burnishing   The act of polishing the surface of a floor with a high-speed (350+ rpm) floor machine to achieve an extremely high gloss (wet look) surface.

capital assets   Long-term tangible or intangible assets such as land and buildings. See also *current assets; fixed assets.*

capital expenditure budget   Financial statement of estimated capital expenditures over a given period of time.

capitalize   Convert an expenditure into a capital item or charge the cost of an item to a capital expenditure account. See also *expense; capital expenditure budget; fixed assets.*

carcinogen   A substance that causes cancer.

card entry system   Technically superior system for gaining regular entry into a hotel guestroom. Most systems use plastic devices (cards) with changeable electronic signatures that activate door locks, eliminating the need for a metal key.

carnuba wax   A high-quality wax obtained from the leaves of the carnuba plant.

cationic   A positively charged ion.

chambermaid   See *section housekeeper.*

checkout (c/o)   Designation assigned to a guestroom in which the guest has permanently left the hotel and the room is waiting to be serviced, or in the process of being readied for the arrival of a new guest. Synonymous with *on change.*

chemical agent   A chemical added to a solution in the correct dosage that will kill bacteria, or at least stop its growth.

civil disturbance   In hotels or hospitals a disturbance caused by one or more people refusing to obey the requests, commands, or demands of those in authority.

classical school   The first great theoretical school of management. Characterized by a systematic approach to the management of the assets and the employees in the corporation. Henri Fayol and Frederick W. Taylor are considered by many to be the founders of this management school.

classification of accounts Arranging various types of revenues, expenses, and costs into meaningful groupings for accounting purposes.

cleaning and guest supply inventory A major segment of operational inventory under the direct control and responsibility of the *executive housekeeper*.

cleaning and maintenance circuits (rounds) Planned sequences for attending to the cleaning of various *public areas*.

clostridium perfringens (clos-TRID-ee-um per-FRIN-gins) No gram stain. An anaerobic spore. "Botulism" is found in feces, sewers, milk improperly sterilized or sealed foods. Also found in untreated wounds (gaseous gangrene).

coach-pupil method A one-on-one training system of assigning one trainee to one instructor.

coccus Bacteria that is round-shaped.

communicate To pass or receive knowledge, instructions, or data and to ensure understanding.

communication symbols A series of written symbols used to communicate the status of guestrooms; for example, R, CO, OCC, DND, RFV, OOO, MR, and T.

competitive shopping Looking critically at the alternative sources and suppliers of items and services purchased to support a hotel or hospital operation.

computer An electronic system of *hardware* components used to store and process data electronically.

conceptual thinking A *management task*. Formulating notions for the resolution of problems.

conference method A training technique whereby students participate in a workshop arrangement for problem solving. An excellent technique for supervisory training.

consolidated room sales summary Document prepared by the sales and marketing department of a hotel indicating rooms expected to be sold during the upcoming fiscal year. Used by other departments to budget salaries, wages, and *controllable costs* in support of expected room sales; a part of the overall budget package.

consumer (market segment) A market segment of hotel guests that is not usually on an expense account; for example, vacationers with or without young children. See also *group market; corporate transient hotel.*

contingency approach Management theory that holds that the appropriate management style is contingent upon the makeup and attitude of the subordinate. Closely related to the *situational leadership* model.

continuous functions of management Related actions (*analyze problems, make decisions, communicate*) that managers do continuously.

control information Data collected and used to maintain control of an operation.

controllable costs Classification of supply and expense accounts under the control of a department manager. See also *wage costs; employee costs.*

controller (also comptroller) Manager in charge of all accounting functions of a hotel or hospital. Duties include overall budget preparation, costing, and internal audit procedures and measuring performance against previously approved plans, procedures, and standards; interpreting and reporting financial data to other members of hotel management; participating in making policy decisions and executive action.

controlling Performing certain activities that ensure progress toward desired objectives according to plan. A *sequential function of management*. See also *in control.*

control profit (loss) What remains after subtracting *controllable costs, wage costs,* and *employee costs* from revenue within a given department. Usually under control of a department manager.

coordinating (efforts of employees) Relating the effort of employees in the most effective combinations. An activity of *directing.*

corporate transient hotel A hotel that is usually used by business people on expense accounts. May have a transient group market in addition to some *consumer* or *resort*-type guests.

count sheet Form used to record results when taking inventory.

coverlet A bedspread that just covers the top of a dust ruffle. It does not reach to the floor.

creating position (job) description Identifying and defining the scope, relationships, responsibilities, duties, and authority of people in an organization. An activity of *organizing*.

critique Statement of performance analysis, usually reserved for elements or areas on a performance statement that are not *in control*. The statement should contain comments as to intended action and how *control* of the elements will be regained. A *standard operating procedure* performed by department managers of well-controlled companies.

current assets *Assets* of a short-term nature such as cash, accounts receivable, and *inventories*. See also *fixed assets*.

cut loop The yarns in a carpet arranged into areas of high-cut tufts and lower loop tufts to form a sculptured pattern of various heights.

daily routine Series of administrative and work-related events that occur between 6:30 A.M. and midnight and form the routine for a housekeeping department in the *guestroom portion* and *public areas* of a hotel. See also *housekeeping day*.

daily work assignment sheet Form that indicates special work tasks required for a given day and are assigned to a specific worker.

damp mopping The use of a damp (not wet) mop for spot cleaning of spills and overall cleaning of light dirt from floors. This technique is not intended to remove heavily embedded dirt or old floor finish.

deep clean Periodic act of cleaning a guestroom in depth. Involves moving heavy furniture, high dusting, turning mattresses, vacuuming draperies and curtains, and other cleaning functions not normally performed in the day-to-day servicing of a guestroom. Synonymous with *general cleaned*.

deficiency of knowledge (DK) Workers could not perform a task even if their lives depended on it. Usually caused by no training or lack of understanding of what has been taught.

deficiency of task execution (DE) Workers fail to perform a task properly after training.

defoamers Chemical added to a fabric cleaner that reduces the amount of suds produced by the detergent in the cleaner. Defoamers are often used in water extraction carpet cleaning chemicals so that the pickup tanks are not inundated with suds.

delegating Creating responsibilities for or assigning tasks to subordinates, passing to them the required authority to act, then exacting accountability for results. An activity of *directing*.

delineating relationships Defining liaison lines within formal organizations that will facilitate relationships. An activity of *organizing*.

demonstration method Training technique in which you show someone how to do something.

denier A unit of weight of silk, nylon, or rayon that is an indicator of fineness. One denier is equal to $5/100$ of a gram in a 450 meter length of thread. The smaller the number, the smaller the circumference of the thread. (Fifteen denier nylon lingerie is more transparent than 25 denier nylon lingerie.)

departmental meetings A technique of communicating with all members of the department at the same time. Housekeeping departmental meetings should be scheduled at least once each month and when unique situations warrant them. Meetings should be interesting, informative, and always under the control of management. Employees should always be allowed time to ask questions, which should receive timely replies.

department staffing guide Document that specifies positions within the organization and the number of people required to fill these positions. Used as a hiring guide.

depreciate Systematically reduce the book value of a *fixed asset* over its estimated useful life.

detergents A chemical that acts like a soap and is used for cleaning numerous surfaces. Detergents can be used effectively in hard water where ordinary soap will not produce suds and will leave a residue.

developing employees Improving the attitudes, knowledge, and skills of employees with a view toward assigning greater responsibilities or effecting promotions. An activity of *staffing*.

developing policies Making decisions that will govern when, where, and how procedures will be implemented; usually of long-standing nature. An activity of *planning*.

developing strategies Deciding how and when to achieve certain goals. An activity of *planning*.

development of subordinates Responsibility of management to assure the professional growth of those placed under the manager.

dilution control Controlling the mixing of certain *all-purpose cleaning agents* with water in prescribed amounts that will enable the performance of various types of cleaning operations. See also *dilution ratio*.

dilution ratio Comparison of the amount of water that is, or must be, added to a specific cleaning agent that is recommended for a specific cleaning task. For example, a 20:1 dilution ratio means 20 parts water to 1 part cleaning agent to perform a specific task. See also *dilution control; all-purpose cleaner*.

diplococcus pneumonia (dip-lo-COCK-us new-MOAN-ee-a) Gram positive. Lobar (lung) pneumonia. Also walking pneumonia. Treatable with antibiotics.

directing Performing certain activities that bring about purposeful action toward desired objectives. A *sequential function of management*.

discrepancy A situation occurring when the reported status of a guestroom by the front desk is different from the status actually observed by the housekeeping department during A.M. or P.M. *room checks*. For example, front desk holds a room to be *occupied* and housekeeping views the room to be a *ready* room or a *checkout* room. Discrepancies must be resolved by the front desk or the room must be *rechecked* by housekeeping.

disinfectants A substance or means used to destroy *pathogenic microorganisms*.

disinfection A condition existing when infectious material or infection(s) are removed.

disinfection (concurrent) Process used while disease is still in progress.

disinfection (terminal) Process used when disease is ended.

dissatisfiers Items peripheral to a job, such as pay, working conditions, company policies, and quality of supervision, that if not properly attended to will demotivate employees. The positive effects on motivation caused by properly attending to dissatisfiers are usually short lived. See also *satisfiers*.

division of work document A report prepared by the *executive housekeeper* as a result of inspection and investigation of a new facility before opening. The report indicates areas that will require cleaning and contains recommendations as to who should be responsible for cleaning each area. Forms the basis for development and promulgation of the *area responsibility plan*.

documented Recorded event, happening, or inspection result.

do not disturb (DND) A verbal or written notation by a guest that he or she is not to be bothered. Refers to the guest, not the guestroom. Guest usually makes the request by hanging a small sign, which says "do not disturb" on the hall side of a guestroom door.

double double (DD) Guestroom having two double beds.

double occupancy Guestroom occupied by two guests. See also *single occupancy; multiple occupancy*.

double rooming Front desk accidentally rooms two separate guests or guest parties in the same room; usually occurs as a result of an unresolved *discrepancy*.

drying capacity Optimum weight of linen that should be placed in an automatic commercial dryer; for example, 50-pound, 100-pound, 200-pound, 300-pound dryers. Used in the *sizing of laundries*. See also *washing capacity, handling capacity*.

eighteen-room workload Size of the room-cleaning workload assigned daily to *section housekeepers* in the model hotel in this text. A typical workload that would be assigned to well-equipped section housekeepers in a *corporate transient* hotel.

electronic data processing (EDP) Processing of data by *computer* when *input* and *output hardware* are connected *on-line* to a computer *processor*. Opposed to *automatic data processing* (ADP) where data to be fed to a computer is stored on tape or punch cards.

electrowriter Electromechanical device used for transmitting facsimile handwritten messages, usually among housekeeping, front desk, and engineering.

elements of management   See *management elements*.

emergencies   Unpredictable combination of circumstances or resulting states that call for immediate enlightened action; can often be anticipated but seldom foreseen.

employee absenteeism   See *absenteeism*.

employee appearance   Aspect of employee behavior or training having to do with personal and uniformed appearance. A concern of management and supervision.

employee claims of unfairness   Statements by workers that indicate less than harmonious relations with management; related to the manner in which employees are being treated. A major cause of worker attempts and desire to unionize.

employee contamination   Corruption of relatively inexperienced or impressionable employees through the observance of the dishonest acts of others.

employee costs   Costs occurring as a result of having employees; exclusive of per/hour *wage costs;* includes costs of health and welfare, sick leave, meals, and other benefits. See also *controllable costs; wage costs*.

employee handbook   Collection of facts, rules, regulations, and guidelines about a hotel, hospital, or a specific department; usually given to an employee at the time of hiring to assist in employee orientation.

employee hygiene   Personal cleanliness habits of employees that may be of concern to other employees or guests.

employee problems   Problems that cause employees to have difficulties on the job; employees who cause interruptions or inefficiencies in work.

employee profile   Concise biographical sketch of an employee indicating certain traits, characteristics, and personality.

employee requisition   Document initiated by a department and forwarded to the personnel office requesting that hiring procedures be started to fill a vacancy or a newly created position.

employee theft prevention   Positive program or plan that anticipates the possibility of employees stealing.

employee turnover   See *turnover*.

employment checklist   Document used during the acquisition phase of hiring new employees; used to guarantee that no steps are omitted or overlooked in the hiring process.

employment history   Written record of prior employment status; usually a part of an employment application indicating chronologically where the applicant has worked in the past, inclusive dates of employment, name of employee's supervisor, and reason for leaving the employment.

entomological   Relating to insects, especially those that can cause or carry diseases.

epoxy   A synthetic, seamless flooring material. Very long lasting and extremely durable.

escherichia coli (ee-shear-EEK-ee-ah COAL-i)   Gram negative. Can grow in soap. Never use bar soap in a public washroom. Bacteria can be contracted in the droppings of animals.

establishing organizational structure   Developing the formal organization plan for the accomplishment of tasks within a company. An activity of *organizing*.

establishing position qualifications   Defining qualifications and preparing specifications for people who will fill positions in an organization. An activity of *organizing*.

establishing procedures   Deciding and specifying how a task is to be done. An activity of *planning*.

executive committee   Usually the highest level of operations management on a hotel property. Includes but is not necessarily limited to the general manager, resident manager, director of food and beverage, controller, and director of sales and marketing. Ex officio members may include the director of personnel, chief engineer, and security director. The top policy-making body on the property.

executive housekeeper   Person in charge of management and administration of a housekeeping department or operation within a hotel. Synonymous titles include *director of services, director of internal services,* and *director of environmental services* (in hospitals).

exit interviews   Management's attempt to gain information regarding working conditions and reasons for voluntary separations from former employees of the organization.

expense to To write off as an expense or expenditure or to charge to an expense account as cost of doing business on an *operating statement* over a given period of time. See also *capitalize.*

face weight The number of ounces of yarn per square yard in a carpet.

filling The threads of yarn that run the width of the fabric (also known as the *weft*).

financial statement Summary of accounts, showing a balance as of the beginning of business on a given date, the credits and the debits made, and the balance remaining at the end of the accounting period. See also *operating statement; balance sheet.*

finish Final coat(s) of either wax or a synthetic product that is intended to protect the floor from abrasion, provide a seamless and smooth top layer for the floor, and when polished, will provide a glossy and reflective surface.

finished sheet A sheet size that includes the top and bottom hem.

fire Chemical decomposition of a fuel element through combustion or burning. For fire to occur and sustain itself, there must be four elements—fuel, oxygen, heat, and a chemical reaction.

fire byproducts The side effects or results of fire. They include heat, smoke, toxic gas, and fumes.

first-line supervisor One who supervises one or more *first-line workers.*

first-line worker A trained worker who performs hands-on work at the lowest level of the organization; works for a *first-line supervisor.*

fixed assets Tangible assets of a long-term nature such as land, buildings, machinery, and equipment. See also *assets; capital assets; current assets.*

fixed positions Positions that are fixed in terms of work and man-hour requirements; positions not subject to being reduced in hours due to fluctuations in occupancy.

flash point The temperature at which the vapor from a flammable substance will ignite momentarily in the air, in the presence of a small flame.

floorplan layout Engineering or architectural drawing of the layout of machinery, furniture, fixtures, and equipment.

forecasting Establishing where present courses of action will lead. An activity of *planning.*

forecasting man-hour requirements A short-run statement of need for the utilization of man-hours to accomplish a specific task.

foundation The primary coat(s) of sealer applied to a floor. A foundation's intended purpose is to prevent spilled liquids that may cause staining and other damage from penetrating into the floor.

fourteen point theft prevention program Fourteen guidelines for managerial and supervisory action that may reduce employee theft and dishonesty.

fresh look Inspections conducted by people not regularly associated with the area; allows for observing and reporting deficiencies not noticed by someone regularly in contact with the area.

front office manager Person in charge of front office operations in a hotel. One of several principal assistants to a *resident manager,* relates equally with the *executive housekeeper.* Person in charge of the front desk, bell services, transportation, and other related activities in a hotel.

full-time employment Incumbent has attained full-time status, usually after successfully completing training and a probationary period of employment. In union-free environments, infers that the employee is committing to work and the company is committing to schedule the employee 30 or more regular hours of work each week.

function room sheet Form upon which special instructions are given for setting up, arranging, or rearranging a guestroom for a special function. See also *parlor; hospitality; hospitality suite; function room.*

functions Management duties and activities. Can be divided into sequential and continuous functions.

fungus Simple plants lacking chlorophyll. Bread mold is an example.

furniture, fixtures, and equipment (FFE)   Classification of *fixed assets* of a hotel or hospital that have specified depreciable lives, usually ranging from three to seven years.

general clean   See *deep clean.*

gray goods   Unfinished fabric directly from the loom.

gram (positive/negative)   Refers to the color staining of test samples of certain bacteria. Gram "positive" is a "blue" test result when certain bacteria are treated with testing reagents. Gram "negative" is a "red" test indication.

ground warp   Yarn threads that run lengthwise in a towel. They are used as the backing for the pile warp threads. The ground warp is usually a poly-cotton blend.

group market   Market segment of hotel business, usually defined by the sale of 10 or more *room nights* in one group.

guest essentials   *Guest supplies* that are essential in guestrooms but that the guest would not normally be expected to use up or remove upon departure. Examples include water glasses, ice buckets, and clothes hangers. See also *guest expendables; guest loan items.*

guest expendables   *Guest supplies* that guests would normally be expected to use up or take away upon departure. Examples include stationary, toilet tissue, and soap. See also *guest essentials; guest loan items.*

guest loan items   *Guest supplies* not normally found in a guestroom but available upon request. Examples include hair dryers, razors, ironing boards, and irons. Guests sign a receipt and specify a time that the item may be picked up by the housekeeping department. See also *guest expendables; guest essentials.*

guest receipt log book   Log book in which guests sign for the use of *guest loan items.*

guest request   Any special request not normally included in the regular servicing of a guestroom, such as for extra towels, hair dryer, razor, roll-away bed, or baby crib.

guestroom   Numbered room in a hotel provided specifically for occupancy by one or more regular or transient guests; is most often rented but can be complimented to special guests; is located in a major subsection of a hotel known as the *guest-room portion of the hotel.*

guestroom attendant (GRA)   See *section house-keeper.*

guestroom portion of the hotel   Specific area of a hotel in which guestrooms are located; also includes guest corridors, elevators, stairwells, vending areas, and some service areas. Not included are *public areas,* restaurants, lounge areas, *recreation areas,* or major service areas.

guestroom types   A differentiation among *guestrooms* based on types of sleeping accommodations or equipment; usually identified by specific symbols as follows: T, room with one twin bed; TT, room with two twin beds; D, room with one double bed; DD, room with two double beds; ST, studio, room with a day bed or convertible sofa; Q, room with one queen bed; K, room with one king bed; P, parlor sitting room usually having hidden sleep equipment, may be set for a small meeting or *hospitality* function; S, suite, two or more rooms that connect internally and are sold as one unit; CON, rooms that are adjacent and connect internally; BS, bi-level suite, a suite on two levels having an internal stairway between levels; ES, executive suite, a high-quality suite, usually having two or more rooms but only one with access to the hotel corridor.

guest supplies   Supplies specifically needed because guests are staying in a hotel. See also *guest expendables; guest essentials; guest loan items.*

handling capacity   Measure of the design of a laundry facility that relates to the amount and ease of handling of linen within the facility. See also *washing capacity; drying capacity.*

hardware (computer)   Physical components of a computer system; includes *input* and *output* devices, *processor,* printing devices, and video monitors (CRTs).

HazComm   Hazardous Communication Standard for chemicals and toxic wastes established by the Occupational Safety and Health Administration.

homogeneous   Uniform throughout. Made up of the same elements.

hospitality suite   Guestroom that has been temporarily set up to accommodate a small party; may require the movement of some furniture; more appropriately set in a *suite* or *parlor.*

house breakout plan Document specifying the division of the *guestroom portion of a hotel* into meaningful work units for cleaning and servicing. The plan is usually a line drawing of the floorplans of the rooms section, appropriately divided into *room sections* and *house divisions* to delineate supervisory responsibilities.

house division Group of four to six *room sections* with associated and/or specified corridors, elevators, stairwells, and service and storage areas; may be assigned a color or letter designation and placed under the control of a *senior housekeeper* (supervisor).

housekeeper's report A report made daily to the front desk by the housekeeping department and signed by a manager indicating the correct status of all guestrooms in a hotel as visually noted at about 3:00 P.M. each day. Compilation of results obtained from P.M. *room checks* conducted of the entire *guestroom portion of the hotel*. Specifies which rooms are *ready* for occupancy, *occupied* by a guest or contain luggage, and/or *on-change* (being serviced for newly arriving guests).

housekeeping central Synonymous with main linen room. Central physical point of administrative and operational activity for a housekeeping department. Usually contains or is adjacent to the offices of the *executive housekeeper* and principal assistants. Under the supervisory control of the *linen room supervisor* and/or *night supervisor*. Central point of control for all communications emanating from and received by the housekeeping department. A point of issue for selected and special items of supply. See also *satellite linen room*.

housekeeping day That period of a 24-hour day when the housekeeping department is open and operating; usually from about 6:30 A.M. until midnight.

housekeeping manager Manager who is the principal assistant to the *executive housekeeper;* person who is directly responsible for guestroom cleaning. May also be the person in charge of the housekeeping department in a small property.

housekeeping standing rotational scheduling form Form used to create and display a system of standing rotational scheduling, specifying regular days off for *housekeeping teams* and other individuals within the department. See *standing rotational scheduling system*.

housekeeping team (regular or swing) Group of housekeeping employees consisting of one *senior housekeeper* (supervisor), several *section housekeepers,* and a *section housekeeping aide* who work together as a regular team or designated swing team within an assigned *house division*. The team is usually identified by a color or number similar to that of the house division where it is assigned to work.

hypochlorite A salt or ester of hypochlorous acid. Hypochlorous acid is an unstable, weak acid that is used as a bleach and disinfectant.

idophors A variety of disinfectants.

individual development (ID) program Development program for managers being groomed for greater responsibilities and/or promotion by the Marriott Hotel Corporation.

input (computer) Data entered into a computer for processing.

inspection day One particular day of the work week when regular inspections of *guestrooms* and other sections of the hotel are performed. See also *zone inspection program*.

inspection program Regular inspection of specified areas of a hotel or hospital. Usually formalized and specified through *standard operating procedures*. See also *property inspection program; zone inspection program*.

inspectress Person who does nothing but inspect *guestrooms* in a hotel or hospital to ensure that *standards of cleanliness* are being maintained.

intermediate host A transmitter of disease who is not affected by it. Also known as an "immune carrier." An example would be the anopheles mosquito; it can bite a person infected with malaria, then bite another victim, thus transmitting the disease.

inventories Quantities on hand of various items of value; recorded in the *books of account* as *current assets*.

inventory (verb) To count and record the quantity of items of value.

inventory control Management function of classifying, ordering, receiving, storing, issuing, and accounting for items of value.

inventory record book Record of amounts of specific items on hand; also contains pricing information and valuation of total *inventory*.

ironers Commercial pieces of machinery used for ironing linens in a commercial or *on-premises laundry*.

JCAHO Joint Commission of Accreditation of Health Care Organizations.

job descriptions Documents describing the work to be done in each of several unique jobs within a department. Specify working hours, special qualifications of the worker, if any, responsibilities and duties of incumbents to the positions to which they refer. Usually prepared for workers who do hands-on work and first-line supervising. See also *position descriptions*.

jute A strong smooth fiber that comes from plants in Asia. It is used to make rope, canvas, and carpet backing.

key control program Plan of control for the prevention of loss of keys used by employees in the daily performance of their work functions.

key pouch Leather container for storing keys. Pouch usually contains an identifying mark or number to facilitate easy reference to a specific area of the facility and ease in subcustody reference and key control inventory.

labor costs See *wage costs*.

laundry consultant Expert in the development of laundry facilities and operations.

laundry supervisor Working supervisory position in a hotel or hospital *on-premise laundry;* reports to a laundry manager.

leadership *Management task* of influencing people to accomplish desired goals.

leadership style The observed behavior of the leader in an organization. Commonly observed styles have been categorized and given labels by management theorists. Examples would include MacGregor's *"theory x"* manager who has a high concern for production but little concern for the welfare of subordinates in the organization, and the *"theory y"* manager who has a high concern for both production and a high concern for people in the organization.

leave-of-absence (LOA) Authorized period of time away from work without pay; granted by management to an employee during which time seniority is protected.

leveling technique Enlightened style of conducting a *performance appraisal* when poor, questionable, or unsatisfactory performance is the subject of the appraisal.

level loop A type of carpet in which the pile loops are of uniform height.

linen broker Person who deals in linen; may represent several *linen mills;* has knowledge and access to sources of immediate linen supplies.

linen count sheet Form used to record the results of counting items of linen. See also *count sheet*.

linen in use Specific amount of linen in circulation or being used by a housekeeping department to service *guestrooms* at the time a linen *inventory* is taken. See also *linen (new) on hand; linen on hand*.

linen (mills) Places where linens are woven. Linen mills usually sell to hotels and hospitals through *linen brokers,* but large or well-managed hotel organizations deal directly with mills.

linen, new, on hand Specific amount of new and unused linen that is stored in cases on the property and is available when needed; as a part of total *linen on hand*.

linen on hand Total amount of linen as reflected by *inventory* of all linen. Includes new linen on hand and linen in use.

linen poundage requirements Specified amount of linen by weight, generated from linen demands of a specific hotel or hospital based on the size of the facility (number and type of beds). Used to determine *washing capacity* and *drying capacity* and in *sizing laundries*.

linen room supervisor Working supervisor in charge of *main linen room* activities; assistant to the *executive housekeeper*. Person is in charge of the central or main linen room, linen room operations, and communications with the housekeeping department, the front desk, engineering, and the guests.

linens Traditionally a cloth made from flax fiber, but now it is used to indicate sheets, pillow cases, washcloths, cloth bath mats, towels, tablecloths, and napkins.

linen valuation Monetary value of the linen *inventory,* including both *new* and *in-use linens*. Calculation is determined by multiplying specific linen counts of each item of linen by the last known purchase price of the linen item. A value of the asset linen inventories as a part of total *inventories*.

line organization The organizational structure parallels the duties and activities involved in the production of a good or service. Follows the principle of *span of control* and unity of command (every employee answers to just one supervisor).

lobby housekeeper See *public area (PA) housekeeper*.

lobby housekeeping aide See *public area (PA) house- keeper*.

lock cylinder That portion of a door locking mechanism that contains the key-way; houses the pins that match the indentation of a particular key being used to open a door. Cylinders are removable and thus interchangeable.

loss-prevention program A plan or procedure under which action may be taken to eliminate or minimize the loss of life or property.

MacGregor, Douglas Educator, author, management psychologist; noted for the development of the *theory x* and *theory y* models for managers.

maid See *section housekeeper*.

main linen room See *housekeeping central*.

maintenance checklist Document used as a guide in the performance of a *maintenance inspection*.

maintenance inspection Inspection conducted for the sole purpose of uncovering repair needs, as opposed to cleaning needs; also conducted to ensure that preventive maintenance is being regularly performed on machinery and equipment.

maintenance work request form A three-part document used for recording the need for repairs; is transmitted to the engineering department. Form allows for the control and progressing of work and the recording of man-hours and materials involved in the repairs performed.

make ready (MR) The act of servicing a *guestroom* for occupancy. Making a room ready prepares the room for a change of status from *checkout (CO)* or *tidy (T)* to a *ready (R)* room.

management continuous functions *Analyzing problems, making decisions,* and *communicating*.

management elements Those things that a manager has to work with: ideas, material resources, money, and people.

management science The modern-day derivation of *"scientific management."* Management science attempts to apply mathematical models to aid in solving management decisions.

management sequential functions Group of related actions (*planning, organizing, staffing, directing,* and *controlling*) that a manager may be seen to do in a given sequence. This sequence is most appropriate when managing a project.

management tasks Continuous objectives imposed on a person who manages, such as *conceptual thinking, administration,* and *leadership*.

management triangle Relationship among three aspects of managerial activity; concern for the accomplishment of work, concern for the people who perform the work, and application of scientific techniques to the field of management.

manager (as a leader) Leadership skills of person assigned to manage or supervise a group of employees.

managerial grid Graphical presentation of five classical styles of behavior exhibited by managers when thinking through decisions in a group setting.

managerial styles See *leadership styles*.

managing change Stimulating creativity and innovation among subordinates which will foster cooperation when changes in policies and procedures are necessary. An activity of *directing*.

managing differences Encouraging independent thought among workers and resolving conflict; commonly thought of as *problem solving*. An activity of *directing*.

man-hour justification Statement explaining the need for and how man-hours will be used in support of revenue-generating operations.

material Broad classification of items including furniture, fixtures, equipment, and supplies used in or under the control of a housekeeping or other department within a hotel, hospital, or health care institution.

material safety data sheets   Informational sheets available from manufacturers of chemicals that describe the toxic effect of these chemicals and the proper procedures to use when handling these chemicals. The HazComm Standard demands that these sheets be made available to all employees who might be exposed to a potentially hazardous chemical.

measuring results   Ascertaining whether or not there have been, and the extent of, deviations from goals and standards. An activity of *controlling.*

mercerizing   A fabric finishing process that treats cotton with sodium hydroxide (a caustic soda). This process strengthens the cotton and enables dyes to better penetrate the fabric. Patented by John Mercer (1791–1866), an English fabric printer.

metal cross-linked polymer finishes   Floor finishes that contain heavy metals, such as zinc. These finishes have fallen into disfavor because of their potential harm to the environment.

microbiology   A natural science that began with the discovery of the microscope. It had been suggested since the thirteenth century that "invisible" organisms were responsible for decay and disease. In the latter quarter of the nineteenth century the term *microbe* was coined to describe these organisms, all of which were thought to be related. Bacteriology, protozoology, and virology are three subdisciplines.

micron   A unit of measure—10^{-6} meter, or 1/25,000 of 1 inch. (Bacteria are usually in the range of 1 to 300 microns.)

microorganisms   Bacteria, rickettsiae, small fungi (such as yeasts and molds), algae, and protozoans, as well as problematical forms of life such as viruses.

mineral   A solid homogeneous crystalline chemical element or compound that results from the inorganic processes of nature having a specific chemical composition.

miscellaneous charge   Nonstandard charge (as opposed to a charge for room rent, food, or beverage) of a hotel guest for services rendered or product purchased.

molecule   A compound created by combining a certain group of *atoms.*

morning activities   Group of activities occurring from about 6:30 A.M. until about 1:00 P.M. during the *housekeeping day.* They include *opening the house,* commencing the assigned work, conducting an A.M. *room check,* receiving information about *checkout rooms,* making up guestrooms, and providing *ready rooms* to the front desk throughout the day for reassignment to new guests.

motivating employees   Creating an atmosphere whereby employees are persuaded or inspired to take a desired action. An activity of *directing.*

multiple occupancy   Guestroom is occupied by more than two guests. See also *single occupancy; double occupancy.*

mycobacterium diptheria (my-co-back-TEER-ee-um dip-THE-ree-ah)   Gram positive. Transmitted in milk. Not too prevalent due to vaccination now available against disease.

mycobacterium tuberculosis (my-co-back-TEER-ee-um too-BER-cue-LOW-sis)   Gram negative. Acid fast (cannot be killed with acid).

napery   Tablecloths, napkins, and doilies.

natural disaster   Event capable of causing loss of life, great material damage, destruction, and distress. May be caused by fire, flood, earthquake, hurricane, or tornado.

needles   Refers to hypodermic needles.

new linen on hand   See *linen, new, on hand.*

night clerk's report to housekeeping   Report prepared by the night clerk for the housekeeping department at the end of the night's activity; prepared at the front desk; indicates guestrooms that will require service during the upcoming workday.

night housekeeping supervisor   Supervisor in charge of evening housekeeping operations; an assistant to the *executive housekeeper.*

night supervisor's report of evening activities   Report maintained by the night supervisor in charge of the second work shift, indicating the volume and type of activity performed by the evening shift. Includes a record of *checkouts* and *tidies* made ready, *rechecks* made and the results thereof, and a summary of special requests made by guests.

no-iron linens Specific type of linen manufactured with a certain percentage of polyester fiber. Also identified as blend linen; for example, 50-50 blend has 50 percent cotton content and 50 percent polyester fiber. If properly handled in laundering, it will appear wrinkle free.

nonionic detergent A detergent that does not ionize in solution.

nonresilient flooring Flooring materials that do not "give" to any degree underfoot. Examples include concrete, ceramic tile, epoxy, marble, terrazzo, and all other stone floors.

nosocomial infection An infection that results from a stay in a hospital and the exposure to germs present in that hospital.

occupancy forecast Short-range estimate of guest-room occupancy expected over a given period of time, such as a day, a week, or other accounting period of usually not more than 90 days.

occupancy type Manner in which a registered guest or group of guests will occupy a room; *single occupancy* is one person only to a room; *double occupancy* is two people to a room, *multiple occupancy* is more than two people in a room.

occupied (OCC) The status of a guestroom indicating that a guest or guests are in residence; the presence of luggage in the room indicating the probable presence of a registered guest.

odor-pair neutralization Molecules of gas from a chemical stimulate receptor cells deep inside the nose and thus cancel out unpleasant odors being caused by other gas molecules.

once-around method Method of cleaning a guestroom whereby unnecessary steps and transportation of supplies and equipment are eliminated or minimized.

on-change See *checkout.*

one par of linen Quantity of linen required to meet certain requirements; usually the total amount required to cover beds and to handle bath needs in all guestrooms.

one-stroke solution *Dilution ratio* of an *all-purpose cleaner* that provides a proper cleaning agent for certain operations in approximately one wipe; for example, 4:1 dilution ratio of a specific cleaning agent is used to sanitize a toilet in one wiping stroke. See also *three-stroke solution.*

on-line computer equipment Computer equipment (*input* and *output* devices and the *computer processor*) that are electronically connected and ready to operate at all times on demand of an operator; as opposed to off-line equipment, which requires the mechanical or time-scheduled entry of data into the system.

on-premises laundry Also called the in-house laundry. A laundry that is built, owned, or operated by the user of the linens processed; usually on the same premises where linens will be used, but facility may be detached.

on-scene commander Member of local fire or police protection organization or other technically competent municipal official having authority over local law or police services who takes charge at the scene of an *emergency.*

on-the-job training (OJT) Training technique whereby one or more trainees are shown what to do on the job. Employees practice the skill and are observed by the instructor. Work is then critiqued by the instructor. When only one trainee receives instruction at a time, the technique is referred to as the *coach-pupil* method of training.

opening the house A daily operational planning procedure whereby rooms requiring service are assigned to *section housekeepers* specifically scheduled to work that day. Procedure becomes more or less complicated depending on occupancy levels and number of guestrooms that must be reassigned as *pick-up rooms.* This is the first of several *morning activities* performed each day and should be completed before workers arrive for work.

open section A specific *room section* created for the regular assignment to a *section housekeeper* for cleaning but, due to lack of occupancy, has no *section housekeeper* assigned. Occupied rooms in the open section must be reassigned as *pick-up rooms* to a *section housekeeper* on that day.

operating budget A financial statement of a plan giving an estimate of operating revenues, expenses, and profit (or loss) expected for a given period of time. See also *budgeting; capital expenditure budget.*

operating cost Expenses associated with generating revenues. See *operating statement; operating budget.*

operating statement Periodic financial report indicating actual performance (results) as compared to budgeted performance; reports revenues, expenses, and profit (or loss) over a given period of time; may also report utilization of other *assets* such as labor, man-hours, and material.

operational budget cycle Chronological expression of time involving budget preparation, activation, and operation. Budget cycles usually start three to six months before the beginning of the fiscal year. They include expectations of annual sales revenues and planned utilization of salaries, wages, and controllable supplies. Time is then allowed for review and critique of the new budget. Finally, budget approval precedes the beginning of the new budget year. As the year proceeds, plans are made to start the next budget cycle.

operational budget for the housekeeping department Housekeeping segment of the total *operational budget* of a hotel or hospital. In hotels, that portion of the operating budget dealing with guestroom revenue, housekeeping department salaries and wages, employee costs and *controllable costs* related to the servicing of *guestrooms* and *public areas* of a hotel.

organic A substance or a product of substances of plant or animal origin. Chemically, organic compounds contain carbon "r" strings of molecules attached to one or more hydrogen molecules.

organizing Performing certain activities that arrange and relate people and work for effective accomplishment of objectives. A *sequential function of management.*

orienting new employees Familiarizing new employees with their situation and surroundings. An activity of *staffing.*

osmological Relating to soils of organic or inorganic matter which emit unpleasant odors.

out of order (room) (OOO) Designation assigned to a guestroom that for some mechanical or repair reason cannot be occupied by a guest. Authority for such designation usually rests with the chief engineer.

output (computer) Data generated by a computer as a result of *input* data being fed into a *computer processor,* which in turn responds to the direction of a computer program.

padding A layer of material placed under carpet to increase resiliency. It can be made from a number of natural and synthetic materials.

panic emotion Uncontrolled psychological departure from responsible action or behavior when experiencing fear or sudden widespread fright as a result of not knowing what to do in an emergency situation.

par A standard, specific, or normal level of stock.

parlor (P) Sitting room usually having hidden sleep equipment; may be set up for a small meeting or *hospitality function.*

participative management Act of involving workers in discussions regarding decisions that ultimately affect the workers.

part-time employee In the hotel industry, one who regularly commits to and is scheduled to work by the company 29 hours or less per week. See also *steady extra; regular employee; temporary employee; pool employee.*

pathogenic Disease causing, disease producing.

pathogenic microorganisms Disease-causing bacteria and viruses.

pay increases A stepped increment of pay normally awarded to an employee for satisfactory performance during a specified time period, for outstanding performance, or in recognition of cost-of-living increases.

pay scale A published table of compensation offered for jobs performed; usually indicates increments of pay based on seniority and minimum and maximum compensation to be offered for each job. Usually developed by personnel departments as a result of wage surveys of the surrounding area, degree of difficulty of jobs surveyed, availability of labor markets, and company policies.

percale A cotton cloth that is closely woven so as to give a smooth finish.

performance analysis Breaking apart a job into its various elements of work to evaluate how the elements affect each other.

performance appraisal Formal act of notifying employees about the observed quality of their performance. May be verbal but is usually written and become an official part of the employee's record.

performance standards Conditions that will exist when key duties are done well. An activity of *controlling*.

period Segment of time in which performance will be demonstrated and measured against a plan or budget.

period linen inventory count record Log or similar record of all items of linen counted as reported on *linen count sheets* during *period inventories*. See also *inventory; inventory control; inventory record log*.

period statements *Financial statements* of an operational nature covering a set period of time; indicating revenue, *expenses,* and *control profit (or loss);* usually show comparisons to budget for the same period; require critique of out-of-control elements. See also *operating statements.*

personal development of managers Responsibility of managers to develop subordinates or junior managers for future assignments.

personal plan Document prepared by a manager indicating how he or she intends to carry out assigned responsibilities and meet commitments or stated objectives.

personnel action form (PAF) Standardized document used for recording details about an employee such as name, address, job classification, rate of pay, and record of past performance with the company for company reference; may be computerized.

petroleum naptha solvents Fabric cleaners and spot removers made from distilled petroleum or coal tar products.

phenolic compounds Any one of a series of aromatic hydroxyl derivatives of benzene, of which carbolic acid is the first member.

physical agents Nonchemical agents that will affect the growth of bacteria or will destroy it. Examples of nonchemical agents are sunlight, temperature, heat, moisture, and pressure.

physical linen inventory Actual count or supply of various items of *linen on hand.*

pick-up room Occupied room in an *open section* that must be assigned to a *section housekeeper* in a nearby section for servicing.

pile The threads of yarn found on the surface of the rug. The nap. Pile density and weight are indications of quality.

pile warp Yarn threads that run lengthwise in a towel that make the terry loops on both sides of the towel. These are normally 100 percent cotton fibers.

planning Performing certain activities that predetermine a course of action. A *sequential function of management.*

P.M. report A document used for noting the status of guestrooms in a *room section* in the late afternoon, usually about 3:00 P.M. Report forms are developed daily for every section in the hotel to indicate whether rooms are *occupied (OCC), ready (R),* or *checkouts (C/O).* P.M. reports form the basis of the *housekeeper's report.*

P.M. room check Visual inspection of every guestroom in a hotel to determine observed status of rooms. Results of the room check are recorded on the P.M. report.

polygraph examination Inconclusive examination of a person that may give indications as to the honesty or dishonesty of that person. Federal law forbids their use for pre-employment testing in all but a few occupations and has effectively limited their use to but a handful of other applications.

polypropylene A lightweight resin. It is used for making carpet backing, molded plastics, and insulation.

polyurethane A strong plastic resin that resists fire, acids, and decay. It is used in a number of applications, including insulation, a substitute for foam rubber, and a substitute for varnish.

pool employee or employment Classification of employee or employment where the worker is called in to work when needed. No regular schedule of work is expected or promised.

poor performance Appraisal indicating that quality of performance is less than satisfactory but not unsatisfactory.

portion control Specifying and providing to workers specific quantities of chemicals, cleaning solutions, or other measurable agents used in housekeeping operations. Some cleaning agents are prepackaged in measured proportions and may be issued to *section housekeepers* for cleaning tasks.

position descriptions Similar to *job descriptions* but written for management positions. Documents that set forth the manager's basic function, scope of activities, specific responsibilities, and reporting relationships; also indicates where the manager should apply his or her time. See and compare *job descriptions*.

preopening budget Plan for the use of certain fixed and variable cost items before opening a hotel or hospital. See also *preopening cost or expense*.

preopening cost or expense Those costs or expenses normally associated with opening a hotel or hospital (before revenue generation commences). Such costs are usually *amortized* over a several-year period after operation has begun. May include the cost of certain *fixed assets* as well as preoperating costs.

primary backing The primary backing is the surface into which carpet fibers are stitched in a tufted carpet. The backing is normally made from polypropylene.

probationary period of employment Usually the first three or four months of employment when training is being conducted and suitability for full-time employment is being established. A period of employment before the inauguration of all employment rights and benefits.

problem solving Act of seeking solutions to professional and personal problems. The end result of *analyzing problems*.

problem-solving temperament The personal and psychological emotion and attitude displayed by a manager when involved in *problem solving*.

processor (computer) The heart of a computer hardware system; stores a *computer program;* accepts *input* data, processes data according to the program, and provides *output* data on demand of the operator.

productivity The ability to produce. Management theory is concerned with increasing productivity.

pro forma An imaginary balance sheet or system of accounts containing figures for illustrative pur-

poses; usually provides retroactive indications of how an operation will run.

program (computer) The electronic intelligence stored in a computer that controls the processing of data. See also *software (package)*.

programming Scheduling of a group of tasks in a desired order. An activity of *planning*. The act of developing a *software program* for a computer.

progressing work Act of keeping track of work completed by a *section housekeeper* during the *housekeeping day*.

project Element of work to be performed that is not routine or part of a *daily routine*.

property inspection program Formalized program for the inspection of an entire hotel or hospital property. See also *inspection program; zone inspection program*.

pseudomonas aeruginosa (sue-doe-MOAN-us air-o-gin-O-sa) Gram negative. Very resistant to disinfectants. A major problem in public restrooms. Disease is more prevalent in women. Bacteria will grow in standing water.

public area housekeeper One who works in *public areas* as opposed to the *guestroom portion* of the hotel.

public areas Physical areas of a hotel where the general public may congregate or walk; includes lobby area, public sitting area, public restroom, and public thoroughfare. Does not include *guestrooms* or the *guestroom portion* of the facility. Also excluded are restaurants, lounges, offices, and service areas.

purchasing Management function of researching and ordering items of value used in the production of revenue. Some companies have *purchasing agents* who do all purchasing; others require department managers to perform purchasing functions for their departments, allowing for better departmental accountability for expenditures.

purchasing agent Person who performs the purchasing function for all departments within an organization. See also *purchasing*.

purify the room rack Correcting the front desk room rack to reflect the correct status of all guestrooms; usually done about 4:30 P.M. each day by reference to the *housekeeper's report.*

quality circle Group of people consisting of managers, supervisors, and workers, all having an equal responsibility for quality of work or production output.

quaternary ammonium compounds Any derivative of ammonium in which the four hydrogen atoms have been replaced by organic radicals. Quaternary ammonium compounds are used as disinfectants and in various medicines.

ready to rent (R) Status of a guestroom indicating that the room is vacant and has been serviced for occupancy. See also *checkout; occupied.*

reagents A group of testing solutions used to identify certain bacteria and their properties. Such tests can help determine what chemicals should be used to kill certain bacteria.

reasonable security for guestrooms A level of quality in the attributes or physical items in a guestroom that provide the guest with a reasonable measure of protection from uninvited guests.

rechecks Guestroom or rooms that have been identified by the front desk as *discrepancies* and that cannot be readily resolved at the front desk; requires that the housekeeping department take a second visual look at the guestroom to ascertain the correct status of the room.

red tag system Control system using a red tag (form) to administer the legal removal of property from a hotel or hospital facility. The form indicates what material is being removed and who the rightful property owner is; it is signed by a manager. A receipt (second copy) of the form is collected by a door security person as the item is removed and is returned to the authorizing manager for control.

regular employee One who has attained *full-time employment* status; usually attained after successfully completing a probationary period of employment.

relief team See *swing team.*

repair and physical maintenance Correction of a physical defect in a facility; occurs under the direction of the head of the repair and maintenance department (chief engineer).

reporting systems Determining critical data that will be needed, by whom, and how often in order to follow the conduct of an operation. An activity of *controlling.*

resident manager Person in charge of hotel operations exclusive of food and beverage operations; principle assistant to a hotel manager. An executive committee member. Usually the immediate supervisor for a *front office manager* and the *executive housekeeper.*

resilient floors Floors that "give" underfoot. When dented, a resilient floor will eventually rebound wholly or partially to its original form. Resilient flooring materials include asphalt tile, carpet, linoleum, rubber, vinyl tile, and wood.

resort hotel A hotel with fine amenities and luxury flair located near or organized about social settings, geographical points of interest, or centers of activity. May be frequented by *corporate transients* and *consumer* guests but is primarily a vacation destination.

rewarding employees Praising or disciplining employees as necessary to show acceptance or rejection of performance. A part of *performance appraisal;* an activity of *controlling.*

room check Visual check of guestrooms by an employee to determine the status of the room. Room is either *ready (R), occupied (OCC),* or *checkout (C/O).*

room found vacant (RFV) Status of a guestroom as observed by housekeeping that was thought to have been occupied according to the front desk. This is not an unusual occurrence when guest having made prior arrangements for payment of bills depart without notifying the front desk. Also, guests who pay in advance may depart without notifying the front desk. This creates a discrepancy that must be resolved by rechecking the room.

room inspections Periodic inspections of *guestrooms* to ensure that *standards of cleanliness* and servicing are being maintained.

room revenue Gross monies generated from the sale of guestrooms in a hotel.

room section Group of 13 to 20 guestrooms reasonably contiguous to each other that may normally be cleaned and serviced by one person in one eight-hour shift. The room section is normally assigned a number and assigned to a *section housekeeper*.

sales per man-hour Performance ratio of two statistics maintained by the hotel industry that can act as a measure of operational performance; reflects the amount of revenue received for the sale of guestrooms for every man-hour used in support of the hotel occupancy that generated the revenue; can be budgeted or forecast in preparation of a comparison to actual performance. See also *target statistics*.

salmonella choleraesuis (sal-moe-NELL-a coller-ah-SUE-iss) Gram negative. A form of food poisoning. Body can usually tolerate and throw off. The bacteria is used to test germicides.

sanforizing A patented process that preshrinks cotton, linen, or rayon fabric. The process was invented by Sanford L. Cluett (1874–1968).

sanitizer A sanitizing substance or product. To sanitize is to prevent the spread of disease.

satellite linen room One of several service areas located in the *rooms portion* of the hotel used as central work station for a *housekeeping team;* a storage area for bed and bath linens and other supplies used regularly by *section housekeepers* and aides in the performance of their work tasks. See also *housekeeping central*.

satisfiers Experiences intrinsic in a job or work that create positive attitudes and act to enhance motivation. See also *dissatisfiers*.

scenario An outline of possible events or happenings.

scientific management Systematic way of thinking about management based on obtaining information from which to derive facts, form conclusions, make recommendations, and take action.

sealer A product intended to fill in the holes in the porous surface of a floor. It protects the floor from spilled liquids.

secondary backing A second backing on the carpet that provides additional strength, usually made from polypropylene or jute.

second request Second *maintenance work request form* submitted to the maintenance department for work called for on a prior request and not yet completed.

seconds Linens and clothing that have imperfections. Most imperfections are not noticeable and have no effect upon the product's use.

section housekeeper Person regularly assigned to clean guestrooms in a hotel. Synonymous with maid, chambermaid, room attendant.

section housekeeper's daily work report Form designed for a specific (numbered) room section that is used by a *section housekeeper* during the day. A copy of this form will be used to make a P.M. *room check* and will become a P.M. *report*.

section housekeeping aide Worker who is a member of and assists workers in a housekeeping team. Must be capable of lifting heavy objects and operating heavy machinery in the servicing and cleaning of major areas in the guestroom portion of a hotel; is not directly involved in regular and routine guestroom cleaning.

security Quality or condition of being free from danger, fear, anxiety, uncertainty, doubt, or care.

selecting employees Recruiting and acquiring qualified people for each position in an organization. An activity of *staffing*.

selvage The side edge of a towel. There is no pile warp present in the selvage. It is finished off to prevent unraveling.

senior housekeeper Hourly supervisor who is in charge of a *house division* and division personnel; supervises several *section housekeepers* and a *section housekeeping aide;* performs supervisory functions and ensures that division workers perform to standards; inspects guestrooms cleaning when necessary.

senior housekeeper's daily work report form A document indicating every room within a *house division* broken down into sections. Allows the senior housekeeper to progress work of section housekeepers throughout the day within the assigned division.

senior housekeeping aide Working supervisor assistant to the *executive housekeeper;* is in charge of all public area cleaning, project work, storeroom inventories, and training section and utility housekeeping aides.

sequential functions of management See *management sequential functions.*

setting objectives Determining desired end results. An activity of planning.

shams Decorative pillow covers used on a bed. Shams are often made from the same material as the bedspread.

sharps A small plastic case outfitted for flow-through cleansing agent which is used to clean and sanitize needles, scalpels, and other sharp instruments.

shellac A *varnish* made from alcohol and refined lac. Lac is a sticky substance made from the deposits of insects.

simulation training A training technique whereby a guestroom is set aside for training purposes and various situations are presented to the trainee for resolution.

single occupancy Guestroom is only occupied by one guest. See also *double occupancy; multiple occupancy.*

situational leadership Management theory that asserts that the leadership style of the manager must vary according to the situation, that being the skill level and attitude of the subordinate.

sizing laundries Determination of proper *washer, dryer,* and *handling capacities* for *on-premises laundries.*

skip To leave a hotel without paying a bill.

snoop Someone hired to work undercover for the purpose of gathering evidence against people guilty of dishonest acts.

software items Fixtures found in a hotel or hospital room that are normally considered a part of depreciable *fixed assets,* such as mattresses, curtains, draperies, pillows, and other items of soft nature; does not include bed and bath linens.

software package The program by which a computer processes data; as opposed to computer hardware, the physical components of a computer system.

sours A substance that is used to lower the pH level of the laundry wash water to enhance the bleaching process.

spalling The chipping or breaking up of a stone floor surface.

span of control The number of subordinates that can be adequately supervised by a superior. Factors that have an influence on this number include the complexity of the task, the level of skill of the subordinates, distance, and time.

spirochete Corkscrew-shaped microorganisms.

spores Microorganisms that are in a restive, protective shell.

spot check Selective inspection of guestrooms and other sections of a hotel to ensure that *standards of cleanliness* and maintenance are being maintained.

spray buffing The application of a finish solution while polishing a floor's surface to retouch worn spots and to restore a glossy look to the floor's surface.

staffing Performing certain activities that result in selecting competent people for positions in an organization. A *sequential function of management.*

standard operating procedure (SOP) A formal document of a standing nature that specifies a certain method of operating or a specific procedure for the accomplishment of a task.

standards of cleanliness Statement of the conditions that will exist when work has been performed satisfactorily. Used sometimes as a basis for constructing inspection forms. See also *standards setting.*

standards setting Prescribing the conditions that will exist when work has been done satisfactorily.

standing rotational scheduling system A continuous system of scheduling workers or teams of workers for regular days off in each week of a seven-week period. Regular days off in each *workweek* rotate forward (or back) as each week passes through the seven-week cycle. See also *tight scheduling.*

staphylococcus aureus (staff-ill-i-COCK-us OAR-ee-us) A grapelike cluster organism which can cause boils, skin infections, purulent discharge, and/or peritonitis.

steady extra Classification of employee or employment for people who work in a steady but part-time manner; used mostly in union operations. See also *part-time employee.*

sterilization A process whereby all bacteria are killed by heat.

stock-outs A depleted item that is normally found in inventory.

streptococcus pyogenes (strep-tow-COCK-us pie-O-jeans) Chainlike round organism which causes the strep throat infection. Gram positive. Bacteria found in public places; wound and throat infections. Also associated with scarlet fever and rheumatic fever.

stripper A product designed to remove old floor finish and sealer. The product often has an ammoniated base.

styrene butadiene rubber A synthetic rubber made from petroleum and used as a floor surface material.

subroutine A routine series of events or activities performed periodically in a housekeeping department, different from the *daily routine* but of equal importance. Involves controlling operations, purchasing, personnel administration, communications and training, and long-range planning.

suite (S) Two or more guestrooms that are sold as a unit and that connect internally. See also *guestroom types.*

swing team Housekeeping team that works in relief of one or more *regular housekeeping teams* that have been assigned a regular day off. Swing teams work in place of regular house division teams according to predetermined scheduling on a *standing rotational schedule.*

syringe Refers to a hypodermic syringe.

systemeering A term coined by Baring Industries (laundry consultants) relating to the service provided by their consultants when studying and establishing laundry equipment requirements for a user (customer). Service includes recommendations for equipment purchases, bid service, and mechanical rough-in drawings for utility service.

table of personnel requirements Management tool used to describe the number of guestrooms that

constitute a certain percentage of rooms occupancy at each level (0–100 percent); the number of *section housekeepers* and the number of worker hours per day, per week, and per accounting period required to clean or service a certain percentage or level of occupancy.

taking corrective action Adjusting plans and counseling as necessary to attain standards. May require replanning and a repeat of the *sequential functions of management.* An activity of *controlling.*

target statistics Numerical items of data that become goals for the measurement of performance.

Taylor, Frederick W. Noted industrialist, author, and consultant recognized as the father of scientific management.

team scheduling System of scheduling whereby a group of employees organized into a permanent team is scheduled to perform work as a unit. See also *team staffing.*

team staffing System of staffing whereby employees are hired and combined into identifiable teams for the purpose of performing units of work that have been combined into logical relationships. See also *team scheduling; housekeeping teams.*

team system of organization System of formal organization whereby several similar organizational groups may be identified and recognized as performing identical types of work tasks. See also *team scheduling; team staffing; housekeeping teams.*

temporary employee Classification of employee or employment where the period of employment will only be temporary. Employment termination date is usually established at the time of employment.

tensile strength An indicator of fabric quality. The degree of tensile strength is determined by the amount of weight that it takes to tear a $1'' \times 3''$ piece of fabric.

terminal cleaning The action of cleaning a patient room or surgical suite upon completion of its use.

terrazzo A composition flooring material made from chips of marble, granite, travertine, or other materials, and portland cement.

theory x A way of thinking about employees that infers that there is no intrinsic satisfaction found in work; that human beings avoid it as much as possible; that positive (authoritative) direction is needed to achieve organization goals; and that workers possess little ambition or originality. A theory x manager is recognized by the manner in which he or she communicates.

theory y Managerial thinking that infers that work is natural and to be enjoyed by the worker; that the committed worker will exercise self-discipline and direction; that avoidance of responsibility, lack of ambition, and emphasis on security are general consequences of experience—not inherent human characteristics.

theory z Japanese management model that asserts that productivity can be enhanced in the organization by involving all employees in the planning and decision-making process. Term coined by Thomas Ouchi in his management text, "Theory Z." See *participative management*.

thermoplastic Certain resins that have the potential of becoming soft when heated.

thread count The total number of threads in a one-inch square piece of cloth. It is one of a number of quality indicators.

three-stroke solution Refers to the dilution (with water) ratio of an *all-purpose cleaner* that provides a proper agent for certain cleaning operations in approximately three wipes; for example, 40:1 dilution of specific cleaning agent is used to clean mirrors and windows in three wiping strokes. See also *one-stroke solution*.

ticking A strong cloth used to cover mattresses and pillows.

tidy (tidies) (T) The act of tidying or identifying rooms that require tidying in order to *make ready* to rent. Tidies require only light service and usually do not require the full making of a bed or heavy service. Tidies are also rooms that have already been serviced once before a guest departs but then requires light service to make the room ready for reoccupancy.

tight schedule System of scheduling whereby a *standing rotational schedule* may be or is modified on a daily basis to accommodate a specific guestroom occupancy.

time card control The act of *controlling* use of time cards by employees so as to conform to company policy and government regulations.

time in the hole An expression of calendar days between the time a worker completes a workweek and the time that paychecks or pay will become available; ranges between three and fourteen days depending on payroll processing and delivery procedures.

time sheets, weekly or periodic Documents on which time from employee time cards are recorded; forms the basis for calculation of earned or benefit pay. A basis for payroll. May contain other forms of pay besides time actually worked.

torn sheet size Torn sheet size is the length and width of a sheet before the top and bottom hems are added. Top and bottom hems will subtract approximately five inches from the length of the sheet.

total linen on hand See *linen on hand*.

training employees Making employees proficient in the performance of a task through instruction and practice. An activity of *staffing*.

tricophyton interdigitale (tri-CO-fi-ton inter-digit-ALL-ee) No gram stain. A fungus (athlete's foot). The fungus can be used to evaluate a germicidal.

tung oil A poisonous oil from the seeds of the tung tree. It is often used in finishing wood surfaces.

turnover The number of employee separations in an organization over a period expressed as a percentage. Calculated by taking the total number of separations that occur in a year and dividing by the average number of total positions in the organization (the total number of positions in the organization at the beginning of the year plus the total number of positions at the end of the year divided by two). This ratio is expressed as a percentage. High turnover is costly to an organization.

turnover rate See *turnover*.

uniforms Distinctive clothes worn by employees so that they can be recognized by the general public as being part of the business.

varnish A liquid that gives a shiny, hard, transparent surface to wood or metal. It is made from resins that have been dissolved into oil, turpentine, or alcohol.

virus A part of the protist kingdom, includes influenza (a flu virus), herpes simplex, vaccine (cow pox), adeno virus type 2, and AIDS. Gram positive (blue stain). Major cause of infections (boils, carbuncles, ear infections) and food poisonings. Size is .8 to 1 micron. It is resistant to antibiotics. Best cure is heat.

wage costs Classification of labor based on the calculation of hours worked times a given or assigned wage rate depending on the classification of the employee. See also *controllable costs, employee costs.*

wage department Classification system for the identification of various types of man-hours used by departments in hotels and hospitals. Classifications usually refer to the types of work that are to be performed.

warp Lengthwise threads of yarn in a fabric.

wash formula Quantitative determinants of how long a specific type or piece of linen is to be washed, rinsed, and extracted; includes temperatures of wash and rinse solutions and quantities of detergents, bleaches, and softeners to be used during the various wash cycles.

washing capacity Optimum weight of linen that should be placed in an automatic commercial washing machine; for example, 50-pound, 100-pound, 200-pound washer; used in the *sizing of laundries.* See also *drying capacity; handling capacity.*

weekly maintenance Identified housekeeping service or repair type maintenance that is to be performed each week on schedule.

weekly wage analysis Breakdown of expended wages by departments, showing comparisons to budgeted and forecast wages; identifies out-of-control areas and indicates corrective measures to regain control of costs if necessary.

weekly wage forecast Document prepared weekly by housekeeping management indicating how many man-hours will be required or expended and in what *wage departments* (classifications) to support a specified forecast of guestroom occupancy.

weft The threads of yarn that run the width of a fabric.

"What-If" publication Interesting presentation of emergency situations a person might encounter in a hotel or hospital. Presentation is in the form of questions asking "what if" and enlightened alternative responses.

work-centered theory of management Classical theory of management that revolves around a concern for production. Two major principles emerge from this theory: authority—the right to command and the power to exact obedience—and the task of decision making are vested in those who must ensure production.

work calendar Seven-week period of time divided into workweeks; indicating regular workdays and regular days off in each week as presented in the *standing rotational scheduling system.*

workshop training Training technique used primarily for supervisors. Involves the presentation of managerial problems and allows the participants to work out one or more solutions, which are then critiqued.

workweek Seven consecutive days with an identifiable beginning and ending used to separate and identify one week from another in a continuous daily operation. Workweeks may begin on any day of the week and end six days later. The identification of workweeks is imperative in continuous daily operations for scheduling and accounting purposes.

zero-based budgeting A concept of budgeting that requires the planner to start the entire budgeting process from scratch each year. No prior assumptions regarding past years are made. While extremely accurate in its approach, it is time consuming and difficult to attempt in an extremely complex and/or large organization.

zone Segmented part of a facility subject to zone inspection. See *zone inspection program.*

zone inspection program A form of *property inspection* where various sections of a hotel are divided into zones and assigned to several zone inspectors; usually conducted once each week.

Index

A

X

X theory of management, 6

Y

Y theory of management, 6

Yeasts, 244, 245

Z

Zero-base budgeting, 28
Zinc cross-linked polymers, 97
Zone inspection, 212